THE ROUGH GUIDE TO

Southwest USA

There are more than one hundred and fifty Rough Guide titles
covering destinations from Amsterdam to Zimbabwe

Forthcoming titles include

Alaska • Copenhagen • Ibiza & Formentera • Iceland

Rough Guide Reference Series

Classical Music • Country Music • Drum 'n' bass • English Football
European Football • House • The Internet • Jazz • Music USA • Opera
Reggae • Rock Music • Techno • Unexplained Phenomena • World Music

Rough Guide Phrasebooks

Czech • Dutch • Egyptian Arabic • European Languages • French
German • Greek • Hindi & Urdu • Hungarian • Indonesian • Italian
Japanese • Mandarin Chinese • Mexican Spanish • Polish • Portuguese
Russian • Spanish • Swahili • Thai • Turkish • Vietnamese

Rough Guides on the Internet

www.roughguides.com

Rough Guide Credits

Text Editor:	Polly Thomas
Series Editor:	Mark Ellingham
Editorial:	Martin Dunford, Jonathan Buckley, Jo Mead, Kate Berens, Amanda Tomlin, Ann-Marie Shaw, Paul Gray, Helena Smith, Judith Bamber, Orla Duane, Olivia Eccleshall, Ruth Blackmore, Geoff Howard, Claire Saunders, Gavin Thomas, Alexander Mark Rogers, Joe Staines, Lisa Nellis, Andrew Tomičić, Richard Lim, Duncan Clark, Peter Buckley, Sam Thorne (UK); Andrew Rosenberg, Mary Beth Maioli, Don Bapst, Stephen Timblin (US)
Online Editor:	Kelly Cross, Anja Mutic-Blessing (US)
Production:	Susanne Hillen, Andy Hilliard, Link Hall, Helen Ostick, Julia Bovis, Michelle Draycott, Katie Pringle, Robert Evers, Niamh Hatton, Mike Hancock, Robert McKinlay
Cartography:	Melissa Baker, Maxine Repath, Nichola Goodliffe, Ed Wright
Picture Research:	Louise Boulton, Sharon Martins
Finance:	John Fisher, Gary Singh, Edward Downey, Mark Hall, Tim Bill
Marketing & Publicity:	Richard Trillo, Niki Smith, David Wearn, Jemima Broadbridge (UK); Jean-Marie Kelly, Myra Campolo, Simon Carloss (US)
Administration:	Tania Hummel, Demelza Dallow

Acknowledgements

Thanks especially to Sam Cook, for her love, support and encouragement. On the road, Edie Jarolim provided generous hospitality and help, and Jean McKnight, Marian DeLay, Pamela Westwood, Steve Lewis and Jennifer Franklin offered valuable assistance, while back home, Jules Brown, Rob Humphreys and Rob Jones gave me a healthy perspective on things.

At Rough Guides, I greatly appreciate all the hard work put in by Polly Thomas as editor, and would also like to thank Melissa Baker for her maps, Russell Walton for proofreading, Mike Hancock for typesetting and Paul Gray for the overview.

The editor would like to thank Greg for being such a joy to work with.

This second edition published September 2000 by Rough Guides Ltd, 62–70 Shorts Gardens, London WC2H 9AH.

Distributed by the Penguin Group:
Penguin Books Ltd, 27 Wrights Lane, London W8 5TZ.
Penguin Putnam, Inc. 375 Hudson Street, New York, NY 10014, USA.
Penguin Books Australia Ltd, 487 Maroondah Highway, PO Box 257, Ringwood, Victoria 3134, Australia.
Penguin Books Canada Ltd, 10 Alcorn Avenue, Toronto, Ontario M4V 1E4, Canada.
Penguin Books (NZ) Ltd, 182–190 Wairau Road, Auckland 10, New Zealand.
Printed in England by Clays Ltd, St Ives PLC
Typography and original design by Jonathan Dear and The Crowd Roars.
Illustrations throughout by Edward Briant.

592pp. Includes index

ISBN 1-85828-556-9

THE ROUGH GUIDE TO

Southwest USA

Written and researched by
Greg Ward

**ROUGH
GUIDES**

Help us update

We've gone to a lot of trouble to ensure that this second edition of *The Rough Guide to Southwest USA* is accurate and up-to-date. However, things inevitably change, and if you feel we've got it wrong or left something out, we'd like to know: any suggestions, comments or corrections would be much appreciated. We'll credit all contributions and send a copy of the next edition – or any other Rough Guide if you prefer – for the best correspondence.

Please mark letters "Rough Guide to Southwest USA" and send to:
Rough Guides, 62–70 Shorts Gardens, London WC2H 9AH or
Rough Guides, 4th Floor, 345 Hudson St, New York, NY 10014.

Email should be sent to:
mail@roughguides.co.uk

Online updates about Rough Guide titles can be found on our Web site at *www.roughguides.com*

The Author

Greg Ward has worked for Rough Guides since 1985, in which time he has also written *Rough Guides* to Las Vegas, Hawaii, Honolulu, Maui, the Big Island, Brittany and Normandy, and Essential Blues CDs, edited and co-written the *Rough Guide to the USA*, contributed to books on China, Mexico, California, France, Spain and Portugal, and edited several more. He has also written travel guides for several other publishers, and is currently writing a biography of one of the many unusual characters mentioned in this book.

Readers' letters

Many thanks to the readers of the first edition who took the time to write in with their comments and suggestions:
Gary Bowden, Rachel Gawith, Jennifer DeSelle-Milam and Garrett Milam, Dario Pellegrini and Simon Skerritt.

Rough Guides

Travel Guides • Phrasebooks • Music and Reference Guides

We set out to do something different when the first Rough Guide was published in 1982. Mark Ellingham, just out of University, was traveling in Greece. He brought along the popular guides of the day, but found they were all lacking in some way. They were either strong on ruins and museums but went on for pages without mentioning a beach or taverna. Or they were so conscious of the need to save money that they lost sight of Greece's cultural and historical significance. Also, none of the books told him anything about Greece's contemporary life – its politics, its culture, its people, and how they lived.

So with no job in prospect, Mark decided to write his own guidebook, one which aimed to provide practical information that was second to none, detailing the best beaches and the hottest clubs and restaurants, while also giving hard-hitting accounts of every sight, both famous and obscure, and providing up-to-the-minute information on contemporary culture. It was a guide that encouraged independent travelers to find the best of Greece, and was a great success, getting shortlisted for the Thomas Cook travel guide award, and encouraging Mark, along with three friends, to expand the series.

The Rough Guide list grew rapidly and the letters flooded in, indicating a much broader readership than had been anticipated, but one which uniformly appreciated the Rough Guides' mix of practical detail and humor, irreverence and enthusiasm. Things haven't changed. The same four friends who began the series are still the caretakers of the Rough Guide mission today: to provide the most reliable, up-to-date and entertaining information to independent-minded travelers of all ages, on all budgets.

We now publish 150 titles and have offices in London and New York. The travel guides are written and researched by a dedicated team of more than 100 authors, based in Britain, Europe, the USA and Australia. We have also created a unique series of phrasebooks to accompany the travel series, along with the acclaimed series of music guides, and a best-selling pocket guide to the Internet and World Wide Web. We also publish comprehensive travel information on our Web site: *www.roughguides.com*

Contents

Chapter 5 Flagstaff and Central Arizona   272

Chapter 6 The Grand Canyon   318

Chapter 7 Southern Utah   359

Chapter 8 Las Vegas and Salt Lake City   486

Part Three Contexts   517

Index   550

List of maps

MAP SYMBOLS

Symbol		Symbol	
━━━	Railway	⚶	Viewpoint
▬⟨15⟩▬	Interstate	🜨	Butte
═⟨89⟩═	U.S. Highway	◠	Cave
─⟨21⟩─	State Highway	♥	Museum
- - - - -	Footpath/Track	⌇	Waterfall
────	Waterways	◆	General point of interest
━ ━ ━	Chapter Division Boundary	(i)	Tourist Office
■━■━■	International Borders	⊠	Post Office
━ ▪▪ ━	State Borders	◉	Hotel
✈	Airport	▪	Building
⌒⌒	Mountains	➕	Church
▲	Peak	▦	National Park
⌒	Arch	▦	Park
⚠	Campsite	▨	Indian Reservation
∴	Ruin		

Introduction

The Southwest is the most extraordinary and spectacular region of the United States. The splendor and scale of its scenery consistently defies belief – a glorious panoply of cliffs and canyons, buttes and mesas, carved from rocks of every imaginable color, and enriched here by groves of shimmering cottonwoods and aspens, there by cactuses and agaves. In addition, the Southwest is unique in being the only part of the United States whose original inhabitants remain in residence. Though century after century has brought fresh waves of intruders, somehow none has managed to entirely displace its predecessors, leaving all to coexist in an intriguing blend of cultures and traditions.

The area covered by this book roughly corresponds to the former Spanish colony of **New Mexico**, which has belonged to the US for a mere 150 years, and is now divided between the modern states of New Mexico, Arizona, Utah, Colorado and Nevada. Though rainfall is scarce everywhere, not all the region is **desert**; indeed, the popular image of the Southwest as consisting of scrubby hillsides studded with many-armed saguaro cactuses is true only of the Sonoran Desert of southern Arizona. Towering snow-capped **mountains** rise not only in southern Colorado and northern New Mexico, at the tail-end of the Rockies, but are scattered across Utah and Arizona as well, while dense **pine forests** cloak much of northern Arizona.

The most dramatic landscapes are to be found on the **Colorado Plateau**, an arid mile-high tableland, roughly the size of California, that extends across the **Four Corners** region of Arizona, Utah, Colorado and New Mexico. Atop the main body of the plateau, further layers of rock are piled level upon level, creating a "**Grand Staircase**" of successive cliffs and plateaus. During the last dozen or so million years, the entire complex has been pushed steadily upwards by subterranean forces. As it has risen, the earth has cracked, warped, buckled and split, and endless quantities of crumbling sandstone have been washed away by the Colorado River and its tributaries. The **Grand Canyon** is simply the most famous of

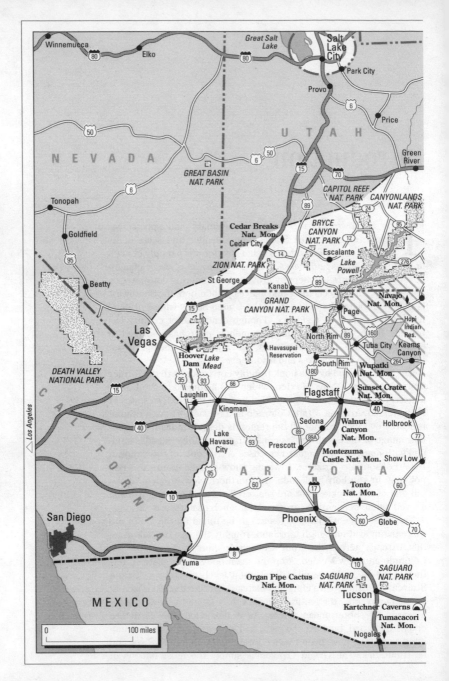

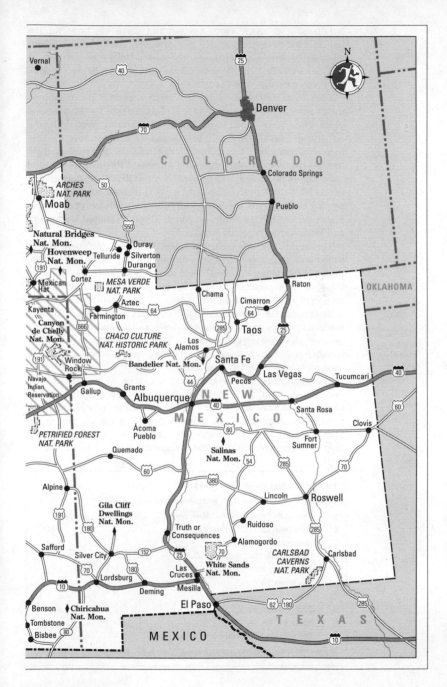

hundreds of dramatic **canyons**, and can seem too huge for the human mind to appreciate. No one, however, could fail to be over-whelmed by the sheer weirdness of **southern Utah** – the red rocks of **Monument Valley**, the fiery sandstone pinnacles of **Bryce Canyon**, the endless expanses of **Canyonlands**.

Though, to outsiders, such harsh terrain appears inhospitable in the extreme, it has been home to **Native Americans** for ten thousand years. These days, much of the Colorado Plateau is taken up by the self-styled "**Navajo Nation**", the largest of the Southwest's fifty Indian reservations. Until around 1300 AD, however, it was occupied by a people now remembered as the **Ancestral Puebloans** (the term "Anasazi" is no longer widely used; see p.520). Their magnificent adobe "cliff dwellings", squeezed like eagles' nests into crevices in soaring canyon walls, are now major tourist attractions, preserved in places such as the gorgeous **Canyon de Chelly National Monument** and **Mesa Verde National Park**.

The immediate descendants of the Ancestral Puebloans estab-lished new settlements to the south and west of the Four Corners, most notably along the Rio Grande valley of northern New Mexico. Many of their villages, as seen by the sixteenth-century Spanish explorers who first called them "**pueblos**", are still there today, with their architecture and ceremonial life all but unchanged. Visiting a modern Pueblo community such as **Ácoma** – the amazing "Sky City", perched on a glowing golden mesa – **Taos**, or the **Hopi mesas** offers a unique opportunity to experience indigenous American cultures in their most authentic surviving form.

The **Spaniards**, the **Navajo** and the **Apache** all carved out their own domains in the Southwest from the seventeenth century onwards, and have shared the region – not always peacefully – with the Pueblo peoples and other Native American groups ever since. They were joined in the nineteenth century by the **Mormons**, who through utter determination and communal effort colonized modern

---

Top Ten Southwest Destinations

A completely subjective list of ten Southwestern places you *must* see:

1	**Canyon de Chelly National Monument**, AZ	p.51
2	**Havasupai Indian Reservation**, AZ	p.342
3	**Monument Valley**, AZ/UT	p.45
4	**Canyonlands National Park**, UT	p.443
5	**Mesa Verde National Park**, CO	p.69
6	**Las Vegas**, NV	p.486
7	**Ácoma Pueblo**, NM	p.94
8	**Zion National Park**, UT	p.374
9	**Santa Fe**, NM	p.100
10	**Bryce Canyon National Park**, UT	p.396

Further "Top Ten" lists are scattered through the Index, beginning on p.550.

Utah, and by the **Americans**, who swiftly outnumbered everyone else.

In the early years of US rule, the Southwest was very much the **Wild West**; that era is now recalled in towns such as **Lincoln**, New Mexico, where Billy the Kid blazed his way out of jail, and **Tombstone**, Arizona, where the Earps and the Clantons fought it out at the OK Corral. The century since Utah, Arizona and New Mexico achieved statehood has been characterized by attempts to transform the landscape on an unprecedented – not to say unnatural, let alone unsustainable – scale. A series of monumental **water** projects – including the construction of the **Hoover Dam**, the damming of Utah's Glen Canyon to form **Lake Powell**, and the creation of a network of canals across hundreds of miles of the Arizona desert – has brought the region prosperity as the **Sunbelt**.

While the proximity of the wilderness remains the supreme attraction for most visitors, certain Southwestern **cities** make worthwhile destinations in their own right. **Santa Fe** is the best example, with its 400-year history, top-quality museums and galleries, and superb array of hotels and restaurants; **Tucson** holds an enjoyable combination of desert parks, Hispanic history, restaurants and ranch resorts; and **Las Vegas**, entirely and quintessentially a product of the twentieth century, is far too amazing to miss. **Phoenix**, on the other hand, is one to avoid; it's possible to have a good time there, but you'd have to have a *very* long vacation before there'd be much point bothering.

Though most of the region's **smaller towns** are best treated as overnight pit-stops, some have blossomed into appealing bases for a few days' stay. **Moab** is a welcome exception to the typical monotony of southern Utah farming communities; the college town of **Flagstaff** is a lively enclave within easy reach of the Grand Canyon; and **Taos** still has the feel of the artists' colony that attracted Georgia O'Keeffe and D.H. Lawrence.

Planning your itinerary

The only way to explore the Southwest in any detail is to **drive** yourself around; the very limited public transport options are outlined on p.20. However long your vacation may be, aim to spend most of your time on the Colorado Plateau, seeing as much as possible of the Four Corners region and southern Utah.

Your exact itinerary will depend largely on which city serves as your starting point. In **one week**, you could fly into **Las Vegas**, and loop around the Colorado River to Grand Canyon, Zion and possibly Bryce Canyon national parks; into **Phoenix**, to reach Canyon de Chelly, Monument Valley and the Grand Canyon; into **Albuquerque**, and see Santa Fe, Taos and Ácoma Pueblo; or to **Salt Lake City**, and make a lightning tour of all southern Utah's national parks.

With **two weeks**, you can extend any of the above itineraries to cover most of the Colorado Plateau, making sure you get to Canyon de Chelly, Monument Valley and Mesa Verde. Only if you have three weeks or more are you likely to manage any large-scale hiking – for example into the stunning Havasupai Indian Reservation, or down to Phantom Ranch in the Grand Canyon – or to detour south into southern New Mexico or southern Arizona.

When to go

Summer is the peak tourist season for most of the Southwest, though temperatures in excess of 100°F render cities such as Phoenix and Tucson all but unbearable, and make it an ordeal even to get out of your car in many of the national parks. Hikers, bikers and rafters do better to come either between mid-September and mid-October,

Average Temperature and Rainfall												
	Jan	Feb	March	April	May	June	July	Aug	Sept	Oct	Nov	Dec
Grand Canyon (South Rim)												
Av High °F	41	45	51	60	70	81	84	82	76	65	52	43
Av Low °F	18	21	25	32	39	47	54	53	47	36	27	20
Rainfall (in)	1.3	1.5	1.4	0.9	0.7	0.4	1.8	2.3	1.6	1.1	0.9	1.6
Las Vegas, NV												
Av High °F	56	67	68	77	87	98	104	101	94	81	66	57
Av Low °F	33	37	42	49	59	68	75	73	65	53	41	33
Rainfall (in)	0.5	0.5	0.4	0.2	0.2	0.1	0.5	0.5	0.3	0.3	0.4	0.3
Phoenix, AZ												
Av High °F	65	69	75	84	93	102	105	102	98	88	75	66
Av Low °F	38	41	45	52	60	68	78	76	69	57	45	39
Rainfall (in)	0.8	0.8	0.8	0.5	0.3	0.3	0.7	0.9	0.6	0.6	0.6	0.8
Salt Lake City, UT												
Av High °F	37	43	51	61	72	83	93	90	80	66	50	38
Av Low °F	20	27	30	37	45	53	62	60	50	39	29	22
Rainfall (in)	1.4	1.3	1.7	2.2	1.5	1.0	0.7	0.9	0.9	1.1	1.2	1.4
Santa Fe, NM												
Av High °F	40	44	51	60	69	79	82	80	74	63	50	41
Av Low °F	19	22	28	35	43	52	57	56	49	38	27	20
Rainfall (in)	0.6	0.8	0.8	0.9	1.2	1.1	2.4	2.3	1.7	1.1	0.7	0.7
Tucson, AZ												
Av High °F	64	67	71	80	89	99	99	96	94	84	72	65
Av Low °F	38	40	44	50	58	67	74	72	67	57	45	39
Rainfall (in)	0.8	0.6	0.7	0.3	0.1	0.2	2.4	2.1	1.3	0.9	0.6	0.9
Zion National Park												
Av High °F	52	57	63	73	83	93	100	97	91	78	63	53
Av Low °F	29	31	36	43	52	60	68	66	60	49	37	30
Rainfall (in)	1.6	1.6	1.7	1.3	0.7	0.6	0.8	1.6	0.8	1.0	1.2	1.5

when the crowds are gone and dazzling fall colors brighten the canyons, or in April and May, when wildflowers bloom in the desert.

If your timings aren't flexible, however, don't worry. It's always possible to escape the heat – the thermometer drops by 3°F for every thousand feet above sea level, so Santa Fe, for example, is always relatively cool – and the summer is also peak period for the region's festivals, as detailed on p.187.

Winters can be seriously cold, and snowfalls close down certain areas altogether – don't reckon on seeing Mesa Verde, or the North Rim of the Grand Canyon, between October and April. Those parks that remain open are often at their most beautiful when frosted with snow, however, while ski resorts like Telluride and Taos are in full swing, and Tucson and Phoenix fill up with sun-seeking "snowbirds" from colder states.

The Basics

Getting There from the US and Canada

For US and Canadian travelers who live too far from the Southwest simply to drive there, the most cost-effective way to visit is to fly to one of the four major cities described in this book,

rent a car, make a loop tour, and fly back from the same airport.

Las Vegas, Nevada, is probably the best bet, as it offers low air fares and rental-car rates, and makes an exhilarating starting point for tours to the Grand Canyon and the national parks of southern Utah. Sky Harbor International Airport in **Phoenix**, Arizona, is equally well served by the major carriers, and although Phoenix itself is a less appealing destination it's convenient for both the Grand Canyon and the deserts of southern Arizona. New Mexico's principal airport, in **Albuquerque**, receives fewer long-distance flights, but it's the obvious point of arrival if you want to see Santa Fe and Taos, and it's also the closest airport to the Four Corners region. Finally, **Salt Lake City** may be in Utah's mountainous northwest corner, but it's only half a day's drive from fashionable Moab and national parks such as Canyonlands and Arches.

AIRLINES SERVING THE SOUTHWEST			
Air Canada *www.aircanada.ca*	☎ 1-800/776-3000	**Mesa Airlines** *www.mesa-air.com*	☎ 1-800/637-2247
Canada	☎ 1-800/263-0882	**Northwest Airlines** *www.nwa.com*	☎ 1-800/225-2525
Alaska Airlines *www.alaska-air.com*	☎ 1-800/426-0333	**Scenic Airlines** *www.scenic.com*	☎ 1-800/634-6801
America West *www.americawest.com*	☎ 1-800/235-9292	**Skywest** *www.skywest.com*	☎ 1-800/453-9417
American Airlines *www.aa.com*	☎ 1-800/433-7300	**Southwest** *www.iflyswa.com*	☎ 1-800/435-9792
American Trans Air *www.ata.com*	☎ 1-800/435-9282	**TWA** *www.twa.com*	☎ 1-800/221-2000
Continental Airlines *www.continental.com*	☎ 1-800/525-0280	**United Airlines** *www.ual.com*	☎ 1-800/241-6522
Delta Air Lines *www.delta-air.com*	☎ 1-800/221-1212	**US Airways** *www.usairways.com*	☎ 1-800/428-4322
Frontier Airlines *www.frontierairlines.com*	☎ 1-800/432-1359		
Hawaiian Airlines *www.hawaiianair.com*	☎ 1-800/367-5320		

DISCOUNT TRAVEL COMPANIES IN THE US AND CANADA

Council Travel, 205 E 42nd St, New York, NY 10017; ☎ 1-800/226-8624; *www.counciltravel .com*. Student/budget travel agency with branches in many US cities.

Educational Travel Center, 438 N Frances St, Madison, WI 53703; ☎ 608/256-5551 or 1-800/747-5551; *www.edtrav.com*. Student/ youth and consolidator fares.

STA Travel, 7810 Hardy Drive, Suite 109, Tempe, AZ 85284; ☎ 1-800/777-0112; *www.sta-travel.com*. Discount travel firm specializing in student/youth fares and related services, with branches in many US cities.

Travel Avenue, 10 S Riverside Plaza, Suite 1404, Chicago, IL 60606; ☎ 1-800/333-3335;

www.travelavenue.com. Full-service travel agent offering 7–12 percent rebates off airfares, car rentals and hotels.

Travel CUTS, 187 College St, Toronto, ON M5T 1P7; ☎ 416/979-2406 or 1-800/667-2887 (Canada only); *www.travelcuts.com*. Student fares, IDs and other travel services.

Travelers Advantage, 3033 S Parker Rd, Suite 900, Aurora, CO 80014; ☎ 1-800/548-1116; *www.travelersadvantage.com*. Full-service travel club.

Worldtek Travel, 111 Water St, New Haven, CT 06511; ☎ 1-800/243-1723; *www.worldtek.com*. Discount travel agency.

SOUTHWEST TOUR OPERATORS

AmeriCan Adventures/Roadrunner Worldwide Hosteling Treks ☎ 1-800/864-0335; *www.americanadventures.com*. Active camping tours and hosteling treks for 18- to 35-year-olds. Most, like the ten-day, $769 "Canyons and Indians" trip, include transportation by small van, campground accommodations, guide services and park and attraction entrance fees.

Backroads, Inc ☎ 1-800/462-2848; *www.backroads.com*. Luxury hotel or camping, hiking or biking tours covering New Mexico, Arizona and southern Utah; 5 nights in Zion and Bryce costs $1700.

Contiki Tours ☎ 1-800/CONTIKI; *www.contiki.com*. 18-day Southwest camping tours, for 18- to 35-year-olds only, at $1175–1450.

Delta Certified Vacations ☎ 1-800/872-7786; *www.deltavacations.com*. Flight and hotel packages, especially to Las Vegas.

Grand Canyon Field Institute ☎ 520/638-2485; *www.grandcanyon.org/fieldinstitute/*. Park-sponsored program of hikes and educational expeditions in the Grand Canyon; a 4-day backpacking tour costs $275.

Green Tortoise ☎ 1-800/867-8647; *www.greentortoise.com*. California-based,

youth-oriented bus tours; 9-day tours to the Grand Canyon from San Francisco for around $400.

Holidaze Ski Tours ☎ 1-800/526-2827; *www.holidaze.com*. Four- to seven-night moderate to upscale ski packages to Telluride, CO for $400–1000.

Kemwel's Premier Selections ☎ 1-800/234-4000; *www.premierselections.com*. Seven-night vintage train tour from Santa Fe to Phoenix via the Grand Canyon for $1700.

REI Adventures ☎ 1-800/622-2236; *www.rei.com/travel*. Small-group Utah hiking trips; 5 nights based at ranch near Zion for $100.

Saga Holidays ☎ 1-800/343-0273; *www.sagaholidays.com*. 14-night national park bus tours for over-50s from $1800.

Smithsonian Odyssey Tours ☎ 1-800/258-5885; *www.si.edu/tsa/sst/internat/odyssey.htm* 14-night guided tours of geological wonders, with stops in Santa Fe, the Grand Canyon and Zion, from $2599.

Suntrek ☎ 1-800/292-9696; *www.suntrek.com*. Three-week camping adventure tour of the Southwest; $1089–1154.

Fares

Flights are at their most expensive in summer, which despite soaring temperatures is the **peak season** for travel to the Southwest. Prices drop during the "**shoulder**" **seasons** – September to December, and March through May – and are cheapest during the **low season**, from January to February, excluding New Year. Fares also vary widely according to how far in advance you make a reservation. **Finding the best price** of course involves shopping around; any travel agent should be prepared to check with several different airlines, and it's easy to do so yourself on the Internet, through sites such as *www.travelscape.com* or *www.travelocity.com*.

A good first call is to contact **Southwest Airlines**, which in recent years has set out to establish itself as the lowest-price carrier to the region, traveling to Phoenix, Las Vegas, Tucson, Salt Lake City and Albuquerque from around fifty other US cities. While regular fares are competitive, travelers who plan in advance can take advantage of special promotions, such as sixty percent off published fares, with no fare higher than $99 one way. Check your local paper for promotions if Southwest flies from your home town.

More generally, a round-trip from New York to **Phoenix** should cost around $350; equivalent figures for Chicago might be $300, and for Los Angeles, just under $100. Sample fares from Montréal to Phoenix start from CAN$600, and from Vancouver CAN$350.

Fares to **Albuquerque** are similar, with a round-trip from New York or Chicago costing around $340; a round-trip between New York and **Salt Lake City** starts at around $300. In general, the best bargains tend to be on routes to **Las Vegas**, although the only airline that has a regular nonstop service there from New York is America West. It should be possible to find fares to Las Vegas for under $200 from Seattle, and around $300 from New York; even a two-week **fly-drive** trip from New York to Las Vegas can cost well under $500 per person.

Regional and commuter airlines

Commuter airlines connect each of the Southwest's major airports with lesser communities in the region. Thus several airlines link Phoenix with towns such as Tucson, Flagstaff, Yuma and Lake Havasu City – America West has the most extensive service – while Salt Lake City is connected with airports in southern Utah such as St George and Moab. Mesa Airlines, who operate America West, use Albuquerque as their hub for flights to destinations including Carlsbad, Farmington, Silver City and Alamogordo. Las Vegas has the best connections of all, including direct flights to (and over) the Grand Canyon; operators are detailed on p.328.

Few of these flights are particularly suited to the needs of tourists, however. The cheapest fares tend to be on the scale of $50–100 for a one-way trip, and it's far easier to drive from

place to place than to have to rent another car every few days.

Much the best plan if you need to get somewhere that only has a minor airport is to fly to the Southwest with a specialist **regional carrier** that will also be able to fly you to your ultimate destination for a small additional cost. Thus America West serves all four principal regional airports, and if you fly into Phoenix with them it can cost as little as $30 extra to continue to Tucson, whereas an ordinary round-trip flight between Phoenix and Tucson can cost a ludicrous $540. Similarly, Skywest, Delta's commuter airline, fly into Salt Lake City and Albuquerque, and have connections for Yuma, St George and Cedar City.

By rail

Amtrak **rail service** to and within the Southwest is restricted to three completely separate east–west routes, two of which pass through Arizona and New Mexico on the way to and from Los Angeles, while the other crosses northern Utah.

The daily Southwest Chief originates in Chicago and crosses from Colorado into northern New Mexico near Raton, passing close to Santa Fe (connected by a bus service from tiny Lamy) and through **Albuquerque** before heading due west via Gallup and **Flagstaff**, where connecting buses run north to the Grand Canyon. Between Albuquerque and Gallup, an onboard Native American interpretive guide describes natural and Native American sites.

The thrice-weekly Sunset Limited service from New Orleans reaches southern New Mexico via El Paso, Texas, then calls at **Tucson** and Yuma as it heads across Arizona. There is no longer any rail service to **Phoenix**, though Amtrak run connecting buses from both Flagstaff and Tucson, or to **Las Vegas**, which is linked by bus with Barstow, California. However, it is possible to reach **Salt Lake City** and **Thompson** in Utah by rail, on the daily California Zephyr between Chicago, Denver and San Francisco.

For fares and schedules, call ☎1-800/USA-RAIL or visit *www.amtrak.com*; do not contact individual stations.

By bus

If you're happy to sit on a **bus** for days on end, Greyhound usually offers the cheapest possible way to get to the Southwest. A one-way trip to Albuquerque from Los Angeles costs $68 and takes around twenty hours; the ride from Milwaukee takes a day and a half, and costs $133; and the two-day cross-country trek from New York costs $140.

For full details of routes and fares, and to make reservations, contact Greyhound on ☎1-800/231-2222 or visit *www.greyhound.com*.

Insurance

Before buying an **insurance policy**, check that you're not already covered – some homeowners'

or renters' policies are valid on vacation, and credit cards such as American Express often include some medical or other insurance, while most Canadians are covered for medical mishaps overseas by their provincial health plans. If you only need trip cancellation/interruption coverage (to supplement your existing plan), this is generally available at around $6 per $100. If you aren't already covered, however, you should consider taking out specialist **travel insurance**, such as the Rough Guides scheme detailed on p.8.

Getting There from Britain and Ireland

There are only two direct, nonstop flights from Britain or Ireland to any of the cities covered in this book: British Airways has a daily service from London Gatwick to Phoenix, Arizona, and Virgin Atlantic offers a twice-weekly service from London Gatwick to Las Vegas, Nevada. Most other transatlantic carriers can get you to Phoenix, Las Vegas, Salt Lake City or Albuquerque, but all require at least one stop en route.

From **Britain**, you can either fly nonstop to the West Coast and then double back towards the Southwest, or touch down on the East

Coast and then fly west; time-wise, it makes little difference. For the cheapest possible deal, and the shortest flight, it makes sense to fly nonstop to **Los Angeles** – British Airways and Virgin fly twice daily from London, while American, United and Air New Zealand fly once daily – and **drive** to the Southwest from there, taking advantage of California's low rental-car rates. **San Francisco** is another possibility, though the drive is a little longer; British Airways and United fly there twice daily, American and Virgin fly at least once daily, depending on the day of the week.

From **Ireland**, you can fly to New York, Boston, Chicago or Los Angeles with Aer Lingus, or to New York or Atlanta with Delta, or fly to London and take your pick of transatlantic routes.

Fares and airlines

Britain remains one of the best places in Europe to obtain **flight bargains**, but fares vary widely according to season, availability and the current level of inter-airline competition. Shop around carefully for the best offers by checking the travel ads in the weekend papers, on the holiday pages of *Teletext*, *Time Out* and the *Evening Standard* in London, or free papers like *TNT*. You

AIRLINES, FLIGHT AGENTS AND TOUR OPERATORS IN BRITAIN AND IRELAND

AIRLINES

	BRITAIN	IRELAND
Aer Lingus *www.aerlingus.ie*	☎ 0645/737747	☎ 01/844 4777
Air New Zealand *www.airnz.co.uk*	☎ 020/8741 2299	
American Airlines *www.aa.com*	☎ 0345/789789	
British Airways *www.british-airways.com*	☎ 0345/222111	
Continental *www.continental.com*	☎ 0800/776464	
Delta *www.delta-air.com*	☎ 0800/414767	☎ 01/676 8080
Northwest *www.nwa.com*	☎ 08705/561000	
TWA *www.twa.com*	☎ 0345/333333	
United *www.ual.com*	☎ 0845/844 4777	
Virgin Atlantic *www.virgin-atlantic.com*	☎ 01293/747747	☎ 01/873 3388

FLIGHT AGENTS

Joe Walsh Tours Dublin ☎ 01/676 0991

North South Travel Chelmsford ☎ 01245/608291

STA Travel *www.statravel.co.uk*. London ☎ 020/7361 6262; Bristol ☎ 0117/929 4399; Cambridge ☎ 01223/366966; Manchester ☎ 0161/834 0668; Leeds ☎ 0113/244 9212; Oxford ☎ 01865/792800

Trailfinders *www.trailfinders.co.uk*. London ☎ 020/7938 3366; Birmingham ☎ 0121/236123; Bristol ☎ 0117/929 9000; Glasgow ☎ 0141/353 2224; Manchester ☎ 0161/839 6969

Travel Bug *www.flynow.com*. London ☎ 020/7835 2000; Manchester ☎ 0161/721 4000

USIT *www.usitcampus.co.uk*. London ☎ 020/7730 2101; Belfast ☎ 028/9032 4073; Cork ☎ 021/270900; Dublin ☎ 01/679 8833

TOUR OPERATORS

AmeriCan Adventures *www.americanadventures.com*. Tunbridge Wells ☎ 01892/512700

American Holidays Belfast ☎ 028/9031 0000; Dublin ☎ 01/679 8800

Bon Voyage Southampton ☎ 023/8024 8248

British Airways Holidays *www.baholidays.co.uk*. Crawley ☎ 0870/242 4245

Destination USA *www.destination-group.com*. London ☎ 020/7400 7000

Dragoman *www.dragoman.co.uk*. Stowmarket ☎ 01728/861133

Explore Worldwide *www.explore.co.uk*. Aldershot ☎ 01252/760000

Greyhound International *www.greyhound.com*. East Grinstead ☎ 01342/317317

North America Travel Service Leeds ☎ 0113/246 1466

Trans Atlantic Vacations Horley ☎ 01293/789400

TrekAmerica *www.trekamerica.com*. Banbury ☎ 01295/256777

Unijet Haywards Heath ☎ 08705/114114

United Vacations Heathrow Airport ☎ 020/8313 0999

Virgin Holidays Crawley ☎ 01293/456789

can also search on the Net at sites like *www.travelscape.com*, *www.cheapflights.co.uk* and *www.lastminute.co.uk*.

Generally, the most expensive time to fly – **high season** – is from mid-June to the end of September, and around Easter and Christmas. Between March to mid-June and during October, **shoulder season** fares are slightly less pricey; the rest of the year is considered **low season** and is cheaper still. Check the exact dates of the seasons with your operator or airline; you might be able to make major savings by shifting your departure date by a week – or even a day. **Weekend rates** for all return flights tend to be around £30 more expensive than those in the week.

For an overview of the various offers, and of unofficially discounted tickets, go straight to an **agent** specializing in low-cost flights. Such agents may be able to knock up to thirty percent off the regular fares, especially if you're under 26 or a student. In low or shoulder season, you should be able to find a return flight to California, Las Vegas or Phoenix for under £300 – students may get closer to £200 – while high-season rates are more likely to be between £400 and £450.

With an **open-jaw** ticket you can fly into one city and out of another; fares are calculated by halving the return fares to each destination and adding the two figures together. Remember, however, the high **drop-off fee** for returning a rental car in a different state to the one where you picked it up (see p.19).

Packages

Packages can work out cheaper than arranging the same trip yourself, especially for a short-term stay. **Fly-drive** deals, which give cut-rate (sometimes free) car rental when buying a transatlantic ticket from an airline or tour operator, are always cheaper than renting on the spot and give great value if you intend to do a lot of driving. On the other hand, you'll probably have to pay more for the flight than if you booked it through a discount agent.

Several of the operators listed in the box on p.7 go one stage further and book accommodation for **self-drive tours**; some travelers consider having their itineraries planned and booked by experts to be a real boon. Bon Voyage, for example, arranges tailor-made packages in the Southwest; the cost of two weeks in Arizona, including the flight to Phoenix and standard hotels, ranges from £1000 per person in low season up to £1250 in high season. Schemes under which you buy **prepaid hotel vouchers** in advance, and then have to seek out hotels that will accept them, tend to be more bother than they're worth, and seldom save any money.

Companies such as TrekAmerica and AmeriCan Adventures organize **camping tours** of the Southwest, usually starting in California or Las Vegas, and circling through Utah's national parks and the Grand Canyon. Typical rates for a two-week trip – excluding flights – range from £600 in low season up to £750 in midsummer.

Entry requirements

Citizens of **Britain**, **Ireland** and most European countries in possession of full passports do not require **visas** for trips to the United States of less than ninety days. Instead, you are simply asked to fill in the **visa waiver form** handed out on incoming planes; immigration control takes place at your initial point of arrival on US soil. Visitors on the visa waiver scheme are entitled to cross the land border into Mexico and return to the US. For further details, contact the **American embassies** in Britain (5 Upper Grosvenor St, London W1A 1AE; ☎020/7499 9000; premium-rated visa information service ☎0891/200290; *www.usembassy.org.uk*), or Ireland (42 Elgin Rd, Ballsbridge, Dublin; ☎01/668 7122).

Rough Guides travel insurance

Rough Guides now offer their own travel insurance, customized for our readers by a leading UK broker and backed by a Lloyds underwriter. It's available for anyone, of any nationality, traveling anywhere in the world, and we are convinced that this is the best-value scheme you'll find.

There are two main Rough Guide insurance plans: **Essential**, for effective, no-frills cover, starting at £11.75 for 2 weeks; and **Premier** – more expensive but with more generous and extensive benefits. Each offer European or Worldwide cover, and can be supplemented with a "Hazardous Activities Premium" if you plan to indulge in sports considered dangerous, such as skiing, scuba-diving or trekking. Unlike many policies, the Rough Guides schemes are calculated by the day, so if you're traveling for 27 days rather than a month, that's all you pay for. You can alternatively take out annual multitrip insurance, which covers you for all your travel throughout the year (with a maximum of 60 days for any one trip). For a policy quote, call the Rough Guides Insurance Line on UK freefone ☎0800/015 0906, or, if you're calling from outside Britain on (+44) ☎1243/621046. Alternatively, get an online quote at *www.roughguides.com/insurance*.

There's a British **consulate** in the Southwest at 15249 N 59th Ave, Glendale, AZ 85306 (☎602/978-7200), and an Irish one at 6186 Squires Lane, Reno, NV 89509 (☎702/829-0221).

Insurance

Though not compulsory, **travel insurance** including medical cover is essential in view of the high costs of health care in the US. Credit cards (particularly American Express) often have certain levels of medical or other insurance

included, especially if you use them to pay for your trip; in addition, if you have a good "all risks" home insurance policy it may well cover your possessions against loss or theft even when overseas, and many private medical schemes also cover you while abroad. If you plan to participate in potentially dangerous activities such as watersports or skiing, you'll almost certainly have to pay an extra premium; check carefully that your policy will cover you in case of an accident.

Getting There from Australia and New Zealand

There are no direct flights from Australia or New Zealand to any of the Southwestern cities, so you'll have to fly to one of the main US gateway airports and pick up onward connections – or a rental car – from there.

The cheapest route, and the one with the most frequent services from Australia and New Zealand, is to **Los Angeles**, which also has plenty of onward flights to Phoenix, Las Vegas, Salt Lake City and Albuquerque. Air New Zealand and Qantas fly to LA at least twice daily, while

United fly once a day; other airlines that serve LA include America West and Japan Airlines.

Fares and tickets

Whatever kind of ticket you're after, start by calling one of the travel agents listed overleaf for the latest fares and special offers. If you're a student or under 26, you may be able to undercut some of the prices given here; STA is a good place to start.

The most expensive time to fly, peak season, is during the northern summer (mid-May to end Aug) and over the Christmas period (Dec to mid-Jan); shoulder seasons cover March to mid-May and September, while the rest of the year is low season. Exact dates vary slightly between the airlines, so it's worth shopping around, especially if you have the flexibility to change your departure date by a day or two.

Los Angeles is the main US gateway airport for flights from Australia; when they have surplus capacity, airlines frequently offer special fares to LA, which can be as low as A$1499 from the eastern states. Otherwise, the best you're likely to find are the regular Air New Zealand, Qantas and United flights: low-season return fares to LA cost around A$1599 from the eastern states, rising to A$1629 from Western Australia; flying during

AIRLINES

	Sydney	Auckland
Air New Zealand *www.airnz.co.nz*	☎ 13 2476	☎ 09/357 3000
America West Airlines *www.americawest.com*	☎ 02/9290 2232	
American Airlines *www.aa.com*	☎ 1300/650 747	☎ 0800/887 997
British Airways *www.british-airways.com*	☎ 02/8904 8800	☎ 09/356 8690
Japan Airlines *www.jal.com*	☎ 02/9272 1111	☎ 09/379 3202
Qantas *www.qantas.com.au*	☎ 13 1313	☎ 0800/808 767
United Airlines *www.ual.com*	☎ 13 1777	☎ 09/379 3800

peak season will add at least another A$500. Fares from New Zealand start at NZ$1799.

If you want to cover a lot of ground in a short time, US **air passes** can be a worthwhile add-on. America West's Tri-State Pass, available in conjunction with any international ticket, is valid for travel within California, Nevada and Arizona only; two coupons (the minimum purchase) cost approximately A$250 (prices fluctuate with the exchange rate), and additional coupons (up to a maximum of nine) cost A$85.

Packages and tours

Package deals available to travelers in Australia and New Zealand range from fly-drive deals to fully escorted bus tours and camping treks, and can work out significantly cheaper than making the same arrangements yourself; some of the no-frills flight and car-rental packages, for example, can cost less than a flight alone. Insight's eight-day "West Coast" **bus tour** costs A$1180, while tours from Creative Holidays start at A$1750 for seven days, including all your accommodation, but excluding flights.

Specialist **hotel** and **camping tours** for small groups can get you further off the beaten track. TrekAmerica offers several itineraries ranging from one to three weeks; its ten-day "Wild West" tour, starting and ending in LA, takes in Death

---

TRAVEL AGENTS AND TOUR OPERATORS IN AUSTRALIA AND NEW ZEALAND

Anywhere Travel *anywhere@ozemail.com.au* Sydney ☎ 02/9663 0411

Budget Travel Auckland ☎ 09/366 0061 or 0800/808 040

Destinations Unlimited Auckland ☎ 09/373 4033

Flight Centres Sydney ☎ 13 1600; Auckland ☎ 09/358 4310

Northern Gateway *www.norgate.com.au* Darwin ☎ 08/8941 1394

STA Travel *www.statravel.com.au*. Nearest branch in Australia ☎ 13 1776; fastfare telesales ☎ 1300/360 960; Auckland ☎ 09/309 0458; fastfare telesales ☎ 09/366 6673

Thomas Cook Nearest branch in Australia ☎ 13 1771; direct telesales ☎ 1800/801 002; Auckland ☎ 09/379 3920

SPECIALIST AGENTS

Adventure Specialists Sydney ☎ 02/9261 2927

Adventure Travel Company Auckland ☎ 09/379 9755

Adventure World Sydney ☎ 02/9956 7766; direct telesales ☎ 1800/221 931; Auckland ☎ 09/524 5118

Canada & America Travel Specialists Sydney ☎ 02/9922 4600

Creative Holidays Sydney ☎ 02/9386 2111

Insight Sydney ☎ 02/9512 0767

Peregrine *www.peregrine.net.au*. Melbourne ☎ 03/9662 2700

Qantas Holidays book through travel agents (see above)

TrekAmerica book through STA (see above)

Wiltrans Sydney ☎ 02/9255 0899

Valley, Las Vegas and the Grand Canyon, and costs from A$944/NZ$1170, excluding flights.

Entry requirements

Australian and New Zealand citizens who have full passports do not require **visas** for trips to the United States of less than ninety days; simply fill in the **visa waiver form** handed out on incoming planes. Immigration control takes place at your initial point of arrival on US soil. Visitors on the visa waiver scheme are also entitled to cross the land border into Mexico and return to the US. For further details, contact the **American embassies** in Australia (21 Moonah Place, Canberra; ☎02/6270 5000; premium-rated visa informa-tion service; ☎1902/262 682) or New Zealand (29 Fitzherbert Terrace, Thorndon, Wellington; ☎04/472 2068).

The closest Australian **consulate** to the Southwest is at 2049 Century Park E, Los Angeles, CA 90067 (☎310/229-4800). New Zealand has one at 12400 Wilshire Blvd, Los Angeles, CA 90025 (☎310/207-1605).

Travel insurance

A typical **insurance policy** for travel in the United States costs A$130/NZ$145 for two weeks, A$190/NZ$210 for a month, and A$280/NZ$310 for two months. For details of Rough Guides' own policies, see p.8.

Information and Maps

Each state covered in this book has its own tourist office, accessible online as well as by phone or mail, which can provide prospective visitors with a colossal range of free maps, leaflets and brochures. Contact them in advance of your departure, and be as specific as possible about your interests.

Visitor centers in most towns – often known as the "Convention and Visitors Bureau", or CVB, and listed throughout this book – provide details on the area. Most also have their own Web presence, usually with extensive links to local busi-nesses and attractions. In cities such as Las Vegas, Phoenix and Santa Fe, **free newspapers** carry dining and entertainment listings. In addition, you're likely to come across the useful **Welcome Centers**, along the interstates close to the state borders, which dispense maps and information on the entire state. For details on national and state parks, and other public lands, see p.21.

The **USTTA** – United States Travel and Tourism Administration – has offices all over the world, usually in US embassies and consulates. These serve mainly as clearing houses, stocking vast quantities of printed material, but are unable to help with queries on specific states or cities. In Britain, you can only contact them by telephone, on ☎020/7495 4466 (Mon–Fri 10am–4pm).

Maps

By far the best general-purpose **map** for the principal areas covered by this book is the *Guide to Indian Country*, available free to members of the American Automobile Association (see p.19), and sold throughout the Southwest at $3.95. It focuses on the Four Corners region, however, and does not extend into southern Arizona, southern New Mexico, or Nevada. Each individual state also issues a free **highway map**, which

STATE TOURIST OFFICES

STATE TOURIST OFFICES

Arizona Office of Tourism 2702 N Third St, Suite 4015, Phoenix, AZ 85004; ☎602/230-7733 or 1-800/842-8257, fax 602/542-4068; *www.arizonaguide.com*.

Colorado Tourism Board 1625 Broadway, Suite 1700, Denver, CO 80202; ☎303/592-5510 or 1-800/433-2656; *www.colorado.com*.

Nevada Commission on Tourism Capitol Complex, Carson City, NV 89710; ☎702/687-

4322 or 1-800/638-2328, fax 702/687-6779; *www.travelnevada.com*.

New Mexico State Tourism 491 Old Santa Fe Trail, Santa Fe, NM 87501; ☎505/827-4000 or 1-800/545-2040; *www.newmexico.org*.

Utah Travel Council Council Hall, Capitol Hill, Salt Lake City, UT 84114; ☎801/538-1030 or 1-800/200-1160, fax 801/538-1399; *www.utah.com*.

is fine for general driving and route planning, and can be obtained either direct from the tourist office or from local visitor centers. Free **town maps** are generally available at local visitor centers.

All **national parks**, and most state parks, national forests and the like – as detailed on p.21 – provide reasonable maps to visitors. Both these, and the maps throughout this book, are adequate for day-hikes on the most popular trails. Serious hikers and backpackers, however, should equip themselves with detailed **topographical maps**. Among the best are the waterproof and tearproof maps of individual national parks published by Trails Illustrated (PO Box 4357, Evergreen, CO 80437; ☎303/670-3457 or 1-800/962-1643; *www.trailsillustrated.com*), who

also produce state maps of Colorado, Utah and New Mexico.

Rand McNally produce good **commercial maps**, bound together in their *Rand McNally Road Atlas*, or printed separately for each state. They also run 24 stores across the US; call ☎1-800/333-0136 (ext 2111) or look on the Net (*www.randmcnally.com*) for their locations, or for direct mail maps. Britain's best source of maps is Stanfords, at 12–14 Long Acre, London WC2E 9LP (☎020/7836 1321; *www.stanfords.co.uk*), who have a mail-order service.

In **Australia**, try the Travel Bookshop, 3/175 Liverpool St, Sydney, NSW 2000 (☎02/9261 8200); the best resource in **New Zealand** is Specialty Maps, 58 Albert St, Auckland (☎09/307 2217).

Costs and Money

This book contains detailed price information for lodging and eating throughout the Southwest. Accommodation rates are coded according to the system explained on p.15, which excludes any local taxes that may apply, while restaurant prices include food only and not drinks or tip. For museums and similar attractions, the entrance fees quoted are for adults; unless specified otherwise, assume that children get in half-price. Naturally, costs will increase slightly overall during the life of this edition.

Costs

North American travelers find **prices** in the Southwest broadly similar to the rest of the US, with food and lodging generally cheaper than in major US cities and tourist regions, and gas and groceries, especially in out-of-the-way places, a little more expensive. Most visitors from Europe and Australasia feel that their money goes further in the US than it does at home. However, if you're used to traveling in the less expensive countries of Europe, let alone in the rest of the world, you can't expect to scrape by on the same minuscule budget in the US.

As explained on p.18, the only way to reach most of the places described in this book is to drive. If you can't bring your own vehicle, your least avoidable major expense will be **car rental**,

at around $150 per week. What you spend on **accommodation** is more flexible. For most of the year, in most places, you should have no problem getting a motel room for under $50, though even the cheapest peak-season rates in or near certain national parks, or in downtown Santa Fe, are more like $75. Although **hostels** offering dorm beds – usually for $12 to $15 – are reasonably common, they're by no means everywhere, and in any case they save little money for two or more people traveling together. **Camping** is not only cheap, with federal and state park campgrounds ranging from free to perhaps $12 per night, but for many wilderness areas it's the only option.

As for **food**, $20 per day is enough to get an adequate life-support diet, consisting of perhaps one full-scale meal in a local diner supplemented by a stash of groceries, while for a daily total of around $30 you can eat pretty well. If you're visiting a significant number of **national parks** and monuments, buy a National Parks pass (see p.21); the $50 fee covers all passengers in your vehicle. You'll probably also average another $5 or $10 a day on admissions to state parks, museums and the like.

The most economical possible vacation, therefore, with two people sharing a rental car, camping in state and federal parks most nights, and eating one restaurant meal per day, will work out at a minimum of $250 per person per week.

For advice on **tipping** and **taxes**, see p.26 and p.33.

Taking, changing and accessing money

Expect to pay most of your major expenses by **credit or debit card**; hotels and car rental agencies usually demand a credit card imprint as security, even if you intend to settle the bill in cash, and you'll be at a serious disadvantage if you don't have one. Visa, MasterCard, Diners Club, American Express and Discover are the most widely used.

You'll also need to carry a certain amount of **cash**. If you have a MasterCard or Visa, or a cash-dispensing card linked to an international network such as Cirrus or Plus – check with your

Money: A Note for Foreign Travelers

US currency comes in bills of $1, $5, $10, $20, $50 and $100, plus various larger (and rarer) denominations. All are the same size and same green color, making it necessary to check each bill carefully. The dollar is made up of 100 cents in coins of 1 cent (known as a penny), 5 cents (a nickel), 10 cents (a dime) and 25 cents (a quarter); there's also a gold one-dollar coin. Change – especially quarters – is needed for buses, vending machines and telephones, so always carry plenty.

Generally speaking, one **pound sterling** will buy between $1.50 and $1.70; one **Canadian dollar** is worth between 70¢ and 90¢; one **Australian dollar** is worth between 70¢ and 80¢; and one **New Zealand dollar** is worth between 60¢ and 70¢.

home bank before you set off – you can withdraw cash from appropriate automatic teller machines (**ATMs**). For both American and foreign visitors, **US dollar travelers' checks** are a better way to carry money than ordinary bills; they offer the great security of knowing that lost or stolen checks will be replaced. Checks issued by American Express, Visa and Thomas Cook are universally accepted as cash in shops, restaurants and gas stations, and change from your transactions will be rendered in hard currency. Be sure to have plenty of $10 and $20 denominations, and don't be put off by "no checks" signs, which only refer to personal checks. Foreign travelers should *not* bring travelers' checks issued in their own currencies; it can be hard to find a bank prepared to change them, and no other business is likely to accept them.

Emergencies

Assuming you know someone who is prepared to send you money in a crisis, the quickest way is to have them take the cash to the nearest **American Express** office and have it instantaneously **wired** to the office nearest you, by means of a **Moneygram**. In the US this process should take no longer than ten minutes; call ☎1-800/543-4080 to locate the closest outlet. American Express charge according to the amount sent (ranging from $12 to wire $100, to $66 for $1000). The fees are slightly different if the money is being sent from outside the US (from the UK, for example, it costs $20 to wire $100, and $50 to wire $1000). **Western Union** offers a similar service, at slightly higher rates (US ☎1-800/325-6000; UK ☎0800/833833; Ireland ☎1800/395395; Australia ☎1800/649 565; New Zealand ☎0800/270 000); if credit cards are involved they charge an extra $10.

If you have a few days' leeway, it's cheaper to mail a **postal money order**, which is exchangeable at any post office. The equivalent for foreign travelers is the **international money order**, for which you need to allow up to seven days in the mail before arrival. An ordinary check sent from overseas takes two to three weeks to clear.

Foreign travelers in real difficulties also have the final option of throwing themselves on the mercy of their nearest national consulate, who will – in worst cases only – repatriate you, but will never, under any circumstances, lend money.

To report stolen traveler's checks and credit cards, call:

American Express checks	☎1-800/221-7282
American Express cards	☎1-800/528-4800
Citicorp	☎1-800/645-6556
Diners Club	☎1-800/234-6377
MasterCard	☎1-800/826-2181
Thomas Cook/ MasterCard	☎1-800/223-9920
Visa checks	☎1-800/227-6811
Visa cards	☎1-800/336-8472

Accommodation

For advice on **camping**, see the "Outdoors" section beginning on p.21.

On the whole, accommodation in the Southwest is relatively inexpensive. Most travelers simply want a bed for the night before moving on the next day, so motels everywhere provide clean, no-frills places to sleep without bothering to offer additional amenities. Basic room rates in rural areas start as low as $30 per night, while prices along the principal highways and interstates tend to range upwards from $45. Only in the most popular summer destinations – cities such as Santa Fe, or "gateway" towns near the major national parks – will you find it hard to get a room for under $60. If you prefer a bit more comfort, it's almost always available, and in most areas covered by this book you can get a room in a top-class hotel for under $100.

At the lower end of the spectrum, a fair number of budget **hostels** are scattered across the region, though with a single dorm bed usually costing between $12 and $15, groups of two or more will find them little cheaper than motels. Many motel rooms hold two double beds, and will accommodate three or four guests for slightly over the normal two-person rate. On the other hand, the lone traveler has a hard time of it: a "single" room is just a double at a fractionally reduced rate.

Wherever you stay, you'll be expected to pay in advance, at least for the first night and perhaps for further nights too. Most places ask for a credit card imprint when you arrive, but they'll also accept cash or dollar traveler's checks. Reservations – essential in busy areas in summer – are only held until 5pm or 6pm unless you've warned the hotel you'll be arriving late.

Hotels and motels

It is consistently easy to find a basic **motel** room in the Southwest. Drivers approaching any significant town are confronted by lines of motels along the highway, while the choice along major cross-country routes is phenomenal. Most of the towns mentioned in this book hold more motels than there's room to review; the very few that have none at all are clearly indicated.

Hotels and **motels** are essentially the same thing, although motels tend to be located beside main roads away from city centers, and thus are much more accessible to drivers. The budget ones are pretty basic affairs, but in general there's a uniform standard of comfort everywhere – each room

---

ACCOMMODATION PRICE CODES

Throughout this book, **room rates** in hotels, motels and B&Bs are indicated with the symbols below, according to the cost of their least expensive double rooms, **excluding taxes**, which can add between five and fifteen percent. Significant seasonal variations are indicated as appropriate, as are establishments that hold rooms at widely differing prices. The cheapest price code, ①, is also used to indicate hostels which offer individual dorm beds, in which cases specific rates are also included.

① up to $30	④ $60–80	⑦ $130–175
② $30–45	⑤ $80–100	⑧ $175–250
③ $45–60	⑥ $100–130	⑨ $250+

HOTEL, HOSTEL AND MOTEL CHAINS

Best Western (③–⑥) *www.bestwestern.com*	☎ 1-800/528-1234	**Howard Johnson** (②–④) *www.hojo.com*	☎ 1-800/446-4656
Comfort Inns (③–⑤) *www.hotelchoice.com*	☎ 1-800/221-2222	**La Quinta Inns** (④) *www.laquinta.com*	☎ 1-800/531-5900
Days Inn (③–⑤) *www.daysinn.com*	☎ 1-800/329-7466	**Marriott Hotels** (⑥ and up) *www.marriott.com*	☎ 1-800/228-9290
Econolodge (②–④) *www.econolodge.com*	☎ 1-800/424-4777	**Motel 6** (②) *www.motel6.com*	☎ 1-800/466-8356
Fairfield Inns (④/⑤) *www.marriott.com*	☎ 1-800/228-2800	**Ramada Inns** (④ and up) *www.ramada.com*	☎ 1-800/272-6232
Hampton Inns (④/⑤) *www.hampton-inn.com*	☎ 1-800/426-7866	**Sleep Inn** (③) *www.sleepinn.com*	☎ 1-800/627-5337
Hilton Hotels (⑤ and up) *www.hilton.com*	☎ 1-800/445-8667	**Super 8** (②–④) *www.super8motels.com*	☎ 1-800/800-8000
Holiday Inns (③ and up) *www.holiday-inn.com*	☎ 1-800/465-4329	**Travelodge** (②–③) *www.travelodge.com*	☎ 1-800/578-7878
Hosteling International – American Youth **Hostels** (①) *www.hiayh.org*	☎ 1-800/909-4776	**YMCA** (②–③) *www.ymca.net*	☎ 212/308-2899

comes with a double bed, a TV, a phone to which it's usually possible to hook up a computer, and an attached bathroom – and you don't get a much better deal by paying, say, $65 instead of $45. Over $65 or so, the room and its fittings simply get bigger and more luxurious, and there'll probably be a swimming pool which guests can use for free.

The very cheapest properties tend to be family-run, independent motels, but there's a lot to be said for paying a few dollars more to stay in motels belonging to the national **chains**. After a few days on the road, you should find that a particular chain consistently suits your requirements (Super 8 is a personal recommendation). You can then use its central reservation number, listed above, to book ahead, and possibly obtain discounts as a regular guest.

During off-peak periods many motels and hotels struggle to fill their rooms, and it's worth haggling to get a few dollars off the asking price. Staying in the same place for more than one night will bring further reductions. Additionally, look out for **discount coupons**, especially in the free magazines distributed by local visitor centers and interstate welcome centers. These can offer amazing value – $30 for a double room in a comfortable mid-range chain – but read the small print, as rates are often limited to midweek.

Not many budget hotels or motels bother to compete with the ubiquitous diners and offer **breakfast**, although many provide free self-service coffee and sticky buns.

Bed and breakfasts

Over the last couple of decades, **bed and breakfast** has become an ever more popular option, often as a luxurious – if not necessarily any more expensive – alternative to conventional hotels. Some B&Bs consist of no more than a couple of furnished rooms in someone's home, and even the larger establishments tend to have no more than ten rooms, without TV and phone but often laden with flowers, stuffed cushions and an almost over-contrived homely atmosphere.

The price you pay for a B&B – which varies from around $50 to $130 – always includes a huge and wholesome breakfast. The crucial determining factor is whether or not each room has an en-suite bathroom; most B&Bs feel obliged to provide private bath facilities, although that can damage the authenticity of a fine old house. Those that do tend to cost between $60 and $80 per night for a double. At the top end of the price spectrum, the distinction between a "hotel" and a "bed and breakfast inn" may amount to no more than that the B&B is owned by a private individual rather than a chain.

many areas, B&Bs have grouped together to form central **booking agencies**, making it much easier to find a room at short notice; we've given addresses and numbers for these where appropriate. Statewide organizations include the Arizona Association of B&B Inns (PO Box 7186, Phoenix, AZ 85011; ☎1-800/284-2589; *www.arizona-bandbs .com*); B&B Inns of Utah (PO Box 3066, Park City, UT 84060; ☎435/645-8068; *www.bbiu.org*); and the New Mexico B&B Association (PO Box 2925, Santa Fe, NM 87504-2925; ☎505/766-5380 or 1-800/661-6649; *www.nmbba.org*). In addition, B&B business has been booming since the advent of the **Internet**; simple searches will usually throw up a myriad of possibilities.

Ys and youth hostels

Around twenty **hostels** provide accommodation for backpackers and budget travelers in the Southwest. Most work out little cheaper than motels, so there's little point staying in hostels unless you prefer their youthful ambience and sociability. Note also that many are not accessible on public transport, or particularly convenient for sightseeing in the towns and cities, let alone in rural areas.

Hostels belonging to the official **HI-AYH** (Hosteling International–American Youth Hostels) network tend to impose curfews and limited daytime hours, and segregate dormitories by sex. Most expect guests to bring sheets or sleeping bags. Rates range from $10 up to around $15 for HI members; nonmembers generally pay an additional $3 per night.

There's also a growing number of **independent hostels**, of which some may have failed to meet

the HI's (fairly rigid) criteria, but most simply choose not to be tied down by HI regulations. Many are no more than converted motels, where the "dorms" consist of a couple of sets of bunk beds in a musty room, which is also let out as a private unit on demand; others may be purpose-built rural properties, or at least converted and modernized to a high standard.

In addition, **YMCA/YWCA** hostels (known as "Ys"), provide mixed-sex or, in a few cases, women-only accommodation, at prices ranging from around $12 for a dormitory bed to $20–35 for a single or double room. Ys offering accommodation (and many do not, being basically health clubs) are often in older buildings in less than ideal neighborhoods, but facilities can include a gym, a swimming pool and an inexpensive cafeteria.

Especially in high season, it's advisable to **reserve ahead** by writing to the relevant hostel and enclosing a deposit. The maximum stay is often restricted to three days, though this rule tends to be ignored if there's space. Few hostels provide meals but most have cooking facilities. Bear in mind that as the accommodation price codes used in this book relate to the least expensive double room in each establishment, we have given prices as well as codes for hostels throughout.

All the information in this book was accurate at the time of going to press; however, youth hostels are often shoestring organizations, prone to changing address or closing down altogether. Similarly, new ones appear each year; check the noticeboards of other hostels for news. The *Hostel Handbook for the USA and Canada*, produced each May, lists over four hundred hostels

OUTHWEST YOUTH HOSTELS

Southwest Youth Hostels

Albuquerque, NM	p.174	Phoenix, AZ	p.220
Antonito, CO	p.163	Pilar, NM	p.139
Cedar Crest, NM	p.125	Salt Lake City, UT	p.511
Cuba, NM	p.132	Santa Fe, NM	p.105
Durango, CO	p.76	Sedona, AZ	p.297
Flagstaff, AZ	p.286	Silver City, NM	p.208
Hurricane, UT	p.372	Silverton, CO	p.77
Kanab, UT	p.392	Taos, NM	p.150
Las Vegas, NV	p.494	Torrey, UT	p.418
Moab, UT	p.466	Truth or Consequences, NM	p.204
Oscuro, NM	p.187	Tucson, AZ	p.238
Page, AZ	p.432	Williams, AZ	p.311

ACCOMMODATION

17

and is available for $3 from Jim Williams, *Sugar Hill International House Hostel*, 722 St Nicholas Ave, New York, NY 10031 (☎212/926-7030; *www.hostelhandbook.com*). *Hosteling North America*, the HI guide to hostels in the USA and Canada, is available free of charge to any overnight guest at HI-AYH hostels, or direct from the HI National Office, 733 15th St NW, Suite 840, Washington, DC 20005 (☎202/783-6161; *www.hiayh.org*).

Overseas travelers will find a comprehensive list of hostels in the *International Youth Hostel Handbook*. In the **UK**, it's available from the Youth Hostel Association (YHA), Trevelyan House, 8 St Stephen's Hill, St Albans, Herts AL1 2DY (☎01727/855215; *www.yha.org.uk*), from whom annual HI membership costs £9.50 (under-18s £3).

In **Australia**, membership fees are A$49 (under-18s A$15). The office is at 11 Rawson Place, Sydney, NSW 2000 (☎02/9281 9444; *www.yha.org.au*). Adult New Zealanders pay NZ$40, but membership for under-18s is free; contact PO Box 436, Christchurch (☎03/379 9970; *www.yha.org.nz*).

Getting Around

Attempting to tour the Southwest by public transport is an extremely bad idea. While buses and planes – and trains to a much lesser extent – connect the major urban areas, the national parks and wide-open landscapes that are the region's greatest attractions simply cannot be explored without your own vehicle. Even public transport within the cities is minimal. Unless you're an *extremely* energetic cyclist, therefore, you'll need a motorbike or car.

If you can't drive, the only itinerary that makes much sense is to cross northern Arizona and northern New Mexico by bus or train, flying in or out of **Albuquerque** in the east or **Las Vegas** in the west. Obvious stops would include **Flagstaff**, with a side-trip by bus to the Grand Canyon, and **Santa Fe**, the only city small enough to be seen on foot. Phoenix and Tucson are no fun at all without a car, while what little public transport exists in southern Utah is no use for seeing the parks. **Hitchhiking** is not recommended under any circumstances.

By car

To **rent** a car, you're supposed to have held your licence for at least one year; drivers under 25 years old may encounter problems, and have to pay higher than normal insurance premiums. Rental companies expect customers to have credit cards; if you don't, they may let you leave a cash deposit (at least $200), but don't count on it.

All the major rental companies have outlets at the main regional airports. Reservations are handled centrally rather than locally, so calling their national toll-free numbers is the best way to shop around for **rates**. Potential variations are endless; certain cities and states are consistently cheaper than others, while individual travelers may be eligible for corporate, frequent-flier or AAA discounts. In low season, you might find a tiny car (a "subcompact") for as little as $100 per week, but a typical budget rate would be more like $35–40 per day, and $150 per week. A car rented in Las Vegas, Nevada, can easily cost $100 less per week than one rented in Colorado, and prices in Arizona, New Mexico and Utah are ranged between the two.

Don't automatically go for the cheapest rate. Little-known local rental companies may offer appealing prices, but if you break down several hundred miles from their offices it may be hard to get assistance. Even between the major operators, there can be a big difference in the quality of cars.

Industry leaders like Hertz and Avis tend to have newer, lower-mileage cars, often with air-conditioning and stereo cassette decks as standard equipment – no small consideration on a 3000-mile desert drive. Always be sure to get free **unlimited mileage**, and remember that leaving the car in a different city to the one where you rent it can incur a drop-off charge of as much as $200.

When you rent a car, read the small print carefully for details on **Collision Damage Waiver** (CDW), sometimes called Liability Damage Waiver (LDW), a form of insurance which often isn't included in the initial rental charge but is well worth considering. This specifically covers the car that you are driving yourself; you are in any case insured for damage to other vehicles. At $10–15 a day, it can add substantially to the total cost, but without it you're liable for every scratch to the car – even those that aren't your fault. Some credit card companies offer automatic CDW coverage to anyone using their card; contact your issuing company for details.

Your rental papers should include an emergency number to call in case of breakdown or accident; contact the rental company before you arrange, or pay, for any repairs. Women in particular should also consider renting a **mobile telephone** with their car – you often only have to pay a nominal amount until you actually use it, and it can be a lifesaver should something go terribly wrong.

The **American Automobile Association**, or AAA (4100 E Arkansas Drive, Denver, CO 80222; ☎1-800/222-4357; *www.aaa.com*), provides free maps and assistance to its members, and to members of affiliated associations overseas, such as the British AA and RAC.

Renting an RV

RVs, or Recreational Vehicles – can be rented at prices which start at around $400 per week (plus mileage charges) for a basic camper on the back of a pickup truck, with sleeping room for two adults. If you're looking for one of those huge juggernauts that rumble down the highway complete with multiple bedrooms, bathrooms and kitchens, you'll have to pay at least double that rate. Though good for groups or families traveling together, RVs can be unwieldy on the road, and as people tend to own their own, rental outlets are not as common as you might expect. On top

of rental fees, you'll also have to take into account the cost of gas (some RVs do twelve miles to the gallon or less) and any drop-off charges. It's rarely legal simply to pull up in an RV and spend the night at the roadside; you are expected to stay in designated parks that cost up to $20 per night.

The Recreational Vehicle Dealers Association, 3251 Old Lee Highway, Fairfax, VA 22030 (☎703/591-7130 or 1-800/336-0355; *www.rvda.com*), publishes a newsletter and a directory of rental firms. Among the larger companies offering RV rentals are Cruise America (☎1-800/327-7799; *www.cruiseamerica.com*), Go! Vacations (☎1-800/845-9888) and Grand Travel Systems (☎602/939-6909 or 1-877/478-7368).

Driving for foreigners

Foreign nationals from English-speaking countries – which includes UK, Irish, Australian and New Zealand citizens – can drive in the US using their full domestic **driving licences** (International Driving Permits are not always regarded as sufficient). Fly-drive deals are good value if you want to rent a car (see pp.8 & 10), though you can save up to sixty percent simply by booking in advance with a major firm. If you choose not to pay until you arrive, be sure you take a written confirmation of the price with you. Remember that most standard rental cars have automatic transmissions, and that it's safer not to drive immediately after a long transatlantic flight.

It's also easier and cheaper to book **RVs** in advance from Britain. Most travel agents who specialize in the US can arrange RV rental, and usually do it cheaper if you book a flight through them as well. A price of £400 for a five-berth van for two weeks is fairly typical.

Buying a **secondhand car**, and selling it at the end of your trip, might sound like a money-saving idea. Quite apart from finding a reliable vehicle, however, registering and insuring it is a complicated and expensive business. Each state has different regulations; contact the AAA for details.

By bike

While riding a bike in the Southwest can be absolutely exhilarating, long-distance cyclists face a fearsome challenge, above all in the heat of summer. Neighboring towns can be as much as a hundred miles apart, along desert highways that offer neither food, water nor shade. Quite

---

For advice on **driving in the desert**, see p.24.

CAR RENTAL COMPANIES			
	USA	**UK**	**Australia**
Alamo *www.goalamo.com*	☎1-800/354-2322	☎0800/272200	
Avis *www.avis.com*	☎1-800/331-1212	☎08705/900500	☎1-800/225 533
Budget *www.drivebudget.com*	☎1-800/527-0700	☎0800/181181	☎13 2727
Dollar *www.dollar.com*	☎1-800/800-6000	☎01895/233300	
Enterprise *www.enterprise.com*	☎1-800/325-8007		
Hertz *www.hertz.com*	☎1-800/654-3131	☎08705/996699	☎13 3039
Holiday Autos *www.kemwel.com*	☎1-800/422-7737	☎08705/300400	
National *www.nationalcar.com*	☎1-800/227-7368	☎08705/365365	
Rent-a-Wreck *www.rent-a-wreck.com*	☎1-800/535-1391		
Thrifty *www.thrifty.com*	☎1-800/367-2277	☎08705/168238	
US Rent-a-Car *www.us-rentacar.com*	☎1-800/777-9377		

apart from the high mountains and deep canyons, most areas covered in this book are a mile or more above sea level, so the altitude alone can be a real problem. The only road from A to B may well turn out to be a major interstate; when there's no alternative, cyclists are generally allowed to ride on interstate shoulders, but they have to battle the slipstream of mighty trucks.

> Commuter flights within the Southwest are detailed on p.5.

If you have a good bike and know how to maintain it, however, and time your trip for the cooler months, it is feasible to explore the Southwest by bike. Specific regions that lend themselves to **cycle touring** are north-central New Mexico, where countless routes radiate from Santa Fe; the vicinity of Flagstaff and Sedona in Arizona; and southwest Utah, around Zion National Park. Other areas have seen a recent boom in **mountain-biking**, such as Moab, Utah – home of the grueling Slickrock Bike Trail (see p.468) – and Durango, Colorado.

For general **information** and advice, contact the New Mexico Touring Society, 4115 12th St NW, Albuquerque, NM 87107 (☎505/298-0085), the Arizona Bicycle Club, PO Box 7191, Phoenix, AZ 85011 (☎602/264-5478), or ask the Utah Travel Council (see p.12) for a free *Bicycle Utah Vacation Guide*. The national, nonprofit **Adventure Cycling Association** (formerly Bikecentennial), at 150 E Pine St, Missoula, MT 59807 (☎406/721-1776; *www.adv-cycling*

.org), publishes maps ($10.50 each) of several 400-mile routes, detailing campgrounds, motels, restaurants, bike shops and sites of interest. Their Southwest America Bicycle Trail runs from Yuma up to Flagstaff and the Grand Canyon, then crosses the Navajo and Hopi reservations to Gallup. Backroads Bicycle Tours, 1516 Fifth St, Berkeley, CA 94704 (☎510/527-1555 or 1-800/462-2848; *www.backroads.com*), and the HI-AYH hosteling group (see p.18) also arrange group tours.

Greyhound, Amtrak and major airlines all carry passengers' bicycles – dismantled and packed into a box – for a small additional fee.

By train

Details of the very limited Amtrak **rail service** to and across the Southwest appear on p.5. There are also a number of **historic** and **scenic rail-roads** in the region – some of them steam-powered or running along narrow-gauge mining tracks – including the Cumbres and Toltec line in northern New Mexico (see p.162); the Grand Canyon Railway between Williams and the Grand Canyon in northern Arizona (see p.325); the San Pedro and Southwestern Railroad in southern Arizona (see p.254); and the Durango & Silverton Narrow Gauge Railroad in Colorado (see p.75).

By bus

Greyhound buses link all major cities and many smaller towns in the Southwest; for fares, schedules and reservations, call ☎1-

800/231-2222, or access the Web site at *www.greyhound.com*. Routes that are particularly useful for tourists – as well as services offered by other operators – are detailed at the relevant points in this book.

While scheduled buses can get you from city to city, they're of no use when it comes to enjoying the great outdoors. **Tour buses**, however, do set off into the wilderness from most major towns; they too are detailed throughout this book.

Outdoors

Cut by deep canyons, coated by dense forests and capped by great mountains, the Southwest glories in some of the most fabulous wilderness areas in the United States.

By far the easiest way for visitors to enjoy this natural wonderland is to plot an itinerary that samples the countless **national, state and county parks**. These are not necessarily the most beautiful places of all – after all, some are simply lands that pioneer farmers, Indian tribes and mining corporations alike never bothered or managed to grab – but they do offer the campgrounds and hiking trails that make backcountry exploration possible even for the least experienced tourists.

National parks and monuments

The **National Park Service** (NPS) administers both national parks and national monuments monuments. However, it's sadly underfunded; in most instances, it doesn't even get to keep park entrance fees, which are absorbed into the general Federal treasury. In style and design, most of its visitor centers and other facilities still date conspicuously from the 1950s. Nonetheless, park rangers do a superb job of providing information and advice to visitors, maintaining trails and organizing such activities as free guided hikes and campfire talks.

For up-to-the-minute information on the national park system, access the official National Park Service **Web site** at *www.nps.gov*. It features full details of national parks and monuments, including opening hours, the best times to visit, admission fees, hiking trails and visitor facilities.

Most parks and monuments charge an admission fee of between $4 and $20, which covers a vehicle and all its occupants for up to a week. They also sell the **Golden Eagle pass**, which for $65 gives a named driver, and all passengers in the same vehicle, a year's unlimited access to (almost) all public lands in the country, and the $50 **National Parks Pass**, which covers national parks and monuments only and should be sufficient for most users of this guide. Separate passes are available for disabled travelers and senior citizens – see p.32 and p.33 respectively.

In theory, a **national park** preserves an area of outstanding natural beauty, encompassing a wide range of terrain as well as sites of historic interest, while a **national monument** is much smaller, focusing perhaps on just one archeological site or geological phenomenon and thus holding a narrower appeal for tourists. In practice, however, the distinction between the Southwest's national parks and national monuments is somewhat blurred. Most of the **parks** cover desert regions that have barely known human occupation, and thus boast little historic significance, and while the **Grand Canyon** and **Zion** are huge and very varied, parks such as **Bryce Canyon** and **Carlsbad Caverns** are essentially one-trick wonders. Many of the **monuments** do consist of a single Indian ruin or nineteenth-century fort, but several more are as diverse and spectacular as the parks. Arizona's **Canyon de Chelly** would surely be a national park were it not on the Navajo reservation, while the new **Grand Staircase-Escalante** monument in Utah is larger than any park.

Hotel-style **lodges** are found only in the major parks – specifically, the Grand Canyon, Zion,

Adventure Travel

The opportunities for **active traveling** in the Southwest are all but endless. In the last few years, the former uranium mining town of **Moab**, Utah, has grown to become the region's major base for adventure travel of all kinds. Mountain biking is its specialty, with rafting and four-wheel-driving (universally abbreviated to 4WD) as close rivals; full listings can be found on p.468. Other towns popular with energetic visitors include **Durango**, Colorado (see p.75) and **Sedona**, Arizona (see p.294); guides, outfitters and local tour operators are recommended throughout this book.

Bryce and Mesa Verde. However, both parks and monuments tend to offer at least one well-organized **campground**. With appropriate permits – subject to fees and number restrictions in popular parks – backpackers can also usually camp in the **backcountry** (a term for areas inaccessible by road, as opposed to the frontcountry).

While national parks tend to be perfect places to **hike** – almost all have extensive trail networks – they're all far too large to tour on foot. Canyonlands in Utah is an extreme example, with its different sections lying a hundred miles apart, but of all the parks in this book, only the Grand Canyon could conceivably be visited using **public transport**. If you don't have a vehicle of your own, your only option is to join a sightseeing tour from a nearby town.

Other public lands

National parks and monuments are often surrounded by tracts of **national forest**, which are also federally administered, but are much less protected. While these too tend to hold appealing rural campgrounds, each is in the words of the slogan a "Land Of Many Uses," and usually allows some limited logging and other land-based industry – ski resorts more often than strip mines, fortunately.

Further government departments administer a wildlife refuges, national scenic rivers, recreation areas and the like – such administration consisting basically of leaving the natural landscape alone. The **Bureau of Land Management** (BLM) has the largest holdings of all, most of it open rangeland, such as in Utah, but also including some enticingly out-of-the-way reaches.

State parks and state monuments are a mirror-image of the federal system, preserving sites of more limited, local significance. Many are explicitly designed for recreational use, and thus hold better campgrounds than their federal equivalents.

Camping and backpacking

The ideal way to see the Southwest – especially if you're on a low budget – is to tour the region by car, and **camp** at night in state and federal campgrounds. These may lack the luxury of the commercially run campgrounds, found in abundance near the larger towns, but they tend to be far more peaceful, far more scenic and far better positioned for days of hiking and canyoneering. Typical public campgrounds range in **price** from free (usually when there's no water available, which may be seasonal) to around $12 per night; commercial fees are more like $15–25, for campgrounds that can be more like open-air hotels, with shops, restaurants and washing facilities.

There may be plenty of campgrounds, but there are also plenty of people who want to use them: if you're camping during public holidays or the high season, you should either reserve in advance or avoid the most popular areas. By contrast, basic campgrounds in isolated areas may well be completely empty whatever time of year you're there, and if there's any charge at all you'll be expected to pay by leaving the money in the bin provided.

Backcountry camping in the national parks is usually free, by permit. Before you set off on anything more than a half-day hike, and whenever you're headed for anywhere at all isolated, be sure to inform a ranger of your plans, and ask about weather conditions and specific local tips. Carry sufficient food and drink to cover emergencies, as well as all the necessary equipment and maps. In summer in the national parks, you have to carry so much water – see p.24 – that you'll need to lighten your load as much as possible, perhaps by sleeping in a lightweight sack rather than a sleeping bag.

When camping rough, check that **fires** are permitted before you start one; even if they are, try to use a camp stove in preference to local materials – in some places firewood is scarce, although you may be allowed to use deadwood. In wilderness areas, try to camp on previously

CAMPING ON PUBLIC LANDS

Mailing and Web site addresses for individual **national parks** are given throughout this book. For more general maps, and information on camping on public lands, visit the Public Lands Information Center Web site (*www.publiclands.org*), which contains information on both BLM and forest-service lands, or the following organizations:

Arizona State Parks Office, 1300 W Washington, #150, Phoenix, AZ 85007; ☎620/542-4174; *www.pr.state.az.us.*

Bureau of Land Management Arizona State Office, 222 N Central Ave, Phoenix, AZ 85004; ☎602/417-9200

Bureau of Land Management New Mexico State Office, 1474 Rodeo Rd, Santa Fe, NM 87505; ☎505/438-7400

Bureau of Land Management Utah State Office, PO Box 45155, 324 S State St, #301, Salt Lake City, UT 84145-0155; ☎801/539-4001

National Forest Service, Southwest Regional Office, 517 Gold Ave SW, Albuquerque, NM 87102; ☎505/842-3898

National Forest Service Intermountain Regional Office, 324 25th St, Ogden, UT 84401; ☎801/625-5306

New Mexico State Parks Division, PO Box 1147, Santa Fe, NM 87504-1147; ☎505/827-7173; *www.emnrd.state.nm.us.*

Utah State Parks and Recreation, 1636 W North Temple, #116, Salt Lake City, UT 84116-3156; ☎801/538-7221

---

used sites. Where there are no toilets, bury human waste at least six inches into the ground and a hundred feet from the nearest water supply and campground. Burn what trash you can, and take the rest away.

Desert survival

If you plan to go **hiking in the desert**, it's crucial to plan ahead. Tell somebody where you are going, and write down all pertinent information, including your expected time of return. Carry an extra two days' food and water and never go anywhere without a map. Try to cover most of your ground in early morning: the midday heat is too debilitating, and you shouldn't even think about it when the mercury goes over 90°F.

Stick to official trails in the national parks, as described throughout this book, and you shouldn't face any serious **technical difficulties**. However, many trails are marked only by occasional stone cairns, and if your concentration starts to wander your feet may do so too. If you do get lost, try your utmost to retrace your steps; if that fails, find some shade and wait. As long as you've registered, the rangers will eventually come and fetch you. There are two good reasons not to try to blaze your own trail. The first is the **cryptobiotic crust** – what looks like a faint coating of dead moss on the sand is the building block on which all desert life depends, and merely treading on it has serious ecological con-

sequences. The other is the risk of becoming **rim-rocked**; picking your way across even a shallow gully, it's much easier to climb up than down, and you may well find yourself stuck above a drop you're unable to negotiate.

On a day-hike down into a **canyon**, allow more time to hike back up – when you're already tired, and the temperature is likely to be hotter – than you do to go down. Turn back after a third of your allotted time; if you plan a six-hour hike, reckon on two hours hiking down and four hours to hike up.

To stay cool during the day, wear full-length sleeves and trousers. Shorts and a vest will expose you to far too much sun – something you won't be aware of until it's too late. A wide-brimmed hat and a pair of good sunglasses will spare you the blinding headaches that can result from the desert light. You may also have to contend with flash floods, which can appear from nowhere: one innocent-looking dark cloud can turn a dry wash into a raging river. Never camp in a dry wash, and don't attempt to cross flooded areas until the water has receded.

Bear in mind too that much of the Southwest – such as the Colorado Plateau, home to the Grand Canyon and Utah's national parks – is more than a mile above sea level, and the **altitude** alone can impose severe demands on even the fittest of athletes. Be prepared for below-freezing temperatures at high elevations at night.

FLORA AND FAUNA ■

Water

It's essential to carry – and **drink** – large quantities of liquid in the desert. An eight-hour hike in typical summer temperatures of over 100°F would require you to drink a phenomenal **thirty pints** of water. Loss of appetite and thirst are early symptoms of heat exhaustion, so it's possible to become seriously dehydrated without feeling thirsty. Watch out for signs of dizziness or nausea, and if you feel weak and stop sweating, it's time to get to the doctor. You should always know whether water will be available on your chosen trail – park rangers keep abreast of the latest conditions – and carry at least a quart per person even if you do expect to be able to pick up more en route. Just to confuse things, there's also a risk of **water intoxication**, which can happen if you drink too much without eating; you must have regular snacks as well. Finally, watch your **alcohol** intake: if you must booze during the day, compensate heavily with pints of water between each drink.

Backpackers should never drink from rivers and streams, however clear and inviting they may look; you never know what unspeakable acts people – or animals – have performed further upstream. **Giardia** – a water-borne bacteria that causes an intestinal disease, characterized by chronic diarrhoea, abdominal cramps, fatigue and weight loss – is a serious problem. Water that doesn't come from a tap should be boiled for at least five minutes, or cleansed with an iodine-based purifier (such as Potable Aqua) or a Giardia-rated filter, available from any camping or sports store.

Insects and allergies

Mosquitoes and biting insects are rarely a problem in the Southwest, though in springtime you may encounter them near rivers in parks such as Zion. Avon Skin-so-soft handcream or anything containing DEET are fairly reliable repellents. **Ticks** – tiny beetles that plunge their heads into your skin and swell up – can be a hazard. They sometimes leave their heads inside, causing blood clots or infections, so get advice from a park ranger if you've been bitten.

Beware, too, of **poison oak**, an allergenic shrub that grows all over the western states, usually among oak trees. Its leaves come in groups of three and are distinguished by prominent veins and shiny surfaces. If you come into contact,

wash your skin (with soap and cold water) and clothes as soon as possible – and don't scratch. In serious cases, hospital emergency rooms can give antihistamine or adrenaline jabs.

Desert driving

Whenever you **drive** in the desert, be sure to have two gallons of water per person in the car. You should also carry flares, matches, a first-aid kit and a compass, plus a shovel, air pump and extra gas. If the car's engine **overheats**, don't turn it off; instead, try to cool the engine quickly by turning the front end towards the wind. Carefully pour some water on the front of the radiator, and turn the air conditioning off and heating up full blast. In an emergency, never panic and leave the car: you'll be harder to find wandering around alone.

Flora and fauna

Though the popular conception of the Southwest sees it as an arid wasteland, in fact it holds a broad spectrum of plant and animal life. Scientists divide the earth into "life zones" according to climate and distance from the equator, each of which holds a different assortment of species. In the Southwest, altitude substitutes for latitude; the higher the elevation, the cooler the temperature. Within the Grand Canyon alone, the range of habitat is equivalent to that experienced in a trip from the deserts of Mexico to the forests of the Canadian mountains.

It's the lowest, hottest level, the **Lower Sonoran** zone, that's home to the rattlesnakes and cactuses you're probably expecting. Southern Arizona is the obvious example, with its dramatic saguaro and organ-pipe cactuses, but a similar ecosystem can be found in the depths of the Grand Canyon.

By the time you reach a mile above sea level – the height of most of Utah's national parks – you're in the **Upper Sonoran** zone. This is characterized by smaller prickly pear cactuses and sagebrush, mammals such as rabbits and prairie dogs, and predators like coyotes and mountain lions (not that tourists are at all likely to encounter lions). Low rainfall results in a "pigmy forest" where gnarled, long-lived trees such as the piñon (also spelled pinyon) pine and Utah juniper grow to a maximum height of little more than twenty feet.

Around ten thousand feet up in the mountains of southern Colorado, northern New Mexico and cen-

Top Ten Southwest Hikes		
Mesa Arch Trail, Canyonlands National Park	one hour	p.446
Delicate Arch Trail, Arches National Park	two hours	p.460
White House Trail, Canyon de Chelly National Monument	two hours	p.55
Calf Creek Falls, Grand Staircase-Escalante National Monument	four hours	p.416
Betatakin Trail, Navajo National Monument	five hours	p.43
Horseshoe Canyon, Canyonlands National Park	five hours	p.449
Chesler Park Loop Trail, Canyonlands National Park	one day	p.454
West Rim Trail, Zion National Park	one day	p.383
Havasupai Indian Reservation	two days	p.342
Grand Gulch Primitive Area	one week	p.480

tral-southern Utah, the **Canadian** zone is even more densely forested, with Douglas firs joining the aspen and ponderosa, and bighorn sheep making an appearance in remoter areas. The Colorado Rockies, and Utah's Henry and La Sal ranges, rise higher still into the **Hudsonian** zone, between eleven and twelve thousand feet. Before the tree cover gives out altogether, ultra-resilient species such as the bristlecone pine, which can live for literally thousands of years, cling to the slopes.

The highest summits in the Southwest – places like the San Francisco Peaks near Flagstaff in Arizona (12,633ft), Wheeler Peak near Taos in New Mexico (13,161ft), and Uncompahgre Peak near Ouray in Colorado (14,309ft) – belong to the **Arctic** or **Alpine** zone, where the occasional tiny mammal scuttles through the tundra-like grasses and mosses.

Wherever and whenever **water** is abundant, however, the position changes. Southwestern riverbeds are lined with magnificent **cottonwood** and **aspen** trees, so many a canyon buried deep in the desert still manages a superb display of fall colors, while spring snowmelts help bring the mountain hillsides and the meadows of Zion alive with wildflowers.

Snakes and creepy-crawlies

Though the Southwestern deserts are home to an assortment of **poisonous creatures**, these are rarely aggressive towards humans. By observing obvious **precautions**, you should be able to avoid trouble. Don't attempt to handle wildlife; keep your eyes open as you walk, and watch where you put your hands when scrambling over obstacles; shake out shoes, clothing and bedding before use; and back off if you do spot a creature, to give it room to escape.

If you are **bitten** or stung, current medical thinking rejects the concept of cutting yourself open and attempting to suck out the venom; whether snake, scorpion or spider is responsible, apply a cold compress to the wound, constrict the area with a tourniquet to prevent the spread of venom, drink lots of water, and bring your temperature down by resting in a shady area. Stay as calm as possible and seek medical help immediately.

Food and Drink

The international craze for contemporary Southwestern cuisine has done little to turn the Southwest itself into a gourmet's paradise. In Santa Fe, dozens of top-class restaurants have followed in the footsteps of Mark Miller's trail-blazing *Coyote Cafe* – see p.118 – while the upscale resorts of Phoenix, Tucson, Taos and Sedona all offer opportunities for fine dining.

Out there on the road, however, the great American **diner** still holds sway. With typical dinner prices starting well below $10, travelers happy to eat the same old steak or chicken, with baked potato and salad bar, can get excellent value for money. That said, southern Utah, for example, is the last place to go if lingering over an exquisite meal in atmospheric surroundings ranks high on your vacation wish list. Vegetarians in particular are in for a rough ride, unless macaroni strips with jelly bits consistently hit your spot.

The **Hispanic** regions of New Mexico and southern Arizona do at least have their own indigenous cuisine, broadly similar to **Mexican** food but influenced by the Pueblo Indians. The essential ingredient is the **chile** (New Mexicans insist it should never be spelled *chili* or *chilli*). You'll soon become familiar with the bright-red *ristras*, strings of dried peppers, that adorn doorways throughout the region, and are festooned on restaurant entrances as warnings of the fiery

delights awaiting within. Both **green** and **red** chiles grow on the same plant; in principle the red is the mature version of the green, but confronted with a plateful there's no guarantee which will be the hotter variety. They in turn go to make spicy **salsa**, which at its most basic is simply dried peppers mixed with water, but more usually contains tomato and onion, *cilantro* (coriander) and other herbs, oil and lemon juice, plus other secret ingredients. If it's too hot for you, the best remedy is to drink milk.

A basic meal in a New Mexican cafe or diner is broadly similar to what you'd eat south of the border, though it may well make more use of fresh meats and vegetables. The essentials are: lots of rice and pinto beans, often served refried as *frijoles* (ie boiled, mashed and fried), with variations on the **tortilla**, a very thin corndough or flour pancake that can be wrapped around the food and eaten by hand (a burrito); folded, fried and filled (a taco); rolled, filled and baked in sauce (an enchilada); or fried flat and topped with a stack of filling (a tostada). Meals are usually served with complimentary nachos (chips) and salsa dip, or with *sopaipillas*, deep-fried air-filled pastry "pillows", often sweetened with honey. The chile relleno is a good vegetarian option – a green pepper stuffed with cheese, dipped in egg batter and fried.

Here and there, you'll also find **Native American** restaurants, both on and off the reservations. The most ubiquitous dish, generally known as a **Navajo taco**, consists of a piece of **fry-bread** – a puffy deep-fried slab of bread – smothered with beans, lettuce and cheese. A Hopi taco, an Apache taco and a Pueblo taco are all surprisingly similar. **Corn** or maize, the first

---

Tipping

Whatever you eat and wherever you eat it, service is usually enthusiastic – thanks in large part to the American institution of **tipping**. Waiting staff depend on tips for the bulk (and sometimes all) of their earnings; fifteen to twenty percent is the standard rate.

crop cultivated in the Americas, comes in some amazing multicolored varieties. Blue corn chips have spread beyond the Southwest, but you may also encounter blue cornflakes and wafer-thin *piki* or *piiki* bread made with blue cornflour.

Drinking

In general, to buy and consume **alcohol** in the US, you need to be aged 21 or over; you may be asked for ID even if you look much older. In **New** **Mexico** and Arizona, most restaurants have liquor licences, and it's always easy to find a drink. In Mormon-dominated **Utah** – whose drinking laws are outlined on p.362 – things are a bit more complicated, though it's not quite the "dry" state of popular legend. Most small towns have at least one restaurant licensed to sell beer or wine to diners. On **Indian reservations**, however, alcohol is prohibited altogether; you can't have beer in your car, let alone in your motel room.

Communications

Telephones

It's usually easy to find a public **payphone** in the Southwest. As a rule, local calls cost between 25¢ and 35¢, but you may have to feed in nine or ten quarters just to call the next town down the high-way, and long-distance calls can cost far more. Some budget **motels** offer guests free local calls, but in general calls from **motel rooms** are even more expensive.

If you make a lot of calls when you're on the road, it's well worth getting a **charge card** or **pre-paid phone card** of some kind, perhaps from your phone service provider at home. Americans can obtain these from AT&T (☎1-800/874-4000 ext 359); British travelers should contact BT (☎0800/800838) or Swiftcall (☎020/7488 2001 or 0800/769 0800). Such cards also make it possible for foreigners to call **toll-free** (☎1-800) numbers in America before they arrive in the US.

Gas stations and other outlets throughout the Southwest sell prepaid phone cards of various denominations. Almost without exception, these offer sizeable savings on conventional phone rates – not least because they're normally accessed via a toll-free number that incurs no additional charge when called from a motel room – and are thoroughly recommended.

US mail

Post offices in the Southwest are usually open Monday to Friday from 9am until 5pm, and Saturday from 9am to noon, and there are blue mail boxes on many street corners. Ordinary mail within the US costs 33¢ for a letter weighing up to an ounce. Air mail between the US and Europe or Australia costs 55¢ for postcards, 60¢ for aerograms

---

International Telephone Calls

The telephone code to dial **TO THE US** from the outside world (excluding Canada) is 1.

To make international calls **FROM THE US**, dial 011 followed by the country code:

Australia 61	Ireland 353
New Zealand 64	United Kingdom 44

---

or letters weighing up to half an ounce (a single thin sheet), and generally takes about a week.

The last line of the address consists of two letters to denote the state (Utah is "UT", New Mexico is "NM", etc), and a five-figure **zip code**; you should also write a return address on the envelope. Mail that doesn't carry the zip code is liable to get lost or at least delayed. The additional four digits you sometimes see appended to zip codes are not essential.

Letters can be sent c/o General Delivery (what's known elsewhere as **poste restante**) to the relevant post office in each city, but must include the zip code and will only be held for thirty days before being returned to sender. If you're receiving mail at someone else's address, it should include "c/o" and the regular occupant's name.

Rules on sending **parcels** are very rigid: packages must be in special containers bought from post offices and sealed according to their instructions. To send anything out of the country, you'll need a green customs declaration form, available from a post office.

Internet access

Public **Internet access** at Net cafes and the like is not (yet) as widely available in the Southwest as you might expect, though of course that situation may change. Hostels that cater for international travelers tend to have a computer or two where guests can send and pick up email, and here and there a self-styled "alternative" cafe lets customers go online. On the road, however, it's not as easy to stay in touch as it is in many a backpacker destination in the developing world.

If you're carrying a portable machine with you, on the other hand, it's almost always possible to hook up your modem in even the cheapest motel (though you may have to shift a supposedly immovable bed to reach the socket). The big issue for international travelers is whether your Internet service provider can be accessed with a toll-free or at least local call in the US, or if you have to make an international call just to log on. That's when it pays to be with one of the larger service providers, such as AOL.

Useful Numbers

Emergencies ☎ 911; ask for the appropriate emergency service: fire, police or ambulance

Long-distance directory information ☎ 1-(Area Code)/555-1212

Directory enquiries for toll-free numbers ☎ 1-800/555-1212

Festivals and Public Holidays

The box below lists the Southwest's major annual festivals. Specific annual events are described in the relevant town accounts, and you'll also find a full calendar of events in the pueblos of New Mexico on p.135. In addition, tourist offices for each state (see p.12) can provide full lists, or you can call local visitor centers ahead of your arrival and ask what's coming up. As a rule, only the Indian Market in Santa Fe and the Balloon Fiesta in Albuquerque attract large enough crowds to place a serious strain on accommodation and other facilities.

Annual Festivals and Events

Jan to mid-Feb	Gem & Mineral Show	Quartzsite, AZ
Early Feb	Festival of the Arts	Tubac, AZ
Late May	Zuni Artists Exhibition	Flagstaff, AZ
Late May	Iron Horse Bicycle Classic	Durango, CO
Early June	Bluegrass Festival	Telluride, CO
Late June	New Mexico Arts & Crafts Fair	Albuquerque, NM
June to mid-Oct	Utah Shakespeare Festival	Cedar City, UT
Early July	Hopi Artists Exhibition	Flagstaff, AZ
July 4	Nambe Falls Celebration	Nambe Pueblo, NM
July–Aug	Santa Fe Opera	Santa Fe, NM
July (second week)	Taos Pueblo Pow-wow	Taos Pueblo, NM
July (last week)	Spanish Market	Santa Fe, NM
July (last week)	Navajo Artists Exhibition	Flagstaff, AZ
Aug (second week)	Inter-Tribal Indian Ceremonial	Gallup, NM
Aug (third week)	Indian Market	Santa Fe, NM
Late Aug	Central Navajo Fair	Chinle, AZ
Sept 2	San Esteban Feast Day	Ácoma Pueblo, NM
Labor Day (first Mon in Sept)	All-American Futurity (horse race)	Ruidoso, NM
Early Sept	New Mexico State Fair	Albuquerque, NM
Early Sept	Hatch Chile Festival	Hatch, NM
Early Sept	Navajo Nation Fair	Window Rock, AZ
Sept (second week)	Fiestas de Santa Fe	Santa Fe, NM
Sept (last week)	Jazz on the Rocks	Sedona, AZ
Early Oct	International Baloon Fiesta	Albuquerque, NM
Early Oct	Northern Navajo Fair	Shiprock, NM
Mid Oct	Western Navajo Fair	Tuba City, AZ
Oct (third week)	Helldorado Days	Tombstone, AZ
Late Oct	Fat Tire Festival	Moab, UT
Early Dec	National Finals Rodeo	Las Vegas, NV
Early Dec	Shalako Ceremony	Zuni Pueblo, NM

Public holidays

On national **public holidays** shops, banks and offices are liable to be closed all day. The traditional **summer season** for tourism runs from Memorial Day to Labor Day; some tourist attractions are only open during that period.

Jan 1	**New Year's Day**
Jan 15	**Martin Luther King's Birthday**
3rd Mon in Feb	**President's Day**
	Easter Monday
Last Mon in May	**Memorial Day**
July 4	**Independence Day**
1st Mon in Sept	**Labor Day**
2nd Mon in Oct	**Columbus Day**
Nov 11	**Veterans' Day**
Last Thurs in Nov	**Thanksgiving Day**
Dec 25	**Christmas Day**

Traveling in Indian Country

There are around fifty separate Indian reservations in the Southwest, ranging in size from the vast Navajo Reservation (or "Navajo Nation"), which extends across three states in the Four Corners region, to the nineteen autonomous pueblos of New Mexico, many of which consist of one single village.

Some reservations make no effort to attract or inform visitors; some do the bare minimum to sate tourists' curiosity; some eagerly encourage paying guests to stay in tribal-run motels and campgrounds. Among the most compelling attractions on Native American soil are **Monument Valley**, and **Canyon de Chelly** and **Navajo national monuments**, all on the Navajo Reservation; the stupendous waterfalls of the **Havasupai Reservation**, deep in the Grand Canyon; and the adobe pueblos of **Taos** and **Ácoma** ("Sky City") in New Mexico.

Many outsiders – Americans and non-Americans alike – feel uncomfortable about entering Indian land, but so long as you behave with due **cultural sensitivity** you will almost always be made to feel welcome. In particular, travelers in "Indian Country" should respect the laws that bar the sale, possession and consumption of **alcohol** on the reservations. Always request permission before drawing or **photographing** people or personal property, and accept that you may be asked for a fee. As well as obeying explicit signs that ask you not to enter specific areas, such as shrines or *kivas*, you should also be aware that **off-road driving**, and **off-trail hiking** or **climbing**, is forbidden. If you have to drive up to someone's home or *hogan*, stay in your car and wait to be approached, rather than blundering in.

On a more general note, attempts to make friends may run contra to what Native Americans regard as good **manners**. In the words of a leaflet issued by the Navajo, "the general exuberance many cultures define as friendliness is not considered such by the American Indians." Most Southwestern Indians regard **eye contact** as rude, and will avoid meeting your eye; they may also prefer not to shake hands. Your **clothing** may also be an issue; the Hopi, for example, request visitors not to wear shorts or hats, or to use umbrellas. Persistent, intrusive questioning is obviously liable to offend. In Pueblo communities especially, don't ask about religious matters when children are present, as children are only initiated into religious secrets at the appropriate age.

Buying Indian crafts

For many tourists, the quest to buy **Indian crafts** becomes a major focus of their visit to the Southwest. Museums and galleries throughout the region display beautiful Pueblo pots, Navajo rugs, Apache baskets, and silver and turquoise jewelry of all kinds, stimulating a desire for affordable gifts and souvenirs that stores everywhere can barely keep up with.

Much of what's widely seen as traditional Indian craftwork has in fact only developed in the last hundred years or so. The collapse of traditional tribal economies coincided with the nineteenth-century arrival of the railroads, and with them the Southwest's first wave of tourists. Enterprising traders encouraged Indians to adapt or learn craft techniques to make souvenirs; as one anthropologist put it, the resultant hybrid was "the Indian's idea of the trader's idea of what the white man thought was Indian design."

To ensure good prices and good quality, you should ideally buy specific Indian crafts as near as possible to where they're made. On the Navajo Reservation, head for the **Hubbell Trading Post** (see p.58); on the Hopi Reservation, try the **Hopi Cultural Center** and the nearby stores; **Ácoma**, **Taos** and **San Ildefonso** pueblos are also good bets. More accessibly, the Indian traders in front of the Palace of the Governors in **Santa Fe** are a reliable source, while that city's summer **Indian Market** is a showcase for the entire region. In addition, the Northern Arizona Museum in Flagstaff, the Heard Museum in Phoenix and the Millicent Rogers Museum in Taos all have excellent stores.

If you want to be sure that whatever you're buying was individually crafted by a Southwestern Indian, you're entitled to ask the vendor for a written Certificate of Authenticity. Only the phrase "Authentic Indian hand-made" has any legal force. "Indian hand-made" means that the object was designed and assembled by American Indians; "Indian crafted" means that American Indians had a hand in the process; and words such as "real" and "genuine" mean nothing. The **Indian Arts & Crafts Association** (122 La Veta NE, Suite B, Albuquerque, NM 87108; ☎505/265-9149) can provide further detailed advice.

Jewelry

Jewelry is perhaps the oldest Southwestern craft of all. The Ancestral Puebloans made necklaces of disks cut from seashells; a single specimen unearthed near Kayenta was 36 feet long and held over fifteen thousand beads. Such necklaces are now known as *heishi*, and are the speciality of New Mexico's Santo Domingo pueblo.

Turquoise has always been prized by Southwestern Indians; the prehistoric city at Chaco Canyon (see p.84) was probably founded on the proceeds of the turquoise trade, while to

Another Hopi specialty, the carving of the wooden statuettes known as *kachina* dolls, is described on p.60.

this day the Navajo see turquoise as symbolizing the state of harmony and beauty known as *hozho*. Necklaces of raw and polished turquoise beads are widely available, and it also adds color and character to the **silver** jewelry made by the Hopi, Zuni and Navajo in particular.

Silversmithing is a relatively recent tradition, probably introduced from Mexico in the mid-nineteenth century. For many years, acquiring chunky silver bracelets, or belts studded with solid-silver conches, was the standard Navajo way of accumulating wealth. Such items could be pawned for cash at trading posts on the reservation, and then redeemed when times got easier; now known as pawn jewelry, they count as valuable collectors' pieces. Casual buyers tend to prefer – and to be more able to afford – the more delicate **overlay** style, in which a stencilled design is cut from a thin sheet of silver then soldered onto a solid backing sheet. This originated in 1947, when returning Hopi servicemen were trained in the technique as a means of earning a living, and the Hopi remain its finest exponents. Overlay designs can be seen on earrings, belt buckles, rings, and, especially, the clasps of *bola* (bootlace) ties.

Weaving

The best **weavers** in the Southwest are generally acknowledged to be the Navajo. In legend, they acquired the craft from Spider Woman, who lives atop Spider Rock in the Canyon de Chelly; in fact, they were probably taught by the Pueblo peoples after the Pueblo Revolt of 1680. That was also when they began to raise sheep, which had been introduced by the Spanish a century earlier.

Originally the Navajo wove blankets and clothing; **Navajo rugs** were the brainchild of nineteenth-century traders, who also suggested that using "earth" colors such as brown would appeal to tourists expecting a "natural" look. Many individual Navajo communities or families weave designs named for their own area, such as Teec Nos Pos, Ganado or Two Gray Hills. As a rule, the patterns have no religious significance, but most include an "escape route" or "spirit line," a line that runs to the very edge of the rug and ensures that the weaver's spirit is not trapped within it. Traditional rugs also left a hole in the center, as in a spider's web.

Authentic Navajo rugs take months to create, and sell for thousands of dollars; anything you see cheaper is probably a mass-produced Mexican imitation. The monthly Navajo Rug Auction at Crownpoint in New Mexico (see p.88) is the best opportunity to pick up a genuine bargain.

Pottery

Spanish explorers in 1540 spoke of Pueblo women as making "jars of extraordinary labor and workmanship, which were worth seeing". The **ceramic** tradition of northern New Mexico's pueblos remains as strong as ever, having been revitalized in the twentieth century by the San Ildefonso potter **Maria Martinez**. Although she consciously modeled her earlier work on designs found in ancient archeological sites, the black-on-black museum pieces for which she became famous are a far cry from the popular conception of Native American crafts. Many tourists prefer either the straightforward pots and jars, painted with rectilinear "pueblo motifs", created at Ácoma Pueblo, or the ubiquitous **"storyteller"** figures, showing a mother surrounded by children, that were first created at Cochiti Pueblo. A representative cross-section of styles can be seen at the roadside store run by **Pojoaque Pueblo**, twelve miles north of Santa Fe (see p.132).

Directory

AIRPORT TAX This is invariably included in the price of your ticket.

BANKS As explained on p.32, if you carry an ATM card and/or US dollar travelers' checks, you won't need to visit a bank in the Southwest. However, normal banking hours are from 9am or 10am until 3pm or 4pm Monday to Thursday, and slightly longer on Friday.

DATES In the American style, the date 1.8.2002 means not August 1, as in Europe, but January 8.

DISABLED TRAVELERS For information on specific states, contact the tourism departments listed on p.12; New Mexico, for example, produces the free *Access New Mexico* guide (☎505/827-6328). SATH (☎212/447-7284; *www.sath.org*), is a non-profit travel-industry referral service that passes queries on to its members as appropriate; allow plenty of time for a response. Travel Information Service (☎215/456-9600) is a telephone information and referral service. Mobility International USA (☎541/343-1284; *www.miusa.org*) offers travel tips to members ($35 a year) and operates an exchange program for disabled people. The Golden Access Passport, issued without charge to permanently disabled US citizens, gives free lifetime admission to all national parks. *Easy Access to National Parks,* published by the Sierra Club ($15; ☎415/977-5653; *www.sierraclubbookstore.com*), details access facilities in every national park for people with disabilities, senior citizens and families with children. Various other useful publications are produced by Twin Peaks Press (☎360/694-2462 or 1-800/637-2256; *www.pacifier.com/~twinpeak*).

ELECTRICITY The US electricity supply is 110 volts AC. Plugs are standard two-pins – foreign visitors will need an adaptor and voltage converter for their own electrical appliances.

EMERGENCIES Dial ☎911.

FLOORS The first floor of a building in the US is what would be the ground floor in Britain; the second floor would be the first floor, and so on.

GAY AND LESBIAN TRAVELERS Resources for gay and lesbian travelers in the Southwest include the Gay and Lesbian Community Center, 24 W Camelback Rd, Suite C, Phoenix (☎602/265-7283); Wingspan, 300 E Sixth St, Tucson; (☎520/624-1779; *www.wingspanaz.org*); Utah Stonewall Center, 770 South 300 West, Salt Lake City (☎801/539-8800); and the Gay and Lesbian Center of Las Vegas, 912 E Sahara Ave (☎702/733-9800), or the Gay Las Vegas Web site (*www.gayvegas.com*).

HEALTH MATTERS Most travelers do not require inoculations to enter the US, though you may need certificates of vaccination if you're en route from cholera- or typhoid-infected areas in Asia or Africa – check with your doctor before you leave. The "mystery illness" that killed around fifty people in the Four Corners region in 1993 was eventually traced to a hantavirus spread by the droppings of deer mice; backpackers should take care to avoid camping near rodent nests.

ID You should carry ID at all times. Two pieces should suffice, one of which should have a photo: a passport and credit card(s) are your best bets. Not having your license with you while driving is an arrestable offence.

MEASUREMENTS AND SIZES US measurements are Imperial, though American pints and gallons are about four-fifths of Imperial ones. Clothing sizes are two figures less than in the UK – a British women's size 12 is a US size 10 – while British shoe sizes are half below American ones for women, and one size below for men.

PHOTOGRAPHY In the bright Southwestern sun, you should get better photographs if you use slower film; an ASA speed of 100 is recommended.

SENIOR TRAVELERS Anyone over the age of 62, who can produce suitable ID, can enjoy certain discounts. Amtrak and Greyhound, for example,

offer (smallish) percentage reductions on fares to older passengers. US residents aged over 50 can join the American Association of Retired Persons, 601 E St NW, Washington, DC 20049 (☎202/434-2277 or 1-800/424-3410; *www.aarp.org*), which organizes group travel for senior citizens and can provide discounts on accommodation and vehicle rental. Golden Age passports, available to US citizens or residents aged 62 or older, allow free admission to national parks for life, for a one-off $10 fee.

TAX Sales tax is added to virtually everything you buy in a shop, but isn't included in the marked price. The actual rate varies from place to place, but in the states covered in this book it ranges between around five and seven percent – except on Indian reservations, which do not levy sales tax. Most towns also charge lodging taxes of between five and fifteen percent.

TEMPERATURES Always given in Fahrenheit.

TIME ZONES New Mexico, Utah, Colorado and Arizona all operate on **Mountain Standard Time**, which is two hours behind Eastern Standard Time and seven hours behind Greenwich Mean Time, so 2pm in Santa Fe is 4pm in New York City, and 9pm in London. Nevada and California are on **Pacific Standard Time**, another hour behind. Between the first Sunday in April and the last Sunday in October, New Mexico, Utah, Colorado and Nevada switch to **Daylight Savings Time**, and advance their clocks by one hour. Arizona, however, does not, so in summer it joins Nevada in being an hour behind New Mexico and Utah. Confusingly, the **Navajo Nation** in northeast Arizona does shift to Daylight Savings Time, making it one hour later than the rest of Arizona in summer, while the Hopi Reservation, entirely surrounded by the Navajo Nation, stays put. The time in the part-Navajo, part-Hopi town of Tuba City, Arizona – see p.41 – varies from street to street.

VIDEOS The standard format used for video cassettes in the US is different from that used in Britain. You cannot buy blank videos in the US compatible with a video camera bought in Britain.

The Guide

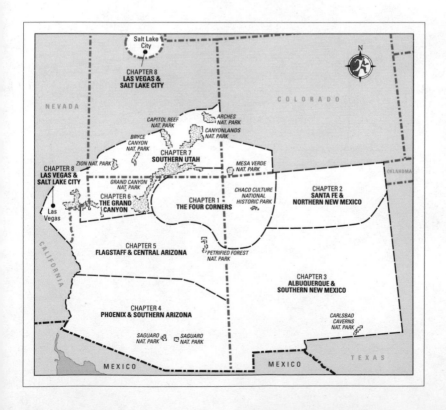

Chapter 1

The Four Corners

The **Four Corners** region is the heartland of the Southwest, not because the states of Arizona, Utah, Colorado and New Mexico happen to meet here, but because it remains dominated by **Native American** cultures to an extent that's unique in the modern United States.

Quite possibly, the uplands of the Colorado Plateau – said to be the highest inhabited plateau in the world, bar Tibet – are now home to a smaller population than a thousand years ago. At that time, the people now known to historians as the **Ancestral Puebloans** occupied settlements scattered throughout the region. They're chiefly remembered for their fabulous "**cliff dwellings**," which cling like eagle-nests to the walls of soaring red-rock canyons, but in fact they lived everywhere, from the valley floors to the mesa tops. Seven centuries ago, the Ancestral Puebloans moved away from the plateau, for reasons that are still not fully understood, and in due course the nomadic **Navajo** took their place. Now 250,000 strong, the Navajo are the largest single Native American group in the United States, and their reservation occupies the bulk of the Four Corners area. Contrary to popular legend, however, the Ancestral Puebloans did not vanish completely. Some of their descendants still live nearby, in the **Hopi** villages of Arizona, and the pueblos of **Zuni** and **Ácoma**, across the border in New Mexico.

For a history of the peoples now known as the Ancestral Puebloans – and an explanation of why the name "Anasazi" is no longer widely used – see p.520.

The ruins left by the Ancestral Puebloans have become the Four Corners' prime tourist destinations. Among the most significant are those at **Mesa Verde National Park** in southwest Colorado, where dozens of graceful pueblo complexes are tucked into high rocky alcoves, and the fully-fledged cities of New Mexico's remote **Chaco Canyon**, where Ancestral Puebloan civilization reached its peak. For sheer beauty, however, **Canyon de Chelly National Monument** in Arizona, where Navajo farmers live alongside the ancient remains, far surpasses both. Elsewhere, the main appeal is the **scenery**, which

For general advice on "Traveling in Indian Country", see p.30.

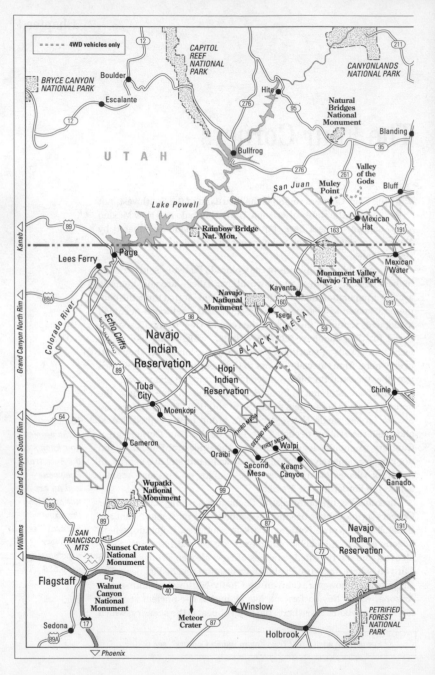

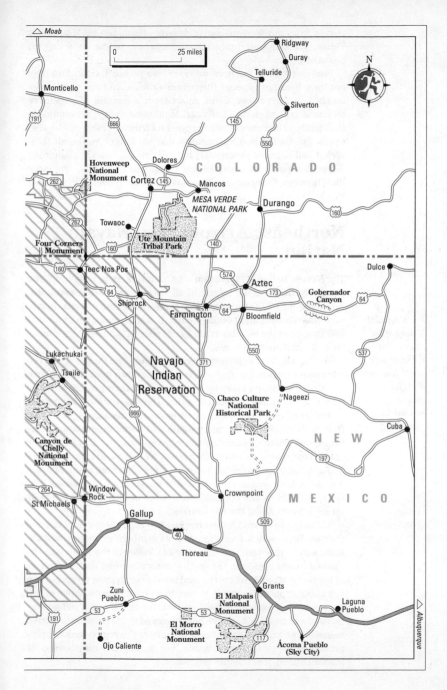

ranges from the Western-movie deserts epitomized by **Monument Valley**, via lone outcrops such as **Shiprock**, to the snow-capped peaks of Colorado.

Planning a Four Corners itinerary can be hard work. You may not have heard of most of the region's towns, and you won't miss much if you never see them. Apart from a handful of expensive motels near Canyon de Chelly and Monument Valley, **accommodation** tends to be concentrated around its fringes. "Edge-of-the-res" towns like Gallup and Farmington may no longer be the alcohol-fueled hell-holes of yesteryear, but they're not exactly glamorous either, and you'd do better to stay slightly further afield, in places like **Durango**, Colorado, or **Flagstaff**, Arizona (covered in Chapter Five).

Northeast Arizona: the Navajo Nation

The **Navajo Indian Reservation** – or, as it prefers to style itself, the **Navajo Nation** – is the largest of all Native American reservations, extending for 27,000 square miles across northeast Arizona, northwest New Mexico, and southern Utah. It has a population of around 250,000, of whom two thirds are aged under 21, and between a quarter and a half are Christians.

For a detailed history of the Navajo, see p.538; there's also lots of useful information on the Net at www .navajo.org.

The Navajo, who call themselves the *Diné* ("the People"), are relative newcomers to the region. They drifted down from the far North less than a thousand years ago, and occupied their present territory within the last three or four centuries. They have always been great assimilators, quick to adapt to new environments and acquire skills from their neighbors. Navajo religion and social organization draw heavily on Pueblo examples, while many "traditional" crafts, now sold in roadside stalls and trading posts, were learned from outsiders and adapted in response to tourist demand. Above all, contemporary Navajo culture was shaped by the acquisition of the **horses** and **sheep** brought by the Spanish, which were originally seized in raids on settlements along the Rio Grande.

Although the Navajo Nation has just two major year-round rivers – the **San Juan**, which forms much of its northern boundary, and the **Colorado** to the west – only Monument Valley in the north and the Painted Desert region in the south technically count as desert. Most of the rest is **steppe**, where the land is too poor to grow crops but can just about support livestock. It used to be covered with native grasses, but having evolved in tandem with the Southwest's indigenous fauna, these could not survive being gnawed to the roots by imported animals. The sagebrush that now dominates the region looks appropriately Western to most visitors, but is, like the tumbleweed or Russian thistle, just another interloper.

While a declining proportion of Navajo are now farmers or shepherds, their nomadic origins remain evident. Most Navajo choose not to live in urbanized areas, so what few towns there are on the reservation tend to be ugly modern accretions, consisting of trailer homes gathered around a few disheveled lots.

For travelers, a day or two's driving across the Navajo Nation carries a real sense of adventure. Whether at supermarket checkouts or on the radio, you're sure to hear spoken Navajo, a language of such complexity that it was adapted during World War II as an uncrackable military code. You'll also get a chance to try the ubiquitous **Navajo taco**, a piece of open-topped fry-bread smothered with chile and/or refried beans that's another cultural borrowing, this time acquired during the years of exile in New Mexico.

Between early April and late October, when the Navajo Nation joins Utah and New Mexico on Daylight Savings Time, it's one hour later than the rest of Arizona, including the Hopi Reservation.

The tourist infrastructure is relatively minimal, however, with only half a dozen widely-scattered towns offering even a single motel. As a result, most visitors confine their attentions to the region's trio of indisputably top-class attractions – the stunning sandscape of **Monument Valley**, the Ancestral Puebloan remains and Navajo *hogans* of the beautiful **Canyon de Chelly**, and the ancient cliff dwellings of **Navajo National Monument**.

Tuba City

Though it's the largest community on the western side of the Navajo Nation, you're only likely to stop at **TUBA CITY**, ten miles up US-160 from US-89, if you're too tired to drive any further (if you're feeling weary, spare a thought for the Hopi runner reported as having run to Flagstaff and back from Tuba City – a total of 156 miles – in under 24 hours.) Don't expect any brass bands; the town was named for Tuuvi, a Hopi from nearby Moenkopi, who upon converting to Mormonism in 1877 invited a group of Mormon families to settle here. Soon the Mormons were monopolizing the site's precious springs – fed by an aquifer that reaches to Monument Valley – and they were forced to move out when the area was added to Navajo lands in 1903.

Tuba City hosts the three-day Western Navajo Fair in mid-October.

Tuba City has two unusual claims to fame. The first is a set of petrified **dinosaur tracks**, near the highway five miles southwest of town. These widely spaced 65-million-year-old sandstone imprints were left by a ten-foot creature known as Dilophosaurus. They were hugely significant in proving that dinosaurs could run, but there's no evidence to support the suggestion in *Jurassic Park* that Dilophosaurus also spat venom. It's hard to spot the tracks on your own – in truth, they're not all that riveting – but waiting Navajo guides can lead you to them for a small donation. Second, Tuba City straddles two separate **time zones**. Most businesses along the highway, such as Basha's supermarket, operate on Mountain Standard Time, while clocks in the town proper, a block or two north, are set in summer to Daylight Savings Time, an hour later.

*The price
codes used
here are
explained on
p.15.*

Practicalities

In the center of Tuba City, a mile north of the US-160/Hwy-264 intersection, a complex of buildings focused around the *hogan*-shaped Tuba City Trading Post services most visitor needs. A large, relatively modern *Quality Inn* (☎520/283-4545, fax 283-4144; winter ③, summer ⑤) has reasonable rooms, with RV spaces also available; the *Hogan Restaurant* (☎520/283-5260) features a long, inexpensive Mexican-American menu; and a gift store sells rugs, jewelry, books and groceries.

Back at the intersection, the *Tuba City Truck Stop Cafe* (☎520/283-4975) is renowned for its cheese-and-chile-topped Navajo tacos. In summer, **Grey Hills High School** – turn left off US-160, half a mile northeast – becomes the *Grey Hills Inn* (☎520/283-6271; ①/③). Its thirty basic twin-bedded rooms, which share bathrooms, are normally rented by the room, but members of hosteling associations can rent a bed for $16 per night.

Navajo National Monument

Despite its name, **NAVAJO NATIONAL MONUMENT**, reached via a ten-mile spur road that runs north from US-60 fifty miles northeast of Tuba City and twenty miles southwest of Kayenta, has little to do with the Navajo. Instead, it's among the most beautiful ancient sites in the Southwest, with each of its three separate parcels preserving a long-lost Ancestral Puebloan **cliff dwelling**.

Betatakin, set in an enormous rocky alcove, can be admired from an overlook near the visitor center, or entered on a six-hour ranger-led hike. The even larger **Keet Seel** is a seventeen-mile round-trip from the road, on foot or horseback, and thus only seen by a dedicated few. Finally, fragile **Inscription House** – named not for ancient petroglyphs, but for the date "1661" carved on a wall, suggesting that some seventeenth-century Spaniard passed this way – has been closed to visitors for over thirty years.

Archeologists divide the Ancestral Puebloans of the Four Corners into three subgroups. One centered on Mesa Verde (see p.69), another on Chaco Canyon (see p.84); **Tsegi Canyon**, the focus of Navajo National Monument, is the definitive **Kayenta** site. Its inhabitants are seen as conservative, in that they still lived in pithouses long after the people of Chaco and Mesa Verde started to construct sophisticated pueblos. They were fine potters, however, and Kayenta ceramics are now much-prized museum pieces. Tree-ring dating pinpoints their move into the alcoves of Tsegi Canyon to around 1250 AD. The first three of the still-standing dwellings in Betatakin were erected in 1267; another was added in 1268, and a further ten or more, plus a *kiva* (see p.520), in 1275. By 1300 AD, intensive irrigation had lowered the water table and rendered farming impossible, and the canyon had been abandoned.

What became of the Kayenta people is no mystery. According to the Navajo, Keet Seel was built by settlers from Navajo Mountain, and Betatakin by a group from Chaco. That dovetails with the **Hopi** legend that as many as eight of their clans lived here for around fifty years, just before their migrations ended at the Hopi Mesas, fifty miles south. A pictograph at Betatakin – consisting of a bird-like figure within a large white circle – shows Masaw, the symbol of the Hopi Fire Clan. Hopis regularly return for ceremonies honoring their ancestors, and at the time of the Oraibi dispute, in 1905 (see p.536), the breakaway Hopi faction that eventually founded Hotevilla seriously considered resettling here.

Navajo National Monument was established in 1909, after Navajo guides led members of the Wetherill family (of Mesa Verde fame; see p.71) to Keet Seel. Betatakin was "discovered" a year or two later, by chance already within the monument boundaries.

Practicalities

The paved section of Hwy-564 ends ten miles north of US-160, at the monument's **visitor center** (daily: May to early Sept 8am–6pm; early Sept to mid-Dec & April 8am–5pm; mid-Dec to March 8am–4.30pm; ☎520/672-2366 or 672-2367). You can't see the ruins from here, but interesting displays include a traditional Navajo forked-stick *hogan* (see p.56) in the forest at the back.

The lovely little **campground** nearby is open year-round; all its first-come, first-served sites are free, but water is only available from May to September. The closest **motel** is the rudimentary *Anasazi Inn*, whose individual turquoise-roofed cabins are located in the town of **TSEGI** on US-160 ten miles east of the turnoff, halfway to Kayenta (☎520/697-3793, fax 697-8249; winter ③, summer ⑤). It has a small restaurant and no neighbors apart from its derelict predecessor.

Admission to Navajo National Monument is free; ordinary vehicles should not continue along the unpaved extension of Hwy-564, beyond the monument.

The Sandal Trail

If you only have time for a brief visit, all you can do is gaze across the canyon to **Betatakin** from the end of the **Sandal Trail**. This easy one-mile round-trip hike, which doubles as a nature trail, runs partly on a boardwalk and partly over level open rock.

The view at the end, where a sumptuous orange recess in the canyon wall arches above the hundred-room cluster of dwellings, is quite amazing. Their straight walls rise in tiers from a ledge above the canyon floor; hence the Navajo name Betatakin, or "house on ledges." It's all in such good condition – everything you see is original, except for the ladders and a few of the roof beams – that it's hard to believe the 120 or so inhabitants left not seven years but seven centuries ago.

The best time to photograph Betatakin from the Sandal Trail is late afternoon, when direct sunlight penetrates the alcove.

Hiking to Betatakin

While it's worth visiting the monument for the long-distance view alone, to get any closer to Betatakin you have to join a free, ranger-guided **hike**, which is also a great opportunity to learn more about the land and its history. The precise schedule depends on funding, but in principle, hikes depart daily at 9am and noon between Memorial Day and Labor Day, and at 10am only during early May and from Labor Day until some time in October; remember the time difference if you're hurrying here from beyond the Navajo Nation. Only the first 25 people to register at the visitor center each day get to go; there are no advance reservations.

All hikers are expected to bring enough food and water (at least half a gallon) to last the six-hour round-trip. The hike starts not at the visitor center but a mile or two's drive away, along a trail that drops steeply into the canyon from the top of Skeleton Mesa. Betatakin itself only comes into sight right at the end, as you head up a steadily narrowing side canyon, filled with delicate aspens that turn a gorgeous yellow in the fall. Closely monitored by the rangers, you climb right up into the alcove, whose full dimensions – 452ft high, 370ft wide and 135ft deep – are overwhelming. Anyone lacking a head for heights may well prefer to stay below. Most of the dwellings are off limits in any case, but sitting in the plaza of the ancient pueblo is an extraordinarily evocative experience.

Keet Seel

Getting all the way to **Keet Seel** – Arizona's largest cliff dwelling – is a major undertaking. The grueling seventeen-mile self-guided round-trip **hike** is too much to attempt in a single day, so **hikers** have to spend the night at the primitive campground near the ruin. The alternative is to go on **horseback** with a Navajo guide, which can be arranged through the visitor center for $60 per person.

Unlike Betatakin, all hikers *must* make reservations through the visitor center, at least one day (but not more than two months) in advance. Up to twenty permits per day are issued between Memorial Day and Labor Day. There's no drinkable water en route, though you may well have to wade through muddy streams.

Visitors to Keet Seel can only enter the ruins with the ranger stationed nearby. The village reaches deep back into the hillside, so well sheltered that its 150-plus rooms have barely deteriorated. No more than half a dozen are *kivas* – the Kayenta were not relentless *kiva*-builders like their neighbors at Mesa Verde. Keet Seel was a longer-lasting and more dynamic settlement than Betatakin; its cliff dwellings date from the same era, but people lived in the vicinity from around 950 AD, and migrating groups came and went for the next few hundred years. Little now survives of the large free-standing pueblo that stood on the valley floor not far away.

Black Mesa

Immediately opposite the Navajo National Monument turnoff, a broad but poorly-surfaced road sets off south to climb **Black Mesa**. Only 4WD vehicles can get more than a mile or two down here, so few tourists see the gaping **strip mines** where the Peabody Western Coal Company extracts the prodigious coal deposits for which the mesa is named. While you may well pass one of the endless trains that ferry coal up to the **Navajo Generating Station** at Page (see p.431), neither will you see the underground pipeline that uses an extravagant billion gallons of pure water per year to slurry crushed coal on a three-day trip around the Grand Canyon and into Nevada. For many Navajo and Hopi, the mining of Black Mesa remains a deeply controversial issue, although the meager payments the two tribes formerly received from Peabody increased after the mineral leases were renegotiated during the 1980s.

Kayenta

KAYENTA, where US-160 meets US-163 twenty miles northeast of Navajo National Monument, is not in any sense an historic town. Having begun life in the 1950s as a dormitory community for workers in the uranium mines to the north, it later became the main base for the miners of Black Mesa. Just twenty miles south of Monument Valley, it now also caters to ever-increasing numbers of tourists, but remains little more than a conglomeration of trailer homes, with barely a two-story building to its name.

Practicalities

Kayenta's *hogan*-shaped **visitor center**, at the highway intersection (daily 10am–9pm; ☎520/697-3572), carries information on the whole Navajo Nation, holds several crafts stalls, and stages Navajo dances on summer Tuesdays (from 8pm). The *Burger King* next door has a large display on the wartime Navajo Code Talkers.

Kayenta's zip code is AZ 86033.

Kayenta is also home to three upscale **motels**. Immediately south of the junction, facing drivers arriving from Monument Valley, the large *Holiday Inn* (☎520/697-3221 or 1-800/HOLIDAY, fax 520/697-3349; winter ④, summer ⑥), houses the distinctive and good-value *Wagon Wheel* **restaurant**, as well as its own pool. A little to the west, beyond the *Burger King*, the smart new *Hampton Inn of Kayenta* also has a pool and a restaurant (☎520/697-3170, fax 697-3189; winter ④, summer ⑥). The *Best Western Wetherill Inn*, a mile north on US-163 (☎520/697-3231, fax 697-3233; winter ③, summer ⑤), is less fancy, but the fact that it's run by the same people as *Goulding's* in Monument Valley makes it handy for arranging tours, and the routine *Golden Sands Cafe* stands alongside (☎520/697-3684). There's also a reasonable deli counter at the central Basha's supermarket.

The price codes used here are explained on p.15.

Monument Valley

The classic Wild-West landscape of stark sandstone buttes and forbidding pinnacles of rock, poking from an endless expanse of

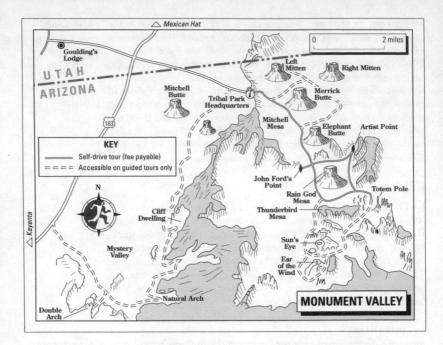

drifting red sands, has become an archetypal image. Only when you arrive at **MONUMENT VALLEY** do you realize how much your perception of the West has in fact been shaped by this one spot. Such scenery does exist elsewhere, of course, but nowhere is it so perfectly concentrated and distilled. While movie-makers have flocked here since the early days of Hollywood, the sheer majesty of the place still takes your breath away. Add the fact that it remains a stronghold of **Navajo** culture, little affected by tourism, and Monument Valley may well prove to be the absolute highlight of your trip to the Southwest.

Monument Valley Tribal Park straddles the Arizona–Utah state line, 24 miles north of Kayenta and 25 miles southwest of Mexican Hat. You can see the buttes for free – silhouetted on the skyline from fifty miles away, and towering alongside US-163 – but the four-mile detour to enter the park is rewarded with much closer views, while the tours beyond the end of the road are unforgettable.

A history of Monument Valley

Monument Valley is not really a valley. There's no permanent stream, nor higher ground to either side, and no valley has buttes along its floor. This whole region was once a flat plain, concealing the top of what are now the tallest "monuments." In the last ten million years, the Monument Uplift – part of the general upthrust of the Colorado Plateau

– has pushed that plain up from below, bulging to create cracks that have since eroded to leave only isolated nuggets of harder rock.

On the surface, thanks to annual rainfall of under ten inches, this looks like an unpromising region in which to live. However, sand dunes are surprisingly efficient at conserving moisture, and a huge aquifer deeper down stretches all the way to Tuba City. Beneath the small **cliff dwellings** that burrow into the rocks, the slopes are littered with ancient potsherds, indicating an Ancestral Puebloan presence that lasted until around 1300 AD. After that, the area may have remained unoccupied until a band of Navajo retreated here to avoid Kit Carson's round-up in 1864 (see p.539). Their leader, **Hoskinnini**, is said to have discovered silver nearby. Two white prospectors sneaked some of the metal away in 1880, but were killed – by passing Paiutes, according to the Navajo – when they returned, at the bases of **Mitchell** and **Merrick** buttes respectively.

The Navajo, who named Monument Valley *Tse 'bü'ndisgaü'*, or "there is a treeless area amid the rocks," see the whole place as a *hogan*, with its "door" facing east at the visitor center, and the butte behind *Goulding's Lodge* as its central hearth. They say the whole area has become drier during the last century, perhaps because the spirit of the Totem Pole formation, which was regarded as a line of prayersticks capable of granting rain, was offended when it was climbed during the filming of *The Eiger Sanction* (see p.49).

Park practicalities

The park's $2.50 **admission fee** is payable a short way down the approach road off US-163, which ends about four miles along at the **visitor center** (daily: May–Sept 7am–7pm; Oct–April 8am–5pm; Thanksgiving 8am–noon; closed Christmas Day and New Year's Day; ☎435/727-3353). As well as holding a small museum and staging **dances** on summer evenings (from 8pm), this is the site of the *Haskeneini* **restaurant** (daily: April–Oct 6am–10pm; Nov–March 6.30am–6pm; ☎435/727-3312), which serves reasonable conventional meals, plus Navajo fry-bread. The exposed, summer-only *Mitten View* **campground** nearby operates on a first-come, first-served basis, with sites costing $10.

In the parking lot, among the crafts stalls, several Navajo-run outfits tout for takers on their **valley tours**, by jeep or horse. These are very highly recommended; all can be booked in advance, but it's usually easy to turn up and get on a tour straight away. The going rate per person for a **jeep tour**, with operators such as Roland's Navajoland Tours (☎435/727-3313 or 1-800/368-2785) or Daniel's Guided Tours (☎435/727-3227) is around $20 for up to two hours, $25 for up to three hours, and $50 for a whole day. Typical **horseback tours** cost $35 (1hr 30min), $40 (2hr 30min), or $100 all day; possibilities include Ed Black's Monument Valley Trail Rides (☎435/739-4285 or 1-800/551-4039) and Navajo Country Trail

Monument Valley and the Mythic West

*The real star of my Westerns has always been the land . . . My
favorite location is Monument Valley. It has rivers, mountains,
plains, desert, everything that land can offer . . . I consider this
the most complete, beautiful, and peaceful place on earth.*

John Ford, *Cosmopolitan*, March 1964

In 1937, Harry Goulding, the owner of *Goulding's Lodge*, heard talk that
Hollywood producers were planning to shoot Western-themed movies in
the Southwest. Armed with a portfolio of photographs of Monument
Valley, he set off for California, and started knocking on doors. Within a
year, John Ford had brought a crew to Goulding's remote desert outpost,
and was filming *Stagecoach*.

From their first moment on screen, Monument Valley's emblematic
buttes served as a visual shorthand for the Wild West. The geographical
reality was irrelevant. *Stagecoach* supposedly followed a coach heading
through Apache territory from Tonto in southern Arizona to Lordsburg in
New Mexico. In fact, it did no more than duck in and out of Monument
Valley; as John Wayne put it, "there's some things a man just can't run
away from." Wayne was at it again in *The Searchers* (1956), when he
spent five years scouring Texas for Scar's band of Comanche, although in
reality both he and they were within the same five-mile radius of The
Mittens all along. In *My Darling Clementine* (1946), Henry Fonda as
Wyatt Earp drove his cattle across the floor of Monument Valley and into
Tombstone, somehow transplanted from southern Arizona complete with
(potted) saguaro cactuses; the OK Corral perched on a mesa nearby.
Monument Valley consistently symbolized the untamed wilderness that lay
beyond the ramshackle towns, beleaguered forts, isolated cabins or crude
fences of the West's earliest white pioneers.

In total, John Ford made seven movies in Monument Valley, including his increasingly turgid "cavalry trilogy" of *Fort Apache* (1948), in

Rides (☎435/727-3210). Roy Black's Hiking and Van Tours
(☎435/739-4226), also do **hiking trips**, charging $75 for either a
six-hour hike or an **overnight** backpack.

Guided jeep tours are also run from *Goulding's Lodge* (see p.50),
and the associated *Wetherill Inn* in Kayenta. Call ahead for the latest schedules, but as a guideline, **all-day** trips (adult $60, under-8s
$45) start from *Goulding's Lodge* daily at 9am in season; **half-day**
tours (3hr 30min; adult $30, under-8s $18) leave daily at 9am and
3.30pm; and there are shorter trips at 1.30pm daily (2hr 30min;
adult $25, under-8s $15).

Seeing the valley

The most prominent of the buttes visible from outside the visitor center are the pair known as **The Mittens**, of which the Left or West
Mitten is in Arizona and the Right or East Mitten is in Utah. Rising a
thousand feet from the desert floor, each has a distinct "thumb" that
splinters off from its bulkier central section.

which both Wayne and Fonda played opposite the adult Shirley Temple, *She Wore A Yellow Ribbon* (1949), and *Rio Grande* (1950). He worked closely with the Navajo, who featured as all-purpose Indians whenever necessary, camping out in wigwams in *The Searchers*, for example, at what's now known as John Ford's Point. Medicine man Hosteen Tso is said to have been kept on hand to control the weather, and is credited with producing a snowstorm and a sandstorm to order for *Stagecoach*. The construction of Monument Valley's first road, in the 1950s, spoiled Ford's hitherto pristine landscape, but he carried on filming here until *Cheyenne Autumn* (1963). He died shortly after announcing plans to make *Appointment at Precedence* in the valley, in 1972.

The spectacle of Henry Fonda's son smoking marijuana in Monument Valley, in *Easy Rider* (1969), may have marked an end to the days of the classic Western, but the valley itself has remained in demand. Clint Eastwood had some perilous moments on top of the Totem Pole in *The Eiger Sanction* (1975), and Michael J. Fox's souped-up DeLorean out-gunned pursuing Indian warriors in *Back to the Future III* (1989). Other visitors have included Mick Jagger in *Freejack* (1992) and Tom Hanks in *Forrest Gump* (1994), while in Mario van Peebles' hip-hop Western *Posse* (1993), Monument Valley was almost bursting with Sioux Indians, gold mines, railroads and buffalo soldiers.

Monument Valley's starring role as the setting for many *Roadrunner cartoons* probably stems from its appearances in the wildly popular *Krazy Kat* syndicated comic strip of the 1920s and 1930s. Despite the opinions of learned critics such as e e cummings, who referred to the strip's "strictly irrational landscape," and Umberto Eco, who spoke of "surrealistic inventions, especially in the improbable lunar landscapes," artist **George Herriman** was a regular visitor to *Goulding's Lodge*. The adventures of Krazy Kat and Ignatz Mouse – set in Coconino County – were played out against a backdrop of realistic depictions of Monument Valley formations.

A rough, **unpaved road** drops from the western end of the visitor center parking lot to run through Monument Valley. Taking a guided tour is infinitely preferable, but the 17-mile loop marked as the **self-drive** route makes a bearable if bumpy ride in an ordinary vehicle, and takes something over an hour to complete (daily: summer 8am–6pm; winter 8am–4.30pm). You're allowed to stop en route to stretch your legs, but not hike for any distance.

At the main halt, **John Ford Point**, you can browse a few jewelry stalls, enter a *hogan*-cum-gift store, and enjoy the classic wide-screen valley panorama. A Navajo man normally poses on horseback at the tip of the nearby promontory, while closer at hand, children in traditional dress invite you to photograph them for a dollar or two. The road goes on to pass near the **Totem Pole** before heading back via **Artist Point** to the visitor center.

Guided tours with the operators listed on p.47 follow the same route, but also take visitors "behind the scenes" beyond the main road, and offer a fascinating Navajo perspective on the place. Likely stops on longer tours include the **Sun's Eye** – a high natural arch, with petroglyphs of bighorn sheep at its base – and the similar, even more dramatic **Ear of the Wind**, as well as an obligatory visit to a *hogan* for a weaving demonstration. The most striking **Ancestral Puebloan remains** are in adjacent **Mystery Valley**, which you're only likely to see if you take a full-day tour.

Goulding's Lodge

The price codes used here are explained on p.15.

The only **accommodation** within twenty miles of Monument Valley is two miles west of US-163, along a road that starts immediately opposite the park approach road. **Goulding's Monument Valley Lodge** (PO Box 360001, Monument Valley, UT 84536; ☎ 435/727-3231, fax 727-3344; *www.gouldings.com*; Jan to mid-March & mid-Oct to Dec ④, mid-March to May ⑤, June to mid-Oct ⑦) rises in tiers at the foot of a large sandstone bluff, with superb views across the valley. It began life as a 1920s trading post, opened by Harry Goulding and his wife "Mike," and has expanded to incorporate an upscale motel, a restaurant, an indoor pool, a general store and a gas station. All the motel rooms have balconies, as well as VCRs to watch the *Lodge*'s library of Westerns; dinner at the *Stagecoach Dining Room* (daily 6.30–9pm) will set you back up to $20. There's also a **campground** (mid-March to mid-Oct; ☎ 435/727-3235), where sites cost $14 per night.

Alternative bases for Monument Valley, further afield, include Mexican Hat (see p.484), Bluff (see p.483) and Kayenta (see p.45).

The original lodge building has been preserved much as the Gouldings left it, and holds a small but entertaining **movie museum** (April–Nov daily 7.30am–9pm), where visitors are invited to make a $2 donation towards scholarships for Navajo students. Behind it stands the cabin used by John Wayne, as Captain Nathan Brittles, in *She Wore A Yellow Ribbon*. The nearby store, incidentally, sells John Wayne Toilet Tissue: "it's rough, it's tough, and it doesn't take crap off anyone."

From Monument Valley to Canyon de Chelly

The most direct – and also the most scenic – route between the Navajo Nation's two major tourist attractions, Monument Valley and Canyon de Chelly, is **Arrowhead Hwy-59**. This gorgeous drive heads south off US-160 eight miles east of Kayenta, and then spends almost fifty miles skirting the northern flanks of Black Mesa.

For most of the way, it runs across flat desert grasslands, like a slightly more fertile version of Monument Valley, with cracks in the plains to either side hinting at unfathomable canyons. Occasionally, off to the south, villages such as **Chilchinbito** and **Rough Rock** nestle against the mesa, but the road steadfastly ignores them. When it finally drops down **Carson Mesa** to reach Chinle Valley, you're confronted by the unlikely waters of **Many Farms Lake**. The road meets US-191 at the community of **Many Rivers**, fourteen miles north of Chinle.

Canyon de Chelly

A short way east of **Chinle**, halfway between Kayenta and Window Rock, twin sandstone walls emerge abruptly from the desert floor, then climb with phenomenal speed to become the thousand-foot cliffs of **CANYON DE CHELLY NATIONAL MONUMENT**. Between these sheer sides, the cottonwood-fringed Chinle Wash meanders through an idyllic oasis of meadows and planted fields. Here and there, a *hogan* stands in a grove of fruit trees, a straggle of sheep is penned in by a crude wooden fence, or ponies drink at the water's edge. And everywhere, perched above the valley on ledges in the canyon walls and dwarfed by the towering cliffs, are the long-abandoned stone and adobe dwellings of the **Ancestral Puebloan** peoples.

The monument in fact holds two main canyons, which branch apart a few miles upstream: **Canyon de Chelly** to the south and **Canyon del Muerto** to the north. Each twists and turns in all directions, scattered with immense rock monoliths, while several smaller canyons break away. The whole labyrinth threads its way upwards for thirty miles into the Chuska Mountains.

Canyon de Chelly is a magnificent place, easily on a par with any of the Southwest's national parks. Its relative lack of fame owes much to the continuing presence of the **Navajo**, for whom the canyon retains enormous symbolic significance, despite the fact that they did not themselves build its cliff dwellings. Casual visitors are restricted to peering into the canyon from above, from overlooks along the two "rim drives." There's no road in, and apart from one short but superb hike, you can only enter the canyons with a Navajo guide.

A history of Canyon de Chelly

Ancestral Puebloan Basketmakers first occupied Canyon de Chelly around 300 AD, digging primitive pithouses into the valley floor. Over the next thousand years, their descendants moved first into freestanding "pueblo" apartment-style blocks (from 700 AD), and then into elegant cliff dwellings, starting in 1100 AD. Virtually all these canyon-wall complexes face south to catch the sun, with cool storage chambers set in deep recesses. Many now look more inaccessible than they actually were, thanks to rock falls and the erosion of toe- and hand-holds in the soft sandstone. The valley's population peaked at roughly one thousand, shortly before drought drove the Ancestral Puebloans out around 1300 AD.

For the next few centuries, **Hopis** from the west farmed the canyon floor in summer, but no permanent inhabitants returned before the Pueblo Revolt of 1680 (see p.526). As the Spanish reasserted control over New Mexico, the first **Navajo** arrived in the region, quite possibly accompanied by Pueblo refugees. From then on, the Navajo and Spanish were locked in a bloody cycle of armed

Northeast Arizona: the Navajo Nation

Canyon de Chelly is pronounced "de shay"; the name is a corruption of the Navajo tségi, meaning "rock canyon."

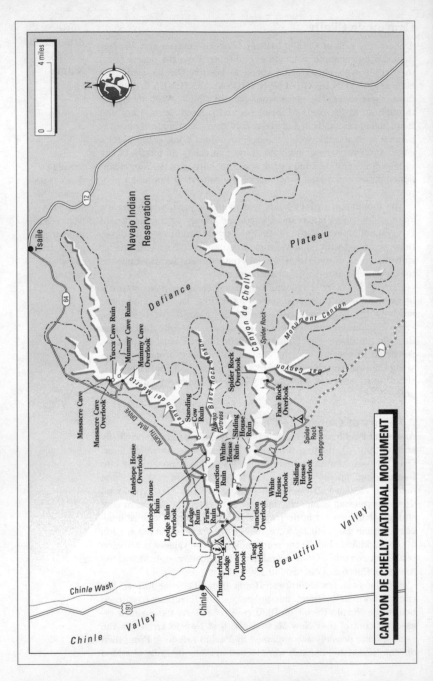

CANYON DE CHELLY NATIONAL MONUMENT

clashes and slave raids. As the "stronghold of the Navajo," Canyon de
Chelly became the target of punitive **Spanish** expeditions. In 1805,
Lieutenant Antonio Narbona's party gunned down over a hundred
Navajo in the Canyon del Muerto. According to the Spanish, ninety of
them were warriors; the Navajo say that the warriors were away at
the time, and that all the dead were women, children and elders.

After the Yankees replaced the Mexicans in Santa Fe, the US Army
in turn set about dislodging the Navajo. The process culminated in
1864, when General Carleton's men dispatched all the Navajo they
could round up on the "**Long Walk**" to Fort Sumner (see p.539). In
Canyon de Chelly, **Kit Carson** starved the last Navajo warriors down
from the natural Navajo Fortress and destroyed their homes, livestock and beloved peach orchards. Within a few years, however,
Congress allowed the Navajo to return from their barbaric imprisonment. To this day, 25 Navajo families still farm the Canyon de Chelly
in summer, the land having passed down from mother to daughter –
as is usual for the Navajo – from the women between whom it was re-
apportioned in the 1870s.

Arrival and information

The monument's **visitor center** is a little over two miles east of
Chinle and US-191 (daily: May–Sept 8am–6pm; Oct–April 8am–5pm;
☎520/674-5500). Set on the mound where Kit Carson signed the
"treaty" that ended his siege of the canyon in 1864, it holds useful
displays, and is the place to arrange unorthodox hiking or motorized
expeditions (see p.55). No **public transport** runs closer to the
canyon than the Greyhound buses and Amtrak trains that ply the
I-40 corridor to the south.

*No entrance fee
is charged at
Canyon de
Chelly.*

Accommodation and eating

For the moment, Canyon de Chelly remains remarkably unspoiled,
but nearby facilities are overstretched in summer, when it's essential
to book **accommodation** well in advance. None of the three options
could be considered cheap. Much the best is *Thunderbird Lodge*,
just past the visitor center near the canyon entrance (☎520/674-
5841 or 1-800/679-2473, fax 520/674-5844; mid-Nov to March ④,
April to mid-Nov ⑤). Its conventional motel rooms surround a century-old trading post, which houses a large and reasonably priced if
deeply boring self-service **cafeteria** (daily 6.30am–9pm) that's festooned with rugs from the well-stocked **giftshop** next door (daily
7.30am–9pm). If you take a *Thunderbird* sightseeing tour on the
day you leave, check out of your room first; they charge $5 per hour
extra after 11am.

*Chinle's zip
code is AZ
86503.*

*No alcohol is
sold in Chinle.*

Locals had hoped the former **Garcia Trading Post**, half a mile
short of the monument entrance, would be restored as an historic
attraction. Instead, the site now holds the ersatz adobe *Chinle
Holiday Inn* (☎520/674-5000 or 1-800/HOLIDAY, fax 520/674-

8264; winter ⑤, summer ⑥). This comfortable hundred-room complex adjoins *Garcia's Restaurant*, which serves a breakfast buffet, full lunches (Mon–Fri only), and good quality dinners. The *Best Western Canyon de Chelly*, just east of the US-191 intersection in Chinle (☎520/674-5875 or 1-800/327-0354, fax 520/674-3715; winter ④, summer ⑥), is an adequate but somewhat characterless alternative, again with its own restaurant.

Chinle itself is a brief nondescript straggle on the highway, with service stations, *Taco Bell*, *Kentucky Fried Chicken*, a post office and a laundromat. In late August, it hosts the **Central Navajo Fair**.

It's also possible to spend the night in one of several traditional *hogans* in the vicinity that belong to the Coyote Pass clan, and offer basic **B&B** lodging together with the opportunity for guided hikes (c/o Will Tsosie Jr, PO Box 91, Tsaile, AZ 86556; ☎520/724-3383 or 602/674-9655; ⑤). In addition, the Navajo Tourism Department in Window Rock (☎520/871-6436) can provide details of the reservation's ever-changing roster of local B&Bs.

No **camping** is permitted in the canyons. However, the first-come, first-served *Cottonwood Campground* spreads among the trees beside *Thunderbird Lodge*. All sites are free, with a five-day maximum stay, but there are no showers, and when the water is cut off from November to March, no restrooms either. The equally primitive and much less convenient Navajo-owned *Spider Rock RV & Campground* (☎520/674-5261) is near the end of South Rim Drive.

The view from above: the rim drives

The monument's two rim drives are equally superb. The dead-end **South Rim Drive** traces the south rim of the Canyon de Chelly, while the **North Rim Drive** follows the north rim of the Canyon del Muerto and then heads off to the northeast. Both involve a round-trip drive of roughly forty miles from the visitor center, punctuated by overlooks where short walks across the mesa-top lead to views of natural or archeological wonders. Even if you don't stop at them all, each drive takes around half a day. Thefts from cars have been a major problem, so follow the prominent warnings.

To take the best photographs, tour the North Rim in the morning, the South Rim in the afternoon.

The South Rim Drive

The first stop along the South Rim Drive – **Tunnel Overlook**, two miles up from the visitor center – is a trailhead for guided hikes; unaccompanied travelers have no reason to stop. **Tsegi Overlook**, just beyond, stands high above a sweeping curve in the canyon. Though the wash itself is seldom more than a trickle, its broad sandy floor clears a wide gap between the fringe of cottonwoods. Behind the *hogan* near the stream, fields and paddocks reach to the cliffs.

By now, as you look back west, Chinle is visible spreading across the valley, with the full stretch of Black Mesa beyond. Four miles up, **Junction Overlook** marks the meeting of the two main canyons.

Canyon de Chelly Tours

With the exception of the White House Trail (see below), taking a **guided tour** is the only way to get a close-up view of Canyon de Chelly's amazing Ancestral Puebloan remains, or to see the rock art that lines its walls. It's also unforgettable for the scenery alone, with the glorious, glowing cliffs towering far above you, and tranquil Navajo farms to either side.

The most popular are the **4WD trips** organized by *Thunderbird Lodge* (see p.53), which zigzag into either or both canyons following the washes, which vary from two or three feet deep during the spring thaw to completely dry in summer. For most of the year, these "shake'n'bake" tours are in open-top flatbed trucks, lurching over the rutted riverbed, and the heat can be incredible; in winter they carry on in glass-roofed army vehicles with caterpillar tracks. A **half-day** trip (daily: summer 9am & 2pm, winter 9am & 1pm; adults $36, under-13s $27) enables you to see a wide variety of sites and terrain, but to reach as far as Spider Rock, you have to take the **full-day** tour (late spring to early fall only, daily 9am; $58, no reductions). At the visitor center, you can also hire a Navajo guide to accompany you in your own 4WD vehicle for $10 per hour.

The visitor center arranges highly recommended 4.5-mile, four-hour **group hikes**, which enter the canyon via the White House Trail and cost $10 per person. The precise schedule varies, but usually includes a morning and an afternoon trip each day; separate **night hikes** last just two hours but cost slightly more. You can also hire your own personal guide through Canyon de Chelly Tours (☎520/674-3772), at a fee of $20 per hour for hiking trips or $15 per hour for expeditions in your own jeep or one of theirs.

Both Justin's Horse Rental (☎520/674-5678) and Twin Trail Tours (☎520/674-8425) organize **horseback** trips for around $10 per person per hour, plus $10 an hour for a guide.

Canyon de Chelly narrows off to the right, behind a large monolith, while Canyon del Muerto to the left is much less conspicuous. Two tiny ruins indent the base of the canyon walls opposite.

At **White House Overlook**, six miles from the visitor center, Canyon de Chelly is 550ft deep, with its rim topped by strange whorls of slickrock. Pale and majestic, the cliff that drops on the far side of the wash forms a stupendous backdrop for the photogenic **White House Ruin**. Squeezed into a tiny recess, well above the fields, this cluster of rooms originally stood above a larger pueblo on the valley floor, roughly half of which has now eroded away; it was probably reached by ladders on the roofs of the topmost towers.

The **White House Trail**, to the right of the viewing area, offers the sole opportunity for visitors to hike alone into the canyon. A beautiful if slightly precarious walk – some of it runs along ledges chiseled into the rock – it reaches the canyon floor through a tunnel that perfectly frames a Navajo *hogan* and its glowing attendant cottonwood. Thus far the ruin has been hidden from view, but once across the wooden footbridge that spans the wash you can admire it close up, separated only by a protective fence. Sixty feet above you, the

Allow at least two hours for the 2.5-mile round-trip hike on the White House Trail; 30 to 45 minutes to get down, and a good hour to get back up.

ancient dwelling appears to be in almost perfect condition, still with the dazzling coat of plaster that gave it its name. Navajo traders nearby sell sodas and trinkets while keeping an eye out for hikers tempted to wander any further than the permitted hundred yards in either direction.

From **Sliding House Overlook** – separated from the road by a couple of hundred yards of cairned slickrock, twelve miles along – the **Sliding House Ruin** appears to be tucked into the slenderest of crevices in the cliff face. It's now steadily slipping down towards the ploughed Navajo fields below.

South Rim Drive ends after roughly twenty miles at the astonishing double monolith of **Spider Rock**, where Monument and Bat canyons split away from Canyon de Chelly. These eight-hundred-foot twin pinnacles of rock soar to within two hundred feet of the canyon rim, and are said by the Navajo to be home to Spider Woman. She taught them the art of weaving, but also steals misbehaving children; their bleached, chewed bones lie strewn across the top.

The North Rim Drive

The **Ledge Ruin Overlook**, five miles along the North Rim Drive, does not rank among the monument's more significant moments, but

---

The Navajo Hogan

The traditional dwelling known as a *hogan* (pronounced *ho-wun*), as seen throughout Canyon de Chelly, is the focus of Navajo life, and the venue for all sacred ceremonies. Few Navajo may actually live in a *hogan* year-round, but every family has at least one, and those who still farm and raise sheep in the backcountry are likely to have several.

The earliest *hogans*, described by the Spanish in the sixteenth century and still widely used until the 1940s, were known as "male *hogans*." They consisted of three vertical forked sticks propped against each other, aligned to the north, south, and west, covered with logs, brush and mud, and with a door that faced east to greet the rising sun.

Virtually all the *hogans* on the reservation today are "female," larger six- or eight-sided structures made of cribbed horizontal logs and once again covered with mud. These became more popular at the end of the nineteenth century, with the advent of steel saws to cut the timber, and wagons to haul it; in fact many were made from salvaged railroad ties. The doorway still faces east, with a floor of hard-packed dirt to provide contact with the earth, and a smoke hole in the center of the domed roof for access to the sky. Each area of the *hogan* has a particular significance; the south side "belongs" to the women and the north to the men, while the male head of the household sits to the west. Food is prepared and stored on the northeast side, and the southwest is the sleeping area.

Since the 1970s, more and more Navajo have chosen to live in trailers rather than face the labor of constantly renewing a *hogan*'s protective mud coating. It's also said that as many Navajo now die in hospital, the custom that a dwelling place in which a death has occurred must be abandoned has become less of a deterrent against building elaborate homes.

---

both the viewpoints at **Antelope House Overlook**, five miles beyond that, are well worth seeing. The first faces across to **Navajo Fortress**, at the tip of the mesa that divides Canyon del Muerto from Black Rock Canyon. It took Kit Carson's besieging forces three months, from December 1863 onwards, to starve down a group of defiant Navajo warriors who had reached the summit of this solitary tower of rock by means of ladders which they then drew up behind them.

The other viewpoint looks down on **Antelope House Ruin**, at the base of a huge white overhang in a separate twist of Canyon del Muerto. This site was first occupied in 693 AD, and grew to comprise two square towers to the rear, plus a central plaza that held half a dozen dwellings. It's named after an antelope pictograph painted by the Navajo artist Dibé Yazhi, or Little Sheep, in the 1830s. He was also responsible for the "Spanish Mural" a little further along, which shows a Spanish lieutenant, priest and troops advancing through the canyon. Across the wash, in the **Tomb of the Weaver**, the embalmed body of an old man was found wrapped in golden eagle feathers.

The next, final spur road off the North Rim Drive splits to reach two separate overlooks. To the south, **Mummy Cave Overlook** offers a clear view of the single most striking ruin in the monument – **Mummy Cave Ruin**, which the Navajo call **House Under The Rock**. Inhabited for over a thousand years, from 300 AD until 1300 AD, it consists of two pueblo complexes deep in the shade of adjacent alcoves, with a prominent **Central Tower** on the spur in between. As the masonry of the tower is more sophisticated than the rest, and its construction has been dated to 1284 AD, archeologists believe it may have been built by migrants from Mesa Verde.

In the "cave" visible from **Massacre Cave Overlook**, to the north, Narbona's expedition of 1805 (see p.53) killed more than a hundred Navajo. It's less of a cave than a pitifully exposed ledge, far above the canyon floor, on which the huddled group were easily picked off by the Spanish, using ricochets off the overhang above. A short walk away – there's no sign or trail to guide you there – you can also see **Yucca House Ruin**, which unlike the rest of the monument's Ancestral Puebloan sites is very near the mesa-top. It's an amazing location, set in a hollow in the rock above a sheer drop, with no conceivable way down to the valley floor, but almost none of the buildings survive.

As Hwy-64, the North Rim Drive continues for fifteen more miles to meet Arrowhead Hwy-12 in the small town of **TSAILE**. The upper floors of Diné College here hold the stimulating **Ned Hatathli Museum** of Navajo history (Mon–Fri 9am–4pm; free), which also sells craft items, and there are even a few B&B rooms available in a mocked-up *hogan*, the *Rainbow Inn* (☎520/724-6830 or 1-888/HOGAN-4U; ④). It's possible to hike into Canyon del Muerto from this end, with a guide hired in Chinle.

Ganado and the Hubbell Trading Post

The village of **GANADO**, halfway between Chinle and the interstate, and thirty miles west of Window Rock, was named after Chief Ganado Mucho ("Won a lot"), one of the twelve signatories of the 1868 treaty that ended the Navajo's imprisonment at Fort Sumner.

After the Navajo returned from New Mexico, independent white entrepreneurs set up trading posts at the edge of the reservation, supplying the Indians with goods from the world beyond in return for craft items such as blankets and jewelry. The **Hubbell Trading Post**, founded by John Hubbell a mile west of Ganado, still functions today, now run by the Park Service (daily: summer 8am–6pm; winter 8am–5pm; ☎520/755-3475). Located at the end of a tree-lined avenue beside the Pueblo Colorado Wash, it's a fascinating living museum, where you can watch Navajo weavers at work and wander out to the old stables, piled with hay and filled with venerable wooden wagons. Serious collectors pay premium prices for the best rugs and silverwork, but the groceries in the general store – pretty historic in themselves – make less expensive souvenirs.

Ganado has no **motels**, but the *Cafe Sage* makes a good lunchtime stop. To the east, Hwy-264 climbs onto the thickly wooded Defiance Plateau and heads for Window Rock, while US-191 undulates for forty miles due south, through more forests, to Chambers on I-40.

Window Rock

On the first weekend after Labor Day, Window Rock hosts the Navajo Nation Fair (☎520/871-6478).

The capital of the Navajo Nation, **WINDOW ROCK**, sits on the Arizona–New Mexico border 25 miles northwest of Gallup. It only became capital in the 1930s, and remains much more of an administrative headquarters than a lively town. Most casual visitors simply pass through on Hwy-264, and spot a few malls and gas stations plus the showpiece *Navajo Nation Inn*. Technically, if you do that, you're not in Window Rock at all; you also won't see the rock itself.

Both "town" and rock are a mile or two north on Arrowhead Hwy-12. The **Window Rock**, an impressive, almost circular hole in a golden sandstone cliff, used to surmount a spring where water was collected for use in the Water Way ceremony. With the spring now dry, it has become the focus of a landscaped area with picnic tables, dedicated as the Navajo Nation Veterans Memorial in November 1995. Nearby stands the octagonal **Council Chamber** where the **Navajo Tribal Council** meets at least four times yearly.

Back on Hwy-264, the large new **Navajo Nation Museum and Visitor Center** (winter Mon–Fri 8am–5pm; summer Mon–Sat 8am–5pm; donation) stands a short distance east of the *Navajo Nation Inn*. This is a good spot to pick up tourist information, and ask any questions you may have about the Navajo themselves, but surprisingly enough, it doesn't hold permanent displays covering

Navajo history and culture. Instead, most of its exhibitions are temporary; they tend to be well conceived, but it's impossible to say whether there will be anything to capture your interest. Tucked among the rocky outcrops across the parking lot, a small **zoo** (same hours; free) holds specimens of local wildlife, including a bald eagle and a growling cougar that endlessly eyes the neighboring elk. The captions are in Navajo, so visits double as language lessons.

Northeast Arizona: the Navajo Nation

Practicalities

Regular **buses**, run by the Navajo Transit System (☎520/729-5449), connect Window Rock with Gallup, New Mexico (see p.88) as well as Tuba City and the Hopi mesas. The **Navajoland Tourism** office, in the Economic Development Building on Hwy-264 a couple of miles west of town, can supply general information on the region (PO Box 663; Mon–Fri 8am–5pm; ☎520/871-6436, fax 871-7381; *www.navajo.org*).

The zip code for Window Rock is AZ 86515.

Much of the Navajo's day-to-day business is conducted in the **restaurant** and coffeeshop of the *Navajo Nation Inn*, at 48 W Hwy-264 (☎520/871-4108 or 1-800/662-6189, fax 520/871-5466; ④), which is open for all meals daily. Ask at the desk for details of their program of local **tours**, which can incorporate pretty much anything you're interested in doing, but start at an expensive $100 per day. The rooms are good value, but can be hard to come by in summer; if you're stuck, continue two miles west to the *Navajoland Days Inn* in St Michaels (☎520/871-5690; ④), which has an indoor pool.

The Hopi Indian Reservation

The ten thousand inhabitants of the **Hopi Indian Reservation** can trace their ancestry back well over a thousand years, to the **Ancestral Puebloan** people who dominated the entire Four Corners region. What's more, almost uniquely in the United States, the Hopi have occupied the same spot for at least eight hundred years.

For a detailed history of the Hopi, see p.534.

To outsiders, it's not obvious why, with the whole Southwest to pick from, the Hopi should have chosen to live on three barren and unprepossessing fingers of rock, poking from the southern flanks of **Black Mesa** in the depths of northeast Arizona. There are two simple answers. The first is that while Black Mesa has no perennial streams, its subterranean rocks are tilted at just the correct angle to deliver a tiny but dependable trickle of water, and that the "black" in its name comes from the coal that gives the Hopi limitless reserves of fuel. The second is that the Hopi used to farm and hunt across a much wider area, and have only been restricted to their mesa-top villages by the steady encroachment of their Navajo neighbors. While the Hopi are celebrated for their skill at "**dry farming**," managing to preserve enough precious liquid to grow

The Hopi
Indian
Reservation

HOPI RELIGION: THE KACHINAS

The Hopi feel neither the urge nor the obligation to divulge details of their **religious beliefs** and practices to outsiders. To that end, they have resisted attempts to make Hopic a written language, or to expose it to scrutiny by teaching it in schools. Missionaries and anthropologists have gleaned what they can, but well-known accounts of Hopi spirituality, such as Frank Waters' *Book of the Hopi*, are based on the reports of informants not themselves initiated into the innermost secrets of the *kiva*. Inevitably, Hopi spirituality has been repeatedly misrepresented to the world, whether as barbarous devil-worship or New Age guff.

There is in any case no single unified Hopi religion; ceremonials vary from clan to clan and village to village. The most basic common element is the role of the **kachina** (often spelled *katsina*, with the plural *katsinum*). These "spirit messengers," which may represent the spirits of the dead, live in the San Francisco peaks north of Flagstaff, and return to the Hopi mesas in the form of rain-bearing clouds.

There are over three hundred different *kachinas*. At one time, they visited the mesas in person; now they come in the form of masked dancers. Not every village follows the same **ceremonial calendar**, but in general the *kachinas* arrive each year in early February for the *Powamuya* ceremony, or **Bean Dance**. Each matriarch receives a bundle of fresh bean sprouts to plant for the coming year, and the threats of the *so'so'yoktu* ogres to eat disobedient (*ka-hopi*) children are placated by gifts of food from their parents. The *kachinas* continue to visit throughout the growing season, before returning home after the *Niman* ceremony or **Home Dance** in July.

The Hopi do not worship the *kachinas*; their main significance is as examples and allegories for the children. All Hopi babies receive a *tihu* – what outsiders know as a **kachina** doll – at their first *Niman* ceremony, and the girls receive further dolls at each *Powamuya* and *Niman* ceremony thereafter. Most boys and girls alike are initiated into a **kachina society** at around the age of ten, when they discover that the *kachina* dancers are their own relatives, and begin to participate themselves.

All the Southwestern pueblos had some form of *kachina* cult, which is occasionally suggested to have arisen as a post-Hispanic mimicry of Catholicism. However, pottery, murals and rock carvings point to an earlier origin, around 1300 AD. Anthropologists have tended to argue that it spread east from the Hopi mesas or Zuni rather than west from the Rio Grande, though the *kachina* cult's virtual disappearance along the Rio Grande is probably due to vigorous Spanish attempts to stamp it out. In fact, it seems to have reached both regions from the **Mimbres** culture to the south, and to have developed in **Mexico**.

The role and iconography of specific Hopi *kachinas* strongly echo **Aztec** deities such as **Tlaloc**, the god of rain, and **Quetzalcoatl**, the plumed serpent, who was also the bringer of rain and corn. For the Aztec preoccupation with death, blood and human sacrifice, however, the Hopi and other Southwestern people substituted an obsessive focus on **rain**.

ATTENDING HOPI CEREMONIES

For much of the twentieth century, Hopi ceremonies were promoted as tourist attractions. Even after cameras were banned in 1916, occasions such as the **Snake Dance**, when members of the Snake clan dance with live snakes between their teeth, attracted as many as 2500 observers. In recent years, however, the Hopi have moved towards the **exclusion** of non-Indians. By 1989, Second Mesa had closed all its ceremonies to outsiders, and it was joined by all the First Mesa villages in 1992 after the publication of a *Marvel* comic that characterized the *kachinas* as violent avengers.

While spectators are now very unlikely to be allowed at any *kachina* dances, however, some **social dances**, held between August and January when the *kachinas* are away from the mesas, may still be "open." Held in the village plazas, these usually take place at the weekend, so that Hopi who live off the reservation can return. Specific timings tend not to be announced until a few days in advance; for information, ask at the Cultural Center (see p.63) or call ☎520/734-2441.

KACHINA DOLLS

Kachina masks, worn by the dancers, are sacred objects, and the Hopi have successfully petitioned to remove them from museum displays. However, because a *tihu* (the plural is *ti'tihu*) is just an instructional tool, it has become acceptable for *kachina* dolls to be sold to outsiders as collectors' items.

The *ti'tihu* given to Hopi children were originally flat dolls that were intended to hang from beams or walls within the home. Made from kaolin clay, and thus white in color, the basic shape was painted to show a head, plus a pair of arms folded over a kilt that represented rain. Local trading posts were stocking these simple dolls in the 1890s, and by 1900 they were being made specifically for sale.

Since then, they have acquired a much greater complexity of form and color, as well as feet to enable them to stand. Most are carved from cottonwood roots; the carving is seen as a prayer for water, symbolizing the root's own search for water. The artists themselves – who thanks to the art market's desire for signed pieces are no longer anonymous – became more interested in representing human anatomy, and also began to tailor their designs to suit the tastes of white collectors. Strictly speaking, only men should carve *ti'tihu*, but the rewards are great enough for some women now to be making them as well.

Not all *ti'tihu* represent *kachinas*. Some of the most popular designs depict the clowns who also appear during ceremonies, such as the black-and-white-striped *koshares*, and the knobbed "mudheads" or *koyemsi*. Just as the clowns may devise costumes to mock tourists, for example, certain *ti'tihu* caricature of recognizable figures, like basketball players or anthropologists.

The Hopi do however draw the line at attempts by others to cash in on the commercial success of the *kachina*-doll business. During the 1960s, the tribal council failed in a bid to copyright the word "*kachina*," and thus stop Navajo and other non-Indian copyists from using the name. Genuine hand-carved dolls are both exquisite and expensive, and a top-class carver will produce fewer than fifty per year, while fake *kachinas* are mass-produced in New Mexico at the rate of over 100,000 per year. People from Ácoma pueblo recently acceded to a Hopi request to stop working in one such factory, but the Navajo have refused to do so.

Good places to buy a *kachina* doll include the Hopi Cultural Center on Second Mesa, the Museum of Northern Arizona in Flagstaff (see p.287), and the Pueblo Cultural Center in Albuquerque (see p.177), though it's hard to find a reasonable-sized piece for under $300. The best bet of all is to take a tour of Walpi, and see what you're offered.

The Hopi
Indian
Reservation

If you do get the chance to attend a Hopi ceremony, wear clothing that fully covers your body, keep your distance, and do not photograph, sketch or question either dancers or audience.

corn, beans and squash on hand-tilled terraces laid out beneath the villages, this precarious and difficult way of life has nonetheless been forced upon them.

The Hopi **language**, Hopic, belongs to the Uto-Aztecan group of languages, and is spoken in different dialects on each of the three mesas. While it bears similarities to the Ute and Paiute languages, the Hopi themselves have little in common with either tribe. Their culture and beliefs are instead closely related to those of the Pueblo peoples of New Mexico, to the east. Until the 1920s, the Hopi were known by a name coined by the people of Ácoma: **Moki**, or Moqui. Because that sounded too much like a Hopic word meaning "to have died," they then changed to *Hopi*, which means "well-behaved."

The Hopi are a matriarchal society, with homes, land and clan affiliation passing down the female line. They are not a united people; each of the thirteen villages or settlements, which belong to five main clusters, is an independent entity. As required by federal law, there is a Hopi Tribal Council, but it's currently recognized by the religious leaders of only two of the villages.

By their very survival, not to mention the persistence of their ancient beliefs and ceremonies in the heart of modern Arizona, the Hopi have long been a source of fascination to outsiders. Visitors are welcomed, but the Hopi have no desire to turn themselves into a **tourist** attraction. Two motels make it possible to stay on the reservation, and stores and galleries provide plenty of opportunity to buy much-prized Hopi **crafts** such as pottery, basketwork, silver overlay jewelry and hand-carved *kachina* dolls. However, tourists who arrive in the hope of extensive sightseeing – let alone spiritual revelations – are likely to leave disappointed, and quite possibly dismayed by what they perceive as conspicuous poverty.

*For more
about Hopi
crafts, see
p.31.*

Since 1986, when increased mining revenues finally placed the tribal economy on a relatively secure footing, non-Indians have been barred from almost all Hopi ceremonies. These days, the only way visitors can get a sense of traditional Hopi life is to take a guided tour of the magnificently situated village of **Walpi**, on First Mesa.

Arrival and information

The Hopi mesas – three distinct spurs along a 25-mile stretch of Black Mesa, numbered from east to west as **First**, **Second** and **Third** mesas – are roughly fifty miles north of I-40, fifty miles east of Tuba City, and ninety miles southwest of Canyon de Chelly.

Both the roads from the interstate up to the mesas, **Hwy-87** from Winslow and **Hwy-77** from Holbrook, run through a superbly desolate butte-studded segment of the Navajo reservation, on the western fringes of the Painted Desert. If you're coming from the Grand Canyon, take **Hwy-264** east from US-160. Once beyond the Hopi outpost of **Moenkopi**, just outside Tuba City (see p.41), this traverses some rugged canyonlands and then climbs onto Third Mesa after around fifty miles.

The essential first stop is the roadside **Hopi Cultural Center** below Second Mesa, which serves as motel, restaurant, gift store and information center. If any forthcoming events are open to tourists, the friendly staff should be able to tell you about them. Otherwise, check out the wide-ranging historical exhibits, and the choice displays of Hopi arts and crafts, in the adjoining **museum** (summer Mon–Sat 8am–5pm, Sun 9am–4pm; winter Mon–Fri 8am–5pm; $3). The large single-story shop next door is particularly good for silver.

Touring the Hopi mesas

Each of the mesa-top Hopi villages centers around a **plaza**, where successive generations have built new houses on top of the old ones as they crumble into sand. Often the main entrance is via the roof, itself reached by a wooden ladder. A few buildings are now constructed of grey concrete blocks, but they still blend almost imperceptibly with the ruins that trail away down the slopes. Several villages stand on open seams of coal, and large chunks of coal lie scattered around. Outhouses are dotted across the hillsides; all waste was traditionally thrown over the edge of the mesa to tumble down and fertilize the terraces. That conservationist policy works less well now that refrigerators and old bedsteads are being thrown over too.

For tourist information about the Hopi Reservation, but not motel reservations, call ☎ 520/734-2441.

Fortunately, the most impressive village, **WALPI**, is the only one that offers **guided tours** to visitors (daily: winter 9.30am–4pm, summer 9am–6pm; $5; ☎520/737-2262). By Hopi standards, Walpi is not in fact that old; it was hastily thrown together in the immediate aftermath of the Pueblo Revolt of 1680, when the people of First Mesa decided to move to a more secure site in the face of possible Spanish or Navajo attack (see p.535). The spot they chose is absolutely stunning, standing alone at the narrow southernmost tip of the mesa, and connected to the other First Mesa villages by the merest slender neck of stone, with a drop of three hundred feet to either side. It's now home to around 35 people, who live without electricity or running water.

To see Walpi, take Hwy-264 to modern **POLACCA**, at the foot of First Mesa, then drive a mile up the twisting paved road until it ends in **SICHOMOVI**. Although you can't tell where one village stops and the next begins, you've just passed through **HANO**. Its inhabitants arrived during the Pueblo Revolt to offer their services as the defenders of First Mesa, and still speak the Tewa language.

The tours assemble in Sichomovi's small Ponsi Hall Community Center, setting off at regular intervals for a half-hour walk to and around Walpi. Depending on the time of year, you'll either be in a group of twenty or so, or on your own, but either way there's plenty of opportunity to ask questions, and to buy pottery, *kachina* dolls, and fresh-baked *piiki*, a flatbread made with blue cornflour.

Accommodation and eating

The best place to **stay** on the Hopi Reservation is the modern, mock-Pueblo *Hopi Cultural Center Motel* (☎520/734-2401, fax 734-6651; winter ④, summer ⑤); in summer, its unexotic but adequate rooms are usually booked solid a week or more in advance. The cafeteria serves good, substantial meals, but be warned that there's precious little to do between the time it closes, at 9pm, and 7am the next morning, when you can indulge your curiosity by having blue cornflakes for breakfast.

The price codes used here are explained on p.15.

Extremely basic double rooms are also available at the *Keams Canyon Motel* (☎520/738-2297; ②), twenty miles along Hwy-264 at the eastern edge of the reservation. There's a free campground here too, as well as a popular **cafe**, open until 8pm on weekdays and 6pm on weekends and dishing up local-style fast food (watch out for *noqkwivi*, an exceptionally tough mutton stew).

Southwest Colorado

In ancient times, of course, the straight-line boundaries that divide the states of Arizona, New Mexico, Utah and Colorado – and mark the northeastern limits of the Navajo Nation – did not exist. As a result, while Colorado might not spring to mind as a "Southwestern" state, its far southwest corner holds some of the region's most fascinating archeological sites. **Mesa Verde National Park** is absolutely unmissable, and **Ute Mountain Tribal Park** offers adventurous travelers an even more exhilarating sense of discovery.

Once you've crossed the border into Colorado, it's hard to resist the lure of the Rockies, looming along the skyline to the north. There's no scope in this book to do more than sketch out a brief tour, looping up the **San Juan Skyway** from lively **Durango** to historic mining towns such as **Silverton** and **Ouray**.

Four Corners Monument Navajo Tribal Park

The **Four Corners Monument Navajo Tribal Park** (daily: May–Aug 7am–8pm Sept–April 8am–5pm; $2.50), reached by a short spur road half a mile northeast of US-160, is the only place in the United States where four states meet at a single point. However exciting you may find the concept, the reality is bleak and dull. A steady stream of visitors mooch around the pivotal brass plaque, ponderously contorting a limb into each state for demeaning photographs. Navajo stalls on all sides sell crafts, T-shirts and frybread.

Ute Mountain Tribal Park

For a couple of centuries after **Ute Indians** acquired horses from the Spanish, their hunting territory extended east from Utah as far as what's now Nebraska. As miners pushed the Victorian-era frontier westwards, however, the Ute were confined to ever-decreasing areas of poorer land. The creation of reservations split them into three separate groups: the **Northern Utes**, who now live in the mountains near Utah's border with Wyoming; the **Southern Utes**, who occupy a strip of southern Colorado south of Durango; and the **Ute Mountain Utes**. These latter take their name from a long, low mountain ridge in Colorado's far southwestern corner, known to outsiders as **Sleeping Ute Mountain** because of its uncanny resemblance, when seen from the east, to a slumbering warrior.

Among the Southwest's poorest peoples, the Ute Mountain Utes draw their income from mineral leases and a casino near the main settlement of **Towaoc**. They also run the inaccessible but utterly enthralling **Ute Mountain Tribal Park**, which abuts against Mesa Verde National Park and preserves an equally extraordinary but far less visited assortment of ancient **Ancestral Puebloan** remains.

The only way to see the park is to join a **Ute-guided tour**. In principle, these leave at 8.30am daily from the tribe's **visitor center**-cum-museum (no fixed hours), housed in a former gas station at the intersection of US-160 and US-666, twenty miles up from the Four Corners Monument. That schedule varies according to demand, however, and while in season it's usually possible to take the tour by turning up at the meeting point around 8am, it's much safer to arrange things in advance (☎970/565-3751 ext 282 or 1-800/847-5485; *utepark@fone.net*). As this phone line is not connected to the visitor center itself, however, you can't call on the day you want to take a tour; in fact, you may well find difficulty in getting through at all.

If you don't have the time to take a full-day tour, which costs $30 and gets you back to the highway around 4pm, the half-day tour at $17 makes a very poor alternative. On the half-day trip, you simply leave the group at the end of the morning, having seen a couple of potsherd-scattered mounds, concealing ancient surface-level pueblos, at the foot of the cliffs. On the full-day tour, on the other hand, you continue along a remote and circuitous dirt road to the top of the mesa, and then inch down a succession of ladders onto a three-mile ledge footpath skirting **Lion Canyon**. This leads to three beautifully preserved **cliff dwellings**, built at the same time as those on Mesa Verde: Tree House Ruin, the eighty-room Lion House, and the precarious Eagle's Nest, perched in a colossal natural alcove. The whole expedition demands a fair amount of walking and something of a head for heights, but only the final ascent to Eagle's Nest is difficult for vertigo sufferers – you can admire it from below if you prefer.

Visitors are expected to drive their own sturdy vehicles on the tour, and to bring food and drink for the day. However, the tour leader's van will accommodate half a dozen passengers, and if there's room, you're welcome to pay an extra $5 to ride along, which means you get the benefit of that much more informed commentary on what you're seeing.

Hovenweep National Monument

Hidden in the fifty-mile-wide swath of no-man's-land that straddles the Utah–Colorado border, the Ancestral Puebloan ruins at **HOVEN-WEEP NATIONAL MONUMENT** lack the scale and setting of the Mesa Verde cliff dwellings or similar Four Corners sites. Instead, sprouting from the rims of shallow desert canyons and dwarfed by the distant mountains, they offer a haunting sense of timeless isolation. They also have one distinctive and unusual feature, in the shape of the tall round **towers** that many archeologists regard as early astronomical observatories.

There is no admission fee at Hovenweep, which is named after a Ute word meaning "deserted valley."

Whatever most tourist maps may suggest, almost all the roads that lead to Hovenweep have now been paved, thanks largely to companies such as Mobil drilling for oil and gas around Aneth. The monument is best reached by driving 35 miles due west from Cortez, leaving US-160 near the airport at the south end of town, or 25 miles east from US-191 via Hwy-262, which branches off halfway between Bluff and Blanding in Utah; it's also possible to follow a dirt road southwest from Pleasant View in Colorado.

Although Hovenweep preserves six distinct conglomerations of ruins, easy public access is restricted to the **Square Tower Group**, behind the monument's small **ranger station** (daily: March–Oct 8am–6pm; Nov–Feb 9am–4.30pm; ☎435/459-4344). Until a few years ago, it was possible to walk among and even into several different structures, but the trail system now keeps visitors at a safe distance.

The shorter of the two main routes, the half-mile **Tower Loop Trail**, offers good views of the largest ruins at the head of Little Ruin Canyon. The grandly named **Hovenweep Castle**, a four-square building just a few yards from the ranger station, was constructed around 1200 AD. It may well have stood guard over a much larger pueblo complex that nestled on the sandy floor of the canyon a mere thirty feet below, clustered around the perennial spring that was the site's only source of water. Only **Square Tower Ruin** now survives down there, while Hovenweep Castle has endured, a perfect illustration of the biblical admonition that only a house built on rock shall stand.

The **Square Tower Ruins Trail** continues along the far side of the canyon, and eventually dips across it and loops back to the ranger station, a circuit that takes a little less than an hour to complete. Highlights along the way include a number of ruins perched on solitary boulders and pinnacles, as well as the fortress-like **Stronghold House** and the prosaically-named **Unit-type House**, where niches in the walls appear to line up with the angle of the sun at the summer and winter solstices.

No accommodation, gasoline or food is available at or anywhere near Hovenweep, but (funding permitting) the 31-site **campground** beside the ranger station remains open all year ($10; no reservations). In winter, water is only available at the ranger station.

Cortez

The town of **CORTEZ**, twenty miles north of the US-160/US-166 intersection, consists of little more than a long curve of over-developed highway. Were it not so close to Mesa Verde National Park, there would be no reason to visit; as it is, Cortez offers a large if not exactly broad selection of roadside motels and diners.

Practicalities

The local **visitor center**, on the edge of City Park at 928 E Main St (daily 8am–6pm; ☎970/565-4048 or 1-800/253-1616) has information on the entire state. Both Mesa Verde Tours (☎970/565-1278 or 1-800/626-2066) and Four Corners Tours (☎970/882-8880 or 1-800/884-0591) offer full-day **tours** of Mesa Verde for around $60.

The zip code for Cortez is CO 81321.

A couple of dozen very similar **motels** line the main strip of Cortez; the *Budget Host Inn*, 2040 E Main St (☎970/565-3738; ③), is among the best value, with the *Arrow Motor Inn*, 440 S Broadway (☎970/565-7778; ③), and *Aneth Lodge*, 645 E Main St (☎970/565-3453 or 1-877/263-8454; ③), as reasonable alternatives. *Kelly's Place*, ten miles west at 14663 County Rd G (☎970/565-3125 or 1-800/745-4885, fax 970/565-3540; ④), has eight en-suite **B&B** rooms, with ancient ruins on site and guided hikes and horse-rides available.

The price codes used here are explained on p.15.

The best **restaurant** in town is unquestionably the *Dry Dock*, 200 W Main St (☎970/564-9404), which dishes up delicious seafood specialties in a garden decorated with underwater-themed murals; they even have fresh oysters. For a cheaper old-time Western diner, head for *Homesteaders*, 45 E Main St (☎970/565-6253; closed Sun in winter), where most of the barbecued meats and fish, and Mexican fry-ups, cost under $10. Newer Western traditions are exemplified by the nearby *Main Street Brewery*, 21 E Main St (☎970/564-9112), a brewpub that's open daily from 3pm for microbrews plus simple meals, and the *Hot Bagel Bakery*, an espresso and snack bar at 31 W Main St (☎970/564-1122; closed Sun). Part cafe, part ramshackle bookstore, *Earth Song Haven*, across the road at 34 W Main St (☎970/565-9125), serves eccentric $5 lunch specials such as *pansit bihan* – containing rice, noodles, choc-chip cookies, melon and gherkins – and good smoothies.

Around Montezuma Valley

Cortez is very much Montezuma Valley's biggest town these days, but a thousand years ago the entire valley was densely populated. Romantic notions of this as a peaceful agricultural community have been dashed by the latest archeological research, which as well as uncovering evidence of warfare and wholesale slaughter has even provided the first conclusive proof of ancient **cannibalism** in the Southwest. Human excrement discovered alongside the butchered remains of 23 Ancestral Puebloans in Cowboy Wash was found to contain proteins that could only have come from eating their flesh.

Several small museums and lesser-known sites dotted around the valley now commemorate its previous occupants. The **Anasazi Heritage Center**, three miles west of **DOLORES** and six miles due north of Cortez, centers on a couple of twelfth-century pueblos. Excavated and stabilized during the construction of nearby McPhee Dam – responsible for turning the Dolores River into a broad lake at this point – they're named for the eighteenth-century Spanish friars Domínguez and Escalante, who first noted the traces of prehistoric Indians in the area. Admission to the well-equipped **Museum of Pueblo Life** costs $3 (daily: summer 9am–5pm, winter 9am–4pm), though access to the trail around the ruins themselves is free (daily 8am–5.30pm).

From **Pleasant View** on US-666, fourteen miles northwest, an undulating straight road leads nine miles to **Lowry Pueblo Ruins** (no fixed hours; free). There's not a tremendous amount to see at this freestanding pueblo, but in summer, it's noteworthy as one of the few sites where at least part of an **Ancestral Puebloan mural** remains in place on the walls of a "Great Kiva." In winter, on the other hand, the mural is taken away for preservation, and the gravel surface of the approach road's last four miles is often impassable to vehicles.

For more about Great Kivas, see p.82.

Also in summer, **Crow Canyon Archeological Center**, five miles northwest of Cortez at 23390 County Rd K, runs day programs for amateur archeologists (June to mid-Sept Wed & Thurs 9am; $45; ☎970/565-8975 or 1-800/422-8975). These provide the chance to assist on digs at Ancestral Puebloan sites in the valley, such as **Sand Canyon Pueblo**, a walled city that once covered the cliff-tops at Crow Canyon, or the 1800-room **Yellow Jacket** further north.

Yucca House National Monument near Cortez, shown on many maps, has never been excavated and remains closed to the public.

The *Rio Grande Southern Hotel*, 101 S Fifth St (PO Box 5162, Dolores, CO 81323; ☎970/882-7527; closed Dec–Feb; ③), is an inexpensive, atmospheric **B&B inn**, not far from the Anasazi Heritage Center in Dolores. There's more accommodation available in little **MANCOS**, ten miles east, including the *Mesa Verde Motel*, 191 Railroad Ave (PO Box 552, Mancos, CO 81328; ☎970/533-7741 or 1-800/825-MESA; winter ②, summer ③), which has its own restaurant.

Mesa Verde National Park

MESA VERDE NATIONAL PARK, the only national park in the US
to be exclusively devoted to archeological remains, is set high in the
plateaus of southwest Colorado, off US-160 halfway between Cortez
and Mancos. It's an astonishing place, so far off the beaten track that
its extensive **Ancestral Puebloan ruins** remained unseen by outsiders until late in the nineteenth century.

Mesa Verde itself – the "green table" – is a densely wooded sandstone
plateau, cut at its southern edge by sheer canyons that divide the land
into narrow fingers. Hundreds of natural alcoves, eaten high into the
canyon walls by seeping water, served as homes for over 700 years; by
the time they were abandoned, around 1300 AD, several held multistory **cliff dwellings** that have remained virtually intact to this day.

By Southwestern standards, the mesa is not especially pretty, and
it doesn't offer the same **hiking** opportunities as the region's other
national parks. The relics, however, are compelling enough to make
Mesa Verde an essential stop on any Four Corners itinerary; it has
even been voted as the world's top tourist attraction by readers of
Condé Nast Traveler. As things can get very crowded in summer,
the **best months** to visit are in May, September and October. The
8000ft elevation means that most of the sights become inaccessible
in **winter**, though the park itself, its main museum, and one ruin –
Spruce Tree House – remain open all year round. **Concessions** such
as gas, food and lodging only operate between late April and mid-
October.

A history of Mesa Verde

Although Archaic sites in Montezuma Valley down below date back to
5500 BC, Ancestral Puebloans are thought to have been the only
inhabitants that Mesa Verde has ever had. No one has lived here since
the thirteenth century, and despite repeated searches, the earliest
trace of humans is a Modified Basketmaker pithouse from 550 AD.

People first moved to the mesa, therefore, at around the time they
acquired the skill of pottery. They were not so much farmers as gar-
deners, who continued to gather wild plants and hunt deer and rabbits as well as growing small fields of corn and owning domesticated
dogs and turkeys. For 500 years, they lived in pithouses dug into the
floors of sheltered caves; then, around 1100 AD, they congregated in
walled villages up on the mesa tops. A century later, they returned to
the canyon-side alcoves to build the "palaces" for which Mesa Verde
is now famous.

As some rooms were exclusively used for storage, each settlement probably held roughly as many people as it had rooms. That
would give the largest, Cliff Palace, a population approaching 250.
Two or three people may have slept in a typical living room, measuring six feet by eight feet, while each family had its own *kiva* – see
p.520 – which when not in ceremonial use was used for weaving and

*For a detailed
history of
Ancestral
Puebloan cul-
ture – and an
explanation of
why the name
"Anasazi" is no
longer widely
used – see
p.520.*

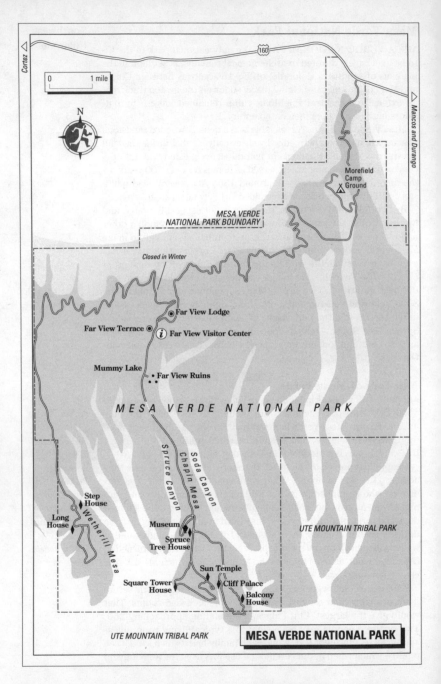

other domestic activities. Neither the architecture, nor the relatively few burials that have been found – some in sealed chambers, and some simply, if reverentially, in the trash heaps – indicate any rigid social hierarchy. Mesa Verde may well have been a **peripheral community**. While its population is thought to have peaked at around 2500, in the middle of the thirteenth century, there were at least eight larger surface pueblos down in Montezuma Valley, whose inhabitants are thought to have been generally hostile to the Mesa Verdeans.

Ironically, archeologists regard the cliff dwellings that seem so elegant to modern visitors as signs of a declining culture. They say the mesa-top pueblos were more sophisticated in both design and construction, while the alcove complexes are haphazard accretions, forced into contortions by the constraints of the rock, and characterized by inferior craftsmanship. These were not ideal homes; older members of the community must have found it impossible to get in or out, while children lived in constant peril of fatal falls. In theory, each complex got its water from the seep or spring that had created its alcove in the first place, but many of those springs had run dry, leaving them with a constant cycle of fetching and carrying.

All of which begs the question of **why** the cliff dwellings were built. Some experts argue that sites such as Balcony House were primarily defensive, though there's little evidence that they were often attacked, and dwellings such as Spruce Tree House lie exposed to assault, while the towers are of little use as lookouts. Agricultural space may have been at a premium, with the entire mesa top crisscrossed by dams, terraces and irrigation channels. In any case, Mesa Verde was completely abandoned by the end of the thirteenth century. The traditional explanation, that a **drought** lasting from 1276 until 1299 drove the Ancestral Puebloans away, only tells part of the story, in that six previous droughts had been just as bad. The likely truth is that both firewood and game animals in the region had become seriously depleted, that the climate had turned too cold to grow crops, and survival became too much of a struggle. The bulk of the Mesa Verdeans migrated into what's now New Mexico, where they established the pueblos where their descendants still live.

Although Mesa Verde was named by the Spanish in the seventeenth century, the ruins themselves went unrecorded for two hundred more years. Photographer William Henry Jackson snapped some lesser sites in 1874, and a passing prospector spotted Balcony House in 1884, but the outside world first took notice when Richard Wetherill stumbled upon Cliff Palace in a snowstorm in 1888. The **Wetherills**, a local ranching family, took to finding and selling Ancestral Puebloan artifacts as a way of life, and helped the Swedish Count Gustaf Nordensköld to ship caseloads of

Thanks to Nordensköld, the National Museum of Finland holds the world's finest collection of Mesa Verde artifacts.

ancient pottery to Europe in 1891. Their activities prompted the Antiquities Act of 1906, which prohibited dealing in archeological treasures, and the creation of Mesa Verde National Park in the same year.

Arrival and information

The access road to Mesa Verde climbs south from US-160 ten miles east of **Cortez**, and 35 miles west of **Durango**. Once past the entrance station – where an **admission charge** of $10 per vehicle, $5 for motorcyclists, cyclists and pedestrians, is payable – it twists and turns for fifteen miles to the **Far View visitor center** (late April to late Oct daily 8am–5pm; ☎970/529-4461). Exhibits inside cover Navajo, Hopi and Pueblo crafts and jewelry. Immediately beyond, the road divides to the two main constellations of remains: Chapin Mesa to the south, and Wetherill Mesa to the west.

Advance information on Mesa Verde National Park is available from PO Box 8, Mesa Verde, CO 81330; or by visiting www.nps.gov /meve.

To tour any of the three major ruins, as opposed to simply skimming around the overlooks, you must first buy **tickets** at the visitor center. The exact seasons and times of the tours vary according to both funding and climate; each costs $1.75, with tickets valid for one specific time only. On **Chapin Mesa**, as a rule, **Cliff Palace** is open daily between 9am and 5pm from late April until early November, with tours every half-hour in midsummer and every hour in low season, and **Balcony House** is open for hourly tours from late April until mid-October, during the same hours. You may well not be allowed to tour Balcony House and Cliff Palace on the same day (though many couples circumvent the regulations by queuing separately for tickets). If you're forced to choose, Cliff Palace can at least be seen from a distance without joining a tour, but on the other hand, the Cliff Palace tours are much less strenuous than those of Balcony House. On **Wetherill Mesa**, which is generally accessible between late May and early September, hourly tours of **Long House** operate between 9am and 4pm daily. Allow several hours between tours on Chapin and Wetherill mesas. After the visitor center closes in late fall, tour tickets are sold for the remainder of the season at the museum on Chapin Mesa (see opposite).

Mesa Verde tours from Durango are detailed on p.76, from Cortez on p.67.

Park **bus tours** start daily in season from *Far View Motor Lodge* and *Morefield Campground* (adults $16 for a half-day, $21 for a full day; under-12s $8 on either); contact either for details.

Accommodation and eating

The only **rooms** at Mesa Verde are at the summer-only *Far View Motor Lodge*, near the visitor center (PO Box 277, Mancos, CO 81328; ☎970/529-4421 or 1-800/449-2288; *www.visitmesaverde .com*; winter ☎970/533-7731; late April to mid-June & early to mid-Oct ④, mid-June to early Oct ⑤). It's a peaceful place, away from the bustle of the park; guestrooms, which lack phones or TVs, are in two-story units dotted around the mesa-top. The sweeping views reach into the Rockies to the north, and across nearby slopes blackened by a forest fire in 1996, but no archeological sites are visible. The *Metate Room*, in the mock-adobe main lodge, serves all meals daily.

The park's official **campground** – the very large, never full *Morefield Campground* (late April to mid-Oct; ☎970/529-4421) – is four miles up from the entrance, and thus a long way from the ruins. No reservations are necessary, and a site for one or two vehicles costs $10.

Food is also available in season at the *Far View Terrace*, across from the visitor center – which serves espresso coffees and has a gas station – and all year round at *Spruce Tree Terrace* near the Chapin Mesa museum, which has a pleasant shaded terrace. Light snacks are sold at the end of the road on Wetherill Mesa.

Southwest
Colorado

*Lodging in
Cortez is
detailed on
p.67, and in
Durango on
p.76.*

Chapin Mesa

A couple of miles from the visitor center towards **Chapin Mesa**, you reach **Far View** itself, a mesa-top pueblo abandoned early in the thirteenth century. Thanks to the coal-burning power plants that dominate the middle distance, it seldom lives up to its name these days. Archeologists used to think it drew its water from the artificial **Mummy Lake** nearby; now they wonder whether this large depression, capable of holding half a million gallons, was in fact an open-air plaza.

Another four miles on, **Chapin Mesa Archeological Museum** (daily: summer 8am–6.30pm, winter 8am–5pm) contains the park's best displays on the Ancestral Puebloans, including several dioramas made in the 1930s. Hikers can register at the adjacent **park headquarters** for a couple of unremarkable two- to three-mile nature trails.

This is also the starting point for the short, steep hike down to **Spruce Tree House**, the only ruin that can be seen in winter. Consisting of several well-preserved three-story structures, snugly moulded into the recesses of a rocky alcove and fronted by open plazas, the neat little village was occupied from 1200 AD until 1276 AD. One of its *kivas* has been reroofed, and visitors can enter the dusty, unadorned interior by way of a ladder.

Ruins Road, beyond the museum area, is only open between April and early November, from 8am until sunset daily. The western of its two one-way, six-mile loops is the one to skip if you're pressed for time, but its overlooks are still interesting. At **Square Tower House**, a 500-foot stroll is rewarded by views of an 80-room alcove complex, focused around the four-story Square Tower – at 26 feet, the tallest tower in the park. **Sun Point Overlook** looks across Spruce Canyon to as many as twelve distinct cliff dwellings, including Cliff Palace, making it clear just how crowded the canyon was in its heyday. Unlike the alcove sites, the mesa-top **Sun Temple**, next, was built to a premeditated design, and may have been a ceremonial center for the whole community. It was never finished, however, and its shape and function can only really be appreciated from aerial photos; walking around its walls is not very thrilling.

Details of Cliff Palace tours are on p.72. As with most of the ruins, the best time for photography is late afternoon.

The first stop on the eastern portion of Ruins Road, **Cliff Palace**, is the largest Ancestral Puebloan cliff dwelling to survive anywhere. Tucked a hundred feet below an overhanging ledge of pale rock, its 217 rooms once housed over two hundred people, while its 23 *kivas* suggest they were split between 23 families or clans. If you haven't managed to get a ticket for a tour (see p.72), you can still get a great view from the promontory where the tour groups gather, just below the parking lot. Entering the ruin itself, especially on a quieter day, provides a haunting evocation of a lost and little-known world, as you walk through the empty plazas and peer down into the mysterious *kivas*. Fading murals can still be discerned inside some of the structures. As you leave, climbing an unalarming metal stairway through a narrow crevice, you may spot the original toe- and footholds used by the Ancestral Puebloans.

Technically, Ruins Road passes out of the national park just beyond Cliff Palace, and briefly enters **Ute Mountain Tribal Park**, where you can pick up information on tours (see p.65). It then arrives at **Balcony House**. This is one of the few Mesa Verde complexes that was clearly geared towards defence. Built around 1240, it was remodeled during the 1270s to make it even more impregnable; access is very difficult, and it's not visible from above. Guided tours involve scrambling up three hair-raising ladders and crawling through a narrow tunnel, teetering all the while above a steep drop into Soda Canyon. Park authorities present it as being more "fun" than the other ruins, but unless you share the fearless Ancestral Puebloan attitude to heights, you might prefer to give it a miss.

Distant views of Balcony House can be had from three-quarters of a mile along the forested **Soda Canyon Overlook Trail**, which starts a short way further around Ruins Road.

Wetherill Mesa

The tortuous twelve-mile drive onto **Wetherill Mesa** from the visitor center is usually open from late May until early September. Access is then permitted between 8am and 4.30pm daily, though cycles and large vehicles such as RVs are always banned.

From the parking lot at the far end of the road, where there's a ranger station and snack kiosk, a free **miniature train** loops around the tip of the mesa. Priority is given to visitors with tickets for the timed Long House tours (see p.72). Any time spent waiting can be occupied by walking down to examine nearby **Step House**, where a single alcove contains a restored pithouse, dated to 626 AD, as well as a pueblo from 1226 AD.

The mini-train stops at various trailheads from which hikers can walk to early mesa-top sites or alcove overlooks, but its principal destination is the **Long House**. The park's second largest ruin is set in its largest cave; hour-long tours descend sixty or so steps to reach its central plaza, then scramble around its 150 rooms and 21 *kivas*. These ruins are said to be especially authentic, having been "re-sta-bilized" in recent years, rather than subjected to the same extensive rebuilding as the better-known sites in the early twentieth century. Excavations here uncovered a number of unburied bodies, some of whom had clearly met violent deaths.

Durango

Named after Durango Mexico and also twinned with it, **DURANGO** was founded in 1880 as a rail junction for the gold-rush community of Silverton, 45 miles further north. **Steam trains** still run the same high-mountain route, through the Animas Valley, and are the foundation of the local tourist economy. In addition, Durango has become a new-style Wild-West boom town, attracting a large influx of computerized teleworkers. Combine them with outdoors enthusiasts, who come to ride their **mountain bikes** on the grueling back roads nearby, and in the morning at least the place has a youthful, energetic buzz. Come the evening, most people seem a bit too wiped-out to do anything very much. Despite such recent developments as the construction of the huge Durango Mall at the town's southern end, Durango's **downtown** district, located along Main Avenue between Seventh and Eleventh streets, remains the liveliest urban area in the Four Corners, and is worth an hour or two of anyone's time.

Steam Trains and River Trips

Between May and October, the **Durango & Silverton Narrow Gauge Railroad** operates up to four daily return trips along a spectacular route through the mountains that parallels the gorgeous San Juan Skyway. All leave in early morning, from the depot at 479 Main Ave at the south end of town, and allow time for lunch in Silverton at the far end. The round trip costs $53, and reservations should be made at least two weeks in advance (☎970/247-2733; *www.durangotrain.com*). Shorter excursions, on the scenic section as far as Cascade Canyon, run between November and early May (daily 10am; $42).

Durango's visitor center can also supply details of the many operators which run **river-rafting** excursions on the Animas River. Brief float trips with Flexible Flyers (☎970/247-4268) cost from $10, and a one-hour ride through the nearest set of rapids is just $12, but it's also possible to take a full-day expedition.

Durango's zip code is CO 81301.

Arrival and information

Durango's **visitor center** is a block or two south of downtown near the train station (summer Mon–Fri 8am–7pm, Sat 10am–6pm, Sun 11am–5pm; winter Mon–Fri 8am–6pm, Sat 8am–5pm, Sun 10am–4pm; ☎970/247-0312 or 1-800/525-8855). Greyhound **buses** between Denver and Albuquerque call in at 275 E Eighth Ave.

   Mountain bikes can be rented for $25 per day from Southwest Adventures, 12th Street and Camino del Rio (☎970/259-0370), or Mountain Bike Specialists, 949 Main Ave (☎970/247-4066), while the cheapest **4WD rentals** are from RentAWreck, 21760 US-160 W (☎970/259-5858). Mesa Verde Tours (☎970/247-4161 or 1-800/626-2066) and Durango Transportation (☎970/259-4818) pick up from Durango motels at around 8am daily for $60 **Mesa Verde tours**.

Accommodation

The price codes used here are explained on p.15.

Very few of Durango's many **motels**, and none of the budget ones, are in walking distance of downtown, though a **free trolley** (Mon–Fri 7am–7pm) loops up and down forty blocks of Main Avenue. Almost all the motels double their rates in summer.

Durango Youth Hostel, 543 E Second Ave; ☎970/247-9905. Shabby downtown private hostel, with $13 dorms and a few basic private rooms. ①/②.

Scrubby Oaks, 1901 Florida Rd; ☎970/247-2176. Good-value mountain-view B&B, three miles east of town. ④.

Siesta, 3475 Main Ave; ☎970/247-0741. Very inexpensive motel, at the curve in the highway well north of the center. Winter ②, summer ③.

Strater Hotel, 699 Main Ave; ☎970/247-4431 or 1-800/247-4431, fax 970/259-2208; *www.strater.com*. Major downtown landmark not far from the railroad depot, with almost a hundred antique-furnished rooms. Winter ④, summer ⑥.

Vagabond Inn, 2180 Main Ave; ☎970/259-5901, fax 247-5345. Inexpensive but adequate motel, which looks smarter on the outside than it does once you're inside. Winter ②, summer ③.

Eating

Main Avenue downtown, and the streets to either side of it, are filled with places to **eat** and **drink**, some with their sights set on affluent train passengers, others aimed at young bikers. There's at least one **espresso bar** on every block.

Buzz House, 1019 Main Ave; ☎970/385-5831. Funky little coffeehouse, open daytime only and opposite *Carver's*, which serves lots of vegetarian snacks along with the usual espressos and smoothies.

Carver's Bakery & Brewpub, 1022 Main Ave; ☎970/259-2545. Bustling brewpub, open Mon–Sat 6.30am–10pm, Sun 6.30am–1pm, with a good menu of big breakfasts and grilled specials during the day, and beer at night.

Lady Falconburgh's Barley Exchange, Century Mall, 640 Main Ave; ☎970/382-9664. Popular pub between Sixth and Seventh in the heart of downtown, open daily 11.30am–2am, with snacks of all kinds and over a hundred beers.

Seasons Rotisserie & Grill, 764 Main Ave; ☎970/382-9790. Smart modern bistro that's as close as Durango comes to offering contemporary Southwestern cuisine, with sandwiches and pasta for lunch (Mon–Fri only) and $15–20 dinner entrees (daily except Sun) such as semolina-crusted trout or spit-roasted chicken.

Steaming Bean Co, 915 Main Ave; ☎970/385-7901. Early-morning espressos and pastries, as well as specialty drinks, sandwiches and live music later on.

Steamworks Brewing Co, 801 E Second Ave; ☎970/259-9200. Large brewpub just off Main Avenue, open for lunch and dinner daily.

Silverton

North of Durango, the **San Juan Skyway** sets off to loop over two hundred miles through the Rockies, up US-550 and then back via Hwy-145 and US-160. Its first stretch, across invigorating high passes, is known as the **Million Dollar Highway**, for the amount of gold in the ore-bearing gravel that was used in its construction. As you skirt around the bald, red-striped **Engineer Mountain**, just beyond the Purgatory Ski Area, the views are utterly spectacular.

The Continental Divide runs along the mountain-tops east of Silverton, with the source of the Rio Grande on the far side.

The first town along the way, **SILVERTON**, spreads across a small flat valley in the heart of the mountains fifty miles up, and marks journey's end for the narrow-gauge railroad from Durango. It's one of Colorado's most atmospheric mountain towns, with wide dirt-paved streets leading off towards the hills to either side of the one main road. Silverton's zinc and copper mining days only came to an end in 1991; the population has dropped since then, but those that remain have resisted suggestions that its future lies in legalizing gambling to draw in tourists. Meanwhile, the falsefront stores along "Notorious Blair Street," paralleling the main drag, recall the days when Bat Masterson was the city marshal – and are the scene of a daily shoot-out at 5.30pm.

Without a 4WD vehicle, it's hard to explore the mountains away from the main highway, but it's possible to continue several miles beyond Silverton in an ordinary car if you simply keep going beyond the end of the main street along the Animas River. The dirt road usually starts to get difficult around the ruins of **EUREKA**, seven miles along, which make a good starting point for hikes to nearby waterfalls.

Practicalities

Silverton is heavily dependent on tourism, which makes it pretty quiet in off season. It's also geared more towards day-trippers than overnight guests, so to spend a night here is to step back a century. Bargain **accommodation** is to be had in the tin-walled *Silverton Hostel*, 1025 Blair St (check-in daily 8–10am & 4–10pm; ☎970/387-0015; ①), which offers dormitory accommodation only,

Silverton's zip code is CO 81433.

for $11 per bed per night, or at the ugly but well-maintained *Triangle Motel*, 848 Greene St (☎970/387-5780; winter ②, summer ③), at the south end of town, which also offers good-value two-room suites and jeep rental. The central *Grand Imperial Hotel*, 1219 Greene St (☎970/387-5527 or 1-800/341-3340; winter ②, summer ④) has far more historic ambience without being much more expensive, though its old-style rooms are not exactly comfortable. You can get a bit more luxury at the *Teller House Hotel*, across the road at 1250 Greene St (☎970/387-5423 or 1-800/342-4338; winter ③, summer ④), where the *French Bakery* downstairs (☎970/387-5976), serves food from sandwiches to full meals. *Romero's*, at 1151 Greene St (☎970/387-5561), is an enjoyable Mexican *cantina*, while *Avalanche Coffee House*, 1067 Blair St (☎970/387-JAVA), is a friendly hangout offering fresh coffee, pastries and snacks.

Ouray

The equally attractive mining community of **OURAY** lies 23 miles north of Silverton, on the far side of the 11,018-foot **Red Mountain Pass**, where the bare rock beneath the snow really is red, thanks to mineral deposits. The Million Dollar Highway twists and turns, passing abandoned mine workings and rusting machinery in the most unlikely and inaccessible spots; back roads into the mountains offer rich pickings for hikers or 4WD drivers.

Ouray itself squeezes into an impossibly slender verdant valley at the head of the Uncompahgre River, with the commercially run **Ouray Hot Springs** ranged alongside the river at the north end of town. A mile or so south, a one-way loop dirt road leads to **Box Cañon Falls Park** (daily 8am–7pm; $2), where a straightforward 500-foot trail, partly along a swaying wooden parapet, leads into the dark, narrow Box Cañon. At the far end, the falls thunder through a tiny cleft in the mountain.

Practicalities

Ouray's zip code is CO 81427.

Ouray's **visitor center** is outside the hot springs (daily 8am–6pm; ☎970/325-4746 or 1-800/228-1876). Switzerland of America, 226 Seventh Ave (☎970/325-4484 or 1-800/432-5337), and Red Hot Ryders, 700 Main St (☎970/325-4444 or 1-800/325-4385), rent **4WD vehicles**.

At *Box Canyon Lodge*, an old-style timber **motel** at 45 Third Ave below the park (☎970/325-4981 or 1-800/327-5080; ③), you can bathe in natural hot tubs. The luxurious *St Elmo Hotel* **B&B**, 426 Main St (☎970/325-4951, fax 325-0348; *www.stelmohotel.com*; ⑤), adjoins the good *Bon Ton* **restaurant**, where Cajun-tinged Italian entrees cost $12–20. The central *Grounds Keeper Coffee House and Eatery*, 524 Main St (☎970/325-0550), serves espresso coffees and pizzas, while the *Ouray Coffee House*, next to the

springs at 960 Main St (☎970/325-4001), has an appealing patio for
light lunches.

Southwest
Colorado

Telluride

As you head north beyond Ouray, the scenery changes abruptly, with
the canyon of the Uncompahgre being characterized by red rocks
and sparse sagebrush. To complete the loop of the San Juan Skyway,
turn west on Hwy-62 after eight miles at **RIDGWAY**. This enables
you to circle around the northern limits of the San Juan Mountains,
which stand as a magnificent serrated ridge along the southern skyline.

When you reach the junction of Hwy-62 and Hwy-145, 23 miles
southwest of Ridgeway, doubling back eastward along Hwy-145
takes you along the pretty, well-wooded valley of the San Miguel
River to reach another former mining village, **TELLURIDE**. It's a
total drive of 74 miles from Silverton, though as the crow flies,
straight across the mountains, the two towns are barely ten miles
apart.

In the 1880s, Telluride was briefly home to the young Butch
Cassidy, who robbed his first bank here in 1889. These days it's better known as a **ski resort**, rivaling Aspen and Vail as a winter destination for the stars. Telluride has, however, achieved this status
without losing its character – the wide main street, a National
Historic District with low-slung buildings on either side, still heads
directly up towards one of the most stupendous mountain views in
the Rockies. Healthy young bohemians with few visible means of
support but top-notch ski equipment form the bulk of the 1200 citizens, while most of the glitzy visitors hang out two miles above the
town in **Mountain Village**, which is reached by a free year-round
gondola service.

Telluride's winter season, which starts as the fall colors fade, usually in late November, continues until early April. Prospective **skiers**
should contact Telluride Central Reservations, 666 W Colorado Ave
(winter Mon–Fri 9am–5pm; summer daily 9am–7pm; ☎970/728-
4431 or 1-800/525-3455), who co-ordinate lodging and package
deals, and provide free lift tickets for the first month of the season
for guests in certain lodges. Alternatively, skiing comes half-price if
you stay in any of seven neighboring towns; otherwise lift tickets
range between $30 and $43 per day. In recent years, the town has
also become a premier **snowboarding** destination, and regularly
hosts the US national championships. The world championships
have also been staged here. Many former ski trails are now reserved
exclusively for snowboarders, and expert instruction is available
from the Telluride Ski and Snowboard School (☎970/728-7533).
Over a dozen operators rent out ski and snowboarding equipment,
with the largest being Telluride Sports (☎970/728-4477 or 1-
800/828-SKIS).

In summer, the **hiking** opportunities are excellent. One three-mile round-trip walk, which also makes a great if grueling bike ride, switchbacks up a bumpy 4WD road from the head of the valley to reach Colorado's highest waterfall, the 365-ft **Bridal Veil**. To take the hike, follow the main highway all the way through town, park where it ends at Pioneer Mill, and set off uphill. Don't expect to be able to cool off with a swim in the falls, however; it's far too perilous a spot for that.

Practicalities

Telluride's zip code is CO 81435.

Accommodation in Telluride is much less expensive in summer than during ski season, though prices do go up for the Bluegrass Festival in June, the Jazz Festival at the beginning of August and the Film Festival at the start of September. Telluride Central Reservations, detailed overleaf, doubles as the town's official **information** service.

Of specific places to stay, the 1895 *New Sheridan Hotel*, 231 W Colorado Ave (☎970/728-4351 or 1-800/200-1891, fax 970/728-5024; winter ⑥, summer ③), offers some bargain rooms with shared bath, and the *Victoria Inn*, 401 W Pacific Ave (☎970/728-6601 or 1-800/611-9893; ⑤), has clean doubles and its own sauna.

Eddie's, 300 W Colorado Ave (☎970/728-5335), serves good Italian food and home-brewed ales, while *Smugglers Brewpub and Grille*, San Juan and Pine (☎970/728-0919), is a lively evening hangout with a wide-ranging menu. Healthy daytime snacks can be had from the *Magic Market Juice Bar*, 225 S Pine Ave (☎970/728-0919).

Northwest New Mexico

Although **northwest New Mexico** formed the heart of the Dinetah, the Navajo's original homeland in the Southwest, the Navajo territories here are now less visited than their more scenic equivalents in Arizona. Archeology buffs are drawn to **Chaco Canyon** and **Aztec Ruins**, which while among the most significant Ancestral Puebloan sites anywhere are – unfortunately for tourists – less photogenic than their better-known rivals. None of the towns nearby, whether on or off the reservation, holds any lasting interest.

Instead the region is notorious as the home of the **Four Corners Power Plant**, near Farmington. After this coal-fired generating station opened in the 1960s, it was said to be the single greatest source of pollution in the United States, emitting more noxious gases than either New York City or Los Angeles. Regulations have been tightened since then, but with the Navajo Mine, the largest open-pit coal mine in the West, just a mile away, and several other generating plants in the immediate neighborhood, there's no incentive for outsiders to linger. For the Navajo, of course, who provide much of the industry's workforce, it's a different story.

Shirock

By far the most striking landmark in the dusty red plains of New Mexico's far northwestern corner is the craggy monolith known as **Shiprock**. In Navajo legend, as *Tsé bit'a'i* or "Rock Wing," this awesome 1500-foot peak was home to one or two monstrous birds, which were either killed by the hero Monster Slayer, or turned into an eagle and an owl. To Anglo eyes, it resembled instead a mighty ocean-going ship. Navajo medicine men continued to use it in sacred ceremonies until 1939, when it was defiled through being climbed by Sierra Club members including David Brower, the "Arch-Druid" who later founded Friends of the Earth (see p.429).

In early October, the town of Shiprock plays host to the Northern Navajo Fair.

US-666 runs within a few miles of Shiprock's vast, eerie bulk. Signs at a roadside pullout explain that the mountain is a volcanic plug, the hard central core of a volcano that has itself eroded away. There's no point trying to approach it any closer – you can't walk up to the base, let alone climb it – or in stopping at the sprawling mining town six miles north, also known as **Shiprock**.

USA Today rates US-666 between Shiprock and Gallup – which bears the Number of the Beast – as the most dangerous highway in the country.

Farmington

FARMINGTON, the largest town in northwestern New Mexico, lies roughly fifty miles east of the Four Corners Monument and fifty miles southwest of Durango, Colorado. Once you know that it was founded as "Farmingtown," in 1876, you know enough of its past; now that it's a mere ten miles west of both the Navajo Mine and the Four Corners Power Plant, you can imagine its present.

When the mineral boom was getting going, from the 1950s onwards, Farmington acquired a dreadful reputation as a definitive "edge-of-the-res" community, rife with racism and violence. In recent years, it has cleaned itself up and prospered accordingly, with new developments such as the **Animas Valley Mall**, 4601 E Main St, making it the principal business center of a wide area.

Farmington's one concession to tourism is its **museum**, on the northern edge of downtown at 302 N Orchard St (Tues–Fri noon–5pm, Sat 10am–5pm; free), which traces its history from the geological "New Mexico Seacoast" up to trading-post times.

The **Bisti Wilderness**, thirty miles due south of Farmington on Hwy-371, is an area of weirdly eroded desert badlands where the Bureau of Land Management encourages hikers to indulge in "primitive types of recreation." If you want to exploit its considerable oil deposits, on the other hand, you'll need a permit.

Practicalities

The local **visitor center** is at 203 W Main St (Mon–Sat 8am–5pm, Sun noon–4pm; ☎505/326-7602 or 1-800/448-1240). TNM&O Coaches, 101 E Animas St (☎505/325-1009), run **buses** to

Farmington's zip code is NM 87401.

Durango and Albuquerque, while the Four Corners Airport, west of town, has **flights** to Albuquerque (Mesa Airlines; ☎505/326-3338 or 1-800/637-2247), Denver (United Express; ☎505/326-4495 or 1-800/242-6522), and Phoenix (America West Express; ☎505/326-4494 or 1-800/235-9292).

You may not set out with the intention of spending a night in Farmington, but with over twenty **motels** to choose from, including two *Motel 6*'s, you might as well stay. The best budget choice is the *Super 8*, southeast on US-64 at 1601 Bloomfield Hwy (☎505/325-1813 or 1-800/800-8000; ②). Upscale alternatives include *La Quinta*, 675 Scott Ave (☎505/327-4706 or 1-800/531-5900; ④), and the nearby *Best Western Inn at Farmington*, 700 Scott Ave (☎505/327-5221 or 1-800/528-1234; ④), which has a reasonable if predictable **restaurant**. *Clancy's Pub*, 2703 E 20th St (☎505/325-8176), is a youth-oriented pseudo-Irish **bar**, serving simple meals, and there's slightly better food at the *Three Rivers Eatery and Brewhouse*, 101 E Main St (☎505/324-2187).

Aztec

The town of **AZTEC**, fourteen miles northeast of Farmington, is the county seat of San Juan County, but it's a lower-key and more enjoyable place to visit. On its leafy central thoroughfare, the homely **Aztec Museum**, 125 N Main Ave (summer Mon–Sat 9am–5pm; winter Mon–Sat 10am–4pm; $1) incorporates a pioneer village with frontier-style buildings such as a schoolhouse, a jail and a bank.

The main reason anyone comes to Aztec, however, is to see **Aztec Ruins National Monument**, across the Animas River a mile north of town (daily: summer 8am–6pm; winter 8am–5pm; $4; ☎505/334-6174). This preserves an **Ancestral Puebloan pueblo** erroneously attributed by early Anglo settlers to ancient Mexicans. In fact it's a large "outlier" settlement, built from 1111 AD onwards by people from the Chaco culture (see p.82), and connected with Chaco Canyon, 64 miles south, by a die-straight road now only visible from the air. Aztec stands halfway between Chaco and Mesa Verde, and is thought to have been remodeled by a new wave of settlers from Mesa Verde around 1225 AD.

From the visitor center, which holds a handful of interesting ancient artifacts, a short trail leads around and through the **West Ruin**, the only part of the site to have been excavated. This 500-room E-shaped structure was entirely walled, with only one entrance. The trail leads through room after room (you'll have to stoop to get through the succession of low doorways) before culminating in the awesome **Great Kiva** – the technical term for a *kiva* used by an entire community rather than an individual clan or family. Reconstructed in 1934, this is the only Great Kiva in the Southwest that can be seen in anything approaching its original state. Aspects of the restoration remain conjectural, but there's no disputing the

The Pueblitos of Dinétah

Although they lie beyond the present-day boundaries of the Navajo Nation, the remote Largo and Gobernador canyons to the east of Farmington and Aztec were the original cradle of the Dinétah, the traditional Navajo homeland. The earliest known trace of a Navajo presence is a *hogan* in Gobernador Canyon that has been tree-ring dated to 1541, but the most significant era in its history followed the Pueblo Revolt of 1680. Refugees from the Rio Grande pueblos fled west during the immediate aftermath of the revolt, to be joined by further waves of migrants when the Spaniards returned to reconquer New Mexico from 1692 onwards.

Between 1680 and 1750, Navajo and Pueblo Indians combined to build around 130 stone fortresses in the region, known as the **Pueblitos of Dinétah**. Perched on high eminences close to the canyon rims, or tucked into alcoves just below them, these "little pueblos" are clearly reminiscent of older Ancestral Puebloan sites such as those at Hovenweep (see p.66). Most were too small to house an entire community for any length of time; instead they were intended as lookouts, retreats for elders and religious leaders, and, above all, as shelters during raids. The Spaniards sent punitive expeditions into the area every summer between 1705 and 1716, while from the 1720s Ute war parties threatened Navajo and Spaniard alike.

The real importance of the pueblitos, however, was their role in forging a new synthesis of Navajo and Pueblo cultures. Many of the modern hallmarks of Navajo identity, both in terms of practical skills such as rug-weaving and sheep-herding, and of religious beliefs, were acquired during this period. The main agent in the process seems to have been the intermarriage of Navajo men with women from the pueblo of Jemez. Their union created the Coyote Pass People, still one of the most prominent Navajo clans. Influences were also absorbed from further afield. Not only were Spanish metalworking techniques introduced, but in Three Corn Pueblito, which was abandoned in the 1750s, archeologists have even unearthed a Qing dynasty plate from China.

It's possible to drive into both Largo and Gobernador canyons, along good-quality dirt roads maintained by the companies who drill there for natural gas, but without expert assistance you'll have no chance of reaching or even spotting the pueblitos themselves. The Bureau of Land Management office at 1235 La Plata Hwy in Farmington (☎505/327-5344) can provide detailed directions to sites located on BLM lands. A better idea is to join an **organized tour** with either the archeologists at Salmon Ruin (☎505/632-2013), who charge $220 for an all-day 4WD trip for up to four people, or M.A.R. (☎505/334-6675), which offers half-day trips for one or two people for $85 and full-day trips for $180.

circular chamber's sheer size. It measured fifty feet across, with each of the four pillars that held up its 95-ton roof resting on four 375-pound limestone disks, carried here from forty miles away. Archeologists say that the *kiva* may have been in use when the *kachina* religion was first being developed, and that the fifteen side rooms, now connected with the main chamber by ladders, may have served as changing rooms from which masked figures would emerge during ceremonies.

For more about kachinas, *see* *p.60.*

*Aztec's zip
code is NM
87410.*

*The price
codes used
here are
explained on
p.15.*

Practicalities

Aztec's well-stocked visitor center, east of the river at 110 N Ash St
(Mon–Fri 9am–noon & 1–5pm; ☎505/334-9951), even sells an
Aztecopoly board game.

Only two of the local motels are currently worth considering: the
shiny modern *Step Back Inn*, where US-550 meets Main Avenue at
103 W Aztec Blvd (☎505/334-1200 or 1-800/334-1255; winter ③,
summer ④), and the smaller old-fashioned *Enchantment Lodge*,
1800 W Aztec Blvd (☎505/334-6143 or 1-800/847-2194; ③). The
Aztec Restaurant, 107 W Aztec Blvd (☎505/334-9586), is a venerable steak-and-pancake diner opposite the *Step Back*, while
Giovanni's, 300 S Main Ave (☎505/334-3452), serves tasteful
lighter midday meals.

Bloomfield

BLOOMFIELD, eight miles south of Aztec or twelve miles east of
Farmington, is an unattractive little desert crossroads notable
only for its **Salmon Ruin**, two miles west (April–Oct daily
9am–5pm; Nov–March Mon–Sat 9am–5pm, Sun noon–5pm; $3;
☎505/632-2013). This outlying Chacoan pueblo was constructed
between 1088 and 1094, roughly twenty years before its neighbor
at Aztec. Salmon Ruin may mark the first attempt to build a "new
Chaco," which failed when the San Juan River proved too unruly
to tame at this point, whereupon Aztec was built as a replacement. Salmon Ruin certainly went through a similar cycle of abandonment and reoccupation by migrants from Mesa Verde as did
Aztec.

Homesteader George Salmon discovered the ruin on his land during the 1880s, and his family spared it the usual looting until they
sold it to the county in 1979. Excavations since then have unearthed
well over a million artefacts, the best of which are displayed, together with reconstructed dwellings, in the on-site museum.

Practicalities

*Bloomfield's
zip code is NM
87413.*

If you find yourself in Bloomfield for the night, much the best of its
few motels is the *Super 8*, at 505 W Broadway (☎505/632-2113 or
1-800/800-8000; ②). The *Triangle Cafe*, across the highway at 506
W Broadway (☎505/632-9918), is a traditional, friendly local diner.

Chaco Canyon

*For a full
explanation of
the Chaco cul-
ture, see p.86*

For casual visitors, the long, bumpy ride to the **Ancestral Puebloan**
ruins of CHACO CANYON, twenty miles off the nearest paved road,
may seem more bother than it's worth. True, the site protected as the
Chaco Culture National Historic Park is the **largest pre-Columbian**
city in North America. For beauty and drama, however, it can't compete with lesser settlements such as Canyon de Chelly. The low-

walled canyon is a mere scratch in the scrubby high-desert plains, and the Chaco Wash that runs through it is often completely dry.

Once you accept that you won't have amazing photos to show the folks back home, there's still plenty about Chaco to take your breath away. Over 3600 separate sites have been logged in the canyon, of which the thirteen principal ones are open to visitors. Six of these, arrayed along the canyon's north wall, are what's known as **Great Houses** – self-contained pueblos, three or four stories high, whose fortress-like walls concealed up to eight hundred rooms. The largest, **Pueblo Bonito**, is claimed to have been the largest single building in America until structural steel was developed in 1898.

Arrival and information

Both the routes to Chaco Canyon entail driving twenty miles over rough but passable dirt roads. Open all year, these should not be attempted during, or within a day of, a rainstorm. Whether you approach from the south – by following Hwy-57 up from **SEVEN LAKES**, eighteen miles northeast of **Crownpoint** – or from the north or east – by turning off Hwy-44 at **NAGEEZI**, 36 miles south of **Bloomfield** – you'll enter the park at its southeast corner.

Admission to Chaco Canyon costs $8 per vehicle.

Park maps and brochures, plus schedules of summer-only ranger-led tours, are available from the **visitor center** where the two routes meet (daily: summer 8am–6pm; winter 8am–5pm; ☎505/786-7014). Rangers also shows videos such as *Sundagger*, which explains how carefully sited rocks and petroglyphs atop nearby **Fajada Butte** plotted not only the annual solstices but also the moon's 18.5-year cycle.

The basic first-come, first-served *Gallo* **campground** ($10), a short way east of the visitor center, is the only visitor facility the park has to offer; from April to October it's usually full by 3pm. Bring any firewood you require. Backcountry camping is forbidden.

Seeing the park

The gates of the canyon's eight-mile one-way **loop road** are immediately north of the visitor center, and open the same hours. The major stop is at the far end, where **Pueblo Bonito** ("Beautiful town" in Spanish), can be explored on an easy half-mile trail. Work on this four-story D-shaped structure, which is almost perfectly aligned east–west, started in 850 AD, and continued for around three hundred years. Speculation that hordes of slaves were forced to build it have been deflated by precise dating of its parts; even at its busiest time, a workforce of just thirty men, cutting and hauling trees for a full month each year, and quarrying and shaping stone for four months every two years, could have done the job.

The trail leads around the back of Pueblo Bonito, passing the spot where Threatening Rock, a colossal boulder whose collapse its ancient inhabitants staved off with prayer sticks and supporting

The Chaco Phenomenon

To archeologists, Chaco Canyon represents the apogee of Ancestral Puebloan achievement. However, what they call the **Chaco Phenomenon** remains one of the Southwest's greatest puzzles. How can the canyon's apparent unsuitability for large-scale occupation – if anything it was slightly drier in Ancestral Puebloan times than it is today – be reconciled with its massive structures, and demonstrable influence over an "empire" that covered at least 25,000 square miles?

Pithouses built by early Ancestral Puebloan Basketmakers are scattered around the canyon, but Chaco's surface pueblos began to appear during the ninth century. Sophisticated masonry techniques were either developed, or brought here by migrants from the Mesa Verde region, around 1000 AD, enabling the construction of larger multistory apartments. The canyon's heyday was between around 1050 AD and 1125 AD; its last definite tree-ring date is 1132 AD, and by 1200 AD it was abandoned altogether. A prodigious amount of work went into its construction; upwards of 200,000 tree trunks, mostly ponderosa pines and corkbark fir, were carried here from hillsides fifty or more miles away, without the use of animals or the wheel.

When Chaco became a national monument in 1907, archeologists estimated that it was once home to twenty thousand people. That figure was later revised down to five thousand, based on the number of rooms in the pueblos. Now, in view of the low number of burials that have been found, the lack of signs that the upper floors were ever inhabited, and the canyon's poor soil, modern theories suggest that Chaco never held more than two thousand inhabitants. By that reckoning, the Great Houses were not homes, but some combination of warehouses, temples and palaces.

Thus Chaco was not a residential community so much as a **ceremonial center**. Huge quantities of **turquoise** have been discovered – harvester ants, who for some reason collect blue and green turquoise to adorn their nests, scavenged fifty thousand pieces in Pueblo Bonito alone. Turquoise, still precious to contemporary Indian cultures, was the most valuable trading commodity in the ancient Southwest. The Chacoans shipped in raw turquoise from distant mines – mostly to the east, in the Cerrillos region (see p.124) – and crafted it into sacred and ornamental objects. Ultimately, turquoise from Chaco passed from hand to hand down trading networks into the heart of Mexico; ninety percent of the turquoise found in the Aztec capital of Tenochtitlan was of Southwestern origin. Similarly, the parrots and scarlet macaws whose skeletons have been found here must have come from southern Mexico or beyond.

However, Chaco's primary significance was much more local. Having started as a small settlement that specialized in trading turquoise, it prob-

walls, finally destroyed thirty rooms in 1941. Entering the ruin via its lowest levels, the path reaches its central plaza, which held at least three **Great Kivas** of the kind restored at Aztec (see p.82). From there, you can walk through the passageways and chambers of the pueblo proper, where the rows of neatly finished doorways, each framed by the next, are Chaco's most photographed feature.

ably became a place of pilgrimage, where individuals came, with appropriate rituals, to obtain the sacred stone. From there, it's a small step to picture regional **festivals**, held at regular intervals, when large crowds would assemble for public ceremonies. For most of the year, Chaco held a relatively small, high-caste population, and the upper floors of its pueblos were empty or used for storage; at festival times, they accommodated a large influx of temporary guests.

Evidence for this ceremonial role includes the extraordinary 450-mile network of **roads** that link Chaco with around 75 "**outlier**" communities. Averaging thirty feet in width, they were far wider than ordinary human foot-traffic could require; in fact they were often more like causeways, built of hard-packed stone and running arrow-straight across cliffs, mesas and canyons. Most are now only visible from the air. The longest to have been identified stretched all the way to Aztec Ruins, 64 miles north (see p.82), but if that same line is extended *south*, it makes a virtually perfect alignment with the site known as either **Casas Grandes** or **Paquimé**, over 300 miles away in Mexico. Roadside beacons may have been lit to summon pilgrims to major festivals.

Navajo legends relate that Chaco was ruled by the despotic **Great Gambler**, who was born to a poor Chacoan woman, taught to gamble by his father, the Sun, and won control over the canyon and all it held. When he was eventually defeated, he was shot into the sky, where he once more accumulated great wealth, and returned to the region in the shape of the Spaniards. Meanwhile, freed of their oppressor, the people of Chaco had dispersed.

Recently, ferocious archeological debate has focused on explaining the signs of large-scale **violence** at Chaco. Human remains found in two-thirds of the Great Houses appear to have been mutilated in a manner that suggests **cannibalism**. In the absence of evidence of warfare, they're seen as possible victims of ritual slaughter. The leading exponent of this theory, Christy Turner III, has even argued that a wandering group of Toltec refugees entered the region from the south around 900 AD, and established a reign of terror at Chaco by introducing the bloodthirsty Mexican practice of **human sacrifice**.

Trying to guess **why** the Chacoans left the canyon when they did – from 1230 AD onwards – is probably futile, although only a tiny reduction in rainfall might have been enough to drive them out. **Where** they went, however, is no great mystery. Both Aztec, at its peak between 1110 AD and 1275 AD, and Casas Grandes, an even richer commercial center occupied from 1250 AD to 1500 AD, can be seen as successive "capital cities," possibly even belonging to a single city. In addition, Ácoma Pueblo (see p.94) is among many modern pueblos that show a clear continuity with Chacoan culture, while the Zuni say a medicine society known as the Sword Swallowers joined them from Chaco.

A separate trail from the same parking lot heads to the smaller complex of **Chetro Ketl**, a quarter of a mile to the east. Constructed over the course of a century, from 1010 AD onwards, this shows Chacoan masonry at its most sophisticated – or as some archeologists put it, at its most obviously influenced by Mesoamerican models. Its horizontal rows of large, squared-off stones are chinked with smaller, flatter stones and set into a bed of adobe mortar with a mosaic-like precision. Many of the original beams (*vigas*) remain in place, and a vivid fragment of an ancient mural is protected behind a glass panel.

Pueblo del Arroyo, the next stop along the loop road, is the only Great House to stand right beside Chaco Wash. Although it rarely holds much water, the stream channel is much deeper and broader than it was in Ancestral Puebloan days, thanks to erosion of its bank caused by overgrazing. The pueblo, raised on a small hillock, was occupied between 1070 AD and 1105 AD. Only half of it has been excavated.

Casa Rinconada, perched on another mound not far beyond, is the canyon's largest **Great Kiva**, at 62 feet across. It now lies open to the sun, the subtleties of its precise astronomical alignments lost but its central features still clearly identifiable. Archeologists are unsure whether the two large vaults in the *kiva* floor served as foot drums, or to propagate seedlings; both usages are suggested by modern Pueblo and especially Hopi practices. Minor house sites and unexcavated mounds are scattered on the canyon floor nearby.

Crownpoint

CROWNPOINT, almost forty miles southwest of Chaco Canyon and 24 miles north of the I-40 town of **THOREAU**, is the principal town along the eastern flank of the Navajo Nation. Its only conceivable appeal for tourists is as the site of the **Navajo Rug Auction**, held on the third Friday of each month at Crownpoint Elementary School. Viewing is from 3pm until 6pm, with the auction at 7pm, and prices range from $100 up to perhaps $2000. For more details, contact Crownpoint Rug Weavers (☎505/786-7386).

Western New Mexico

Although the reality of today's **I-40** may not match the romance of its predecessor, **Route 66**, crossing **western New Mexico** still has its rewards. The interstate passes through some memorable desert scenery, while successive detours to the south lead to crucial sites in Southwestern history. At **Zuni Pueblo**, Spanish *conquistadores* first encountered the region's indigenous inhabitants, and **El Morro National Monument** records centuries of further incursions. Above all, **Ácoma Pueblo**, the superbly sited "Sky City," makes it worth spending a night in the dreary interstate towns of **Gallup** or **Grants**.

Gallup

As the largest town in I-40's 300-mile run between Albuquerque and Flagstaff, you might expect the famous Route 66 halt of **GALLUP**, 25 miles from the Arizona state line, to offer a diverting break in a long day's drive. Don't get your hopes up; cheap motels make it a handy overnight pitstop, but there's nothing to hold your interest.

Gallup sprang into being when the railroad arrived in 1881, and its role as the major railhead for the Navajo Nation has since been augmented by the construction of first Route 66, and later I-40. The interstate and the railroad tracks still run east–west through the heart of town, paralleled by a ten-mile stretch of the former Route 66 that's lined with endless budget motels and fast-food outlets.

In the week leading up to the second weekend in August, the Navajo and other local Native Americans come together in Gallup for the **Inter-Tribal Indian Ceremonial**, a six-day extravaganza centered on Red Rock State Park, four miles east of town. A two-day powwow is followed by four days of rodeo, craft shows and dancing, culminating in a Saturday morning parade through town. For information and tickets, call ☎505/863-3896 or 1-800/233-4528.

During the Inter-Tribal Indian Ceremonial, motel reservations are a must.

During the rest of the year, Gallup remains a major commercial center for the Navajo. An estimated eighty percent of all **jewelry** sold in the Southwest passes through the hands of traders like Shush Yaz, 1304 W Lincoln Ave (☎505/722-0130), Richardson's Trading Company, 222 W 66 Ave (☎505/722-4762), and Tobe Turpen's, 1710 S Second St (☎505/722-3806 or 1-800/545-7958). For more mundane shopping, head to the **Rio West Mall**, near exit 20 off I-40, which has the usual mall stores and a movie theater.

Practicalities

The Amtrak station at 201 E 66 Ave has one daily **train** to Flagstaff (7pm) and one to Albuquerque (9.55am). **Buses** along I-40 call in at the Greyhound station at 105 S Dean St (☎520/863-3761), which is also used by Navajo Transit System (☎520/729-4115) services to Window Rock, Arizona (see p.58). Gallup's **visitor center** is a mile from downtown, across the railroad tracks and the interstate at 701 Montoya Blvd (summer daily 8am–5pm; winter Mon–Fri 8am–5pm; ☎505/863-3841 or 1-800/242-4282).

Absolutely *the* place to **stay** is *El Rancho Hotel and Motel*, 1000 E 66 Ave (☎505/863-9311 or 1-800/543-6351; ③/④), built in 1937 by the brother of movie mogul D.W. Griffith. From the murals in its opulent Spanish Revival lobby, to the photo gallery of celebrity Hollywood guests – John Wayne, Humphrey Bogart and Ronald Reagan among them – this sumptuous Route 66 roadhouse is bursting with atmosphere. Its **restaurant** serves burgers named after Wayne and Bogart, plus (separate) Lucille Ball and Errol Flynn sandwiches, and the usual range of barbecue, steaks, and shrimp. There's also a bar and a gift store. Some guestrooms are in the original ranchhouse, the rest in a less characterful two-story motel building alongside.

El Rancho's original slogan was "The Charm of Yesterday and the Convenience of Tomorrow."

Even if you avoid the scuzziest of Gallup's other 1600 motel rooms, you can pay under $30 per night at places like the *Colonial*, 1007 W

Coal Ave (☎505/863-6821; ①), and the *Ambassador*, 1601 W 66 Ave
(☎505/722-3843; ①). The *Super 8*, 1715 W Hwy-66 (☎505/722-
5300 or 1-800/800-8000; winter ②, summer ③), is not quite up to the
chain's usual standards, but it's still a reliable option. The best place to
camp is Red Rock State Park – see p.89 – where a fully equipped site
for the night costs $8 (☎505/722-3829). The *Chili Pepper Cafe*, 206
W Coal Ave (☎505/726-1401; closed Sun) serves reasonable Mexican
and Italian meals in the heart of town. If you all want is a **snack** or
espresso, head instead for the *Coffee House*, across the road at 203 W
Coal Ave (☎505/729-0291; closed Sun).

*Gallup's zip
code is NM
87301.*

Zuni Pueblo

Although few tourists now bother to visit the dusty and unenthralling **ZUNI PUEBLO**, a short way west of Hwy-602 35 miles
south of Gallup, it occupies a pivotal role in Southwestern history.
Here, in 1539, the black African **Esteban** became the first outsider
to enter the Pueblo world, and was promptly killed and cut into
strips by the Zuni. Fray Marcos de Niza, following close behind
him, fled for his life back to Mexico, to report "this land . . . is the
greatest and best of all that have been discovered." The Zuni call
themselves *A:shiwi*, "the flesh," and their country *Shi:wona*, "the
land that produces flesh." Fray Marcos, who garbled that name into
Cíbola, announced that the six Zuni towns were the **Seven Cities of
Cíbola**. Spanish *conquistadores* had long sought the legendary
Seven Cities of Antilla, founded by bishops who sailed west to
escape the Moorish invasion of Portugal in 714 AD, and rich in
gold. In 1540, therefore, a Spanish expedition led by Francisco
Vasquez de **Coronado** returned to Zuni. Turned back from the now-
vanished town of Hawikkuh, the Spaniards defeated its inhabitants
in the first battle ever fought between Europeans and Native
Americans.

*Esteban's
extraordinary
life story, and
the full tale of
the Coronado
expedition, are
told on p.524.*

There was no gold at Zuni. The region had by that time been occupied for eight hundred years, and had become a major Pueblo trading center, where the peoples of the Rio Grande exchanged turquoise
for birds, feathers and shells brought up from the south. Life went on
after Coronado departed, but, like the Hopi, the Zuni thereafter
found themselves restricted to an ever smaller area by Navajo,
Apache, Spanish and Anglo newcomers. Today's **Zuni Indian
Reservation** encompasses around three percent of ancestral Zuni
lands, and with agriculture rendered marginal by erosion and overgrazing, the Zuni now depend for most of their livelihood on the
recently acquired skill of making **silver overlay jewelry**.

Visiting Zuni Pueblo

The dominant feature on the Zuni reservation is the red-and-white-
striped mesa of **Towayalane** or **Corn Mountain**, a traditional refuge
for the Zuni people in times of trouble. Immediately below, strad-

dling Hwy-53 three miles west of Hwy-602, stands the main **village**, which was founded as *Halona*, or "Middle Anthill," around 1700 AD, when the Zuni came down from Corn Mountain after the Pueblo Revolt.

Western New Mexico

On the eastern edge of town, the **A:shiwi A:wan Museum and Heritage Center** (Mon–Fri 9am–4pm; ☎505/782-4403; donation), holds interesting displays on Zuni history and culture, and is the best place to pick up information of all kinds. The next few blocks west are lined with jewelry outlets, and there's also a supermarket, a *Taco Bell*, and a local diner, the *Seventh City of Cíbola*. There are, however, no motels on the reservation.

General advice on visiting New Mexico's nineteen pueblos, and a calendar of annual events, appears on pp.134–135.

Turn south from the main road in the heart of town onto Malani Street, and a walk or drive of two hundred yards brings you to **Our Lady of Guadalupe Mission Church**. This adobe church, erected by the Spanish in 1629, was derelict in the 1960s, but has now been restored to more or less its original appearance. In line with historical accounts, the interior once more holds "life-sized" murals of Zuni *kachinas* (Mon–Fri 8am–4.30pm; for a guide, call ☎505/782-4481; donation). An ancient five-story "apartment block" still stands nearby, but it's completely concealed beneath modern additions; the only examples of traditional pueblo architecture you'll see are the beehive-shaped bread ovens scattered around the plaza.

On a typical day, few visitors make it to Zuni, and even fewer stay very long. Special events can draw crowds, however, most notably the **Zuni Tribal Fair** in late August, and the all-night **Shalako** dance, held in late November or early December. Anthropologists believe that this winter-solstice celebration, in which the *kachina* cult appears to blend with Aztec elements, was introduced by Mexican Indians left behind by Coronado.

As for long-abandoned **Hawikkuh**, the mound that conceals its remains is roughly 12 miles southeast of Zuni, just west of the dirt road leading to the agricultural community of **Ojo Caliente**. You're only allowed to visit with permission from the Heritage Center in Zuni, which appears to be up to the whim of whoever's on duty there. There's precious little to see, apart from multicolored potsherds poking from the rubble, but once you know the history it's an extraordinarily evocative site. Standing at the edge of the Pueblo world, you get a real sense of what a shock it must have been when first Esteban, and later Coronado, appeared across the infinite grasslands from the west.

El Morro National Monument

Hidden away on Hwy-53 south of the Zuni mountains, 25 miles east of Zuni Pueblo and 42 miles west of Grants, **EL MORRO NATIONAL MONUMENT** feels as far off the beaten track as it's possible to be in the modern United States. It seems incredible, therefore, that this

*The admission
fee at El Morro
is $4 per vehi-
cle, or $2 per
person.*

sheer sandstone cliff was a regular rest stop for international travelers before the Pilgrims landed at Plymouth Rock. The evidence is
plain to see, however. It was first recorded by Spanish explorers in
1583 – *el morro* means "the headland" – and in 1605, **Don Juan de
Onate**, the founder of New Mexico, carved the first of the many messages that earned it the American name of **Inscription Rock**.

Translations and explanations of El Morro's graffiti are displayed in the **visitor center** (daily: summer 9am–7pm; winter
9am–5pm; ☎505/783-4226). You can see the real thing on a half-
mile **trail**, which stays open until an hour before the visitor center
closes.

El Morro is technically a cuesta, a long sloping mesa terminating
in an abrupt bluff. The trail's first stop is the reason so many people
passed this way: a cool, perennial pool of **water**, collected beneath a
waterfall that tumbles through a cleft in the pale pink cliffs. In such
a self-evidently sacred spot, it's no surprise to see ancient **petroglyphs** scraped into the desert varnish nearby.

Not far beyond, Don Juan's chiseled signature celebrates "the discovery of the South Sea"; he was returning from an expedition that
had taken him all the way to the mouth of the Colorado. Further
inscriptions follow thick and fast, some detailing the minutiae of
minor campaigns on the Spanish frontier, others recording
moments such as the Reconquest after the Pueblo Revolt. Many
inscriptions from later years were deleted by national park employees when the monument was first created, for not being historic
enough, but surviving oddities include the autograph of P. Gilmer
Breckenridge, who led a caravan of 25 **camels** past El Morro in
1857 (see p.270).

An optional and much more demanding two-mile hike climbs the
cliff beyond the last of the inscriptions to see the recently excavated
A'ts'ina Ruins, up on top. Its builders, who abandoned it in 1350 AD,
were among the ancestors of the modern Zuni.

El Malpais National Monument

If you had to pick one federal park in the Southwest *not* to visit, **EL
MALPAIS NATIONAL MONUMENT** would be the obvious choice.
There was more than a whiff of the pork-barrel about its creation in
the 1980s, which was bitterly opposed by neighboring Ácoma
Indians. They lost, in part, because they preferred not to reveal the
locations of shrines they wanted to remain inviolate. For tourists,
however, the problem with El Malpais is more basic: it's **dull**.

El Malpais is Spanish for "the **Badlands**," and preserves a tract of
territory covered by **lava flows** from a volcanic eruption two or three
thousand years ago – recent enough for the landscape to remain
blackened and barren. Potholers delight in underground "lava tubes"
up to seventeen miles long, but hiking any distance across the rough
rock above is a pretty miserable business.

The map of El Malpais is a peculiar patchwork of desolate lava interspersed with pockets of grassland that the eruption somehow missed. Confusingly, only the lava areas belong to the **national monument**, which is run by the National Park Service, and served by a **visitor center** twenty miles east of El Morro on Hwy-53. The rest is administered as a **National Conservation Area** by the Bureau of Land Management, which has a **ranger station** on Hwy-17, nine miles south of I-40 exit 89. Each of those roads skirts the periphery of the badlands; in an ordinary vehicle you can only get from one to the other via Grants.

On **Hwy-17**, the more interesting drive of the two, **Sandstone Bluffs Overlook** near the ranger station, commands views westwards across the flatlands to the jagged peaks of the **Cerritos de Jaspe**, and north to Mount Taylor. Displays at the viewpoint illustrate the difference between the two main kinds of lava, known to geologists the world over by their Hawaiian names of *aa* and *pahoehoe*. Not far beyond, **La Ventana Arch** is a chunky natural window three-quarters of the way up a cliff face east of the highway.

Grants

In general, **GRANTS**, sixty miles east of Gallup on I-40, looks a lot better by night than it does by day. Daylight exposes an air of dereliction along its old Route 66 frontage that's concealed when the neon signs come on after dark. Even so, Grants feels more characterful than Gallup, and is a handy base for detours off the interstate.

Like Gallup, Grants started out as a railroad town. In the 1950s, just as a half-hearted **carrot** boom fizzled out, it struck it rich in a rather less wholesome way. A Navajo shepherd, Paddy Martinez, picked up some yellow rocks on nearby Haystack Mountain, and Grants found itself sitting on half the US's reserves of **uranium**. Both the Anaconda mining company, which opened an enormous mine, and the Santa Fe Railroad, who owned the land, made a fortune; Martinez got a monthly pension and the title "official uranium scout."

Grants' uranium years have receded into history, but they're enjoyably recalled in the **New Mexico Museum of Mining** at 100 N Iron Ave (May–Sept Mon–Sat 9am–5pm, Sun 9am–4pm; Oct–April Mon–Sat 9am–4pm; $3). Visits consist of a faked descent into a mock-up mine, where you can poke around with no fear of radiation.

Practicalities

Grants' **visitor center** (☎505/287-4802 or 1-800/748-2142), in the same building as the museum (see above), opens during the same hours. Most of the town's more salubrious **motels** – the ones that charge by the night, not the hour – congregate east of downtown,

The zip code for Grants is NM 87020.

across the railroad near exit 85 off the interstate. These include a
good *Super 8*, 1604 E Santa Fe Ave (☎505/287-8811 or 1-800/800-
8000; ②), and a slightly more upmarket *Holiday Inn Express*, 1496
E Santa Fe Ave (☎505/285-4676; ③). Back in town, the *Sands
Motel*, 112 McArthur Ave (☎505/287-2996 or 1-800/424-7679) is a
presentable budget option.

The most popular place to eat is *Grants Station*, a railroad-
themed family restaurant at 200 W Santa Fe Ave (daily
5.30am–11pm; ☎505/287-2334), which serves full dinners, including soup and salad bar, for under $10. The tiny *Uranium Cafe*, 519
W Santa Fe Ave (☎505/287-7540), is a vintage adobe diner opposite
the mining museum, open from Wednesday to Sunday for breakfast
and lunch only.

Ácoma Pueblo

*General advice
on visiting
New Mexico's
nineteen
pueblos, and a
calendar of
annual events,
appears on
p.134.*

The amazing ÁCOMA PUEBLO, south of I-40 fifteen miles east of
Grants and fifty miles west of Albuquerque, encapsulates a thousand
years of Native American history. Focused around the ancient village
known as "Sky City," perched atop a magnificent mesa, it has adapted to repeated waves of invaders while retaining its own strong identity. The Acomans have long been happy to take the tourist dollar –
they run a large casino beside the interstate, and have hosted the
Miss America swimsuit pageant – so visitors seldom feel the awk-
wardness possible at other Pueblo communities. Nonetheless,
Ácoma is the real thing, and its sense of unbroken tradition can
reduce even the least culturally sensitive traveler to awestruck
silence.

A history of Ácoma Pueblo

Only certain Hopi villages (see p.59) can rival Sky City's claim to be
the **oldest inhabited settlement** in the United States. This isolated
mesa, 367 feet high and 7000 feet above sea level, was probably
occupied by Chacoan migrants between 1100 and 1200 AD, when
the great pueblos of Chaco Canyon were still in use.

The **Coronado** expedition of 1540 described the Acomans as "robbers, feared by the whole country round about." Noting the mesa's
redoubtable defences – it could only be reached by climbing ladders
through a narrow crevice – the Spaniards commented that "no army
could possibly be strong enough to capture the village."

In October 1598, Don Juan de **Oñate** visited Ácoma in peace,
while exploring his recently proclaimed colony of New Mexico. A
month later, however, his nephew Juan de **Zaldivar**, following with
reinforcements, arrived at the foot of the mesa, demanded food, and
was rejected. Depending on which version you believe, the Spaniards
either tricked their way onto the mesa, or the Acomans invited them
up and then ambushed them. In the ensuing fight, all the Spaniards
were killed, save four who survived being hurled off.

A punitive force of seventy men, equipped with cannons, stormed into the village in January 1599, and over eight hundred Acomans died in a three-day house-to-house battle. Five hundred women and children, and eighty men, were taken prisoner. All were sentenced to twenty years of penal servitude, and each man had a foot publicly chopped off, in the plazas of the Rio Grande pueblos. Bitterness persists among the Pueblo peoples to this day; a statue of Oñate erected in Alcalde, New Mexico, in 1999 had its right foot removed within days by unknown attackers.

Oñate was eventually called back to Mexico City and removed from office, in punishment for his savagery. By 1629, Ácoma had a resident Spanish friar – Fray Juan Ramírez is said to have been accepted after he caught a child who fell off the mesa – and the Acomans were hard at work building a huge mission church. Ramírez's successors were driven out during the Pueblo Revolt, and a tyrannical eighteenth-century priest was thrown to his death, but in theory the pueblo was permanently converted to Catholicism.

The people of Ácoma clearly never felt inclined to follow the architectural example of the mission, whose mighty beams were carried 25 miles from Mount Taylor without once being permitted to touch the ground. Instead they went on constructing the same multistory stone and adobe houses that can still be seen today.

The **Ácoma Indian Reservation** now has a population of six thousand, most of whom live in three communities that were originally sited for their proximity to fresh water, but now stand conveniently close to I-40 – **ACOMITA, McCARTYS** and **ANZAC**. Only ten or twelve families, thirty people in all, live on the mesa itself, but others make daily trips to sell pottery or fry-bread, and many more return to their ancestral homes for feast days and other ceremonies. Eighty percent of Acomans call themselves Catholic, but the old religion endures; there are fourteen separate clans, and the Antelope Clan are still, as they have always been, in charge of everything. Even today, the non-Indian priest can only visit the mesa once a week, on Wednesdays.

Arrival and information

Sky City is twelve miles south of the interstate, via any of three connecting roads. For the most dramatic approach, come in from the west, leaving I-40 at exit 102. When the mesa comes into view, glowing in the sunlight as you drop down a hillside roughly three miles distant, you'll understand why the first Spanish explorers spoke of cities of gold.

Ácoma is closed to all visitors July 10–13, and during the first or second weekend in October.

Before you take any photographs, however, you must first pay the relevant fees at the **visitor center**, at road's end below the mesa. You can only see Sky City itself on an hour-long **tour**; buses take groups up at regular intervals (daily: April–Oct 8am–7pm; Nov–March 8am–4.30pm; admission $8, plus $10 for photo permit, no video tripods; ☎505/470-4966 or 1-800/747-0181). There's a small museum and snack-bar, and a gift store sells exquisite pottery.

Sky City

While the original walls of **Sky City's** oldest houses lie concealed beneath several centuries of replastering, the overall appearance of the village can have changed little in the last millennium. The high windowless wall of the main pueblo, at the northern edge of the mesa, protected its inhabitants against both the chill north wind and potential invaders. Three or four stories of terraced "apartments" face south to maximize the winter sun. Just one room still has its original tiny "windowpane" of translucent crystal. Digging *kivas* down into the sandstone requires too much labor, so seven of the above-ground rooms are *kivas*, each shared by two clans and entered by a tall ladder pointing to the north. Ácoma's sparse rainfall collects in natural depressions in the rock; beside the largest of these cisterns is the mesa's only tree, a slender cottonwood.

Tour groups stroll more or less at will around the mesa-top, with plenty of opportunities to buy handmade pottery or ears of multi-colored corn. Don't expect to enter any individual dwellings, however. The main stop is the still-active mission church of **San Esteban del Rey**, which measures 120 feet long by forty feet wide, with seventy-foot-high walls that taper from ten feet thick at the base to six feet at the top. The floor is made of hard-packed earth, while the white-washed interior walls are decorated with a mixture of Christian images and Pueblo motifs. Ácoma's greatest treasure hangs above the altar – a painting of **St Joseph**, said to grant prayers for rain, which was borrowed by Laguna Pueblo in 1800, and only returned after the Acomans took Laguna all the way to the US Supreme Court. As no photography is permitted, you won't be prepared for the sublime view as you turn around from the altar, and look back across the cavernous space to the glorious New Mexican light that streams in through the doorway.

There's no soil on the mesa-top, so all the adobe bricks of the church were made with mud carried up from below, and its **cemetery** was filled with endless basket-loads of sand. Only honoured elders can now be buried here – not in coffins, but "replanted," facing east. At first, the churchyard wall looks crenellated, but in fact the bumps are "warriors," placed to guard the dead.

Legend has it that the forbidding **Enchanted Mesa**, visible to the east, once held its own Pueblo community. The only access to the top was via a spider's-web of ropes strung between the mesa itself and an adjoining rock pillar. When that pillar collapsed one day while the men were away from the village, the women and children on top were left stranded, their cries for help fading as they starved.

If you prefer, you can walk rather than ride back down from Sky City, following the ancient footpath through clefts in the rock.

Laguna Pueblo

LAGUNA PUEBLO, just north of the interstate six miles east of
Ácoma and 44 miles west of Albuquerque, is the **youngest** of the
New Mexican pueblos. It was established in 1698 by refugees from
several different pueblos, driven here by the disruption of the
Pueblo Revolt and the increasing threat of Navajo and Apache
raids. It's also the **richest** pueblo, thanks to the presence of the
world's largest **uranium mine**, Anaconda's Jackpile mine. That
closed in 1982, after operating for thirty years, but the Laguna people are still living off the royalties. They're also having to cope with
the **pollution** it caused, having burrowed its way under the main
Pueblo village; birth defects and cancers have become a major
problem.

All of Laguna Pueblo, including its **San José Mission Church**, is
visible from a rest stop on the westbound side of the interstate,
where traders sell crafts. There's no reason to explore any further.

Chapter 2

Santa Fe and Northern New Mexico

B asking in the magical "light" that artists – and tourist boards – rave about, and stretching beneath the flame-red peaks of the Sangre de Cristo mountains, **Northern New Mexico** is the New Mexico of popular imagination, with its pastel colors, vivid desert landscape and adobe architecture. Quite apart from its ravishing **beauty**, nowhere else in North America can boast such a sense of unbroken **history**. Native American pueblos and Hispanic colonial settlements have stood side by side along the Rio Grande for four hundred years, and the Yankees who arrived on the Santa Fe Trail still seem like relative newcomers.

Adobe

For many visitors, the defining feature of New Mexico is its adobe architecture, as seen on homes, churches, and even shopping malls and motels. Ancient pueblo villages were constructed using blocks of mud, cut from the riverbeds and mixed with grass, but early Franciscan missionaries introduced molded adobe bricks. The Spaniards had themselves learned the technique from the Arabs, in which a mixture of earth, sand, charcoal and chopped grass or straw is left to bake in the sun in a wooden frame known as an adobero. Built into walls, they are set with a mortar of much the same composition, and then plastered over with mud and straw. The color of the soil used dictates the color of the final building, and thus subtle variations can be seen all across the state. However, adobe is far from being a convenient material: it needs replastering every few years, and turns to mud when water seeps up from the ground, so that many buildings must be sporadically raised and bolstered by the insertion of rocks at their base.

These days, most of what looks like adobe is actually painted cement or concrete, but even this looks attractive enough in its own semi-kitsch way, while hunting out such superb old adobes as the remote **Santuario de Chimayó** on the High Road between Santa Fe and Taos, the formidable church of **San Francisco de Asis** in Ranchos de Taos, or the multitiered dwellings of **Taos Pueblo**, can provide the focus of an enjoyable tour.

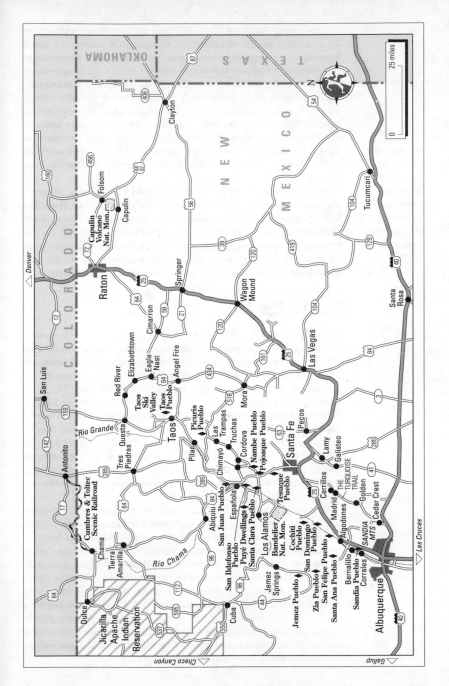

State capital Santa Fe, the only city in the region, more than lives up to its high-profile image as the epitome of Southwestern style, bursting with top-class museums, galleries and restaurants. Nonetheless, it remains less than a tenth of the size of Albuquerque, and its central plaza is still recognizable as the frontier marketplace that welcomed trade caravans from Mexico and the Mississippi. Taos, 75 miles northeast and even smaller, has become almost equally celebrated thanks to a remarkable twentieth-century influx of artists and writers such as Georgia O'Keeffe and D.H. Lawrence. It too has its share of museums and amenities, and is a near-neighbor to the most striking of the Rio Grande pueblos, multistory Taos Pueblo.

An introduction to the pueblos of New Mexico, together with a calendar of major events, appears on p.134.

Both Taos and Santa Fe are surrounded by spectacular scenery, and detours away from the river and into the mountains are rewarded with glimpses of countless fascinating communities. These range from the ancient **cliff dwellings** of **Bandelier** and **Puyé** on the Pajarito Plateau west of the river, to Hispanic villages such as **Chimayó** on the **High Road** to the east, Wild-West towns like **Las Vegas**, and even the high-tech home of the H-Bomb, **Los Alamos**.

Santa Fe

Since the early 1980s, **SANTA FE** has ranked among the chicest destinations in the US, repeatedly voted the country's most popular city with upmarket travelers. That appeal rests on a very solid basis; it's one of America's **oldest** and most **beautiful** cities, founded by Spanish missionaries a decade before the Pilgrims reached Plymouth Rock. Spread across a high plateau at the foot of the stunning **Sangre de Cristo** mountains, New Mexico's capital still glories in the adobe houses and Baroque churches of its original architects, and they're now joined by museums and galleries that attract art-lovers from all over the world. The busiest season is **summer**, when temperatures usually reach into the eighties Fahrenheit; in winter, the average daytime high is a mere 42°F, though with snow on the mountains the city looks more ravishing than ever.

With upwards of a million and a half tourists every year descending upon a town of just sixty thousand inhabitants, Santa Fe has inevitably grown somewhat overblown; long-term residents bemoan what's been lost, while first-time visitors are inclined to wonder what all the fuss is about. The depressing urban sprawl as you approach town from the interstate makes a lousy introduction, while the rigorous insistence that every downtown building should look like a seventeenth-century Spanish colonial palace takes a bit of getting used to. This is the only city in the world where what on first glance appears to be a perfectly preserved ancient adobe turns out to be a multistory parking lot, and it would be illegal to build a gas station that didn't resemble an Indian prayer chamber.

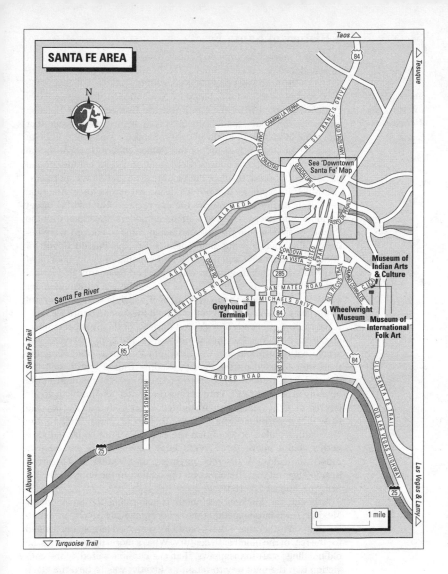

SANTA FE AREA

N

Taos △

Tesuque ▽

CAMINO LA TIERRA

CAM DE LAS CRUCITAS

N ST FRANCIS DRIVE

OLD TAOS HWY

GUADALUPE ST

See 'Downtown Santa Fe' Map

ALAMEDA

PASEO DE PERALTA

Santa Fe River

AGUA FRIA

OSAGE RD

CERRILLOS ROAD

CORDOVA

ALTA VISTA

GALISTEO

GASPAR

CAMINO CARLOS

OLD PECOS TRAIL

C. LEJO

Museum of Indian Arts & Culture

SAN MATEO ROAD

ST. MICHAELS DRIVE

Greyhound Terminal

Wheelwright Museum

Museum of International Folk Art

S ST FRANCIS DRIVE

RODEO ROAD

RICHARDS ROAD

OLD SANTA FE TRAIL

OLD LAS VEGAS HIGHWAY

△ Santa Fe Trail

△ Albuquerque

▽ Turquoise Trail

Las Vegas & Lamy ▽

0   1 mile

There's still a lot to like about Santa Fe, however. Santa Fe style may have become something of a cliché, but even the clichés are changing; the pastel-painted **wooden coyotes** that were the obligatory souvenir a few years ago have been replaced by cast-iron sculptures of Kokopelli, the hunch-backed Ancestral Puebloan flute-player. In a town where the *Yellow Pages* list over 250 art galleries, you'll get plenty of opportunities to buy one.

A History of Santa Fe

The first homes of **La Villa de Santa Fe** were erected on the ruins of an abandoned pueblo in around 1604. In 1610, after previous settlements to the northwest had been deemed unsuitable, it became the third capital of the infant colony of **New Mexico**. Its name, "Holy Faith," was taken from the camp outside Granada where Spanish monarchs Ferdinand and Isabella stayed before the assault that drove the Moors from Spain in 1492. Santa Fe was laid out as an imposing administrative city; as the **Palace of the Governors**, the *casas reales* or "royal houses" that commanded its parade-ground plaza were to house Spanish, Pueblo, Mexican and American rulers.

For a detailed history of New Mexico, see p.525.

It was from Santa Fe that **horses** dispersed across North America, and during its first two centuries the city presented an inviting target for mounted Apache, Ute and Comanche raiders. Relations with the **Pueblo** peoples whom the Spaniards had come to convert were initially stable, but growing antagonism led to the **Pueblo Revolt** of 1680, when Santa Fe was besieged and conquered by an alliance of many different Indian groups. One thousand Spaniards fled south, and lived in exile for twelve years at El Paso before returning under a new Governor, **Don Diego de Vargas**. Their fight to regain control of the city is still celebrated in the annual **Fiestas de Santa Fe**.

Santa Fe was always a neglected outpost of the Spanish empire; at the time of Mexican independence in 1821, its garrison was armed with bows and arrows. Attempts to improve the economy thereafter focused on the ever-expanding United States, and the dispatch of a trade delegation to St Louis in 1824 resulted in the opening of the **Santa Fe Trail** across the plains. As American goods poured in, US citizens were forbidden to settle in the city, in a bid to avoid a repetition of the Yankee takeover of Texas. In 1843, the Mexican president ordered that the Santa Fe Trail be closed altogether, but a mere three years later New Mexico passed into American hands. A discreet payment of $50,000 to Governor Armijo ensured that there was no opposition to the entry of the US Army on August 18, 1846.

Although the Yankees set about transforming the squat, dusty Mexican town into something more conspicuously American, building in wood rather than adobe, Santa Fe remained largely unchanged for the rest of the nineteenth century. What's more, no sooner did the old buildings start to disappear, than the city was seized by the conviction that the only way to retain its identity was to turn the clock back again – ironically the campaign was largely inspired by Anglo newcomers with their own romantic visions of how Santa Fe ought to look. Since the 1930s, city mandates have ensured that almost every structure within sight of the plaza has been designed or redecorated to suit the Pueblo Revival mode. As a result, Santa Fe today – at least at its core – looks much more like its original Spanish self than it did a hundred years ago.

Getting to Santa Fe

Despite its fame, Santa Fe is surprisingly far off the beaten path. Most out-of-state visitors fly into Albuquerque – see p.170 – and either rent a vehicle at the airport for the hour's drive up to Santa Fe, or catch one of the half-dozen daily Gray Line shuttle vans ($25; ☎505/242-3880 or 1-800/256-8991). Santa Fe's **municipal airport**, ten miles southwest of town, is served only by commuter planes, including flights from Denver on United Express (☎505/473-4118 or 1-800/242-6522).

Buses from all over the Southwest to the Greyhound terminal at 858 St Michael's Drive (☎505/471-0008), a long way from the plaza, include four daily buses to and from Albuquerque, which cost $12. There's no direct **rail** link. Amtrak trains arrive every afternoon at **Lamy**, seventeen miles southeast, from Albuquerque and Chicago – to be met by Lamy Shuttle vans ($8 one-way; ☎505/982-8829).

Information

Santa Fe's **visitor center**, two blocks northwest of the plaza in the lobby of the Convention Center, 201 W Marcy St (Mon–Fri 8am–5pm; ☎505/984-6760 or 1-800/777-2489; *www.santafe.org*), stocks a very limited selection of brochures. By contrast, the **New Mexico Department of Tourism**, in the Lamy Building at 491 Old Santa Fe Trail (Mon–Fri 8am–5pm; ☎505/827-4000 or 1-800/545-2040; *www.newmexico.org*), has racks of material on the whole state, and in summer, there's a small information kiosk in the plaza itself.

The main **post office** is also northwest of the plaza, at 120 S Federal Place (Mon–Fri 8am–4pm, Sat 9am–1pm; ☎505/988-6351).

Getting around

Most of what there is to see in Santa Fe lies within walking distance of the central plaza, but to get there from your hotel, or to see the further-flung attractions, you may need to use the Santa Fe Trails **bus** service. All nine routes start from the **Sheridan Transit Center**, a block northwest of the plaza on Sandoval Street (Mon–Fri 6.30am–10.30pm, Sat 8am–8pm; ☎505/438-1464), with a standard adult fare of 50¢, and monthly passes for $10. The most useful for visitors are routes #21–23, which run up **Cerrillos Road**, and route #10, which loops between the plaza and the **outlying museums**, roughly half-hourly in summer and hourly in winter.

The only **taxi** company in town is Capital City Cabs (☎505/438-0000), while **bikes** can be rented at Palace Bike Rentals, 409 E Palace Ave (☎505/986-0455).

Tours and excursions

Two-hour **walking tours** of town are conducted by the Friends of the Palace of the Governors, setting off from the Palace's blue gate on

Lincoln Ave (Mon–Sat 10.15am; $10; ☎505/476-5093), and by Afoot in Santa Fe, based at the *Inn at Loretto*, 211 Old Santa Fe Trail (daily 9.30am & 1.30pm; $10; ☎505/983-3701), who also operate Loretto Line bus tours at similar prices.

Gray Line, 1330 Hickox St (☎505/983-9491), run ninety-minute ($9) and three-hour ($16) city **bus tours**, plus half-day trips to the ancient ruins at Bandelier ($45) and Puyé ($50), and full-day trips to Taos ($55). Nambe Pueblo Tours (☎505/820-1340 or 1-800/946-2623) have an extensive program of trips to modern and ancient Pueblo sites, and up to what they call O'Keeffe Country.

Excursion trains down to Lamy, drawn by diesel not steam, leave from the old Santa Fe Southern Railway depot at 410 S Guadalupe St (April Tues–Thurs 10.30am, Sat 10.30am & 6.15pm, Sun 1pm; May–Oct Tues–Thurs 10.30am, Fri sunset, Sat 10.30am & 6.15pm, Sun & Mon 1pm; Nov–March Tues, Thurs & Sat 11am, Sun 1pm; round-trip $25; ☎505/989-8600). The idea is for passengers to eat at Lamy's *Legal Tender* restaurant, but you can take a picnic if you prefer.

Accommodation

Even in winter, you won't find a room within walking distance of downtown Santa Fe for under $50, and in summer – when every bed in town is frequently taken – there's little under $80. **Cerrillos Road** (US-85), the main road in from I-25, holds most of the town's **motels** and its one **hostel**. Everything gets more expensive as you approach the center, though **B&Bs** make an attractive alternative to paying the sky-high prices demanded by the plush plaza-area hotels. If you get stuck, contact Santa Fe Central Reservations (☎505/983-8200 or 1-800/776-7669; *www.taoswebb.com/nmresv*) or Accommodations Hotline (daily 4–10pm; ☎505/983-6565 or 1-800/338-6877; *www.sfdetours.com*).

Commercial **campgrounds** in the Santa Fe area, charging around $20 for a tent site, include *Los Campos*, 3574 Cerrillos Rd (mid-May to Sept; ☎505/473-1949 or 1-800/852-8160), and the *KOA*, further east at I-25 exit 290 (March–Oct; ☎505/466-1419). Camping nearby in the **Santa Fe National Forest** is a cheaper and much more appealing prospect. The *Black Canyon* site ($8; ☎505/982-8674) is seven miles up Hwy-475, northeast of town, *Big Tesuque* (free; ☎505/438-7840) is five miles beyond that, and *Aspen Basin* (free; ☎505/438-7840) is another three miles on, at the ski area. All open in summer only; for more information, call the relevant campground, or contact the Public Lands Information Center, 1474 Rodeo Rd (Mon–Fri 8am–5pm; ☎505/438-7542; *www.publiclandsinfo.org*).

Unless otherwise specified, properties listed here share the zip code Santa Fe NM 87501.

Inexpensive

El Rey Inn, 1862 Cerrillos Rd at St Michael's Drive, Santa Fe, NM 87502; ☎505/982-1931 or 1-800/521-1349, fax 505/989-9249. This white-painted adobe is the most characterful and best-value of the Cerrillos Rd motels, with surprisingly stylish Southwestern rooms, some nice suites, a pool and a large garden. ④.

Santa Fe International Hostel, 1412 Cerrillos Rd at Alta Vista, Santa Fe, NM 87505; ☎505/988-1153; *sfih@santafe.net*. Old-style HI-AYH hostel, housed in a ramshackle former motel a couple of miles from the plaza. Young international travelers enjoy the enforced intimacy of the dorm beds ($15), but in winter it can be pretty damp and cold. ①/②.

Silver Saddle, 2810 Cerrillos Rd at Siler Rd; ☎505/471-7663, fax 471-1066; *www.home.earthlink.net/~silversaddle*. Busy, down-to-earth but surprisingly characterful motel, well out from downtown. Winter ③, summer ④.

Super 8, 3358 Cerrillos Rd at Richards Ave; ☎505/471-8811 or 1-800/800-8000, fax 505/471-3239. Thanks to its half-hearted adobe exterior, this hundred-room chain motel, four miles from downtown, looks pretty strange, but it's a dependable bargain. Winter ③, summer ④.

Western Scene Motel, 1608 Cerrillos Rd at Cochiti, Santa Fe, NM 87505; ☎505/983-7484. Presentable two-story adobe motel, a short way south of the hostel. Winter ③, summer ④.

Mid-range

Budget Inn of Santa Fe, 725 Cerrillos Rd at Don Diego; ☎505/982-5952 or 1-800/288-7600, fax 505/984-8879. The most centrally located of the chain motels; large, clean and a mile or so from the plaza. Winter ④, summer ⑤.

Fort Marcy Compound Hotel Suites, 320 Artist Rd; ☎505/988-3400 or 1-800/745-9910, fax 505/984-8682; *www.santafehotels.com*. Plush one-, two- and three-bedroom suites an easy walk north of downtown, located on a mountain-view knoll once occupied by the city's first US Army fort. Winter ⑤, summer ⑥.

Garrett's Desert Inn, 311 Old Santa Fe Trail; ☎505/982-1851 or 1-800/888-2145, fax 505/989-1647; *garrett@roadrunner.com*. Large, rather dull-looking two-story motel, but the rooms are well equipped, there's a pool and a cafe, and the rates are good for such a convenient location. Nov–Feb ④, March–Oct ⑤.

Hotel Santa Fe, 1501 Paseo de Peralta at Cerrillos Rd; ☎505/982-1200 or 1-800/825-9876, fax 505/984-2211; *www.hotelsantafe.com*. Run and majority-owned by Picuris Pueblo, this attractive, very comfortable adobe hotel on the edge of downtown is just within walking distance of the plaza, has its own *Blue Corn Cafe*, and stages free lectures by local experts. Winter ⑤, summer ⑦.

Hotel St Francis, 210 Don Gaspar Ave; ☎505/983-5700 or 1-800/529-5700, fax 505/989-7690; *www.historicstfrancis.com*. Very tasteful hotel in the center of town, where the ambience is deliberately European rather than Southwestern, with individually themed antique-furnished rooms that go for bargain rates at quieter times. Winter ⑤, summer ⑥.

La Quinta Inn, 4298 Cerrillos Rd at Rodeo Rd; ☎505/471-1142 or 1-800/531-5900, fax 505/438-7219. Comfortable chain motel, a long way south from the center near the Villa Linda Mall. Winter ④, summer ⑤.

Santa Fe Motel, 510 Cerrillos Rd at N Guadalupe St; ☎505/982-1039 or 1-800/745-9910, fax 505/986-1275; *www.santafehotels.com*. Small, quiet and pleasant adobe motel near downtown. No connection to the *Hotel Santa Fe* next door. Winter ④, summer ⑤.

As explained on p.15, accommodation prices, excluding taxes, are indicated throughout this book by the following symbols:

① *up to $30*
② *$30–45*
③ *$45–60*
④ *$60–80*
⑤ *$80–100*
⑥ *$100–130*
⑦ *$130–175*
⑧ *$175–250*
⑨ *$250+*

Santa Fe

Downtown
hotels and
B&Bs are
marked on the
map on p.108.

Expensive

La Fonda de Santa Fe, 100 E San Francisco St; ☎505/982-5511 or 1-800/523-5002, fax 505/988-2952; *www.lafondasantafe.com*. Gorgeous old inn on the southeast corner of the plaza, marking the end of the Santa Fe Trail; guests have ranged from Kit Carson to John F. Kennedy. Built in 1920 to replace the century-old original, it features hand-painted murals and stained glass throughout. Each opulently furnished room is different, with some lovely suites in the newer *La Terrazza* section, and there's a good restaurant plus the *Bell Tower* rooftop bar. ⑨.

Hilton of Santa Fe, 100 Sandoval St, Santa Fe NM 87504; ☎505/988-2811 or 1-800/336-3676, fax 505/986-6439. Attractive luxury hotel, a short walk west of the plaza, which incorporates three rooms of the 250-year-old adobe Casa de Ortiz as B&B-style honeymoon suites; there's also a good restaurant, and the airy *Chamisa Courtyard Cafe*. Winter ⑥, summer ⑦; suites ⑨.

Hotel Loretto, 211 Old Santa Fe Trail; ☎505/988-5531 or 1-800/727-5531, fax 505/984-7988. Upmarket hotel designed to resemble Taos Pueblo, rising in seven tiers between the plaza and the river, and adjoining the Loretto Chapel (see p.113). ⑧.

Inn of the Anasazi, 113 Washington Ave; ☎505/988-3030 or 1-800/688-8100, fax 505/988-3277; *www.innoftheanasazi.com*. No-expense-spared hotel just north of the plaza, modeled on an ancient cliff-dwelling and featuring a superb restaurant; a fabulous place to stay, although most rooms offer no views to speak of. ⑧.

La Posada de Santa Fe, 330 E Palace Ave; ☎505/986-0000 or 1-800/727-5276, fax 505/982-6850; *www.laposadadesantafe.com*. Downtown's most peaceful option, with individual adobe *casitas* (cottages) set in spacious gardens. Sizes and furnishings vary, but the smaller cottages offer excellent value. Winter ⑦, summer ⑧.

B&Bs

Rural B&Bs
within easy
reach of Santa
Fe include the
charming
Hacienda
Vargas (p.122).

Alexander's Inn, 529 E Palace Ave; ☎505/986-1431 or 1-888/321-5123, fax 505/982-8572. Romantic Victorian inn with barely a Southwestern touch in sight, offering ten en-suite rooms plus two guest cottages. Winter ④, summer ⑤.

Dancing Ground of the Sun, 711 Paseo de Peralta; ☎505/986-9797 or 1-800/645-5673, fax 505/986-8082; *www.dancingground.com*. B&B inn that offers a choice of five separate Southwestern-themed *casitas* set in a tranquil garden. Winter ④, summer ⑤.

El Paradero, 220 W Manhattan Ave; ☎505/988-1177, fax 988-3577; *www.elparadero.com*. Converted Spanish-era farmhouse near Guadalupe St. Twelve rooms are en-suite, four share baths. ④.

Grant Corner Inn, 122 Grant Ave; ☎505/983-6678 or 1-800/964-9003, fax 505/983-1526; *www.grantcornerinn.com*. Incongruous New England-style house, two blocks northwest of the plaza, where guests enjoy considerable luxury, and lavish breakfasts – Sunday brunch in summer features a string quartet. Not all rooms are en suite. ⑤.

Preston House, 106 Faithway St; ☎505/982-3465, fax 988-2397; *www.bbonline.com/nm/preston*. Large Queen Anne inn in a peaceful garden behind the cathedral, with a mixture of rooms (not all en suite) and cottages, all furnished with Pueblo and Mexican artworks. Winter ③, summer ④.

Although it can be almost impossible to distinguish genuine historic buildings from modern counterfeits, there's a definite, romantic continuity between today's Santa Fe and the Spanish settlement of four hundred years ago. The most enjoyable way to start a visit is simply to stroll the narrow streets of the old town, but before long you'll find plenty of specific goals to capture your interest.

Once you've got your bearings in the **plaza**, the best places to get a sense of local history and culture are the four components of the Museum of New Mexico: the **Palace of the Governors** and the **Museum of Fine Arts** downtown, and the museums of **Indian Arts and Culture** and **Folk Art** a couple of miles southeast – plus the **Georgia O'Keeffe Museum**, which though privately run works in conjunction with the Museum of New Mexico. Alternatively, set about exploring Santa Fe's distinct neighborhoods, such as the old **Barrio Analco** just southeast of downtown, home to the **San Miguel Mission**; the **Canyon Road** arts district, just beyond; and the funkier **Guadalupe Street** district to the west.

The plaza

Santa Fe's central **plaza** has been the heart of the city ever since 1610, though the original rectangular parade ground of the Spanish garrison was twice as large as the neat, leafy square of today. It has witnessed many turning points of New Mexican history, from the public hanging of three Indian "witchdoctors" in 1675 (which helped to trigger the Pueblo Revolt five years later, when Pueblo Indians filled the plaza to lay siege to the Palace of the Governors), to the nineteenth-century celebrations of Mexican independence and annexation by the United States, and served as journey's end for countless weary travelers on the Santa Fe Trail. Just how contentious the city's history remains is illustrated by the **obelisk** at the center of

---

The Festivals of Santa Fe

The first of the three major events in Santa Fe's annual calendar is the **Spanish Market**, during the last week in July, when examples of the traditional folk arts of Hispanic New Mexico are sold on the plaza, and contemporary works are on sale in the Palace of the Governors.

The **Indian Market** fills the plaza on the weekend after the third Thursday in August, attracting over 100,000 buyers and craftspeople from all over the world for *the* premier showcase of Southwestern Native American arts and crafts.

September's **Fiestas de Santa Fe**, which take place during the weekend after Labor Day, have been held annually since 1712 to celebrate the Spaniards' return after the Pueblo Revolt. The ceremonial burning of *Zozobra* ("Old Man Gloom") in the plaza on the Thursday, which kicks off the parades and processions, is not a Catholic tradition; it was invented in the 1920s by atheist American intellectuals.

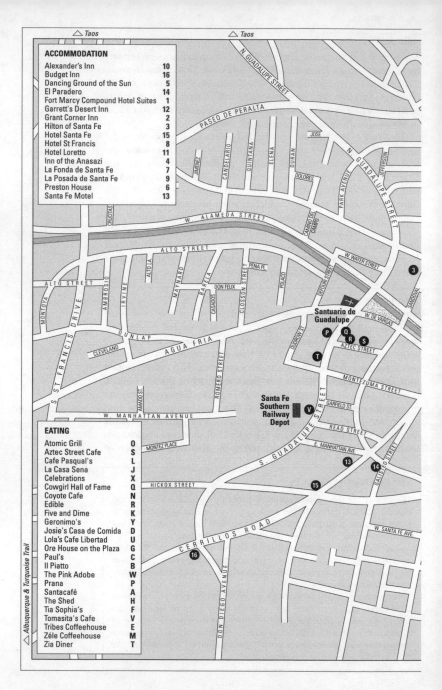

THE GUIDE: CHAPTER 2

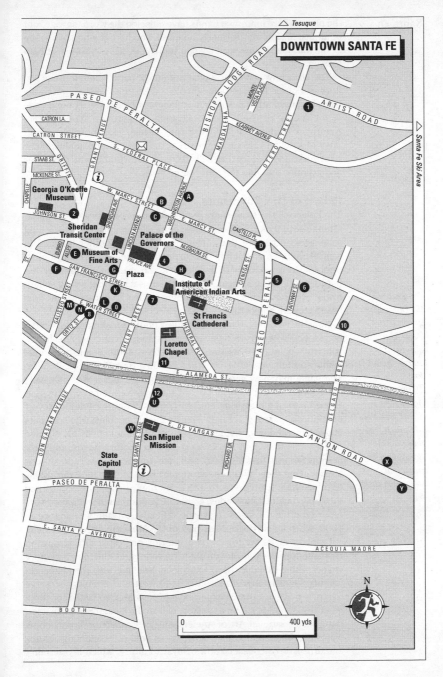

DOWNTOWN SANTA FE

△ Tesuque
△ Santa Fe Ski Area

Georgia O'Keeffe Museum

Sheridan Transit Center

Museum of Fine Arts

Palace of the Governors

Plaza

Institute of American Indian Arts

St Francis Cathederal

Loretto Chapel

San Miguel Mission

State Capitol

PASEO DE PERALTA
CATRON LA.
CATRON STREET
STAAB ST.
McKENZIE ST.
JOHNSON ST.
GRIFFIN
GRANT AVENUE
S. FEDERAL PLACE
W. MARCY STREET
E. MARCY ST.
SHERIDAN AVE
CHAPELLE
SAN FRANCISCO STREET
E. WATER STREET
GALISTEO STREET
ORTIZ ST.
SHELBY STREET
DON GASPAR AVENUE
LINCOLN AVENUE
PALACE AVE
NUSBAUM ST.
CASTILLO PL.
CIENEGA ST.
PASEO DE PERALTA
FAITHWAY ST.
CATHEDRAL PLACE
E. ALAMEDA ST.
E. DE VARGAS
OLD SANTA FE TRAIL
ORCHARD DR.
DELGADOS STREET
CANYON ROAD
ACEQUIA MADRE
PASEO DE PERALTA
E. SANTA FE AVENUE
BOOTH
BISHOP'S LODGE ROAD
MONTE VISTA PLACE
MAGDALENA
KEARNEY AVENUE
OTERO STREET
ARTIST ROAD

0   400 yds

N

the plaza, where unknown hands have chiseled the word "savage" out of an inscription that formerly honored "the heroes who have fallen in the various battles with savage Indians in the territories of New Mexico."

The plaza now serves as a pleasant public park, where tourists visitors and office workers alike picnic on the grass as they watch the latest bemused arrivals spill out of their tour buses. Under the arcade of the Palace of the Governors, along its northern flank, **Native American traders** shelter from the summer sun or winter wind. They're strictly licensed, so the price, authenticity and quality of the craftworks and jewelry they sell all compare favorably with the stores and galleries that line the other three sides.

Palace of the Governors

The **Palace of the Governors**, which fills the north side of the plaza, often fails to make an immediate impression on visitors. It's a long single-story structure that looks much like every other building in central Santa Fe – which is not surprising, since it served as a blueprint for the remodeling of the city. It's also as much of a fake, in that until 1913, it was a typical, formal, territorial building with a square tower at each corner; its subsequent adobe "reconstruction" was based on pure conjecture.

The Palace of the Governors is open Tues–Thurs & Sat–Sun 10am–5pm, Fri 10am–8pm. Admission is $5, or free Fri 5–8pm; a four-day ticket to Santa Fe's five principal museums costs $10.

Nonetheless, the palace is the oldest public building in the United States, and now serves as a fascinating **historical museum**. It was constructed in 1610 as the headquarters of the Spanish colonial administration, and first occupied by Governor **Pedro de Peralta**. The name may now seem misleadingly grand, but it was originally much larger, an imposing adobe, with two towers and a sod roof, that formed part of a bigger defensive complex. After the **Pueblo Revolt** of 1680, the palace was taken over by Pueblo peoples, who sealed its doors and windows, divided its rooms and dug still-visible storage pits into the floor, but it was soon back in Spanish hands, and later became home to first Mexican, and then American, governors of New Mexico. One, **Lew Wallace**, wrote part of *Ben Hur* here during his term of office from 1878 to 1881. By then, the palace had turned Victorian, but its balustrades, elaborate windows and wallpaper were removed after it ceased to be the official Governor's residence in 1909, when it was restored as part of the **Museum of New Mexico**.

Displays in its well-preserved interior are especially strong on Hispanic New Mexico, featuring a reproduction nineteenth-century chapel with a genuine 1830 altarpiece. Starting with the sixteenth-century Spanish *entrada* into the Southwest, the exhibits also serve to stress that the frontier experience of New Mexico lasted for three centuries, far longer than anywhere else in the United States. In addition, the sensational Art of Ancient America collection boasts some wonderful Maya and Olmec artifacts as well as fascinating figures and urns from the lesser-known Nayarit culture, which if you didn't know better could easily convince you that the Chinese beat Columbus to Central America by a millennium. Be sure to visit the well-stocked bookstore, and to wander into the peaceful open-air courtyard beyond, where the restrooms still have their antique fittings, and the Palace Print Shop (daily 9am–4.30pm), which sells handprinted cards and booklets.

Museum of Fine Arts

Across Lincoln Avenue from the palace, on the northwest corner of the plaza at 107 E Palace Ave, Santa Fe's **Museum of Fine Arts** is housed in a particularly attractive adobe, with ornamental beams and a cool central courtyard. Erected in 1917, this was Santa Fe's first example of the "Pueblo Revival" school of architecture, and remains unsurpassed to this day. It was also one of the few major art museums to be established by artists rather than educators or collectors, and concentrates on painting and sculpture by mostly local artists. Since the Georgia O'Keeffe Museum opened, it has focused more than ever on changing exhibits of contemporary work, though intriguing older pieces in the selections from the permanent collection displayed upstairs usually include an O'Keeffe or two.

As part of the Museum of New Mexico, the Fine Arts museum opens Tues–Thurs & Sat–Sun 10am–5pm, Fri 10am–8pm. Admission is $5, or free Fri 5–8pm; a four-day, five-museum ticket is $10.

Georgia O'Keeffe Museum

Santa Fe's showpiece **Georgia O'Keeffe Museum** is a block northwest of the Museum of Fine Arts at 217 Johnson St. Its ten galleries house the world's largest collection of O'Keeffe's work, including many of the desert landscapes she painted near **Abiquiu**, forty miles northwest of Santa Fe (see p.138), where she lived from 1946 until her death in 1986. In its permanent collection, housed in the first two galleries, some New York cityscapes make a surprising contrast among the more familiar sun-bleached skulls and iconic flowers, as sold in print galleries throughout the Southwest. There's such an abundance of material that entire rooms can be set aside to concentrate on paintings of particular flowers, or pink seashells, or whatever, all characterized by such a similar voluptuousness that it can be hard to tell one subject from the other. However, most of the museum is given over to touring exhibitions devoted to differing aspects of O'Keeffe's work, typically on show for three to four months, so there's little guarantee as to which precise pieces may be displayed at any one time.

The O'Keeffe museum opens Tues–Thurs & Sat–Sun 10am–5pm, Fri 10am–8pm. Admission is $5, or free Fri 5–8pm; a four-day, five-museum ticket is $10.

Guadalupe Street

A few blocks southwest of the plaza, the stretch of **Guadalupe Street** that runs south from the tiny Santa Fe River has become the focus of one of Santa Fe's most characterful little districts, catering more to local students and artists than passing tourists. It centers around the small **Santuario de Guadalupe** at Guadalupe and Agua Fria (May–Oct Mon–Sat 9am–4pm, Sun noon–4pm; Nov–April Mon–Fri

9am–4pm; donation), a shrine built between 1776 and 1795 to mark the end of the Camino Real highway from Mexico City. Remodeling in the 1880s added an incongruous New England-style spire and tall windows, and the church was further restored to become a small museum of its own history to mark its (and the nation's) bicentennial in 1976. It's still used for Masses on the 12th of each month, though, and also hosts dance and music performances.

In the late nineteenth century, the surrounding neighborhood became the point of arrival into Santa Fe for trains on the Atchison, Topeka and Santa Fe, and Denver and Rio Grande railroads. Old warehouses and small factory premises nearby have been converted to house stores such as a large branch of Borders, as well as art galleries and restaurants.

For details of excursion trains on the Santa Fe Southern Railway, see p.104.

St Francis Cathedral

Santa Fe only acquired its first Catholic bishop in 1851, after New Mexico joined the United States and ceased to belong to the Mexican diocese of Durango. As described in Willa Cather's novel, *Death Comes For The Archbishop*, the arrival of **Jean Baptiste Lamy** – a Frenchman, previously resident in Kentucky – threw the overwhelmingly Hispanic church in New Mexico into turmoil.

Lamy's most lasting achievement, **St Francis Cathedral**, now makes an unlikely spectacle, looming at the top of San Francisco Street two blocks east of the plaza. Eschewing adobe, the first church west of the Mississippi to be designated a cathedral was built of solid stone, between 1869 and 1886, in the formal – and, frankly, dreary – Romanesque style of France. To enable services to continue during construction, its walls rose over and around those of its eighteenth-century predecessor, which was progressively removed as rubble. The only part of that structure to survive, the side chapel of **Our Lady of the Rosary**, gives pride of place to a statue of the Virgin known as **La Conquistadora**. Originally brought from Mexico in 1625, she was credited by the Hispanic population of Santa Fe with facilitating both their escape from the Pueblo Revolt in 1680, and their subsequent reconquest of the province. The statue itself looks more like a Victorian doll than a venerated religious artifact – an effect enhanced by the practice of dressing it in different clothes at different times of the year – and is still paraded through the city each June, on the Sunday after Corpus Christi.

Institute of American Indian Arts

The stimulating **Institute of American Indian Arts** (June–Sept daily 9am–5pm, Oct–May Mon–Sat 10am–5pm, Sun noon–5pm; $4) is housed in a modern building that faces the cathedral. Don't confuse it with the Museum of Indian Arts and Culture on the edge of town (see p.114); as they insist on telling you before you come in, "we're contemporary, not historical," and most of the artwork on show is likely to be less than a year old. Ranging across paintings, installations, collages and mixed-media pieces, it's all a long way from the usual stereotyped images of Native Americans. The sculpture garden is especially recommended.

Loretto Chapel

A block away from the plaza, at the start of Old Santa Fe Trail, the **Loretto Chapel** was built for the Sisters of Loretto under the auspices of Archbishop Lamy, from 1873 onwards (winter Mon–Fri 9.30am–4.30pm, Sun 10.30am–5pm; summer daily 9am–5pm; $2). Work was directed by Projectus Mouly, the 18-year-old son of the French architect responsible for St Francis Cathedral. In different accounts, he either drank himself to death, unable to take criticism of his design, or was killed by Lamy's cousin. Either way, when the chapel was completed it lacked any means of reaching the choir loft, twenty feet above the nave. Hence the legend of its **Miraculous Staircase**, an elegant wooden spiral – more of a spring, in a sense – which makes two complete 360° turns as it rises, and was built without a single nail, or any support at either the center or the sides. It's said to be the work of a mysterious carpenter who arrived in answer to the nuns' prayers, and disappeared without demanding payment.

The story is more entertaining than the reality, however. The chapel is now deconsecrated, and belongs to the upmarket *Hotel Loretto*, with direct access from the hotel, so it's always packed with irreverent tourists. What's more, the nuns found the staircase too frightening to climb, so they disfigured it by adding banisters, while the whole thing is now propped up with a metal brace.

San Miguel Mission

Two blocks south of the **Loretto Chapel**, across the river along the Old Santa Fe Trail, **San Miguel Mission** is said to be the oldest church in the United States to have remained in continuous use (Mon–Sat 10am–4pm, Sun 2–4.30pm; $1). The site is known to have been occupied in 1300 AD, while the church was built by Tlaxcalan Indians from central Mexico, who accompanied New Mexico's earliest Spanish settlers in 1610. Although its roof was destroyed during the 1680 Pueblo Revolt, parts of its graceful, sloping adobe walls survived. A hole in the floor beneath the altar reveals the foundations of an ancient pueblo, as well as the original steps of the sanctuary, while the pale-green reredos or altar-piece above was painted in 1798 to frame a statue of San Miguel brought by missionaries from Mexico. The mission also holds buffalo hides and deerskins, painted with religious scenes, that date from around 1630.

The claims of a nearby adobe – part of which is a pizzeria – to be the **Oldest House in the United States** are generally dismissed, though it too probably stands on the ruins of the former pueblo. This whole district, the **Barrio de Analco**, is now an appealing residential neighborhood, abounding in two-hundred-year-old houses.

Canyon Road and Acequia Madre

Before Santa Fe ever existed, **Canyon Road**, which climbs a steady but shallow incline east from Paseo de Peralta, a few hundred yards east of San Miguel Mission, was an Indian trail that led to the pueblo at Pecos. Later it was the main route by which firewood from the mountains was brought to the city. Since the 1920s, however, it has been famous as the center of Santa Fe's **art colony**. It's now dominated by snooty galleries and expensive stores – some of which are reviewed on p.120 – but even if you don't plan to buy anything it makes for an enjoyable half-day stroll out from downtown.

Like the rest of the Museum of New Mexico, the Indian Arts and Culture museum opens Tues–Thurs & Sat–Sun 10am–5pm, Fri 10am–8pm. Admission is $5, or free Fri 5–8pm; a four-day, five-museum ticket is $10.

At Canyon Road's far eastern end, the 1940 **Cristo Rey** church is the largest adobe building in the US, and holds a huge carved-stone altarpiece from the long-demolished La Castrense chapel that once stood on the plaza. It's over three miles out, however, and most walkers prefer either to double back along Canyon Road at some earlier point, or return to town via **Acequia Madre**, one block south. The name of this ancient unpaved street literally means the "mother ditch"; following the course of the city's first irrigation canal, it's lined with beautiful adobe homes.

Museum of Indian Arts and Culture

The excellent **Museum of Indian Arts and Culture** is located on a raised plateau two miles southeast of downtown, with extensive views of the hills and mountains that almost entirely surround the city. Displays provide comprehensive coverage of all the major Southwest tribes, including the 'O'odham, Navajo, Apache, Pai, Ute and Pueblo peoples, and include a superb array of Native American pottery, from pristine thousand-year-old Ancestral Puebloan and Mimbres pieces up to the works of twentieth-century revivalists. It's intended as much for Native Americans themselves as for tourists – hence the taped messages at the start of the Ancestors section, which warn Navajo and Tewa visitors to proceed no further in order to avoid religiously proscribed contact with the world of their dead forebears. Myth and history are explained in copious detail, while contemporary realities are acknowledged in such forms as the inclusion of Nintendo games in the exhibit on the modern Apache way of life.

Santa Fe Trails bus #10 loops between the plaza and the museums described here, half-hourly in summer and hourly in winter.

Museum of International Folk Art

The delightful **Museum of International Folk Art**, across the parking lot from the Indian Arts and Culture Museum, centers on the huge **Girard Collection** of paintings, textiles, and, especially, **clay figurines**, gathered from all over the world. These are arranged in colorful dioramas that include a Pueblo Feast Day, complete with dancing *kachinas* and camera-clicking tourists, and street scenes from countries such as Poland, Peru, Portugal and Ethiopia featuring fabulously ornate churches and cathedrals.

An equally eclectic array of oddities is on show in the Cotsen Gallery, which ranges from the prows of Venetian gondolas to translucent walrus-skin parkas from Alaska, while the traditional New Mexican crafts in the **Hispanic Heritage Wing** are also fascinating. Alongside the expected *santeros* and *retablos*, you'll find more recent works like *paños* – handkerchiefs, decorated with religious and secular images in magic marker or pencil by often-anonymous prison inmates.

Wheelwright Museum of the American Indian
The large, private **Wheelwright Museum of the American Indian** (Mon–Sat 10am–5pm, Sun 1–5pm; $2 donation) stands behind the folk art museum. Designed to resemble a Navajo *hogan* (see p.56), its original purpose was to record Navajo sand paintings and ceremonials. These days, however, its permanent collection is seldom on show, and it concentrates instead on changing exhibitions, usually of contemporary art and little different to what you'll see in the galleries in town. The Case Trading Post downstairs sells jewelry, rugs and *kachinas* of very high quality, at very high prices.

Rancho de las Golondrinas
The **Rancho de las Golondrinas**, fifteen miles south of Santa Fe, was once a fortified *paraje* (or stopping place) on the Camino Real, and is now run as a living history museum (June–Sept Wed–Sun 10am–4pm; $4). To reach it, turn right onto Hwy-599 from exit 276 on I-25, then left onto Frontage Road, and then right onto Los Pinos Road, which you follow for three more miles.

The adobe farmstead at the center of the complex is thought to have welcomed the governor of New Mexico in 1698, and strongly resembles Pueblo architecture of the period. Topped by a tall *torreon* or watchtower, it incorporates a covered well and plenty of stabling for animals within its strongly defensive walls, while planted fields reach down to the river beyond. Other early Hispanic structures on the "Ranch of the Swallows," many of them brought from elsewhere in New Mexico, include a watermill, a replica Penitente *morada* or chapel (see p.142), a smithy and smaller farmhouses. The whole place is staffed by well-informed but unobtrusive "villagers" in period costume, with different sections maintained in the style of the seventeenth, eighteenth and nineteenth centuries. On top of all that, it's an absolutely lovely spot in its own right, ranged across the meadows and woodland to either side of the river, and bursting with wildflowers and sweet-smelling herbs. The best time to visit is during one of the monthly **theme weekends** ($5), starting with the Spring Festival in June and ending with October's Harvest

Santa Fe

The Folk Art museum is the fourth part of the Museum of New Mexico; hours and prices are as above. Its gift store stocks some of the best souvenirs in town.

Between April and October, guided tours of the ranch can be arranged by calling ☎505/473-4169.

Festival, but throughout the summer, the ranch provides an authentic evocation of New Mexico's early days.

Eating

Santa Fe has been renowned as one of America's most exciting places to eat since the early 1980s, when a quite stupendous feat of marketing managed to make dishes such as banana-crusted sea bass seem quintessentially Southwestern. It's now said to have more quality restaurants per head than any US city – but that doesn't make it any easier to get a reservation at the latest hot spot in summer. In addition, the presence of so many tourists, and the fact that their clientele is constantly changing, makes it hard for restaurants to develop much character. Nonetheless, there's some memorable dining to be had, even if you don't pay the wallet-busting prices of the big-name attractions, and the sheer inventiveness of the city's menus makes up for its lack of interesting non-American alternatives (though you will find the odd adobe sushi bar here and there). The main cause for regret in recent years has been the closure of several of the most characterful local coffeehouses.

The **Santa Fe School of Cooking**, in the Plaza Mercado at 116 W San Francisco St (☎505/983-4511), holds lunchtime classes in preparing Southwestern specialties, culminating in the opportunity to eat the lot (2hr 30min; $38–60 depending on ingredients).

Coffeehouses

Aztec Cafe, 317 Aztec St; ☎505/983-9464. Counterculture hangout in the Galisteo St district, offering a travelers' noticeboard and a nice patio, as well as coffees, pastries, light meals and occasional live music. Open until well into the evening from 7.30am on weekdays, 8am weekends.

Tribes Coffeehouse, 139 W San Francisco St; ☎505/982-7948. Spacious downtown mall gallery that serves espresso coffees, plus soup, salad and sandwich lunches.

Downtown restaurants are marked on the map on p.108.

Zélé Coffeehouse, 201 Galisteo St; ☎505/982-7835. Central, roomy downtown coffeehouse, with plate-glass windows to watch the world go by.

Inexpensive

Atomic Grill, 103 E Water St; ☎505/820-2866. Snack-oriented restaurant, with patio seating, one block south of the plaza, which squeezes burgers, sandwiches and some reasonable pizzas onto a menu that holds over fifty microbrews. Mon–Sat 7am–3am, Sun 7am–midnight.

Edible, 323 Aztec St; ☎505/983-4699. Inexpensive deli with seating, where the wide range of wholesome dishes, from organic vegetables to pecan chicken or salmon and corn fritters, are sold by the pound, and you can get a sizeable meal for under $10. Tues–Sat 11am–7pm.

Five and Dime, 58 E San Francisco St; ☎505/982-1062. An only-in-Santa-Fe institution; right on the plaza, the lunch counter at what was (until the lease expired) the world's only adobe Woolworth's has remained in business to sell its famous $3.50 *frito* pies – spicy red chile poured over a bag of corn chips and topped with cheese. Mon–Sat 8.30am–4.30pm, Sun 9am–4.30pm.

Josie's Casa de Comida, 225 E Marcy St; ☎505/983-5311. Legendary local diner in a tiny whitewashed house near the plaza. Open for weekday lunches only: spicy chiles, tamales and enchiladas, and an endless array of desserts.

mu du noodles, 1494 Cerrillos Rd; ☎505/983-1411. Largely but not exclusively vegetarian place near the hostel. Its Asian-flavored menu may not always be authentic, but it's still tasty. Dinner entrees cost around $10. Open daily except Sun for lunch and dinner.

The Shed, 113 E Palace Ave; ☎505/982-9030. Classic (New) Mexican diner just northeast of the plaza, serving a steady diet of chile enchiladas, blue-corn tortillas and even low-fat specialties. Mon & Tues 11am–2.30pm, Wed–Sat 11am–2.30pm & 5.30–9pm.

Tecolote Cafe, 1203 Cerrillos Rd at Cordova; ☎505/988-1362. This inconspicuous joint, a couple of miles south of downtown, is renowned for magnificent breakfasts – burritos, *huevos rancheros*, creamy eggs Benedict or shirred eggs (poached on a bed of chicken livers). Open daily except Mon 7am–2pm.

Tia Sophia's, 210 W San Francisco St; ☎505/983-9880. Spicy, very inexpensive Mexican diner, a block or two west of the plaza, that's so popular with lunching locals that you can expect to have to wait in line. Mon–Sat 7am–2pm.

Tomasita's Cafe, 500 S Guadalupe St; ☎505/983-5721. Lively, unpretentious place in the old railroad station, cranking out quickfire platefuls of tasty Mexican food for under $10, plus margaritas by the liter. Mon–Sat 11am–10pm.

Mid-range

Cafe Pasqual's, 121 Don Gaspar Ave; ☎505/983-9340. All purpose Old/New Mexican bakery/restaurant that serves predictable if tasty (and large) eggy breakfasts, salads and Mexican standards for lunch, and fancier dinner entrees costing either side of $20. Open for all meals daily.

Celebrations, 613 Canyon Rd; ☎505/989-8904. Lively mock-adobe bistro, very popular with Canyon Rd employees, specializing in inexpensive but good Southwestern dishes with a definite Cajun twist; they even do crawfish *etouffé* for $11. Open for breakfast and lunch daily, dinner Wed–Sat only.

Cowgirl Hall of Fame, 319 S Guadalupe St; ☎505/982-2565. Probably the liveliest restaurant in town, with lots of well-priced barbecued or grilled meat dishes, plus Mexican specialties and cookhouse-style stews. There's lashings of beer for adults and a play area for kids, plus live music most nights. Mon–Fri 11am until late, Sat & Sun 8am until late.

Il Piatto, 95 W Marcy St; ☎505/984-1091. Well-priced and very good Italian restaurant, festooned with cooking utensils and serving pasta galore, such as a calamari spaghetti for $10, plus specials like a $14 *cioppino* (a sort of Italian *bouillabaisse*). Open Mon–Fri for lunch and dinner, Sat dinner only.

La Casa Sena, 125 E Palace Ave; ☎505/988-9232. Lovely courtyard restaurant, a block from the plaza; zestful Southwestern lunches, with entrees around $10, are the best deal, though the $42 set dinners are consistently good. *La Cantina*, adjoining, is a little cheaper and its staff perform Broadway showsongs as they work. Mon–Fri 11.30am–10pm, Sat & Sun 11am–10pm.

Lola's Cafe Libertad, 311 Old Santa Fe Trail; ☎505/983-8372. Modern, attractively decorated Cuban-themed restaurant just south of the river, offering inexpensive lunches and delicious dinners; the chocolate-flavored *molé* sauce, served on chicken or pork for $13.50, is superb. Closed Mon.

Ore House on the Plaza, 50 Lincoln Ave; ☎505/983-8687. "Nueva Latina" restaurant, where the menu ranges from $5 green chile stews or an $8 *ceviche* up to elaborate $26 dinner entrees such as rack of lamb. The location is unbeatable: from the tiled tables on its *ristra*-garlanded balcony, on the southwest corner of the plaza, you can watch all the life of the city. Lunch and dinner daily.

Paul's, 72 W Marcy St; ☎505/982-8738. Unpretentious but adventurous and well-priced downtown bistro, with delicious breads and salads, and entrees such as baked salmon in a pecan herb crust, for under $20. Open for dinner daily, lunch Mon–Sat.

The Pink Adobe, 406 Old Santa Fe Trail; ☎505/983-7712. This 300-year-old adobe provides a deeply romantic setting for a hybrid New Mexican/Cajun menu that's not wildly inspiring. Open for lunch on weekdays only, with salads and sandwiches for around $8, and dinner nightly, when entrees such as *poulet Marengo Pink Adobe* – a half chicken cooked in wine and brandy – cost $20.

Prana, 320 S Guadalupe St; ☎505/983-7705. Small, redbrick restaurant close to the Santuario de Guadalupe that serves huge platefuls of delicious "pan-Asian" food for under $20, including a Burmese seafood stew bursting with prawns and clams, and smaller "Asian tapas" appetizers like curried hummus or tuna carpaccio for under $10. Lunch and dinner daily.

Zia Diner, 326 S Guadalupe St; ☎505/988-7008. Stylish Art Deco diner with some tasteful steel trimmings, offering all-American meat and fish dishes, plus breads and pastries from its own bakery. Daily 11am–10pm.

Expensive

The Anasazi Restaurant, *Inn of the Anasazi*, 113 Washington Ave; ☎505/988-3236. Very plush Pueblo-style hotel dining room, open for all meals daily and placing an emphasis on organic ingredients. The eclectic dinner menu features entrees such as filet mignon encrusted with chiles, or halibut with plantain, at well over $20; lunchtime specials serve as cheaper samplers.

Coyote Cafe, 132 W Water St; ☎505/983-1615. Celebrity chef Mark Miller's showcase restaurant, just off the plaza, remains as super-trendy as ever. The à la carte prices are ferocious, but the $39.50 set meal features signature dishes such as lamb fig sausage tamale and fried red-banana-crusted sea bass. It's possible to plot a vegetarian course through the menu, if a *polenta torta* is worth $40 to you and you can cope with the cowhide seats. For a cheaper taste, try the rooftop *Cantina* upstairs. Both serve lunch and dinner daily in summer, but in winter only the *Cantina* is open for lunch.

Geronimo's, 724 Canyon Rd; ☎505/982-1500. With its separate small dining rooms, this converted ancient adobe is Santa Fe's most intimate upmarket restaurant, with a streetfront patio and a cool inner courtyard. The menu is mostly contemporary fusion with the odd Mexican touch, but the $10.50 blue-cheese buffalo burger, topped with sensational spiced fries, makes a great lunch. Open for dinner daily, lunch daily except Mon.

Santacafe, 231 Washington Ave; ☎505/984-1788. Downtown courtyard cafe with a not entirely deserved reputation for gourmet cuisine; the menu's blend of Asian and Southwestern styles certainly looks enticing, but the quality can be patchy, and the service snooty in the extreme. So long as you're happy to spend well over $20 per entree, and you steer clear of the seafood, you may come out smiling. Open for dinner daily, lunch daily except Sun.

Nightlife and entertainment

Santa Fe has the range of **nightlife** you'd expect in a small city rather than a major metropolis, though its **cultural scene** livens up during the summer tourist season. For full **listings** of what's going on, check the free weekly *Reporter* or the "Pasatiempo" section of Friday's *New Mexican*.

Santa Fe's major annual festivals are detailed on p.107.

The much-anticipated **Santa Fe Opera** season runs through July and August in a magnificent amphitheater seven miles north of town (☎505/986-5900 or 1-800/280-4654); tickets are sold in the *Eldorado Hotel*, 309 W San Francisco St. July and August is also the time to catch the six-week **Santa Fe Chamber Music Festival** (☎505/983-2075 or 982-1890), and the free **Shakespeare in Santa Fe** alfresco productions held on weekend evenings at St John's College, 1160 Camino de la Cruz Blanca (☎505/982-2910). The Jean Cocteau Coffee House and Cinema, at 418 Montezuma St in the Guadalupe District (☎505/988-2711), programs interesting repertory **movies**, and offers the best prospect in Santa Fe of finding fellow Bohemians to admire your beret.

Some of the most atmospheric places to **drink** in town are in the old hotels – the downstairs *La Fiesta* lounge and rooftop bar in *La Fonda* on the plaza spring to mind – but otherwise conventional bars are surprisingly few and far between.

Clubs and bars

Catamount Bar, 125 E Water St; ☎505/988-7222. Downtown bar with plenty of microbrewed beers on tap, and live rock or blues most nights.

El Farol, 808 Canyon Rd; ☎505/983-9912. Historic bar-cum-restaurant that serves Spanish tapas to a musical accompaniment from blues to flamenco.

Evangelo's, 200 W San Francisco St; ☎505/982-9014. The only good barebones bar in easy walking range of the plaza, with a pool table and a jukebox.

The Paramount and Bar B, 331 Sandoval St; ☎505/982-8999. Santa Fe's premier live music venue and club is housed in the postmodern hangar that previously held the *Double A* restaurant; the adjoining, much smaller *Bar B* hosts some separate events.

Second Street Brewery, 1814 Second St; ☎505/982-3030. This lively brewpub is too far from the center to attract many tourists, which is half the reason it's so popular with young locals; there's also live music several nights a week.

Shopping

Secure in the knowledge that many visitors come specifically to **shop**, central Santa Fe is bursting with (generally high-priced) stores and galleries. The galleries alone turn over more than $200 million each year. The city remains largely the preserve of independents, however; few of the international names that move in seem to last long, so you'll have to familiarize yourself with what's around.

Almost everyone agrees that the best place to buy **Indian crafts**, such as silver and turquoise **jewelry**, is from the Native American sellers outside the Palace of the Governors, ideally during August's Indian Market (see p.107). If you're interested in **Hispanic folk art**, take a look at the gift store in the Museum of International Folk Art before you shop around downtown.

The two main **malls**, neither of which is particularly large or interesting, are the **Villa Linda Mall**, southwest at 4250 Cerrillos Rd, and the **De Vargas Mall**, ten minutes' walk northwest of the plaza at North Guadalupe Street and Paseo de Peralta; there's also a huge new Borders **bookstore** at 500 Montezuma in the Guadalupe District.

For general advice on buying Indian crafts, see p.30.

Downtown Santa Fe

Artesanos, 222 Galisteo St; ☎505/983-1743. Lots of tin mirrors and glassware, *ristras*, furniture, Mexican ceramics, and a roomfull of tiles of all sizes.

The Chile Shop, 109 E Water St; ☎505/983-6080. Chile products galore – sauces, intricate *ristras*, etc – plus tasteful Anasazi- and Mimbres-influenced ceramic tableware.

Mira, 101A W Marcy St; ☎505/988-3585. Tongue-in-cheek religious kitsch (Virgin Mary snowstorms and the like), plus antique clothing and oddments, at very inexpensive prices. One block north of the plaza.

Móntez Gallery, 125 E Palace Ave; ☎505/982-1828. Friendly little store near the plaza, specializing in good-quality antique Hispanic religious art, plus attractive and very inexpensive reproductions.

Don't expect to make an early start when you're shopping in Santa Fe; most stores and galleries don't open until 10am.

Canyon Road

Hahn Ross Gallery, 409 Canyon Rd; ☎505/984-8434. Enjoyable fine-art gallery, run by a children's book illustrator and specializing in very bright paintings that blend the fantastic with the naive.

Kania-Ferrin Gallery, 662 Canyon Rd; ☎505/982-8767. Native American antiques, with baskets, rugs and, especially, superb old Hopi *kachinas*, at prices that run into thousands of dollars.

Nambé Showroom, 924 Paseo de Peralta; ☎505/988-5582. Factory outlet at the foot of Canyon Rd with a large stock of Nambé ware – shiny, futuristic table- and ovenware made from a local alloy that looks like silver but has unique heat-retaining properties.

Pachamama, 223 Canyon Rd; ☎505/983-4020. Unusually cheap Hispanic craftworks, mainly from Mexico, including *retablos*, statues, and lots of tin.

Off the Wall, 616 Canyon Rd; ☎505/983-8337. Eccentric assortment of contemporary art objects, mostly functional, largely ceramic, many tea-oriented. There's a weird influence of medieval Judaica – and an espresso bar.

Silver Sun, 656 Canyon Rd; ☎505/983-8743. Native American arts and crafts, with a standout collection of beautiful turquoise jewelry.

South to Albuquerque

Travelers embarking on the sixty-mile drive southwest from Santa Fe
to Albuquerque have a choice of two routes. The **interstate**, I-25, is
fast and reasonably scenic, but for atmosphere and Old-West charm
it doesn't begin to match the **Turquoise Trail**, which squeezes
between the Sandia and Ortiz mountains to the east.

The interstate route

Commuters may not give it a second thought, but the hour-long
journey from Santa Fe to Albuquerque on I-25 represents a major
transition. When it drops down the escarpment known as **La
Bajada**, twenty miles from downtown Santa Fe, the interstate leaves
the Rocky Mountains and enters the desert. To the north, the Rio
Grande was traditionally known as the **Rio Arriba**, or Upper River,
and cuts through a deep rocky gorge; to the south, the **Rio Abajo** or
Lower River meanders across a broad floodplain.

La Bajada also marks the dividing line between the northern and
southern **pueblos**. Below it, the interstate runs through three separate Indian reservations. In 1996, when state legislators seemed
poised to outlaw the Indian gaming that has finally brought the pueblos a degree of prosperity, Pueblo authorities retaliated by threatening to place **toll-gates** on the interstate at every boundary.

*Advice on visit-
ing the pueblos,
as well as con-
tact numbers
and a calendar
of major feast
days, appears
on p.134.*

Cochiti Pueblo

COCHITI PUEBLO, ten miles west of the interstate on Hwy-16, at
the foot of La Bajada, is home to a thousand Keresan-speaking
Indians who trace their ancestry back to the cliff dwellers of
Bandelier (see p.128). Visitors have free access to the pueblo in daylight hours, but while you may find some inhabitants selling crafts
outside their houses, it holds no formal stores. The mission church of
San Buenaventura still incorporates vestiges of its original adobe
form, but has been greatly modified over the years, and the contemporary frescoes within are not all that enthralling.

A Cochiti potter, Helen Cordero, fashioned the first ceramic "**storyteller**" here in 1946. Each depicting a mother with up to thirty children, these rank among New Mexico's best-selling souvenirs, and are
made by over two hundred Indians, including around fifty Cochiti.

In the 1970s, the tribe leased land to the federal government for
the creation of nearby **Cochiti Lake**, which attracts a million recreational visitors each year. A planned residential community went
bankrupt, however, and the loss of Cochiti agricultural land has left
the pueblo skeptical about further "developments."

*In the Keresan
language,*
Kotyete *means
"stone kiva."*

Santo Domingo Pueblo

Six miles on from Cochiti, **SANTO DOMINGO PUEBLO** is the
largest Keresan pueblo. For many centuries, its people have been

renowned for making **jewelry**, and especially necklaces of delicate shell and turquoise *heishi* beads. By some accounts, the Santo Domingans taught the art of silversmithing to the Navajo in the nineteenth century, and they're now prominent among the Indian traders of Santa Fe.

The **visitor center** in the plaza at Santo Domingo doubles as a crafts store and tribal museum (daily 8am–5pm; ☎505/465-2214), while the all-purpose Santo Domingo Trading Post to the north ranges from food to jewelry.

San Felipe Pueblo

SAN FELIPE PUEBLO, the next of the southern pueblos, stands another half-dozen miles downriver from Santo Domingo. Until 1250 AD, the San Felipeans were a single tribe with the fellow Keresan speakers now known as the Cochiti. Their subsequent migrations only ended in 1693, when they settled here for good after the Pueblo Revolt.

Daytime visits are always permitted here, but photography is not. On the pueblo's **feast day**, May 1, its bowl-shaped plaza is thronged with dancers performing a daylong corn dance.

Algodones

The village of **ALGODONES**, stretching languidly beside the river five miles southwest of San Felipe, makes a tranquil base for visits to both Santa Fe and Albuquerque. *Hacienda Vargas*, 1431 El Camino Real (☎505/867-9115; ④), is one of New Mexico's most relaxing rural **B&Bs**, set in a lovely adobe trading post.

Bernalillo and Coronado State Monument

BERNALILLO, five miles on from Algodones, is an unexciting satellite community at the edge of Albuquerque's urban sprawl, principally noteworthy as the site of **CORONADO STATE MONUMENT** (daily 8.30am–5pm; April–Oct $3, Nov–March $2). In a spectacular setting on the west bank of the Rio Grande, a mile west of the interstate, this preserves what remains of the ancient pueblo of **Kuaua**. The Spaniards knew this region as **Tiguex**, and described it as a "broad valley planted with fields of maize and dotted with cottonwood groves"; Francisco de Coronado may well have spent the winter of 1540 here. Kuaua was then a thriving community of well over a thousand rooms; now it's a ruin, of which a few eroded adobe walls have been exposed by archeologists. The central feature is a restored *kiva*, decorated with vivid reproductions of its multicolored **murals**. The faded originals, preserved in the visitor center, include scenes of a rabbit hunt – the animals are still abundant in the undergrowth by the river.

Rabbits often represent the moon in Pueblo art, as Pueblo peoples see a "rabbit in the moon" rather than a "man in the moon."

Near the monument entrance, the state maintains a large but attractive riverfront **campground** (☎505/867-5589), where rates

South to
Albuquerque

depend on what degree of comfort you require. Bernalillo also boasts a couple of New Mexico's finest **restaurants**. At the south end of town, east of the river – and, being close to exit 240 off I-25, an easy evening excursion from Albuquerque – the *Range Cafe*, 925 Camino del Pueblo (☎505/867-1700), is a brightly decorated hall that serves all meals daily, with huge Mexican-style appetizers like *chimichangas* for $8 or less, and strongly chile-flavored main dishes garnished with blue corn chips for little more. Across the Rio Grande, a mile or so northwest of the monument, the *Prairie Star*, 1000 Jemez Canyon Dam Rd (☎505/867-3327), opens nightly for dinner only, offering contemporary Southwestern cuisine at upwards of $20 per entree.

Opposite the monument entrance, the enormous Jackalope outlet (☎505/867-9813) is utterly unabashed about selling "Folk Art by the Truckload"; if you're looking for a large, cheap **souvenir**, this is the place to come.

*Santa Ana
Pueblo, near
Bernalillo, is
described on
p.132.*

Sandia Pueblo

SANDIA PUEBLO, between Bernalillo and Albuquerque, dates back to around 1300 AD, and was visited by Coronado in 1540. *Sandía* is the Spanish for watermelon; the Spaniards mistook the squashes they saw growing here for watermelons. The village's Tiwa name – **Nafiat**, meaning "dry or sandy place" – seems more appropriate to its dusty central plaza. After it was destroyed in 1692, by Spaniards returning after the Pueblo Revolt, many of its inhabitants took refuge with the Hopi, far to the west, and the settlement was not rebuilt for fifty years. The main preoccupation of the three hundred present-day Sandians is the protection of their sacred sites in the nearby mountains from blundering hikers, but being so close to Albuquerque, they're also among the chief beneficiaries of the legalization of Indian gaming, operating the 24-hour **Sandia Casino** alongside the interstate. Other tribal concerns include the *Bien Mur Trading Post* **crafts center** and **restaurant**, on Tramway Road nearby (☎505/821-5400), which has a herd of buffalo.

The Turquoise Trail

The **Turquoise Trail** – less glamorously known as **Hwy-14** – is a modern name for what may be one of the oldest thoroughfares in North America, connecting **mines** along the eastern flanks of the Sandia Mountains with the settlements of the Rio Grande Valley. In the last two hundred years, these mines have yielded considerable quantities of copper, coal, and even gold, but **turquoise** production dates back perhaps ten times as far. Long before the coming of the Spaniards, traders carried local stone all over the Southwest and down into Mexico, and wealthy pueblos lined the nearby streams.

Until a recent influx of artists, craftworkers and small-scale entrepreneurs, communities along the trail had dwindled to become little

more than **ghost towns**, but now **Madrid** in particular is one of the
most appealing day-trip destinations for visitors to Santa Fe.

Cerrillos

The northernmost Turquoise-Trail town, **CERRILLOS** is just over
twenty miles south of Santa Fe, reached simply by continuing south
on Cerrillos Road, which becomes Hwy-14, for fifteen miles beyond
its intersection with I-25. The dusty rolling hillocks that surround it
– the "little hills" of its name – hold one of the world's greatest concentrations of **turquoise**.

Archeologists have estimated that ninety percent of the fabled
turquoise treasures seized by the Spaniards from the Aztec capital of
Tenochtitlan came from this unprepossessing spot. With basic tools,
prehistoric miners scooped a hundred thousand tons of rock from
Mount Chalchihuitl, two miles northeast, leaving a cavern 300 feet
wide and 200 feet deep. Early Spanish settlers may have forced the
Indians to work for them; it's said that a mine collapse around 1680,
which killed up to eighty Indians, helped to precipitate the Pueblo
Revolt. By the time the Spaniards returned, the Indians had deliberately hidden many of the shafts, and tales of fabulously wealthy "lost
mines" still abound.

*The unpaved
streets and
falsefront
wooden build-
ings of
Cerrillos made
it an ideal
location for the
1988 bratpack
Western Young
Guns.*

Today's Cerrillos, nestled amid the giant cottonwoods along the
bank of the broad but usually dry Galisteo River, has changed little
since its last boom in the 1890s. Mining not only turquoise but gold,
silver, copper and lead, it was briefly rich enough to support eight
daily newspapers and numerous hotels and saloons. There's still a bit
of life in the old town; as recently as 1983, robbers made off with
$500,000 worth of gold from the nearby Ortiz Mines. Tourists, how-
ever, have to content themselves with the **Casa Grande Trading
Post, Turquoise Mining Museum and Petting Zoo**, an endearing
shop-cum-museum that offers a random assortment of old bills and
letters, porcupine quills, rattlesnake skins and petrified wood, plus
the chance to pet a llama or pull on a string to make a plaster Indian
hammer on a rock.

Madrid

Between 1869 and 1959, the village of **MADRID** (pronounced *MAD-
rid*), three miles south, made a good living from mining **coal**. The
hills here are unusual in holding deposits of both bituminous (soft)
and anthracite (hard) coal, which in the early days was hauled by
wagon as far as St Louis, and later was consumed in vast quantities
by the Santa Fe Railroad. Tunnels ran directly beneath the main
street, while a mine shaft that burrows straight into the hillside can
now be seen in the **Old Coal Mine Museum** at the south end of town
(daily 9am–5.30pm; $3). The rest of the museum consists of several
barns stuffed with ancient junk like obsolete X-ray machines and
decrepit Model "T" Ford trucks, plus the Engine House Theater,

which stages the moustache-twirling **Madrid Melodrama** on summer weekends (performances May–Sept Sat 3pm & 8pm, Sun 3pm; $9; ☎505/982-1237).

After the mine closed down, the whole town was auctioned off piecemeal, and the straggle of wooden cottages to either side of the narrow highway have progressively been taken over by New-Agey newcomers. Several hold genuinely interesting crafts and antiques stores; if you're close enough to home to carry **furniture**, there are some real bargains to be had. Among the best stores are Primitiva, on the raised boardwalk at 500 Main St, which has two spacious floors of artifacts from around the world, including plenty of novelty stuff, and the Turquoise Trail Trading Post nearby, which concentrates more on Pueblo crafts.

One attractive old mining home, *Java Junction* (☎505/438-2772; ③), houses a **coffeeshop** downstairs and a **B&B** apartment upstairs, with kitchen and bathroom; *Back Street Pizza* (☎505/474-5555) serves more substantial food; and the lively *Mine Shaft Tavern*, in front of the museum (☎505/473-0743), claims to have the longest **bar** in New Mexico, and puts on live **music** at weekends.

Golden

In 1825, **GOLDEN**, fifteen miles beyond Madrid, was the site of the Wild West's first-ever gold rush. It has yet to revitalize to any great extent, and you might hardly notice it was there as the highway races down its former main street. Look out, however, for the tumbledown **adobe church** on the hill at the north edge of town, which served the mining camp of **Tuerto**, and has preserved its pioneer graveyard.

Sandia Crest and Cedar Crest

Ten miles on from Golden, the **Sandia Crest Scenic Byway** branches west from Hwy-14, to climb for eight tortuous miles up to the razorback ridge atop the Sandia Mountains. From the mile-high **observation deck** at road's end, you can survey the sprawling city of **Albuquerque**, with the Rio Grande flowing in from the north, and also look east across the endless plains, beyond the Ortiz Mountains. The adjacent *Sandia House* sells tasteless snacks and useless gifts. A fee of $3 is charged for day-use of the nearby trails, but most visitors stay for barely ten minutes before heading back down the hill; there's no through route to Albuquerque.

In winter, **skiers** exploring the eastern Sandia slopes base themselves down below, in **CEDAR CREST** at the foot of the Scenic Byway. *Elaine's*, 72 Snowline Estates (☎505/281-2467 or 1-800/821-3092; *www.elainesbnb.com*; ⑤) is a very comfortable B&B set in spacious grounds, while the *Sandia Mountain Hostel* (☎505/281-4117) offers dorm **accommodation** at $12 per bed, and the *Kokopelli Cafe* (☎505/281-2002) serves all **meals**. The Turquoise Trail ends six miles south at the intersection with I-40, which sweeps the final dozen miles west to Albuquerque through **Tijeras** – "Scissors" – **Canyon**.

West of Santa Fe

The **Jemez Mountain Trail**, which loops through the mountains west of Santa Fe, can be enjoyed as a long day's excursion, or a round-about route down to Albuquerque. Communities along the way range from modern **Los Alamos** – the top-secret Town That Never Was – to the ancient dwellings of **Bandelier National Monument**; the scenery encompasses mountain meadows and desert canyons.

Pajarito means "little bird" in Spanish; it's a direct translation of the Tewa tsirege, the name of an abandoned local pueblo.

The **Pajarito Plateau**, the dominant feature of the landscape, was created just over a million years ago, when colossal **volcanic eruptions** buried four hundred square miles of land beneath a thousand feet of ash. This solidified into the easily-eroded rock known as **tuff**, which has been eaten away by wind and rain ever since to form an intricate tangle of deep gorges and forested mesas. Only one road climbs onto the plateau, **Hwy-502**, which branches west from US-84 near Pojoaque Pueblo, fifteen miles north of Santa Fe.

Los Alamos

LOS ALAMOS, eighteen miles up Hwy-502, is not so much a town as the overgrown campus of the **Los Alamos National Laboratory**. Home during World War II to the **Manhattan Project**, which first developed the atomic bomb, it has remained the leading US center for the research and development of nuclear weapons. With the laboratory now run by the University of California, Los Alamos has become New Mexico's wealthiest enclave.

*This book went to press before the long-term effects on Los Alamos and Bandelier of May 2000's huge **Cerro Grande forest fire** had become clear. Early indications were, however, that tourism to both areas will remain largely unaffected*

It's a confusing place to visit. The layout – sprawling along several "fingers" at the edge of the Pajarito Plateau, separated by deep canyons – is bizarre in the extreme, and the fact that most of the complex is off limits to the public doesn't help. Most tourists call in at one of the two local **museums**, then head on to Bandelier.

The **Bradbury Science Museum**, at Central and 15th (Tues–Fri 9am–5pm, Sat–Mon 1–5pm; free), presents the authorized version of the laboratory's history. Opponents of nuclear proliferation are given space to state their case, but visitors inevitably gravitate towards the central exhibits – full-sized 1940s replicas of "Little Boy," which devastated Hiroshima, and "Fat Man," dropped on Nagasaki. The **visitors' book** is fascinating enough to have been published in the past. Americans tend to be resolutely gung-ho; international travelers – of which a sizeable percentage seem to come from Hiroshima and Nagasaki – rather less so. The excellent Otowi Station **bookstore**, alongside, is open daily for varying but consistently longer hours.

Los Alamos Historical Museum, adjoining the visitor center at 2132 Central Ave (winter Mon–Sat 10am–4pm, Sun 1–4pm; summer Mon–Sat 9.30am–4.30pm, Sun 11am–5pm; free), is housed in the former dining hall of Los Alamos Ranch School. As well as displays on the school, and local geology and prehistory, it too covers the bomb in some detail. Exhibits range from a 360° aerial photo of

---

The Town That Never Was: Los Alamos and the Bomb

In 1942, the American and British governments decided to amalgamate the nine research efforts then racing to build the **atomic bomb**. Albert Einstein had suggested the idea to President Roosevelt three years earlier, and a team led by Enrico Fermi was achieving promising results in a laboratory beneath a disused football stadium in Chicago. The search was on for a suitable location, in a sparsely populated area, away from the sea, with a reasonable year-round climate. **J. Robert Oppenheimer**, the scientific chief of the **Manhattan Project**, had backpacked before the war in New Mexico. He recommended the Los Alamos Ranch School, an exclusive private school on the Pajarito Plateau, and the site was duly bought out. When its final class graduated in February 1943, the scientists moved in.

It took just over two years, working in the utmost secrecy – the words "Los Alamos" were forbidden, and newcomers were told merely to report to 109 Palace Avenue in Santa Fe – for the bomb to become a reality. The first successful test took place at the **Trinity Site**, two hundred miles south (see p.187), on July 16, 1945. Three weeks later, bombs were dropped on the cities of **Hiroshima**, on August 6, and **Nagasaki**, August 9; a complete Japanese surrender followed immediately.

For Oppenheimer, who described the development of the bomb with a quotation from the Bhagavad Gita, "I am become Death, the shatterer of Worlds," Los Alamos had served its purpose, and the laboratory could now close. Instead, as the Cold War set in, its energies were devoted towards the construction of the **H-Bomb**. Though security was more paramount than ever, ideologically motivated spies such as **Klaus Fuchs** and **David Greenglass** (whose sister and her husband, **Ethel** and **Julius Rosenberg**, were later executed) soon betrayed Los Alamos' secrets to the Russians. Paranoia grew to the point that employees were instructed to "Watch Your Liberal Friends," and Oppenheimer himself was barred by his successor Edward Teller from access to privileged information.

The gatehouse on the road up from Santa Fe that denied outsiders access to Los Alamos was finally removed in 1957, and the ownership of private property on the plateau was allowed in 1962. The laboratory business is still booming, however, and still spending well over half its billion-dollar annual budget. Of its 1993 budget of $1,122 million, just over half, $589 million, was spent on the research and development of nuclear weapons. While the lab has also drilled a 12,000-foot hole to "mine" heat from hot rocks deep in the earth, and worked on the Human Genome project which aims to map the entire DNA structure of human beings, its public image remains firmly linked with nuclear experimentation – recent revelations concerning spies operating on behalf of China have hardly helped – and constantly changing plans for the disposal of its radioactive waste are among New Mexico's hottest political issues.

Visitors to Los
Alamos should
avoid the rush
hour traffic
that heads up
Hwy-502 until
around 9am,
and comes back
down again
from 3pm
onwards.

Los Alamos' zip
code is NM
87544.

Hiroshima, to classic examples of atomic kitsch, such as a picture of the commander of the 1946 tests at Bikini cutting a mushroom-cloud shaped cake, some earrings made with "atomsite" fused glass from the Trinity site, and an A-bomb-shaped lamp.

Practicalities

Los Alamos' visitor center is a couple of blocks west of the Bradbury Museum, at 2132 Central Ave (Mon–Fri 9am–4pm, Sat 10am–4pm; ☎505/662-8105). As well as a couple of nondescript upmarket motels that cater largely for visiting scientists – the *Best Western Hilltop House*, 400 Trinity Drive (☎505/662-2441 or 1-800/831-2381, fax 505/662-5913; *www.losalamos.com/hilltophouse*; ④), and *Los Alamos Inn*, 2201 Trinity Drive (☎505/662-7211 or 1-800/279-9279; ④) – the town has a handful of B&Bs, such as the *Orange Street Inn*, 3496 Orange St (☎505/662-2651 or 1-800/279-2898; ③). The *Trinity Sights Restaurant*, upstairs in *Hilltop House*, is the best place to eat in town, though the *Cafe Allegro*, 800 Trinity Drive (☎505/662-4040), serves a mean espresso.

Bandelier National Monument

Long before the scientists descended upon Los Alamos, the "finger canyons" of the Pajarito Plateau were home to Native Americans. At BANDELIER NATIONAL MONUMENT, ten miles south of Los Alamos – a fifty-mile drive from Santa Fe – Ancestral Puebloans enlarged natural cavities in the soft volcanic rock to create cliff dwellings, and built freestanding pueblo communities beside the streams on the valley floors. Set amid delightful woodlands and framed against the rose-pink canyon walls, Bandelier's intriguing remains provide an ideal introduction to New Mexico's prehistoric roots.

For details of
Gray Line bus
tours to
Bandelier from
Santa Fe, see
p.104.

Although the Ancestral Puebloans are often said to have "disappeared" around 1300 AD, there's little mystery about where they went. Bandelier is a "missing link," occupied between roughly 1150, at the time the Four Corners region was being abandoned, and 1550, when many of today's pueblos were established. As successive itinerant groups streamed in, perhaps fleeing drought or invasion, they may have amalgamated here to create the modern Pueblo culture. The peoples of Cochiti and San Ildefonso in particular trace their ancestry back via Bandelier to Mesa Verde, and it was a Cochiti guide who led amateur archeologist Adolph Bandelier to this site in 1880.

Frijoles Canyon

The major sights of Bandelier are concentrated along a 1.5-mile loop trail through Frijoles ("Beans") Canyon. The visitor center, at the bottom of a narrow switchback road down from Hwy-4 (daily: winter 8am–5pm; summer 8am–6pm; ☎505/672-3861), gives an excellent overview, with displays of pottery and jewelry, models of the ruins, full-scale reconstructions of pueblo interiors and century-old photographs of Indian life.

Beyond the visitor center, the trail leads swiftly to the remains of **Tyuonyi**, a circular, multistory village of four hundred rooms, of which only the ground floor and foundations survive. Its name means "place of agreement," and it's seen as a center for trade and storage, common to the **Keresan**-speaking peoples, whose pueblos lay to the south, and the **Tewa** speakers to the north. Local obsidian was traded as far as the Dakotas and the Mississippi. Tyuonyi may have still been in use when Coronado's soldiers became the first Spaniards to penetrate the Southwest (see p.524), though they didn't reach this far.

A side path from Tyuonyi leads up to dozens of **cave dwellings**, their rounded chambers scooped into the warmer, south-facing wall of the canyon. Ladders and walkways mean visitors can scramble up to, and even enter, some of them, to peer out across the valley.

The main trail continues to the **Long House**, an 800ft series of two- and three-story houses built side by side against the cliffs. Though most of the upper stories have collapsed to expose the plastered walls, you can still see the mortised holes that held up their pine roof beams or *vigas*. Above these are rows of petroglyphs and pictographs, mostly depicting figures and abstract symbols.

Though the main trail doubles back to the visitor center, keen hikers can follow the stream for another half-mile, to the point where **Ceremonial Cave** nestles in a rocky overhang 150 feet above the canyon floor. Reaching it entails climbing three hair-raising ladders, as well as steep stairways hacked into the crumbling rock. At the top, you can see by the *viga*-holes that the cave once held several structures, but it's now bare except for a reconstructed *kiva*, set down in its sloping sandy floor, and entered by ladder.

Another trail drops south from the visitor center, coming out after a mile and a half at the **Lower Falls** – at their best in late spring – and then reaches the Rio Grande in another ten minutes.

Tsankawi

The small, separate **Tsankawi** section of Bandelier is located a dozen miles northeast of the monument visitor center, just off Hwy-502 as it climbs from the Rio Grande valley up to Los Alamos. Visits consist of an hour-long loop hike onto and around an isolated mesa-top that holds the almost indiscernible ruins of another ancient pueblo. If the site itself is disappointing, however, the trail is not; following the same route once used by the Ancestral Puebloans, it's worn waist-deep into the soft turf in places, and includes a number of prehistoric "stairways." Assuming you're happy to negotiate a couple of short ladders, you're also rewarded with lovely views down into the valley, as well as glimpses of the mysterious Los Alamos laboratories closer at hand.

Admission to Bandelier National Monument is $10 per vehicle, and the Frijoles Canyon trails are open daily from dawn to dusk.

If Bandelier captures your imagination, don't miss the similar Puyé Cliff Dwellings (see p.137).

Practicalities

Snacks and sodas are available at the monument visitor center, but
there's no **accommodation** at Bandelier itself apart from the very
pleasant *Juniper Campground*, just off Hwy-4 up on Frijoles Mesa
(March–Nov; first-come, first-served; $10). Tsankawi, however,
stands close to the tiny community of White Rock, which holds the
smart little *Bandelier Inn* motel, 132 Hwy-4 (☎505/672-3838 or 1-
800/321-3923, fax 505/672-3537; ④).

Valle Grande and Spence's Hot Spring

Hwy-4 climbs west of Bandelier and Los Alamos, bursting unexpectedly out of the forests to skirt the long rim of **Valle Grande**. This
500-foot-deep, 176-square-mile basin is the world's largest extinct
caldera, and its wide meadows form a lush counterpoint to the dry-
as-dust terrain of most of New Mexico. At some point, it's hoped that
the huge **Baca Ranch** here will become a new public park, but for the
moment, the Valle Grande remains primarily a drive-through experience.

However, vestiges of the volcanic past can be seen in the form of
the numerous **hot springs** that bubble from beneath the ground.
Among the most irresistible is **Spence's Hot Spring**, on a promontory above the Jemez River between mileposts 24 and 25, half an
hour out of Los Alamos. Half a dozen waterfall-connected pools provide a range of temperatures to suit anybody, from the high 90°sF in
the lower pools to a blissful 104°F at the top; local custom calls for
bathing suits on weekend nights, otherwise it's clothing optional. To
get there, cross the river over a fallen tree and then climb up the
canyon, keeping to the left for about ten minutes' walk uphill.

Jemez Springs

Five miles down from Spence's Hot Spring, Hwy-4 runs past the
bizarre **Soda Dam**, where calcified deposits all but block the Jemez
River, to enter **JEMEZ SPRINGS**. This appealing hamlet, where the
river is lined by glowing cottonwoods and flows between high canyon
walls that flame gold and red, was once the site of the Towa-speaking pueblo of **Giusewa**, the "Place of the Boiling Waters."

What little remains of the mission church of **San Jose de los
Jemez**, built by Franciscans in 1621 only to be destroyed almost
immediately by Navajo raiders, is now preserved in **Jemez State
Monument** (daily 8.30am–5pm; April–Oct $3, Nov–March $2).
Walls that once held bright frescoes are now just ruined stumps, but
the principal doorway has been reconstructed.

Practicalities

Jemez Springs offers several small-scale **accommodation** options,
including the beautiful riverview *Dancing Bear B&B* (PO Box 128;

☎505/829-3336 or 1-800/422-3271, fax 505/829-3395; ④–⑥), and the *Jemez River B&B Inn*, 16445 Hwy-4 (☎505/829-3262 or 1-800/809-3262; ⑨), which doubles as a hummingbird sanctuary. The *Laughing Lizard Cafe* (☎505/829-3692; ④) holds yet more rooms, and serves espresso coffee and full meals on a nice terrace above both highway and river, while the late-opening *Los Ojos Restaurant and Saloon* (☎505/829-3547) has food, pool tables and cheap beer.

West of
Santa Fe

*Jemez Springs'
zip code is NM
87025*

Jemez Pueblo

After Giusewa Pueblo was abandoned in 1630, its inhabitants built **JEMEZ PUEBLO**, fifteen miles downstream. There they participated in the Pueblo Revolt of 1680, sacking their church and killing its priest; when the Spaniards returned, they briefly retreated northwest, establishing cultural and family links with the Navajo that endure to this day. They also assimilated the last twenty survivors of Pecos Pueblo in 1838 (see p.144). Jemez now has a population of around 3000, and is the only surviving Towa-speaking pueblo. Its people successfully resisted plans to develop a geothermal power plant in the Jemez mountains in 1982.

*Advice on visiting the pueblos,
and a calendar
of major feast
days, appears
on p.134.*

In honor of the surrounding scenery, the Jemez Indians call themselves **Walatowa**, "people of the canyon," and that's also the name of their village. A **visitor center**, three miles north on Hwy-4 at **Red Rock** (daily 8am–5pm; ☎505/834-7235), holds displays on their history and crafts, but the pueblo itself is only open to visitors on feast days such as August 2, November 12 and December 12. On weekends between April and mid-October, the **Jemez Pueblo Open Air Market**, also at Red Rock, sells food and artworks.

Cuba

Turning right rather than left when Hwy-4 meets US-550 at **San Ysidro**, just beyond Red Rock, would carry you away from the Rio Grande, and northwest towards Chaco Canyon (see p.84) or Mesa Verde (see p.69). It's also possible to complete an even larger loop than the one along Hwy-4 by circling around north of the mountains on Hwy-96 before dropping back down to the river at Española. That route takes you through the truly spectacular ranching country west of **COYOTE**, where the highway is paralleled to the north by a magnificent escarpment of striated red rock, and then past Abiquiu Lake and Abiquiu itself (see p.138).

*Hwy-96 also
makes a good
route if you're
driving
between Santa
Fe and
Durango or
Chaco.*

Whichever direction you ultimately choose, you'll have to head first to the lonely farming community of **CUBA**, reached after a 43-mile drive through Indian lands. Not much more than a curve in the highway, Cuba is nonetheless home to three **motels**, of which the *Frontier* (☎505/289-3474; ①) at the north end of town across the Rio Puerco, is the most salubrious. Alongside it, the friendly

Frontier Cafe, 6478 Hwy-44 (☎505/289-3130), is smarter than it
looks from the outside, and makes an excellent stop for a Mexican
lunch or dinner: a delicious *posole* stew, with chile and *sopaipillas*,
costs just $4. Set in the hills nearby, the appealing *Circle A Ranch*
hostel (PO Box 2142; May to mid-Oct; ☎505/289-3350; ①–③), is
an adobe *hacienda* that offers dorm beds for $13 as well as private
rooms with and without baths.

*Cuba's zip code
is NM 87013*

Zia and Santa Ana pueblos

Reached by a short spur road off Hwy-44, little **ZIA PUEBLO**, which
also overlooks the Jemez River a dozen miles further downstream, is
best known for the **sun symbol** that features on New Mexico's flag
and licence plates. Now 750 strong, the Zia Indians have occupied
this spot since the sixteenth century, when they were visited by early
Spanish explorers. Their neighbors at the equally small **SANTA ANA
PUEBLO**, eight miles southeast along Hwy-44, are also Keresan
speakers, who moved in after the Pueblo Revolt. There's little reason
for outsiders to visit either pueblo; the road into Santa Ana, in fact,
is barred except for the occasional feast day.

The Jemez Mountain Trail ends ten miles on from Santa Ana, when
Hwy-44 meets the I-25 interstate at **Bernalillo**, home to the
Coronado State Monument (see p.122). Downtown Albuquerque is
a sixteen-mile drive south – though the suburbs start almost immediately – while Santa Fe is forty miles northeast, a drive described on
p.121 onwards.

From Santa Fe to Taos:
the northern pueblos

*For a detailed
history of the
Pueblo peoples,
see p.523; gen-
eral advice on
visiting the
pueblos
appears on
p.134.*

The quickest route between Santa Fe and Taos follows US-84 as far
as the Rio Grande, then continues northeast beside the river on **Hwy-
68** – not that the switch from one to the other, at **Española**, is discernible to the naked eye. US-84 passes through the heartland of the
northern pueblos, a cluster of tiny Tewa-speaking villages that have
survived for over five hundred years. The most interesting for casual
visitors are **Santa Clara**, where the **Puyé Cliff Dwellings** are among
the Southwest's least-known ancient ruins, and **Nambe**, near the
impressive **Nambe Falls**. **Pojoaque** on the highway can provide a
quick taste of Pueblo culture and a souvenir or two, but serious collectors head instead for **San Ildefonso** and its famous pottery.

Tesuque Pueblo

Nine miles north of Santa Fe, west of US-84, and overlooked by the
remarkable **Camel Rock**, the traditional community of **TESUQUE
PUEBLO** studiously turns its back on the city. Its name means "place

of the cottonwood trees," and its people were the first to strike against the Spaniards during the Pueblo Revolt. They now operate a **campground**, geared mainly towards RVs (☎505/455-2661).

Pojoaque Pueblo

POJOAQUE PUEBLO, twelve miles out of Santa Fe, was once one of the largest pueblos, but its original settlement was abandoned after a smallpox epidemic in 1895. Though some ceremonial activities have resumed in the last twenty years, most of the tribe's attention is

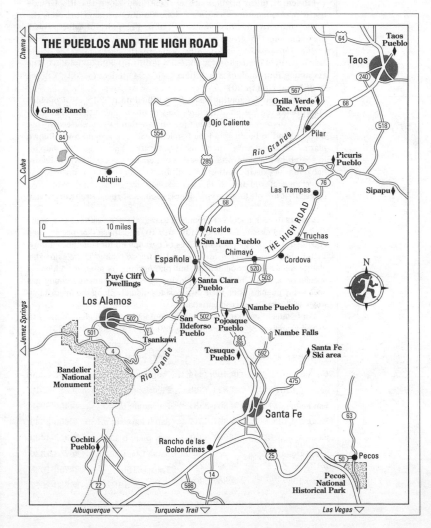

THE PUEBLOS AND THE HIGH ROAD

Visiting the Rio Grande Pueblos

In 1540, the first Spaniards to explore what's now New Mexico encountered a settled population of around a hundred thousand people, living in a hundred or so villages and towns. They named them the **Pueblo Indians**, pueblo being the Spanish for "village." Smallpox, war, and general disruption have taken their toll, but New Mexico is still home to around forty thousand Pueblo Indians who live in nineteen autonomous pueblos, each with its own laws and system of government.

Fifteen of those pueblos are concentrated along the Rio Grande north of Albuquerque. There's a longstanding division between the seven southern pueblos, south of Santa Fe, most of which speak Keresan, and the group to north, which mostly speak Tewa (pronounced *tay-wah*), and jointly promote themselves as the Eight Northern Indian Pueblos (☎505/852-4265 or 1-800/793-4955). The remaining four pueblos are Ácoma (see p.94), Isleta (p.202), Laguna (p.96), and Zuni (p.90).

Despite their fascinating history – outlined on p.523 – most pueblos aren't really the tourist attractions they're often touted to be. The best-known, **Taos** and **Ácoma**, retain their ancient defensive architecture, but the rest tend to be dusty adobe hamlets scattered around a windblown plaza. Unless you arrive on a feast day, or are a knowledgeable shopper in search of Pueblo crafts (most have their own specialties), visits are liable to prove disappointing. In addition, you'll certainly be made to feel unwelcome if you fail to behave respectfully – don't go "exploring" places that are off limits to outsiders, such as shrines, *kivas* or private homes.

Visitors to each pueblo are required to register at a visitor center; some charge an admission fee of from $3 to $10, and those that permit such activities at all charge additional fees of perhaps $5 for still photography, $10–15 for video cameras, and up to $100 for sketching. There's no extra charge for feast days or dances, but photography is often forbidden on special occasions. The recent explosion of Native American gaming has seen many pueblos open their own casinos, usually along the major highways, well away from residential areas.

For details of **guided pueblo tours**, contact Nambe Pueblo Tours (112 W San Francisco St, Santa Fe; ☎505/820-1340 or 1-800/946-2623).

Southern Pueblos		Northern Pueblos	
Cochiti; p.121	☎465-2244	Nambe; p.136	☎455-2036
Jemez; p.131	☎834-7235	Picuris; p.139	☎587-2519
San Felipe; p.122	☎867-3381	Pojoaque; p.133	☎455-2278
Sandia; p.123	☎867-3317	San Ildefonso; p.136	☎455-3549
Santa Ana; p.132	☎867-3301	San Juan; p.138	☎852-4400
Santo Domingo; p.121	☎465-2214	Santa Clara; p.137	☎753-7326
Zia; p.132	☎867-3304	Taos; p.156	☎758-1028
		Tesuque; p.132	☎983-2667

All the above numbers share area code ☎505

A Pueblo Calendar

Jan 1	Transfer of Canes	Most pueblos
Jan 6	Three Kings Day	Most pueblos
Jan 22–23	San Ildefonso Pueblo Feast Day	San Ildefonso
Jan 25	St Paul's Feast Day	Picuris
Feb 2	Candelaria Day	Santo Domingo, San Felipe
March 19	St Joseph's Feast Day	Laguna
April 1	Spring Corn Dance	Many pueblos
Easter	Dances	Most pueblos
May 1	Green Corn Dance	San Felipe
May 3	Santa Cruz Feast Day	Cochiti, Taos
June 8	Buffalo Dance	Santa Clara
June 13	Sandia Pueblo Feast Day	Sandia
June 13	St Anthony's Feast Day	Most pueblos
June 20	Governor's Dance	Isleta
June 23–24	San Juan Pueblo Feast Day	San Juan
June 24	Corn Dances	Santa Ana, Taos
June 29	San Pedro Feast Day	Most pueblos
July 4	Nambe Falls Celebration	Nambe
July 14	San Buenaventura	Cochiti
July (2nd wk)	Taos Pueblo Powwow	Taos
July (3rd wk)	Northern Pueblo Artist & Craftsman Show	Varying northern pueblos
July 25–26	Corn Dances	Taos
July 25–26	Santa Ana Pueblo Feast Day	Santa Ana
Aug 2	Pecos Bull Dance	Jemez
Aug 4	Corn Dance	Santo Domingo
Aug 9–10	San Lorenzo Feast Day	Picuris
Aug 12	Santa Clara Pueblo Feast Day	Santa Clara
Aug 15	Zia Pueblo Feast Day	Zia
Aug (3rd wk)	Indian Market	Santa Fe
Aug 28	St Augustine Feast Day	Isleta
Sept 2	San Esteban Feast Day	Ácoma
Sept 4	Isleta Pueblo Feast Day	Isleta
Sept 19	Laguna Pueblo Feast Day	Laguna
Sept 22	Harvest Dance	San Juan
Sept 29–30	Feast of San Gerónimo	Taos
Oct 3–4	San Francisco Feast Day	Nambe
Nov 12	San Diego Feast Day	Jemez, Tesuque
Early Dec	Shalako ceremony	Zuni
Dec 12	Guadalupe Feast Day	Jemez, Pojoaque
Dec 25	Matachina Dance	Most pueblos
Dec 26	Turtle Dance	San Juan
Dec 26	Children's Dances	Picuris, Santa Clara

devoted to running a busy roadside complex just east of US-84. As
well as a visitor center covering all the Tewa peoples (Mon–Sat
9am–6pm, Sun 9am–4pm), which sells a wide range of Native
American artifacts, this includes the Poeh Museum (Tues–Sat
8am–noon & 12.30–4.30pm; $1), whose displays are little different
from those in the store, and the *Po Suwae Geh* restaurant (daily
7am–8pm; ☎505/455-7493). On summer Saturdays and Sundays,
it's also the venue for dance performances at 11am and 1pm. The
Cities of Gold casino, which stands alongside, has proved so lucrative that the tribe was able to buy the nearby Santa Fe Downs racetrack, adjoining the pueblo, in order to close it down.

Nambe Pueblo

The most beautifully sited of the northern pueblos is NAMBE
PUEBLO, reached by turning right on Hwy-503 just beyond
Pojoaque. Keep going up the hillside beyond the Sacred Heart
church, and after a total of three verdant miles, you'll come to a turning on the right. Three road signs in quick succession here suggest
that Nambe lies five miles, six miles, and eight miles further on. In
fact, the actual pueblo is 1.5 miles along, and is not visible from the
road; in any case, apart from a large *kiva*, not much remains in its
old plaza area. The signs actually refer, respectively, to a tribal
ranger station that controls access to the triple-decker Nambe Falls;
to the falls themselves; and to the reservoir that stands above them,
reached by a separate fork of the road.

Seeing Nambe Falls requires a steep five-minute hike from the far
end of the picnic area and campground just beyond the ranger station; the admission fee is just $2, but a still photography permit costs
a hefty $18 extra (daily March, Sept & Oct 7am–7pm; April and May
7am–8pm; June–Aug 6am–8pm). At the top of the climb, you can
admire the waters as they tumble through a jagged cleft in the surrounding red rocks, but the view is somewhat marred by the colossal
concrete dam that towers above. There's no way to reach the foot of
the falls, let alone swim there. Camping back at the picnic area costs
$8 per night.

San Ildefonso Pueblo

*The finest col-
lection of pot-
tery made by
the Martinez
family is in
Taos' Millicent
Rogers
Museum; see
p.155.*

Five miles west of Pojoaque, before Hwy-502 crosses the Rio Grande
and climbs up to Los Alamos, SAN ILDEFONSO PUEBLO is best
known as the former home of potter Maria Martinez. From 1919
onwards, together with her husband Julian, she was responsible for
revitalizing the Pueblo ceramic tradition. The people of San
Ildefonso trace their ancestry back to Mesa Verde, by way of the
Pajarito Plateau. In 1694, when the Spaniards returned after the
Pueblo Revolt, refugees from San Ildefonso and its neighbors held
out on a nearby mesa, Black Rock, until they were starved down.

San Ildefonso now consists of two distinct plazas, one of which holds a replica of its original mission church. Individual artisans sell pottery from their own homes – look out for signs – or you can buy from the selection in the **visitor center** (Feb–Oct daily 8am–5pm; Nov–Jan Mon–Fri 8am–4.30pm) when you pay your $3 pueblo admission fee. The nearby **tribal museum** (Mon–Fri 8am–4pm; no additional charge) holds some of Martinez' original works.

Santa Clara Pueblo and Puyé Cliff Dwellings

Five miles north of San Ildefonso, or five miles west of Española, **SANTA CLARA PUEBLO** is known to its 1500 inhabitants as Kapo, "where the roses grow near the water." They too now sell black pottery from houses around the central plaza, but the main reason to visit is to see where they *used* to live: the dramatic **PUYÉ CLIFF DWELLINGS** in Santa Clara Canyon, an eleven-mile drive on paved roads west of the pueblo (daily: April–Sept 8am–8pm; Oct–March 8am–4pm; $5, or $7 for a guided tour, summer Mon–Fri 9am).

Puyé means "where the rabbits meet" in Tewa.

Like the similar but better-known ruins at Bandelier (see p.128), the ancient community of Puyé was set against the south-facing cliffs at the edge of the Pajarito Plateau, and occupied, presumably by descendants of the Mesa Verdeans, between 1250 and 1550. Two tiers of "apartments" were hollowed into the upper canyon wall – so soft that it could be shaped with wooden tools – while a large free-standing pueblo occupied the mesa-top just above. The trail up from the visitor center is easy at first, but seeing the whole thing involves climbing at least one steep ladder, plus some deeply worn "staircases" in the rock. What seem like cozy little cave dwellings were originally interior rooms in larger complexes; each was fronted by several adobe-walled rooms, as the countless holes that once supported roof-beams now testify. Intriguingly, petroglyphs above the entranceways appear to mark specific homes.

If you're reluctant to tear yourself away from this gorgeous spot, there's a **cafe** in the visitor center that serves snacks on weekdays, and it's even possible to **camp** six miles further along Santa Clara Canyon (April–Oct; $8; ☎505/753-7326).

Española

The only sizeable Hispanic settlement between Santa Fe and Taos is **ESPAÑOLA**, roughly halfway between the two and immediately south of the confluence of the Rio Chama and the Rio Grande. While most highway traffic continues northeast at this point on Hwy-68 towards Taos, US-84 veers west across the river towards Chama (see p.162) and Colorado.

Other than watching the local youth cruising the streets in their customized "low-riders," or joining them in one of the dozens of neighborhood fast-food joints, Española has little to offer tourists. However, it's central enough to make an inexpensive alternative

base, with a strip of budget **motels** that includes a *Super 8*, 298 S
Riverside Drive (☎505/753-5374 or 1-800/800-8000, fax 505/753-
5339; winter ②, summer ③). Typical New Mexican **restaurants** in
town include *Angelina's*, 1226 N Railroad Ave (☎505/753-8543),
and *La Paragua*, where Hwy-76 meets US-285 (☎505/753-3211).

Abiquiu and Ghost Ranch

Twenty miles up US-84 from Española towards Chama, the landscape erupts into a riot of red-rock splendor. Cliffs and mesas of
Chinle, Entrada and Windgate sandstone soar above corrugated
hillocks of gray, brown and red clays, all strongly reminiscent of
southern Utah and the Navajo badlands of northeast Arizona.
Surprisingly few visitors pass this way, but it's hardly little-known. If
it now appears definitively Southwestern, that's largely because the
paintings of Georgia O'Keeffe have done so much to shape contemporary notions of the Southwest – and it was this very terrain that
inspired those paintings.

*Of the
Pedernal, near
Abiquiu,
O'Keeffe said
"God told me if
I painted that
mountain
enough, I could
have it."*

From 1946 until she died, aged 98, in 1986, O'Keeffe lived and
worked in the pretty adobe village of **ABIQUIU**, originally a settlement of *genízaros* (the Christianized descendants of Plains peoples
captured by eighteenth-century Spaniards). Her former home,
perched on a hilltop south of the highway, is open for guided tours,
for which reservations need to be made several weeks in advance at
the very least (April–Nov, Tues, Thurs & Fri 9.30am, 11am, 2pm &
3.30pm; $20; ☎505/685-4539). The tours set off from the *Abiquiu
Inn* (☎505/685-4378 or 1-800/447-5621; ④), which features twenty comfortable guestrooms and a good restaurant.

The village itself was a trading center on a par with Taos in the late
eighteenth and early nineteenth centuries, and grew to become New
Mexico's third largest town. These days, it consists of little more than
a small plaza, surrounded by tumbledown adobes and focusing on
the beautiful, restored church of **Santo Tomás**; photography is not
permitted.

Several religious groups have established retreats in the Abiquiu
region, including the international Moslem community that erected
the **Dar al-Islam mosque** on the mesa above the village, and the
Presbyterian ministry at **Ghost Ranch**, fourteen miles north, where
there's also a **Living Museum** of local natural history (daily except
Mon 8am–4.30pm; $3). The Benedictine brothers of the **Monastery
of Christ in the Desert**, thirteen miles west of Ghost Ranch on the
unpaved Hwy-151, have attracted a lot of recent attention by selling
their services designing Web sites.

San Juan Pueblo

SAN JUAN PUEBLO, the largest of the Tewa pueblos, is set amid the
cottonwoods on the east bank of the Rio Grande off Hwy-68, five

miles north of Española. It's the third village to have stood in this vicinity since 1250, all of which have been called **O'ke**, meaning "we are the brothers." The first two capitals of the colony of New Mexico were also built here in 1598. Before they relocated to Santa Fe in 1610, the Spanish started out by taking over O'ke and calling it **San Juan**, and then occupied nearby Yunge and renamed it **San Gabriel**. Later that century, San Juan was the birthplace of **Po'pay** ("ripe squash"), the medicine man who led the Pueblo Revolt.

From Santa Fe to Taos: the northern pueblos

The centerpiece of the plaza today is the much-restored **mission church**, which was the first building in the Southwest to be made with adobe bricks as opposed to simple chunks of mud. It's flanked by two rectangular *kivas*, as well as a smaller Catholic chapel. Admission is free in daylight hours, but photography is by permission only. The *Tewa Indian Restaurant* serves weekday lunches.

Alcalde

The previously low-profile community of **ALCALDE**, a couple of miles further up the Rio Grande from San Juan Pueblo, hit the local headlines in 1999. Shortly after the unveiling of a statue of New Mexico's first governor, Don Juan de Oñate, unknown assailants amputated its right foot – an obvious reference to the barbaric punishment Oñate meted out to the defeated menfolk of Ácoma Pueblo in 1599 (see p.95).

Picuris Pueblo

Tiny **PICURIS PUEBLO**, tucked away in a side valley ten miles off the Rio Grande, twenty miles south of Taos, was the last pueblo to be "discovered" by the Spanish, and proudly insists that it has never signed a treaty with any other government, the US included. Its population has never risen much above two hundred, and Picuris today remains no more than a cluster of adobe houses spreading across the hillside around a whitewashed church.

Picuris Pueblo owns and runs the excellent Hotel Santa Fe *in Santa Fe; see p.105.*

There's a model of the pueblo and a reconstructed *kiva* in the village **museum** (daily 11am–8pm; free). The same building also holds a gift store and the *Hidden Valley Restaurant*, a snack bar with views over a small blue lake. A self-guided **pueblo tour**, which leads past a few active *kivas*, costs $1.75, or $5 with a photo permit.

Pilar

Once an Apache farming village, later occupied by Hispanic settlers, **PILAR**, perched above the Rio Grande fifteen miles southwest of Taos, is now a base for summer **rafting** trips run by the operators listed on p.150. **Accommodation** at the attractive *Rio Grande Gorge Hostel*, perilously close to the highway (☎505/758-0090; ①), consists of two six-bed dorms, where a bed for the night costs $9.50 in summer and $11.50 in winter, two private en-suite rooms (①), and

two strange domes in the garden that cost $23 per night.
Reservations are essential in summer, when the little *Pilar Cafe* next
door serves basic meals.

Orilla Verde Recreation Area

The main objective of the gleaming new Bureau of Land Management
visitor center, on the east side of Hwy-68 at Pilar (daily
8.30am–5pm; ☎505/751-4899), is to inform travelers about the
Orilla Verde Recreation Area. Reached by a minor road that drops
from the far side of the highway, this consists of a stretch of publicly-
owned land that runs to either side of the southern end of the **Upper
Rio Grande Gorge**. Six miles along, there's a developed riverside
campground charging $7 per vehicle.

Whatever your map may suggest, landslides have long since precluded continuing towards Taos at this level, along the east bank of
the river. However, it's possible to meet up with US-285 by following
the dirt road that crosses the river beyond the campground. More to
the point, the **Vista Verde Trail** shortly after the bridge is an enjoyable 1.25-mile hiking trail that leads across the sagebrush-topped
west-bank mesa to an overlook above the Rio Grande Gorge. There's
also a longer trail, slightly further up the hillside, that runs all the
way to the Rio Grande Gorge Bridge (described on p.161); at around
seven miles one way, it's better tackled on a bike or a horse than on
foot.

The High Road

Though the most direct route from Santa Fe to Taos heads straight
up the Rio Grande Valley – see p.132 onwards – the "**High Road**"
over the forested Sangre de Cristo Mountains to the east makes a
rewarding alternative if you have a couple of hours to spare. Winding
its way through timeless **Hispanic villages**, it passes some splendid
old **adobe churches**, and offers good opportunities to buy locally
produced folk art, or sample traditional New Mexican food.

Chimayó

The first and most famous of the High Road towns, **CHIMAYÓ** is 25
miles north of Santa Fe, eight miles northeast of **Pojoaque Pueblo**
via Hwy-592 and Hwy-503, or eight miles east of **Española** on Hwy-
76. Stretching luxuriantly through the fertile upland meadows that
line the Santa Cruz River, and backed by scrubby red-tinged hills, it
feels more of a piece with the Rio Grande Valley below than with the
mountains in the distance to the east.

Chimayó was founded in 1740, as a sort of penal colony for
Hispanic troublemakers. In Tewa, the word *tsimayo* means "good
flaking stone," and Indians from San Juan Pueblo quarried obsidian

here, which they chipped to form sharp blades. They held a dried-up hot spring nearby sacred, claiming that the mud from around it, when eaten, had healing properties. That spring, in the *barrio* (district) at Chimayó's southern end known as **El Potrero**, is now the site of a spellbinding colonial chapel, the **Santuario de Chimayó** (daily: May–Sept 9am–6pm; Oct–April 9am–4pm).

The church was built between 1813 and 1816, after the landowner, **Bernardo Abeyta**, was told by a visiting priest of the shrine at Esquipulas in Guatemala, which had arisen at a similar spring venerated by Guatemalan Indians. As a result, Abeyta's church also centered on a crucifix known as **Nuestro Señor de Esquipulas**, supposedly found locally in 1810 (conceivably it had been buried during the Pueblo Revolt).

The church, the crucifix, and the still-exposed *posito*, or dust pit, swiftly became the focus of **pilgrimages** not only by Hispanic peasants, but also by Pueblo Indians, for whom the sacred hole in the earth clearly echoed the ancient concept of the *sipapu* (see p.520). To this day, it remains the "**Lourdes of America**." Devout New Mexican Catholics resent state advertising campaigns that seem to reduce festivals such as the Good Friday ceremonies, and the re-enactment of the conquest of Spain by Santiago Matamoros (Saint James the Moor-killer), held during the fourth weekend in July, to the status of picturesque tourist attractions.

*Mass is said in
the Santuario
at noon on
Sun, and 11am
Mon–Sat.*

However, the Santuario is an undeniable delight to visit, a ravishing little round-shouldered, twin-towered, tin-roofed adobe beauty set in a walled churchyard beneath the rolling Sangre de Cristo foothills. At the heart of the altar within, the crucifix is framed by a gorgeous **reredos** painted by the nineteenth-century *santero* Molleno, with a small equestrian statue of Santiago to the right. Two smaller **side chapels** are filled with a mind-boggling array of votive offerings – paintings, photographs, statues, press cuttings, even discarded crutches. The hole containing the "Holy Dirt" is in the floor at the rear; pilgrims are allowed to take a scoop, as it's replenished regularly with earth from the hills.

The smaller and more ramshackle **Santo Niño Chapel** (same hours), across the plaza, contains a diminutive statue of Santo Niño, the Lost Child – more of a doll, if truth be told – to whom expectant mothers bring offerings such as tiny pairs of shoes.

Chimayó has specialized in **weaving** since 1805, when two weavers sent as teachers from Spain chose to live here in preference to Santa Fe. Outlets scattered through the village sell hand-woven goods; other galleries concentrate on woodcarving and religious art.

Practicalities

Two properties belonging to the long-established Jaramillo family make Chimayó an appealing overnight destination. The *Rancho de*

The Penitentes

During the nineteenth century, the remote hills above Chimayó were renowned as the heartland of the mysterious Hispanic Catholic sect known as the **Penitentes**. Anglo newcomers claimed to have glimpsed hooded figures filing along the ridges at dawn, **whipping** themselves as they went.

A large grain of truth lay beneath the lurid speculation. Self-mortification – the infliction of pain in order to share the suffering of Christ – was widespread in medieval Europe. The Spanish expedition that founded New Mexico performed public self-flagellation on Good Friday 1598, as it marched up through Mexico, and similar acts by early Franciscan missionaries attracted Pueblo Indian scorn. The Penitentes as such, however, emerged after Mexico achieved independence in 1821. Cut off from Spanish funding, the Franciscans vanished from New Mexico within twenty years, leaving the region almost devoid of priests. Hispanic Catholics formed **lay brotherhoods** to keep their faith alive.

The Penitentes – **Los Hermanos de Nuestro Padre Jesús Nazareno**, or the Brothers of Our Father Jesus of Nazareth – may well have modeled themselves on a Guatemalan example, introduced at the same time as the Guatemalan-influenced pilgrimages to Chimayó. From an initial emphasis on individual prayer and penance, they extended to develop a complex system of rituals. They never administered the sacraments, but brought solace to Catholics forced to live – and die – in the absence of priests. The Penitente brotherhood in each village soon became a mutual-aid society for the community, a cultural and political force as well as a spiritual one.

After the American takeover of New Mexico in 1846, the Penitentes were suddenly outsiders not only in their own country, but even in their own church. The first Catholic bishop of Santa Fe, Jean-Baptiste **Lamy** (see p.112), had little sympathy for the unorthodoxies of his Hispanic flock, and denied the sacraments to their most prominent spokesman, Father **Martínez** of Taos (see p.147). The Penitentes were forced into **secrecy**, and began to gather at night in remote spots. Denied access to official church property, they met instead in plain adobe structures known as ***moradas*** – not necessarily distinguished with crosses or towers, but adorned with the handmade sacred images known as ***santos***.

The focus of ritual activity was **Lent**, when all Catholics practice some form of self-denial, and the Penitentes attempted to experience the passion and death of Christ. For processions, they divided into *Los Hermanos de Luz* – the **Brothers of Light**, responsible for the candles and music – and *Los Hermanos de Sangre*, the **Brothers of Blood**, who scourged themselves with yucca whips or carried giant wooden crosses. Participants were hooded to ensure humility. Some reenacted the **crucifixion**, though tied rather than nailed to the cross, while others dragged a **Death Cart** – a wooden wagon holding an effigy of Death, armed with a bow and arrow – laden with stones. The Death Cart also figured in the Penitentes' elaborate **funeral** processions. The wayside stone cairns, topped with crosses, seen throughout the High Country are not graves, as outsiders supposed, but *descansos* – places where the coffin-bearers would pause to rest.

A century of conflict ended in 1947, when the Penitentes were officially recognized by the Bishop of Santa Fe. Those that remain now regard themselves as members of the **Third Order of St Francis**, a lay branch of the Franciscan monastic order, and the most lasting Penitente legacy in New Mexico is the *santero* tradition of religious folk art.

Chimayó, Hwy-503 (☎505/351-4444), must be the best traditional New Mexican **restaurant** in the state, serving superb *flautas* and a mouthwatering *sopaipilla*, stuffed with meat and chiles, on a lovely sun-drenched outdoor patio. Across the road, the rambling adobe *Hacienda Rancho de Chimayó* (PO Box 11, Chimayó, NM 87522; ☎505/351-2222; ④), has lovely **B&B** rooms.

Truchas

By the time you reach **TRUCHAS**, eight miles up from Chimayó on Hwy-76, you're well into the mountains; the views from the highway down and across the Rio Grande Valley are tremendous. Villagers from Las Trampas, further up, were granted permission to establish Truchas in 1754, on condition that it was enclosed within a walled square, to defend against Comanche attacks. The settlement took on its present form almost immediately, however, consisting of separate individual farms arrayed along a high ridge above the Río de las Truchas, or "river of trout." As one of New Mexico's least changed Hispanic communities, it served in 1987 as the location for Robert Redford's movie of John Nichol's *Milagro Beanfield War* (see p.547).

Hwy-76 makes a right-angle bend to avoid Truchas, but a detour east onto the minor road up the valley takes you along a narrow street of adobe homes and barns – interspersed with the odd incongruous gallery – and past the fields towards the 13,103ft **Truchas Peak**. Besides its gorgeous desserts, the *Truchas Mountain Cafe*, on the highway (☎505/689-2444), fries up fine *sopaipillas*.

Las Trampas

Truchas' parent community, the quiet hamlet of **LAS TRAMPAS**, is another eight miles along Hwy-76. This started life as an outpost used by fur-trappers pursuing beaver – hence its name, "the traps" – which by attracting Comanche raids doubled as an early-warning system for Santa Fe. Though no longer walled, its dusty central plaza, right alongside the highway, still holds the powerfully evocative adobe church of **San Jose de Gracia** (daily 10am–4pm). Built in 1760, it features a choir loft that extends both inside and out, so that singers could accompany ceremonies on the square as well as in the church. Note the unattached *morada* – Penitente meeting place (see box, opposite) – beside the cemetery to the east.

Five miles on from Las Trampas – which holds a couple of gift stores, but nowhere to eat or sleep – Hwy-76 meets Hwy-75 at **Picuris Pueblo** (see p.139), ten miles west of Hwy-68. The quickest route to Taos, twenty miles north, is via Hwy-518 to the east; more Hispanic villages line the way, but none is of interest to tourists.

East of Santa Fe

Modern visitors tend to gravitate northwards after seeing Santa Fe, up the Rio Grande towards Taos. Pueblo Indian traders, pioneers on the **Santa Fe Trail**, and transcontinental train travelers, on the other hand, have all crossed the mountains to the **east**. Now followed by the I-25 interstate, the traditional route between New Mexico and the plains still holds a number of intriguing historical sites, including the ancient pueblo at **Pecos** and the Wild-West town of **Las Vegas**.

Pecos National Historical Park

A short way north of I-25, twenty-five miles east of Santa Fe, a long, low ridge in the heart of the Sangre de Cristo mountains served for over a thousand years as one of the most significant cultural rendezvous in the Southwest. Since 1920s excavations so precisely chronicled changes in pottery and architecture that it became the model for all other such digs, **PECOS NATIONAL HISTORICAL PARK** has been famed as the "birthplace of Southwestern archeology."

Ninth-century Basketmakers (see p.520) were the first to inhabit this spot, but between 1450 and 1550, as the pueblo of **Cicuyé**, it was home to over two thousand people, including five hundred warriors. Protected behind four-story walls, it was a major **trading center**, where Pueblo peoples exchanged turquoise, axes and shells from as far west as the Pacific for bison meat, hides, and wood for bows brought by plains nomads who camped outside the walls. **Coronado** stayed here in 1541, and met a captive from the plains who lured his expedition east in search of the nonexistent gold of Quivira.

The full saga of Coronado's expedition is told on p.524.

After Franciscan missionaries built a church alongside what they called **Pecos Pueblo** sixty years later, Spaniards too came to trade, but Apache and Comanche raids eventually forced Pecos into decline. Its last twenty survivors migrated 65 miles west to join Jemez Pueblo in 1838. Their descendants continue to elect a governor of Pecos Pueblo, and return for ceremonies. One such occurred in May 1999, when following representations from Jemeze over two thousand skeletons were repatriated from Massachusetts, where they'd languished in Harvard's Peabody Museum and the Phillips Academy, and reburied at Pecos.

The whole Pecos story is well told in the **visitor center** (daily 8am–5pm; $4), from where a mile-long trail loops onto the ridge itself. Much of the former pueblo area remains unexcavated, though some walls are exposed, and large buried structures are obvious everywhere. Beyond it, the trail leads around and through the high roofless walls of the **mission church**, stark in the bright sunlight, and surrounded by the ruined *convento* buildings where its priests once lived. The *kiva* in the heart of the church was dug as a deliberate act of sacrilege during the Pueblo Revolt.

Two newly acquired parcels of the park, not expected to open to visitors in the near future, incorporate the site of the **Battle of Glorieta Pass**. Fought on March 28, 1862, it was the turning point of the **Civil War** in the Southwest, when four thousand Union soldiers repelled three thousand Confederate invaders who had already briefly occupied Santa Fe.

Las Vegas

LAS VEGAS, New Mexico, has more in common with its upstart Nevada namesake than may be immediately obvious. Though now a sleepy backwater, it was once a wild, lawless frontier outpost, where almost anything went. It consists of two distinct sections. The **old Plaza** area, above the fertile meadows (*vegas*, in Spanish) that line the Gallinas River, was established in 1835, when Hispanic settlers drove away the Comanche and set about capturing trade on the burgeoning **Santa Fe Trail**. When the **railroad** arrived in 1879, the focus of town shifted across the river to the grid of streets around the new station. Incomers included the legendary "Doc" Holliday, who briefly owned a saloon on Center Street before scurrying back to Dodge City to escape a murder charge, and in one month alone Las Vegas witnessed 29 gunshot deaths.

At the end of the nineteenth century, Las Vegas was the principal city in New Mexico, and almost all its buildings still date from the Victorian era. The conspicuous lack of adobe makes it easy to forget you're in the Southwest, but it ranks among the state's most authentic Wild-West towns, and while it offers no particular standout tourist attractions, it's a real delight to stroll around.

Grand Avenue – the main business drag – and I-25 alike now closely parallel the railroad, leaving the **Plaza** high and dry a mile to the west. Its four-square layout resembles something from the Deep South, though a Victorian bandstand rather than a courthouse stands at its center. The only significant building on the perimeter is the *Plaza Hotel* (see below), but **Bridge Street**, which leads up from the highway, is lined with antique stores and cafes.

Theodore Roosevelt recruited around forty percent of his volunteer **Rough Riders**, who invaded Cuba in 1898, in Las Vegas. Their exploits, plus the minutiae of local history, are recorded in the **City Museum**, 727 Grand Ave (Mon–Fri 9am–noon & 1–4pm, Sat 10am–3pm; free).

Practicalities

Two Amtrak trains still pull into Las Vegas each afternoon, from Albuquerque and Chicago. Brochures at the **visitor center**, in the museum at 727 Grand Ave (same hours; ☎505/425-8631 or 1-800/832-5947), detail **walking tours** of town.

The nicest place to **stay** is a restored, antique-furnished en-suite room at the *Plaza Hotel*, 230 Old Town Plaza (☎505/425-3591 or

1-800/328-1882, fax 505/425-9659; ④), where the *Landmark Grill*
is Las Vegas' classiest **restaurant**. There are also plenty of **motels**,
such as the *Super 8*, 2029 N Grand Ave (☎505/425-5288 or 1-
800/800-8000, fax 505/454-8481; ②), and the *Inn of Las Vegas*,
2401 N Grand Ave (☎505/425-6707; ②). Local students huddle over
lunchtime espressos in the coffeehouse at the back of Meadowlands
Antiques, 131 Bridge St (☎505/425-9502), while the nearby *Rialto*,
141 Bridge St (☎505/454-0037), is more of a traditional diner.

*Las Vegas' zip
code is NM
87701.*

Mora

While I-25 heads northeast into the grasslands from Las Vegas,
towards **Raton** (see p.165), **Hwy-518** leads due north into some of
New Mexico's most appealing mountain scenery, and serves as an
eighty-mile short cut to **Taos**.

The village of **MORA**, thirty miles out, is the seat of Mora County,
which has a population of fewer than five thousand, and has been
ranked by the *Wall Street Journal* as one of the three poorest coun-
ties in the US. Mora itself is the closest thing New Mexico now has to
a traditional, unspoiled Hispanic farming community, and its inhabitants are determined to keep it that way. The one concession to
tourism, the former flour mill preserved in working order as the
Cleveland Roller Mill Museum (May–Sept daily 10am–5pm; $2), is
unlikely to change things.

Sipapu

*The High Road
between Santa
Fe and Taos is
described on
p.140
onwards.*

Twenty miles up from Mora, not long before Hwy-518 is joined by
Hwy-75, the "High Road," for the final run down to Taos, the tiny **ski
resort** of **SIPAPU** is tucked into the pretty mountain valley known as
Tres Ritos Canyon. *Sipapu Lodge*, along the highway to either side
of the Rio Pueblo (Rte Box 29, Vadito, NM 87579; ☎505/587-2240;
①–④), offers every conceivable grade of accommodation, from
$9.50 dorm beds through private camping cabins, motel rooms and
luxury duplexes. Lift tickets in season cost $29.

Taos

*"Taos" rhymes
with "house."*

Part Spanish colonial outpost, part hangout for bohemian artists and
New-Age dropouts, and home to one of the oldest Native American
communities in the United States, tiny **TAOS** has become famous out
of all proportion to its size. Just six thousand people live in its three
component parts: **Taos** itself, around the old plaza; sprawling
Ranchos de Taos three miles south; and the Indian village of **Taos
Pueblo** two miles north.

Like Santa Fe, Taos stretches languidly across a glorious high-desert
plateau. The approach from the south is especially spectacular, as you
cross a final bluff on Hwy-68 to be confronted by the pine-forested

Sangre de Cristo mountains soaring above the sunbleached foothills. This far up, the **Rio Grande** is not yet meandering through a well-watered valley, but lies deep in a craggy canyon west of town, occasionally glimpsed as a crack in the plateau.

Beyond the usual unsightly highway sprawl, Taos is a delight to visit. As well as museums, galleries and stores to match Santa Fe, it still offers the unhurried pace and charm, and the sense of a meeting place between Pueblo, Hispanic and American cultures, that attracted figures such as Georgia O'Keeffe and D.H. Lawrence.

A history of Taos

Taos Pueblo is around a thousand years old, and its first Franciscan mission was established in 1598. However, the modern town of Taos dates from the 1630s, when an uprising at the pueblo induced Spanish colonists to found the separate community of **Fernando de Taos** a few judicious miles south. Although its early history was dogged by Pueblo rebellions, the Spaniards and Pueblos eventually united to resist raids by "horse Indians" such as the Apache and Comanche. In the early nineteenth century, despite attempts by the Mexican authorities in Santa Fe to restrict contact with the outside world, Taos was the venue for annual **rendezvous**, at which "mountain men" and trappers from the Rockies traded with Indians from the Pueblos and Plains and New Mexican merchants.

The history of Taos Pueblo is summarized on p.156.

After the US takeover of New Mexico, Taos' Hispanic and Pueblo citizens once more found common cause. In 1847, the territory's first American governor, Charles Bent, was killed in his Taos home, but the revolt failed to spread to Santa Fe, and the US Army launched an assault on the Pueblo that succeeded in suppressing further resistance. For long after that defeat, local priest **Antonio Jose Martínez** – sometimes alleged to have been complicit in the uprising, and the villain of Willa Cather's *Death Comes For The Archbishop* – continued to champion the rights of the Hispanic population.

Taos' reputation as an **arts colony** began at the end of the nineteenth century, with the arrival of the painter Joseph Henry Sharp. He was soon joined by two young New Yorkers, Bert Phillips and Ernest L. Blumenschein; legend has it that their wagon lost a wheel outside Taos as they headed for Mexico in 1898, and they liked it so much they never got round to leaving. The three men formed the nucleus of the **Taos Society of Artists**, established in 1915. Soon afterwards, society heiress and arts patron Mabel Dodge arrived, and married an Indian from the Pueblo to become **Mabel Dodge Luhan**; she later speculated that perhaps "Taos" was the plural of "tao." In turn, she also wrote a fan letter to English novelist **D.H. Lawrence**, who visited three times in the early 1920s; his widow **Frieda** made her home in Taos after his death. New generations of artists and writers have "discovered" Taos ever since, but the most famous of all was **Georgia O'Keeffe**, who stayed for a few years at the end of the 1920s before moving to Abiquiu (see p.138). Her renditions of the church at Ranchos de Taos in particular were a major influence on contemporary Southwestern art.

An influx of hippies converged upon Taos in the late 1960s, to be followed in subsequent decades by art-loving tourists, gallery-owning entrepreneurs and, it would seem, wealthy divorcees. Even as the urban area has grown, however, the population has remained minimal, and the opening of a small Walmart store in 1999 was seen as a shocking warning that commercialization might finally start to change the place for the worse.

Arrival and information

Hwy-68, the main route up to Taos from Santa Fe and Albuquerque, passes first through Ranchos de Taos, and is then lined by an uninspiring strip of motels as it approaches downtown and becomes **Paseo del Pueblo Sur**. The well-equipped **visitor center**, two miles south of the plaza at the intersection of Hwys 68 and 64 (daily 9am–5pm; ☎505/758-3873 or 1-888/580-8267; *www.taoschamber .com*), stocks all the brochures and maps you could possibly require, including valuable **accommodation discount coupons**.

Greyhound and TNM&O **buses** from Albuquerque ($22) and Santa Fe ($17) arrive at **Taos Bus Center**, at the Chevron station opposite the visitor center on Hwy-68 (☎505/758-1144. Faust Transportation (☎505/758-3410) also link Taos with Santa Fe ($25) and Albuquerque airport (one-way $35, round-trip $65; connection to Taos Ski Valley costs a total of $40 one-way). In addition, you can even **fly** to Taos from Albuquerque, with Rio Grande Air (Mon–Fri only, 3–4 flights daily; $79 one-way, $150 round trip; ☎505/737-9790 or 1-877/I-FLY-RGA).

Taos' **post office** is north of the plaza at 318 Paseo del Pueblo Norte (Mon–Fri 8am–4pm, Sat 9am–1pm; ☎505/758-2081).

Getting around

Walking is the best way to get around the compact center of Taos, though a public **bus** service, the Chile Line (☎505/751-4459), covers the greater urban area. The hourly Red Chile bus runs along a twelve-mile stretch of Hwy-68, between Ranchos de Taos and Taos Pueblo, with a loop around the plaza in the middle (Mon–Sat 7am–9pm; 50¢ one-way, $1 for an all-day pass); Green Chile buses, which circle the residential districts, is less useful for sightseeing. Another option is to rent a **bike**, for $20 per day, from Cottam's, 207A Paseo del Pueblo Sur (☎505/758-2822).

Tours and excursions

For a **guided walk** around town, contact either Taos Historic Walking Tours (June–Aug, Mon–Sat 10am from the Mabel Dodge

Rio Grande

64

150

64

Millicent
Rogers
Museum

MILLICENT ROGERS ROAD

PASEO DEL PUEBLO NORTE

CAMINO DEL PUEBLO

Taos Pueblo

N

BLUEBERRY HILL ROAD

UPPER RANCHITOS ROAD

Taos

CAMINO DE LA PLACITA

VALVERDE ST

Plaza

KIT CARSON ST.

240

RANCHITOS ROAD

Martínez
Hacienda

LOWER RANCHITOS ROAD

See 'Downtown
Taos' Map

CALLEJON

CAMINO DEL MEDIO

CAMINO DE LA MERCED

PASEO DEL PUEBLO SUR

SALAZAR ROAD

SANTE FE ROAD

i

PASEO DEL CAÑON

585

64

△ Angel Fire

RANCHOS
DE TAOS

68

San
Francisco
de Asis

518

ESPINOSA ROAD

| 0 | 800 yds |

TAOS AREA

Luhan House, 240 Morada Lane; ☎505/758-4020; $10) or the *Taos Inn* (Tues–Thurs & Sat 10am & 5pm, Sun, Mon & Fri 5pm; ☎505/776-2562; $15). In summer, open-air **trolley tours** visit the main attractions (Historic Taos Trolley Tours; May–Oct daily 10.30am from visitor center, 10.45am at plaza, and 2pm from visitor center, 2.15pm plaza; ☎505/751-0366; $25, including entry fees).

Out of ski season, from April to mid-October, many visitors go **whitewater rafting** instead, through the Taos Box Canyon of the Rio Grande. Operators based at Pilar, south of town – see p.139 – include Far Flung Adventures (1-day trips $99; ☎505/758-2628 or 1-800/359-2627), and Rio Grande Rapid Transit (half-day $30, full-day $69; ☎505/758-9700 or 1-800/222-RAFT).

Taos Indian Horse Ranch (☎505/758-3212 or 1-800/659-3210) run **horseback** excursions on Pueblo lands, under the slogan "discover the Indian in your cupboard"; short beginners' rides cost from $32 to $95. Rafting, horse riding, and, in winter, snowmobiling can also be arranged through Native Sons Adventures, 1033-A Paseo del Pueblo Sur (☎505/758-9342 or 1-800/753-7559).

Accommodation

Taos has **accommodation** to meet all needs, at prices well below those of Santa Fe. However, midwinter rates are no lower than midsummer, and for properties close to the ski area they can even be considerably higher. There are no real **budget** options near the plaza, but the *Abominable Snowmansion* to the north, and the *Rio Grande Gorge Hostel* to the south both offer bare-bones bunks or simple rooms. Otherwise, chain motels line Hwy-68 south of town, while three or four amusingly adobe-styled motels on Kit Carson Road just east of the plaza provide quieter alternatives; call in at the visitor center first to pick up any discount coupons they may have. For a few dollars more, you can avail yourself of atmospheric B&B inns or luxury hotels. **Agencies** that reserve lodging in advance include Taos Central Reservations (☎505/758-9767 or 1-800/821-2437) and the Taos Bed & Breakfast Association (☎505/758-4747 or 1-800/876-7857).

The Rio Grande Gorge Hostel *at Pilar is only a dozen miles southwest of Taos; see p.139.*

The best places to **camp** in the vicinity are the ten summer-only campgrounds in **Carson National Forest** (☎505/758-6200), reached by following Kit Carson Road east until it becomes Hwy-64.

High season in Taos is Christmas to mid-April and mid-June to mid-Oct; low season is mid-April to mid-June and mid-Oct to Dec.

Hostels, motels and hotels

Abominable Snowmansion Hostel/HI-Taos, Taos Ski Valley Rd, Arroyo Seco; ☎505/776-8298, fax 776-2107; *www.taoswebb.com/hotel/snowmansion*. Pleasant, friendly HI-AYH hostel-cum-ski lodge at a very tight curve in the road as you enter Arroyo Seco village on Hwy-150 up to the ski valley, five miles north of downtown. Office hours daily 8–11am & 4–10pm, so don't arrive at midday; membership not required. Dorm beds $16 in summer, $22 in winter; teepees and camping space out back; and bargain private rooms. ①/③.

Best Western Kachina Lodge de Taos, 413 Paseo del Pueblo Norte; ☎505/758-2275 or 1-800/522-4462, fax 505/758-9207; *www.kachinalodge.com*. Large, tasteful, family-oriented motel at the Taos Pueblo turnoff, with lots of Southwestern art, a good restaurant, live music, and nightly Pueblo dance performances in summer. There's some suggestion it may soon incorporate a casino; check before you book. ⑤.

El Monte Lodge, 317 Kit Carson Rd; ☎505/758-3171 or 1-800/828-8267. Rural 1930s motel half a mile east of the plaza, offering comfortable en-suite accommodation in a complex of adobe cottages. Low ④, high ⑤.

El Pueblo Lodge, 412 Paseo del Pueblo Norte; ☎505/758-8700 or 1-800/433-9612, fax 505/758-7321; *elpueblo@newmex.com*. Southwestern-themed motel, half a mile north of downtown near the Taos Pueblo turnoff. Low ③, high ④.

Historic Taos Inn, 125 Paseo del Pueblo Norte; ☎505/758-2233 or 1-800/826-7466, fax 505/758-5776; *www.taosinn.com*. Gorgeous central Taos landmark, where several ancient adobes have been welded together to create an atmospheric and very Southwestern hotel; the lobby area was originally an open-air courtyard. Both *Doc Martin's* restaurant (see p.159), and the *Adobe Bar* are packed nightly, while each of the 37 rooms plays a variation on the Pueblo theme. ④–⑧.

Indian Hills Inn, 233 Paseo del Pueblo Sur; ☎505/758-4293 or 1-800/444-2346; *indianhills@newmex.com*. The only cheapish highway motel within walking distance of the plaza; if you're sensitive to noise, be sure to get a room well away from the street. ③.

La Fonda de Taos, 108 South Plaza; ☎505/758-2211 or 1-800/833-2211, fax 505/758-8508. Throwback 1930s hotel on the plaza, with a gallery of D.H. Lawrence paintings (see p.153); not the cheapest place in town, but among the most charming. The rooms are not as large or lavish as in modern motels – and lack TVs – but with their bright hand-painted furniture they're infinitely more characterful. Low ④, high ⑤.

Quail Ridge Inn Resort, Ski Valley Rd; ☎505/776-2211 or 1-800/624-4448, fax 505/776-2949; *www.taoswebb.com/hotel/quailridge*. Rooms and suites in luxury adobe cottages near the start of the Ski Valley Rd, five miles north of downtown, with a good on-site restaurant, mountain views, swimming pool and hot tub, tennis courts and fitness center. ④/⑤.

Sagebrush Inn, 1508 Paseo del Pueblo Sur; ☎505/758-2254 or 1-888/449-8267, fax 505/758-5077; *sagebrsh@newmex.com*. Attractive three-story adobe inn, well south of the center near Ranchos de Taos, which was briefly home to Georgia O'Keeffe and is filled with Southwestern arts and crafts. Swimming pool, tennis, and live music in the lobby bar nightly. ④.

Taos Super 8 Motel, 1347 S Hwy-68; ☎505/758-1088 or 1-800/800-8000, fax 505/758-2685. Among the least expensive of the franchise motels that line Hwy-68 south of town, and making a half-hearted attempt to look adobe. Low ③, high ④.

B&Bs

Casa de las Chimeneas, PO Box 5303, 405 Cordoba Rd; ☎505/758-4777, fax 758-3976; *casa@newmex.com*. Grand four-room B&B, set in adobe-walled gardens a couple of blocks southeast of the plaza. ⑥/⑦.

La Doña Luz, 114 Kit Carson Rd; ☎505/758-4874 or 1-800/758-9187, fax 505/758-4541. Hispanic-flavored rooms of differing standards in a peaceful adobe not far east of the plaza. ④–⑥.

Taos

Unless otherwise stated, all the properties listed here share the zip code Taos, NM 87571.

As explained on p.15, accommodation prices, excluding taxes, are indicated throughout this book by the following symbols:
① *up to $30*
② *$30–45*
③ *$45–60*
④ *$60–80*
⑤ *$80–100*
⑥ *$100–130*
⑦ *$130–175*
⑧ *$175–250*
⑨ *$250+*

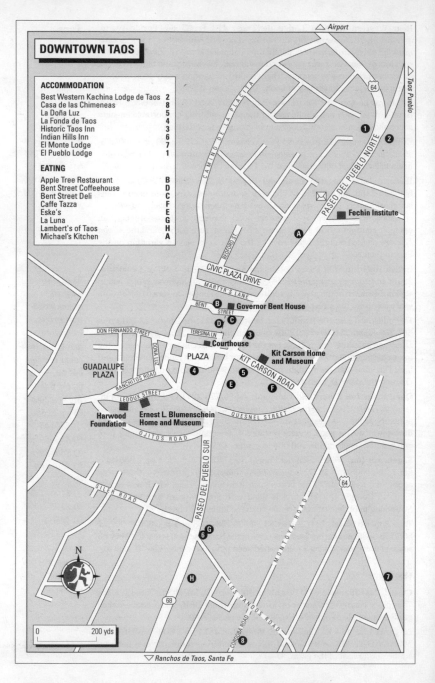

DOWNTOWN TAOS

ACCOMMODATION
Best Western Kachina Lodge de Taos	2
Casa de las Chimeneas	8
La Doña Luz	5
La Fonda de Taos	4
Historic Taos Inn	3
Indian Hills Inn	6
El Monte Lodge	7
El Pueblo Lodge	1

EATING
Apple Tree Restaurant	B
Bent Street Coffeehouse	D
Bent Street Deli	C
Caffe Tazza	F
Eske's	E
La Luna	G
Lambert's of Taos	H
Michael's Kitchen	A

△ Airport

△ Taos Pueblo

64

PASEO DEL PUEBLO NORTE

CAMINO DE LA PLACITA

Fechin Institute

BEDFORD ST

CIVIC PLAZA DRIVE

MARTYR'S LANE

Bent Street

Governor Bent House

DON FERNANDO STREET

TERESINA LN

DOÑA LUZ

Courthouse

PLAZA

GUADALUPE PLAZA

RANCHITOS ROAD

LEDOUX STREET

Kit Carson Home and Museum

KIT CARSON ROAD

QUESNEL STREET

Harwood Foundation

Ernest L. Blumenschein Home and Museum

OJITOS ROAD

PASEO DEL PUEBLO SUR

SILER ROAD

64

N

MONTOYA ROAD

G

H

68

LOS PANDOS ROAD

CORDOBA ROAD

8

0   200 yds

▽ Ranchos de Taos, Santa Fe

Laughing Horse Inn, 729 Paseo del Pueblo Norte; ☎505/758-8350 or 1-800/776-0161, fax 505/758-8350; *www.laughinghorseinn.com*. Former print shop, half a mile north of the plaza, turned 11-room B&B inn. Rooms, suites and cottages of varying degrees of luxury, plus jacuzzi, psychic readings and free mountain bikes. ③–⑥.

Old Taos Guesthouse, 1028 Witt Rd; ☎505/758-5448 or 1-800/758-5448; *www.taoswebb.com/hotel/oldtaoshouse*. Vintage adobe *hacienda*, within a couple of miles west of the plaza, now restored as a spacious B&B complex. Each of the nine en-suite rooms offers different facilities, and there's an outdoor hot tub. ④–⑤.

Taos Ski Valley

Amizette Inn, PO Box 756, Taos Ski Valley, NM 87525; ☎505/776-2451 or 1-800/446-8267, fax 505/776-2451. Small but comfortable ski lodge, with sweeping views from its verandas. Rates include breakfast. Low ③, high ⑤.

Hotel Edelweiss, PO Box 83, Taos Ski Valley, NM 87525; ☎505/776-2301 or 1-800/I-LUV-SKI, fax 505/776-2533; *www.newmex.com/edelweiss*. Intimate, luxurious hotel at the foot of the slopes with its own French restaurant, plus sauna, jacuzzi and in-house masseuse. Summer ④, winter ⑦.

Thunderbird Lodge, PO Box 87, Taos Ski Valley, NM 87525; ☎505/776-2280 or 1-800/776-2279, fax 505/776-2238. Lively ski lodge – south-facing, so sunnier than most – with a few quieter and plusher chalets. Rates include full board. Low ⑥, high ⑧.

The Town

Downtown Taos still centers on the old Spanish **plaza**, which has been remodeled several times over the years, and migrated slightly eastwards in the process. The tiny square is now ringed by galleries and souvenir stores, but its tree-shaded benches make a pleasant spot from which to watch the world go by. The Stars and Stripes have flown day and night from the flagpole at its heart ever since it was erected by Kit Carson during the Civil War; the nearby bandstand was a gift from Mabel Dodge Luhan.

While there's little to see on the plaza itself, apart from the **D.H. Lawrence paintings** in the *La Fonda* hotel and the murals in the old **Courthouse**, a short walk along the narrow, winding streets that stretch away in all directions will be rewarded with glimpses of Taos as it used to be. The best of the central museums is the **Kit Carson House**, but the **Millicent Rogers Museum**, a few miles north, holds a superb collection of Native American and Hispanic artworks.

A $20 ticket, sold at each museum and valid for a year, buys admission to every museum in Taos.

La Fonda

La Fonda hotel, on the south side of the plaza, was built in 1937, well after **D.H. Lawrence**'s death, but a gallery in the lobby holds a unique collection of paintings by the Nottinghamshire novelist (irregular hours; $3). Bought from his widow Frieda's second husband, most were painted in Italy rather than Taos; one, *The Holy Family*, was his first ever canvas, and it shows. Apart from one

La Fonda *hotel is reviewed on p.151; D.H. Lawrence's ashes are held in a memorial chapel north of Taos; see p.163.*

landscape (a "collaboration" with Frieda and their friend Dorothy Brett), they depict sweaty, fleshy wrestlings such as *The Rape of the Sabine Women*. When first exhibited, at London's Warren Gallery in 1929, they were regarded as obscene, and banned from further showing in Britain. They now seem tame, though the *Sunday Times'* original verdict remains accurate: "he can do rather less with a paint-brush than a child of seven without any natural flair."

The Courthouse and the Harwood Foundation

After much of the north side of the plaza was destroyed by a fire in May 1932, Taos' **Courthouse** was rebuilt in the prevalent Pueblo Revival style (Mon–Fri 10am–5pm, Sat 10am–4pm; $3). Four artists, led by Emil Bisttram, a former student of Diego Rivera, were commissioned as part of Franklin Roosevelt's make-work WPA program to decorate its interior with **murals** depicting the use and misuse of law. The Courthouse itself closed in 1970, but the murals have now been restored, and make an interesting diversion as you tour the plaza.

The murals are exhibited under the auspices of the Harwood Foundation, whose **Harwood Museum** is two blocks southwest of the plaza at 238 Ledoux St (Tues–Sat 10am–5pm, Sun noon–5pm; $5). This combines works by twentieth-century Taos artists such as Bert Phillips and woodcarver Patrociño Barelo with *santos* and *retablos* by their nineteenth-century Hispanic counterparts.

Ernest L. Blumenschein Home and Museum

Near the Harwood Museum at 222 Ledoux St, the **Ernest L. Blumenschein Home and Museum** preserves the much-restored 1790 house of the co-founder of the Taos Society of Artists (daily: April–Oct 9am–5pm; Nov–March 11am–4pm; $5). Paintings by Blumenschein, his daughter Helen, and Zuñi and Hopi artists such as Fred Kabotie (see p.276) are on display, but the real star is the house itself. Though Taos has grown to obscure its original uninterrupted views, Blumenschein's studio, made gloriously light by its raised ceiling and enlarged windows, still commands a fine prospect of the mountains.

The Blumenschein Home is one of the three Kit Carson Historic Museums, each of which charges $5 admission, with combined tickets at $10 for three.

Governor Bent House and Museum

Bent Street, a block north of the plaza, takes its name not from any irregularities but from the first American governor of New Mexico, Charles Bent, whose former home at no. 117 is now the **Governor Bent House and Museum** (daily April–Oct 9am–5pm, Nov–March 10am–4pm; $2). The imposition of American rule was resented by Taos' Hispanic and Indian population alike, and Bent was killed here by an angry mob on January 19, 1847. You can still see the hole hacked into the adobe walls through which most of his family attempted to escape; they were captured, but their lives were spared.

The rest of the small house serves as a ramshackle museum of frontier Taoseño life, holding Indian artifacts, antiquated rifles and even an eight-legged lamb.

Kit Carson Home and Museum

Just east of the plaza, across the highway at the end of Taos' sole surviving stretch of wooden boardwalk, is the dusty but evocative adobe home of "mountain man," mason and part-time US cavalry officer **Kit Carson** (daily: May–Oct 8am–6pm; Nov–April 9am–5pm; $5). Born in Kentucky in 1809, Carson left home to join a wagon train to Missouri in 1826 – a one cent reward was offered for the return of the teenage runaway – and spent the ensuing winter in Taos. He was to return repeatedly throughout his life, in between escapades like scouting for the 1840s Frémont expeditions, and campaigning against the Navajo in the 1860s (see p.539).

Carson's house is one of the Kit Carson Historic Museums; see opposite.

Carson bought the house at the heart of today's museum in 1843, upon his marriage to a local woman, Josefa Jaramillo, and it was sold after their deaths in 1868 to support their seven orphaned children. Much of it is now filled with run-of-the-mill Wild-West paraphernalia, such as rifles with crude wooden handles, and the accoutrements of fur trappers. However, press cuttings and photos relating to Carson himself, and the mock-up of a typical Hispanic home of the period, complete with *fogon de campaña* – a bell-shaped adobe fireplace – make for a fascinating hour's visit.

Millicent Rogers Museum

Four miles north of the plaza, well past the Taos Pueblo turning and reached by a dirt road that angles into a tricky five-way intersection, the **Millicent Rogers Museum** (April–Oct daily 10am–5pm; Nov–March Tues–Sun 10am–5pm; $6) is among New Mexico's very finest galleries. Millicent Rogers – a former fashion model who was the granddaughter of a founder of Standard Oil, and is said to have been "close" to Cary Grant – lived here until her death in 1953.

The museum focuses on both Native American and Hispanic art, and traces how those cultures have been perceived. Its undoubted highlight is the family collection of San Ildefonso Pueblo potter **Maria Martinez**, whose black-on-black ceramics are the most famous (and valuable) Native American artworks of the twentieth century. It also outlines the unbroken thousand-year tradition of Pueblo pottery, from pieces produced by the prehistoric Mimbres and Ancestral Puebloan peoples through Rio Grande works from the fourteenth and fifteenth centuries. Other crafts include turquoise jewelry, Navajo blankets, and some amazing *kachinas* (see p.60), such as a Zuni buffalo *kachina* from 1875, made of hide, fur and feathers.

For more on Death Carts and the like, see p.142; see also the Glossary on p.548.

The development of Spanish Colonial religious art in the New World is shown through an array of rugs, looms, carved wooden furniture, *bultos* and *retablos*, plus a couple of "**Death Carts**," in which a skeleton holding a bow and arrow, known as Doña Sebastiana, rides in a rickety wooden carriage. The earliest relic is a faded representation of *Christ Washing the Feet of the Disciples*, painted on buffalo hide by an unknown Franciscan around 1700.

Taos Pueblo

Tiwa-speaking peoples have lived at **TAOS PUEBLO**, just over two miles north of Taos plaza, for almost a thousand years. While they may have originally arrived from the east, across the plains, they have long been at the forefront of the **Pueblo Indian** cultural tradition, which as the name implies can be traced back to the Ancestral Puebloans of the Four Corners. Together with Ácoma (see p.94) and the Hopi mesas (see p.59), the pueblo can claim to be the oldest continuously occupied settlement in the United States. It's also stunningly beautiful, centering on two multistory adobe "apartment blocks" framed beneath the shining forested peak of Taos Mountain.

The northernmost New Mexican pueblo, Taos is among the few not to have been displaced by the coming of the Spaniards in the sixteenth century. Its survival has taken a long hard struggle; the pueblo was abandoned for two years in the 1630s, to escape retaliation after the killing of a priest, and it later played a central role in the **Pueblo Revolt** of 1680. When the Spanish subsequently reconquered New Mexico, Taos Pueblo was almost completely destroyed. It revolted again under both Mexican and American rule. In 1837, Taos Indians cut off the head of the Mexican governor of New Mexico and used it as a football, and their leader José Gonzalez briefly usurped the governorship until he was himself executed. Ten years later, they were heavily implicated in the rebellion against Charles Bent (see p.147); over 150 Taos Indians were killed when the US Army besieged and burned the pueblo's church.

For more on the Pueblo Revolt, see p.526.

In the twentieth century, the pueblo was forced to campaign for the return of the sacred **Blue Lake**, high in the mountains. The source of the Río Pueblo de Taos that flows through the heart of the village, and the focus of an annual three-day pilgrimage, Blue Lake was unexpectedly incorporated into a federal forest reserve in 1906. When Richard Nixon finally handed it back in 1970, it marked the first time that land had ever been returned to Native Americans for religious reasons; access is now forbidden to outsiders.

Visiting the pueblo

Taos Pueblo is reached via two approach roads off Hwy-68. One continues north as the highway veers west at the *Best Western Kachina Lodge*, half a mile north of the plaza, the other branches off at Jackie's Trading Post, another half-mile on. After entering the reservation, they meet and run together to the pueblo plaza, where you pay the **entrance fee** ($10 per person, plus $10 per still camera, $20 per video camera) and park your vehicle. Pueblo residents lead guided **walking tours** at regular intervals, which can help overcome any awkwardness you may feel but won't take you beyond the limited public areas through which you're free to wander alone.

Visits focus on the two large **adobe complexes** – Hlauuma, the north house, and Hlaukwima, the south house – to either side of the Río Pueblo de Taos. In their current form, they almost certainly date from the uncertain years that followed the Pueblo Revolt, at the start of the eighteenth century. This architectural design, consisting of individual dwellings stacked like dice and entered via rooftop ladders, was originally adopted for defense, and has been abandoned as unnecessary by most other pueblos. At Taos, the homes have been adapted to include ground-level doorways and windows, but their hundred or so occupants still choose to live without toilets, running water or electricity. The remainder of the reservation's two thousand inhabitants live in newer homes nearby. Several rooms facing the plaza function as **craft shops**, but you can't penetrate any further, and you'll only glimpse the *kivas* (ceremonial chambers), distinguished by their long ladders, from a distance.

Visitors are encouraged to enter, but not photograph, the pretty little **Church of San Gerónimo** on the edge of the plaza. The latest incarnation of the pueblo's Catholic mission church – the ruins of the previous version stand beside the pueblo cemetery, to the west – is decorated inside with murals that feature traditional corn and sun motifs. In the plaza itself, what look like makeshift awnings to shelter parked cars are in fact *ramadas*, wooden racks used for drying corn and chile peppers.

For most of the year, Pueblo life continues with scant regard for the intrusion of tourists, though (camera-less) outsiders are welcome at certain spectacular feast days and dances. Most of these take place in summer; the biggest are the **Corn Dances** (June 13 and 24, July 25 and 26), the **Taos Pueblo Powwow** (second weekend in July), and the **Feast of San Gerónimo** (Sept 29 and 30).

Taos Pueblo is one of the many pueblos to have rushed to build its own **casino**, located on Hwy-68 several miles northwest of the pueblo itself. As one unapologetic elder remarked, "poverty was never a part of Pueblo life until the Europeans came."

Ranchos de Taos

The distinct community of **RANCHOS DE TAOS**, which spreads to either side of Hwy-68 three miles southwest of central Taos, was originally an area of Indian farmlands. These were later taken over by the Spanish to grow the crops that fed the townspeople of Taos. Each *rancho* or farm had its own main house, or *hacienda*, and even today Ranchos de Taos retains the feel of a rural village; you can still buy fresh hay for your animals from lots along the highway.

Taos Pueblo is generally open daily 9am–6pm, but may be closed for tribal events such as festivals or funerals; call ☎505/758-1028 to check.

For details of horse riding with the Taos Indian Horse Ranch, see p.150.

Taos

The reredos at Ranchos de Taos is the work of the nineteenth-century santero Molleno, who was also responsible for the altarpiece of the Santuario de Chimayó; see p.140.

San Francisco de Asis

In Ranchos' small unpaved plaza, the mission church of **San Francisco de Asis** turns its broad shoulders, or more accurately its massive adobe buttresses, to the passing traffic on Hwy-68. Built around 1776, it's one of colonial New Mexico's most splendid architectural achievements, with subtly rounded walls and corners disguising its underlying structural strength. Encountering genuine adobe, which crumbles away after heavy rain or snow, can come as a shock after so much fakery elsewhere in the state; the local congregation is obliged to replaster the whole thing yearly.

Though the ever-changing interplay of light and shade across the church's golden exterior has fascinated painters from Georgia O'Keeffe onwards, its **interior** is equally intriguing. Amid a clutter of devotional objects and artworks, a magnificently ornate green-and-red reredos (altarpiece) frames several individual paintings. The **plaza** outside – remarkably peaceful considering that the highway is thirty yards away – holds a handful of restaurants and gift stores.

Hacienda Martínez

The Hacienda Martínez is one of the Kit Carson Historic Museums; see p.154.

Two miles west of the highway, roughly halfway between San Francisco de Asis and the downtown plaza on Ranchitos Road, the **Hacienda Martínez** is one of the few Spanish *haciendas* anywhere to be preserved in anything approaching its original state (daily: April–Oct 9am–5pm; Nov–March 10am–4pm; $5). It was built in 1804 by Don Antonio Martínez, an early mayor of Taos who was also the father of Padre Antonio Jose Martínez (see p.147). Within its thick, windowless, adobe walls – the place could be sealed like a fortress against still-prevalent Indian raids – two dozen rooms are wrapped around two separate patios, holding animal pens and a well. Trade goods of the kind Don Antonio once carried south along the Rio Grande are displayed alongside tools, looms and simple furnishings of the era.

Taos Ski Valley

Fifteen miles north of Taos, reached via an attractive road that winds up through a narrow gap in the mountains from the village of Arroyo Seco, lie the precipitous slopes of **TAOS SKI VALLEY**. Located on the north flank of **Wheeler Peak** – the highest point in New Mexico at 13,161 feet – the runs are usually open to skiers from late November until early April (daily lift tickets $29 in December, $42 for the rest of the season; information ☎505/776-2291, reservations ☎1-800/776-1111). Experts rate Taos one of the most challenging ski resorts in the Rockies, but the highly-rated Ernie Blake Ski School (same number) teaches novices aged three and upwards on the nursery slopes.

Snowboards are not permitted in Taos Ski Valley.

Several hotels and condos in the Ski Valley remain open year-round, but there wouldn't be a lot of point staying in summer.

Eating and drinking

Taos is too small to offer much **nightlife**, but it does have a fine selection of **restaurants** in all price ranges, and several **coffeehouses**. If your main priority is to **drink**, the *Adobe Bar* in the *Taos Inn* (see p.151), with its roaring log fire and regular live music, is the coziest spot in town, while *Eske's*, a short way south at 106 Des Georges Lane (☎505/758-1517), is a **brewpub**, open nightly until 10.30pm, that also serves simple stews and snacks.

Selected accommodations in Taos Ski Valley are listed on p.153.

Apple Tree Restaurant, 123 Bent St; ☎505/758-1900. Eclectic international cafe, very near the plaza, where the menu ranges from Thai to Mexican, and evening entrees cost up to $20. The courtyard seating is ideal for a summer's evening. Open for lunch and dinner daily, and all afternoon for light snacks.

Bent Street Deli & Cafe, 120 Bent St; ☎505/758-5787. Airy, partly outdoor place, just north of the plaza; good-value breakfasts, sandwich or pasta lunches, and tasty dinners for well under $20. Try the *ceviche* appetizer and the Mexican-style *pollo con molé* (chicken in chocolate). All meals daily except Sun.

Casa Fresen Bakery, 482 Ski Valley Rd, Arroyo Seco; ☎505/776-2969. Unlikely gourmet deli, in a tiny village on the road up to Taos Ski Valley, that serves espresso coffees, pricey but tasty pastries, and sandwiches. Wed–Mon 7.30am–5pm.

Doc Martin's, *Historic Taos Inn*, 125 Paseo del Pueblo Norte; ☎505/758-1977. Delicious, inventive New Mexican food in romantic old adobe inn, on the main road just east of the plaza. Most dinner entrees, such as piñon-crusted salmon or smoked lamb sirloin, are $17–23. Open daily for all meals.

La Luna, 223 Paseo del Pueblo Sur; ☎505/751-0023. Top-quality modern Italian-influenced cooking a few blocks south of the plaza, past *McDonald's*. Good-value wood-fired pizzas for around $10, plus inexpensive specials such as fresh snapper. Lunch Mon–Sat, dinner daily.

Lambert's of Taos, 309 Paseo del Pueblo Sur; ☎505/758-1009. Stylish contemporary diner half a mile south of the plaza, serving New American rather than New Mexican cuisine, with grilled meat or fish entrees for $15–20, and opulent desserts. Open for dinner nightly, lunch Mon–Fri only.

Michael's Kitchen, 304C Paseo del Pueblo Norte; ☎505/758-4178. Inexpensive Mexican and Southwestern dishes in old adobe kitchen a few blocks north of the plaza. Daily 7am–8.30pm, closed April and Nov.

Outback in Taos, 712 Paseo del Pueblo Norte; ☎505/748-3112. Hard-to-find pizzeria tucked in behind another building to the left of the highway a mile north of town, with a welcoming youthful ambience and huge portions of great food – the $8 calzones are amazing.

Downtown Taos restaurants are marked on the map on p.152.

Stakeout Grill and Bar, Outlaw Hill off Hwy-68; ☎505/758-2042. Well-hidden, unpretentious and popular dinner-only restaurant in a truly stunning setting, specializing in big, good-value steaks. Only accessible by car, 4 miles south of Ranchos de Taos up a dirt track east of the highway. Daily 5–10pm.

Tiwa Kitchen, Taos Pueblo; ☎505/751-1020. Indian-run restaurant on the road into Taos Pueblo, serving strong chile-flavored stews, traditional *horno*-baked bread, Indian fry bread, and lots of blue corn meal. Closed Tues.

Coffeehouses

The Bean, 900 Paseo del Pueblo Norte; ☎505/758-7711. Serious coffee roasters, selling espressos and pastries to a clientele composed largely of forty-somethings, including Indians from the nearby pueblo.

Bent Street Coffeehouse, 124-F Bent St; ☎505/751-7184. Small coffee bar just north of the plaza, with a nice sideline on tasty home-baked cookies.

Caffe Tazza, 122 Kit Carson Rd; ☎505/758-8706. Trendy central cafe with nice sunlit terrace, next door to Taos Book Shop, selling coffees and light veggie meals to students and assorted crazies. Live entertainment most evenings, with anarchic open-mike nights.

Shopping

If you're **shopping** for souvenirs, Taos may not have Santa Fe's range of stores, or anything like so many upmarket galleries, but it's just as much fun to walk around. Most of the shops on the plaza itself are very predictable, but the area immediately north, towards Bent Street, is more diverting, and there are some genuine oddities elsewhere. As ever, the **museum stores** – especially at the Millicent Rogers Museum – are among the best in town.

Gift stores and galleries

Blue Rain Gallery, 115 McCarthy Plaza; ☎505/751-0066. The very best in Native American arts and crafts, on the east side of the plaza; unfortunately, the exquisite *kachinas* can run into thousands of dollars.

Coyote Moon, 120C Bent St; ☎505/758-4437. Taos' best selection of Mexican folk art, with plenty of colorful Oaxacan carved animals.

Françoise, 103-H East Plaza; ☎505/758-9255. The plaza's strongest collection of turquoise and silver jewelry, both new and antique.

FX-18, 1018 Paseo del Pueblo Norte; ☎505/758-8590. Quirky crafts, from jewelry to metalwork, plus unusual gifts, a couple of miles north of town.

Hacienda de San Francisco Galeria, 4 St Francis Plaza, Ranchos de Taos; ☎505/758-0477. Also known as Colonial Antiques. Antique *retablos* and furniture, mostly from South America, in gorgeous old adobe beside the church at Ranchos.

Silver Eagle, 113 Paseo del Pueblo Norte; ☎505/758-7709. Enjoyable, inexpensive assortment of mostly South American crafts, just south of *Taos Inn*.

Taos Artisans Co-op, 107A Bent St; ☎505/758-1558. Individually styled jewelry, clothing and sculpture by an assortment of Taoseño artists.

Bookstores

The Brodsky Bookshop, 226 Paseo del Pueblo Norte; ☎505/758-9468. Very helpful store, a couple of blocks north of the plaza, with a huge array of Southwest-related material, and lots of maps.

Moby Dickens, 124A Bent St; ☎505/758-3050. Copious selection of local fiction and history, plus New Age material.

Taos Book Shop, 122D Kit Carson Rd; ☎505/758-3733. Friendly, venerable store with a large stock of rare and out-of-print volumes but a surprisingly small selection of current titles.

West of Taos

While the obvious day-trip drive from Taos follows the **Enchanted
Circle** to the northeast – see p.163 – a longer and wilder route heads
west on US-64, across the Rio Grande and over the dramatic **San
Juan Mountains**. Branching west off Hwy-68 four miles out of downtown Taos, this reaches the awesome, 650-ft-high **Rio Grande Gorge
Bridge** seven miles on. Be sure to take the time to park at the end
and walk out to the middle; otherwise you'll barely get a glimpse of
the narrow chasm as you drive across.

After a magnificent seventy-mile mountain run, punctuated by
scenic overlooks, US-64 finally drops into **Chama Valley**. From
there, either head south into Georgia O'Keeffe country around
Abiquiu, or north to **Chama** itself, the base for excursions on New
Mexico's best-known **steam railroad**.

*The Rio Grande
Gorge Bridge
featured in the
wedding scene
in the movie
Natural Born
Killers.*

Tierra Amarilla

US-64 meets the north–south US-84 in **TIERRA AMARILLA** ("yellow
earth"), at the foot of the sheer, furrowed **Brazos Cliffs**. This pastoral village, founded in 1832 when the valley was prone to constant
Ute, Apache and Navajo raids, provides a classic example of how
New Mexico's Hispanic population suffered after the American
takeover of the territory. In 1860, the US Congress refused to recognize that shared grazing lands belonged to the community as a whole,
and instead sold them off to a Yankee landowner from Santa Fe.

Bitter disputes have raged ever since, culminating in an incident
commemorated by a defaced roadside marker in the heart of the village. In 1967, a group led by Chicano activist **Reies López Tejerina**
– a Texan Protestant – seized a nearby campground in the Kit Carson
National Forest. Declaring independence from the United States,
they burned down Tierra Amarilla's Rio Arriba Courthouse, destroying land-grant records and injuring a policeman and a jailer. The government responded by sending in two hundred military vehicles,
including tanks. After a controversial trial, Tejerina was acquitted of
any involvement by an Albuquerque court. Although he has long
since distanced himself from the campaign, passions still run high –
hence the sign reading *TIERRA O MUERTE* ("Land or Death") on
the outskirts of town.

While Tierra Amarilla remains the county seat, it has suffered a
decline in the last thirty years. Parts are now all but derelict, but the
community continues to resist the construction of weekend homes
for wealthy outsiders, and the possible development of a ski resort
on Brazos Peak. In the nearby village of **LOS OJOS** – the scene of
major civil disobedience in 1989 – one cooperative effort to revitalize the local economy has proved a resounding success. **Tierra
Wools** maintains local **weaving** traditions by breeding Spanish
Churro sheep in the valley, and selling hand-dyed rugs and clothing

from the clearly signposted Los Ojos Trading Post (☎505/588-7231), a mile or so west of US-84.

Chama

Tiny **CHAMA**, set in the meadows at the head of the Chama Valley, a dozen miles north of Tierra Amarilla and a total of 85 miles northwest of Taos, is a former mining camp that has reinvented itself as a base for summer hunters and winter skiers.

Chama's major appeal for out-of-state visitors is that the pretty yellow station just below the town center is the western terminus of the narrow-gauge **Cumbres and Toltec Scenic Railroad** (Memorial Day to mid-Oct; ☎505/756-2151). This exhilarating, if not wildly comfortable, 64-mile steam-train ride – the highest such railroad in the nation – crosses the High Brazos mountains into Colorado by way of **Cumbres Pass**, then runs through the deep **Toltec Gorge** and out onto the plains at **Antonito**. You can't do the entire round-trip by train in one day; passengers either go by van to Antonito, and return by train (depart Chama 8am; $52), or take the train through the most scenic segment as far as Osier, and pick up a return train there (depart Chama 10.30am; $34).

Wrap up warm if you ride the Cumbres and Toltec train; it gets pretty cold in the mountains.

Practicalities

Chama's **visitor center**, half a mile south of town at the junction of US-64 and Hwy-17 (daily 8am–5pm; ☎505/756-2235), can provide details on the whole state, as well as the many **riverfront lodges** along US-64/84 to the south, such as the comfortable, modern *Vista del Rio* (☎505/756-2138 or 1-800/939-9943; ④). Back in town, *Gandy Dancer*, 299 Maple St (☎505/756-2191 or 1-800/424-6702; ⑤), is a **B&B** in a purple-clapboard mansion with seven en-suite rooms and a hot tub; "gandy dancer" was railroad slang for a track laborer. Opposite the rail station, the menu at the cheerful, inexpensive *Whistle Stop Cafe* (☎505/756-1833), includes a few vegetarian options. The most convenient place to **camp** is the *Rio Chama RV Campground*, beside the river at the north end of town (☎505/756-2303).

Chama's zip code is NM 87520.

The Cumbres Pass and Antonito, Colorado

North of Chama, **Hwy-17** follows much the same route as the railroad, first climbing far above the single track and then crisscrossing it repeatedly as it makes its way up to the 10,022-foot **Cumbres Pass**. In July 1848, legendary "mountain man" Bill Williams was injured here in a confrontation between the US Army and a combined force of Utes and Apaches.

Beyond the pass, highway and railroad part company, not to meet again until they reach **ANTONITO**, Colorado, fifty miles out of Chama – a dreary, depressing little town that's home to the reasonable *Narrow Gauge Railroad Inn* (☎719/376-5441 or 1-800/323-9469; ②) and a few basic cafes. If you're looking for a place to stay in the vicinity, the *Conejos River Hostel* (☎719/376-2518; ①) – a cluster of green cabins on the far side of the Conejos River, ten miles west of Antonito where forest-service road FDR-103 branches south from Hwy-17 – is a far more enticing prospect than anywhere in Antonito itself.

Dulce

US-64 and US-84 join forces for twelve miles **west of Chama**, then once across the Continental Divide (not at all dramatic at this point), US-64 continues alone for another fifteen miles to DULCE, the headquarters of the **Jicarilla Apache Indian Reservation**. Today's three-thousand-plus Jicarilla are descended from separate Apache groups who lived further east, some as Plains nomads in the Cimarron area, and some in adobe villages near the pueblos of the Rio Grande. Their name is often said to come from the little baskets (*jicarillas*) they now sell to tourists, but the Jicarilla themselves suggest that they started making baskets when they were confined to this remote reservation in the nineteenth century, and that the name comes from a Mexican word connected with chocolate.

There's little for tourists to see or do on the Jicarilla reservation, whose economy is based on oil and gas revenues and raising sheep. Dulce itself is little more than a very sharp right-angle turn in the highway, where US-64 is forced to turn south rather than climb onto sheer Archuleta Mesa; after a few miles the road turns west again to head through Vaqueros Canyon and Gobernador Canyon (see p.83). However, the roomy and attractive *Best Western Jicarilla Inn* in Dulce (☎505/759-3663 or 1-800/742-1938, fax 505/759-3170; ④), is regarded as a model for Indian-owned businesses. It has a good restaurant, and offers special deals on train trips from Chama.

The Enchanted Circle

The driving circuit through the Sangre de Cristo range northeast of Taos doesn't quite live up to its tourist-brochure billing as the **Enchanted Circle**, though it does pass a handful of long-abandoned ghost towns amid the mountain scenery. While Oklahomans and Texans flock to the closest **ski slopes** to home, visitors from further afield are more likely to make the brief detour east to the hard-bitten frontier town of **Cimarron**.

The Lawrence Ranch

Starting seventeen miles north of Taos on Hwy-222, a rutted, muddy road climbs for five miles east to the **Lawrence Ranch**. The English novelist **D.H. Lawrence** made three six-month visits to Taos in the early 1920s, having been enticed across the Atlantic by Mabel Dodge Luhan (see p.147). Staying at her mountain cabin, then known as Kiowa Ranch, he wrote "there are all kinds of beauty in the world, but for greatness of beauty I have never experienced anything like New Mexico." **Georgia O'Keeffe** was also a guest here, in 1929, when she painted the tree right in front of the main cabin as *The Lawrence Tree*. As seen from below, the painting makes the tree look more like a giant squid; it's usually on display in the Georgia O'Keeffe Museum in Santa Fe.

Lawrence died in France in 1930, but five years later his widow Frieda shipped his ashes back to New Mexico. They now rest in a small **shrine** that enjoys panoramic views of the upper Rio Grande valley, at the top of a zigzag cement footpath cleared through the forest. Frieda is said to have acquired the ranch from Mabel Dodge Luhan in exchange for the manuscript of *Sons and Lovers* – which Mabel in turn used to pay her psychiatrist – and lived in it until her death in 1956. It now belongs to the University of New Mexico, which holds weekend retreats in the main cabin; only the shrine is accessible to visitors, with no fixed hours or admission fee.

Red River

Half a dozen miles beyond the Lawrence Ranch turnoff, as Hwy-222 gathers itself for the final climb into Colorado, **Hwy-38** follows Red River east from **QUESTA**, an ugly little village ravaged by opencast mining. After twelve more attractive riverside miles, it reaches **RED RIVER** itself, a former gold-mining town whose rough-shod timber architecture is more authentic than it looks. Summer visitors hike in the surrounding forests, but Red River is at its busiest during the winter **ski** season, when there's cross-country skiing down in the valley and a downhill resort in the mountains to the south.

Red River's zip code is NM 87558.

Red River claims to have more **hotel** rooms than Santa Fe, though it's hard to see where they might be. Appealing options include the *Riverside Lodge*, 201 E Main St (☎505/754-2252 or 1-800/432-9999; ③), and the *Lodge at Red River*, PO Box 189, W Main St (☎505/754-6280 or 1-800/915-6343; ④); there's also a central **reservations** service (☎505/754-2223 or 1-800/331-SNOW).

Cimarron

Beyond Red River, Hwy-38 negotiates the 9820-foot **Bobcat Pass** – often closed in winter – then drops by way of the ruins of long-abandoned **Elizabethtown** down to **EAGLE NEST**. Just a cluster of cabins and RV parks, Eagle Nest sprang up around a lake formed when the **Cimarron River** was dammed in 1920, and is popular with fishing enthusiasts. US-64 parallels the river to enter impressive **Cimarron Canyon** four miles east, beneath the towering 800-foot **Palisade Cliffs**. This route provided access to Taos for nineteenth-century travelers who split from the Santa Fe Trail's "mountain branch" at **CIMARRON** itself, 24 miles east of Eagle Nest.

Cimarron means "wild" or "untamed," and in its heyday the town was as wild as the West could be. It stood at the heart of the 1.7-million-acre **Maxwell Land Grant**, the largest private landholding in the United States, accumulated by Lucien Bonaparte Maxwell in the years following the American takeover of New Mexico. Maxwell's main business was cattle ranching, but with gold and silver mines booming and busting all over the mountains, Cimarron lured a vast profusion of gamblers, gunfighters, outlaws and cowboys.

Cimarron's old downtown area now stands relatively intact half a mile or so south of the main highway. Its history is lovingly chronicled in the **Old Mill Museum** (May–Oct Mon–Wed, Fri & Sat 9am–5pm, Sun 1–5pm; $3), where visitors can pick up a walking tour map of other nearby relics. The most famous of all is the **St James Hotel** opposite, at 17th and Collinson (☎505/376-2664 or 1-800/748-2694, fax 505/376-2623; motel ③, hotel ⑤). Built by President Lincoln's former White House chef in 1873, it's said to have witnessed 26 murders; names in the guest register include Jesse James and Buffalo Bill, who stayed here while organizing his Wild West Show. It now has its own grand, atmospheric restaurant, and a less romantic motel annex.

Angel Fire

The Enchanted Circle loops back to Taos from Eagle Nest along US-64, passing, after ten miles, through the part-**golf**, part-**ski** resort of **ANGEL FIRE** in Moreno Valley. First developed in the late 1960s, Angel Fire shows no signs of maturing beyond its current brash, unappealing sprawl, though the creature comforts of its centerpiece, the *Angel Fire Resort* itself, cannot be faulted (☎505/377-6401 or 1-800/633-7463; ④–⑥).

Northeast New Mexico

As I-25 heads north from Las Vegas (see p.145) into New Mexico's **northeast corner**, the Sangre de Cristo mountains gradually recede below the western horizon and the Great Plains begin to unfurl in all their relentless monotony. There's no great reason to stray off the interstate until the Rockies start to loom above **Raton**, a hundred miles on, though with time to spare the detour to **Capulin Volcano** at that point is worth making.

Raton

Appealing little **RATON** is tucked into the foothills of the Rockies around a hundred miles north of Las Vegas on I-25, a mere eight miles south of the Colorado border. Once a way-station on the Santa

Raton's zip code is NM 87740.

*Trinidad,
twenty miles
north of Raton
in Colorado,
makes an
equally divert-
ing stop.*

Fe Trail, it reached its present size after becoming the site of a rail-road repair shop in 1880, and can have changed little since then.

Few passengers now bother to dismount from the sleek Amtrak Starliner that pulls into the Santa Fe Depot around noon daily, but an hour or two's stroll in **downtown Raton** can be fun. Photos and odd-ments in the **Raton Museum**, facing the station at 216 S First St (May–Sept Tues–Sat 9am–5pm; Oct–April Wed–Sat 10am–1pm & 3–5pm; free), recall highlights from Raton's first century. Until 1938, it was dominated by the seven-story *Hotel Swastika*, which then "found it necessary to change its name" to the *Yucca*, and is now a bank.

The *Best Western Sands Motel*, 300 Clayton Hwy (☎505/445-2737 or 1-800/528-1234; closed Feb; ④), is the best hotel in town these days, though you can get a cheaper but perfectly adequate room a few blocks north of the Amtrak station in the *Budget Host Melody Lane Motel*, 136 Canyon Drive (☎505/445-3655 or 1-800/421-5210; ②).

Capulin Volcano National Monument

CAPULIN VOLCANO NATIONAL MONUMENT, thirty miles east of Raton on US-64/87 and then three miles north on Hwy-325, pre-serves the neatest and most symmetrical of a chain of cinder cones that last exploded around ten thousand years ago.

Displays explaining its formation can be examined in the **visitor center** (daily: summer 7.30am–6.30pm; winter 8am–4pm; ☎505/278-2201; $4 per vehicle), but most visitors drive straight on up the two-mile spiral of road that leads to its summit. Once there, a thousand feet above the surrounding plains, you can **hike** for a mile around the rim, enjoying views to the Sangre de Cristo mountains in the west and Oklahoma to the east, or pick your way down to the vent where it all began.

FOLSOM, six miles north of the volcano, is renowned in scientific circles as the place where 1920s archeologists first identified a type of spearpoint known as the **Folsom point**. Some were found wedged between the ribs of a species of bison that has been extinct for ten thousand years, proving that Paleo-Indians were here around 9000 BC – much earlier than had previously been thought. Such points have since been found at sites all over the Southwest. The original excavation site at Folsom is not open to the public.

Clayton

The town of **CLAYTON** stands fifty miles on from Capulin in the far northeast corner of the state, just short of both Oklahoma and Texas. Early Spanish explorers named this region the **Llano Estacado**, or "Staked Plains," on the basis that they could only find their way through the high grasslands by hammering a trail of wooden stakes into the ground. Clayton itself was founded when the railroad came through in the 1880s, and it's still hard to imagine that anyone would set out on a journey with this as their goal.

The fenced-in dinosaurs on the lawn of the local **visitor center**, 1003 S First St (Mon–Fri 9am–5pm; ☎505/374-9253) – they're named "Moonbeam" and "Spike," if you must know – are a reference to the dinosaur footprints in the fossilized lakeside muds at **Clayton State Park**, twelve miles north. As well as rock-bottom **motels** in town, like the *Clayton Motel*, 422 Monroe St (☎505/374-2544; ①), there's a *Super 8* to the south at 1425 US-87 (☎505/374-8127 or 1-800/800-8000, fax 505/374-2598; winter ②, summer ③).

Chapter 3

Albuquerque and Southern New Mexico

C entral and southern New Mexico are not wholly devoid of interest, but it's not surprising that they see fewer visitors than the prime tourist destinations to the north. Despite being the state's largest city, **Albuquerque** holds less to encourage a long stay than Santa Fe or Taos, while few of the towns that lie along the monotonous I-40 highway to the **east**, or in the endless desert expanses to the **south**, are worth going out of your way to see.

Much of the region remained under the domination of the nomadic Apache until well into the nineteenth century. Even Albuquerque was founded long after Santa Fe, while towns such as **Silver City**, **Mesilla** and **Lincoln** didn't really get going until New Mexico joined the United States in 1846. All three went on to play significant roles in the career of **Billy the Kid**, and all still look today much like the frontier outposts Billy must have known. Together with the pre-Columbian remains of the **Gila Cliff Dwellings** in the remote southwest corner, they're the most appealing historic attractions in the region, but there are also a couple of **geological** wonders. The subterranean labyrinths of **Carlsbad Caverns National Park** lure a million tourists across the plains each year, while the dazzling dunes of **White Sands National Monument** make an extraordinary spectacle against the San Andres Mountains. Top-secret missile tests and bomb blasts give this desolate landscape an added sense of mystery, making its role in popular myth as the site of the notorious **Roswell Incident** a tiny bit more plausible.

Albuquerque

Sprawling at the heart of New Mexico, where the main east–west road and rail routes cross both the Rio Grande and the old road south to Mexico, **ALBUQUERQUE**, with half a million people, is the state's only major metropolis. Though many tourists race straight from the

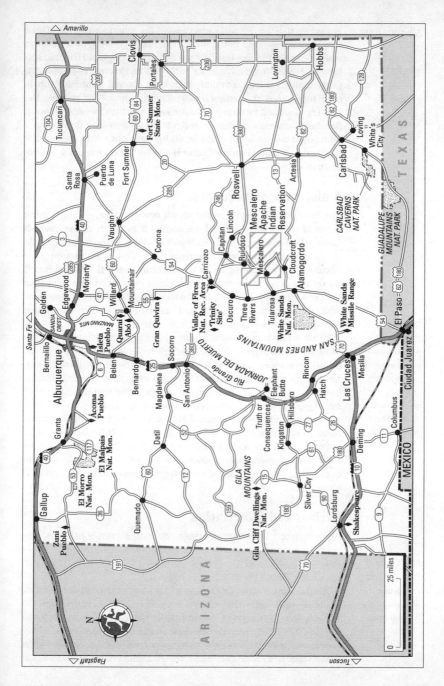

airport up to Santa Fe without a thought for Albuquerque, the "Duke City" has a good deal going for it. Like Phoenix, it's grown a bit too fast for comfort in the last fifty years, but the original Hispanic settlement is still discernible at its core, and its diverse, cosmopolitan population gives it a rare cultural vibrancy. Even if its architecture is often uninspired, the setting is magnificent, sandwiched between the Rio Grande, lined by stately cottonwoods, and the dramatic, glowing **Sandia Mountains**. Specific highlights for visitors include the intact **Spanish plaza**, the neon-lit **Route 66** frontage of Central Avenue, the fascinating **Indian Pueblo Cultural Center**, and October's **hot-air balloon** extravaganza.

A history of Albuquerque

The Spanish colonists who founded a new town beside a sweeping curve of the Rio Grande in 1706 named it in honor of the Spanish **Duke of Alburquerque**. Its earliest surviving adobe buildings, still the nucleus of **Old Town**, date from the 1790s, when Albuquerque occupied a pivotal position on the **Camino Real** – the "Royal Road" from Chihuahua to Santa Fe – which later connected with the **Santa Fe Trail** from the Mississippi. Modern Albuquerque began to grow with the arrival of the railroad in 1880, when its epicenter shuffled a couple of miles east towards the new station.

The extra "r" in Alburquerque got lost somewhere along the way, possibly thanks to a misspelling by a railroad signpainter.

What really transformed Albuquerque was the decentralization of **defense** industries during World War II. Weapons research at **Sandia National Laboratories**, on the Kirtland Air Force Base, brought a massive influx of money and jobs. In the 1950s, "Atomic City" was the best educated city in the nation, in terms of PhDs per capita, and acquired enough federal offices to earn the nickname "Little Washington." It also achieved the dubious distinction of surviving an **H-bomb**: in 1957, a B-36 bomber accidentally dropped a 42,000-pound nuclear device near the air base. Its conventional explosives went off, creating a sizeable crater, but failed to trigger the intended one-megaton thermonuclear blast.

Arrival and information

Albuquerque's **International Sunport**, New Mexico's principal airport, is four miles southeast of downtown. Mesa Airlines (☎1-800/637-2247) and Southwest Airlines (☎1-800/435-9792) run commuter flights throughout the state.

For details of flights to and within the Southwest, see p.3 onwards.

All the **rental car** chains (see p.20) have outlets at the airport, while a **taxi** into the center with the Albuquerque Cab Co (☎505/883-4888) costs around $10; Checker Airport Express (☎505/765-1234) run door-to-door shuttles at similar rates. Many hotels and motels also have their own free shuttles, while half a dozen daily Gray Line vans make the 70-minute drive north to Santa

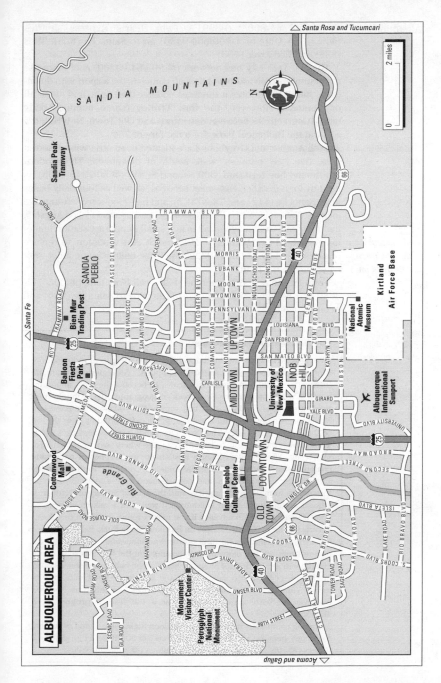

△ Santa Rosa and Tucumcari

SANDIA MOUNTAINS

N

2 miles

0

Sandia Peak
Tramway

SANDIA
PUEBLO

TRAMWAY BLVD

JUAN TABO
MORRIS
EUBANK
MOON
WYOMING
PENNSYLVANIA

ACADEMY ROAD
SPAIN ROAD
PASEO DEL NORTE
END ROAD

△ Santa Fe

Bien Mur
Trading Post

TRAMWAY ROAD
ROY

Balloon
Fiesta
Park

25

JEFFERSON ST

SAN FRANCISCO
SAN ANTONIO DR

MONTGOMERY BLVD
INDIAN SCHOOL ROAD
CONSTITUTION
LOMAS BLVD

40

66

CENTRAL AVENUE

Kirtland
Air Force Base

National
Atomic
Museum

LOUISIANA

COMANCHE ROAD
CANDELARIA ROAD
MENAUL BLVD

SAN PEDRO DR

SAN MATEO BLVD

CARLISLE

MIDTOWN

UPTOWN

University of
New Mexico

NOB
HILL

GIRARD

YALE BLVD

ZUNI ROAD

GIBSON BLVD

KATHRYN

Albuquerque
International
Sunport

✈

ALAMEDA BLVD
EDITH BLVD
SECOND STREET
FOURTH STREET
CHAVEZ OSUNA ROAD

Cottonwood
Mall

GOLF COURSE ROAD
PARADISE BLVD
N. COORS BLVD
Rio Grande
RIO GRANDE BLVD
12TH ST
MANTANO RD
GRIEGOS ROAD

Indian Pueblo
Cultural Center

OLD
TOWN

DOWNTOWN

TINGLEY DR

BROADWAY
SECOND STREET

25

UNIVERSITY BLVD

66

COORS ROAD

BRIDGE BLVD
ARENAL ROAD
ISLETA BLVD
BLAKE ROAD
RIO BRAVO BLVD
S. COORS BLVD

SQUAW ROAD
UNSER BLVD
SCENIC ROAD
GILA ROAD
MANTANO ROAD
ATRISCO DR

Monument
Visitor Center

Petroglyph
National
Monument

UNSER BLVD

LADERA DRIVE
COORS BLVD

98TH STREET

40

TOWER ROAD
SAGE ROAD

CENTRAL AVENUE

△ Acoma and Gallup

ALBUQUERQUE
AREA

Albuquerque

Fe ($25; ☎1-800/256-8991). Twin Hearts Express shuttles (☎505/751-1201 or 1-800/654-9456) go to Santa Fe ($25), Taos ($35) and Red River ($50).

The Sun Tran **city bus** network (☎505/843-9200) is of more use to commuters than tourists; bus #50 connects the airport with downtown, but like all routes it operates no later than 6pm, and not at all on Sundays. However, the **Sun Trolley** (same number; daily 6am–10pm) circles between downtown and Old Town, Nob Hill, the zoo and the Biological Park, for a flat fare of 75¢.

Both Amtrak and Greyhound are located in an otherwise deserted area, five easy minutes' walk south of downtown. The modern Greyhound **bus terminal**, 300 Second St SW (☎505/243-4435), is used by long-distance east–west services, as well as four daily buses up to Santa Fe ($12) and Taos ($22), and has good-sized left-luggage lockers. Two daily Amtrak **trains** – one heading west to Los Angeles, the other east to Chicago – call in at a small temporary station immediately behind Greyhound, at 214 First St. A new station, to replace one destroyed by fire in 1993, is due to be built at some indeterminate point in the future.

Walking tours of the Old Town are detailed on p.176.

For a **city tour** of Albuquerque ($23), call Gray Line (☎505/242-3880 or 1-800/256-8991); they also run trips to Santa Fe ($36) and Ácoma Pueblo ($30).

The Balloons of Albuquerque

First held in 1972 as a 50th anniversary stunt for a local radio station, when it featured just thirteen balloons, Albuquerque's annual **International Balloon Fiesta** has grown to become the most important event in world ballooning. By a freak of geography, the "**Albuquerque Box**" offers ideal conditions for balloonists. After take-off, the prevailing winds consistently blow balloons towards the east, until they clear the top of the Sandia Mountains. Then stronger winds propel them back westwards, making it possible to land more or less where they were launched. As a result, Albuquerque regularly hosts major gas and hot-air ballooning championships, such as the unlikely-sounding Coupe de Gordon Bennett.

A photographer's dream, and now sponsored by Kodak, the Balloon Fiesta lasts from the first Saturday until the second Sunday of October. It attracts around a thousand balloons and well over a million visitors, so book several months in advance if you need a room, or even a rental car, in early October. The fun focuses on **Balloon Fiesta Park**, half a mile west of I-25 and seven miles north of downtown. Admission costs $4, and the busiest times are the dawn mass launchings on the four weekend mornings, as well as the "Special Shapes" events, when balloons in shapes ranging from beer bottles to dumptrucks, and dragons to doughnuts, take to the air. Volunteers are always welcomed to help set the things up, and may be rewarded with a quick flight. For a full festival program, call ☎505/821-1000.

Among companies running hot-air balloon flights year round, at around $100 per person, are Discover Balloons (☎505/842-1111), Rainbow Ryders (☎505/293-0000) and World Balloon (☎505/293-6800).

Information

Free listings magazines and brochures are available from the **visitor center** downtown in the Galeria mall, 20 First Plaza at Second and Tijeras (Mon–Fri 8am–5pm; ☎505/842-9918 or 1-800/733-9918; *www.abqcvb.org*). Americana enthusiasts will also enjoy their *Historic Route 66* map. Further **information kiosks** can be found in Old Town, in the Plaza Don Luis on Romero NW (daily: April–Oct 9am–5pm; Nov–March 9.30am–4.30pm); at the Cottonwood Mall (Mon–Sat 10am–6pm, Sun 11am–6pm); and at the airport (daily 9.30am–8pm). The city's main **post office** is at 1135 Broadway NE (daily 7.30am–6pm).

Accommodation

The easiest way to find a place to stay in Albuquerque is to cruise the twenty-mile length of **Central Avenue**, the old Route 66, which is lined with the flashing neon signs of dozens of $30-a-night motels. Try to have a good look in daylight, to spot those that may turn scary at night. If you want to escape your car for a while, you'll have to pay a little extra to stay in the heart of Old Town – which holds few accommodation options – or downtown. Larger convention hotels are congregated along the interstates, and near the airport – look out for discount coupons in New Mexico's welcome centers – while a handful of B&Bs are scattered across the city.

As explained on p.15, accommodation prices, excluding taxes, are indicated throughout this book by the following symbols:
① *up to $30*
② *$30–45*
③ *$45–60*
④ *$60–80*
⑤ *$80–100*
⑥ *$100–130*
⑦ *$130–175*
⑧ *$175–250*
⑨ *$250+*

Albuquerque Hilton, 1901 University Blvd NE, Albuquerque, NM 87102; ☎505/884-2500 or 1-800/274-6835, fax 505/889-9118; *www.hilton.com*. Midtown high-rise near the intersection of I-40 and I-25. Good rooms, three restaurants – the *Casa Chaco* serves tasty Southwestern cuisine – and several busy bars. ⑥.

Barcelona Suites Uptown, 900 Louisiana Blvd NE, Albuquerque, NM 87110; ☎505/255-5566 or 1-800/ABQ-SUITES; *www.barsuites.com*. Spacious suite-only hotel, three miles east of downtown and two blocks south of I-40 at exit 162. All the units have kitchens, and there are indoor and outdoor pools. ⑤.

Best Western Airport Inn, 2400 Yale Blvd SE, Albuquerque, NM 87106; ☎505/242-7022 or 1-800/528-1234, fax 505/243-0620; *www.bwairportinn.com*. Pleasant courtyard motel, quieter than you might expect and offering a free airport shuttle. ④.

Casa del Granjero, 414 C de Baca Lane NW, Albuquerque, NM 87114; ☎505/897-4144 or 1-800/701-4144, fax 505/897-9788; *www.innewmexico.com*. Adobe farmhouse in three-acre gardens, well north of Old Town, that's been converted into a tasteful, upmarket nonsmoking B&B inn, with three rooms and four suites plus a sauna. ④–⑦.

Casas de Sueños, 310 Rio Grande Blvd SW, Albuquerque, NM 87104; ☎505/247-4560 or 1-800/242-8987, fax 505/842-8493; *www.casasdesuenos.com*. Beautifully furnished, exotic – as in the extraordinary Caracol room coiled above the entrance – and friendly B&B, very close to Old Town, with themed cottages and smaller rooms. One of New Mexico's most appealing places to stay. ⑤–⑨.

Comfort Inn–Airport, 2300 Yale Blvd SE, Albuquerque, NM 87106; ☎505/243-2244 or 1-800/221-2222, fax 505/247-2925. Good-value motel, served by free shuttles from the airport across the road, and offering complimentary breakfasts. ④.

Crossroads Motel, 1001 Central Ave NE, Albuquerque, NM 87102; ☎505/255-7586. Simple, good-value budget motel, immediately east of I-25 between Old Town and the University on Route 66, and complete with a pool. ②.

Crowne Plaza Pyramid, 5151 San Francisco Rd NE, Albuquerque, NM 87109; ☎505/821-3333, fax 822-8115; *ljpyr@aol.com*. Gigantic pyramid (stepped not smooth) near exit 232 off I-25 north of town, with a waterfall in the lobby and over three hundred rooms. President Clinton holed up here in 1996. ⑥.

El Vado Motel, 2500 Central Ave SW, Albuquerque, NM 87104; ☎505/243-4594, fax 836-1981. Vintage adobe Route 66 motel, within easy reach of Old Town. ②.

Conrad's
*restaurant in
La Posada is
reviewed on
p.180.*

La Posada de Albuquerque, 125 Second St NW, Albuquerque, NM 87102; ☎505/242-9090 or 1-800/777-5732, fax 505/242-1945; *www .historychanneltours.com/hotels/newmexico1.html*. Historic, elegant hotel in a convenient downtown location, built in Mexican style by Conrad Hilton in 1939. Plush, renovated rooms, a beautiful wood-paneled lobby, a superb restaurant and a spacious, atmospheric bar. ⑥.

Monterey Nonsmokers Motel, 2402 Central Ave SW, Albuquerque, NM 87104; ☎505/243-3554 or 1-877/666-8379, fax 505/243-9701. Clean, fifteen-room motel, two blocks west of Old Town, with pool, laundry and a strict non-smoking policy. ③.

Old Town Bed and Breakfast, 707 17th St, Albuquerque, NM 87104; ☎505/764-9144 or 1-888/900-9144; *www.inn-new-mexico.com*. Friendly, very small-scale B&B in mock-adobe home a couple of blocks from the heart of Old Town; one of the two guestrooms has its own bathroom, the other is a more extensive suite but shares a bathroom. ④/⑤.

Route 66 Hostel, 1012 Central Ave SW, Albuquerque, NM 87102; ☎505/247-1813; *ctaylor939@aol.com*. Albuquerque's only hostel, a friendly place on the outskirts of Old Town, a mile west of downtown, offers dorm beds for $14 ($12 members), kitchen facilities, and bargain private doubles. Office hours daily 7.30–10.30am & 4–11pm. ①.

The City

Albuquerque consists of several distinct districts, interspersed between anonymous residential areas, and threaded through by the twenty-mile artery of **Central Avenue**, the most authentic surviving remnant of the classic Route 66, alive with flashing neon. **Old Town** remains the most interesting area for visitors, with **downtown** two miles to the east, and the **university district** and the fashionable **Nob Hill** area beyond that. Further east, the **Sandia Mountains** finally call a halt to the Sunbelt sprawl. The city has begun instead to push west of the Rio Grande, where only **Petroglyph National Monument** holds any interest for tourists.

Old Town

Albuquerque's tree-filled **Old Town Plaza** may lack the cachet of its Santa Fe equivalent, but it makes an appealing focus for explorations

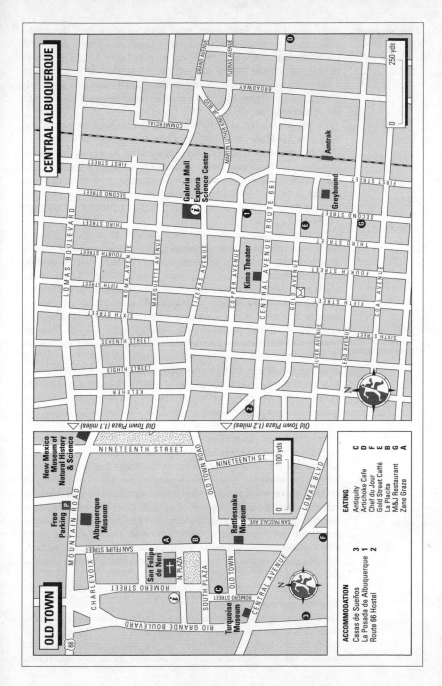

CENTRAL ALBUQUERQUE

250 yds

Galeria Mall
Explora
Science Center

Kimo Theater

Amtrak

Greyhound

GRAND AVENUE
TIJERAS AVENUE
BROADWAY
COMMERCIAL
MARTIN LUTHER KING JR BLVD
FIRST STREET
SECOND STREET
THIRD STREET
FOURTH STREET
FIFTH STREET
SIXTH STREET
SEVENTH STREET
EIGHTH STREET
KELEHER
LOMAS BOULEVARD
ROMA AVENUE
MARQUETTE AVENUE
TIJERAS AVENUE
COPPER AVENUE
CENTRAL AVENUE (ROUTE 66)
GOLD AVENUE
SILVER AVENUE
LEAD AVENUE
COAL AVENUE
FIRST STREET
SECOND STREET
THIRD STREET
FOURTH STREET
FIFTH STREET
SIXTH STREET

Old Town Plaza (1.1 miles)
Old Town Plaza (1.2 miles)

N

OLD TOWN

New Mexico
Museum of
Natural History
& Science

Free
Parking P

Albuquerque
Museum

San Felipe
de Neri

Rattlesnake
Museum

Turquoise
Museum

NINETEENTH STREET
NINETEENTH ST.
OLD TOWN ROAD
MOUNTAIN ROAD
CHARLEVOIX
ROMERO STREET
SAN FELIPE STREET
N PLAZA
SOUTH PLAZA
OLD TOWN
RIO GRANDE BOULEVARD
CENTRAL AVENUE
ROMERO STREET
SAN PASCALE AVE
LOMAS BLVD

66

N

100 yds

ACCOMMODATION

Casas de Sueños	3
La Posada de Albuquerque	1
Route 66 Hostel	2

EATING

Antiquity	C
Artichoke Cafe	D
Chef du Jour	F
Gold Street Caffè	E
La Placita	B
M&J Restaurant	G
Zane Graze	A

of the old Spanish settlement. After decades of decline, the adobe buildings on all four sides have been restored as souvenir stores and tourist restaurants, and they're still presided over by the twin-towered facade of **San Felipe de Neri church** to the north. Inside the church, the main features are a crucified Christ lying in a glass coffin to the right of the altar, and a *retablo* commissioned to celebrate the Bicentennial in 1976.

To get a sense of the city's past, spend an hour or two at the **Albuquerque Museum**, a couple of blocks northeast of the plaza at 2000 Mountain Rd (Tues–Sun 9am–5pm; free). As well as an impressive array of the armor and weaponry carried by the Spanish conquistadors, it holds delicate religious artifacts, plus paintings and photos showing Albuquerque through the centuries. It's also the starting point for Old Town **walking tours** (mid-April to mid-Nov Tues–Sun 11am; $2).

Another two blocks east, the **New Mexico Museum of Natural History and Science**, 1801 Mountain Rd NW (daily 9am–5pm; closed Mon in Jan & Sept; $5), primarily appeals to kids. Star attractions include full-size animatronic dinosaurs, a simulated volcanic eruption, and a replica of an Ice Age snow cave, plus an engaging, handleable collection of fossils and dinosaur bones. A Dynamax theater shows the usual limited array of giant-screen movies for an additional charge.

Southeast of the plaza at 202 San Felipe St NW, the bizarre **American International Rattlesnake Museum** has live rattlers on display and rattlesnake curios for sale (daily 10am–6.30pm; $2). It advertises itself with leaflets that show snakes being handled, but in fact a visit is more likely to consist of walking through a small room at the back of the gift store, where spiders and scorpions as well as snakes are kept in tiny glass cases. Gus' Trading Post, across the highway nearby at 2026 Central Ave SW, stocks a well-priced assortment of Indian crafts and jewelry.

Still on Central Avenue, in the Old Town Shopping Center at 2107 Central Ave NW, half a block west of the plaza, the intriguing little **Turquoise Museum** (Mon–Sat 9.30am–6pm; $2) looks like just another mall store. Once you step inside, you find that in fact you've entered a fortified bank vault, filled with rare and beautiful turquoise nuggets. The story of worldwide turquoise production is told in copious detail, and there's lots of useful advice on the tricks of the trade; unfortunately, the only way to tell if a piece of turquoise is genuine involves destroying it. Of course, visits end with the chance to buy a few trinkets.

The riverfront

The Rio Grande has shifted its course in the last three hundred years, so there's an unexpectedly low-key gap west of Old Town, much of it left undeveloped in deference to the unruly river. Along the wooded eastern riverbank, north of where Central Avenue crosses the river, the **Albuquerque Biological Park** holds two attractions that focus on the natural world.

Not for the squeamish, the **Albuquerque Aquarium** (June–Aug Mon–Fri 9am–5pm, Sat & Sun 9am–6pm; Sept–May daily 9am–5pm; $6.50) offers such diverse experiences as eating in a restaurant beside a glass-walled tank filled with live sharks, and walking through a tunnel surrounded on all sides by fierce-eyed moray eels. The whole place was designed with a great eye for aesthetics, with lots of sculpture outside and beautifully lit tanks filled with ethereal, wispy jellyfish within. Across the central plaza, the **Rio Grande Botanic Garden** (same hours, same ticket) consists of two large conservatories – one holding rare plants from the Sonoran and Chihuahua deserts, the other more temperate Mediterranean species – plus a series of formal walled gardens. Disappointingly, the river itself is not visible from either section.

Two miles north of Old Town, by way of Rio Grande Boulevard, the lower-key **Rio Grande Nature Center** (daily 10am–5pm; $1) has informative displays describing local wildlife. Two short but very welcome nature trails follow the riverside, feeling far removed from the city.

Indian Pueblo Cultural Center

The **Indian Pueblo Cultural Center**, at 2401 12th St NW, across I-40 a few blocks north of Old Town (daily 9am–5.30pm; $4; ☎505/843-7270 or 1-800/766-4405), is a stunning museum and crafts market collectively run by the nineteen New Mexican pueblos. Its horseshoe-shaped design deliberately echoes the architecture of the Ancestral Puebloan city of Pueblo Bonito, in Chaco Canyon (see p.85).

The good-quality Pueblo Kitchen cafe in the Cultural Center is reviewed on p.180.

This is New Mexico's one major museum about Native Americans to be curated by Native Americans, and the displays downstairs, under the banner Our Land, Our Culture, Our Story, have a clear and distinct point of view. The shared heritage at the root of Pueblo culture is explained in detail, as is the impact of the Spanish conquistadors. Describing the Pueblo Revolt of 1680 as the "first civil war," it states that by allowing the defeated Spaniards to leave unharmed, the Pueblo peoples "showed them more mercy than they showed us." There's also as good an explanation as you're ever likely to get of a topic Pueblo Indians rarely discuss with outsiders; how indigenous Pueblo religion has managed to coexist with imported Catholicism. Videos illustrate modern Pueblo life, and an outstanding selection of pottery and jewelry is sold in the stores upstairs. On weekends throughout the year, **Pueblo dances** take place in the central courtyard (Sat & Sun 11am & 2pm; free).

Downtown

Downtown Albuquerque may be where New Mexico's largest city conducts its daily business, but it holds little that's likely to detain tourists for long. If you call at the visitor center in the small **Galeria**

mall (see p.173), you might also stop by the **Explora Science Center** in the same building (Tues–Fri 9am–4pm, Sat 9am–5pm, Sun noon–5pm; $4). Its hands-on displays and experiments are mainly designed to keep kids occupied while their parents shop.

The University District

A couple of miles east of downtown, the campus of the **University of New Mexico** stretches along the northern side of Central Avenue. The 25,000-strong student body keeps the southern side of the highway – lined with funky hangouts of all kinds, from bookstores to laundromats by way of cafes and diners – lively right around the clock, but there's not all that much scope for sightseeing.

Of the six museums on campus, non-academic visitors are most likely to enjoy the **Maxwell Museum of Anthropology** (Mon–Fri 9am–4pm, Sat 10am–4pm, Sun noon–4pm; free), which holds a wide range of displays on the Peoples of the Southwest, past and present. There's some fine Mimbres pottery (see p.210), as well as material from Chaco Canyon, while the Ancestors segment traces human evolution from the three-million-year-old Lucy, just 3ft 7in tall, unearthed in Ethiopia.

The National Atomic Museum

Ensconced within the giant Kirtland Air Force Base, southeast of the city, the **National Atomic Museum** (daily 9am–5pm; $2) delights in its "impressive array of American fission weapons." Since the US Embassy bombings of 1998, security constraints have meant that visitors are not allowed to drive onto the base; instead you have to park and register at either of its main gates, on Wyoming and Gibson boulevards, and wait an average of twenty minutes for a shuttle bus to take you on to the museum itself. En route, you'll find that the base is effectively a self-contained city, with its own schools and even a *McDonald's*.

Manzano Mountain, entirely enclosed by Kirtland Air Force Base, is said to be hollow, stuffed full of more nuclear weapons than any other site on earth.

Assorted Titan ICBMs and Cruise and Polaris missiles stand baking in the sun outside the museum. Displays inside trace the history of radiation and nuclear weapons from the early discoveries of Madame Curie, via newspaper advertisements promoting the health-giving properties of drinking the Radithor brand of radioactive water and a 1953 *Life* magazine cover reading "*WE ARE IN A LIFE AND DEATH BOMB RACE,*" up to modern robotic devices such as the "truck-killing standoff weapon" Fireant.

You'll be soothed to learn how much more precise and sophisticated today's weapons are compared to the "primitive city-busting concepts" of the Cold War era, just how surprisingly safe nuclear waste disposal can be, and a host of other little-known facts.

The Sandia Mountains

The forested 10,500ft peaks of the **Sandia Mountains** tower over Albuquerque to the east; the view from the summit is especially beautiful at and after sunset, when the city lights sparkle below. In summer it's a good 25°F cooler up here than in the valley, while in winter you can go downhill or cross-country **skiing** (mid-Dec to mid-March; lift tickets $33 per day; ☎505/242-9133).

The most exciting way to reach the top is by riding the world's longest tramway, the 2.7-mile **Sandia Peak Aerial Tram**, which departs from the end of Tramway Road a dozen miles northeast of town. During the uppermost 1.5 miles of its exhilarating 15-minute climb, not a single support tower interrupts the progress of the cable car (summer daily 9am–10pm; spring and fall Thurs–Tues 9am–8pm, Wed 5–8pm; winter Mon, Tues, Thurs & Fri 9am–8pm, Wed noon–8pm, Sat & Sun 8.30am–8pm; $15).

If you'd rather **drive** to the top of the mountains, you have to circle around the back and approach from the east, by way of the Turquoise Trail – a route described on p.123.

High Finance, *the restaurant at the top of the tramway, is reviewed on p.181.*

Petroglyph National Monument

Beneath a chain of burned-out cinder cones thrown up by a 150,000-year-old volcanic eruption, a low seventeen-mile escarpment west of the Rio Grande has been designated as the **PETROGLYPH NATIONAL MONUMENT**, to protect its unusually accessible ancient Indian **rock art**. Apart from the spectacular views of the valley and the Sandia Mountains, there's no great need to go to its **visitor center** (daily: summer 9am–6pm; winter 8am–5pm; ☎505/899-0205), reached by crossing the river on I-40 then driving four miles north on Unser Boulevard. Instead, continue to the petroglyphs themselves, another mile north in **Boca Negra Canyon** (same hours; Mon–Fri $1 per vehicle, Sat & Sun $2 per vehicle).

Three short trails off the canyon's one-way loop road lead up to the escarpment, which on close inspection turns out to consist of tumbled black lava boulders; only the half-hour **Mesa Trail** demands any energetic climbing. Most of the crudely scratched images you'll pass, ranging from simple spirals to masked figures and eagles with Bart Simpson hairdos, date from 1300 to 1680 AD. During the eighteenth century, shepherds from the nearby Hispanic settlement of Atrisco added a number of Christian crosses and symbols.

Petroglyph National Monument is currently the focus of intense controversy, thanks to repeated campaigns to allow the construction of a new highway through its heart. City boosters argue that the only direction in which Albuquerque can expand any further is westwards, and that the monument is therefore a crucial obstacle to future progress. The snag is, of course, that the whole point of a national monument is to prevent such development.

Eating

The chefs of Santa Fe may be trying to redefine Southwestern cuisine, but Albuquerque still knows what it likes – mountainous

Mexican meals. This is the place to get to grips with what real New Mexican food is all about, with family diners all over the city competing to create the spiciest *chile rellenos*, enchiladas and *sopaipillas*. If you prefer to stick with the familiar, there are also 25 branches of *McDonald*'s, and a number of gourmet restaurants where prices are generally well below those in Santa Fe.

Budget restaurants and diners

Chef du Jour, 119 San Pasquale St SW; ☎505/247-8998. Sandwiches and inventive light meals in a plain cafe an easy walk from Old Town Plaza, with some outdoor seating. Mon–Thurs 11am–2pm, Fri 11am–2pm & 5.30–8.30pm, Sat 5.30–8.30pm.

Duran Central Pharmacy, 1815 Central Ave NW; ☎505/247-4141. Mexican dining counter attached to a working drugstore, not far from Old Town, with delicious, inexpensive tortillas, enchiladas and plenty of chile. Mon–Fri 9am–6.30pm, Sat 9am–2pm.

Frontier, 2400 Central Ave SE; ☎505/266-0550. Legendary 24-hour diner across from the university, where an unceasing parade of characters chow down on burgers, burritos and great vegetarian enchiladas.

Kanome, 3128 Central Ave NE; ☎505/265-7773. Bright, colorful, modern pan-Asian diner near the University, where few of the Thai, Chinese or Japanese entrees cost over $10. Open for lunch and dinner on weekdays, dinner only on weekends.

La Placita, 208 San Felipe St NW; ☎505/247-2204. Attractive centuries-old adobe hacienda on the Old Town Plaza, where a predominantly tourist crowd enjoy Mexican meals at surprisingly reasonable prices. Open daily 11am–9pm, with live Mexican music most evenings.

M&J Restaurant, 403 Second St SW; ☎505/242-4890. Family-run Mexican diner near the Greyhound station, boasting fresh-made tortillas and *sopaipillas*, blue-corn enchiladas and pork *adovada*. Mon–Fri 9am–4pm.

Pueblo Kitchen, Indian Pueblo Cultural Center, 2401 12th St NW; ☎505/843-7270. Indian fry-bread and other Pueblo specialties, plus good guacamole burgers. Daily 7.30am–3.30pm.

Albuquerque restaurants are marked on the map on p.175.

66 Diner, 1405 Central Ave NE; ☎505/247-1421. Classic Fifties diner near the university, with white-capped waiting staff, a soda fountain and a lively late-night clientele. Lunch and dinner daily, breakfast on weekends only.

Fine dining

Antiquity, 112 Romero St NW; ☎505/247-3545. Old Town cottage turned romantic Mediterranean/New Mexican restaurant, with a changing menu of gourmet dishes at around $20. Dinner only, nightly from 5pm.

Artichoke Cafe, 424 Central Ave SE; ☎505/243-0200. Simple but classy restaurant in the heart of downtown, with indoor and outdoor seating. Good, varied menu of California-influenced modern American cuisine; most entrees well under $20. Open for dinner daily except Sun, lunch on weekdays only.

Conrad's, *La Posada de Albuquerque*, 125 Second St NW; ☎505/242-9090. Classic Thirties ArtDeco hotel diner, modernized and serving excellent Hispanic-influenced dishes, including tasty salads and tapas, plus the signature dish, a superb seafood paella, complete with lobster and saffron rice, at $20 for one person or $34 for two. Open daily for all meals.

High Finance, 40 Tramway Rd NE; ☎505/243-9742. Pricey seafood and steak place in unparalleled location (at the top of the Sandia Peak Tramway – see p.179) with eagle's-eye views of sunset over Albuquerque. Entrees range from $15 to $35. Open daily: summer 4.30–10pm, winter 4.30–8pm.

Monte Vista Fire Station, 3201 Central Ave NE; ☎505/255-2424. Upmarket haunt, housed in one of Nob Hill's unlikeliest buildings – a restored ArtDeco Pueblo Revival fire station. The menu concentrates on a different themed cuisine each month, but in principle you can expect fancy grilled meats and fish at under $20 per entree, with specialties like crab cakes and even ostrich fajitas. Dinner nightly, lunch on weekdays only.

Coffeehouses

Double Rainbow, 3416 Central Ave SE; ☎505/255-6633. Nob Hill coffee bar, with indoor/outdoor seating, a lively student clientele, a stupendous array of breads and pastries, full cooked breakfasts, and a huge stock of magazines. Daily 6.30am–midnight.

Gold Street Caffé, 218 Gold Ave SW; ☎505/765-1633. Oddly formal downtown espresso cafe, offering "a unique coffee experience" and wonderful pastries. Tues–Fri 7am–2pm, Sat & Sun 8am–2pm.

Zane Graze, 308 San Felipe NW; ☎505/243-4377. Old Town coffee bar, open for breakfast and lunch daily, with salads and desserts as well as espressos.

Drinking and nightlife

Most of Albuquerque's best **nightclubs**, theaters and music venues are concentrated within a couple of blocks along Central Avenue downtown; the recently restored **KiMo Theater** in particular should not be missed. There are also a few **brewpubs** around, while oddly enough, many of the larger chain hotels hold reasonable **bars**. Two free magazines, the weekly *Alibi* and the monthly *On The Scene*, can tell you everything you need to know about what's coming up or going down.

Assets Grille & Brewing Company, 6910 Montgomery Blvd NE at San Pedro; ☎505/889-6400. Lively microbrewery with indoor and outdoor seating – the latter overlooked by a giant steel vat – plus Italian food. Dinner nightly, lunch daily except Sun.

Brewster's Pub, 312 Central Ave SW; ☎505/247-2533. Raucous downtown bar, where on any night except Monday – reserved for football – you've a good chance of hearing live jazz or blues.

Caravan East, 7605 Central Ave NE; ☎505/265-7877. Enormous honky-tonk, where tenderfeet can do the two-step with throngs of urban cowboys.

Club Rhythm and Blues, 3523 Central Ave NE; ☎505/256-0849. Upmarket University District bar that plays host to swing and jazz bands as well as blues. Closed Sun.

Club 211, 211 Gold Ave SE; ☎505/766-9601. Extravagant, outrageous downtown dance club.

El Rey Theater, 620 Central Ave SW; ☎505/243-7546. Live music from salsa to country, and all points in between.

Further fine dining options within easy reach of Albuquerque include the Range Cafe and Prairie Star in Bernalillo; see p.122.

Golden West Saloon, 620 Central Ave SW; ☎505/764-2624. The venue of choice for Albuquerque's metal maniacs, and host to touring indie bands.

KiMo Theater, 423 Central Ave NW; ☎505/848-1370. Gorgeous city-owned "Pueblo Deco" theater, dating from the late 1920s, which puts on an eclectic program of opera, dance and theater performances, kids' movie shows, and also regular live bands.

The Launchpad, 618 Central Ave SW; ☎505/764-8887. Dance and live music space that showcases touring indie bands and also has a cluster of pool tables.

University Draft House, 318 Central Ave SW; ☎505/843-7078. Hectic no-cover downtown bar, always packed with students, open Tues–Sat until 2am.

East of Albuquerque

The first twenty miles of I-40's eastward run from Albuquerque are deceptively scenic, as the interstate threads its way between the Sandia Mountains. Once through the hills, however, unless you then turn north onto the **Turquoise Trail** towards Santa Fe – see p.123 – you're in for a long hard slog out into the plains. The only place before Texas which might conceivably pique your curiosity is **Fort Sumner**, which played a heartrending role in Navajo history and also holds the grave of **Billy the Kid**.

Santa Rosa

A hundred unutterably boring miles east of the Sandia Mountains, weary drivers reach their first potential overnight stop. South and west of the interstate, a four-mile stretch of the former Route 66 runs through **SANTA ROSA**. As **Parker Avenue** in the small downtown, and **Will Rogers Drive** further east, it's dotted with diners and motels, but there's nothing worth going out of your way to see. **Scuba-divers** desperate for a desert dip cross the plains to plunge into Santa Rosa's **Blue Hole**, a crystal-clear natural pool that's sixty feet across and eighty feet deep, though to anyone who's seen the ocean it may come as an anticlimax. You'll find it by turning left off Fifth Street, south of the main drag, onto Blue Hole Road.

In 1541, the first Spanish expedition into the Southwest is said to have crossed the Pecos River at **Coronado's Bridge**, ten miles south of Santa Rosa on the dead-end Hwy-91. Following the lush river-banks makes a welcome break from the interstate, and the village of **PUERTO DE LUNA** at road's end is pretty enough, but of the bridge itself not a trace remains.

Practicalities

Santa Rosa's **visitor center** is at 486 Parker Ave (Mon–Fri 9am–5pm, Sat 9am–1pm; ☎505/472-3763 or 1-800/450-7084). Of its dozen or so **motels**, the *Super 8*, 1201 Will Rogers Drive (☎505/472-5388 or 1-800/800-8000; winter ②, summer ③) is large, clean and comfortable, while the *Sun'n'Sand*, 1120 Will Rogers Drive (☎505/472-5268; ②), is cheaper and has its own predictable but reasonable diner next door. The best place to **camp** is in the Santa Rosa Lake State Park, seven miles north of town on Hwy-91 (☎505/472-3110; $7).

Santa Rosa's zip code is NM 88435.

The *Lake City Diner*, downtown at 101 Fourth St (☎505/472-5253), is a spotless cafe straight out of a Norman Rockwell painting. Housed in a converted bank, and run by a dynamic young man enthused by a year in Barcelona, Spain, it serves an enticing menu of sandwiches, daily specials, Coca Cola cake and espresso coffees.

Tucumcari

Sixty miles east of Santa Rosa, **TUCUMCARI** is the definitive Route 66 pit-stop. If you expect its abundant truck stops, diners, and motels to yield a kitsch fascination, you'll be sorely disappointed, but their glittering neon signs make a welcome sight as dusk descends on the plains. No one in their right mind stays two nights in Tucumcari; an hour spent admiring the barbed-wire collection of the **Tucumcari Historical Museum**, 416 S Adams St (June–Aug Mon–Sat 9am–6pm, Sun 1–6pm; Sept–May Tues–Sat 9am–5pm, Sun 1–5pm; $2), should convince you it's time to hit the road again.

Practicalities

Tucumcari Boulevard cuts a broad five-mile swath through town, passing 34 motels along the way, as well as the local **visitor center** at 404 W (Mon–Fri 8am–noon & 1–5pm; ☎505/461-1694). Among the more salubrious places with **rooms** for well under $30 are the *Palomino*, 1215 E (☎505/461-3622; ①), and the *Blue Swallow*, 815 E (☎505/461-9849; ①). Classier options include the *Super 8*, 4001 E (☎505/461-4444 or 1-800/800-8000; ②), and the more central *Rodeway Inn East*, 1023 E (☎505/461-0360; ②).

Tucumcari's zip code is NM 88401.

More fun than the plentiful highway fast-food outlets is the *Big Dipper*, an old-fashioned diner and soda-fountain in the heart of the old downtown at 101 Second at Main (☎505/461-4430). A popular local rendezvous, it opens daily around 9am.

Fort Sumner

A 45-mile detour south of I-40 between Santa Rosa and Tucumcari brings you to modern **FORT SUMNER**, a small town named after a nineteenth-century Army outpost that stood seven miles southeast, on what's now **Fort Sumner State Monument** (daily 8.30am–5pm; $1). The fort was infamous as the headquarters of the **Bosque Redondo Indian Reservation**, where nine thousand Navajo and Mescalero Apache captives were incarcerated during the 1860s (see p.539). The idea was for the reservation to be self-sufficient, and for the Indians to become accustomed to an agricultural lifestyle. In fact,

East of Albuquerque

the Pecos River proved too salty to drink, let alone use for irrigation. Over three thousand prisoners died before the experiment was abandoned in 1868, and the survivors were allowed to return home. In the words of Navajo headman Barboncito:

> *Whatever we do here causes death. Some work at the acequias, take sick and die; others die with the hoe in their hands; they go to the river to their waists and suddenly disappear; others have been struck and torn to pieces by lightning. A rattlesnake bite here kills us; in our country a rattlesnake before he bites gives warning which enables us to keep out of its way and if bitten, we readily find a cure – here we can find no cure.*

A low ridge of adobe bricks on the eastern riverbank is all that remains of the fort the Navajo built for their captors, while the dead are honored by a brass plaque nearby inscribed in Navajo.

After the reservation closed down, the fort and the surrounding land was bought by rancher Lucien Maxwell. **Billy the Kid** was hiding in his son Peter's bedroom here in 1881 when **Pat Garrett** tracked him down and shot him dead. His **grave** is located in the backyard of the **Old Fort Sumner Museum**, a few hundred yards east of the fort (daily 9am–5pm; $3). Billy was buried alongside two fellow outlaws Tom O'Folliard and Charlie Bowdre; all remain imprisoned to this day, as their joint tombstone, poignantly inscribed "*PALS*," is protected from would-be thieves behind steel bars. The museum itself holds a jumble of items that may or may not have belonged to Billy, together with displays relating to local history. In that respect, it's indistinguishable from the rival **Billy the Kid Museum**, back in town at 1601 E Sumner Ave (mid-May to mid-Sept daily 8.30am–5pm; mid-Sept to mid-May Mon–Fri 8.30am–5pm, Sun 11am–5pm; $4).

For the full saga of Billy the Kid, see box p.188.

Practicalities

If you're trapped by a desert thunderstorm, you might choose to shelter in one of Fort Sumner's two rudimentary **motels** – the *Oasis*, 1704 E Sumner Ave (☎505/355-7414; ①), or the *Coronado*, 309 W Sumner Ave (☎505/355-2466; ①). Later on, you'd probably end up eating a cheap Mexican **meal** at the *Rodeo Cafe*, 112 E Sumner Ave (☎505/355-9986).

Clovis

The mid-sized railroad and ranching community of **CLOVIS**, on the border with Texas sixty miles east of Fort Sumner and 85 miles southeast of Tucumcari, has twice entered the history books. In 1932, the remains of prehistoric mammoth hunters found at nearby **Blackwater Draw** provided the first firm evidence that humans were present in North America as much as twelve thousand years ago. Although archeologically speaking it was a sensational discovery, the

Blackwater Draw Museum, en route to **PORTALES** a dozen miles southwest of town on US-70 (summer Mon–Sat 10am–5pm, Sun noon–5pm; winter closed Mon; $2), is not wildly exciting. The excavation site, ten miles east on Hwy-467, is open to visitors in summer (same hours and ticket).

Clovis' other brush with fame came in 1958, when a bespectacled teenager, **Charles "Buddy" Holly**, crossed the state line from Lubbock, Texas, to record a few tunes with his band, the Crickets – *Peggy Sue, That'll Be the Day* and a dozen others. Call the visitor center in advance (see below), to arrange a tour of Norman Petty's original **studio** – which also gave Roy Orbison his first break – at 1313 W Seventh St.

Practicalities

Clovis' **visitor center** is downtown at 215 N Main St (Mon–Fri 9am–5pm; ☎505/763-3435), near the huge, derelict old *Hotel Clovis*. **Motels** interspersed between the Mexican diners and fast-food specialists along US-60/84 further east include the *Days Inn*, 1720 Mabry Drive (☎505/762-2971; ②), and the *Clovis Inn*, 2922 Mabry Drive (☎505/762-5600; ②).

Southeast of Albuquerque

While the Rio Grande Valley, south of Albuquerque – and covered on p.202 onwards – has always held a larger human population, the terrain that lies **southeast** of the city is of far greater scenic and historic appeal. Here you'll find the ancient pueblos of **Salinas National Monument**, the eerie gypsum wastelands of **White Sands**, and the mountain resorts of **Ruidoso** and **Cloudcroft**. Most compelling of all, however, is the rough-hewn frontier town of **Lincoln**. Scene of the bloodiest exploits in the saga of **Billy the Kid**, it has remained all but untouched in the century since his death.

Salinas National Monument

The precious salt deposits of **Salinas Valley**, east of the Manzano Mountains around seventy miles southeast of Albuquerque, were regarded by early Spanish colonists as one of New Mexico's greatest treasures. Franciscan missionaries targeted the Pueblo peoples of the valley, erecting massive churches atop their existing settlements, but thanks to epidemics and Apache raids, the entire region had been abandoned by the time of the Pueblo Revolt of 1680. Three separate ruined pueblos now form **SALINAS NATIONAL MONUMENT**. Each has its own "contact station" (all daily 9am–5pm; free), and they share a **visitor center** (daily 8am–5pm; free; ☎505/847-2585) in **MOUNTAINAIR**, 36 miles

*Visiting Gran
Quivira in
1598, Juan de
Oñate reported
that its inhabi-
tants painted
stripes on their
noses.*

east of I-25 on US-60. Mountainair itself is a small community whose one claim to fame is that fifty years ago it was the "Pinto Bean Capital of the World."

The largest of the Salinas pueblos, **Gran Quivira**, stands on a low hill 26 miles south from Mountainair along Hwy-55. It's the only one where the pueblo itself has been more than minimally excavated, to reveal an impressive 300-room structure complete with hidden *kivas*, built in secret to avoid the wrath of the Spanish priests. The adjoining Mission of San Buenaventura church was probably not yet completed by the time the pueblo was abandoned.

The main feature of **Quarai**, a mile west of Hwy-55 eight miles north of Mountainair, is the fortress-like stone church of La Purísima Concepción, whose golden walls tower above the rubble-strewn mounds that conceal the pueblo village. At **Abó**, just north of US-60 nine miles west of Mountainair, the church of San Gregorio dominates an even more tantalizing expanse of ruins.

Carrizozo and the Valley of Fires

Fifty miles southeast of Gran Quivira, where US-54 meets US-380, **CARRIZOZO** is a parched desert outpost that replaced better-known Lincoln as the seat of Lincoln County in 1909. Apart from a couple of **motels** – the *Four Winds*, at the crossroads (☎505/648-2356; ②), has its own restaurant – there's nothing much to it.

The **Valley of Fires Recreation Area**, four miles northwest (daily dawn–dusk; $6; ☎505/648-2241), preserves a jet-black river of lava that poured for over forty miles down the Tularosa Valley around 1500 years ago. Though it ranges from four to six miles wide, and up to 150 feet deep, the one trail across the lava is less than a mile long. It's so rough underfoot, and so exposed to the sun, that you're unlikely to want to hike any further, but there's a good **campground** alongside ($8).

*At its southern
end, the lava
flow abuts the
utterly con-
trasting White
Sands National
Monument; see
p.195.*

Three Rivers Petroglyphs

Five miles east of US-54, halfway from Carrizozo to Alamogordo, an extensive if not wildly enthralling collection of pre-Columbian **rock art** now forms the **Three Rivers Petroglyph National Recreation Area** (daily dawn–dusk; $3). Between 1000 and 1400 AD, agricultural Mogollon villagers hacked over twenty thousand petroglyphs into boulders at the foot of the Capitan Mountains, depicting bighorn sheep, stylized masks and geometric patterns. A representative sample can be admired from a half-mile trail, while a separate, easier trail leads to the remains of three Mogollon dwellings. This area once belonged to Susan Barber, "Cattle Queen of New Mexico" and widow of Alexander McSween, killed in the Lincoln County War (see box p.188). She's said to have "rode as hard and shot as straight as any man."

Trinity Site

Twice each year, sightseers make a peculiar pilgrimage to the **Trinity Site**, out on the **White Sands Missile Range** in the desert thirty miles west of Carrizozo, where the first **atomic bomb** was detonated at 5.30am on July 16, 1945. Brought by road from Los Alamos (see p.126), in the back of a '42 Plymouth, the bomb, code-named **Fat Man**, was not dropped, but placed atop a steel tower. As well as destroying a nearby "doom town" built to study its effects, the blast was strong enough to shatter windows in Silver City, 120 miles west, and to fuse the sands below "Ground Zero" into a thick slab of radioactive green glass known as **trinitite**. It made a crater that was eight feet deep, which was subsequently filled in to minimize radiation.

The Missile Range has witnessed thousands more weapons tests since then, and remains off limits to non-military personnel except for the first Saturdays of April and October. Visitors on those days can either join a "caravan" of vehicles that sets off from **Alamogordo** at 8am, or enter the range unaccompanied via the **Stallion Gate** (9am–2pm), on US-380 fifty miles west of Carrizozo. You're forbidden to stop or take photos other than at the site itself, or to make political speeches, and encouraged to resist the temptation to pick up any trinitite you may spot. Not only is it part of a National Historic Landmark, it's radioactive.

For full tour information, contact Alamogordo's visitor center. If you'd like to know more about the range itself, drop in at the White Sands Missile Range Museum, described on p.196.

The closest lodging is in one of New Mexico's few budget **hostels**, in **OSCURO**, a dozen miles north on US-54. The *High Desert Hostel Ranch* (PO Box 798, Carrizozo, NM 88301; ☎505/648-4007; *oscuro@nm.net*; ①), has $14 dorm beds and $27 private rooms. Its friendly owners run local tours, and offer a weekly shuttle service to their *Route 66 Hostel* in Albuquerque.

Capitan

A twenty-mile drive up into the mountains east of Carrizozo brings you to the crossroads known as **CAPITAN**, and notable only as the birthplace of a little bear named **Smokey**. Rescued from a forest fire in 1950, the five-month-old Smokey was taken to the National Zoo in Washington DC, where he survived another 26 years. His words of wisdom, seen on anti-fire billboards across the country – "Only YOU Can Prevent Forest Fires" – live on. Smokey's grave is the centerpiece of **Smokey Bear Historical State Park**, which also features exhibits on his life, and a short nature trail (daily 9am–5pm; 50¢).

Capitan is plagued by a running feud between people who say "Smokey Bear" (good), and wilful misfits who insist on "Smokey the Bear" (bad).

Capitan's adobe *Hotel Chango* has no guestrooms; it's a top-class **restaurant**, serving a changing menu of gourmet Southwestern delicacies amid an eclectic collection of folk art (Tues–Sat, dinner only; ☎505/354-4213). The small *Smokey Bear Motel* (☎505/354-2253; ②), does however offer basic **accommodation** near the park.

Lincoln

Though not strictly speaking a ghost town, tiny **LINCOLN**, twelve
miles east of Capitan on Hwy-380, is as perfectly preserved a Wild-
West settlement as it's possible to imagine. During the late nineteenth century, as a cattle-ranching center and the site of the Army
outpost of **Fort Stanton**, it was home to around 750 people, including the legendary Billy the Kid. Bypassed by the railroads, however,
it lost its role as seat of Lincoln County to Carrizozo in 1909; the pop-

---

Billy the Kid and the Lincoln County War

The Hispanic farming community of Las Placitas del Río Bonito, founded
during the 1850s, was renamed **Lincoln** in 1869. It became the seat of
Lincoln County, which occupied a quarter of New Mexico – itself much
larger than it is today – and was, at 27,000 square miles, the largest
county in the United States. At that time, rival Anglo ranchers and their
political allies were competing for economic control throughout the Wild
West. What some historians call the **Western Civil War of
Incorporation** pitted large cattle-raising conglomerates, federal lawmen
and Republican capitalists against small-scale Democrat ranchers and
cowboys. Such tensions were everywhere exacerbated by individual
antagonisms; Tombstone's **Gunfight at the OK Corral** is a classic example (see p.188).

Lincoln in the 1870s was dominated by a "ring" of men that centered on
the mercantile (store) of **Lawrence G. Murphy**, an Irish former theology
student (and an alcoholic) whose business affairs were run by **James J.
Dolan**. Their racketeering included rustling cattle from local rancher,
John Chisum, to supply beef at knock-down prices to the US Army at
nearby Fort Stanton. The arrival of a wealthy 23-year-old Englishman,
John Tunstall, who opened a rival mercantile in Lincoln with lawyer
Alexander McSween, triggered the **Lincoln County War**.

On February 18, 1878, Tunstall was murdered on the road to Ruidoso
by a posse of Dolan's men. Among Tunstall's hired hands who witnessed
the slaying was the gunslinger history remembers as **Billy the Kid**. Born
Henry McCarty in Brooklyn in late 1859, he had been brought west by his
mother, who married William Antrim in Santa Fe in 1873. Within a year,
she had died in Silver City, and young Billy Antrim was cast adrift. A life of
petty teenage crime culminated with the shooting in August 1877 of a bul-
lying Irish blacksmith in Fort Grant, Arizona. Now calling himself **Billy
Bonney**, the fledgling outlaw fled to Lincoln.

After Tunstall's death, his men formed the **Regulators**, and were dep-
utized by the local justice of the peace to seek out his killers. Ten of
them, including Billy, killed the two chief culprits in March, then gunned
down **Sheriff William Brady**, a Dolan man, on Lincoln's main street on
April 1. That July, forty of Dolan's supporters laid siege to the
Regulators in the adobe home of Alexander McSween; after five days,
they summoned soldiers from Fort Stanton, who trained a Gatling gun on
the house and set it ablaze. McSween and three Regulators were killed
trying to escape the flames, but Billy and around ten others sprinted to
safety.

---

ulation soon dwindled to well under a hundred, and time seems to have stood still ever since. No new buildings have joined the venerable false-front structures that line Main Street, and the entire town is now **Lincoln State Monument**. Visitors can stroll its length at any time, while admission to its various historical sites is via a joint ticket sold at each (all open daily 8.30am–5pm; $5; ☎505/653-4372).

The **Lincoln County Historical Center**, towards the east end of town, is the most modern museum, and its short opening video makes a good introduction to Lincoln's complicated story. After

---

Billy spent two years on the run, mostly rustling cattle near Fort Sumner, where he also dealt cards in the saloon of Texan buffalo hunter **Pat Garrett**. In 1880, New Mexico's governor **Lew Wallace** offered an amnesty to all participants in the Lincoln County War who would testify against Dolan. Billy accepted the deal and surrendered, only to escape when he realized that Wallace – then busy writing *Ben Hur* – was not going to keep his word. Later that year, Pat Garrett was elected as sheriff of Lincoln County, on a pledge to recapture Billy (who naturally lobbied for his opponent). Garrett knew exactly where to look. Just before Christmas, after ambushing and killing two of Billy's friends at Fort Sumner, he duly captured Billy himself at nearby Stinking Springs. Reporting his arrest, the *Las Vegas Gazette* made the first-ever reference to "Billy the Kid."

Billy was taken by train to Santa Fe and on to **Mesilla** (see p.205), where he was convicted of Sheriff Brady's murder in the only successful prosecution relating to the Lincoln County War. As he awaited the hangman's noose in Lincoln's courthouse – which ironically was the former Murphy store, its owner James Dolan having by now taken over the Tunstall mercantile down the street – Billy committed his most daring **escape**, on April 28, 1881. Taking advantage of a trip to the outhouse, he shot Deputy J.W. Bell with his own gun. Meanwhile, Marshal Bob Olinger, a long-time Dolan ally, was having lunch with a group of prisoners in the *Wortley Hotel*. Hearing the shots, he raced across the street, to be felled by a blast from an upper window. Eyewitness accounts relate how Billy struggled unsuccessfully for an hour to break his shackles, and repeatedly fell off the horse he was attempting to commandeer, watched all the while by a crowd of onlookers who dared not intervene.

With a $500 reward on his head, Billy fled back to Fort Sumner. Late on the night of July 14, Pat Garrett crept into Pete Maxwell's bedroom to ask if he had seen his friend Billy. Moments earlier, Billy had climbed through the window to find out if Maxwell knew Garrett's whereabouts. Garrett recognized the voice that called "*quien es?*" (who's there?), and shot him dead.

The next year, Garrett wrote a bestseller, *The Authentic Life of Billy The Kid, the Noted Desperado of the Southwest*. He was not reelected as sheriff, however, and embarked on a life of wandering that saw him ranching in Texas, a guest of Theodore Roosevelt at the White House, and a customs collector in El Paso, before he was eventually murdered for no apparent reason near Las Cruces in 1908. Strangely enough, the man who shot him, William Brazel, was the uncle of the main "witness" of the Roswell UFO crash in 1947 (see p.196).

---

displays covering Hispanics, cowboys, "Buffalo Soldiers" – the black cavalrymen stationed at Fort Stanton – and Apaches, the museum moves on to the Lincoln County War. Prize exhibits include Billy the Kid's knife, holster and what may have been his gun, as well as the coroner's handwritten report on the men shot during his April 1881 escape. Movie posters celebrate celluloid Billies such as Paul Newman, Kris Kristofferson and Val Kilmer, and the museum store has a fun selection of Western souvenirs.

Alongside the museum stands Lincoln's oldest building, the **Torréon**. This circular masonry tower may resemble the handiwork of Ancestral Puebloans, but was in fact erected by Hispanic settlers during the 1850s, as a refuge against Apache raids. It's too small to admit visitors; a glance from the street makes it easy to imagine quite how cramped and airless it must have been, and speaks volumes about the miserable, unglamorous reality of frontier life.

A few yards further west, the **Tunstall Store** is an extraordinary time capsule. The "mercantile" over which the Lincoln County War was fought – and which passed from the Tunstall to the Dolan factions as a result – must have failed to sell a single item in the ensuing century. It remains stocked with dusty date-expired groceries, plus Victorian storekeeping paraphernalia like weighing scales and cash registers, cases of photos and artifacts, and even Lincoln County's first-ever light bulb, installed in 1914 and allegedly still capable of burning. The wounded Billy the Kid is said to have hidden beneath the floorboards after shooting Sheriff William Brady on the street outside, on April 1, 1878.

After Dolan took over Tunstall's operation, L.G. Murphy's original store, across the road and a hundred yards west, became the **Lincoln County Courthouse**, and served as Billy's prison when he was brought back from Mesilla to be hanged. It's hardly surprising that Billy felt he was being railroaded, as evidenced by his increasingly bitter letters to Governor Lew Wallace, displayed downstairs. A bullethole at the foot of the stairs shows where he shot Deputy Bell during his famous escape, while you can stand at the upstairs window through which he then shot Marshal Olinger. Stones in the garden mark where the two men died. That the Courthouse is now so old and musty merely adds to the atmosphere of it all.

Practicalities

Lincoln doesn't have its own visitor center; call the monument offices for general information. On the first weekend of August, the town fills up, and its streets echo with gunfire once again, during the three-day **Old Lincoln Days** festival.

Near the courthouse, the *Wortley Hotel* – once owned by Pat Garrett – had to be rebuilt to its original appearance following a fire in the 1930s (PO Box 96; ☎505/653-4300; ④). It now offers eight plain but appealing hotel rooms, furnished with functional rather

Lincoln's zip code is NM 88338.

than twee Victorian antiques, and its dining room serves simple stews and sandwiches at lunchtime only. If you like a bit more comfort, head to the *Casa de Patrón* (PO Box 27; ☎505/653-4676 or 1-800/524-5202, fax 505/653-4671; *www.casapatron.com*; ④–⑥), another former store and hideout of Billy the Kid that's now a friendly, romantic B&B, with three en-suite rooms in an 1860 house, two more in a modern annex, and a couple of individual *casitas*.

Ruidoso

For visitors from the flatlands of West Texas and Oklahoma – not to mention valley towns like Alamogordo – the hilltop community of **RUIDOSO**, nestling at an altitude of almost 7000 feet amid the forested Sacramento Mountains thirty miles southwest of Lincoln, offers an enticing weekend retreat from the heat of summer. As a result, it's the fastest-growing resort in the Southwest, with motels and mountain lodges lining several miles of the Ruidoso ("Noisy") River. Tourists from further afield, however, may well find it lacking in interest, though it makes a reasonable overnight stop en route to Carlsbad.

Ruidoso's major claim to fame is the **All-American Futurity**, which was, until the 1980s, the world's richest **horse race** of any kind, and with prize money totalling over $2.5 million remains the highest-paying event for quarter horses. The race takes place each Labor Day at the **Ruidoso Downs** racetrack, just east of town, as the climax of a 77-day season that runs from early May.

Quarter horses are the world's most popular breed, and are so called because they excel at quarter-mile races.

All matters equine are celebrated in the **Museum of the Horse**, alongside the racetrack (daily: May to Labor Day 9am–5.30pm; Labor Day to April 10am–5pm; $5). Displays on the natural and human-related history of horses plot their arrival in North America – which was really a return, as horses had become extinct on the continent around 7000 BC – and there's a selection of memorabilia from around the world, such as horse-drawn Russian sleighs, English road coaches and Wild West stagecoaches. By the time you reach "Anne's Attic," holding collector Anne Stradling's riding trophies and copies of *Black Beauty*, it's all getting a bit sickly, while the huge statue that stands outside – *Free Spirits of Noisy Water*, portraying eight lifesize horses – is too sentimental for words.

In winter, attention turns to the 12,000ft slopes of **Ski Apache** (☎505/336-4356), a downhill ski area northwest of town where lift tickets cost around $40 per day. Though operated by the Mescalero Apache, it's not on tribal land – they bought it as a going concern.

Practicalities

Brochures from Ruidoso's **visitor center**, 720 Sudderth Ave (Mon–Sat 9am–5pm, Sun 1–4pm; ☎505/257-7395 or 1-800/253-2255; *www.ruidoso.net*), list dozens of **motels**, but supply still fails to meet demand on big race days. Among inexpensive options are the

Southeast of
Albuquerque

Ruidoso's zip
code is NM
88355.

Apache Motel, 344 Sudderth Ave (☎505/257-2986 or 1-800/426-0616; *apache@lookingglass.net*; ②), and the *Super 8*, beside US-70 at 100 Cliff Drive (☎505/378-8180 or 1-800/800-8000; ②), which has separate male and female saunas. **B&Bs** in the immediate vicinity include the welcoming *Sierra Mesa Lodge*, ten miles north near the ski area at Fort Stanton Road in the village of Alto (PO Box 463, Alto, NM 88312; ☎505/336-4515; ⑥).

The real local showpiece, however, is the glitzy *Inn of the Mountain Gods*, three miles southwest of town on Carrizo Canyon Road (PO Box 269, Mescalero, NM 88340; ☎505/257-5141 or 1-800/545-9011, fax 505/257-6173; winter ⑤, summer ⑥). Owned and run by the Mescalero Apache, and overlooking a lovely large lake, it offers ski packages, gambling in the **Casino Apache**, golf, fishing, tennis and horse riding. The excellent *Dan Li Ka* ("good food") **restaurant** serves steak and seafood entrees for under $20, and nightly specials with a more thoroughly Southwestern (read hot) twist.

Other dining possibilities range from the classy French cuisine of *La Lorraine*, 2523 Sudderth Ave (closed Sun; ☎505/257-2954), to the steaks at the *Inncredible*, near Ski Apache on Hwy-48 in Alto (☎505/336-4312) and the wholesome snacks at the *Hummingbird Tearoom*, in the Village Plaza at 2306 Sudderth Drive (lunch only, closed Sun; ☎505/257-2100).

Mescalero Apache Indian Reservation

Immediately south of Ruidoso, US-70 runs for around fifteen miles through the highlands of the **Mescalero Apache Indian Reservation**. The Mescalero trace their history as a distinct Apache group back to the early eighteenth century, when like the Jicarilla of northern New Mexico (see p.163), they were driven from the plains by the Comanche and turned to a lifestyle partly of farming and partly of raiding Pueblo and Hispanic settlements. After being rounded up by Kit Carson in 1862 and confined with the Navajo at Fort Sumner (see p.183), they were granted this small reservation in 1872, which was too high to grow or gather many of their traditional foods. The Mescalero were later joined by other Apache refugees, such as those remnants of Geronimo's Chiricahua who chose to return to the Southwest in 1913 from their enforced exile in Oklahoma.

Thanks both to their successful investment in Ski Apache, and latterly the revenues from gaming at the *Inn of the Mountain Gods* (see above), the Mescalero's tribal economy has greatly strengthened in recent years. Tourists don't get to see much from the highway, while most of the roads leading off it are barred to outsiders. It's well worth driving through the open range country between Ruidoso and Cloudcroft, however, where wildflowers dot the quasi-alpine meadows and Apache cowboys gallop in pursuit of their errant cattle.

Cloudcroft

Much smaller and cozier than Ruidoso, the picturesque mountain village of **CLOUDCROFT** – forty miles further south, and almost two
thousand feet higher – has been a vacation resort from the word go.
It was built in 1898, after a railroad spur was pushed up into the
Sacramento Mountains in order to carry mountain timbers down to
El Paso, and immediately began to attract day-trippers from the
sweltering valley below. These days, the railroad has gone, so drivers
who have never rounded a curve in their lives now twist their wary
way up US-82 from Alamogordo, leaving behind the bare sandstone
hills, scattered with creosote bushes, as they penetrate the forested
uplands.

Though it lacks any great history or significance, Cloudcroft itself
is a pretty little Western community that makes a nice enough place
in which to while away an afternoon. The souvenir stores and cafes
that line the boardwalk of **Burro Avenue**, one block north of the
highway, do seem to be getting that bit more twee with each year that
passes, however, and you may well enjoy your visit more if you do a
little **hiking** as well. Cloudcroft stands at the heart of the southern
segment of the Lincoln National Forest, which features maintained
and waymarked trails of varying lengths. Starting near the west end
of town, the **Cloud Climbing Rail Trail** follows the old railroad route
for a mile down to a vast ruined trestle which drivers on US-82 may
have already noticed. Spectacular views extend right across the valley; it's usually possible to glimpse the White Sands (see p.195), in
the form of the thin white line at the foot of the San Andres
Mountains on the far side.

Practicalities

Cloudcroft's **visitor center** is housed in a log cabin beside US-82 on
the eastern approaches to town (daily 10am–5pm; ☎505/682-2733;
www.cloudcroft.net); for information on this section of Lincoln
National Forest, you can also call in at the local ranger station on
Chipmunk Avenue (summer Mon–Fri 8am–5pm, closed winter;
☎505/682-2251). The rangers are also responsible for several
nearby **campgrounds**; the closest to town, about a mile northeast of
the center along Hwy-244, is *The Pines* ($7; mid-May to mid-Sept;
☎505/682-2551).

Most of the visitors who come to Cloudcroft are here to experience
the mountains, and thus choose to rent their own individual **cabin** in
one of the many such complexes. Usually rented for a minimum of two
nights, the cabins always have heating and en-suite facilities, while
many also offer kitchenettes or extra bedrooms. *Buckhorn Cabins*
(PO Box 276; ☎505/682-2421; ②–⑤) is on the highway in the town
center – and has a sideline in selling large carved wooden bears – while
Spruce Cabins (PO Box 315; ☎505/682-2381; ③–⑤), and *Tall
Timber Cabins* (PO Box 402; ☎505/682-2301 or 1-888/682-2301;

③–⑤) are tucked up in the hills further east. The *Aspen Motel* (☎505/682-2526; ③), on the main road at the east end of town, provides more conventional accommodation.

South of the highway, a mile up Hwy-130, *The Lodge at Cloudcroft* (PO Box 497; ☎505/682-2566 or 1-800/395-6343, fax 505/682-2715; ④–⑨) ranks among the Southwest's most prestigious historic hotels. As well as surprisingly well-priced B&B rooms, it features some absurdly plush suites and private cottages, and is home to *Rebecca's*, an attractive continental restaurant with panoramic views. The choice of restaurants in town is more limited, with the *Western Cafe* on Burro Avenue (☎505/682-2445) as the best alternative to the fast-food outlets on the highway.

Cloudcroft's zip code is NM 88317.

Alamogordo

ALAMOGORDO, sprawled at the foot of the Sacramento Mountains seventy miles northeast of Las Cruces, is like Los Alamos a child of the Bomb. Once a quiet ranching center, it has grown since World War II to a town of thirty thousand inhabitants, most of whom owe their living to the various military bases and research facilities tucked away in the surrounding deserts. Its original central streets remain oddly atmospheric, but they're now a neglected backwater compared to the frenzy of commercial activity along the five-mile strip of US-54, here known as White Sands Boulevard.

Given pride of place at the Alamogordo Museum, 1301 N White Sands Blvd (Mon–Sat 10am–4pm; free), an old electric toaster from *Howards Cafe* bears witness to quite how little ever happens round these parts. Other exhibits include a headdress worn by Geronimo, and the stuffed head of a grizzly bear.

Any five-story building in Alamogordo would probably be a tourist attraction; that the gleaming glass cube on the hillside east of town holds the International Space Hall of Fame is gilding the lily (daily: summer 9am–6pm; winter 9am–5pm; museum $2.50, movie theater $5.50 or $9 for two shows). Displays inside trace the history of rocketry from eleventh-century China onwards, covering New Mexico-based pioneers Robert Goddard (see p.197) and Wernher von Braun (see p.196) – one snap of von Braun's cheery crew sitting astride a V-2 rocket is straight out of *Dr Strangelove* – up to the futuristic Delta Clipper, designed to replace the Space Shuttle and offer the first commercial space flights. A diorama depicts the unfortunate Ham, who became the first chimp in space in 1961, and was trained at Alamogordo by receiving electric shocks or banana-flavored pellets according to which lever he moved. There's also a mock-up Martian landscape – not something it's all that hard to create in New Mexico. The adjoining Clyde W. Tombaugh Omnimax Theater shows giant-screen movies and doubles as a state-of-the-art planetarium, and there's a "garden" of abandoned rockets outside.

Practicalities

Alamogordo's **visitor center** is alongside the local museum at 1301 N White Sands Blvd (summer Mon–Sat 8.30am–5pm, Sun 1–5pm; winter Mon–Fri 8.30am–5pm, Sat 9am–3pm; ☎505/437-6120 or 1-800/826-0294 in NM, 1-800/545-4021 elsewhere; *www.alamogordo.com*). **Motels** along US-54 range from the *Super 8*, north of town at 3204 N White Sands Blvd (☎505/434-4205 or 1-800/800-8000; ②), and directly opposite the huge White Sands Mall (and movie theater), to the large, low, stylish *Holiday Inn*, to the south at 1401 S White Sands Blvd (☎505/437-7100 or 1-800/465-4329; ④).

As for **food**, *Keg's Brewery*, a mile west of the highway at 817 Scenic Drive (☎505/437-9564), is a Fifties-themed diner that has successfully reinvented itself as a microbrewery while still serving good meals. If a snack will do, head for *Hatsue's Japanese Kitchen*, downtown at 804 New York Ave (☎505/437-2323), which sells simple soup and noodle dishes, but not sushi.

White Sands National Monument

The glistening, three-story dunes of **White Sands** fill 275 square miles of the broad Tularosa Basin, between the Sacramento and San Andres Mountains. Though their whiteness is beyond dispute, they're not in fact sand, but fine **gypsum**, deposited on an ancient seabed 250 million years ago. Anywhere else, they'd have dissolved, and been carried off by rivers; here, however, they're trapped in a riverless ring of mountains. The southern portion of this surreal landscape has been set aside as **WHITE SANDS NATIONAL MONUMENT**, entered north of US-70 fourteen miles west of Alamogordo. One of the very few unmissable attractions in southern New Mexico, it also provides a wonderful opportunity for photographers, though the bright light of midday is likely to bleach out almost any make of film.

Roughly twice each week, both US-70 and the Dunes Drive close for up to two hours while missile tests are underway.

Beside the highway, the **visitor center** (daily: summer 8am–7pm; winter 8am–4.30pm; ☎505/479-6124) illustrates the unique bleached life-forms that have adapted to suit this pallid environment. From there, it takes five more miles along the paved portion of **Dunes Drive** (daily: summer 7am–10pm; winter 7am–sunset; $3), before you reach the heart of the dunes. At first, as you drive beyond the entrance station and get your first glimpses of white sand beneath the scrubby vegetation, you may wonder what the fuss is about. Gradually, however, the plants thin out, and you come to an utterly bizarre world of dazzling white knife-edge ridges and graceful slopes. The drive now loops around a six-mile one-way labyrinth, where the roadway is at times hundreds of yards wide, and then narrows again to a slender channel, as the west winds that constantly replenish the dunes pile sand in your path in luxuriant drifts. Plentiful pull-outs, some of them equipped with fabulous 1950s-style curving picnic shelters, enable you to leave your vehicle and plow through pristine sand to the top of the ridges, which offer long-range mountain views. Slipping and sliding back down again is even better.

There's no developed **campground** at White Sands, but backcountry camping is allowed, by permit only (available at the monument visitor center). Once or twice a year, rangers also lead vehicle convoys up to Lake Lucero, the actual source of the sands; call ahead to see if one is currently scheduled.

White Sands Missile Range Museum

A couple of miles north of the national monument boundary, on the top-security White Sands Missile Range – said to be the largest military installation in the United States – the **White Sands Space Harbor** holds one of the three seven-mile runways where the **Space Shuttle** is able to land. A back-up facility to the regular landing sites in California and Florida, it has only been used once, in 1982.

For the full story, head for the **White Sands Missile Range Museum**, thirty miles west of the monument en route to Las Cruces, and four miles south of US-70 (Mon–Fri 8am–4.30pm; free). The open-air **Missile Park** alongside offers a chance to inspect "the weapons that won the Cold War and Operation Desert Storm," and displays all the missiles ever tested at White Sands. These date back to "Vengeance Weapon 2," the V-2 rocket, almost four thousand of which were fired across the English Channel by the Nazis during World War II. After the war, the weapon's designer, Dr Wernher von Braun, directed the firing of sixty more V-2s at White Sands – one went astray and crashed across the border near Ciudad Juarez, Mexico – before he moved on to Huntsville, Alabama in 1950.

The southeast corner

East of the mountains, at the edge of the Great Plains, **southeast New Mexico** has little in common with the rest of the Southwest. It's not quite as dull as it looks, however; all its treasures are tucked away under the ground, in the shape not only of the oil and mineral wealth that keeps its economy ticking over, but also of the fairy-tale labyrinth of **Carlsbad Caverns National Park**. Traditionally, Carlsbad has been the only reason tourists ever stray this way, but these days, a steady influx of pilgrims also make the trek to contemplate the extraterrestrial wonders of **Roswell**.

Roswell

Seventy-five miles north of Carlsbad, the small ranching town of **ROSWELL** is renowned as the spot near which an **alien spacecraft** supposedly crash-landed on the night of July 4, 1947. The commander of the local air force base authorized a press statement announcing that they had retrieved the wreckage of a flying saucer, which had been taken away for examination. Despite a follow-up denial within a day, claiming that it was in fact a weather balloon, the story has kept running. As 100,000 *X-Files* fanatics descended upon Roswell for a six-day festival to mark the "Incident's" fiftieth anniversary, in 1997, the US Air Force revealed that the errant balloon had been monitoring the atmosphere for evidence of Soviet nuclear tests. Witnesses were also said to have confused the balloon crash with a series of parachute experiments in 1953, which involved the dropping of dummies from high-altitude planes. UFO theorists, however, remain unconvinced. Incidentally, considerable vagueness surrounds exactly where the crash took place. Since a local entrepreneur bought up one purported site, the original witnesses have started to "remember" that it all happened somewhere else entirely.

A new generation of conspiracy freaks has been descending on Roswell since the success of the X-Files teen spin-off TV series Roswell High.

Each of the two **museums** in town devoted to the "Roswell Incident" has its own particular lunacies to offer. Despite its best intentions, and the wishful thinking of the truly weird clientele who drift in from the plains, the central **International UFO Museum**, 114 N Main St (daily 10am–5pm; free), inadvertently exposes the whole tawdry business as transparent nonsense. Run by the military press officer responsible for the 1947 announcement, it reveals such gems as that John Kennedy was shot because he was about to reveal the secret, and that Neil Armstrong, astonished at encountering flying saucers on the moon, blurted out "Boy, were they beige!" (You'd have to assume that "big" was the word he was fumbling for.) Its showpiece is a model of the "**alien autopsy**," said to have taken place at the Wright-Patterson Airforce Base in Dayton, Ohio, later the venue for the Bosnian peace talks (conspiracy theorists see that as no coincidence). Built for the movie *Roswell*, you can't help suspecting it also featured in the grainy "documentary" autopsy footage that created a brief international sensation in 1995.

Responding to a child as he switched on Belfast's Christmas lights in 1995, President Clinton declared "No, an alien spacecraft did not crash in Roswell, New Mexico in 1947."

There's another chance to have your photo taken with a "little gray", as those who know their aliens like to call them, at the even tackier **UFO Enigma Museum**, a long way south at 6108 S Main St (Mon–Sat 9am–5pm, Sun noon–5pm; $1). Here it's not dead on a slab, but alive and keen to make friends – unlike two of its unfortunate hand-knitted companions, which lie strewn in silver jumpsuits beside their disabled spaceship nearby.

By way of contrast, the longstanding **Roswell Museum**, 100 W 11th St (Mon–Sat 9am–5pm, Sun 1–5pm; free), boasts an excellent, multifaceted collection with nary an alien corpse to be seen. Its most sensational section celebrates pioneer rocket scientist **Robert Goddard** (1882–1945), one of whose early experiments prompted the newspaper headline *'Moon Rocket' Man's Test Alarms Whole Countryside*. His entire laboratory has been reconstructed, and an

The
southeast
corner

*Roswell's zip
code is NM
88201.*

entertaining video shows him wheeling a rudimentary rocket in a wagon to the launch pad, then racing to escape the blast in a model T Ford. Elsewhere, historical artifacts range from armor and pikes brought by Spanish conquistadors, to an Apache Ghost Dancer's shirt and astronaut Harrison Schmitt's spacesuit. There's also a huge, top-quality **art gallery**, displaying Southwestern landscapes by Henriette Wyeth and Peter Hurd, and Georgia O'Keeffe's *Ram's Skull With Brown Leaves*.

Practicalities

Roswell's **visitor center** is near the Roswell Museum at 912 N Main St (Mon–Sat 9am–5pm; ☎505/624-6860). The finest **motel** in town, the *Best Western Sally Port Inn*, 2000 N Main St (☎505/622-6430 or 1-800/548-5221, fax 505/623-7631; ④), also has a good restaurant; if you just want a place to lay your head, the *Super 8*, 3575 N Main St (☎505/622-8886 or 1-800/800-8000; ②), and the *Frontier Motel*, 3010 N Main St (☎505/622-1400 or 1-800/678-1401; ②), are cheaper. The *Cattle Baron*, 1113 N Main St (☎505/622-2465), is a large, good-value **steakhouse** with an extensive salad bar, while the *Blues Coffee Bar*, 305 N Main St, serves a decent espresso.

Carlsbad

Considering that a million tourists per year pass through **CARLS-BAD** en route to Carlsbad Caverns National Park – covered opposite – the town itself is astonishing in its mundanity. A century of ranching and potash mining has given it a sizeable if characterless downtown area, but the one significant attraction is the **Living Desert State Park**, a couple of miles northwest (daily: summer 8am–8pm; winter 9am–5pm; last admission 1hr 30min before closing; $3). This botanical garden of desert plants doubles as a zoo that houses elk, bear, rattlesnakes and a prairie dog village.

Practicalities

*Carlsbad's zip
code is NM
88220.*

Carlsbad's **visitor center**, at 302 S Canal St (Mon–Fri 8am–5pm; ☎505/887-6516 or 1-800/221-1224; *www.caverns.com/~chamber*), can supply copious lists of local motels. Central options include the *Holiday Inn*, 601 S Canal St (☎505/885-8500 or 1-800/742-9586, fax 505/887-5999; *www.caverns.com/~chamber/lodging3.htm*; winter ④, summer ⑤), while cheaper alternatives like the clean, comfortable *Super 8*, 3817 National Parks Hwy (☎505/887-8888 or 1-800/800-8000; winter ②, summer ③), line US-62/180 to the southwest.

Decent places to eat are much harder to find, but at least *Beaver's Restaurant*, 1620 S Canal St (closed Mon & Tues; ☎505/885-4515), has a big menu, with three-course dinners for just $7, and lots of breaded seafood. *Lucy's*, 701 S Canal St (closed Sun; ☎505/887-7714), is a popular Mexican alternative.

Carlsbad Caverns National Park

CARLSBAD CAVERNS NATIONAL PARK consists of a tract of the Guadalupe Mountains that's so riddled with underground caves and tunnels as to be virtually hollow. Tamed in classic park-service style with concrete trails and electric lighting, this subterranean wonderland is now a walk-in gallery, where tourists come in droves to marvel at its intricate limestone tracery. Before you decide whether to join them, however, be sure to grasp that the park is a *long* way from anywhere else – three hundred miles southeast of Albuquerque, and 150 miles northeast of El Paso, Texas.

The Guadalupe Mountains are the remnants of the **Capitan Reef**, a 400-mile-long horseshoe-shaped reef that formed beneath the waters of a primeval ocean. Made up of algae and sponges rather than coral, it was thrust above the plains a mere three million years ago. In the process, cracks were created through which surface moisture has trickled ever since, gnawing at the rock within. Almost all park visitors confine their attention to the main cave, **Carlsbad Cavern** itself, and the summer crowds can get pretty intense. In a strange way, though, that's part of the fun – coming to Carlsbad feels like a real throwback to the great 1950s boom in mass tourism. If you're not convinced, wait until you see the gloriously kitsch Underground Lunchroom.

Arrival and information

The park headquarters are reached by driving twenty miles southwest of the town of Carlsbad on US-62/180, then turning west at **White's City** to climb another seven miles. This narrow, twisting road ends atop the mountains, with sweeping views east across the plains. Part of a complex that includes a restaurant, a gift store, a crèche and even a kennel, the **visitor center** is the place to pay entrance fees, and pick up details of the day's program of tours (daily: June to mid-Aug 8am–7pm; mid-Aug to May 8am–5.30pm; ☎505/785-2232).

The standard park fee of $6 for three days covers access to **Carlsbad Cavern** by elevator or on foot. For additional fees that range from $7 to $20 you can also join guided tours to otherwise inaccessible parts of the main cavern, or of **Slaughter Canyon Cave**, as detailed overleaf. Some tours require participants to carry flashlights, or even to wear kneepads. All tours can be reserved in advance, using Visa or MasterCard, on ☎1-800/967-2283.

Carlsbad Cavern

The centerpiece of Carlsbad Cavern, the **Big Room**, lies 750 vertical feet below the visitor center – though being inside the mountain, in places it's also 400 feet horizontally from the open air. Measuring up to 1800 feet long and 250 feet high, it's festooned with stalactites, stalagmites and countless unnameable shapes of swirling liquid rock. All are a uniform stone gray; the rare touches of color are provided by slight red or brown mineral-rich tinges, improved here and there

The southeast corner

Note that there's no camping at the national park; the nearest campgrounds and motels are at White's City and Carlsbad.

For advance information, write to Carlsbad Caverns National Park, 3225 National Parks Hwy, Carlsbad, NM 88220, or visit www.nps.gov/cave.

National Parks passes (see p.21) are not accepted at Carlsbad Caverns; Golden Access and Golden Age passes (see p.32 and p.33) earn fifty percent discounts.

with gentle pastel lighting. Most visitors take an hour or so to complete the reasonably level trail around its perimeter. Whatever the weather up top – and summer highs exceed 100°F – the temperature down here is always a cool 56°F, so dress warmly.

Direct **elevators** drop to the Big Room from the visitor center (summer first down 8.30am, last up 6.30pm; winter first down 8.30am, last up 4.55pm). They arrive alongside the **Underground Lunchroom**, a vast formation-free side cave paved over in the 1950s to create a diner-cum-souvenir-store that sells indigestible lunches in polystyrene containers, plus Eisenhower-era souvenirs like giant pencils and Viewmaster reels. To modern eyes, this strange installation seems absurd, but moves to close it down have been stymied by its place in popular affections.

To get a better sense of the cavern's depth, eschew the elevator and **walk** down via the **Natural Entrance Route** (last entry summer 3.30pm, winter 2pm). This steep paved footpath switchbacks into the guano-encrusted maw of the cave, a short way from the visitor center, taking fifteen minutes to reach the first of the formations and another fifteen to reach the Big Room itself. $3 buys you a recorded "audio tour," if you'd like a commentary as you go.

All visitors to the cavern are obliged to ride the elevator back out.

The main appeal of walking down used to be that the trail meandered through beautiful side caves such as the **King's Palace** and the **Queen's Chamber**, filled with translucent "draperies" of limestone. However, these were closed to casual visitors in 1993, as formations were being broken at the rate of two thousand per year. They're now open on guided tours only, which start from the Big Room (daily 9am, 11am, 1pm & 3pm; $8).

The rest of the park

The park's other readily accessible cave is **Slaughter Canyon Cave**, 25 miles southwest of the visitor center. Much less frequented, and much

---

The Bats of Carlsbad

The recesses of Carlsbad Caverns are the summer home of around a million Mexican free-tailed **bats**. Each evening, having slept all day suspended from the ceiling of the imaginatively titled **Bat Cave** – to which there's no public access – they emerge in cloud-like spirals at dusk and a little later, and disperse across the desert in search of delectable insects. Park visitors watch the spectacle from the amphitheater seating that faces the cave mouth, while rangers give a free and informative "Bats aren't as bad as you think" presentation.

It was the bats that first brought the caves to human attention, in the 1890s. Miners employed to dig bat dung or **guano**, which was greatly prized as fertilizer, started to explore what lay beyond the cave mouth. As word of their discoveries spread, sightseers began to arrive. Early visitors were dropped down in buckets and guided through on ropes, with the present trail system being constructed after the caverns became a national park in 1930.

less developed, it can only be explored on two-hour guided tours (usually summer daily 10am & 1pm, winter Sat & Sun 10am & 1pm; call ☎505/785-2232 for exact schedule; $15). To get there, drive five miles south of White's City on US-62/180, then eleven miles west on Hwy-418, and finally hike the steep half-mile up to the cave entrance.

Slaughter Canyon Cave still appears as "New Cave" on some maps, but it's been renamed to avoid confusion since the discovery of **Lechuguilla Cave**. Revealed after cavers cleared a thirty-foot plug of bat dung and rubble in 1986, the astonishing Lechuguilla cave system is not only deeper than Carlsbad Cavern but, at 1600 feet, has turned out to be the deepest in the US. Sixty miles of tunnels have been mapped so far, but they're so dangerous that Lechuguilla is off limits to all but the experts. It's expected to remain a "wilderness cave" – even its location is kept secret – so the rest of us will have to content ourselves with the marvelous pictures of its delicate crystalline formations in the visitor center.

White's City

WHITE'S CITY, twenty miles southwest of Carlsbad at the turnoff for Carlsbad Caverns, is not a town but a privately owned tourist complex that provides the closest accommodation and camping to the national park. A notorious eyesore, it was opened in 1926 by entrepreneur Charlie White, who cannily anticipated the imminent advent of automobile tourism and bought up the land at this crucial road junction without ever having seen it. The park service has deplored its very existence ever since, and has attempted to avoid the same situation arising at parks elsewhere.

All the current components of White's City share the same address and phone number (17 Carlsbad Caverns Hwy, White's City, NM 88268; ☎505/785-2291 or 1-800/CAVERNS). They include the mock-adobe *Best Western Cavern Inn*, on both sides of the highway (*bestwest@caverns.com*; winter ③, summer ④), the *White's City RV Park*, which has tent camping space, and the *Velvet Garter Restaurant*. The minivan shuttles up to the park ($15 round-trip) might be convenient for passengers arriving on the thrice-daily Carlsbad–El Paso Greyhound **buses** (☎505/887-1108).

White's City also boasts the ultratacky **Million Dollar Museum** (daily 7am–8pm; $2.50), an assortment of decrepit dolls' houses, two-headed snakes, old shoes, arrowheads, the twelfth largest moose ever shot in Wyoming, and even a human corpse, in the nauseating form of a "7000-year-old cliff dwelling baby."

Hobbs

Unless it's on your route home, it's hard to know what impulse might carry you seventy miles east of Carlsbad to **HOBBS**, in New Mexico's far southeastern corner. Surrounded by endless dusty flatlands punctuated only by dementedly bobbing oil-pumps, this 30,000-strong community holds nothing to divert visitors. If you're sure there must be more to it than meets the eye, a handful of cheap motels – such as the *Super 8*, 722 N Marland Blvd (☎505/397-7511 or 1-800/800-8000; ②) – will be baffled to accept your custom.

The Rio Grande valley

The 260-mile route **south from Albuquerque**, to El Paso, Texas, and the Mexican border, follows one of America's oldest and most romantic trails. For 250 years, the **Camino Real** or "Royal Road" beside the Rio Grande gave the Hispanic colonists of New Mexico their one tenuous link with the outside world. Now, however, it's a monotonous four-hour drive on I-25, with little to divert the eye apart from distant views of the mountains that rear to either side. You don't even see much of the river itself, except where it's been dammed to form incongruous turquoise lakes around the town of **Truth or Consequences**. Of the old way-stations en route, only **Socorro** in the north and **Mesilla** in the south are particularly worth visiting.

Isleta Pueblo

The only New Mexican pueblo south of Albuquerque, **ISLETA PUEBLO** lies just off the interstate a dozen miles from downtown. The sole survivor of the many pueblos encountered by early Spanish explorers along the lower Rio Grande, it served in the seventeenth century as a refuge where Tiwa peoples gathered to resist the threat of Apache raids. At the time of the Pueblo Revolt, those Isletans who chose not to accompany the Spanish retreat southwards – where they founded the pueblo of **Tigua**, outside El Paso – fled west to join the Hopi in what's now Arizona. Isleta itself was repopulated in 1718, and remains home to almost four thousand people.

For more about visiting New Mexico's pueblos, and a full calendar of festivals, see box p.135.

Although the tribal lands mark a verdant interruption amid the dormitory communities that line the interstate's first fifty miles, the reservation is plagued by river-borne pollution from the industries of Albuquerque. Economically, though, it's dependent on its huge neighbor; a high proportion of Isletans work in the city, and the tribe also runs a 24-hour **casino** (11000 Broadway Blvd SE). Every day during daylight hours, visitors have free access to the principal pueblo village – also known as **SHIAW-IBA** – where the main attraction is the white-walled **mission church** of San Agustín de Isleta. In addition, Isleta stages major festivals on August 28 and September 4.

Socorro

Historic **SOCORRO**, eighty miles south of Albuquerque, received its unusual name – "help," in Spanish – from Don Juan de Oñate in 1598, after local Pueblo peoples fed his expeditionary party from their reserves of corn. The first Hispanic settlement was destroyed during the Pueblo Revolt of 1680, whereafter the site was abandoned for over a century. Both the picturesque **plaza** at its core, and the imposing adobe church of **San Miguel** a couple of blocks north (daily 6am–6pm; free), were rebuilt during the 1820s. Sixty years later, triggered by the arrival of the railroads and the discovery of extensive **silver** deposits nearby, Socorro briefly became New Mexico's largest town. When the silver ran out, so too did most of the population, leaving behind some fine Victorian architecture.

Practicalities
For a self-guided walking tour of Socorro, call in at the **visitor center**, north of the center at 103 Francisco de Avondo (Mon–Fri 8am–5pm, Sat 9am–5pm; ☎505/835-0424; *www.socorro-nm.com*). The most central **budget motel** is the *Sands*, 205 California St NW (☎505/835-1130; ②); the smarter *Super 8* is further out at 1121 Frontage Rd NW (☎505/835-4626 or 1-800/800-8000; winter ②, summer ③), while *Eaton House*, 403 Eaton Ave (☎505/835-1067; ⑤), is a luxurious central **B&B** with three en-suite rooms and two guest *casitas*. As for **food**, the atmospheric *Val Verde Steak House*, housed in a former hotel east of the plaza at 203 Manzanares Ave (☎505/835-3380), is open daily for lunch and dinner.

Socorro's zip code is NM 87801.

The Jornada del Muerto
Early Hispanic travelers on the Camino Real were so prone to Apache attack if they followed the curve of the Rio Grande between Socorro and Las Cruces that they preferred to take a hundred-mile shortcut behind the mountains that lie east of the river. This route too had its perils – not least a complete lack of water – and became known as the **Jornada del Muerto**, or Dead Man's Route, after Juan de Oñate's chaplain Fray Cristóbal de Salazar died here in the early 1600s. A long litany of subsequent deaths gave it a terrible reputation, and to this day there's no north–south road through the desert.

The point where the old trail crossed the river, twenty miles south of Socorro on Hwy-1, is now the **Bosque del Apache Wildlife Refuge**, the Southwest's most spectacular **bird-watching** site (Nov–March daily 7am–5pm; April–Oct Mon–Fri 7am–5pm; ☎505/835-1828; $3 per vehicle). As migratory birds arrive for the winter, in early December, it can hold as many as twenty thousand sandhill cranes and almost fifty thousand snow geese; even in summer, its riverine marshes and forests are bursting with birds and mammals.

Truth or Consequences
Until 1950, the minor spa town seventy miles south of Socorro was appropriately known as **Hot Springs**. Then the radio show *Truth or Consequences* promised that any community prepared to change its

name would receive the meager reward of hosting its tenth anniversary edition. Hot Springs prostituted itself for fifteen minutes of fame, and **TRUTH OR CONSEQUENCES** was saddled with the world's worst name – though locals habitually abbreviate it these days to "**T or C.**"

Many of the region's **thermal springs** – where Apache warriors such as Geronimo once soaked away the worries of the warpath – are now run as private bathhouses, with prices starting at around $3 for a twenty-minute session. Native American memorabilia, including Mimbres pottery (see box p.210) form a prominent part of the historical collection at the **Geronimo Springs Museum**, 211 Main St (Mon–Sat 9am–5pm; $2). You can also learn fascinating snippets about **Ralph Edwards**, presenter of the long-defunct *Truth or Consequences* show, who still returns each year for the **Truth or Consequences Fiesta**, on the first weekend in May.

Practicalities

T or C's small downtown consists of a couple of blocks sandwiched between two busy one-way streets, Broadway and Main Street. That's where you'll find the **visitor center**, just off Main Street at 201 Foch St (Mon–Fri 9am–5pm; ☎505/894-3536 or 1-800/831-9487), but most of the better **motels** are well to the north, near interstate exit 79. These include the *Best Western Hot Springs Inn*, 2270 N Date St (☎505/894-6665 or 1-800/528-1234; ③), where there's a pool and a steakhouse, and the *Super 8*, 2151 N Date St (☎505/894-7888 or 1-800/800-8000, fax 505/894-7883; ③). Beside the Rio Grande in the heart of town, however, the lovely *Riverbend Hot Springs Hostel*, 100 Austin St (☎505/894-6183; ①/②), offers $13 dorm beds, private rooms and suites, and even individual tepees, and also has spring-fed hot tubs. *La Cocina*, 280 Date St (☎505/894-6499) is a good Mexican **restaurant**, while *Touch of Seattle*, 1806 S Broadway (closed Sun; ☎505/894-9460), is an appealing coffee- and snackbar adjoining the Downhome Laundry in the suburb of Williamsburg.

T or C's zip code is NM 87901.

Hillsboro

Hwy-152 branches west from I-25 fifteen miles south of T or C, crossing the Mimbres Mountain en route to **Silver City** (see p.207). **HILLSBORO**, less than twenty miles off the interstate in the fertile foothills, is a former gold-mining settlement that has since turned its hand to apple-growing instead. Now no more than a village, with a small crop of arts-and-crafts galleries, it also boasts the *Enchanted Villa* (PO Box 456, Hillsboro, NM 88042; ☎505/895-5686; ④), a bright and attractive whitewashed adobe **B&B**.

Hatch

Forty miles south of T or C, halfway down I-25 towards Las Cruces, tiny **HATCH** is noteworthy only as the home of New Mexico's leading **chile farms**. All year, roadside stalls sell fresh peppers and the dried garlands known as *ristras*, while Labor Day weekend sees a **Chile Festival** with fiercely competitive chile cook-offs. *Dora's*, 401 E Hall St (☎505/267-9294), is renowned for fiery Mexican cuisine.

The Rio Grande valley

For advance details of the Chile Festival, call ☎*505/267-5050.*

Las Cruces

Named after "the Crosses" that marked the graves of early travelers killed by the Apache, **LAS CRUCES** is now a major crossroads, where the east–west I-10 meets the north–south I-25. Once a riverside farming community, it has grown beyond recognition in recent years – it's even rumored to be the prospective site of a **spaceport** designed for commercial space travel – but the boom in industrial and military employment has been at the expense of any scenic beauty it may once have possessed. Now Las Cruces is simply a place to hurry through, with any time you can spare for sightseeing better spent in neighboring Mesilla.

Practicalities

Las Cruces' downtown **visitor center**, 211 N Water St (Mon–Fri 8am–5pm, Sat 9am–1pm; ☎505/541-2444 or 1-800/343-7827; *www.lascruces.org*), has lists of all the **motels** you'd expect, including a couple of *Super 8*s – the handiest is at 245 La Posada Lane (☎505/523-8695 or 1-800/800-8000; ②) – and the surprisingly attractive *Best Western Mission Inn*, 1765 S Main St (☎505/524-8591 or 1-800/390-1440; ③). *Lundeen's Inn of the Arts*, 618 S Alameda Blvd (☎505/526-3326 or 1-888/526-3326; ④), is a **B&B inn** where each room is named for regional artists such as Maria Martínez or Georgia O'Keeffe, and furnished appropriately.

Las Cruces' zip code is NM 88005.

The slogan of *Nellie's Cafe*, 1226 W Hadley Ave (☎505/524-9982) – "Chiles with Attitude" – tells you what to expect: sublimely spicy Mexican food. Blander snacks are readily available in the fast-food court of **Mesilla Valley Mall**, west of I-25 at Lohman Avenue, while University Avenue, which marks the northern limits of the New Mexico State University campus at the south end of town near the interstate intersection, is buzzing with student-oriented **coffeehouses**.

Mesilla

The little-changed Hispanic village of **MESILLA** stands just south of I-10 two miles west of Las Cruces, an easy drive down the Avenida de Mesilla from downtown. When New Mexico passed into American hands in 1846, the Mesilla Valley still belonged to Mexico, and Mesilla itself was founded in 1850 by New Mexicans who preferred to remain Mexican. Under the **Gadsden Purchase**, however, signed here in 1853, it passed to the US, and soon became one of the

Southwest's largest towns, with over eight thousand inhabitants. During the Civil War, Mesilla even served briefly as the Confederate capital of the territory of Arizona, but it went into swift decline when the railroad bypassed it in favor of Las Cruces in 1881.

Mesilla's delightful Old-West **plaza** has a real frontier feel to it, even though most of the old adobes that surround it – including the former courthouse where **Billy the Kid** was tried and sentenced to death in 1881 – now house art galleries and souvenir shops. Gift stores such as La Zia and Del Sol stock interesting Southwest souvenirs and jewelry leavened with some much cheaper Mexican crafts, while the Mesilla Book Center has an excellent selection of local literature. Two blocks east, the small **Gadsden Museum** (Mon–Sat 9–11am & 1–5pm, Sun 1–5pm; $2), recounts the town's history and details the events that lead to the Gadsden Purchase.

*For more on
Billy the Kid,
see box p.188.*

Practicalities

The *Mesón de Mesilla*, 1803 Avenida de Mesilla (PO Box 1212, Mesilla, NM 88046; ☎505/525-2380 or 1-800/732-6025; ③–⑥), is a luxury thirteen-room **B&B** five minutes' walk east of the plaza, offering gorgeous mountain views, an outdoor pool and a top-class gourmet dining room. **Restaurants** on the plaza itself include the *Double Eagle* (☎505/523-6700), which has indoor and outdoor seating and serves steaks, shark and even ostrich for lunch and dinner daily, and *El Patio*, a Mexican *cantina* in the former offices of the Butterfield Stage Coach (closed Sun; ☎505/524-0982).

Southwest New Mexico

Most of New Mexico's sparsely populated **southwest corner** – also known as the "**Bootheel**," for the way it steps down into Mexico – consists of open rangeland that's devoid of interest for travelers. Interstate towns like **Deming** and **Lordsburg** are entirely forgettable, though a detour north into the mountains takes you to the mining town of **Silver City**, and the ancient **Gila Cliff Dwellings**.

Deming

A bonanza of roadside billboards sixty miles due west of Las Cruces announces your arrival at **DEMING**, a typical desert outpost scattered with motels and diners. Half-hearted attempts at agriculture have left their traces on the surrounding landscape, but the main sign of activity comes from the ever-present swirling dust devils. If you're ready for a break, however, the **Deming Luna Mimbres Museum**, 301 S Silver Ave (Mon–Sat 9am–4pm, Sun 1.30–4pm; free), has some surprisingly good displays, including cabinets of Mimbres pottery (see box p.210) and a great show of minerals and gemstones.

Assuming you have a pickax handy, you're allowed to take away whatever agates, onyx or geodes you can prise from the arid slopes of **Rock Hound State Park**, ten miles southeast (daily 7.30am–dusk; $4). Any easy pickings have long since been carted away however, to leave this as perhaps the most frighteningly boring park in the whole Southwest.

Southwest New Mexico

Practicalities

Deming is served by Amtrak **trains** which call at the central railroad station daily except Friday, in alternate directions but always at around 2.30pm – and more frequent Greyhound **buses**, which use a depot at 300 E Spruce St (☎505/546-3881). The **visitor center**, 800 E Pine St, is at the east end of downtown (Mon–Sat 9am–5pm; ☎505/546-2674 or 1-800/848-4955). Budget **motels** along the main drag, parallel to the the interstate, include a *Super 8*, 1217 W Pine St (☎505/546-0481 or 1-800/800-8000; ②), and the *Anselment's Butterfield Stage*, 309 W Pine St (☎505/544-0011; ①), but the large, newly renovated *Holiday Inn* at the eastern interstate exit (☎505/546-2661; ③) is the best of the bunch, and has a decent **restaurant** too.

Pancho Villa State Park

In sleepy **COLUMBUS**, thirty miles south of Deming, just north of the Mexican border, the site where the thousand-strong forces of Mexican revolutionary Pancho Villa did battle in 1916 against the US cavalry, is now **Pancho Villa State Park** (daily 8am–5pm; $4). A small museum chronicles the last invasion of the US, and the adjoining sixty-acre desert botanical garden makes a nice place to **camp** (except in summer, when it's baking hot).

If you fancy a *cerveza* or two, the frontier with neighboring **LAS PALOMAS**, three miles south in Mexico, remains open day or night. Border formalities are minimal, though foreign travelers must be sure to carry their passports.

Silver City

Six thousand feet up in the Mogollon mountains, **SILVER CITY** stands roughly fifty miles northwest and northeast respectively from the I-10 towns of Deming and Lordsburg. As you drive up from the interstate, however, it's easy not to notice that you're climbing – the region has been so extensively **mined** that many of the hills that once lay to the south of Silver City have now been completely carved away.

Ancient peoples knew this region as a source of top-quality **turquoise**, but the Hispanic settlement of La Cienaga de San Vicente was only founded in 1804, soon after some friendly Apaches showed the Spanish soldier Jose Manuel Carrasco where to find **copper**. The Santa Rita copper mine was repeatedly attacked by the Apache, however, and was abandoned altogether in 1838. Only when **silver** was discovered after the Civil War was the town reestablished, with a new name and a rip-roaring reputation. **Billy the Kid** spent most of his childhood here; according to some stories he committed his first robbery – of a Chinese laundry – in Silver City, and also his first murder.

Things calmed down when the silver ran out, so Silver City today is a somewhat run-down, but nonetheless appealing, Victorian relic, scattered with ornate old buildings. The two thousand students of Western New Mexico University, whose campus is on the western edge of downtown, keep things reasonably lively for most of the year, and they're replaced in summer by a large influx of tourists. Copper mining, meanwhile, continues unabated; neighboring Santa Rita, which had become a fully-fledged community in its own right, and was the birthplace of Apollo 17 astronaut Harrison Schmitt, disappeared into the bowels of an open-pit copper mine in 1966.

Arrival and information

Silver City's **visitor center** is on Hwy-90 as it enters downtown, at 201 N Hudson St (April–Oct Mon–Sat 9am–5pm, Sun noon–4pm; Nov–March Mon–Fri 9am–5pm; ☎505/538-3785 or 1-800/548-9378). For information on the town's annual **Blues Festival**, which attracts big names at the end of each May, call ☎1-888/758-7289.

Accommodation

Room rates are surprisingly inexpensive in Silver City, but with most of the **motels** strung along US-180 east of town there's a dearth of options within walking distance of downtown.

Bear Mountain Guest Ranch, Bear Mountain Rd; ☎505/538-2538 or 1-800/880-2538; *www.zianet.com/mccormick*. A 1920s ranch house four miles northwest of downtown, charging all-inclusive rates to stay in very pleasant rooms and eat three full meals per day. Myra McCormick, who has run the place for almost forty years, regularly guides bird-watching trips and can suggest or arrange multiday cycling, mountain-biking, or cross-country skiing tours of the surrounding area. ⑤.

The Carter House B&B, 101 N Cooper St; ☎505/388-5485. Downtown HI-AYH youth hostel that doubles as a B&B, with $13 dorm beds ($16 nonmembers) and some nice little private rooms. ①–④.

Holiday Motor Hotel, 3420 US-180 E; ☎505/538-3711 or 1-800/828-8291. Good-value motel rooms on the eastern approaches to town, with a pool and a good Italian restaurant, *Michael's*. ③.

Palace Hotel, 106 W Broadway; ☎505/388-1811. Small, nicely restored nineteenth-century hotel, downtown. Some rooms have showers rather than baths, and they all have historic rather than contemporary fittings, but the ambience – and the rates – are great. ②.

Super 8, 1040 US-180 E; ☎505/388-1983 or 1-800/800-8000. Reliable chain motel near the Gila Cliff Dwellings turnoff. Winter ②, summer ③.

The Town

A massive flood ripped the heart out of downtown Silver City in 1895, washing away its original Main Street. As a result, disappointingly, no buildings survive from the days of **Billy the Kid**; Western devotees have to settle instead for inspecting the places where they *used* to be. The former site of Main Street is now occupied by **Big Ditch Park**; stand on its eastern edge, at 11th and Hudson, and you're on the spot where Billy grew up, in a simple one-room cabin. His mother is buried in the town cemetery, on Memory Lane a couple of miles east. After her death, Billy found work as a busboy in the *Star Hotel*, which survives in much-altered form at Broadway and Hudson, but soon turned to crime. The jail where he was imprisoned, and from which he made the first of his many escapes, stood at 304 N Hudson St.

Two good museums explore local history in considerable depth. The **Silver City Museum**, 312 W Broadway (Tues–Fri 9am–4.30pm, Sat & Sun 10am–4pm; free) concentrates on the boom-and-bust mining years, with photos of the frontier era and personal accounts of the vanished community of Santa Rita, though it also holds Indian pottery, rugs and basketry. The emphasis at the **Western New Mexico University Museum**, 12th and Alabama (Mon–Fri 9am–4.30pm, Sat & Sun 10am–4pm; free), is on a remarkable collection of **Mimbres pottery**, tracing its development over a thousand-year period.

Eating

Inexpensive **diners** are two-a-penny in the downtown area – not to mention a few hair-raising **bars** – but don't expect to find anything more exciting along the highways further out.

Buckhorn Saloon, 62 Main St, Pinos Altos; ☎505/538-9911. Enjoyable Wild-West-themed steakhouse in the ghost town of Pinos Altos, seven miles north of Silver City (see overleaf). Open Mon–Sat for dinner only, with accompanying live music every night except Tues.

Jalisco Cafe, 100 S Bullard St; ☎505/388-2060. One of the few options in the heart of downtown, serving Mexican meals daily except Sun.

Red Barn Family Steakhouse, 708 Silver Heights Blvd; ☎505/538-5666. Exactly what it sounds like; a large steakhouse, painted a lurid red, on Hwy-180 near the Gila turnoff at the eastern end of town. They have their own herd of cows, so the meat is good, and the $4 salad bar is a real bargain.

Silver Cafe, 514 N Bullard St; ☎505/388-3480. New Mexican dishes in atmospheric saloon surroundings. Mon–Sat 7.30am–7.30pm.

Into the mountains

North of Silver City, the volcanic **Mogollon** and **Mimbres mountains** are among the remotest wilderness areas in the US. Until the late nineteenth century, they were an Apache stronghold; **Geronimo** was born at the headwaters of the Gila River, and returned throughout his free adult life. Before that, they were home to the **Mogollon** peoples,

*Southwest
New Mexico*

As explained on p.15, accommodation prices, excluding taxes, are indicated throughout this book by the following symbols:
① *up to $30*
② *$30–45*
③ *$45–60*
④ *$60–80*
⑤ *$80–100*
⑥ *$100–130*
⑦ *$130–175*
⑧ *$175–250*
⑨ *$250+*

For more about the Mogollon, see the box overleaf.

and the main reason to make the fifty-mile dead-end trip into the mountains on **Hwy-15** these days is to see the dramatic Mogollon ruins of the **Gila Cliff Dwellings National Monument**.

Hwy-15 is however a beautiful drive in its own right, albeit a slow one. It's never especially steep, let alone dangerous, but the twists and turns seem endless. Potential stops along the way include **Pinos Altos** – a fun little semi-ghost town in the woods just a few miles out of Silver City, that's home to one or two businesses such as the *Buckhorn Saloon* (see overleaf) – and the **Vista Viewpoint** above the Gila River near the far end. Most of this region belongs to the **Gila National Forest**. If you know what you're doing, it offers mag-

---

The Mogollon and the Mimbres

Archeologists identify the three major cultures of the prehistoric Southwest as the **Ancestral Puebloans** of the Colorado Plateau, the **Hohokam** of the Salt River Valley around modern Phoenix, and the **Mogollon**, based in the **Mogollon mountains** of what's now southwest New Mexico. Thanks to their proximity to Mexico, Mogollon peoples were the first to acquire both **agriculture** – in the shape of corn and squash, around 1200 BC – and **pottery** – around 200 AD.

At its peak, between 100 AD and 1300 AD, the Mogollon culture extended well into modern Arizona and Mexican Chihuahua. Its heartland, however, remained the **Gila** and **Mimbres** rivers, north and east of modern Silver City, and the Mogollon subgroup known as the **Classic Mimbres** culture is considered to represent the ancient Southwest's finest artistic flowering. Above all, the Mimbres people – their name comes from the Spanish for "willows" – were superb **potters**. While the intricate stylized borders of their plates and bowls are typical of many Pueblo peoples, their vivid naturalistic images of birds, insects and animals are quite extraordinary. Usually executed in black on white, they also hint at a complex mythology; some show bees or rabbits juxtaposed with strange humanoid creatures, others what may be prototype *kachina* figures (see p.60), and there are even scenes of decapitation suggesting human sacrifice.

The Mimbres culture reached its apogee around 1100 AD, with around five thousand people farming beside the Mimbres River. As well as a dozen or so walled villages, each of which held up to 200 rooms, they occupied several smaller, more isolated settlements. Depictions of fish that live only in the Pacific would suggest they traveled extensively, but there's little evidence of trade. No Mimbres ceramics have been discovered elsewhere, and it's believed that the finest bowls were created for specific individuals at birth, used in ceremonies throughout their lifetime, and finally **buried** with them. The bowl would be inverted over the head of the corpse, always with a "**kill hole**" punched through it which according to modern Pueblo Indians released its "spirit" to accompany that of the deceased. As a result, undamaged Mimbres bowls are extremely rare, and Mimbres pottery in general is so valuable that the few known Mimbres sites have been extensively looted, rendering the detective work of archeology almost impossible. As far as anyone can tell, the Mimbres stopped producing pottery around 1150 AD, and left the valley soon afterwards, possibly because overuse had depleted its soil.

---

nificent opportunities for wilderness adventure; first-time backpackers, climbers or canoeists would do better to join an expedition with Southwest Mountain Adventures (☎505/538-2338 or 1-888/482-4453).

Gila Cliff Dwellings National Monument

Occupied for just a brief moment in history, between 1270 AD and 1300 AD, the Mogollon pueblo now preserved as the **GILA CLIFF DWELLINGS NATIONAL MONUMENT** is southern New Mexico's most spectacular archeological site. While not on the scale of the Ancestral Puebloan "cities" of the Four Corners region – see Chapter 1 – it's also nothing like so heavily visited, and you may well be lucky enough to have the place to yourself. To modern eyes, ancient Southwestern peoples often seem to have chosen to live in inhospitable places, but here there's no such problem. The dwellings are tucked into sheltered south-facing recesses along the wall of a shallow canyon, just a couple of hundred feet above a perennial creek and thus in earshot of running water and the constant rustle of small game.

Gila is pronounced "heela," and comes from an Apache word meaning mountain.

Even when there's no traffic, driving the full fifty miles from Silver City can take two hours. The final eight miles are along the broad valley of the Gila River, with the monument's **visitor center**, where the $3 entrance fee is collected, poised near the confluence of its Middle and West forks (daily: summer 8am–5pm; winter 8am–4.30pm; ☎505/536-9461).

You won't have time to see the monument if you set off from Silver City later than 4pm in summer, 2pm in winter.

The **trail** to the dwellings (daily: summer 8am–6pm; winter 9am–4pm) starts a mile further on, crossing the Gila on a long footbridge. Only once you've followed the creek for half a mile do you get your first glimpse of the pueblo. What look from below like three separate caves turn out, when you climb the hillside, to be a single deep, long alcove with three entrances. Each was sealed with stones and mortar, but behind them lay around forty interconnected rooms, sharing a communal – and presumably very dark – plaza at the rear. As the trail leads into and through the complex, keep an eye out for the pictographs that mark certain dwellings, as well as a granary that still holds a desiccated cache of tiny corn.

The monument maintains a small free **campground** beside the Gila River, equipped with running water in summer only. There's another pretty campground eight miles south, at the *Gila Hot Springs Vacation Center* (☎505/536-9551; ②), which also rents out basic rooms.

Lordsburg

Sixty miles down the interstate from Deming, forty-four miles southwest of Silver City, and just twenty miles short of Arizona, **LORDSBURG** is southwest New Mexico's last gasp. John Wayne went to a lot of trouble to get here in *Stagecoach*, but seeing its desultory strip

**Southwest
New Mexico**

of gas stations and motels today you wonder why he bothered. Far more redolent of the old West is **SHAKESPEARE**, two miles south, a privately-owned **ghost town** that's only open for infrequent guided tours (every other Sat & Sun, 10am–2pm; $3; ☎505/542-9034). If you go at any other time, there's no access to the site, and nothing to see.

Practicalities

The **New Mexico Welcome Center**, south of the interstate at the west end of town (daily 8am–5pm; ☎505/542-8149), is the best place to pick up information on Lordsburg and the region. If you need a **bed**, the few blocks south of I-10 on Main Street hold much better options than the dismal mom-and-pop motels on Motel Drive, with a reasonable *Super 8*, 110 E Maple St (☎505/542-8882 or 1-800/800-8000; ②), and a big new *Holiday Inn Express*, 1408 S Main St (☎505/542-3666; ③), with large rooms. *Kranberry's*, opposite at 1405 S Main St (☎505/542-9400), is the best of a hum-drum crop of **diners**, and serves a tasty $7 green-chile stew.

Chapter 4

Phoenix and Southern Arizona

S outhern Arizona may lack the compelling scenery of the
state's northern half, but more than makes up for it in sheer
weight of numbers. Despite every conceivable geographic and
climatic disadvantage, ninety percent of Arizonans live here, mainly
concentrated in two of the most ludicrous cities on earth – **Phoenix**
and **Tucson**. What makes them ludicrous is that there's no logical
reason for their existence; neither has anything like enough water to
support itself, but both have accrued sufficient political leverage to
persuade the federal government to spend ever larger amounts of
money on vast canal projects to meet their needs.

Phoenix in particular can be seen as the bloated spider at the center of the web, sucking the juices from the rest of the state. By far the
largest city in Arizona, it holds only minimal appeal for tourists.
Tucson at least has a spark of life, thanks to its long and fascinating
history; it started out as a Mexican frontier outpost, and is still surrounded by relics of the Spanish missionary era such as the churches
of **San Xavier del Bac** and **Tumacácori**. It's also at ease with its
desert surroundings, accessible in **Saguaro National Park** and the
Arizona-Sonora Desert Museum. Scattered among the "sky
islands" of **southeast Arizona** are some evocative Wild-West sites,
including **Tombstone**, now an entertaining if slightly tacky theme
park, and the mining settlement of **Bisbee**.

Phoenix's fragile grip on reality is highlighted by the fact that it was
built on the ruins of a long-lost desert civilization. Until 1350 AD, the
valleys of southern Arizona were home to the **Hohokam** people, and
crisscrossed by a sophisticated network of irrigation canals. It's
thought that the Hohokam eventually overreached themselves, depleting the land too much for their way of life to endure. Their name means
"people who have vanished," in the language of the **'O'odham** (once
known as the Pima and the Papago) who later took their place. The
'O'odham now occupy vast reservations in southwest Arizona, while
their old enemies, the **Apache**, dominate the mountains to the east.

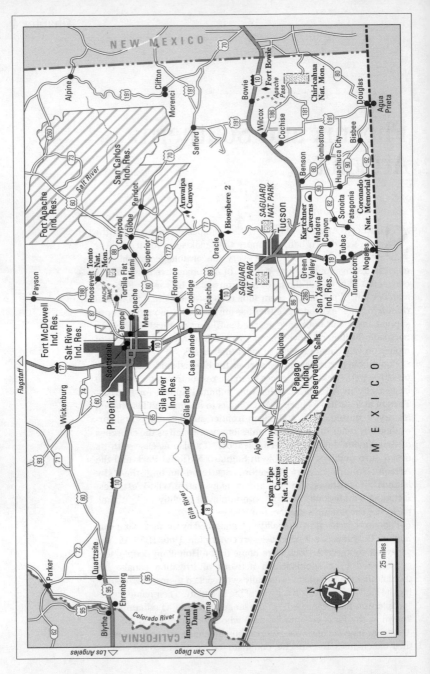

Phoenix

When it began life in the 1860s, **PHOENIX** must have seemed like a good idea. The sweltering little farming town stood in the heart of the **Salt River Valley**, which measures forty miles east to west, and twenty miles north to south, with a ready-made irrigation system left by ancient Indians, and plenty of room to expand. Within a century, however, Phoenix had turned into what writer Edward Abbey called "the blob that is eating Arizona," acquiring as it did so the money and political clout to defy all notions of common sense, and just keep on growing. Today, Arizona's capital has filled the entire valley, and is the eighth largest city in the US. Well over a million people live within the city boundaries, and almost three million people live in the twenty separate incorporated cities that together make up the metropolitan area. The state's financial and industrial epicenter may be just getting into its stride; boosters claim the megalopolis will one day stretch 150 miles, from Wickenburg to Tucson.

Although the entire Phoenix area is known colloquially as the Valley of the Sun, the term has no official meaning.

The city's phenomenal rise was originally fueled by its image as a healthy oasis, where the desert had been tamed and transformed into a suburban idyll. While retirees still flock to enclaves such as **Sun City**, however, it now has a deserved reputation as the most unpleasant city in the Southwest – Las Vegas with no casinos, or LA with no beach. Its endless sprawl has long since covered the "golden fields of ripened grain" described in one 1940s guidebook, and swallowed a host of neighboring communities, such as **Scottsdale**, **Tempe** and **Mesa**, while the TB and asthma sufferers who came to the valley's sanatoriums would now choke on its polluted air. Above all, Phoenix is **hot**; between June and August daytime highs average over 100°F, making it the world's hottest city outside the Middle East.

Phoenix epitomizes the Western maxim that "water flows uphill to money," with a history that revolves around its maneuverings to obtain ever more water, from ever further afield. Despite dams and diversions, the drainage of the Salt River soon proved insufficient, so, absurdly enough, the city is now dependent on aqueducts that cross the deserts from the Colorado River. Since the 1980s, when Phoenicians used a profligate 250 gallons of water per person per day, a note of realism has crept in, and it's no longer legal to adorn your latest real-estate development with an artificial lake. The obsession with liquid remains, though: pedestrians clutch bottled water in the street, and you can't fill your gas tank without the digitized gas pump telling you "Wow it's hot. Wouldn't a cold drink taste good?"

In winter, when temperatures rarely drop below 65°F, **tourists** from colder climes still arrive in Phoenix in large numbers. They pay vast sums to warm their bones in the luxury resorts and spas, concentrated especially in Scottsdale, that are the modern

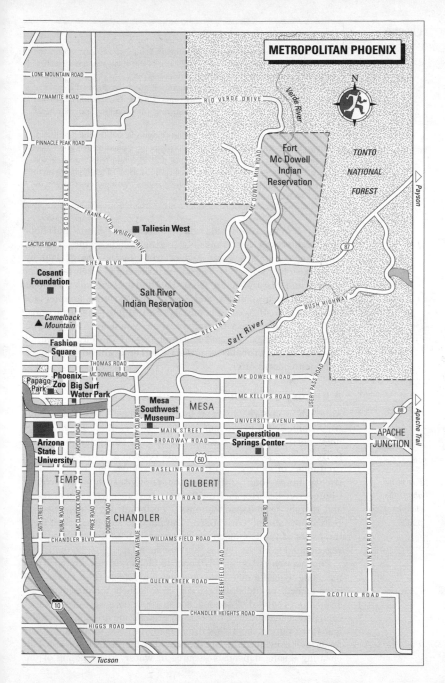

Excursions from Phoenix

If a family visit or business trip to Phoenix brings you to Arizona for the
first time, and you'd like to see a little more of the state, you'll have to rent
a car to get anywhere interesting.

Great **day-trips** include driving a hundred miles north on I-17, and visiting some combination of **Montezuma Castle** (see p.305), **Sedona**
(p.294) and **Jerome** (p.302), or following the **Apache Trail** northeast
from Mesa, as described on p.229.

With a **weekend** to spare, the **Grand Canyon** is an obvious possibility,
though it is a 450-mile round-trip. Alternatively, **Flagstaff** is a good base
for several lesser known attractions (see p.283), while Wild West fans will
enjoy **Tombstone**, 180 miles southeast (p.257). Best of all, if you're up to
driving 300 miles each way, is northeast Arizona's stupendous **Canyon de
Chelly** (p.51).

equivalent of the 1930s dude ranches. Unlike golf, tennis and shopping, **sightseeing** rarely ranks high on the agenda – which is just as
well, since there's a good deal of truth in the charge laid by
Phoenix's older arch-rival, Tucson, that the city is sorely lacking in
culture and history. Apart from the **Heard Museum**'s excellent
Native American displays, and Frank Lloyd Wright's architecture
studio at **Taliesin West**, Phoenix is short of must-see attractions.
In fact, if you're on a touring vacation, you'd miss little if you
bypassed it altogether, and a day at one of the city's plentiful
upscale **malls** is probably as authentic and enjoyable an experience
as Phoenix has to offer.

A history of Phoenix

Although no American settled in the Salt River Valley until **1865**,
when John Smith began supplying hay to Camp McDowell, thirty
miles northeast, it was clear to all that the valley had once supported a large population. Traces still remained of over three hundred miles of **canals** – up to fifteen feet wide, ten feet deep and
twenty miles long – dug by the ancient **Hohokam** people.
Confederate deserter Jack Swilling cleared one such canal in 1867,
and thereby established **Phoenix**. The infant city was named by
British adventurer "Lord" Darrel Duppa, who saw it as rising from
the ashes of the Hohokam civilization much as the mythical bird
regenerated from the flames that consumed it.

*For more
about the
Hohokam, see
p.522.*

Phoenix was laid out in 1870 on a 98-block grid that stretched one
mile long by half a mile wide. Avenues and streets (now numbered)
were named for Indian tribes, and cross streets for presidents. By
1889, it was **capital** of Arizona, and in 1890 there were eleven thousand people in the valley. Catastrophic floods and droughts along the
Salt River during the 1890s drove many farmers to abandon their
fields, and convinced the city-dwellers that their future depended on
ensuring a safe, dependable source of **water**. The building of the

Roosevelt Dam in the mountains to the east, in 1911 (see p.230) was the first step in a process that culminated in the 1990s with the completion of the Central Arizona Project.

By the 1920s, Phoenix was promoting itself as the "winter playground of the Southwest," a healthy refuge from the smog-laden cities of the East that was home to "forty thousand people and the best kind of people, too. A very small percentage of Mexicans, negroes or foreigners." Its citizens were exhorted to landscape their properties with gardens, under the slogan "Let's Do Away With the Desert," and lavish resort hotels began to open. Meanwhile, the black neighborhoods of southwest Phoenix were classified by the federal government as holding the worst slums in the US.

World War II triggered the city's exponential growth, with the acquisition of three major air bases, and industrialization continued apace during the 1950s, when Motorola built a huge plant. The development of air conditioning finally made the desert heat bearable, with half the "evaporative coolers" in the country being made in Phoenix. Between 1950 and 1960 alone, the population swelled from 107,000 to 439,000, and by the time it topped one million, around 1990, the city had grown by over four hundred square miles in forty years. That made it prey to some of the most rapacious speculators in the country, including the infamous Charles Keating, among whose projects were the no-expense-spared *Phoenician Resort* and the "masterplanned community" of Estrella. Keating's arrest and ruin in 1989 coincided with the bankruptcy of ten of Arizona's eleven savings and loans. Eight years later, in a similar scandal, state governor J. Fyfe Symington, was forced to resign after being convicted of fraud in his intricate dealings with downtown developments such as the Mercado Mall.

Arrival, information and getting around

Sky Harbor International Airport (☎602/273-3321), three miles east of downtown, receives flights from all over the US and even direct from Europe. All the major rental car chains, listed on p.20, are represented. Buses on the Valley Metro system (☎602/253-5000) connect the airport with downtown (#13; Mon–Sat), plus Tempe and Mesa (Mon–Fri), but it's easier to take a door-to-door shuttle bus, at $10–12 for downtown destinations and more like $20 for Scottsdale, with SuperShuttle (☎602/244-9000 or 1-800/BLUE VAN). Arizona Shuttle Services (☎520/795-6671 or 1-800/888-2749; $19) run south to Tucson, while Nava-Hopi (☎520/774-5003 or 1-800/892-8687) head north to Flagstaff ($22) and the Grand Canyon ($34.50).

Greyhound buses arrive at 2115 E Buckeye Rd (☎602/389-4200 or 1-800/231-2222), close to the airport. Getting around without a car is not ideal – it can take hours to cross town – but it's not impossible. Valley Metro's commuter bus routes charge $1.25 per ride;

For details of flights to and within the Southwest, see p.3 onwards.

Amtrak trains no longer serve Phoenix, but buses connect with services to Tucson (see p.235) and Flagstaff (p.283).

pick up a schedule at the downtown terminal, at First and Washington. Tourists are more likely to use the purple DASH buses (Mon–Fri 6.30am–5.30pm; 30¢), which ply between the Arizona Center and the Capitol downtown. For a **cab**, call Checker Cab (☎602/257-1818) or Ace Taxi (☎602/254-1999).

Phoenix's main **visitor center** is at Adams and Second downtown (Mon–Fri 8am–5pm; ☎602/254-6500 or 1-877/225-5749; 24hr hotline ☎602/252-5588; *www.arizonaguide.com/phoenix*); there's also an office at 24th Street and Camelback, at the northeast corner of the Biltmore Fashion Park (Mon–Sat 10am–9pm, Sun noon–6pm). The main **post office** is at 4949 E Van Buren St, though the branch at 522 N Central Ave is more convenient for downtown.

Contact Gray Line (☎602/495-9100) for details of city tours.

Accommodation

Metropolitan Phoenix is so huge that it's worth paying a bit extra to ensure that your **accommodation** is near the places you want to visit. Oddly enough, **downtown Phoenix** is not one of the more expensive areas, with cheap motels lining the somewhat run-down West Van Buren Street a few blocks north of the center. Room rates are considerably more expensive in **winter**, when snowbirds from all over the US fill the upscale **resorts** of Scottsdale in particular.

As explained on p.15, accommodation prices, excluding taxes, are indicated throughout this book by the following symbols:

① *up to $30*
② *$30–45*
③ *$45–60*
④ *$60–80*
⑤ *$80–100*
⑥ *$100–130*
⑦ *$130–175*
⑧ *$175–250*
⑨ *$250+*

Central Phoenix

Arizona Biltmore Resort & Spa, 24th St and Missouri Ave, Phoenix, AZ 85016; ☎602/955-6600 or 1-800/950-0086, fax 602/381-7646; *www.arizonabiltmore.com*. Extraordinarily lavish 500-room resort, built under the influence of Frank Lloyd Wright in the 1930s, and renovated while retaining its Art Deco trimmings. June–Sept ⑧, Oct–May ⑨.

Budget Lodge Motel, 402 W Van Buren St, Phoenix, AZ 85003; ☎602/254-7247. Reasonably attractive rooms at very attractive rates – not far from the center, but you'll feel safer if you drive rather than walk here. ②.

HI-Phoenix, *The Metcalf House*, 1026 N Ninth St above Roosevelt St, Phoenix, AZ 85004; ☎602/254-9803. Dorm beds at $12 for HI-AYH members, $15 non-members, a 15min walk north of the Arizona Center. No phone reservations, but space is usually available. No curfew, cheap bike rental. ①.

Howard Johnson Lodge, 124 S 24th St, Phoenix, AZ 85034; ☎602/244-8221. Standard doubles near the airport. Summer ③, winter ④.

San Carlos Hotel, 202 N Central Ave, Phoenix, AZ 85004; ☎602/253-4121 or 1-800/528-5446, fax 602/253-6668; *sancarlos1@aol.com*. Atmospheric, very central 1920s hotel, with tasteful, good-value rooms, a nice cafe (see p.227) and a rooftop swimming pool. June–Sept ④, Oct–May ⑤.

Super 8 Phoenix Airport, 3401 E Van Buren St, Phoenix, AZ 85008; ☎602/244-1627 or 1-800/800-8000, fax 602/275-1126. Dependable chain motel, a mile north of the airport, with free shuttle connection. Summer ④, winter ⑤.

YMCA, 350 N First Ave; ☎602/253-6181. Grungy but central single rooms for men and women, with shared bathrooms. Very low weekly rates. No reservations: first come, first served. ①.

Scottsdale

Days Inn Resort at Fashion Square Mall, 4710 N Scottsdale Rd, Scottsdale, AZ 85251; ☎480/947-5411 or 1-800/325-2525, fax 480/946-1324; *www.daysinnscottsdale.com*. Standard hotel, well priced by local standards and handily located within walking distance of downtown at Fashion Square Mall. Summer ④, winter ⑤.

Phoenician Resort, 6000 E Camelback Rd, Scottsdale, AZ 85251; ☎480/941-8200 or 1-800/888-8234, fax 480/947-4311; *www.thephoenician.com*. Gorgeous 130-acre resort, arrayed at the base of Camelback Mountain at the northern end of Scottsdale, and offering every conceivable luxury, with golf course, waterfalls and lush gardens as well as lavish rooms and restaurants. Mid-June to Aug ⑧, Sept to mid-June ⑨.

Royal Inn Motel, 2934 N Scottsdale Rd, Scottsdale, AZ 85251; ☎480/947-5885 or 1-800/341-8000, fax 480/970-0521. Surprisingly inexpensive, perfectly adequate traditional motel, a few blocks south of Old Scottsdale. Summer ②, winter ④.

Scottsdale Pima Inn & Suites, 7330 N Pima Rd, Scottsdale, AZ 85258; ☎480/948-3800 or 1-800/344-0262, fax 480/443-3374. Relatively inexpensive motel, a few miles northwest of central Scottsdale but offering free local shuttles, with comfortable conventional rooms and pricier suites. Summer ③, winter ④.

Scottsdale's Fifth Avenue Inn, 6935 Fifth Ave, Scottsdale, AZ 85251; ☎480/994-9461 or 1-800/528-7396, fax 480/947-1695. Good-value motel with pool, on the edge of Scottsdale's shopping district. Summer ③, winter ④.

Tempe and Mesa

Arizona Golf Resort, 425 S Power Rd, Mesa, AZ 85206; ☎480/832-3202 or 1-800/528-8282, fax 480/981-0151. Pleasant rooms and suites in individual *casitas*, mainly intended for golfers using the adjoining course, but handy for forays into the mountains to the east. Summer ⑤, winter ⑦.

Fiesta Inn, 2100 S Priest Drive, Tempe, AZ 85282; ☎480/967-1441 or 1-800/528-6481, fax 480/697-0224. Old-style resort, not as plush as its Scottsdale counterparts, but not as expensive either, offering large rooms plus restaurant, pool and spa. Summer ④, winter ⑥.

Motel 6, 630 W Main St, Mesa, AZ 85201; ☎480/969-8111. The most central of Mesa's three *Motel 6*'s; there are three more in Tempe. All offer dull double rooms at budget rates. ②.

Super 8 Mesa Town Center, 3 E Main St, Mesa, AZ 85201; ☎480/834-6060 or 1-800/800-8000. Budget chain motel in the heart of downtown Mesa, a couple of blocks from the Southwest Museum. Summer ②, winter ④.

Super 8 Tempe/Scottsdale, 1020 E Apache Blvd, Tempe, AZ 85281; ☎480/967-8891 or 1-800/800-8000, fax 480/968-7868. Chain motel, within half a mile of the university and five miles of the airport. Summer ③, winter ④.

Central Phoenix

Downtown Phoenix – defined as the few blocks east and west of Central Avenue, and north and south of **Washington Street** – is too hot, too run-down, and too spread out to walk around in any comfort. Nominally it's still the headquarters of Arizona Inc, but the major

ACCOMMODATION

Budget Lodge Motel 3
HI-Phoenix   1
San Carlos   4
YMCA   2

EATING

Alice Cooper'stown C
Pizzeria Bianco   B
Sam's Cafe   A

0   800 yds

DOWNTOWN PHOENIX

corporate offices and institutions are now scattered throughout the
Valley of the Sun. The latest downtown mall – the **Arizona Center**,
on Van Buren Street between Third and Fifth – has finally brought
some retail business back to the center, but it's still a pale imitation
of the megamalls further north (see p.228).

What little remains of Phoenix's nineteenth-century architecture now constitutes **Heritage Square**, a couple of blocks southeast of the Arizona Center at 115 N Sixth St. Rather than original
adobe ranch houses, however, it preserves a twee assortment of
Victorian homes converted into tearooms and toy museums. You
can get a better impression of the early days at the **Phoenix
Museum of History**, across the street at 105 N Fifth St (Mon–Sat
10am–5pm, Sun noon–5pm; $5), which starts with a "calendar
stick" used by Pima Indians, and features the city's first jail – a
rock with a chain attached – as well as early town plans and a
steam-powered bicycle.

Twenty sun-baked blocks west, the sparkling copper dome of the disused **Arizona State Capitol** dominates the low-level sprawl. Documents in the dull, dry **museum** within do little to bring the state's political history to life (Mon–Fri 8am–5pm; free).

Two more significant attractions lie a mile or so north of downtown (and north of I-10, though you won't see the interstate as it burrows beneath Central Ave). Thanks to extensive recent remodeling, the **Phoenix Art Museum**, 1625 N Central Ave (Tues, Wed, Sat & Sun 10am–5pm, Thurs & Fri 10am–9pm; $6, free Thurs 5–9pm), has plenty of space to display its permanent collection, which includes paintings by Georgia O'Keeffe and Rufino Tamayo, as well as de rigueur Western art by Russell and Remington and some middleweight Old Masters, while also maintaining its reputation for controversial temporary exhibitions. A top-quality gift shop stocks Mexican crafts items and jazzy modern ceramics.

Three blocks north and a block east, the **Heard Museum**, 22 E Monte Vista Rd (daily 9.30am–5pm; $7), has also been greatly enlarged in the last few years, while still showcasing the lovely old buildings in which it was originally founded. For first-time visitors to the region, it serves as a fascinating introduction to the culture of the **Native Americans** of the Southwest, and their arts and crafts in particular. There's an especial emphasis on the Hohokam, with plenty of artifacts from the large town, now known as "La Ciudad," which occupied the site of modern Phoenix during the twelfth century. Elsewhere, the superb pottery collection ranges from stunning Mimbres bowls, a parrot-headed and -tailed Salado jar from 1350 AD, and clay dolls made by the Quechan and Mohave peoples as souvenirs for nineteenth-century railroad passengers, to modern Hopi ceramics. You'll also find a complete Navajo *hogan*, some fine old Havasupai baskets, Apache beadwork, and painted buffalo-skin shields from New Mexican pueblos. The real highlight, however, is a refrigerated room filled with *kachina* dolls – 400 of them donated by arch-conservative Arizona senator Barry Goldwater – arranged according to the Hopi sacred calendar. Look for a haunting photo of the *so'so'yoktu*, the ogres who scare Hopi children into good behavior, taken at Walpi in 1900 before photographers were banned from the Hopi reservation.

For more on the Mimbres culture, see p.210; Navajo hogans are discussed on p.56; and the kachina religion is described on p.60.

Scottsdale

Having grown to house well over 150,000 people, and stretch almost twenty miles from north to south, the town of **SCOTTSDALE**, founded ten miles northeast of Phoenix in the 1880s, is a remarkable success story in its own right. Despite being almost wholly subsumed into the metropolitan maw, it has carved itself an eccentric double niche as both the city's chicest destination, home to opulent resorts and designer-led malls, and its most determinedly "Western" quarter.

Phoenix

*If you doubt
whether the
people who
named
Camelback
Mountain had
ever seen a
real camel, see
pp.269–270.*

Southeast of **Camelback Mountain** and the grand **Scottsdale Fashion Square** mall, downtown Scottsdale focuses on a few pleasant blocks of sidewalk cafes and souvenir stores. West of Scottsdale Road counts as the **Main Street Arts and Antiques District**; to the east, **Old Town** plays the Wild West theme for all it's worth.

Whatever its general appearance may suggest, Phoenix has managed to attract some visionary designers. Notable among them is **Frank Lloyd Wright**, who came to the city to work on the *Biltmore Hotel*, and stayed for most of the 25 years before his death in 1959. His winter studio, **Taliesin West** – located at 114th Street and Frank Lloyd Wright Boulevard, at Scottsdale's northeastern edge – is now an architecture school and a working design studio, with multimedia exhibits of the man's life and work (daily: Oct–May 10am–4pm; June–Sept 7.30–11am; ☎480/860-2700). It can only be seen on guided visits; up to five hour-long tours take place each morning ($12), and they're followed on winter afternoons by three 1hr 30min "Insights" ($16).

Less well known, but in many ways more compelling, is the **Cosanti Foundation**, four miles southwest at 6433 Doubletree Rd (daily 9am–5pm; $1 donation). The buildings, designed by **Paolo Soleri**, an Italian-born ex-student of Wright, and constructed out of rammed earth and concrete, have a much more organic feel than Taliesin. Crafts workshops cast bells and bronzes, and a small museum shows drawings and models of Soleri's life work: the planned community of **Arcosanti**, described on p.306.

Papago Park at the south end of Scottsdale is home to the **Desert Botanical Garden** (daily: Oct–April 8am–8pm; May–Sept 7am–8pm; $7), filled with an amazing array of cactuses and desert flora from around the world, and **Phoenix Zoo** (daily: May to Labor Day 7am–4pm; Labor Day to April 9am–5pm; $8.50), which offers four monkey islands and a half-hour ride on a Safari Train. At the **Big Surf water park**, not far east at 1500 N McClintock Ave (May–Sept only, Mon–Sat 10am–6pm, Sun 11am–7pm; $14.25), you can ride five-foot waves or careen down multistory waterslides into a giant freshwater lagoon.

Tempe

As the site of **Arizona State University**, the community of **TEMPE**, across I-60 south of Scottsdale, and around six miles east of downtown Phoenix, is probably the liveliest portion of the Valley of the Sun. Several minor museums and galleries are dotted across the college campus, but the main reason to visit is to hang out in the cafes and clubs of **Mill Avenue**, immediately west. For an overview of local history – Tempe started out as a ferry post for travelers crossing the Salt River – call in at the spruced-up **Tempe Historical Museum** (Mon–Thurs & Sat 10am–5pm, Sun 1–5pm; $2.50).

Navajo *hogan*, Monument Valley, AZ

Santuario de Chimayó, NM

White House Trail, Canyon de Chelly, AZ

Taos Pueblo, NM

Million Dollar Highway, CO

Cliff Palace, Mesa Verde National Park, CO

Navajo National Monument, AZ

Kiva at Coronado State Monument, NM

Monument Valley, AZ

White Sands National Monument, NM

Betatakin, Navajo National Monument, AZ

Petroglyph at Puyé Cliff Dwellings, NM

Mesa

Built on the site of the Mormon settlement of Fort Utah, which lasted for three years from 1877, **MESA**, east of Tempe, is now Arizona's third-largest city. Covering more than a hundred square miles, it has a population of over 300,000. Hidden among its endless broad boulevards are twenty golf courses, several large malls, some of Phoenix's most affordable residential districts, and dozens of cheap motels. With the Superstition Mountains rising to the east, it's not a bad base for passing visitors.

As well as displays on dinosaurs and the Hohokam, the enjoyable **Mesa Southwest Museum**, 53 N MacDonald St (Tues–Sat 10am–5pm, Sun 1–5pm; $4), features a reconstruction of a block of Mesa's Main Street as it looked a century ago. Stars of the show, however, are the crudely carved **Peralta Stones**, believed by some to hold the key to the legendary Lost Dutchman Mine (see p.229); four to six major expeditions each year use them as their guide.

Eating

Most of the **restaurants** in greater Phoenix seem to have retreated to the malls in recent years, so unless you're prepared to pay resort prices, it's hard to find a good restaurant with very much atmosphere. The mall places aren't at all bad, however, and there's plenty of variety. Apart from a block or two in central Scottsdale, no area of the metropolis is small enough to walk around while you look for a place to eat, but if you're happy to drive, neighborhood diners – especially Mexican – can still be found, and the major thoroughfares are the usual fast-food heaven.

Central Phoenix

Alice Cooper'stown, 101 E Jackson St; ☎602/253-7337. Barbecue restaurant-cum-sports bar, owned by the rock star and alongside downtown's America West Arena, where the food's better than you'd expect, and the atmosphere is fun. Lunch and dinner daily.

Ed Debevic's Short Orders Deluxe, 2102 E Highland Ave; ☎602/956-2760. Burgers and fries, malts and cokes, served amid frenetic retro-Americana that includes a mini-jukebox on every table. Open daily for lunch and dinner.

Eddie's Grill, 4747 N Seventh St; ☎602/241-1188. Modern American cuisine served in stylish surroundings north of downtown; lots of seared and blackened meat and fish, with lunchtime entrees priced at $10, and more like twice that in the evening. Open for lunch and dinner Mon–Fri, dinner only Sat.

The Fish Market, 1720 E Camelback Rd; ☎602/277-3474. Two-tier fish restaurant on the way to Scottsdale, which shares its premises with a real fishmonger – always a good sign. The large downstairs dining room, open for lunch and dinner daily, includes an oyster and sushi bar, while the cooking in the pricier dinner-only *Top of the Market* upstairs is more adventurous.

Phoenix

Pizzeria Bianco, Heritage Square, 623 E Adams St; ☎602/258-8300. Good-quality pizzas in very convenient downtown location. Lunch and dinner Tues–Fri, dinner only Sat & Sun.

Roxsand, Biltmore Fashion Park, 2594 E Camelback Rd; ☎602/381-0444. Eclectic, futuristic restaurant in this upmarket uptown mall, where entrees drawn from the major world cuisines – especially Asian, with plenty of spicy Thai and Chinese sauces – start at around $20. Lunch and dinner daily.

Sam's Cafe, Arizona Center, 455 N Third St; ☎602/252-3545. Hectic down-town mall joint, with patio seating, that's nonetheless a great place to try out modern Southwestern cuisine – grilled fish is the best low-cal option – at old-fashioned prices. Lunch and dinner daily.

There's anoth-er Sam's Cafe *in the Biltmore Fashion Park, north of down-town at 24th and Camelback;* ☎602/954-7100.

Scottsdale

Cafe Terra Cotta, Borgata Mall, 6166 N Scottsdale Rd; ☎480/948-8100. Outpost of the long-established Tucson favorite, whose creative Southwestern cuisine – lavishly adorned with chiles, chipotle sauces, and even horseradish – is proving a big hit. Entrees range $12–20. Lunch and dinner daily.

Coyote Grill, 7077 E Bell Rd; ☎480/922-8424. Good, inexpensive Southwestern restaurant, with a healthy menu of grilled meats and fish, and lighter lunchtime snacks. Dinner only Mon–Thurs, lunch and dinner Fri–Sun.

Oregano's Pizza Bistro, 3622 N Scottsdale Rd; ☎480/970-1860. Lively, noisy but fun pizzeria, on the southern fringes of Old Scottsdale, where a good-sized pie costs around $10. Lunch and dinner daily.

Phô Dong Phuong, 8123 E Roosevelt Rd; ☎480/949-5251. Neat, neighbor-hood Vietnamese diner, specializing in great beef or vegetarian noodle soups at very low prices. Lunch and dinner daily.

Roy's, 7001 N Scottsdale Rd; ☎480/905-1155. Huge restaurant in a very chic, busy dining district, where Hawaiian chef Roy Yamaguchi's ravishing Pacific Rim cuisine is cooked before your eyes in the open kitchen area. The blackened ahi (tuna) sashimi makes a great appetizer; meaty entrees, mostly at $20–25, include Szechuan barbecued pork ribs or rack of lamb, while daily specials usually include Hawaiian fish dishes. Open daily for din-ner only.

Windows on the Green, *Phoenician Resort*, 6000 E Camelback Rd; ☎480/423-2530. This bright, attractive resort dining room – overlooking the golf course, it's the *Phoenician*'s "casual" alternative to the formal and very elegant *Mary Elaine's* – is a fine restaurant in its own right. The Southwestern menu concentrates on grilled and roasted fish and meat, at $20–30 per entree. Open Wed–Sun for lunch and dinner.

Tempe

House Of Tricks, 114 E Seventh St; ☎480/968-1114. Tiny little modern-American place in the University district, named for chefs Robin and Robert Trick, with lots of vegetarian options. Most entrees cost around $15. Open Mon–Sat for lunch and dinner.

Monti's La Casa Vieja, 3 W First St; ☎480/967-7594. Tempe's oldest adobe house, built beside the Salt River ferry landing in 1873, is now an atmospheric Western-themed diner, serving a conventional steak-and-chicken menu at extraordinarily low prices. Lunch and dinner daily.

Zipangu, 1066 E Warner Rd; ☎480/839-3924. "Amerasian bistro" featuring a sushi bar (8-piece platter $16), plus skewered *yakitori* meats and assorted noodle dishes. Open for lunch and dinner Mon–Fri, dinner only Sat & Sun.

Mesa

Annabelle's, *Arizona Golf Resort*, 425 S Power Rd; ☎480/832-3202. Attractive resort restaurant, serving good-quality deli lunches for well under $10, and more formal dinners, usually with seafood specials, at $10 and up. Open for all meals daily.

The Landmark Restaurant, 809 W Main St; ☎480/962-4652. Classic mid-American diner housed in a former Mormon church, serving hearty baked and roasted meats for $10–15, including a trip to the excellent salad bar. Open for lunch and dinner Mon–Fri, dinner only on Sat, brunch only on Sun.

The Seafood Market, 1318 W Southern Ave, suite #11; ☎480/890-0435. A feast of fresh fish, flown in from all over the world, and prepared simply at reasonable prices, for lunch and dinner daily.

Coffeehouses

Espresso coffee has swept across Phoenix like wildfire in the last few years, with specialty coffeehouses in the trendier districts and chain outlets in all the malls. The local coffee set even have their own free magazine, *Java Monthly*. As well as the cafes below, look out for the popular *Coffee Plantation* chain, whose locations include the Biltmore Fashion Park, Fashion Square in Scottsdale, Fiesta Mall in Mesa, and 680 S Mill St in Tempe.

Espressions, 4407 N Saddlebag Trail, Scottsdale; ☎480/946-9840. Coffee and tea in every imaginable flavor, at temperatures from frozen to searing.

Orbit Cafe, Uptown Plaza, Central and Camelback; ☎602/265-2354. Large mall cafe doubling as a gallery and performance space, with an emphasis on jazz.

Roma Coffee Co, *San Carlos Hotel*, 202 N Central Ave; ☎602/253-0410. Small downtown cafe set in an historic hotel, with some sidewalk seating.

The Willow House, 149 W McDowell Rd; ☎602/252-0272. Single-story house, a mile north of downtown, that offers snacks and desserts, poetry and comedy, as well as coffee. Open Mon–Fri 7am, Sat & Sun 8am, until late.

Nightlife, entertainment and sports

Not surprisingly, **nightlife** in Phoenix tends toward cowboy dance halls and Top 40 discos in the big hotels. For a rundown of what's on musically, pick up the free weekly *New Times* in local record- or bookstores, or check out the bars and clubs listed overleaf.

Both the **Phoenix Symphony Hall**, 225 E Adams St (☎602/262-7272), and the **Scottsdale Center for the Arts**, 7380 E Second St (☎480/994-2787), put on classical music, theater and ballet. The **Arizona Diamondbacks** have been playing major league baseball beneath the retractable roof of the Bank One Ballpark since 1998 (☎602/514-8500), while the **Phoenix Suns** play NBA basketball at the America West Arena, 201 E Jefferson St (☎602/379-7867), and football's **Arizona Cardinals** are based at the university's Sun Devil Stadium (☎602/379-0102.)

Balboa Cafe, 404 S Mill Ave, Tempe; ☎480/966-1300. Jazz, offbeat rock and acoustic artists near the university.

Char's Has The Blues, 4631 N Seventh Ave; ☎602/230-0205. Phoenix's longest-standing, best-loved blues venue, attracting big-name touring stars.

Coyote Springs Brewing Company, Town & Country Shopping Center, 4883 N 20th St; ☎602/468-0403. Mall microbrewery that puts on R&B several nights of the week.

The Mason Jar, 2303 E Indian School Rd; ☎602/956-6271. Headbanger heaven, hosting mostly metal seven nights a week.

Mr Lucky's, 3660 NW Grand Ave; ☎602/246-0686. Massive country-music honky-tonk, featuring real-life bull riding at weekends.

Phoenix Live!, Arizona Center, 455 N Third Ave; ☎602/252-2502. Anodyne but very central alliance of three separate clubs under a single roof, with a single cover charge.

Shopping

Space does not permit a detailed listing of individual stores in Phoenix, but with the city's great outdoors too hot and sprawling to take for more than a few minutes at a time, you'll probably find yourself looking for a nice cool **mall** at some point.

The biggest of the lot – in the whole Southwest, for that matter – is the **Metrocenter**, just east of I-17 at 9617 Metro Parkway, nine miles north of downtown. The central mall building holds all the usual outlets, plus five large department stores, while countless more stores and restaurants line the oval ring road around it. When you tire of shopping, try the rollercoaster in **Castles and Coasters**, alongside (daily 10am until at least 10pm; pay per ride).

The **Biltmore Fashion Park**, north of Camelback Road at 24th Street, halfway between downtown Phoenix and Scottsdale, concentrates on designer names, but does have a giant Borders bookstore, while the **Scottsdale Fashion Square**, further east at 7000 E Camelback Rd, is (slightly) more affordable. Also in Scottsdale, a couple of miles north, the smaller **Borgata** mall is notable for its extraordinary mock-Italian architecture. Finally, the downtown **Arizona Center** is a bit short on interesting shops but is at least livening the place up a little. Some day, it may be helped in that task by Fyfe Symington's white elephant **Mercado** mall, to build which the former state governor is said to have siphoned off $10 million of the city's pension fund; currently it's all but empty.

East of Phoenix

Almost two hundred miles of mountainous terrain stands between Phoenix and New Mexico to the east, much of it belonging to two huge Apache reservations. Although sweltering Phoenicians spend summer weekends in hill towns such as Payson and Pinetop to the northeast (both covered in Chapter 5), there's little to detain ordinary tourists on the long drive east.

US-60 and US-70 are the quickest routes to New Mexico, but if you want a quick escape from the desert heat, head instead up the Apache Trail into the **Superstition Mountains**. An enduring Arizona legend makes these the site of the **Lost Dutchman Mine**. Two German prospectors, Jacob Waltz and Jacob Weiser, supposedly discovered rich deposits of gold around 1870, and turned up repeatedly in the town of Florence bearing priceless nuggets. Before his death in Phoenix in 1890, Waltz is said to have murdered not only Weiser but another seven men who tried to shadow him back to the motherlode. Ever since, countless expeditions have attempted to follow his deathbed directions to the mine – guarded, according to different accounts, by pygmies or a never-discovered group of Apaches – and an estimated thirty gold-seekers are rumored to have lost their lives.

The Apache Trail

The closest accessible wilderness to central Phoenix lies along **Hwy-88**, which climbs northeast into the Superstition Mountains from Apache Junction, almost twenty miles east of Mesa and a good thirty miles from downtown. This fifty-mile highway was constructed in 1904 to provide a direct route to the site of the Roosevelt Dam, then being built at the confluence of Tonto Creek and Salt River. After the dam's completion in 1911, it was renamed **The Apache Trail** by the Southern Pacific Railroad in a bid to drum up tourists, and became a popular scenic drive. It's still a long, slow haul, tortuous enough to take around two hours end to end.

Just four miles up from Apache Junction, as the cactus-studded foothills start to rise, **Goldfield Ghost Town** provides an appealingly ramshackle photo opportunity, complete with discarded mine machinery and a street of tumbledown timber-frame stores (daily 9am–6pm). Much of what you see is either fake or brought here from somewhere else, but it's all quite atmospheric. **Activities** such as jeep tours, descents into mine shafts, or train rides cost around $4 per person, and the various on-site businesses also have details of horse rides or even helicopter flights in the vicinity. Alternatively, you can pick up a snack or a meal at the *Coffee Cantina and Bakery* (4650 N Mammoth Mine Rd; ☎480/983-8777) or the *Mammoth Steak House*.

Many day-trippers go no further up the Apache Trail than **Canyon Lake**, fifteen miles along. Created by a more recent dam, but nonetheless old enough to look as though it belongs amid the scrubby surrounding hills, it's a bit too narrow to satisfy pleasure-boaters, who find themselves having to turn around every time they get up a bit of speed. However, if you're happy to take it easy, a ninety-minute cruise on *Dolly's Steamboat* is an enjoyable way to pass a morning (☎480/827-9144; $14).

TORTILLA FLAT, at the east end of the lake, is not so much a town as a hundred-yard stretch of boardwalk that holds the County Store, the *Dutchman's Inn* and the *Superstition Saloon*, all operated by the same management (☎480/984-1776). It was named for the nearby flat-topped boulders, not the Steinbeck novella.

Beyond Tortilla Flat, the mountains finally start to get serious, while Hwy-88 responds by turning to gravel. After a few hair-raising hairpin bends, with stomach-lurching views across the saguaro-studded canyons, it returns to undulating gently along beside the river. An optional detour drops down to **Apache Lake**, another busy boating and picnicking spot. Keep going to reach **Roosevelt Dam** itself, which was recently raised and strengthened to cope with Phoenix's bottomless thirst for water.

Tonto National Monument

Three miles east of Roosevelt Dam, the **cliff dwellings** of TONTO NATIONAL MONUMENT (daily 8am–5pm; $4 per vehicle) stand high above Hwy-88, overlooking Theodore Roosevelt Lake. From the **visitor center** (same hours; ☎520/467-2241), a very steep trail, which shuts an hour before closing time, climbs half a mile upwards. Not a walk to schedule for the middle of a summer's day, it leads to the remarkably complete **Lower Ruin**, set in a deep alcove near the top of the rocky ridge, with great saguaro cactuses standing sentinel.

This large pueblo was built in the mid-fourteenth century by a people now known as the **Salado** Indians, who are regarded as less sophisticated than the Ancestral Puebloans to the north. Their masonry is much cruder, using lumps of rock that had fallen from the cliff face and were then thickly plastered with mud that still bears thousands of ancient fingerprints. Visitors can walk right through several rooms of the ruin, some of which retain their original beams and saguaro-rib ceilings. "Shelves" and storage niches are tucked into the cave walls, as well as notches that once supported additional rooms.

Between November and April only, rangers lead guided hikes to the **Upper Ruin**, reached by a separate trail up the next ridge along.

Globe

Hwy-88 rejoins US-60, the direct route east from Phoenix, thirty miles on from Tonto National Monument, just outside GLOBE. This still-functional mining town sprang into being in the 1880s, when a twelve-mile strip of land on which a globe of pure silver had just been discovered was stripped from the Apache reservation; since the silver and gold ran out, it has made its living from copper.

The central few blocks of downtown Globe still hold several brick-built Victorian-era structures, though the claim that these include "the West's oldest Woolworth's" betrays quite how little there is of any great interest. On the northern outskirts, the small **Gila County Historical Museum**, 1330 N Broad St (Mon–Fri 10am–4pm; free), explores local history in punitive detail.

That Native American occupation of the region predated the Apache is shown by the ruins of **Besh-Ba-Gowah**, a mile southeast of town, which were home first to the Hohokam and later to the Salado; their modern Apache name is said to mean "metal-its-house." Visitors can enter reconstructed living quarters and a *kiva* (daily 9am–5pm; $2).

If you like your Wild West to be utterly unvarnished and unromantic, head a mile or two west of Globe to the twin communities of **CLAYPOOL** and **MIAMI**. All but engulfed by monstrous mountains of copper-mine tailings, these flyblown towns are packed with gun stores, all-day saloons and pick-up trucks, and are certainly not a vacation destination to be chosen in preference to Miami, Florida.

Practicalities

Globe's **visitor center** stands in front of the county museum on Hwy-88, at 1360 N Broad St (Mon–Fri 8am–5pm; ☎520/425-4495 or 1-800/804-5623). Of the dozen or so **motels**, the restored, vintage *El Rey*, 1201 E Ash St (☎520/425-4427; ②), and the *Ember*, 1105 N Broad St (☎520/425-5736; ②), which has a pool, offer the best value. Downtown **cafes** include the Mexican bakery *La Luz del Dia*, 304 N Broad St (☎520/425-8400; ②), where the burritos are made with fresh tortillas, while *Java Junction*, at Broad and Center (☎520/402-8926), serves coffee and sandwiches. On the third weekend in October, Native Americans from all over the Southwest pour in for the three-day **Apache Days** fair.

Globe's zip code is AZ 85502.

San Carlos Indian Reservation

The two-million-acre **San Carlos Indian Reservation**, which extends a hundred miles east and north of Globe, was created by President Grant in 1872, to protect the **Apache** from such outrages as the Camp Grant massacre of 1871 (see overleaf). In the words of one tribal member, it was "the worst place in all the great territory stolen from the Apache. If anybody ever lived there permanently, no Apache knew of it . . . The heat was terrible. The insects were terrible. The water was terrible."

Around eight thousand Apache now live on the reservation, which offers few activities for tourists apart from sailing or fishing on **San Carlos Lake**, twenty miles east of Globe, or **camping** beside it at *Soda Canyon Point* (☎520/475-2756; $5). The original reservation town of **SAN CARLOS** was drowned – despite strong Apache opposition – when the lake arose behind the new Coolidge Dam in 1930, whereupon the community previously known as **Rice**, ten miles north, was simply renamed San Carlos. Today, the settlement is just an administrative center; if you want to learn more about the Apache, take time to study the displays on their religion and history at the **San Carlos Apache Cultural Center** in **PERIDOT**, on US-70 nearby (Tues–Sat 9am–5pm, Sun 11am–4pm; $3).

Aravaipa Canyon

One of the most notorious tragedies in the whole sorry tale of Anglo-Apache relations took place in the deceptively beautiful **ARAVAIPA CANYON**, just below the southern boundary of the San Carlos reservation. In 1871, when it was home to a semi-permanent Apache encampment under the nominal protection of the US army, 144 women and children were slaughtered in the **Camp Grant Massacre**. Their killers, an unholy party of Tucson vigilantes who called themselves the Committee of Public Safety, consisted of a hundred Tohono 'O'odham, fifty Hispanics and six Anglos.

Reached along a well-maintained eleven-mile dirt road that heads east from Hwy-77 fifty miles south of Globe, Aravaipa Canyon is now a **wilderness area** managed by the federal government and the Arizona Nature Conservancy. The terrain ranges from sun-drenched hillsides covered with saguaros to the deep red gorge carved by Aravaipa Creek – a rare perennial desert stream – and lined by giant cottonwoods. Visitors keen to experience the desert in its wild state need to come prepared; the canyon has no trails, no established campgrounds and no signs, and is home to rattlesnakes and scorpions. Only fifty people can enter the thirty-square-mile wilderness at any one time; obtain a **permit** ($1.50 per day, with a maximum two-night stay) from the Bureau of Land Management, 711 14th Ave, Safford, AZ 85546 (☎520/428-4040).

Safford

The farming community of **SAFFORD**, 77 miles southeast of Globe, is the only sizeable town north of I-10 in southeast Arizona. There's no significant reason to visit, but if you're ready to stop for the night, it holds around a dozen motels, such as the *Econo Lodge*, 225 E Thatcher Blvd (☎520/348-0011; ②), as well as a pleasant **B&B**, *Olney House*, 1104 Central Ave (☎520/428-5118; *olney@zekes.com*; ⑤).

Morenci and Clifton

At its southern end, the **Coronado Scenic Road** – described on p.278 – twists its way down past a vast tiered pit, where the Gila Mountains still yield 175,000 tons of copper a day. **MORENCI**, at the bottom, is a modern-looking company town that was built in the 1960s to replace a predecessor swallowed up by the mine, and is absolutely dominated by the Phelps Dodge company. The *Morenci Motel and Restaurant* (☎520/865-4111; ③) stands on a knoll opposite the Phelps Dodge Mercantile Company Store.

A few miles further on, the older town of **CLIFTON** has become seriously run-down, and is too derelict to be worth a stop.

From Phoenix to Tucson

The hundred-mile sprint from Phoenix to Tucson along the I-10 interstate is one of Arizona's less inspiring drives, though it is at least over quite quickly. The main interruption en route is the molar-shaped promontory of **Picacho Peak**, at the base of which, the roadside stall of the Rooster Cogburn Ostrich Farm is as good a place to stretch your legs as any, and possibly buy a feather duster. If you don't mind taking a slightly more circuitous route, however, it's possible to break the journey at a couple of equally unlikely and enigmatic structures – ancient **Casa Grande**, and ultramodern **Biosphere 2**.

Casa Grande Ruins National Monument

Near **COOLIDGE**, fifteen miles east of exit 185 on the interstate, or twenty miles north of exit 210, **CASA GRANDE RUINS NATIONAL MONUMENT** preserves the most substantial surviving example of the architecture of the **Hohokam** people (daily 7am–6pm; $4 per vehicle; ☎520/723-3172). The Casa Grande itself – the name is Spanish for "Great House" – is a four-story building that was completed in the early fourteenth century. Made of the concrete-like natural stone known as caliche, it stood at the center of a walled compound in the flood-plain of the **Gila River**. The villagers used a well-developed network of canals to grow crops, harvested fruit from saguaro cactuses, and traded for shells and macaws with peoples from the south. The exact purpose of the Casa Grande is unknown, however; archeologists speculate that it was an astronomical observatory that doubled as a fortress in case of attack. Now protected beneath a spider-like canopy, it's not open to visitors, who have to content themselves with the historical displays in the visitor center and strolling through other less identifiable ruins.

Casa Grande Ruins National Monument shares a name, but little else, with the I-10 pit stop of Casa Grande, thirty miles southwest, and the much larger ancient site of Casas Grandes, far south in northern Mexico.

Biosphere 2

Hwy-79 heads southeast from the small farming community of **FLORENCE**, ten miles west of Casa Grande monument, to meet **Hwy-77** roughly thirty miles north of Tucson. Turning east towards Oracle at this point gives tourists the chance to catch up with the latest developments in the extraordinary science-fiction saga of **BIOSPHERE 2**, at mile-marker 96.5 on Hwy-77 (guided tours daily 8am–5pm; $13; ☎520/896-6200 or 1-800/828-2462).

From
Phoenix to
Tucson

When it was completed, in 1991, this vast complex of plexiglass pyramids was trumpeted as a major laboratory for experiments in applied environmental science. Containing five separate "biomes," or self-contained ecosystems – rainforest, marsh, savannah, desert and a 25-foot-deep ocean – it was designed as a miniature working model of Biosphere 1, planet Earth itself, and stocked like a real-life Noah's Ark with almost four thousand species of plants and animals. Investigative journalists soon revealed, however, that it was staffed largely by ex-actors from an obscure experimental theater group, the "Theater of All Possibilities," assembled by John Allen, or "Johnny Dolphin," at the Synergia Ranch outside Santa Fe, to colonize Mars and thus escape the impending nuclear holocaust on Earth. A hundred million dollars' worth of support from Texas oil tycoon Ed Bass got this far-fetched scheme off the ground, and top academics were recruited to add a veneer of respectability.

Eight "Biospherians" were sealed into Biosphere 2 in September 1991, their "mission" being to survive in isolation for two full years. This they more or less did, although emergency oxygen twice had to be pumped in as carbon dioxide levels rose, and one member briefly exited for medical treatment (and was seen to return with a suspiciously full bag of belongings). They grew 88 percent of their own food, and lost 13.65 percent of their body weight. Much of what transpired was replete with irony; hungry Biospherians soon found themselves planting bananas and papayas in what they had resolved would be the inviolate wilderness of the rainforest, and destroying parts of the desert to boost oxygen, while the ocean proved impossible to keep clean. As for their fellow inhabitants, the bush babies caught the hummingbirds, and the only birds to survive were unwanted sparrows that sneaked in during construction. "Crazy ants" killed all the pollinating insects, so the Biospherians were reduced to the tedious task of pollinating all their plants by hand.

By the time the next crew moved in, conditions at Biosphere 2 had degenerated into farce. Two of the original crew, who had been acrimoniously fired, sneaked back and broke the Biosphere's seals from the outside, thus aborting the second mission after just six months; they later sued and won compensation for their dismissal. Ed Bass remains in charge, but since 1996 Biosphere 2 has operated in conjunction with Columbia University. Presented with this vast, expensive tool – now referred to as a campus – they seem to be trying to think of something to do with it. The line these days is that the problems are what makes it interesting.

In its brief heyday, Biosphere 2 was one of Arizona's most popular tourist destinations. Now that no one is locked inside, the crowds have dwindled, but the two-and-a-half-hour guided tours are still worth taking. Most of that time is spent peering into the greenhouses hoping to spot any sign of life larger than an ant, and marveling at the fact that, whatever you may have assumed, Biosphere 2 is not solar powered but depends on an external natural-gas power plant. Tunnels take you down beneath the "Coral Biome"; the guides insist it isn't an aquarium, but it doesn't half look like one. Only 100,000 gallons of it is authentic ocean water, trucked from the Pacific; the other 650,000 gallons were fresh water, to which a powder known as "Instant Ocean" has been added. Visitors are also allowed into the Biospherians' futuristic living quarters, tacked like a space capsule onto the back of the main block, where they appear to have suffered no privations whatsoever.

From
Phoenix to
Tucson

Should you arrive at the compound after 5pm, paying $5 admission entitles you to a quick look around on your own, and you can redeem your fee against purchases at its all-day *Canyon Cafe*, which serves good **meals** on an appealing terrace, There's also a **cybercafe**, and good-value **lodging** at the on-site *Inn at Biosphere 2* (☎520/825-6222; May–Sept ③, Oct–April ⑤).

Tucson

TUCSON has been southern Arizona's leading city for over two hundred years, during which time it has lived under five separate flags. Spreading across a mountain-ringed basin at the northern limits of the **Sonoran Desert**, its 750,000-plus inhabitants pride themselves on being more cosmopolitan, cultured and liberal than those of its upstart rival Phoenix. Like Phoenix, the "Old Pueblo" has grown way past the point where the flow of the region's rivers, such as the Santa Cruz, is sufficient to quench its thirst. All are now dry sandy washes for most of the year, though flash-floods still rage through the crosstown culverts after summer thunderstorms. However, unlike Phoenix, Tucson embraces rather than denies the desert, eschewing lawns and fountains in favor of directing visitors towards the authentic landscapes of **Sabino Canyon** and the **Arizona-Sonora Desert Museum**, and the cactus-strewn hillsides of **Saguaro National Park**.

Tucson is pronounced too-sawn.

By Southwestern standards, Tucson is a diverse, attractive and lively city, home to the 35,000 energetic students of the **University of Arizona** as well as a large recent influx of retirees, and tempered by its long association with Mexico, a mere sixty miles south. Although it suffers from the same Sunbelt sprawl as Albuquerque and Phoenix, it still has a compact and recognizably historic center, some good parks and museums, affordable accommodation and enjoyable restaurants, and even a pretty good nightlife.

A history of Tucson

The valley of the Santa Cruz had already been inhabited for many centuries by the time Spanish priest Eusebio Kino passed through in 1700, and visited the **Pima Indian** settlement of *Stjukshon*, or "dark spring." In 1776, under the direction of **Hugo O'Conor**, one of the

Catholic "Wild Geese" who had fled English-controlled Ireland to fight for Spain, the Spanish relocated their main Arizonan fortress here from Tubac (see p.250). That forty-mile move northwards brought them closer to **Apache** territory, and the energies of the Hispanic and Pima citizens of **San Agustín de Tucson** were largely devoted to resisting Apache raids and sieges. The severed heads of Apache warriors were displayed as trophies on the city walls.

When Tucson was sold to the US government as part of the **Gadsden Purchase** of 1854, the incoming Anglos were generally welcomed as a stabilizing presence. Not only did most of the valley's Mexican farmers remain in Arizona, but they were joined by more of their former compatriots. Soon, however, travelers were describing Tucson as "a place of resort for traders, speculators, gamblers, horse-thieves and vagrant politicians . . . a paradise of devils."

Although the **Confederates** who occupied southern Arizona in 1862 were swiftly driven away by Union forces from California, suspicions of lingering Confederate sympathies ensured that Tucson was passed over as capital of the new Territory. Conflict with the Apache continued, and a vigilante force of Mexicans, Anglos and 'O'odham Indians from Tucson was responsible for the notorious **Camp Grant Massacre** of 144 Apaches in Aravaipa Canyon in 1871 (see p.232). US army commanders came to believe that a shadowy "Tucson Ring" of businessmen were consistently provoking the Apache, in order to profit from the resultant military spending.

The end of the Apache Wars in the 1880s coincided with the coming of the transcontinental **railroad**, and the reorientation of the commerce of Tucson along east–west routes. Its role as an entrepot for trade with Mexico rapidly declined, and the Mexican merchants who had been its wealthiest citizens were driven out of business. Ever since, Mexican laborers have streamed back and forth across the border as the economy expands and contracts, but Tucson has become ever more American. Outstripped by Phoenix during the 1920s, and home to under forty thousand people (in an area of just nine square miles) as recently as 1940, by conventional standards the city has nonetheless grown at a phenomenal rate.

Arrival, information and city tours

Tucson International Airport, eight miles south of downtown (☎520/573-8100), receives flights from all over the Southwest, but as far as long-distance services are concerned it very much plays second fiddle to Phoenix. It's connected to central Tucson by the slow Sun Tran **bus** #25 (85¢), and the $12 shuttle vans of Arizona Stagecoach (☎520/889-1000). For **taxi** service, call Allstate Cab (☎520/798-1111) or Yellow Cab (☎520/624-6611).

The Amtrak station, downtown at 400 E Toole Ave, is served by three **trains** weekly in each direction between Los Angeles and points east; connecting Amtrak buses run north to Phoenix.

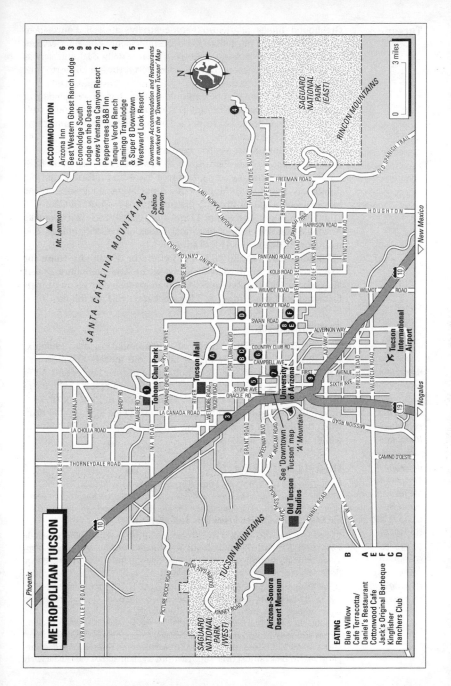

METROPOLITAN TUCSON

See 'Downtown Tucson' map

ACCOMMODATION

Arizona Inn	6
Best Western Ghost Ranch Lodge	3
Econolodge South	9
Lodge on the Desert	8
Loews Ventana Canyon Resort	2
Peppertrees B&B Inn	7
Tanque Verde Ranch	4
Flamingo Travelodge	
& Super 8 Downtown	5
Westward Look Resort	1

Downtown Accommodation and Restaurants
are marked on the 'Downtown Tucson' Map

EATING

Blue Willow	B
Cafe Terracotta/	
Daniel's Restaurant	A
Cottonwood Cafe	E
Jack's Original Barbeque	F
Kingfisher	C
Ranchers Club	D

0   3 miles

Tucson

Greyhound **buses** also stop very centrally, at 2 S Fourth Ave (☎520/792-3475 or 1-800/231-2222). Arizona Shuttle Services (☎520/795-6771 or 1-800/888-2749) run a daily $19 shuttle-van service between Tucson and **Phoenix**'s Sky Harbor airport, with hourly departures, on the hour.

Most of downtown can be explored on foot, but on weekends you can ride the **Old Pueblo Trolley** (Fri 6pm–midnight, Sat noon–midnight, Sun noon–6pm; $1) from Fourth Avenue out to the university, a mile east of the center.

Tucson's downtown **visitor center**, 130 S Scott Ave (Mon–Fri 8am–5pm, Sat & Sun 9am–4pm; ☎520/624-1817 or 1-800/638-8350; *www.visittucson.org*), has free maps and information. The Southwest Parks and Monuments Association bookstore, three blocks away in the El Presidio district, at 223 N Court St (Mon–Fri 10.30am–5.30pm, Sat & Sun 11am–4pm; ☎520/792-0239), stocks Arizona's best selection of historical, hiking and wildlife guides. The main **post office** is at 141 S Sixth Ave.

Tucson Tours (☎520/297-2911) offer 1hr 30min **city tours** for $18, excursions to Mission San Xavier, the Arizona-Sonora Desert Museum, or Old Tucson for $20, and an extensive program of trips further afield from around $30 for a half-day, $60 per full day.

Accommodation

Tucson offers a broader range of **accommodation** than Phoenix, with plenty of reasonably priced **hotels** and **motels** downtown as well as some atmospheric B&Bs both in the historic center and out in the surrounding desert. It also has its fair share of **resorts**, which can be every bit as expensive as their counterparts in Phoenix (if, as a rule, much less stuffy), and **dude ranches**. Once again, rates drop when the mercury rises, and some places are open only in the peak winter and spring seasons.

As explained on p.15, accommodation prices, excluding taxes, are indicated throughout this book by the following symbols:

① *up to $30*
② *$30–45*
③ *$45–60*
④ *$60–80*
⑤ *$80–100*
⑥ *$100–130*
⑦ *$130–175*
⑧ *$175–250*
⑨ *$250+*

Hostels and B&Bs

Casa Tierra, 11155 W Calle Pima, Tucson, AZ 85743; ☎520/578-3058, fax 878-8445; *www.bbonline.com/az/casatierra*. Secluded four-room desert-edge B&B near the Arizona-Sonora Desert Museum, modeled on an adobe *hacienda*, and with an outdoor spa. Sept–May only, ④.

El Presidio Inn, 297 N Main Ave, Tucson, AZ 85701; ☎520/623-6151 or 1-800/349-6151, fax 520/623-2860; *www.azohwy.com/e/elpresdo.htm*. Three tastefully furnished Spanish colonial suites in historic downtown adobe B&B, with spacious wraparound veranda. ⑤.

Hotel Congress, 311 E Congress St, Tucson, AZ 85701; ☎520/622-8848 or 1-800/722-8848, fax 520/792-6366; *www.hotcong.com*. Central, bohemian hotel, an easy walk from Amtrak and Greyhound, with vintage Art Deco furnishings. In the 1930s, bank-robber Dillinger was arrested here after pleading for his strangely heavy luggage to be rescued from a blaze on the third floor; now it offers $15 hostel beds for HI-AYH members (no reservations) and simple private rooms for just over $30. There's a small breakfast cafe and a lively bar downstairs, as well as the *Library of Congress* Internet cafe, and at night it's one of the hottest spots in town, with loud music and dancing. ①–③.

Peppertrees B&B Inn, 724 E University Blvd, Tucson, AZ 85719; ☎ & fax 520/622-7167 or ☎1-800/348-5763; *www.bbonline.com/az/peppertrees*. Upscale B&B in private home very close to the university, with four bedrooms in the main house and two separate guesthouses. Summer ⑤, winter ⑥.

Roadrunner Hostel, 346 E Twelfth St, Tucson, AZ 85701; ☎520/628-4709; *roadrunr@azstarnet.com*. Small and very central independent hostel in a downtown home, offering space in six-bed dorms for $13 per night or $70 per week, plus Internet access and bicycles for rent. ①.

Hotels and motels

Clarion Santa Rita Hotel & Suites, 88 E Broadway Blvd, Tucson, AZ 85701; ☎520/622-4000 or 1-800/448-8276, fax 520/620-0376. Large if anonymous hotel that's an unexpected downtown bargain, and has the good Mexican *Cafe Poca Cosa* (see p.246) downstairs. ③.

Econolodge South, 3020 S Sixth Ave, Tucson, AZ 85713; ☎520/623-5881 or 1-800/623-5881, fax 520/624-2899. Inexpensive motel, northwest of the airport. Summer ②, winter ③.

Flamingo Travelodge, 1300 N Stone Ave, Tucson, AZ 85705; ☎520/770-1910 or 1-800/300-3533, fax 520/770-0750. Attractively renovated motel, barely a mile north of downtown Tucson. Summer ②, winter ④.

Super 8 Downtown, 1248 N Stone Ave, Tucson, AZ 85705; ☎520/622-6446 or 1-800/800-8000. Adequate, if not wildly prepossessing, chain motel, a mile northwest of the university not far from downtown. Summer ②, winter ③.

Ranches and resorts

The Arizona Inn, 2200 E Elm St, Tucson, AZ 85719; ☎520/325-1541 or 1-800/933-1093, fax 520/881-5830. Elegant desert oasis that's been a winter favorite for numerous presidents, Rockefellers and the Duke and Duchess of Windsor, but remains surprisingly unstuffy and not all that expensive in low season. Rates include gourmet breakfast. Summer ⑤, winter ⑦.

Best Western Ghost Ranch Lodge, 801 W Miracle Mile, Tucson, AZ 85705; ☎520/791-7565 or 1-800/456-7565, fax 520/791-3898. Charming old-fashioned resort, roughly ten miles north of the airport, with south-of-the-border stylings, a cactus-filled garden, and amazingly low rates. Summer ②, winter ④.

Lodge on the Desert, 306 N Alvernon Way, Tucson, AZ 85711; ☎520/325-3366 or 1-800/456-5634, fax 520/327-5834; *lodgdesert@aol.com*. 1930s adobe resort a couple of miles east of downtown, tastefully restored to resemble a Mexican *hacienda*, with a good restaurant and large, comfortable rooms. Summer ⑤, winter ⑦.

Loews Ventana Canyon Resort, 7000 N Resort Drive, Tucson, AZ 85750; ☎520/299-2020 or 1-800/234-5117, fax 520/299-6832. Grand redbrick resort, reaching majestically across a hundred acres at the foot of the Santa Catalina mountains northeast of the city, with its own on-site waterfall. Four restaurants, two golf courses, plus tennis and spa, and the desert on your doorstep. Summer ⑥, winter ⑧.

Tanque Verde Ranch, 14301 E Speedway Blvd, Tucson, AZ 85748; ☎520/296-6275 or 1-800/234-DUDE, fax 520/721-9426; *www.tvgr.com*. Arizona's most authentic dude ranch, an irresistibly romantic 400-acre spread adjoining

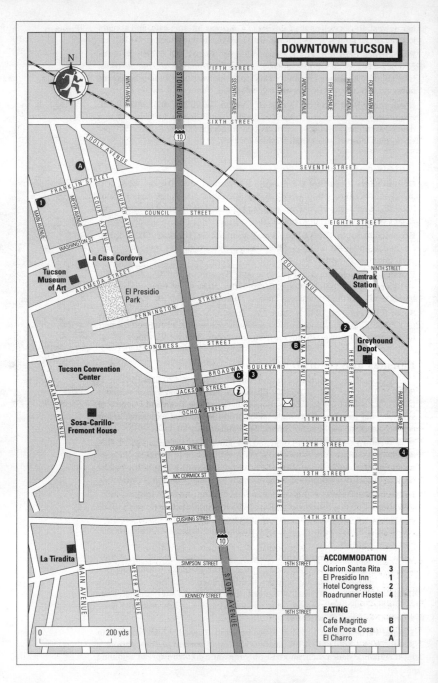

DOWNTOWN TUCSON

ACCOMMODATION

Clarion Santa Rita	3
El Presidio Inn	1
Hotel Congress	2
Roadrunner Hostel	4

EATING

Cafe Magritte	B
Cafe Poca Cosa	C
El Charro	A

Saguaro National Park twenty miles east of downtown, offers luxury accommodation in individual *casitas* and a stable of over a hundred horses. Rates include all meals and a full program of rides, from early-morning cowboy cookouts to all-day pack trips; there's also tennis, swimming and hiking. Summer ⑧, winter ⑨.

Westward Look Resort, 245 E Ina Rd, Tucson, AZ 85704; ☎520/297-1151 or 1-800/722-2500, fax 520/297-9023; *www.westwardlook.com*. Plush modernized resort in attractive landscaped grounds north of the city, offering extra-large rooms and suites in low-slung *casitas*. The emphasis on physical fitness, and tennis in particular, doesn't preclude having a top-quality restaurant. Summer ⑤, winter ⑦.

Downtown Tucson

Downtown Tucson, which centers on the area where the east–west Congress Street and Broadway Boulevard cross the north–south Stone Avenue, is characterized by undistinguished modern architecture. The adobe fortress of San Agustín de Tucson occupied what's now the four-block **El Presidio Historic District**, a couple of blocks northwest. None of its original structures is still standing, but several of their nineteenth-century successors, dating from the period when Tucson passed into American hands, have been restored as cafes, art galleries and B&Bs.

Access to much of El Presidio is controlled by the **Tucson Museum of Art**, alongside at 140 N Main Ave (Sept–May Mon–Sat 10am–4pm, Sun noon–4pm; June–Aug Tues–Sat 10am–4pm, Sun noon–4pm; $2, free Tues). Its oldest house, **La Casa Cordova** at 175 N Meyer Ave (same hours), now contains displays on the city's Mexican heritage, and between October and April, free **walking tours** leave at 11am on Wednesday and Thursday mornings from the museum's tree-shaded courtyard.

The museum itself has an excellent collection of pre-Columbian artifacts, including ceramics with extraordinarily lifelike faces produced from 100 BC onwards by the Mochica culture of northern Peru, textiles from the later Peruvian Chancay culture, and gold from Colombia and Costa Rica. Mexican artifacts range from masks and effigies created by the ancient Olmec and Mixtec peoples, via eighteenth-century religious pieces, to nineteenth-century oil-on-tin family portraits. A large gallery that spirals down into the basement is used for changing exhibitions of modern painting and sculpture, and the gift shop stocks some interesting contemporary crafts.

Three blocks south, engulfed by the Tucson Convention Center complex, the solitary adobe **Sosa-Carrillo-Frémont House** (Wed–Sat 10am–4pm; free) is the sole survivor of a neighborhood torn down during the 1960s in the name of urban renewal. Built for merchant Leopoldo Carrillo in 1858, it was briefly rented by former explorer John C. Frémont when he was Governor of Arizona in 1878. Though much restored, it offers a vivid sense of the more civilized side of frontier life, from the high-quality furniture and the saguaro-rib ceilings to the fig-tree-shaded rear courtyard gardens.

Still within walking distance, **Cushing Street**, three more blocks south, marks the start of the **Barrio Historico**. The city's 1880s business district holds plenty of century-old adobes, but its most notable landmark is the sidewalk shrine of **El Tiradito**, "the castaway." Said to mark where a young man was killed by his father-in-law for committing adultery with his mother-in-law, and was buried where he fell, it's famous as the **Wishing Shrine**. Light a candle that burns through the night, and your prayers will be answered.

The University district

Fruitissimo, *opposite the main university gate at 998 E University Blvd, sells delicious fruit smoothies.*

The other main area of interest in central Tucson is the **University of Arizona**, which spreads between Sixth Street and Speedway Boulevard a mile east of downtown. Park Avenue, on its western flank, is lined with funky cafes and stores that cater to students.

On campus, the highlight is the two-part **Arizona State Museum** (Mon–Sat 10am–5pm, Sun noon–5pm; free). Its southern wing concentrates on archeology, with a diorama of a mammoth hunt and an exhibit on cave-dwellers, plus pottery and a macaw skull unearthed during university-sponsored excavations at the abandoned Hopi site of Homolovi (see p.282). The remodeled north wing is more innovative, housing the fascinating **Paths of Life** exhibition, which illuminates the history and beliefs of all the major Native American peoples of the Southwest.

Just to the north, the **Center for Creative Photography** holds one of the world's finest photography archives (Mon–Fri 11am–5pm, Sun noon–5pm; free). Ansel Adams left his personal negatives, prints and journals to the university on condition that they be available to the public, and his collection has since been complemented by photographs from all eras. Temporary exhibitions can only show a tiny selection, however, and the archive is primarily intended for serious scholars who know what they wish to see. Next door, the eclectic UA **Museum of Art** (winter Mon–Fri 9am–5pm, Sun noon–4pm; summer Mon–Fri 10am–3.30pm, Sun noon–4pm; free) has some morbid Spanish *retablos* and assorted modern pieces, with canvases by Rembrandt, Picasso, O'Keeffe and Warhol, and some fine cubist sculpture by Jacques Lipchitz.

The **Arizona Historical Society Museum**, across Park Avenue at 949 E Second St (Mon–Sat 10am–4pm, Sun noon–4pm; free), is a tired and somewhat humdrum ragbag of a place, currently in the process of being updated, where reconstructed rooms trace the history of Tucson "From Shelter to Showplace."

Northern Tucson and the Santa Catalina Mountains

Metropolitan Tucson's northern boundary is formed by the natural barrier of the **Santa Catalina Mountains**, whose bare, dusty slopes are eventually crowned with pine forests. At the edge of the mountains, eight miles north of downtown, **Tohono Chul Park**, a block west of Oracle Road at Ina Road, is a former private estate that has been converted into a desert garden (daily 7am–sunset; $2 donation). The name means "desert corner" in the Tohono 'O'odham language, and it's now filled with yucca, prickly pear and other cactuses, and a-flutter with hummingbirds.

Tucson

The park's Tohono Chul Tea Room *is reviewed on p.246.*

For an enjoyable taste of the mountains, head to **Sabino Canyon**, at the far end of Sabino Canyon Road in the Coronado National Forest, ten miles northeast of downtown (daily 8am–4.30pm; free; ☎520/749-2861). The canyon was cut into the lower reaches of Mount Lemmon by Sabino Creek, which manages to flow for up to eleven months of the year, and is lined by green vegetation. Assorted trails lace into the hills from the four-mile riverbank road – barred to private vehicles, but served by jump-on, jump-off **tram rides** ($6) – which is popular with early-morning joggers.

The 9157-foot summit of **Mount Lemmon**, which towers above Sabino Canyon, is a two-day hike beyond the canyon, or a one-hour drive on the recently upgraded **Mount Lemmon Highway**. After branching off Tanque Verde Road, an eastward continuation of Grant Road, a few miles east of the Sabino Canyon turnoff, this winds for 25 slow miles up the mountain, with countless panoramic viewpoints to either side.

Western Tucson

Twelve miles west of the university on Speedway Boulevard, en route to Saguaro, **Old Tucson Studios**, 201 S Kinney Rd (daily 9.30am–6pm; $14) is an entertaining if contrived Wild West theme park. Its focus is a movie-set mock-up of the "Old Pueblo" that was constructed for a 1939 western, and has been used for TV shows and movies up to such recent productions as *Tombstone* and *Geronimo*. Visitors can ride a stagecoach or a coal-fired steam train, and watch gunfights on Main Street or a bawdy music-hall show in the saloon. Kids love it, though since Old Tucson had to be almost entirely rebuilt after being gutted by fire in April 1995, it's now even more spurious than ever.

Part zoo, part garden, the much more worthwhile **Arizona-Sonora Desert Museum** stands two miles further west in Tucson Mountain Park (daily: March–Sept 7.30am–6pm; Oct–Feb 8.30am–5pm; adults $8.95, ages 6–12 $1.75). Gallery displays in the museum proper explain regional geology and history, and a series of dioramas are filled with tarantulas, rattlesnakes and other creepy crawlers. In enclosures along the loop path beyond – a hot walk in high summer – bighorn sheep, mountain lions, jaguars and other seldom-seen desert denizens prowl in credible simulations of their natural habitats, and a colony of impish prairie dogs goes about its impenetrable business. Hawks and bald eagles fly about their own large aviary, thankfully separated from the greenhouse full of hummingbirds. The museum also serves as an animal rescue center: almost all the ani-

The outdoor terrace of the museum's Ironwood Tree *restaurant makes a great stop-off for a light lunch; it also has a good coffee bar.*

Tucson

mals you see were injured in some way before ending up here, and would be unable to survive on their own.

Saguaro National Park

Flanking Tucson to either side, the two sections of SAGUARO NATIONAL PARK offer visitors a rare and enthralling opportunity to stroll through strange desert "forests" of monumental, multi-limbed saguaro (pronounced sa-wah-row) cactuses. Both tend to be seen on short forays from the city; in summer, it's far too hot to do more than pose for photographs, dwarfed beneath some especially eccentric specimen, and there is in any case no lodging, or even permanent campground, in either segment.

Saguaro prefer sloping foothills, which offer a little run-off after rain, to level desert, so both sections include rugged mountain tracts. Most of the Rincon Mountain District in the east, which became a national monument in 1933, is much higher, and the one road only penetrates its low-lying fringes. It was joined in 1961 by the Tucson Mountain District in the west, which incorporates the world's densest stand of saguaro. The two together were upgraded to national park status in 1994.

The western park: Tucson Mountain District

For advance information, write to Saguaro National Park, 3693 S Old Spanish Trail, Tucson, AZ 85730, or access www.nps.gov /sagu.

The Tucson Mountain District of Saguaro National Park stretches north from the Desert Museum around fifteen miles west of downtown Tucson, and charges no admission fee to visitors. Beyond the Red Hills visitor center (daily 8am–5pm; ☎520/733-5158), the nine-mile Bajada Loop Drive is not fully paved but is always passable to ordinary vehicles. It loops through a wonderland of weird saguaro, offering plentiful short hiking trails and photo opportunities. The easiest walk is the half-mile Desert Discovery Nature Trail, but the best plan is to make sure that you're further along the road at Signal Hill in time for its magnificent sunset views. You'll know you're not the first to pass this way; boulders at the top are marked with Hohokam petroglyphs. True gluttons for punishment can follow the longer Hugh Norris Trail up a ridge to the 4687-foot summit of Wasson Peak.

Branching onto Golden Gate Road from the northeastern limit of the loop drive brings you in around five miles to Picture Rocks Road, which joins Ina Road a few more miles along and thus makes an alternative route back to northern Tucson.

The eastern park: Rincon Mountain District

Contact park rangers for details of back-country camping (by permit only).

To reach the eastern section of Saguaro National Park, the Rincon Mountain District, drive seventeen miles east of town along first Broadway Boulevard and then Old Spanish Trail. An admission fee of $4 per vehicle is collected at the visitor center at the end of the road (daily 8am–5pm; ☎520/733-5153); national park passes are both sold and accepted.

The Saguaro Cactus; a Desert Saga

As the mighty, multiarmed **saguaro cactus** is unique to the Sonora Desert, and Tucson stands near the desert's northeastern extremity, the Tucson region is one of very few places in the Wild West where real-life saguaro grow. Whatever you may have seen in the movies, you can drive a long way in Arizona without seeing a saguaro; the thrill when you finally encounter a thousand at once is deeply satisfying.

Each saguaro can grow up to fifty feet tall, and weigh up to eight tons, but it reaches that size at the slowest of rates. A teenage cactus is a foot high, a fifty-year-old more like seven feet. At 75, it sprouts the first of what may amount to forty "arms," and it only reaches its full height at around 150, with perhaps another fifty years to go before it dies. Its roots radiate as much as a hundred feet in all directions, barely three inches below the surface, and can draw enough water from one rainstorm to last the plant for two years.

Each year from the age of thirty onwards, between late April and June, a saguaro grows up to a hundred white flowers, each of which blossoms for a single night and dies by the next afternoon. In its lifetime, each saguaro produces as many as forty million seeds, though few if any are likely to germinate and thrive. It's also home to an intricate community of birds, insects, mammals and reptiles. Woodpeckers and owls burrow holes into the trunk for their nests, which the cactus heals over with hardened "scar tissue" to create permanent hollows. The **Tohono 'O'odham** Indians traditionally cut away these depressions for use as bowls; they also mashed the saguaro's succulent crimson fruit to make jam, syrup and even wine, and used its long, wood-like ribs to construct dwellings and fences.

Although short trails such as the quarter-mile **Desert Ecology Trail** lead off the eight-mile **Cactus Forest Drive** (daily: Nov–March 7am–5pm; April–Oct 7am–7pm), many visitors come specifically to hike far from the road, up into the mountains. The saguaro cactuses thin out almost as soon as you start climbing the **Tanque Verde Ridge Trail**, which leads in due course to a hundred-mile network of remote footpaths through thickly forested canyons.

Eating

Though downtown Tucson shuts down pretty early each evening – it's hard to find anywhere open after 9pm – the city has a fine selection of **restaurants**. Mexican joints and cowboy-style Wild West steakhouses abound in the central districts, while fancier restaurants congregate in the exclusive St Philip's Plaza, a few miles north, as well as in the resort hotels.

Coffeehouses

Coffee, Etc, 2830 N Campbell Ave; ☎520/881-8070. Hectic but attractive 24-hr cafe, serving burgers and sandwiches as well as fresh-ground coffee.

Cup Cafe, *Hotel Congress*, 311 E Congress St; ☎520/798-1618. Jazzy downtown cafe, straight out of the 1930s but updated to include an espresso

Tucson

bar, and serving a bewilderingly broad menu from 8am until after midnight daily.

Cuppuccinos, 3400 E Speedway Blvd; ☎520/323-7205. Espresso bar that does its best to turn Tucson into Seattle, with pastries in the week and omelettes at weekends. The specialty "cuppuccino" itself is a double shot, topped with a mountain of froth. Daily until late, from 7am Mon–Fri, 8am Sat & Sun.

Cafes and diners

Blue Willow, 2616 N Campbell Ave; ☎520/795-8736. Tasty, fruity breakfasts and light lunches and dinners, served on a pleasant garden patio. Open daily until late, from 7am on weekdays and 8am weekends.

Cafe Magritte, 254 E Congress St; ☎520/884-8004. Self-consciously arty downtown cafe, with an eclectic – but not expensive – menu to match its off-beat clientele. Great desserts, coffees and digestifs, plus sandwiches and pasta for under $10. Tues–Sat 11am until late, Sun dinner only.

Cafe Poca Cosa, 88 E Broadway Blvd; ☎520/622-6400. Stylish cafe in a central downtown location, serving tasty but inexpensive Mexican cuisine with a contemporary Southwestern twist. Lunch entrees are under $10, at dinner they're more like $15. Daily except Mon for lunch and dinner.

El Charro, 311 N Court Ave; ☎520/622-1922. Housed in the same El Presidio building since 1922, this claims to be the oldest Mexican restaurant in the US, and now has its own lively bar next door. The food is good, though not especially fiery; specialties include fine *chimichangas*, said to be a Tucson invention, and the *topopo* salad, piled like a pyramid atop a tortilla. Open from 11am daily for lunch and dinner.

Jack's Original Barbeque, 5250 E 22nd St; ☎520/750-1280. Drive-in barbecue pit with a fifty-year tradition of serving tangy pork ribs followed by down-home peach cobbler or sweet potato pie. Open daily for lunch and dinner.

Tohono Chul Tea Room, Tohono Chul Park, 7366 N Paseo del Norte; ☎520/797-1222. Attractive adobe cafe in small desert park on the northern fringes of town, operated by the *Cafe Terra Cotta* (see below). Open daily 8am–5pm, and ideal for breakfast, a light lunch or a scones-and-jam afternoon tea.

Fine dining

Cafe Terra Cotta, St Philip's Plaza, 4310 N Campbell Ave; ☎520/577-8100. Inventive Southwestern cuisine in smart mall surroundings. The menu ranges from gourmet pizzas cooked in a wood-burning oven to meats grilled with chiles, all at under $20. Open daily for lunch and dinner, until late.

Cottonwood Cafe, 60 N Alvernon Way; ☎520/326-6000. Large and very popular restaurant, east of downtown, with top-quality Southwestern food at reasonable prices. Mussels steamed with red chilie and tequila for $7 make a great appetizer, while entrees include a huge Sonoran seafood paella for $19, or, if you can bear to eat a bird with eyelashes, ostrich mole rojo with pumpkin polenta for $20. The same food is served in the adjoining *Cottonwood Club*, which features live music nightly. Open daily for lunch and dinner.

Daniel's Restaurant and Trattoria, St Philip's Plaza, 4340 N Campbell Ave; ☎520/742-3200. North Italian specialties served amid stylish black decor, lightened with ArtDeco mirrors. Typical entrees cost around $20; the sauces are kept light, and the breads are delicious. Open for dinner only, daily from 5pm.

Kingfisher, 2564 E Grant Rd; ☎520/323-7739. Upmarket fish restaurant that serves seafood from Maine lobsters and Maryland soft-shelled crabs to Oregon oysters, with an eclectic mix of American cooking styles from Cajun to New Pacific. Most entrees are priced under $20, and strict meat-eaters can opt instead for barbecue chicken or ribs. Open for lunch and dinner daily until midnight.

Ranchers Club, *Sheraton Tucson Hotel*, 5151 E Grant Rd; ☎520/321-7621. Tucson's best and biggest cuts of beef – starting under $20, and rising to 48-oz steaks for $50 – grilled over desert mesquite or cherrywood flame, plus excellent soups and salads, all served beneath the horrified gaze of generations of stuffed animals. Open for lunch and dinner Mon–Fri, dinner only Sat.

Ventana Room, *Loews Ventana Canyon Resort*, 7000 N Resort Drive; ☎520/299-2020. Showcase resort dining room, commanding a panoramic view from the northern foothills. Continental-style grilled meats and fish from $20 per entree, or pick the prix fixe menu. Opens for dinner nightly at 6pm.

Entertainment and nightlife

Tucson **nightlife** focuses on Congress Street downtown, with its gaggle of arty cafes and nightclubs; most venues double as bars or restaurants. A handful of studenty places can be found near the university, and there are half a dozen country-and-western saloons on the outskirts of town. For a full rundown, check the listings in the free *Tucson Weekly*. The Tucson Convention Center Music Hall, 260 S Church Ave (☎520/791-4266), features orchestral concerts, opera and ballet, while the city's prime **drama** venue is the Temple of Music and Art, 330 S Scott Ave (☎520/622-2823). The Tucson Jazz Society (☎520/743-3399) promotes jazz gigs all over town.

Cafe Sweetwater, 340 E Sixth St; ☎520/622-6464. Casual, thirty-something place with regular live jazz.

Club Congress, *Hotel Congress*, 311 E Congress St; ☎520/622-8848. Hectic, trendy, late-opening bar with live music a couple of nights each week.

Cushing Street Bar and Grill, 343 S Meyer Ave; ☎520/622-7984. Nightly live jazz and swing, plus excellent food, in a hundred-year-old Barrio Historico building.

Gentle Ben's Brewing Co, 865 E University Blvd; ☎520/624-4177. Microbrewery, regularly packed out with students, which serves simple food.

The Maverick, King of Clubs, 4702 E 22nd St; ☎520/748-0456. Small but atmospheric old-fashioned country-music honky-tonk, well out from the center and brimming with Stetsons. Live music nightly except Mon.

The Rialto Theatre, 318 E Congress St; ☎520/740-0126. 1920s vaudeville theater that's reopened as Tucson's hottest venue for touring bands.

South to Mexico: the Mission Trail

The tract of southern Arizona that lies between Tucson and the Mexican border was the first part of the state to be settled by the

Spanish, and it remained Arizona's most populous region until well into the nineteenth century. The Spanish called this area **Pimería Alta**, and its scattering of **mission churches** and abandoned forts still testify to their efforts to Christianize its **Pima** inhabitants from 1692 onwards. Epidemics and Apache raids meant that of the early towns, only Tucson grew to any size, but as recently as 1870, the Pima were still Arizona's largest ethnic group.

Twelve thousand Pima – now known as the **Tohono 'O'odham** – survive on the **San Xavier Reservation** a few miles south of Tucson. The magnificent church of San Xavier – the "White Dove of the Desert" – is the prime attraction for modern travelers who drive the 65 miles down to Mexico on the **I-19** interstate, but the artistic community at **Tubac**, and the atmospheric frontier town of **Nogales**, help to make for an entertaining international day-trip.

San Xavier del Bac

Even today, the white-plastered walls and towers of **San Xavier del Bac**, the best-preserved mission church in the United States, seem like a dazzling desert mirage. How much more dramatic they must have been two centuries ago, when to Christian missionaries and

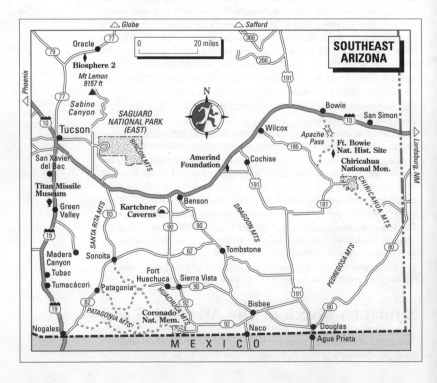

Apache warriors alike they symbolized the Spanish quest to subdue
and convert the native peoples of the Southwest.

Located a mere nine miles south of downtown Tucson, just west of
I-19, the church stands on the eastern fringes of the arid San Xavier
Reservation. It was founded by the Jesuit **Father Eusebio Kino** in
1700, beside the Santa Cruz River and next to the Pima village of
W:ak ("where the water emerges"), which soon became Bac. Kino's
church was destroyed by Apaches in 1767; what survives is its
replacement, built for the Franciscans between 1783 and 1797. No
one knows the name of the architect responsible for its Spanish
Baroque, even Moorish lines – it consists almost entirely of domes
and arches, making only minimal use of timber – let alone the
'O'odham craftsmen who embellished its every feature. The whole
structure has recently been restored to its original resplendence
under the supervision of experts from the Vatican.

Although the church attracts a constant stream of tourists (daily
9am–6pm; donation), the ideal time to come is on Sunday morning,
when Masses at 8am, 11am and 12.30pm attract large congregations
of Indians from the reservation. As you approach the main entrance
across the dusty plaza, with saguaro cactuses to the right and ocotillo
to the left, take a moment to appreciate its ornate facade. On the top
level, a cat squats on the spiral flourish to the right, eyeing a mouse
in the corresponding position on the left. The tower on the right was
never completed, possibly to avoid the need to pay a levy to the
authorities back in Mexico.

Inside the church, the left alcove holds a recumbent, articulated
statue of **St Francis Xavier**, covered with metal *milagros* – images of
healed bodyparts – and photographs of children. Devout Catholics are
permitted to lean in and lift his head. The approach to the main altar is
guarded by two naive gilt-headed lions, representing the royal lions of
Leon and Castille in Spain. The altar itself holds a telling example of
the intermingling of Catholicism with traditional beliefs; the gilded
monstrance used to exhibit the host during communion incorporates a
wickerwork surround bearing the 'O'odham "man in the maze" design.

Still within the mission walls, to the right of the church, a small
museum (Mon–Fri noon–4pm, Sat & Sun 8.30am–4.30pm; donation) displays a gigantic illuminated sheepskin psalter, and photos of
other remote churches on the Tohono 'O'odham reservation.

The little hillock immediately to the east is now topped by a replica of the shrine of Saint Bernadette at Lourdes, France. Juan Mateo
Manje, who accompanied Father Kino to W:ak, described finding a
white stone on top of this hill in November 1699:

> "We guessed it might be some idol that the heathen Indians
> worshipped, so with great effort we pulled out the stone, thereby
> exposing a large hole. At the time, we did not know what it could
> be. While we were coming down the hill, a great and furious hur-
> ricane developed. We could scarcely walk because of the terrific

*The major feast
days at San
Xavier Mission
are those of St
Francis of
Assissi, on
October 4, and
St Francis
Xavier,
December 3.*

windstorm. None of the Indians had gone with us to the top of the
hill; but when the furious wind arose they started to yell, saying in
sort of rebellion, '*Vbiriqui cupioca*', which meant that the House
of the Wind (god) had been opened."

The Titan Missile Museum

Another sixteen miles south of San Xavier, the **Titan Missile
Museum** (May–Nov Wed–Sun 9am–5pm; Dec–April daily 9am–5pm;
$7.50) focuses on an underground silo that, until November 1982,
held two Titan II nuclear missiles. Each was primed and ready to fire
at a choice of three specific targets, as much as five thousand miles
away; what those targets were remains classified even today, but
they never changed during the 22 years that the site was operational.
A total of 54 such missile were deployed at 27 separate locations, in
Arizona, California and Arkansas, but this is the only site to have survived the end of the Cold War. One of its missiles is actually still
down there – no longer primed, of course – and can be examined
close up on hour-long subterranean **guided tours**.

The whole installation was designed to remain functional in the
event of a nuclear war. The vast sliding door of the silo was capable
of opening through eight feet of post-holocaust debris, while the
crew could live beneath the surface for up to thirty days, and the
whole place could even operate on two 28-volt batteries in case of
electrical outage. Tours culminate in the control room, still scattered
with top secret manuals, where two keys had to be turned simulta-
neously in order to fire the missile.

As you might imagine, inspecting colossal rocket launchers and
other military hardware seems to be very much a guy thing. Casual
visitors who take the tours may well run out of steam before the
excitable gun nuts in the crowd find the time to draw breath.

Tubac

TUBAC, fifty miles south of San Xavier, was the first permanent
Spanish settlement in what's now Arizona, founded in 1752 as a **presidio** or fortress to guard against repetitions of the previous year's
Pima Revolt against the Jesuits. In 1775, its commander, Juan
Bautista de Anza, launched the expedition that established **San
Francisco**, but Tubac declined after 1776, when its garrison was
shifted to the new city of Tucson. For the next century, it was alter-
nately abandoned and resettled as Apache raids permitted; in the
1850s, it even spent a brief period as a **Mormon** outpost.

*The highlight
of Tubac's
annual calen-
dar is early
February's
week-long
Festival of the
Arts.*

Since World War II, Tubac has redefined itself as an **arts colony**;
it's a tiny little place, where dust-devils whirl down unpaved streets
filled with crafts and jewelry stores. Most sell folk items from south of
the border, but the **Tubac Center of the Arts**, 9 Plaza Rd (Oct to mid-
Nov and mid-April to May Tues–Sat 10am–4.30pm, Sun 1–4.30pm;

mid-Nov to mid-April Mon–Sat 10am–4.30pm, Sun 1–4.30pm; free), holds exhibitions by local artists.

South to Mexico: the Mission Trail

Although the foundations of the original adobe fortress now lie beneath an earthen mound in the **Tubac Presidio State Historic Park** (daily 8am–5pm; $2), they can be admired from a cool underground viewing gallery. The large museum alongside contains pieces from all periods of Tubac's long history, including some beautiful naive *retablos*, the press used to print Arizona's first newspaper, *The Weekly Arizonan*, in March 1859, and a crucifix depicting the black "Christo Negro" – a Native American Christ.

Practicalities

For information on Tubac, ask at the state park or call the local **chamber of commerce** (☎520/398-2704). The nicest of the **B&Bs** in the old center is the *Tubac County Inn*, a small blue wooden house at 409 Burruel St (☎520/398-3178; closed Aug; ④), with four en-suite rooms. Nearby, the flower-bedecked *Tosh's Hacienda de Tubac*, Camino Otero and Burruel (☎520/398-3008), is a clean Southwestern and Mexican **restaurant**, open daily for lunch and dinner. The *Burro Inn*, west of the interstate at 70 W El Burro Lane (☎520/398-2281; summer ④, winter ⑤), is a steakhouse-cum-motel with a well-priced selection of comfortable two-room suites.

Tubac's zip code is AZ 85646.

Tumacácori National Historical Park

A **Spanish mission** founded by Father Kino in 1691, before its more celebrated neighbor at San Xavier (see p.248), is now the focus of the **TUMACÁCORI NATIONAL HISTORICAL PARK**, three miles south of Tubac and nineteen miles north of the border (daily 8am–5pm; $4 per vehicle; ☎520/398-2341). Like San Xavier, the church here was built at the end of the eighteenth century, but Tumacácori soon proved unable to withstand Apache raids, and was abandoned in 1848, five years before the region passed into US control.

It's now an evocative ruin, topped by a restored whitewashed dome but home only to the birds that fly down from the Patagonia Mountains. Behind its weatherbeaten red-tinged facade, the plaster has crumbled from the interior walls to reveal bare adobe bricks. A few traces of a mural can still be discerned in the raised sanctuary, but little remains of the priests' living quarters alongside.

A fascinating **museum** holds a replica of a banner carried by missionaries; one side depicts the Madonna and Child, the other shows an Indian burning in hell. Opposite the gate, the *Tumacácori Restaurant* serves Mexican and Greek specialties, including deli sandwiches.

Nogales, Arizona and Nogales, Mexico

Twenty miles south of Tumacácori, an hour from Tucson, sits the largest of the Arizonan–Mexican border towns, **NOGALES** – in effect two towns, one in the US and one across the border in Mexico. Known jointly as *Ambos Nogales* (both Nogales), they were founded in 1880 to handle the frontier formalities necessary on the main route between their two countries, and still see vast quantities of freight traffic daily. Tourists too pass through in considerable numbers, though with cheap Mexican crafts now so widely available in the US, the day-trippers these days tend to be looking for cut-price medicines rather than rugs or hammocks.

There's nothing in particular to see on either side of the border, though the contrast between the sedate, ordered streets of the American town and the jumbled whitewashed houses clinging to the slopes in Mexico hits you as soon as you come in sight. Nogales, Arizona – the birthplace of iconoclastic jazz great **Charles Mingus** – is a dreary little community, while Nogales, Mexico is basically a lively, large-scale street market.

Crossing the border is straightforward, as Mexican visas are only required by travelers heading more than 21km south of the border. US citizens should, however, ideally carry their passports or birth certificates – drivers' licences are not always sufficient – while foreign visitors should check that their visa status entitles them to re-enter the US; if you're on or eligible for the Visa Waiver Scheme (see p.8), you're fine. There's no need to **change money**; US dollars are freely accepted by stores and businesses in Mexico.

If you do plan to set off south, pick up a **tourist visa** just beyond the border crossing. Then take a taxi (around $6) a couple of miles to the **long-distance bus station**, from which regular buses head to **Hermosillo**, **Guaymas** on the Pacific (a good overnight stop), and **Los Mochis**, the start of the Copper Canyon Railroad.

Practicalities

*Nogales' zip
code is AZ
85621.*

Nogales' **visitor center** is in Kino Park at the north end of town (winter Mon–Fri 8am–5pm; summer Mon–Fri 8am–1pm & 2–5pm; ☎520/287-3685). Hourly direct **buses** to Tucson are operated by Citizens/Grayline Bus, 35 N Terrace Ave ($6.50; ☎520/287-5628).

None of the Arizona-side **motels** stands within a mile of the border; the closest is the *Best Western Siesta Motel*, 673 N Grand Ave (☎520/287-4671, fax 287-9616; ③), while the cluster near the interstate three miles out includes a *Super 8*, 543 W Mariposa Rd (☎520/281-2242 or 1-800/800-8000; ③).

Most visitors prefer to **eat** in Mexico, where abundant cafes and diners line the busy central streets. Classier dining is offered by the unusual *La Roca*, hollowed into the rocky hillside just east of the railroad, a couple of blocks from the border at c/Elias 91, where a full seafood meal still costs well under $20. The best restaurant on the Arizona side is *Mr C's Supper Club*, above town at 282 W View Point Drive (☎520/281-9000), which specializes in fish.

Sonoita Valley and Patagonia

A longer but even more attractive route back from Nogales to Tucson avoids the interstate by following highways 82 and 83 northeast from Nogales through the lush **Sonoita Valley**, in the craggy mountains of the Coronado National Forest.

Thanks to the **Patagonia-Sonoita Creek Sanctuary** (Wed–Sun 7.30am–4pm; $5 donation; ☎520/394-2000), the mining and cattle-ranching town of **PATAGONIA**, twenty miles up from Nogales, now attracts weekend crowds of **bird watchers**. Located at the far south-western end of a mile-long dirt road that leads off Fourth Street, this dense riverbank stand of oaks and cottonwoods is home to an amazing range of songbirds and raptors, including finches and flycatchers, kingbirds and kestrels, and woodpeckers and cardinals. With all this colorful collection to choose from, the sighting most prized by twitchers from all over the world is a drab little specimen called the northern beardless tyrannulet.

Twelve miles north of Patagonia, Hwy-83 veers northwest to rejoin I-10 two miles east of Saguaro National Park; Hwy-82 cuts east toward Tombstone, 35 miles away (see p.257), passing through **SONOITA** itself after a dozen miles.

Practicalities

Welcoming little **B&Bs** in Patagonia include the three-room *Duquesne House*, a century-old adobe boarding house at 357 Duquesne Ave (☎520/394-2732; ④), while the *Stage Stop Inn*, 303 W McKeown Ave (☎520/394-2211 or 1-800/923-2211 in AZ; ④) is a convenient modern **hotel** with its own restaurant. *Angelo's Espresso Bar and Ice Cream Parlor*, nearby at 319 W McKeown Ave (☎520/394-2097), is handy for a lunchtime snack.

Patagonia's zip code is AZ 85624; Sonoita's is AZ 85637.

Sonoita holds further accommodation options, like the *Vineyard Bed & Breakfast*, 92 S Los Encinos Rd (☎520/455-4749; ⑤), which has three en-suite guestrooms and also a separate *casita*. Just west of town at 3280 Hwy-82, *Cafe Sonoita* (lunch Thurs–Sun, dinner Wed–Sat; ☎520/455-5278) serves high-quality food, with succulent barbecued ribs for $9, pan-seared trout for $8, and some fancier specialties.

The southeast corner

Although the **I-10** interstate somehow manages to plot a dull and monotonous course across **southeast Arizona**, the rugged territory to the south holds some of the state's most spectacular scenery and memorable historic sites. The much-mythologized WildWest outpost of **Tombstone** is the best known, and does its best to entertain the hordes of cowboy fanatics who troop this way, but the mining town of **Bisbee** is in many ways a more evocative relic of frontier times.

Tourism in the region has recently been given a major boost by the opening of **Kartchner Caverns**, which is expected to transform previously quiet interstate towns such as nearby **Benson**.

Further east, the **Chiricahua Mountains** witnessed the final saga of Native American resistance to federal encroachment, in the 1880s guerrilla campaign of Geronimo's **Apaches**. These mountains are merely one of around a dozen separate ranges that soar from the deserts, known as **"sky islands"** because each wilderness harbors its own unique ecosystem of plants, birds and animals.

Benson

Forty miles southeast of Tucson on I-10, sleepy little **BENSON** has recently shaken itself awake in readiness for the anticipated influx of visitors to Kartchner Caverns (see below). Tourists on their way to Tombstone have long been passing through without making any great impact on the town's economy, but now the local community is hoping for an upturn in overnight stays. There's nothing much to do in Benson itself, however, though it does serve as the headquarters of the restored **San Pedro and Southwestern Railroad**. Four-hour steam-driven excursions set off from a station on Country Club Drive, chugging south along the banks of the San Pedro River, with a one-hour stop in the ghost town of **Fairbanks** (departures Oct–May Thurs–Sat 11am, less frequently at other times of year; adults $30, ages 5–17 $20; ☎1-800/269-6314).

A couple of miles north of central Benson, up Ocotillo Road, the Singing Wind **bookshop** (☎520/586-2425) consists of a farmhouse that's bursting with volumes about Southwestern history and culture.

Practicalities

Benson now boasts its very own crop of identikit chain **motels**, including a *Super 8*, 855 N Ocotillo Rd (☎520/586-1530 or 1-800/800-8000; ③) and a *Days Inn*, 621 Commerce Drive (☎520/586-3000; ③). Cheaper mom-n-pop places still line its main thoroughfare, however – the *Benson Motel*, 185 W Fourth St (☎520/586-3346; ②) is an attractive example – while the *Skywatcher's Inn*, four miles southeast of town, is an absolute one-of-a-kind **B&B** (☎520/615-3886; *www.communiverse.com /skywatcher*; ⑤). Located on a hilltop next to the private Vega-Bray **astronomical observatory**, it offers guests (for an additional fee) the chance to have exclusive use of the observatory equipment, including high-power telescopes and even a planetarium.

Back in town, the *Horseshoe Cafe*, 154 E Fourth St (☎520/586-3303), is a quintessential Western **diner**, bedecked with Stetson hats and horseshoes, with a mini-Wurlitzer jukebox on each table.

Kartchner Caverns

The much-anticipated opening of Arizona's newest state park, **Kartchner Caverns** – signposted off both Hwy-90 and Hwy-80 eight miles south of Benson – finally took place in November 1999. The delays in unveiling what's expected to become one of the state's premier tourist attractions were due to the fact the caves here, unlike counterparts such as Carlsbad Caverns (see p.199), are "live." That means they're still being hollowed out of the Whetstone Mountains by each new dose of rainfall, and that the formations within are still growing. What's more, the park authorities intend to keep them that way.

The southeast corner

Kartchner Caverns were discovered in 1974 by local cavers Gary Tenen and Randy Tufts, who were investigating a strange-smelling hole in the mountainside and squeezed their way into what turned out to be a vast open space. Eventually the two explorers mapped out the total subterranean system at over two miles long, with around 13,000 feet of passageways. They told no one of their discovery until 1987, when together with the Kartchner family who owned the land, they invited Arizona state parks to buy the caverns. It took a further twelve years, and $28 million, to prepare them for display, with constant monitoring to ensure that the formations were not damaged by either construction work or the effects of artificial lighting.

Visitors are only admitted to the actual caves on **guided tours**, in carefully controlled numbers. Reservations can be made by phone only, up to a year in advance (Mon–Fri 8am–5pm; ☎520/586-2283). You have to pay the full fee by credit card when you book; the fees are not refundable, though it is possible to change the precise time of your tour. On the day of your visit, you're expected to pick up your tickets an hour ahead of time. Thanks to heavy demand from Tucson-area residents, all tours have so far tended to be fully booked several months ahead. Tourists who arrive without reservations are therefore unlikely to be able to see the caverns themselves, and have to content themselves with the displays in the large **Discovery Center** instead (daily 7.30am–6pm; park information on ☎520/586-4110).

Admission to Kartchner Caverns is $10 per vehicle; tours cost a further $14 for adults, $6 for ages 7–13.

In the first phase of development, a narrow, switchbacking cement trail of a third of a mile was laid through the caverns' two upper "rooms," the **Throne Room** and the **Rotunda Room**. At some point in the future, a separate trail will enable tours of three more rooms on the lower level, but for the moment, there's just one standard tour, lasting for one hour, including the tram ride to the cave entrance and 45 minutes spent underground. Tours starts every twenty minutes, with the first at 8.40am daily, and the last at 4.40pm. Among the formations en route are precarious stalactites (the ones which dangle from the ceiling) and towering stalagmites (which rise from the floor) – to add to the confusion, there's also a hollow soda straw, a combination of both which stretches from floor to ceiling. However, the most spectacular feature is the striated **coloring** of the cavern walls, created by aeons of unseen flooding. As no photography or filming is permitted during the tour, though, you'll have to commit it all to memory.

The Amerind Foundation Museum

If you choose to continue east from Benson on I-10, the one point of interest on the barren run to New Mexico comes a total of 65 miles east of Tucson, in the shape of the excellent **Amerind Foundation Museum** (June–Aug Wed–Sun 10am–4pm; Sept–May daily 8am–4pm; $3). This privately-run anthropological museum is located in remote Texas Canyon, a mile southeast of exit 318 halfway between Benson and Willcox. Not that you'll see anything as vulgar as a roadside billboard to announce its presence: it's a rather high-brow affair, with the declared ambition to "increase the world's knowledge of ancient man by excavation and collection." Displays cover native cultures from North, Central and South America, but specialize in the Southwest, featuring fine Apache, Navajo and Hopi crafts, plus older pieces from the Mimbres and Hohokam peoples, and a gallery of Western art.

Sierra Vista

Heading south from Benson and the caverns on Hwy-90, by contrast, brings you after 25 miles to **SIERRA VISTA**, a characterless modern town that has grown in tandem with the Army base at **Fort Huachuca**. Once home to detachments of Apache scouts and Buffalo Soldiers, and one of the few nineteenth-century military outposts to survive into the modern era, the fort still employs over thirteen thousand people, now working on high-tech electronic early-warning systems and the like. Its oldest buildings house dull displays on its early years (Mon–Fri 9am–4pm, Sat & Sun 1–4pm; free).

A much more enjoyable hour or two can be spent at the **Ramsey Canyon Preserve**, squeezed into a slender gorge in the Huachuca Mountains, off Hwy-92 seven miles south (March–Oct daily 8am–5pm; Nov–Feb Mon–Fri 9am–5pm, Sat & Sun 8am–5pm). Owned by the Nature Conservancy, this well-watered spot is dedicated to safeguarding local wildlife in general, but the reason everyone comes here is for its mind-boggling array of colorful **hummingbirds**. There's so little room for cars that it's essential to call in advance of your visit – as much as a week in summer – to reserve parking space.

Practicalities

Plenty of **motels** in town cater to visiting service families and nature-lovers. The *Windermere Hotel*, 2047 S Hwy-92 (☎520/459-5900 or 1-800/825-4656, fax 520/458-1347; ④) is the newest and largest; the *Super 8*, 100 Fab Ave (☎520/459-5380 or 1-800/800-8000; ③), among the most reasonably priced. Just outside the preserve, seven miles south, the *Ramsey Canyon Inn*, 31 Ramsey Canyon Rd (☎520/378-3010; ⑥), is a plush six-room **B&B** where a battery of sugar-water feeders ensures the constant presence of countless hummingbirds.

Sierra Vista's zip code is AZ 85635.

Coronado National Memorial

The
southeast
corner

Tucked into the southernmost notch of the Huachuca Mountains, five miles off Hwy-92 twenty miles from Sierra Vista, **CORONADO NATIONAL MEMORIAL** commemorates the approximate spot where in May 1540 the expedition of **Francisco Vasquez de Coronado** first entered what's now the United States. A short video and some interesting displays in the **visitor center** (daily 8am–5pm; free; ☎520/366-5515) explain the history, but the memorial basically exists to offer a selection of scenic **hiking trails**.

*The story of
Coronado's
expedition is
told on p.524.*

The best short hike climbs south from **Montezuma Pass**, the highest point along the washboard dirt road west of the visitor center. The 0.4-mile **Coronado Peak Trail** culminates in huge views in all directions, and especially to the pyramidal Mexican mountains across the border. Heading north from the same trailhead, you can hike for twenty miles up the western flank of the Huachucas. If the weather's good enough – check with rangers – ordinary vehicles can continue west on unpaved roads all the way to **Nogales** (see p.251), fifty miles distant beyond the Patagonia Mountains.

Tombstone

Perhaps the most famous town in the Wild West, **TOMBSTONE** lies 22 miles south of I-10 on US-80, 67 miles southeast of Tucson. More than a century has passed since its mining days came to an end, but "The Town Too Tough to Die" clings to an afterlife as a tourist theme park. With its dusty streets, wooden sidewalks and swinging saloon doors, it's surprisingly unchanged. Most adults, however, have seen too many inauthentic replicas and movie re-creations for the real thing to retain much appeal, and so Tombstone is reduced to trying to divert kids with tacky dioramas and daily shoot-outs.

When **Edward Schieffelin** began prospecting in the Dragoon Mountains in 1877, he was told by soldiers stationed nearby that all he'd find would be his own tombstone. Hence the name of the town that rose from the desert when he made Arizona's largest **silver** strike, in March 1878. Schieffelin sold his stake for $500,000, but the mine produced $30 million in the next seven years, and by 1880 Tombstone was home to over ten thousand people. Drifters arrived from the played-out gold fields of Canada and Australia, and gamblers came in from Dodge City, only for the mine to hit water 500 feet below ground in 1886, and be flooded beyond repair.

Most of the buildings that fill modern Tombstone's simple grid date from the early 1880s. Decaying wagons are parked on the street corners, and signs along the boardwalks mark the sites of famous shoot-outs. **Gunslingers** too still pace the streets and snarl at each other, though the prey they're stalking these days are the tourists themselves. Whenever they've rounded up enough customers, usually at around $4 per head, they gun each other down on some appropriate

The Gunfight at the OK Corral

Despite the worldwide fame of the shoot-out with which it ended – the leg-endary **Gunfight at the OK Corral** – how the feud between the **Earps** and the **Clantons** began remains obscure. To Hollywood, the Earps have always been the heroes, with Wyatt played by firm-jawed stars like Henry Fonda and Kevin Costner. They were, after all, officers of the law, although it was **Virgil** who was Tombstone's marshal, and his brothers **Wyatt** and **Morgan** merely temporary deputies. Ike Clanton, his brother Billy and their "gang" were freebooting cattle rustlers, who raided Mexican ranches for beef to feed Tombstone's hungry miners.

Tombstone's Episcopalian minister at the time of the shoot-out, Endicott Peabody, went on to be Franklin Roosevelt's White House chaplain.

Such family-based clans were typical of the West, where it was hard for individuals to prosper alone but trustworthy partners were few and far between. Equally typically, both factions had allied themselves with more powerful forces. The Earps dreamed of establishing their own cattle empire, but in Tombstone they were the hired guns of the town's **Republican** elite. For the owners and managers of the local mines, a fed-erally imposed end to Arizona's frontier anarchy was essential for future investment. Their mouthpiece was the Republican mayor, John Clum, who was also editor of the *Tombstone Epitaph*. The Clantons, like most cow-boys and small-scale ranchers, were aligned with the county sheriff, **Democrat** John Behan.

In the spring of 1881, masked gunmen held up a Wells Fargo stage-coach near Tombstone, and killed two passengers. Some sources say the robbers were Clanton associates; others, that a familiar cough betrayed one to be **John "Doc" Holliday**, a consumptive dentist from Georgia who was close to the Earps, and that the victims were Clanton's men. The hold-up may even have been a joint operation by both groups, who fell out when the plan went awry.

By October, each faction had sworn to shoot the other on sight. The showdown finally came at 2pm on **October 26, 1881**. Virgil, Wyatt and Morgan Earp, together with Doc Holliday, confronted the Clanton broth-ers, Tom and Frank McLaury, and Billy Claiborne, not in the OK Corral itself, but on Fremont Street nearby. Two of the Clanton group were unarmed, whereas all the Earps had pistols, and Holliday was carrying a shotgun. The Earps fired first. When the shooting stopped, Billy Clanton and the McLaury brothers were dead; Virgil and Morgan Earp, and Doc Holliday, had been wounded, and Ike Clanton had fled.

Under the headline "Three Men Hurled Into Eternity in the Duration of a Moment," the next day's *Tombstone Epitaph* reported that "the feeling among our best citizens is that the Marshal was entirely justifiable." However, Wyatt and Holliday were charged with murder, and were held in jail before being acquitted towards the end of November.

In March 1882, Morgan Earp was killed by a shot fired through the win-dow as he played billiards in Tombstone's *Campbell & Hatch* saloon. Three days later, Wyatt Earp shot the chief suspect, Clanton associate Frank Stilwell, in Tucson. He's said to have killed two more of the Clanton gang that summer before leaving Tombstone for good, with his surviving brothers. Warrants were issued for his arrest, but the governor of Colorado refused to authorize his extradition to Arizona on the grounds that he faced lynching if he returned to Tombstone. Instead, Wyatt Earp moved to Los Angeles, where he was lionized by early movie-makers, and died in 1929.

vacant lot. With three or so groups usually in town at any one time, there's seldom long to wait. During **Helldorado Days**, held on the third weekend of each October, you can hardly move for corpses.

Although the real gunfight at the OK Corral in fact took place on Fremont Street, the **OK Corral** itself remains the major attraction for visitors (daily 8.30am–5pm; $2.50). As you enter the corral building, on Allen Street between Third and Fourth, the first thing you see is the hearse used to take the victims away. In the second of two baking-hot adobe-walled courtyards beyond, crude dummies show the supposed locations of the Earps and the Clantons, in complete contradiction to contemporary reports of the fight. The original studio of photographer C.S. Fly stands alongside, displaying his pictures of Geronimo and other Apache warriors, and you can also visit the room from which Big Nose Kate, Doc Holliday's girlfriend, is said to have witnessed the shootings.

A couple of blocks along Allen Street, the **Bird Cage Theater** (daily 8am–6pm; $4) was Tombstone's leading venue for entertainment of all kinds. Seven "bird cages," much like theater boxes but curtained off and said to have been used by prostitutes, hang from either side of the main hall. Those on the left were frequented by the Earps and their cronies, while the ones on the right were the preserve of Sheriff Behan and the Clantons. The theater now holds a motley collection of curiosities, including a revolting foot-long "merman" from China and another ornate hearse, while downstairs you can see the old gaming tables and bordello rooms.

Tombstone's role as the seat of Cochise County – before it was supplanted by Bisbee – is recalled at the **Tombstone Courthouse State Historic Park**, at Third and Toughnut (daily 8am–5pm; $2.50). Among displays on the Apache and early outlaws, the sheriff's office here holds the coroner's report on John Heith, a robber lynched in 1884 by a Bisbee mob: "I find that the deceased died of emphysema of the lungs which might have been caused by strangulation, self-inflicted or otherwise." Upstairs, you can watch a video reconstruction of a notorious 1897 murder trial in the former courtroom, while admiring the gallows in the high-walled yard outside.

Boothill Graveyard, half a mile north on US-80, closed in May 1884, having been filled by 276 burials. In keeping with the souvenir store that now guards the entrance, several of the graves bear dubious jokey epitaphs, and country music is piped from concealed speakers, but you can see where the losers at the OK Corral still rest in peace (daily 7.30am–6pm; free).

Practicalities

Tombstone's **visitor center** is at Allen and Fourth (daily 10am–4pm; ☎520/457-3929 or 1-800/457-3423), while the Territorial Book Trader (☎520/457-3170), at the same intersection, has a fine stock of books on local history.

The
southeast
corner

Tombstone's
zip code is AZ
85638.

Central **motels** include the *Tombstone Motel*, 502 E Fremont St
(☎520/457-3478 or 1-888/455-4578; *tombstonemotel@theriver
.com*; ③), and the *Adobe Lodge*, 505 Fremont St (☎520/457-2241
or 1-888/457-2241; ③). The classier mountain-view *Best Western
Lookout Lodge* is a mile north on US-80 W (☎520/457-2223 or
1-800/652-6772, fax 520/457-3870; summer ③, winter ④).
Priscilla's, 101 N Third St (☎520/457-3844; *priscilla@tomb-
stone1880.com*; ③), and *Buford House*, 113 E Safford St
(☎520/457-3969; *bufordbb@primenet.com*; ④), are similar
antique-filled **B&Bs**.

Among old-style **saloons** serving steaks and beer in as raucous
an atmosphere as they can manage are the *Crystal Palace* at Fifth
and Allen, the *Longhorn Restaurant* at 501 Allen St, and *Big
Nose Kate's* at 417 E Allen St, where you can still join an ongoing
card game. *Pony Espresso*, slightly back from the street at 509
Allen St (☎520/457-2526) serves espresso coffees and pastries.

Bisbee

Crammed into a narrow gorge 25 miles south of Tombstone, the
town of **BISBEE** is rivaled only by Jerome, near Sedona (p.302) as
Arizona's most atmospheric Victorian relic. Like Jerome, its fortunes
were built on a century of mining mundane, dependable **copper** from
the surrounding mountains, rather than a few ephemeral years of
gold and silver. Its solid brick buildings still stand as an enduring testament to the days when Bisbee's population of twenty thousand outstripped both Phoenix and Tucson to make it the largest city between
New Orleans and San Francisco.

George Warren first discovered copper in Mule Pass Gulch, the
site of modern Bisbee, in 1877. So little did he value his claim that he
lost it in a fit of drunken bravado, betting he could outrun a man on
horseback. The Copper Queen and Phelps Dodge companies soon
moved in, then amalgamated rather than face a legal battle over
which owned a vast ore body found between their two mines.

The most notorious incident in local history came at the height of
World War I, when demand for copper was at its peak. On July 12,
1917, two weeks into a miners' strike, a story in the *Bisbee Daily
Review* under the headline "All Women and Children Keep Off
Streets Today," announced the formation of a 2200-strong posse to
arrest "strange men." In the so-called **Bisbee Deportation**, 1286
alleged members of the International Workers of the World – the
"Wobblies" – were packed into railroad boxcars and dumped in the
desert near Columbus, New Mexico. Following a national outcry,
Bisbee's Sheriff Wheeler was tried for kidnapping in 1920, but the
charges were dropped.

Phelps Dodge finally closed down its Bisbee operations in 1975,
having extracted over six billion dollars' worth of metals. As the miners moved away, however, artists and retirees moved in, preserving

Bisbee's original architecture while turning it into a thriving, friendly little community that caters to tourists without being overwhelmed by them.

Walking Bisbee's narrow central streets, lined with galleries and antiques stores, is a pleasure in itself, though you may grow weary of climbing the high staircases built by the WPA during the 1930s. If you'd like to know more about local history, it's well worth calling in at the **Bisbee Mining and Historical Museum**, 5 Copper Queen Plaza (daily 10am–4pm; adults $3, under-18s free). You can also tour the actual mines, with Queen Mine Tours, 111 Arizona St (☎520/432-2071). Hour-long **underground tours** of the Queen Mine leave daily at 9am, 10.30am, noon, 2pm & 3.30pm (adults $10, ages 7–11 $3.50, ages 3–6 $2), while **van tours** of the opencast Lavender Pit, a massive hole that ended up swallowing many of Bisbee's earliest homes, set off at 10.30am, noon, 2pm & 3.30pm ($7 all ages).

Practicalities

Bisbee's **visitor center**, at 7 Main St (Mon–Fri 9am–5pm, Sat & Sun 10am–4pm; ☎520/432-5421), has details of **B&Bs** like the *Inn@Castle Rock*, 112 Tombstone Canyon (☎520/432-4449 or 1-800/566-4449, fax 520/432-7868; *www.theinn.org*; ④), and the quirky *School House Inn*, a mile or two further out in a converted school at 818 Tombstone Canyon (☎520/432-2996 or 1-800/537-4333; ③). A grander alternative is the venerable *Copper Queen Hotel*, in the heart of town at 11 Howell Ave (☎520/432-2216 or 1-800/247-5829 in AZ, fax 520/432-4298; *copperqueen@msn .com*; ④), which has a plush bar and a good restaurant with terrace seating; the only drawback is the antiquated plumbing. For sheer comfort, the equally central *High Desert Inn*, 8 Naco Rd (☎520/432-1442 or 1-800/281-0510; *www.highdesertinn.com*; ④) – a more modern equivalent in the former county jailhouse – has to be recommended. In addition, it offers slightly fancier dining.

Once-notorious **Brewery Gulch**, which runs north from Main Street, still holds a handful of spit-and-sawdust saloons and diners, while the less atmospheric **Bisbee Convention Center** to the south has its own brewpub and espresso cafe. Otherwise, *La Carreta*, 105 Tombstone Canyon (daily except Wed; ☎520/432-6600), is a white-washed cottage where standard Mexican entrees cost just $6; they also serve mesquite-grilled steaks and shrimp.

Douglas

As you'll see from the endless tailings that spill from the canyons to the south, room to build in or near Bisbee was extremely limited. In 1900, therefore, a new town was constructed 25 miles to the east, to hold a smelter to process copper from Bisbee's mines. Nestled against the Mexican border, **DOUGLAS** was equally dependent upon the world demand for copper. Although Douglas has diversified into

The southeast corner

Bisbee's zip code is AZ 85603.

ranching and industry, the relocation of Phelps Dodge following a bitter strike at the end of the 1980s has left the town's economy too depressed for it to make an appealing stop for tourists. Illegal trade with the much larger city of **AGUA PRIETA** across the border – home to almost 100,000 people – is a major source of income. In one recent case, a drug smuggler with houses in both towns hired surveyors and laborers to dig a deep tunnel between the two, and then had them executed to preserve his secret.

Since the US instigated a major national crackdown in 1994, under the code name Operation Hold the Line, Douglas has also supplanted El Paso and San Diego as the number one port of entry for **illegal immigrants** from Mexico. In March 1999 alone, the 275 agents of the Border Patrol stationed in Douglas arrested 61,000 such entrants – a rate of almost one hundred per hour. That's reckoned to be a small proportion of the estimated several thousand people who cross the border each night.

Cars and pedestrians alike cross into Mexico at the foot of Pan American Avenue, a mile or so southwest of downtown Douglas; US citizens don't need to carry passports, but it makes sense to do so. With its whitewashed adobe homes and churches, Agua Prieta is a considerably more attractive place to stroll around than Douglas, and offers plenty of opportunities to eat spicy Sonoran food and buy cheap souvenirs.

Practicalities

The only building of any interest in Douglas is the 160-room *Gadsden Hotel*, 1046 G Ave (☎520/364-4481; *www.theriver.com /gadsdenhotel*; ②–⑤), which opened in 1907 and still boasts an extraordinarily opulent lobby with a white-marble staircase leading to a 42-foot Tiffany glass window. The guest **accommodation** is not nearly so classy, but the *Saddle and Spur Lounge* and *El Conquistador* **restaurant** both have a real frontier-town air about them. A few more downmarket **motels** are scattered along Hwy-80 to the east.

Chiricahua National Monument

Stretching northeast of Douglas towards New Mexico, the **Chiricahua Mountains** were renowned in the nineteenth century as the homeland and stronghold of the **Chiricahua Apache**. Led by such legendary warriors as **Cochise** and **Geronimo**, the Chiricahua were the last Native Americans to hold out against the US Army. The 25-year **Apache Wars** began at Apache Pass in 1861, when Cochise met Lt George Bascom under a flag of truce, and was falsely accused of kidnapping a twelve-year-old boy. He escaped into the mountains, but his brother and two nephews were hanged, precipitating a vicious cycle of raids and killings that only ended with Geronimo's fourth and final surrender in 1886.

*For more
about the
Apache, see
p.541.*

Had the small Chiricahua band not fought so long and hard, they might still be permitted to live on the **Chiricahua Reservation**, which measured 55 miles on each side, and occupied the entire southeastern corner of Arizona. Established during a period of relative peace in 1872, it was disbanded in 1876, when the Chiricahua were forcibly decamped to join their distant cousins on the San Carlos reservation to the north. No visible sign of the Apache presence remains, but the core of the former reservation now constitutes **CHIRICAHUA NATIONAL MONUMENT**, entered off Hwy-186 27 miles southeast of Willcox. The monument was designated not so much to commemorate the Apache, however, as to protect the bizarre **rock formations** created in the 27 million years since colossal volcanic eruptions covered the landscape with a 2000-foot coating of dark rhyolite rock. That layer has now cracked and fragmented into strange towers and columns of stacked and balanced stones, a bewildering maze that always defeated Army attempts to pursue the Apache into the mountains.

Birds in the Chiricahua Mountains include a colony of thick-billed parrots, once common here and re-introduced in 1986.

Chiricahua National Monument is not as spectacular as the desert canyons of Utah, which is presumably why the 1994 movie *Geronimo*, for all its much-vaunted authenticity, was filmed in Moab. However, this remote fastness preserves a tract of barely touched wilderness that conjures up haunting images of the Wild West, and it's also a sanctuary for rare animals and birds.

The monument stays open 24 hours, with an admission fee of $4 per vehicle.

Just one paved road – the eight-mile **Bonita Canyon Drive** – penetrates, but does not cross, the mountains. From the monument entrance it runs for two miles to the **visitor center** (daily 8am–5pm; ☎520/824-3560), then follows Bonita Canyon east before climbing south to reach **Massai Point**, 6870 feet up. This high vantage point looks out over the main concentration of rocky pinnacles, in **Echo Canyon** and **Heart of Rocks**.

Only if you have a few hours to spare, however, does Massai Point make a good spot from which to start **hiking** in the monument; it is possible to walk down into the labyrinth from here, but then you're faced with either a long climb to get back out again, or a one-way walk of over four miles to reach the visitor center. For a shorter and less demanding stroll, set off instead along **Echo Canyon Trail**, which starts half a mile or so back down the road. This level footpath provides almost immediate access to some dramatic formations, with the option of turning back as soon as you've had your fill. The highest peak in the monument at 7310 feet, **Sugarloaf Mountain** can be climbed on a separate mile-long trail, but it's a much less rewarding hike.

No food, gas or lodging is available in the monument, and overnight backpacking is forbidden, but you can **camp** year-round at the small *Bonita Canyon Campground* (first-come, first-served; $7).

Fort Bowie

The ruins of **Fort Bowie**, the original focus of the Chiricahua Reservation, now lie just beyond the northern boundary of Chiricahua

*Allow at least
2hr 30min for
the round-trip
hike to Fort
Bowie.*

National Monument (daily 8am–5pm; free). They're reached by a demanding but exhilarating 1.5-mile trail that starts on the north side of **Apache Pass**, a total of 22 miles from the monument visitor center or, if you're coming from the north, thirteen miles from the somewhat desolate I-10 pitstop of **BOWIE**.

Apache Pass today is an insignificant back route. The central nine miles of the **Apache Pass Road** across it are not even paved, though other than during periods of heavy rain they're usually passable to ordinary vehicles. This low saddle between the Dos Cabezas and Chiricahua mountains is currently overgrown with mesquite bushes, but when the Apache were here it ran through clear, open grassland, and its perennial natural **springs** were a vital resource. Those same springs, however, made it a crucial way-station for the **Butterfield Overland Mail**, which started regular runs through Apache Pass in 1857, as part of a 25-day, 2800-mile service between St Louis and San Francisco. At first, local Apaches were cooperative, but after the Bascom Affair of 1861 (see p.262), the US Army established a permanent military presence at the pass.

The first significant relic along the trail comes after half a mile, in the shape of the stone walls of the **Apache Pass Stage Station**, built in 1858. Shortly after crossing the old stage route, now just a narrow furrow in the soil, you reach a **cemetery**, where Little Robe, the two-year-old son of Geronimo, lies alongside several US soldiers. Not far beyond, the trail reaches the glorious lush creek that flows from **Apache Spring** – the source of all the trouble, but now the preserve of a myriad of playful coati and bobcat.

There are no views to speak of as you climb; instead, the **fort** itself sits in a deep, broad bowl, ringed by mountains and dominated by a granite knob known as **Helen's Dome**. All that survives of the large complex are the rounded, sun-baked stumps of its adobe walls, though a flag still flutters above the parade ground, and there's a visitor center nearby to provide much-needed shade and water. An optional, slightly longer route back continues up the adjacent hillside – finally enabling you to appreciate that this really was a good vantage point on which to build – before circling down to the trailhead. En route, you step over the geological fault responsible for creating the springs, which instantly transforms the surrounding vegetation from yucca and flowering cactuses (on limestone) to beargrass (on granite).

Southwest Arizona

Two interstates, **I-8** and **I-10**, run west across central and southern Arizona towards California, 35 miles apart near Phoenix and more than twice that by the time they reach the state line. There's virtually nothing of interest in these vast desert plains, apart perhaps from the strange prototype military airplanes glimpsed above the Barry M.

Goldwater Air Force Base, which stretches south from I-8 to Mexico. A long detour south will take you to the wild terrain of **Organ Pipe Cactus National Monument**, but the only town you might conceivably want to visit is **Yuma**, a venerable river crossing on the far southwest frontier with California, whose mundane present fails to live up to its wild past.

Papago Indian Reservation

The high country to the east of Tucson, known as **Papaguería** to the Spanish, is now dominated by the **Papago Indian Reservation**. One of three related groups who together call themselves the **'O'odham** – "The People" – the Papago are now known as the **Tohono 'O'odham**, which means "desert people." Unlike the Pima, or Akimel 'O'odham, the "river people" who lived in permanent villages, the Tohono 'O'odham were traditionally "two-villagers," who divided their time between a summer "field" village in the valleys and a winter "well" village near a spring in the foothills. Eighteen thousand Tohono 'O'odham now live on the reservation, which was established in 1916. They share it with the less numerous **Hia C–ed 'O'odham**, formerly known as the Sand Papago – desert nomads who in 1976 accepted $26 million as compensation for the loss of the lands now enclosed by Organ Pipe Cactus National Monument and the Barry Goldwater Air Force Base.

For tourists, the only reward in driving the hundred-mile width of the reservation, which starts 25 miles out of Tucson on **Hwy-86**, is its sheer sense of desolation. The only signs of human occupation are a handful of roadside buildings at **SELLS**, the administrative headquarters, and **QUIJOTOA**.

Organ Pipe Cactus National Monument

Hwy-86 eventually meets **Hwy-85**, fifty miles south of Gila Bend, at a "Y"-shaped intersection that has over the years acquired the formal name of **WHY**. A twenty-mile detour south from here through the straight, flat **Sonoyta Valley**, between the jagged ridge of the dry Ajo Mountains to the east and the lower Puerto Blanco Mountains to the west, climbs in due course to reach **ORGAN PIPE CACTUS NATIONAL MONUMENT**, right on the Mexican border.

Located at the heart of the Sonoran Desert, the five-hundred-square-mile monument is a treasure-trove of rare desert plants and animals, but focuses especially on the **organ pipe**, found almost nowhere else in the United States. Where the saguaro stands alone, the organ pipe grows in clusters of tubular "pipes," thrusting up from a shared central root system.

The $4 per vehicle monument **entrance fee** is payable only if you leave the main road. From the **visitor center**, just west of the highway (daily 8am–5pm; ☎520/387-6849), two separate **scenic drives** loop off into the mountains. Both are unpaved and steep, but generally passable for ordinary vehicles; the 21-mile **Ajo Mountain Drive** takes around two hours to complete, the 53-mile **Puerto Blanco Drive** at least half a day.

In summer, **hiking** anything more than the hundred-yard nature trail at the visitor center would be far too grueling to consider, but between October and April, you might feel more inclined to walk several short trails that lead further afield. The cooler months are also the only time when the **campground** (first-come, first-served; $8), a mile south of the visitor center, is likely to fill up.

Ajo

Thirty miles north of the Organ Pipe monument, almost halfway to Gila Bend and the interstate, **AJO** is a former copper-mining town that belies its ugly outskirts – the huge open-pit mine to the south is a hideous spectacle – by having a spruce and attractive Spanish-style plaza at its core. Hispanic settlers were digging for copper by 1750; they named the town in honor of the garlic (*ajo*) that grows wild in the hills nearby.

Since Phelps Dodge closed the mine in 1984, after a bitter year-long strike, Ajo has defied the skeptics and clung to life by attracting a steady trickle of tourists and retirees. There's a welcoming bustle about its grassy plaza, surrounded by palm trees and holding two whitewashed Spanish-colonial churches, even if the streets behind hold little of interest.

Practicalities

Ajo's zip code is AZ 85321.

Two clean, simple **motels** stand either side of the highway a couple of miles north of town. The *Marine Resort* is tucked behind a screen of cactuses at 1966 N Hwy-85 (☎520/387-7626; summer ②, winter ③), while *La Siesta* is on the west side, a little further along at 2561 N Hwy-85 (☎520/387-6569; summer ②, winter ③). Back in town, the *Guest House Inn*, 3 Guesthouse Rd (☎520/387-6133; ③), is a comfortable **B&B** with four en-suite rooms. The *Copper Kettle* on the plaza is the best **restaurant**, serving mainly Mexican dishes.

Gila Bend

At the intersection of Hwy-85 and I-8, **GILA BEND** is a minor farming community whose hopes of prosperity were dashed when the early twentieth-century spate of dam-building all but dried up the Gila River. What little local history available to be celebrated is recorded in the tiny museum that adjoins its rudimentary **visitor center** at 644 W Pima St (daily 8am–4pm; ☎520/683-2002).

While not a destination in itself, Gila Bend has the widest selection of **motels** in almost 200 miles of interstate, with some run-down options offering rooms for little more than $20. The *Best Western*

Space Age Lodge, 401 E Pima St (☎520/683-2273 or 1-800/528-1234; summer ③, winter ④), however, is an irresistible Fifties motel, where the Sputnik motif extends to a giant neon flying saucer sign. Unfortunately, its adjoining coffeeshop, which featured huge murals of the lunar landings both inside and out, was ignited by a stray spark in 1998, but it may well have been rebuilt in even greater splendor by the time you read this.

Twenty miles west of Gila Bend, the petroglyphs of the **Painted Rock Mountains** are said to mark the boundary between the traditional territories of the Maricopa and Yuma Indians.

Yuma

Although the sheer size of **YUMA**, a hundred miles west of Gila Bend, surprises most visitors – its numbered streets start a full fifty miles out from the center – Arizona's third largest city ranks among the state's oldest communities. Commanding the confluence of the Gila and Colorado rivers, the site's significance was recognized as early as 1540, when **Hernando de Alarcon**, in charge of the naval wing of Coronado's pioneering expedition (see p.524), sailed past its high bluffs. It later became the major river crossing for California-bound travelers, though Spanish attempts to establish a permanent mission settlement were destroyed by the **Yuma Revolt** of 1781, when **Quechan** Indians (known to the Spaniards as the Yuma) massacred over 150 settlers during Mass.

At the height of California's **Gold Rush**, sixty thousand passengers in a single year paid $2 each to be ferried across the Colorado at **Yuma Crossing**. This lucrative trade was at first controlled by the Quechan, but freebooting entrepreneurs wrested it out of their hands, with the US Army at Fort Yuma on hand to stifle Indian resistance. Known initially as Colorado City, and later Arizona City, Yuma took on its current name in 1873, by which time it was experiencing a gold rush of its own.

Cormac McCarthy's novel Blood Meridian *features a phenomenally bloodthirsty account of the struggle to control Yuma's river traffic;* see p.547.

Now that intricate hydraulic engineering has tamed the Colorado – one canal feeding California's Imperial Valley actually siphons beneath the river – it would take a major dam-burst to cause a repeat of the river's formerly devastating floods. As seen in 1993, however, when it inundated Yuma's riverfront to a depth of six feet, the Gila remains as dangerous as ever. In theory, Arizona could use its share of the Colorado's water to irrigate the land around Yuma and create a rival to nearby **Imperial Valley**, one of the world's richest farming areas; instead, it's channeled across the desert to Phoenix and Tucson at absurd expense.

Yuma is not a vacation destination in the usual sense, but its warm, dry winters, when temperatures seldom drop below the mid-70°s F, have made it a goal for hordes of "**snowbirds**," who keep an astonishing 72 local RV and trailer parks busy. During summer, on the other hand, when you can expect daytime highs of over 110°F, Yuma is too much of an inferno for anyone to linger very long.

Arrival and Information

A large proportion of Yuma's **visitor center**, in the oldest part of downtown at 377 S Main St (Oct–April Mon–Fri 9am–6pm, Sat 9am–4pm, Sun 10am–1pm; May–Sept Mon–Fri 9am–5pm, Sat 9am–2pm; ☎520/783-0071), is devoted to local opportunities for square dancing. Amtrak **trains** from LA to Tucson stop nearby at 291 Gila St, at hideously unsocial hours, while Greyhound **buses** run from 170 E 17th Place (☎520/783-4403) to Phoenix, Tucson and San Diego.

Yuma River Tours run Colorado cruises from Fisher's Landing, 32 miles upstream from Yuma (five-hour $52, seven-hour $69, both starting at 9.30am daily; ☎520/783-4400).

Accommodation

As well as a plethora of RV parks, the "business loop" that parallels the interstate for around six miles through the heart of Yuma holds dozens of **hotels** and **motels**, with plusher chains along its east–west segment on **32nd Street**, and old-fashioned budget options on the north–south **Fourth Avenue** closer to the river.

Motel 6, 1445 E 16th St, Yuma, AZ 85365; ☎520/782-9521, fax 343-4941. The cheapest of the chains, within easy reach of downtown. ②.

Radisson Suites, 2600 S Fourth Ave, Yuma, AZ 85364; ☎520/726-4830 or 1-800/333-3333, fax 520/341-1152; *www.radisson.com*. Yuma's plushest option; large, modern and relatively central, with nothing but two-room suites. ⑤.

Super 8, 1688 S Riley Ave, Yuma, AZ 85365; ☎520/782-2000 or 1-800/800-8000, fax 520/782-6657. ③. Dependable chain motel, not far from downtown at interstate exit 2.

Yuma Cabana, 2151 S Fourth Ave, Yuma, AZ 85364; ☎520/783-8311 or 1-800/874-0811, fax 520/783-1126). Traditional roadside motel, with a lovely old neon sign, a couple of miles up from the river. Clean, quiet, and very good value. ②.

The Town

The best place to get a feel for Yuma's tempestuous past is the **Yuma Territorial Prison State Historic Park**, set high above the Colorado a few blocks east of downtown (daily 8am–5pm; $3). Built in 1876, and known as the "Hell Hole of Arizona," this was the state's principal prison for 33 years. The restored wooden guard tower outside gives great views of the green-lined river meandering in from the north; this spot originally marked the precise confluence of the two rivers, but as the Colorado's flow has dwindled, the meeting point has shifted five miles further upstream. The "Ocean to Ocean" bridge here was built in 1915, not only superceding the ferry but also completing the southernmost uninterrupted transcontinental railroad route.

Inside the prison compound's adobe walls, built by the earliest inmates, fascinating displays tell the stories of its three thousand prisoners. These ranged from teenage burglars to Harvard lawyers, and included nine Mormon polygamists, several Mexican revolutionaries, and a handful of women, such as the colorful Pearl Hart, who served five years for committing Arizona's last stagecoach robbery in 1899. You can also enter several individual cells, many of which were occupied by homeless migrants during the 1930s. Each held six bunks, apart from the pitch-black "dark cell," where unruly prisoners, such as women spotted "flirting," were punished with spells in isolation.

The entire riverfront at Yuma is gradually being transformed into **Yuma Crossing State Historical Park**, which will extend from the prison to the former Quartermaster Depot on Fourth Avenue near the river bridge. So far, only the depot and its grounds have been opened (daily 8am–5pm; $3). All Yuma's supplies originally reached the town via a fifty-mile river journey from the ocean at Port Isabel on the Gulf of California; the depot still holds two of the three warehouses where the Colorado paddle steamers used to moor. Various ancient wagons, carriages and even trains have been stabled indoors or set out to pasture on the lawns, but unless transportation history is really your thing, it's not a desperately exciting experience.

Yuma's most unusual attraction has to be the **Saihati Camel Farm**, roughly four miles south of town on Avenue 1E (tours Oct–May Mon–Sat 10am & 2pm, by reservation; $3; ☎520/627-2553). Until you get within smelling distance, it's a fiendishly difficult spot to find: Avenue 1E only starts on the south side of the airport, and even then it's a dirt road at first. Furthermore, the farm gates only open briefly, at the exact time of the tours. Assuming you do manage to get in, you'll be able to inspect a large herd of slobbery, drooling dromedaries, bred here for circuses and zoos – there's no camel riding here – plus a cross-section of other wildlife such as ostriches, water buffalo and Watusi cattle.

Finally, many visitors like to take a day-trip south into **Mexico**, whether to little **Algodones**, across from California a mere ten miles west, or to the much larger city of **San Luis**, 23 miles south. Both offer the usual array of souvenir stores and restaurants, together with cut-price drugstores.

Eating

Yuma is not a place to expect memorable **eating**, though a circuit of the main streets will take you past every fast-food option imaginable.

The Coffee Bean, 2450 S Fourth Ave; ☎520/317-0284. Friendly little coffee-and-pastries joint on the main drag.

The Crossing, 2690 S Fourth Ave; ☎520/726-5551. One of the more upscale diners on the climb up from the Colorado, with inexpensive steak and seafood served daily for lunch and dinner.

Garden Cafe, 250 S Madison Ave; ☎520/783-1491. Tasteful cafe with indoor and outdoor seating, behind a small free museum of pioneer life, that's open for breakfast and lunch only, and serves salads, sandwiches and espresso coffees. Closed Mon & July–Sept.

Lutes Casino, 221 Main St; ☎520/782-2192. This downtown landmark may look like a dull old barn from outside, but inside it's bursting with quirky oddities and paraphernalia, and does a brisk trade in surprisingly tasty hamburgers. There's no gambling, but plenty of pool and domino players.

North from Yuma: Quartzsite

North of Yuma, three **wildlife refuges** – the Kofa, Cibola and Imperial – line the Colorado River. Established to protect herds of mule deer and bighorn sheep as well as migratory Canadian geese, the parks aren't really designed for human visitors and are virtually inaccessible without a four-wheel-drive vehicle.

Granted that you'd rather not get caught up in the tank battles staged by the army in its **Yuma Proving Grounds**, there's nowhere to stop on the main north–south highway, **US-95**, until you reach **QUARTZSITE**, eighty miles out of Yuma.

With the Colorado now twenty miles to the west, Quartzsite is even bleaker and drier than Yuma, and has a nominal population of around two thousand, but it too experiences a major winter influx of snowbirds. Literally hundreds of thousands of RV-owners descend on this desert outpost between early January and mid-February each year, ostensibly to bargain for precious, semi-precious and merely pretty stones, but also to ride out the coldest months with likeminded fellow retirees.

To this day, it remains against the law to shoot a camel in Arizona. In Quartzsite's dusty **cemetery**, north of the main drag in the heart of town, a pyramidal monument topped by a brass camel, commemorates one of the odder episodes in Southwestern history. Inscribed "The last camp of **Hi Jolly**, born somewhere in Syria about 1828, died Quartzsite December 16 1902," it marks the grave of Haiji Ali, who arrived at Indianola, Texas, in February 1856, in charge of 33 **camels** that had been requisitioned by the then Secretary of War, Jefferson Davis. The idea was to see if they might prove suitable for use as beasts of burden; while they adapted well to the desert, army mule handlers and cowboys lacked the patience or inclination to care for them properly, and the experiment petered out during the Civil War. "Hi Jolly" became just another prospector; the abandoned camels continued to breed in the wild into the first years of the twentieth century.

Despite its endless expanse of RV parks, Quartzsite has just three tiny and flyblown **motels**, with fewer than ten rooms each.

Parker

Quartzsite's winter crowds spill over to **PARKER**, beside the river 35 miles north. The main activity here is boating on the placid waters downstream of the **Parker Dam**, a Depression-era project designed to divert Colorado water to the thirsty cities of southern California. Arizona's then-governor, Benjamin Moer, was so indignant at losing precious state resources that he sent a detachment of the Arizona National Guard – six men in a boat, nicknamed the Arizona Navy – to halt its construction in 1934. Such differences were soon resolved, however, and since 1985 the dam has also provided water for the **Central Arizona Project**, whose 336 miles of aqueducts stretch as far as Phoenix and Tucson. Almost twenty miles out of Parker, it's the deepest dam in the world, dug 235 feet into the riverbed. Jet-skiers glide up to its base for a closer look, and it can also be seen on free self-guided **tours** (daily 7.30am–4pm).

Before serving as the headquarters for the building of the dam, Parker started life in 1905 as the principal settlement on the **Colorado River Indian Reservation**. Not far from the dam, clearly signposted from Hwy-95, visitors can examine prehistoric rock art, or **intaglios**, made by "carving" the darker top layer of rock away from the desert floor, to reveal lighter layers of sand beneath (daily 8am–sundown; $3). The figures are so huge (up to 160ft) that it's hard to tell what you're looking at, but gaze long enough and you can discern a four-legged animal, and a human and spiral design.

The most appealing **place to stay** in Parker is the vaguely Moorish *Holiday Kasbah Motel*, not far from the California border at 604 California Ave (☎520/669-2133; Sun–Thurs ②, Fri & Sat ③).

Chapter 5

Flagstaff and Central Arizona

Note that the Navajo and Hopi reservations, north of the interstate, are covered in Chapter 1.

With the state's northernmost hundred miles, from the rugged Navajo and Hopi reservations across to the Grand Canyon, impassable to east–west traffic, the I-40 corridor is the focus of a huge tract of north and central Arizona. Before the interstate was pushed through, legendary Route 66 followed much the same path; before either road, there was the Santa Fe Railroad; and before the railroad arrived, little more than a century ago, there were no significant Anglo settlements in the region at all.

Even today, only **Flagstaff** of the I-40 towns amounts to much more than an overnight pit stop. No doubt the contrast with the deserts to the east makes Flagstaff seem especially attractive, but set in the world's largest stand of sweet-smelling ponderosa **pine forest**, it's one of the Southwest's most characterful and charming towns. It also makes a great base for visits not only to the Grand Canyon (detailed in Chapter 6), but to the dramatic ancient sites of **Wupatki** and **Walnut Canyon** and the superbly positioned (if over-hyped and at times even deranged) New Age mecca of **Sedona**.

The highlight of the long drive from Flagstaff to New Mexico is **Petrified Forest National Park**, where giant fossilized remains lie strewn like matchsticks across the eerie desert badlands. To the west, the road to California is less inspiring, so it makes sense to detour south by way of the historic hilltop mining town of **Jerome**, and pristine Victorian **Prescott**, or, further west, to take a timewarp spin along Route 66 to the ghost town of **Oatman**.

East of Flagstaff

During its 150-mile run west from the New Mexican border to Flagstaff, I-40 passes few towns of any size, let alone of any interest. The **landscape** however, while barren in the extreme, is consistently beautiful, with double rainbows reaching across the desert plain and

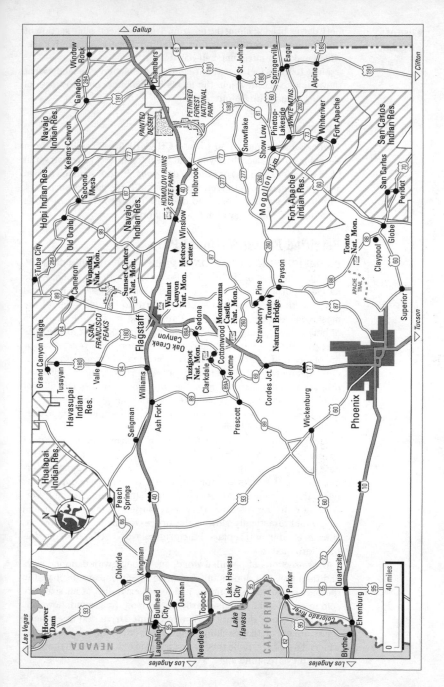

fiery dawns blazing along the horizon. The most accessible section of this **Painted Desert** lies within **Petrified Forest National Park**, which makes an intriguing half-day detour.

Most tourists feel that this relentless desolation is exactly what they came to see; few join the locals in escaping south to the cool uplands of the **White Mountains**.

Chambers

Arizona's easternmost I-40 town – **CHAMBERS**, 25 miles in from New Mexico – is also where you'll hit the interstate as you drive south from Ganado (see p.58) or Canyon de Chelly. It's not so much a town as a speck on the windscreen, consisting of three gas stations, each with its own small grocery, and the *Best Western Chieftain* motel (☎520/688-2754; ④), which has a restaurant.

Petrified Forest National Park

PETRIFIED FOREST NATIONAL PARK, which straddles the interstate 25 miles east of Holbrook, kills two birds with one stone. While its chief purpose is to protect a prehistoric "forest" of fossilized trees, south of I-40, it also stretches north to include some of the most picturesque stretches of the **Painted Desert**, an ill-defined area of multicolored badlands that covers much of northeast Arizona. Its blue-tinged clays and crumbling sands support little vegetation, or life of any kind, but continue to erode at a fearsome rate. Each year, more and more lithified logs are exposed to view, lying in haphazard profusion on the barren slopes. Petrified wood is not in fact all that rare, but its sheer abundance here is extraordinary; the wood-bearing layer, which is also rich in dinosaur bones and other fossils, extends for 300 feet beneath the ground.

The gigantic trees of Petrified Forest, drawn from long-extinct species such as *Auracarioxylon*, *Woodworthia* and *Schilderia*, date back 225 million years. This is not, however, a genuine forest. Its mighty trunks are horizontal, not vertical; they didn't grow here, they accumulated as a vast log jam in an ancient river. Settling onto the riverbed, they were buried by layers of silt and ash, which drastically slowed the processes of decay. Bit by bit, silica seeped in and replaced the original wood cells, then crystallized into quartz.

Cross-sections of petrified wood, cut through with diamond saws and then polished, look stunning; prize specimens are displayed in the park's two visitor centers, and lesser examples of all sizes are sold in commercial outlets nearby. As seen on the ground, however, from trails along the park's **27-mile Scenic Drive**, the trees themselves are not all that exciting. Segmented, crumbling and very dark, when all's said and done they're just a bunch of logs lying in the sand, even if they are stone logs.

Petrified Forest became a national park when large-scale **pilfering** threatened to deplete its stocks of wood altogether. A similar park in the Dakotas had to close in the 1930s after visitors carried off all its fossil treasures, and even today an estimated twelve tons of rock disappears from the Petrified Forest each year. In theory, rangers can search your vehicle as you leave, and impose heavy fines on anyone caught with a pocketful of petrified woodchips. They rarely bother, however, preferring the subtler approach of displaying letters in the visitor centers from repentant rock thieves who have been punished by the loss of hair, health, pets or progeny.

Arrival and information

Although the main road through the park crosses I-40, there's no access to or from the interstate at that point. Instead, where you enter the park will depend on where you're heading afterwards. If you're coming from New Mexico, turn north off the interstate at exit 311, 22 miles west of Chambers, and within a mile you'll come to the **Painted Desert Visitor Center** (daily: summer 7am–7pm; winter 8am–5pm; ☎520/524-6228). Drivers heading east should leave I-40 at Holbrook (see p.277) and take US-180 for twenty miles southeast to the southern entrance, near the **Rainbow Forest Museum** (daily 8am–5pm).

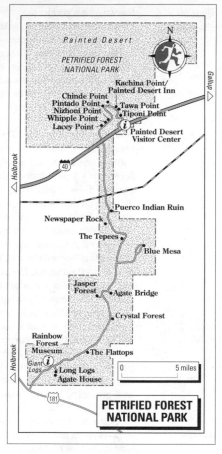

Displays at both visitor centers explain the geology of the park and forest. The **admission fee** of $10 per vehicle, or $5 for motorcyclists, cyclists and pedestrians, is levied at roadside kiosks nearby, where you can also buy the full range of national parks passes (see p.21).

You can pick up simple snacks at the Rainbow Forest Museum, but the Painted Desert Visitor Center holds most of the park's few facilities, including a *Fred Harvey* **restaurant** that serves overpriced cafe meals all day, a large gift store and a gas station. Note that there are no **lodges** or **campgrounds** in the park; the only way to spend a night here is by camping in the backcountry, with a free permit issued at the visitor center.

For advance information, write to Petrified Forest National Park, AZ 86028, or access www.nps.gov/ pefo

Seeing the park

Petrified Forest effectively divides into three sections, with an area rich in ancient Indian remains separating the desert in the north from the forest in the south. To see its full range, you have to complete the entire 27-mile scenic drive, but there's no need to stop at every one of the overlooks along the way.

Assuming you enter the park in the north, beyond the Painted Desert Visitor Center, you'll find that you're soon skirting the edge of a giant mesa, which drops away northwards to reveal long-range views across the **Painted Desert** itself. At different times of day, the undulating expanse of clay-topped mounds takes on different colors, with an emphasis on blueish shades of gray and reddish shades of brown. It's best admired through the panoramic windows of the **Painted Desert Inn** (daily 8am–4pm), a mile or two along. This defunct adobe hotel, now being restored as a museum, holds Mexican-style murals, painted by Hopi artist Fred Kabotie in 1948, of Hopi pilgrimages and dances. A stone slab bears a thirteenth-century petroglyph depiction of a fierce-clawed mountain lion. From the promontory behind the inn, **Kachina Point**, backcountry **trails** drop down into the Painted Desert Wilderness. Walking these is the only way to appreciate the scale of the place, but even the shortest hike involves a hot climb back up again.

After six miles of similar overlooks, the road crosses first the interstate, and then, in quick succession, the Santa Fe Railroad and the broad but usually dry Puerco River. At the **Puerco Indian Ruin**, just beyond, a short trail leads around a small, partially excavated pueblo, abandoned in 1300 AD by its Ancestral Puebloan inhabitants. Patches of black desert varnish on nearby rocks show some well-preserved petroglyphs, including one you'd swear depicted a stork bringing a baby.

*Utah's
Newspaper
Rock is
described on
p.452.*

A little further along, a bunch of bigger petroglyph-covered boulders – known collectively, like many such sites, as **Newspaper Rock** – lie at the foot of a rocky incline. Closer access is forbidden, but free binoculars allow you to peer at the indistinct scribbles. In time, some resolve themselves into male and female figures.

By the time you've passed the bizarre pyramidal hillocks of the **Teepees**, you've finally reached the **Petrified Forest**. At roadside halts from here on, rough concrete walkways have been laid over the terrain – and often over the tree trunks themselves – to enable visitors to ramble through the larger concentrations of logs. At **Blue Mesa**, certain tree-trunks are raised on muddy "pedestals" above the surrounding desert; at **Agate Bridge**, one even spans a little gully.

The park's busiest trail, the **Long Logs Walk** near the southern entrance, is so popular that its parking lot is closed in the mornings, and hikers have to walk an additional few hundred yards up from the Rainbow Forest Museum. Here at the edge of the desert, a little grass manages to survive, which somehow makes the half-mile main trail especially surreal. The large, shattered logs – which when alive resembled ponderosa pines – are simply strewn across the grasslands, with not another stone or rock in sight. A side trail leads in another half mile to a knoll holding the remains of a seven-hundred-year-old Indian pueblo constructed entirely from petrified wood. **Agate House** sounds amazing, but, thanks perhaps to its rather clumsy restoration, it's oddly banal.

Holbrook

Halfway between Gallup and Flagstaff, **HOLBROOK** was for the last two decades of the nineteenth century the rowdy headquarters of the "Hashknife" cattle outfit, the third largest in the country. Not much seems to have happened since then, but Holbrook has been kept ticking over by traffic on Route 66 and I-40.

Unless you're ready to stop for the night, there's no great reason to stray off the interstate, though a romantic patch of Route 66 frontage survives along **Navajo Boulevard**, squeezed between the Little Colorado River and the railroad to the south, and the interstate to the north. The **Historic Courthouse Museum**, 100 E Arizona St (summer Mon–Fri 8am–8pm, Sat 8am–5pm; winter Mon–Fri 8am–5pm; free) is an appealing small-town mélange of Ancestral Puebloan pots, fading photographs and dioramas of Wild West shootouts.

Practicalities

Holbrook's **visitor center** is in the museum (same hours; ☎520/524-2459 or 1-800/524-2459). By far the most unusual, if not exactly luxurious, place to **stay** is the *Wigwam Motel*, 811 W Hopi Drive (☎520/524-3048; ②), a Route 66 relic in which each room is a miniature concrete wigwam. There's also a *Super 8*, up the hill north of the interstate at 1989 E Navajo Blvd (☎520/524-2871 or 1-800/800-8000, fax 520/524-3514; winter ②, summer ③), with a Basha's supermarket nearby, and a dozen other chain motels.

Three of Holbrook's **diners** – including the *Arizona Country Cafe* at Hwy-77 and I-40 (☎520/524-2686), where the menu runs to just about anything – remain open 24 hours a day. The *Butterfield Stage Co*, 609 W Hopi Drive (☎520/645-3447), open for lunch and dinner in summer, and dinner only in winter, serves espresso coffees.

The price codes used here are explained on p.15.

The White Mountains and the Mogollon Rim

Though the spell-binding northern Arizonan desert appears to stretch away forever to either side of I-40, the southern limit of the Colorado Plateau is just beneath the horizon – the 2000-foot escarpment of the **Mogollon Rim**, curving 200 miles from west to east, and extending well into New Mexico. As you approach from the north, it feels as though you're heading into the back of beyond, but you're soon within a hundred miles of the megalopolis of **Phoenix**.

For sweltering city-dwellers, the highland forests – especially in the **White Mountains**, near **Show Low** – make ideal targets for weekend breaks. Visitors from beyond the Southwest rarely stray this way, and unless you're looking to hunt, fish, or, in winter, ski, the only point in doing so is if you want to get to **southern Arizona** without passing through Phoenix. While none of the Mogollon Rim towns amounts to more than the sum of its dreary parts, they do at least offer an abundance of motels. Both roads south, **US-60** and **US-191**, are exhilarating drives, passing through untamed mountainous terrain that evokes the early days of the Wild West.

Springerville and Eagar

The easternmost White Mountain towns, **SPRINGERVILLE** and neighboring **EAGAR**, stand near the edge of the plains in **Round Valley**, just a few miles west of New Mexico. Their only significance is as base camps for trips into the mountains, which you'll encounter a couple of miles south on US-191, or ten miles west on Hwy-260, on the far side of the innocuous Little Colorado River.

Springerville's **visitor center**, 318 E Main St (Mon–Sat 9am–5pm; ☎520/333-2123), can give details of nearby attractions, including a couple of minor Indian ruins. The best value of its half-dozen **motels** is the plain but friendly *Super 8*, Hwy-60 on the north side of town (☎520/333-2655 or 1-800/800-8000, fax 520/333-5450; winter ②, summer ③). As for **restaurants**, the *Safire*, 411 Main St (☎520/333-4512), serves meats and beers to match any hunter's appetite, while *Booga Red's*, 521 Main St (☎520/333-5036), is an all-day diner that offers Mexican specialties such as *chimichangas* as well as steaks.

Coronado Trail Scenic Road

South of Springerville, US-191 is designated as the **Coronado Trail Scenic Road**, though it doesn't so much follow the route taken by Francisco de Coronado in 1540 – see p.524 – as vaguely parallel it. It's such a tortuous high-mountain highway that driving all the way to **Clifton**, 120 miles south (see p.233), can take up to four hours, but so long as you fill up on gas first you're sure to enjoy it.

At the only village to interrupt the pine woods – **ALPINE**, 25 miles south – US-180 branches off west into New Mexico. Just a tiny T-junction in a meadow, Alpine is said to be the chilliest spot in Arizona. It holds a handful of motels, including the *Sportsman's Lodge* near the intersection (☎520/339-4576; ②), and *Tal-Wi-Wi Lodge*, three miles north (☎520/339-4319; summer ③, winter ④).

Beyond Alpine, US-191 is liable to be closed by snow between mid-December and mid-March. When it's open, roadside trailheads, used mainly by hunters, make it possible to hike into the **Apache-Sitgreaves National Forest**, which also holds several rudimentary campgrounds (call ☎520/339-4384 for details). The most scenic spot is the **Blue Vista** pull-out, in the twistiest stretch of road twenty miles south of Alpine, which commands sweeping views of the misty mountains. It lies just south of the **Hannagan Meadow** clearing, where the big red-timber *Hannagan Meadow Lodge* is a restaurant that rents out cabins in summer (☎520/339-4370 or 1-800/547-1416; ④).

Show Low

SHOW LOW, fifty miles south of Holbrook on Hwy-77, and 43 miles west of Springerville, is the largest town on the Mogollon Rim. It stands on the site of a 100,000-acre ranch, whose co-founders played cards in 1876 to decide who should get to keep it. With the game all square, one invited the other to "show low and take the ranch"; his rival drew the deuce of clubs and duly took possession. He went on to sell the ranch to the Mormon church, which built a small settlement before selling it on again.

Show Low today is basically a strip of motels and diners ranged along US-60, or **Deuce of Clubs Avenue**. For a full list, stop by the **visitor center**, 951 W Deuce of Clubs Ave (Mon–Fri 9am–5pm, Sat & Sun 10am–2pm; ☎520/537-2326 or 1-888/746-9569). Inexpensive places to stay include the *Super 8*, 1941 E Deuce of Clubs Ave (☎520/537-7694 or 1-800/800-8000, fax 520/537-1373; winter ②, summer ③), and the more basic *Thunderbird*, 1131 E Deuce of Clubs Ave (☎520/537-4391; ②). No matter how hard you look, there's nowhere distinctive to eat, so you might as well settle for a pizza at the run-of-the-mill *Pat's Place*, 981 E Deuce of Clubs Ave (☎520/537-2337).

Pinetop and Lakeside

Half a dozen miles southeast of Show Low, and a thousand feet higher, the Mormon communities of **PINETOP** and **LAKESIDE** have long since merged into a single amorphous entity. Set deep in the woods, they're a marginally more attractive proposition than Show Low, though once again you have to bring your own entertainment.

The joint **visitor center**, 674 E White Mountain Blvd (summer Mon–Fri 8.30am–5pm, Sat & Sun 9am–3pm; winter Mon–Fri 9am–5pm; ☎520/367-4290), has details of stables, fishing lakes and sporting facilities. There are some pricey luxury ranches around, but if you're just passing through, either the *Blue Ridge Motel*, 2012 E White Mountain Blvd (☎520/367-0758; winter ②, summer ③), or the *Best Western Inn of Pinetop*, 404 E White Mountain Blvd (☎520/367-6667 or 1-800/528-1234, fax 520/367-6672; winter ④, summer ⑤), should match your needs. The best **restaurants** around are *Charlie Clark's Steak House*, 1701 E White Mountain Blvd at Penrod Avenue (open daily for dinner only; ☎520/367-4900), which has a mesquite grill, and the *Christmas Tree Restaurant*, south of central Lakeside at 455 Woodland Rd (closed Tues; ☎520/367-3107), where there's outdoor seating.

Fort Apache Indian Reservation

One reason why the mountains of eastern Arizona are not better
known is that a large proportion of the central massif still belongs to
the **Apache**. As a study of the intricacies of the Apache Wars soon
reveals, the Apache are not a single "tribe" in the way outsiders like
to imagine, and there are two separate but contiguous reservations
here. The **FORT APACHE INDIAN RESERVATION**, which starts
just a mile or two out of Pinetop and Show Low, stretches south to
the Salt and Black rivers, while beyond it the **San Carlos Indian
Reservation** extends for another hundred miles past Globe.

The headquarters of the Fort Apache reservation is in the town of
WHITERIVER, cupped in a mile-high valley twenty miles south of
Pinetop, and home to the *White Mountain Apache Motel &
Restaurant* (☎520/338-4927; ③). What few visitors make it this
far, however, are drawn a few miles further southwest, to **FORT
APACHE** itself, at the confluence of the North and East forks of the
White River. This US Army outpost was founded in 1870 to support
the campaigns of General Crook, who was allied with the White
Mountain Apache but wanted to keep an eye on them nonetheless.
Several buildings survive in reasonable condition, and hold displays
on the period (Mon–Sat 10am–4pm; $3). The **tourist office** in the
post office nearby (Mon–Fri 8am–4.30pm, Sat 8–10.30am;
☎520/338-1230) can direct you towards crafts stores and other
sites.

Two much more contemporary attractions form the backbone of
the reservation's tourist trade. The *Hon-Dah Casino* (☎520/369-
0299 or 1-800/929-8744; ⑤), at the junction of Hwys 260 and 73
three miles southeast of Pinetop, is a 24-hour gaming facility with its
own attached hotel, while the **Sunrise Park Resort** (☎520/735-
7669 or 1-800/554-6835; ③–⑧), at the top of Hwy-273 thirty miles
east, is Arizona's most popular **ski resort**, used by guests staying in
all the neighboring towns and open as a rule between November and
April. Lift tickets cost $35.

Hwy-60, the only north–south road across the reservation, is also
the most direct route between northeast Arizona and Tucson. All of
the 87-mile run from Show Low to **Globe** (see p.230) is awe-inspiring, but the most dramatic moment comes roughly fifty miles along,
where it takes five miles of switchbacks to get the highway down to
the bottom of the gaping **Salt River Canyon**.

Payson

Until 1959, **PAYSON**, ninety miles west of Show Low on Hwy-260,
was a sleepy cowboy town that had started out in a gold-rush frenzy
and then relaxed into a lifestyle where the yearly round of ranching
was punctuated only by the odd rodeo. Then the paving of Hwy-87
placed Payson within two hours' drive of Phoenix, eighty miles
southwest. Ever since then, it has been a mountain retreat whose

population doubles or triples at weekends, as urban refugees flock to
their second homes, or at least rent cabins in the forest.

On first glance, Payson, if not exactly appealing, is at least mildly
impressive, but somehow as you drive down its long, broad streets,
passing representatives of every national fast-food and lodging
chain, you never seem to find a compelling reason to stop. Follow the
signs for "historic Main Street," and it's a fairly sorry story; you can
see that this is a prosperous community with plenty of new residential developments, but its former central thoroughfare, now
bypassed by the highway, is desultory and run-down.

Payson's **visitor center**, at 100 W Main St (Mon–Fri 8am–5pm,
Sat 8am–2pm, Sun 10am–2pm; ☎520/475-4515 or 1-800/672-
9766), can supply details of the town's many **motels**. Among reasonable options are the bright, white, ersatz Alpine *Swiss Village
Lodge* (☎520/474-3241, fax 472-6564; ④), which dominates the
eastern side of Hwy-89 north of town, and the *Payson Pueblo Inn*,
809 E Hwy-260 (☎520/474-5241 or 1-800/888-9828, fax 520/472-
6919; ③).

The garden of *Oaks Restaurant*, 302 W Main St (☎520/474-
1929), is a good spot to **eat** a sandwich lunch or steak or seafood
dinner, or you can pick up coffee and pastries on the patio of the
Pony Espresso (☎520/474-1822), opposite *Swiss Village Lodge*.

Tonto Natural Bridge

The world's widest and longest (but not quite highest) **travertine
bridge** is preserved in **TONTO NATURAL BRIDGE STATE PARK**,
fifteen miles north of Payson on Hwy-87 (daily: winter 9am–5pm;
summer 8am–6pm; $5 per vehicle). In 1877, a Scottish gold
prospector, David Gowan, supposedly hid here as he fled the
Apaches who used the surrounding meadows as a summer camp,
then returned to build a cabin nearby. When a description of the
bridge appeared in an English newspaper in 1896, David Goodfellow
spotted the name of his long-lost uncle and wrote to Gowan, who
offered him the site. Goodfellow's ten-room lodge no longer accepts
guests, but still serves as the park's giftshop and visitor center (same
hours).

The bridge itself, reached by a network of short trails and formed
from minerals deposited by constantly flowing springs, doesn't really
live up to the build-up. Spanning a gully that's roughly 150 feet wide,
it's more of a tunnel, or a dank cave with openings at both ends. With
effort, you can scramble down to a boardwalk at the base, but you
can't go through it.

Pine and Strawberry

It must have taken the Mormon settlers who established a village in
the forest five miles north of Tonto Bridge all of five seconds to hit
on a name – **PINE**. Together with its neighbor and contemporary,

STRAWBERRY, it's not a place you'd go far out of your way to visit, but both these tiny hamlets make very pleasant overnight stops if you're lost in the woods. Pine's *High Country Inn* rents out a couple of nice new **cabins** (☎520/476-2150; ③), and adjoins the friendly *Last Tortilla* **restaurant**, while a little further along Hwy-87, the *Frontier Deli* (☎520/476-3705) does good light lunches.

Winslow

Back on I-40, thirty miles east of Holbrook and 56 miles west of Flagstaff, **WINSLOW** is another Route 66 town that's kept alive by transcontinental truckers. It's also the closest the interstate comes to the Hopi mesas (see p.59), which jut from the desert across sixty miles of butte-studded wilderness to the north.

Winslow was founded as a railroad halt in 1882, not far from the recently-established Mormon community of **Brigham City**, now lying derelict a mile northeast. Such history as it has witnessed since then is recalled in the diverting **Old Trails Museum**, 212 Kinsley St (winter Tues, Thurs & Sat 1–5pm; summer Tues–Sat 1–5pm; free).

Three miles northeast of town, **Homolovi Ruins State Park** (daily 8am–5pm; $4 per vehicle; ☎520/289-4106) holds four pueblo villages, and hundreds of lesser sites, that were occupied by the Hisatsinom people, the ancestors of today's **Hopi**, until perhaps the fourteenth century. Most remain unexcavated, though archeologists are usually hard at work between June and July, when visitors are welcome to join them.

Practicalities

Winslow's Amtrak station still welcomes one daily **train** west to Flagstaff, and one east to Albuquerque. Greyhound **buses** along I-40 stop at 1000 E Third St. The local **visitor center** is near I-40 exit 253, at 300 W North Rd (Mon–Fri 8am–5pm; ☎520/289-2434).

Winslow's zip code is AZ 86047.

1999 saw the reopening of Winslow's grandest **accommodation** option, *La Posada*, 303 E Second St (☎520/289-4366, fax 289-3873; *laposada@igc.org*; ④). Designed during the late 1920s in the style of a Spanish *hacienda* by Mary Jane Colter of Grand Canyon fame (see p.322), this former railroad hotel has been tastefully restored with earthy fixtures and fittings, and feels like a real throwback to the heyday of transcontinental travel. Otherwise, most of the older **motels** in town are now pretty decrepit, so unless you're determined to pay rock-bottom rates you'd do better to head a little further west to either the *Best Western Adobe Inn*, 1701 N Park Drive (☎520/289-4638 or 1-800/528-1234; ③), or the *Super 8*, 1916 W Third St (☎520/289-4606 or 1-800/800-8000; winter ②, summer ③). The pick of the all-day **diners** is the *Falcon Restaurant*, 1113 E Third St (☎520/289-2342), while the best **campground** is at Homolovi Ruins (see above), where water is available in summer only.

Meteor Crater

East of
Flagstaff

Around 22,000 years ago, a meteorite slammed into northern
Arizona, blasting a huge hole, nearly a mile across and over five hundred feet deep, into the scrubby plateau. The site of that impact,
METEOR CRATER (daily: mid-May to mid-Sept 6am–6pm; mid-
Sept to mid-May 8am–5pm; $8, under-18s $2), can now be reached
by a six-mile spur road that heads south of the interstate eighteen
miles west of Winslow and 38 miles east of Flagstaff.

Though the staff dress up in mock Park Service uniforms, Meteor
Crater is privately owned and operated, and frankly offers poor value
for money. A modern gallery beside the parking lot holds the
unimaginative **Astronauts Hall of Fame**, which commemorates the
fact that the first men on the moon were trained on the cavity's otherworldly surface (some skeptics claim that they faked their entire
mission here). Walkways from there climb to the lip of the abyss,
where you'll probably find that there's a limit to how long you can
spend staring at a featureless hole in the ground. You cannot hike
into the actual crater.

Flagstaff

Despite having a population of little over fifty thousand, and barely a
building that rises more than three stories, the likeable college town
of **FLAGSTAFF** is the most important community on Arizona's
major east–west corridor. Its main thoroughfare, Santa Fe Avenue,
was once **Route 66**, and before that, the pioneer trail west, while for
more than a century the Santa Fe Railroad has run right alongside.
All too many tourists race through, en route to the Grand Canyon
eighty miles northwest, but Flagstaff is a worthwhile destination in
its own right, with a couple of good museums, some wonderful
scenery and ancient sites nearby, and, above all, a lively downtown
whose old streets are still redolent with Wild West charm.

Flagstaff's first white settlers arrived in 1876, lured from Boston
by widely publicized accounts of mineral wealth and fertile land.
Although they soon moved on, disappointed, towards Prescott, they
stayed long enough to celebrate the centenary of American independence by flying the Stars and Stripes from a towering pine tree. This
flagpole became a familiar landmark on the route west, and as the
town grew it inevitably became known as Flagstaff. Right from the
start, it was a cosmopolitan place, with a strong black and Hispanic
population working in the (originally Mormon-owned) lumber mills
and in the cattle industry, and Navajo and Hopi Indians heading in
from the nearby reservations to trade.

Today, Flagstaff makes an ideal base for travelers, with hotels,
restaurants, bars and shops aplenty within easy strolling range of the
center, plus outlets of the national food and lodging chains a couple

of miles away beside the interstate. Students from **Northern Arizona University**, whose campus is a mile or so south of downtown, ensure that there's always something going on.

Arrival and information

Though the Santa Fe Railroad is still busy with freight, only two passenger **trains** stop at Flagstaff's venerable wooden stationhouse, in the heart of town – the daily 5.52am for Albuquerque and the nightly 8.49pm to Los Angeles. Connecting **buses** to the Grand Canyon's South Rim, run for Amtrak by Nava-Hopi from their very central depot at 114 W Route 66 (☎520/774-5003 or 1-800/892-8687), are detailed on p.325.

Steam trains to the Grand Canyon still run from Williams, 32 miles west of Flagstaff; see p.325.

Nava-Hopi also run three daily **buses** between Flagstaff and **Phoenix** ($22), a route on which Greyhound, based a few blocks south of downtown at 399 S Malpais Lane (☎520/774-4573 or 1-800/231-2222), operate four daily services at similar rates. Greyhound buses also head west to Las Vegas and LA, and east towards Albuquerque.

The helpful local **visitor center** adjoins the station at 1 E Route 66 (Mon–Sat 7am–6pm, Sun 7am–5pm; ☎520/774-9541 or 1-800/842-7293; *www.flagstaff.az.us*).

Tours and rentals

Nava-Hopi (see above) also operate a wide range of **one-day tours** from Flagstaff, including a $19.50 local trolley tour as well as excursions to the Grand Canyon ($38 by bus, $64 for a combination bus-and-train tour via Williams), Sedona and Jerome ($36), Petrified Forest National Park ($58), Monument Valley ($74), and the Marble Canyon float trips detailed on p.326 ($89). Two local hostels – the *DuBeau* and the *Grand Canyon*, listed on p.286 – arrange inexpensive **excursions for backpackers**. Flagstaff Jeep Tours (☎520/522-0592) run off-road local **jeep tours**, with the possibility of hiking as well, from $20 per person.

The least expensive **car rental**, which for a group traveling to the Grand Canyon should cost less than the bus, is Budget Rent-a-Car, 100 N Humphreys St (☎520/779-0306); Avis, Hertz and National also have outlets.

Cosmic Cycles, 113 S San Francisco St (Mon–Sat 9am–6pm; ☎520/779-1092) rent out **mountain bikes** for $20 per day, or $75 per week. Arizona Mountain Bike Tours (☎520/779-4161 or 1-800/277-7985) run **cycling tours** for $30 (3hr) or $50 (5hr).

Accommodation

Flagstaff is something more than an interstate pit stop, so its dozens of **motels** and **B&Bs** get away with charging higher rates than the Southwest's other I-40 towns. They're still not bad value, however,

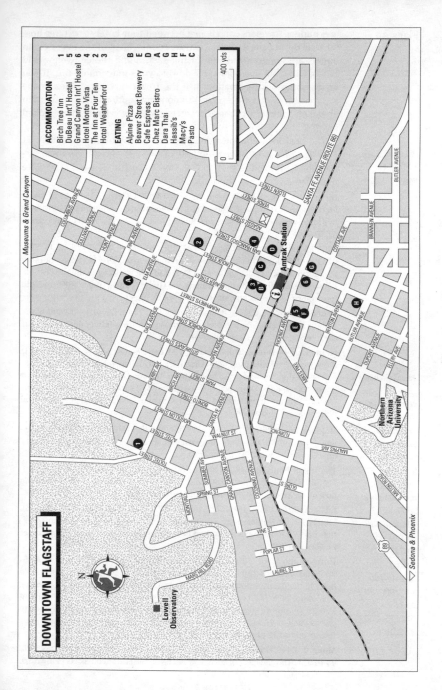

DOWNTOWN FLAGSTAFF

△ Museums & Grand Canyon

N

Lowell Observatory

MARS HILL ROAD

Amtrak Station

Northern Arizona University

▽ Sedona & Phoenix

ACCOMMODATION
Birch Tree Inn   1
DuBeau Int'l Hostel   5
Grand Canyon Int'l Hostel   6
Hotel Monte Vista   4
The Inn at Four Ten   2
Hotel Weatherford   3

EATING
Alpine Pizza   B
Beaver Street Brewery E
Cafe Espress   D
Chez Marc Bistro   A
Dara Thai   G
Hassib's   H
Macy's   F
Pasto   C

0   400 yds

and **budget** travelers can choose between four hotels that offer hostel-style dorm beds as well as private rooms. Most of the major chain motels are congregated well to the east, along Butler Avenue and Lucky Lane, but staying nearer downtown is much more fun. If you arrive without a reservation, use the free **courtesy phones** in the local visitor center (see p.284) to compare options. Above all, **plan ahead** on summer weekends, when everywhere is likely to be booked solid.

Flagstaff's zip code is AZ 86001.

The best local **campground** is three miles south on US-89A, at *Fort Tuthill County Park* (☎520/774-5139), though continue further south and you're soon in Oak Creek Canyon (see p.293), where there are several more options.

Birch Tree Inn, 824 W Birch Ave; ☎520/774-1042 or 1-888/774-1042; *birch@flagstaff.az.us*. Former frat house converted to upmarket B&B, with five tastefully themed guestrooms, fancy breakfasts, and a wraparound veranda. ④–⑥.

DuBeau International Hostel, 19 W Phoenix Ave; ☎520/773-1656, 774-6731 or 1-800/398-7122; *dubeau@infomagic.com*. HI-AYH hostel offering $13 dorm beds, doubles for around $27, and tent camping in the yard for $6. It also runs a $25 round-trip shuttle to the Grand Canyon (tours $38), and $20 tours down to Sedona and Montezuma Castle. ①.

Econolodge West, 2355 S Beulah Blvd; ☎520/774-2225 or 1-800/490-6562. Relatively appealing chain motel, with good facilities, south of downtown near the interstate. Winter ③, summer ④.

Grand Canyon International Hostel, 19 S San Francisco St; ☎520/779-9421; *www.grandcanyonhostel.com*. Clean, friendly independent hostel, housed in a converted motel across the tracks from Amtrak; the towering sign makes it impossible to miss. Dorm beds $8–10 winter, $12 summer, plus private rooms from $25. Tours to the Grand Canyon ($38) and Sedona ($20), plus car rental discounts, are also available. ①.

As explained on p.15, accommodation prices, excluding taxes, are indicated throughout this book by the following symbols:

① *up to $30*
② *$30–45*
③ *$45–60*
④ *$60–80*
⑤ *$80–100*
⑥ *$100–130*
⑦ *$130–175*
⑧ *$175–250*
⑨ *$250+*

Holiday Inn, 2320 E Lucky Lane; ☎520/526-1150, fax 779-2610. Large motel, just off the interstate in a rather characterless area, with a handful of diners nearby. Winter ④, summer ⑤.

The Inn at Four Ten, 410 N Leroux St; ☎520/774-0088 or 1-800/774-2008, fax 520/774-6354; *www.bbonline.com/az/at410/*. Bright ranch home that's now an antique-furnished nine-room B&B. ⑥/⑦.

Little America, 2515 E Butler Ave; ☎520/779-7900 or 1-800/352-4386, fax 520/779-7983. Endearingly 1950s-style motel complex near the interstate, that offers a much higher standard of accommodation than you might expect for the price. ④.

Hotel Monte Vista, 100 N San Francisco St; ☎520/779-6971 or 1-800/545-3068, fax 520/779-2904. Flagstaff's best bargain; a very pleasant little 1920s hotel in the heart of downtown, restored to offer accommodation that ranges from dorm beds ($10 winter, $16 summer) through double rooms of varying sizes, with and without attached bathrooms. Several are named for celebrity guests such as Humphrey Bogart, John Wayne and Jane Russell; room rates rise by up to $15 at weekends. ①–④.

Motel 6, 2440 E Lucky Lane; ☎520/774-8756 or 1-800/466-8356, fax 520/774-2067. The cheapest of several *Motel 6*s on the eastern outskirts of town. ②.

Super 8 Motel, 3725 Kasper Ave; ☎520/526-0818 or 1-800/800-8000, fax 520/526-8786. Standard, good-value motel east of town. Winter ③, summer ④.

Hotel Weatherford, 23 N Leroux St; ☎520/774-2731; *weathtel@infomagic .com*. Very central HI-AYH-approved hostel, upstairs in a once-grand railroad hotel, with $16 dorm beds and private doubles from $35. ①–④.

The Town

Flagstaff's atmospheric **downtown** stretches for a few redbrick blocks north of the railroad. Filled with cafes, bars, and stores selling Route 66 souvenirs and Indian crafts, it's a fun place to stroll around, even if it holds no significant tourist attractions or historic buildings. Your most lasting impression is likely to be of the magnificent **San Francisco Peaks**, rising smoothly from the plains on the northern horizon, and topped by a jagged ridge.

The exceptional **Museum of Northern Arizona**, however, three miles northwest of downtown on US-180 (daily 9am–5pm; $5), rivals Phoenix's Heard Museum as the best museum in the state. Although it covers the geology, geography, flora and fauna of the Colorado plateau, its main emphasis is on documenting **Native American** life. It provides an excellent run-through of the Ancestral Puebloan past and contemporary Navajo, Havasupai, Zuni and Hopi cultures, with a marvellous assortment of pots, rugs, silver and turquoise jewelry, and *kachina* dolls that makes a welcome contrast to the low standards seen in so many of the region's crafts stores. There are also temporary shows of local (not always Native American) arts and crafts, a well-stocked bookstore, and a **nature trail** that runs through the small canyon outside.

Ever since it was established, in 1928, the Museum of Northern Arizona has actively encouraged the development of traditional and even new skills among Native American craftworkers. The exquisite inlaid silver jewelry now made by the Hopi, for example, is the result of a museum-backed program to find work for Hopi servicemen returning from World War II. During its annual Indian Craftsmen Exhibitions, every item is for sale. The **Zuni** show lasts for five days around Memorial Day weekend in late May, the **Hopi** one is on the weekend closest to July 4, and the nine-day **Navajo** event is at the end of July and the start of August.

On the road back towards town, the **Coconino Center for the Arts** is a gallery and concert hall specializing in works by local artists, while just behind it the cooperatively run **Art Barn** (daily 9am–5pm) sells a wide selection of crafts.

Set in the pine forest atop Mars Hill, a mile west of downtown, the **Lowell Observatory** (daily 9am–5pm; $3) is famous as the place where the existence of the planet Pluto was first confirmed. Many of the necessary calculations were performed by Dr Percival Lowell, who founded the observatory in 1894 and deluded himself that he'd discovered canals on Mars. Lowell died in 1916, however – he's buried in a small domed mausoleum of blue glass on the hilltop – and

Call ☎520/774-2096 for details of evening stargazing sessions at the Lowell Observatory, held with varying frequency all year except January.

Flagstaff

the ninth planet was eventually spotted by Clyde Tombaugh in 1930. Tombaugh himself lived on until January 1997.

From the **visitor center**, where only the very technically minded are likely to get much joy from playing with computers or watching explanatory videos, the **Pluto Walk** footpath climbs up to the tiny original observatory. Signs along the way tick off the relative positions of the planets, but in order to show the position of the nearest star, Alpha Centauri, on the same scale, it would have to keep going over 600 miles, beyond Boise Idaho.

Eating

There's enough money around in Flagstaff to support several upscale **restaurants**, but what really gives eating in town an unusual edge is the presence of all those **students**. The area around San Francisco Street, both north and south of the tracks, is filled with vegetarian cafes and espresso bars, while snack places near the university further south include a **Cyber Cafe** in the Bookmans used bookstore at 1520 S Riordan Ranch Rd.

Alpine Pizza, 7 N Leroux St; ☎520/779-4109. Raucous student hangout downtown, with decent pizzas and lots of beer. Open for lunch Mon–Sat, and dinner daily.

Beaver Street Brewery & Whistle Stop Cafe, 11 S Beaver St; ☎520/779-0079. Inventive sandwiches and salads, wood-fired pizzas, and outdoor barbecue in the beer garden in summer, with entrees priced around $8. Ales and lagers are brewed on the premises. Daily 11.30am–midnight.

Black Barts, 2760 E Butler Ave; ☎520/779-3142. Enjoyable Western-themed steakhouse on the east edge of town, with a delicious smell of burning wood and waiting staff who sing and dance on stage in between serving up barbecued steaks, ribs and chickens, for $15–20. Daily 5–10pm.

Cafe Express, 16 N San Francisco St; ☎520/774-0541. Great vegetarian breakfasts, then salads, sandwiches and veggie specials for the rest of the day, plus espresso coffees. Open daily for all meals.

Charly's Pub and Grill, *Hotel Weatherford*, 23 N Leroux St; ☎520/779-1919. Cafe-restaurant which makes a classy if unlikely contrast with the hostel rooms upstairs, serving good, inexpensive meals accompanied by live music (cocktail piano at lunch, bands at night). Daily 11.30am–11pm.

Chez Marc Bistro, 503 N Humphreys St; ☎520/774-1343. Fancy French restaurant, set in a converted historic house on a rise slightly above downtown, with patio seating. Crepes and pasta for lunch, with plenty of vegetarian options, for $6–9; delicious French dinner entrees like veal with lobster, halibut braised with cider, or buffalo with sundried cranberries, all for (just) under $20. Lunch and dinner daily.

Dara Thai, 14 S San Francisco St; ☎520/774-0047. Large Thai place just south of the tracks, where the service is great and a plate of delicious Pad Thai noodles costs just $5 for lunch, $7 for dinner. Mon–Sat 11am–10pm.

Hassib's, 211 S San Francisco St; ☎520/774-1037. Mainly Middle Eastern specialties, like hummus, falafel and pita-pocket sandwiches for around $7; ideal for a cheap, healthy lunch. Mon 11am–4pm, Tues–Fri 11am–7pm.

Macy's European Coffee House & Bakery, 14 S Beaver St; ☎520/774-2243. Not merely superb coffee, but heavenly pastries to go with it, plus more substantial vegetarian dishes such as black bean pizza, all served in an ambience that owes more to Montmartre than Arizona. Mon–Wed 6am–8pm, Thurs–Sat 6am–9pm, Sun 6am–6pm.

Pasto, 19 E Aspen Ave; ☎520/779-1937. Downtown dinner-only Italian joint, with pasta specials plus chicken, shrimp or vegetarian entrees for $11–14. Open daily for dinner only.

Nightlife

Its streets milling with international travelers in summer, and students for the rest of the year, Flagstaff has to be the liveliest **nightspot** between Las Vegas and Santa Fe. Wander a block or two to either side of San Francisco Street downtown, and you can't go far wrong. Hotel bars which feature **live music** most nights include *Charly's* at the *Weatherford*, and the *Monte Vista Lounge*.

Flagstaff Brewing Company, 16 E Route 66; ☎520/773-1442. Popular downtown pub, with outdoor seating, big windows, and live music Wed–Sat. Daily 11am–1am.

The Mad Italian, 101 S San Francisco St; ☎520/779-1820. Highly sociable downtown bar with several pool tables.

Monsoons, 22 E Route 66; ☎520/774-7929. Central downtown music venue, with live local bands most nights, plus barbecue.

The Museum Club, 3404 E Route 66; ☎520/526-9434. A real oddity; this log-cabin taxidermy museum somehow transmogrified into a classic Route 66 roadhouse, saloon and country music venue, that's a second home to hordes of dancing cowboys. Open daily noon–1am. Call ☎520/774-4444 for a free shuttle service from and to your motel.

Around Flagstaff

The area around Flagstaff is extraordinarily rich in natural and archeological wonders, with three national monuments – **Sunset Crater**, **Wupatki** and **Walnut Canyon** – within 25 miles, and the **San Francisco Peaks** overshadowing them all. All are generally seen as day-trips from Flagstaff, however, as no accommodation is available; only Sunset Crater has even a campground.

The San Francisco Peaks

The **San Francisco Volcanic Field**, north of Flagstaff, consists of around four hundred distinct volcanic cones, which have appeared within the past two million years. During that time, the region has also been covered by glacial ice on three separate occasions, shaving around three thousand feet off the top of the volcanoes.

The serrated **SAN FRANCISCO PEAKS**, visible from downtown Flagstaff, are the remnants of a single mountain; their highest

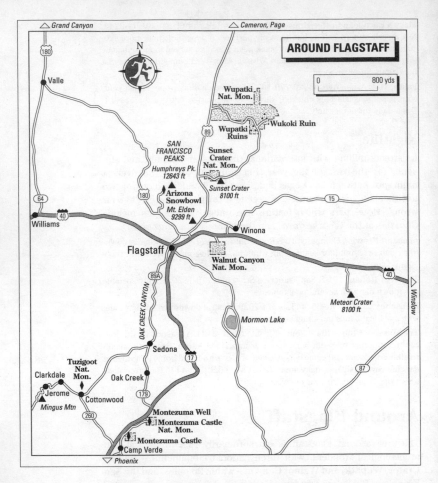

point today, at 12,643 feet, is the summit of **Mount Humphreys**. They were named by Spanish missionaries in honor of St Francis of Assisi, though the Hopi already knew them as *Nuvatukya'ovi*, the home of the *kachina* spirits (see p.60), and to the Navajo they were *Dook'o'oosliid*, one of the four sacred mountains (see p.538). Seen from afar, topped by a semi-permanent layer of clouds, it's obvious why the Hopi and Navajo regarded them as the source of life-giving rain. It's because they were sacred to both that they now belong to neither; federal law dictates that Indian reservations can only include lands of which a tribe can prove it has "exclusive use." The Hopi in particular still make annual pilgrimages on foot from their mesas, 65 miles east, to shrines hidden in the mountains.

Considering that the San Francisco Mountain, which has not erupted for 220,000 years, is dormant rather than extinct, the time may come when the gods decide that the **Arizona Snowbowl** is a desecration no longer to be tolerated. For the moment, it survives, nestling between Mount Humphreys and Mount Agassiz at the end of a seven-mile spur road north of US-180, and featuring ski runs such as "Boo-Boo" and "Bambi." There's not enough water up here to make artificial snow – another early name for the peaks was the **Sierra Sin Agua**, or "waterless range" – so the season typically runs from mid-December to early April. Lift tickets cost $34 per day, and a couple of lodges offer meals and equipment rental, but not overnight accommodation; for more information, call ☎520/779-1951.

In summer, the longest of the Snowbowl's five chairlifts, which climbs to within a few hundred feet of the 12,350-foot summit of Mount Agassiz, remains open as the **Scenic Skyride** (May–Oct daily 10am–4pm; ☎520/779-1951; $10). To protect the fragile vegetation, you can't hike any further from there, but there are plenty of other **trails** in the mountains, all intended for day-use only. One switchbacks right to the top of Mount Humphreys, giving seventy-mile views to the Grand Canyon and beyond.

Sunset Crater National Monument

The focus of SUNSET CRATER NATIONAL MONUMENT, three miles down a side road that heads east off US-89 twelve miles north of Flagstaff, is the youngest of the San Francisco volcanoes. Its most recent eruption, in 1065 AD, had a profound impact on the local population and economy. Thick deposits of ash for miles around opened up previously infertile land to cultivation, accelerating – if not triggering – a land rush that threw different Indian cultures into contact and competition for the first time.

John Wesley Powell named Sunset Crater for its multicolored cone, which swells from a black base through reds and oranges to a yellow-tinged crest. Unfortunately, however, its shifting cinders are too unstable to allow hikers to climb up to the rim. Instead, the one-mile **Lava Flow Trail** at its base offers a close-up look at the jagged black lava that streamed out across the desert, and the steeper one-mile **Lenox Crater Trail** ascends a lesser cone nearby.

All is explained in the **visitor center** near the start of the road (daily 8am–5pm; $3 per person; ☎520/526-0502), opposite the forest service's *Bonito* **campground** (late May to mid-Oct; $10; ☎520/526-0866).

Wupatki National Monument

A dozen miles north of Sunset Crater, the ancient ruins at WUPATKI NATIONAL MONUMENT appear to show different tribal groups living side by side in harmony. After the Sunset Crater eruption, the Sinagua people already present here – who surely witnessed the explosion – were joined by many others, including the Ancestral Puebloans and the Hohokam. When the rich new soil had been exhausted, around 150 years later, they all moved on once more.

The first of the five separate pueblo complexes along the road from Sunset Crater has been named **Wukoki**, a modern Hopi word meaning "big house." Reminiscent of the castle-like structures at Hovenweep (see p.66), it stands within sight of a procession of rounded cinder cones, but was probably positioned for its commanding prospect of the Painted Desert to the north and east. Windows in its central tower, which is molded to the contours of a red-rock outcrop, and built with bricks of the same material, look out in all directions; the floor is deep in crumbling sand. With the Little Colorado River five miles distant, its inhabitants must have been desperately short of water.

The monument's **visitor center** (daily: summer 8am–7pm, winter 8am–5pm; $3 per person; ☎520/679-2365), a short way on, holds some rather antiquated displays, updated via stick-on captions that point out previous shortcomings. Thus an original label that speaks of the Sinagua having "disappeared," is now called "inappropriate," in view of the fact that the Hopi are their obvious descendants.

A paved loop trail leads down from the visitor center to the main three-story, hundred-room pueblo block of **Wupatki** ("tall house") itself. The site's most intriguing features, however, lie a little further along. First comes what seems to be an amphitheater, a walled circular plaza whose purpose remains unknown. Beyond it is an oval **ball court**, the northernmost such court ever found. Similar arenas throughout Central America were used for a game – part ritual, part sport – in which players tried to propel a rubber ball through a stone hoop high on a wall, using their knees and elbows alone. Much like modern basketball; except that the losers were sacrificed at the end. Alongside the ball court, cracks in the ground have created a natural **blowhole**, through which air is either sucked or blown depending on pressure and temperature. The audible "breathing" of the earth clearly made this a sacred shrine for Wupatki's ancient inhabitants.

The loop road past Sunset Crater and Wupatki rejoins US-89 twenty miles south of Cameron (see p.349). Outcrops along its final few miles hold more pueblos, such as one known for obvious reasons as the Citadel, perched on and fully occupying a hilltop.

Walnut Canyon National Monument

Another Sinagua site, even more spectacular than Wupatki, can be seen at **WALNUT CANYON NATIONAL MONUMENT**, just south of I-40 ten miles east of Flagstaff. Between 1125 and 1250 AD, this shallow canyon was home to a thriving Sinagua community, who lived in small family groups rather than in communal pueblos.

Literally hundreds of their **cliff dwellings** still nestle beneath overhangs in the sides of the canyon. They simply walled off alcoves where softer strata of rock had eroded away, and put up partitions to make separate rooms.

A large scenic window in the **visitor center** (daily: June–Aug 8am–6pm; March–May & Sept–Nov 8am–5pm; Dec–Feb 9am–5pm; $3 per person; ☎520/526-3367) gives an excellent overall view. **Walnut Creek** itself, long since diverted to provide Flagstaff's drinking water, now runs very dry, but you can still see how fertile this valley must have been when the Sinagua first arrived. Trees cling to the porous rock to shade the ancient dwellings, and the vegetation thickens down to a valley floor dense with black walnut and oak.

The mile-long **Island Loop Trail** drops steeply down from the visitor center and crosses a narrow causeway to an isthmus of rock high above a gooseneck of the creek. Along the path, you can go inside several Sinagua homes; note the T-shaped doorways, which could only be entered head first, and the ceilings blackened by the smoke of generations of fires. Petroglyphs have been found in the other ruins visible on all sides, but none remain on the trail.

Another trail follows the rim of the canyon. Its main purpose is to provide a less strenuous walk, which leads to a picnic area and to some surface ruins (in the dissimilar pueblo style, consisting of large clusters of rooms), though you could keep going to turn this into a lengthy hike. There is no accommodation, and only minimal snack food, available at the canyon.

Between June and August each year, rangers lead two- to three-hour **guided hikes** to lesser-known and otherwise inaccessible sites within the monument (Wed, Sat & Sun at 10am; call to confirm).

South of Flagstaff

US-89A threads its way south from Flagstaff down **Oak Creek Canyon** to emerge after 28 miles at **Sedona**, on the threshold of the extraordinary **Red Rock Country**. Up from the valley rise giant mesas and buttes of stark red sandstone, where Zane Grey set a number of his Wild West adventures. The boom-and-bust mining town of **Jerome** looks down from a mountainside to the south, while back beside I-17 towards Phoenix are the haunting Sinagua ruins of **Tuzigoot** and **Montezuma Castle**.

Oak Creek Canyon

Claims that **OAK CREEK CANYON**, the largest of several slender chasms that cut into the 2000-foot escarpment of the **Mogollon Rim**, is a serious rival to the Grand Canyon are somewhat exaggerated. However, you *can* drive right through it, and with its sheer walls striped in vivid horizontal bands of color, its sparkling streams and densely wooded glens, and its facilities for camping, eating and generally playing around, this would be an unmissable attraction anywhere else in the world.

Lookout Point, its northern end, appears suddenly a dozen forested miles out of Flagstaff. Native-American craft stalls surround the parking lot, and several overlooks within easy walking distance command prospects of the narrow gorge below. The road then switchbacks sharply down to run alongside **Oak Creek** itself. The lowest level in the rocks to either side, often obscured by maples, cedars, oaks and pine, is the bright red Supai sandstone. Above that, layers of white sandstone, buff limestone, and finally black basalt testify to a geological history which has fluctuated from harsh desert to sea bottom. Temperatures are cool enough to make fishing, picnicking and hiking expeditions welcome escapes.

Seven miles before Hwy-89A reaches Sedona, **Slide Rock State Park** is a natural water chute, where you can swim and slide across smooth boulders set in the river bed (daily: March to mid-May 8am–6pm; mid-May to mid-Oct 8am–7pm; mid-Oct to Feb 8am–5pm; $5 per vehicle). The absence of still water in Oak Creek means that it's almost insect-free.

Practicalities

The canyon floor is quite narrow, and has been heavily developed with leisure facilities, though at least careful landscaping makes most of these inconspicuous; good places to stay include the well-equipped log huts at *Don Hoel's Cabins* (☎520/282-3560 or 1-800/292-4635; ④). **Campgrounds** at river (and road) level include *Bootlegger* and *Pine Flat* (both mid-May to Sept; first-come, first-served; $10; ☎520/282-4119). Despite its tiny size, erratic opening hours and off-the-beaten-track location, the most popular place to eat is the restaurant at *Garland's Oak Creek Lodge*, half a mile north of Slide Rock (April to mid-Nov; closed Sun; ☎520/282-3343; ⑦), a more luxurious log-cabin complex where the dining room features a different small menu each night.

Sedona

Though local boosters make much of its setting, amid some definitive Southwestern canyon scenery, the New Age resort of **SEDONA** adds nothing to the beauty of its surroundings. Architecturally, it's a real mess, with several miles of ugly redbrick sprawl interrupted by the occasional mock-historical mall monstrosity. To the artists, healers, walking wounded and wealthy retirees who have flocked here in the last two decades, however, Sedona is "the next Santa Fe." Whether you love it or hate it will probably depend on whether you share their wide-eyed awe for angels, crystals and all matters mystical – and whether you're prepared to pay over-the-odds prices for the privilege of joining them. Whatever your attitude, however,

Sedona is still a fascinating place to visit, where even the hard-nosed commercial operation can seem a front for the real business of holding earnest conversations about the state of each other's psyches.

Established in 1902 by Theodore Schnebly, and named after his wife, Sedona remained a small farming settlement for most of the twentieth century, unmarked on most maps. German surrealist painter **Max Ernst** moved here in the 1940s – the bizarre backdrops of his later canvases seem less surreal once you've seen where they were painted – and Hollywood movie-makers filmed in the area from the 1950s onwards. However, Sedona's big break came in 1981, when Page Bryant, author and psychic, "channeled" the information that Sedona is in fact "the heart *chakra* of the planet." Since she pinpointed her first **vortex** – a point at which, it is claimed, psychic and electromagnetic energies can be channeled for personal and planetary harmony – the town has achieved its own personal growth, and blossomed as a focus for New Age practitioners of all kinds. Huge crowds came to Sedona in 1987 for the "Harmonic Convergence," paying up to $75 for a seat on Bell Rock at the time when it was supposed to launch itself to the galaxy of Andromeda. (Dissatisfied customers are said to have included one gentleman who brought his mouth organ, under the impression that it was a harmonica convergence.)

Arrival and information

Sedona is 28 miles south of Flagstaff on Hwy-89A, and 120 miles north of Phoenix. It centers on the intersection known as the "**Y**," above Oak Creek, where Hwy-89A branches southwest towards Cottonwood and Prescott, and Hwy-179 continues by way of the village of Oak Creek to meet I-17, fourteen miles south.

Just north of the "Y," in the area known as **uptown** – the one part of Sedona where the stores and businesses are close enough together to make walking a possibility – the **visitor center**, at Hwy-89A and Forest Road, has full listings of lodgings and tour operators (Mon–Sat 8.30am–5pm, Sun 9am–3pm; ☎520/282-7722 or 1-800/288-7336; *www.arizonaguide.com/sedona*).

Three daily **flights** to and from Phoenix are operated by Scenic Airlines (☎520/282-7935 or 1-800/634-6801), with one-way fares starting at around $60. The Sedona–Phoenix Shuttle (☎520/282-2066 or 1-800/448-7988 in AZ), a six-daily **bus** service between Sedona and Phoenix Airport, costs $35 one way. Some Greyhound buses between Flagstaff and Phoenix call in at Sedona.

For a quick overview of the area, pick up either of the two different 45-minute **tours** run by the Sedona Trolley (daily 10am–5pm; hourly tours, $7; ☎520/282-5400), at the visitor center. Companies that rent **bikes** include Mountain Bike Heaven, 1695 W US-89A (☎520/282-1312), Sedona Bike & Bean, 376 Jordan Rd

Sedona's major annual event is the Jazz On The Rocks festival, held on the last Saturday of September; ☎520/282-1985.

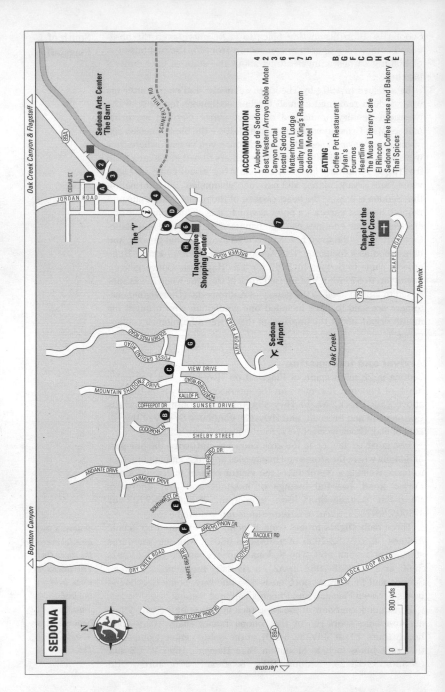

SEDONA

N

ACCOMMODATION
L'Auberge de Sedona 4
Best Western Arroyo Roble Motel 2
Canyon Portal 3
Hostel Sedona 6
Matterhorn Lodge 1
Quality Inn King's Ransom 7
Sedona Motel 5

EATING
Coffee Pot Restaurant B
Dylan's G
Fournos F
Heartline C
The Muse Literary Cafe D
El Rincon H
Sedona Coffee House and Bakery A
Thai Spices E

Oak Creek Canyon & Flagstaff ▷

Sedona Arts Center
'The Barn'

SCHNEBLY HILL RD

89A

CEDAR ST.

JORDAN ROAD

The 'Y'

Tlaquepaque
Shopping Center

BREWER ROAD

Chapel of the
Holy Cross

CHAPEL ROAD

179

▷ Phoenix

SEDBERRY PASS ROAD

POSSE GROUND ROAD

Sedona
Airport

AIRPORT ROAD

Oak Creek

VIEW DRIVE

MOUNTAIN SHADOWS DRIVE

NORTHVIEW ROAD

KALLOF PL.

COFFEEPOT DR.

SUNSET DRIVE

GOODROW LN.

SHELBY STREET

THUNDERBIRD DR.

ANDANTE DRIVE

HARMONY DRIVE

SOUTHWEST DR.

ARROYO PINON DR.

FOOTHILLS DR.

RACQUET RD

DRY CREEK ROAD

WHITE BEAR RD.

RED ROCK LOOP ROAD

BRISTLECONE PINES RD.

89A

◁ Boynton Canyon

▽ Jerome

0   800 yds

(☎520/282-3515), and Desert Jeep and Bike Rentals, 6626 Hwy-179 (☎520/284-1099), who can also provide **4WD** vehicles.

Accommodation

Sedona is an expensive place to **stay**, and apart from the immediate area of the "Y," it's too spread out to walk around in the evening. If you're watching your budget, you can get better deals nearby at Cottonwood, Jerome and Camp Verde (see pp.301, 302 and 306); if you don't mind spending $100 or more, however, Sedona has some extremely fancy options. including at least a dozen upscale **B&Bs** and several full-service resorts. **Agencies** specializing in local accommodations and tours include Sedona Central (☎520/282-1518 or 1-800/445-4128) and Red Rock Reservations (☎520/284-3627 or 1-800/890-0521).

Bell Rock Inn, 6246 Hwy-179, Sedona, AZ 86351; ☎520/282-4161 or 1-800/881-7625, fax 520/284-0192. Upmarket, pastel-painted motel six miles south of town, with two pools and two spas. Winter ④, summer ⑤.

Best Western Arroyo Roble Motel, 400 N US-89A, Sedona, AZ 86339; ☎520/282-4001 or 1-800/7-SEDONA. Comfortable multitiered motel, stacked up above Oak Creek not far north of uptown Sedona. Winter ⑤, summer ⑥.

Canyon Portal, 280 N US-89A, Sedona, AZ 86336; ☎520/282-7125 or 1-800/542-8484, fax 520/282-1825. Freshly renovated, central motel just north of the "Y," which offers some of the best-value rooms in town. ④.

The Canyon Wren, 6425 N US-89A, Sedona, AZ 86336; ☎520/282-6900 or 1-800/437-9736. Individual two-person cabins, each with a whirlpool tub, six miles north of Sedona in Oak Creek Canyon. ⑤.

Cathedral Rock Lodge, 61 Los Amigos Lane, Sedona, AZ 86336; ☎520/282-7608, fax 282-4505. Small, friendly B&B in spacious grounds on the Red Rock Loop Rd, with two double rooms, a suite and a separate cabin. ④.

Cozy Cactus B&B, 80 Canyon Circle Drive, Sedona, AZ 86351; ☎520/284-0082 or 1-800/788-2082. Ranch-house B&B at the edge of the woods near the foot of Castle Rock, offering five themed, en-suite double rooms. ⑤.

Enchantment Resort, 525 Boynton Canyon Rd, Sedona, AZ 86336; ☎520/282-2900 or 1-800/826-4180, fax 520/282-9249; *www.arizonaguide.com /enchantment*. Extremely luxurious resort, equipped with four pools and twelve tennis courts, that has taken over ravishing Boynton Canyon eight miles west of town. Accommodation is in fully equipped one- and two-bedroom adobe *casitas*. ⑧.

Hostel Sedona, 5 Soldiers Wash Drive, Sedona, AZ 86339; ☎520/282-2772. Basic independent hostel, hidden away behind the Tlaquepaque mall, that offers dorm beds for $15 to $18, plus one private double room at $40. Office closed daily 10am–5pm. ①/②.

L'Auberge de Sedona, 301 L'Auberge Lane, PO Box B, Sedona, AZ 86339; ☎520/282-1661 or 1-800/272-6777, fax 520/282-2885; *www.lauberge.com*. Plush two-part resort in the heart of the town, with fancy French-themed motel rooms at road level looking out onto the red rocks and a cable-car connection to the individual guest cottages ranged along the tranquil banks of Oak Creek below. ⑦/⑧.

Matterhorn Lodge, 230 Apple Ave, Sedona, AZ 86336; ☎520/282-7176, fax 282-0727; *www.sedona.net/hotel/matterhorn*. Central motel, on the right

As explained on p.15, accommodation prices, excluding taxes, are indicated throughout this book by the following symbols:

① *up to $30*
② *$30–45*
③ *$45–60*
④ *$60–80*
⑤ *$80–100*
⑥ *$100–130*
⑦ *$130–175*
⑧ *$175–250*
⑨ *$250+*

Within You or Without You: Experiencing Red Rock Country

Dozens of Sedona-based operators compete to offer close encounters with red-rock country. The most popular option is a jeep tour, but you can also take scenic flights, in balloons, airplanes or helicopters, ride on horseback, or trek with a llama. There's also a choice between a traditional tour, on which you'll see formations such as "Snoopy" and "Garfield," and a New Age vision quest, in which the same rock may be a "sacred energy area" or a "beacon vortex." Some guides even eschew vehicles altogether, in favor of taking you on a spiritual journey instead.

Air Safari Charter & Tours; ☎520/204-5939. Quick flights over Sedona – 10min for $19 per person, up to 25min for $45 – plus longer tours by arrangement.

Crystal Light Centers; ☎520/282-2733. Tour the vortex sites; "use the earth energies for personal transformation." Half-day $50, full day with lunch $80.

Don Hanson; ☎520/204-2235. Don "tunes into Universal Intelligence and talks to it out loud"; "you will experience tremendous relief . . . and gratitude."

Earth Wisdom Tours; ☎520/282-4714. "More than ordinary tours, these are journeys. . . in the way of our Native American friends . . . learn of the ancestral secrets of the Medicine Wheel"; costs $40 to $125.

Full Moon Adventures; ☎520/300-4004. "Custom Tours for Couples" at $75 per person for 2hr.

Kachina Riding Stables; ☎520/282-7252. Horseback trips, largely geared around eating (in traditional cowboy style); 3hr rides in the vicinity of Red Rock State Park for $50–60, full-day rides for $128, and multiday customized expeditions at $295 per day.

Legends of Sedona Ranch; ☎520/282-6826 or 1-800/848-7728. "Where horses are free . . . but rides ain't"; 1hr $39, 2hr $49.

Michele Celeste Renee Chaney; ☎520/282-2239. Angelic Visions Emissary, who channels the entity known as "I AM, the one with no name" for $1 per minute.

as you come into town on Hwy-89A from the north, with two tiers of rooms that face across to the red rocks. Winter ③, summer ④.

Quality Inn King's Ransom, 771 Hwy-179, PO Box 180, Sedona, AZ 86339; ☎520/282-7151 or 1-800/228-5151. Predictable upper-range motel, a mile or so south of town, with rather small rooms but a nice garden and a reasonable restaurant. Winter ④, summer ⑤.

Sedona Motel, 218 Hwy-179, PO Box 1450, Sedona, AZ 86339; ☎520/282-7187. Small, relatively inexpensive motel, in an ideal and attractive location close to the "Y" uptown. ③.

Exploring Sedona

Sedona itself has little to detain sightseers, though strolling the two or so blocks that count as uptown, just north of the "Y," is pleasant enough. Even above the roar of the traffic, you can usually still hear the synchronized chirruping of the crickets in Oak Creek down below, while your eyes are repeatedly drawn to the superb red rocks

---

Mystic Tours with Rahelio; ☎520/282-6735. "Inspirational Nature Outing to places of power and beauty," including "vortex empowerments," at $40 for 2hr, $60 for 3hr.

Northern Light Balloon Expeditions; ☎520/282-2274 or 1-800/230-6222. Relatively unspiritual balloon trips, with champagne picnics.

Pink Jeep Tours (☎520/282-5000 or 1-800/8SEDONA). You can't miss this lot in uptown Sedona. Quite exceptionally garish "4-wheelin' vehicles" crunch around in off-road tours lasting 1hr 30min up to 4hr, at $30 to $75 per person.

Sedona Adventures; ☎520/282-3500 or 1-800/888-9494. Tours (2hr 30min; around $50) include hikes to see rock art, while the 3hr Vortex Adventure allows you to "discover your own unique energy and power," for $55.

Sedona Helicopter Adventures; ☎520/282-0904 or 1-800/282-5141. Chopper flights from the 10min Famous Formations ($36) to the 30min Sedona Deluxe ($125).

Sedona Red Rock Jeep Tours; ☎520/282-6826 or 1-800/848-7728. Jeep trips from 1hr ($25) up to 3hr Medicine Wheel Tours ($58). Not only do you get to bomb around the desert, you can "focus on the need to offer love and healing to our earth, as well as each other," and participate in a traditional "smudging" ceremony.

Sedona Vortex Connections; ☎520/204-9355. "Make your dolphin-connection," or "explore the galactic time-concept of 13:20 and timelessness," guided by the Archangel Michael.

Sun Turtle Journeys; ☎520/634-7555. "Learn the real way of the Early People, who do not call them vortexes . . . feel the inner knowing of self" at $45 for 3hr, or take a journey to Hopi Land for $80–95 "depending on numbers."

Touch the Southwest; ☎1-888/CHILAKO. "Luxury Wilderness Experiences" with gourmet picnic lunches from $295.

Way of the Ancients; ☎520/204-9243. "Step back in time to prepare for the future while living in the now" with guide Ted Kills In The Fog; $125.

that tower above the banal buildings along Hwy-89A. A little way south of the "Y," on Hwy-179, **Tlaquepaque Shopping Center** is a very upscale mall, modeled on a Mexican village near Guadalajara, that offers Sedona's most distinctive (and expensive) shopping.

The prevailing pay-no-taxes ethos of Sedona's ardent libertarians has ensured that few of the side roads off the main highways are paved. That dovetails neatly, of course, with the booming business in off-road tours, as listed in the box, above. Nonetheless, a lot of the best scenery is visible from the highway, and in any case many of the jeep roads are perfectly passable in ordinary vehicles. So long as you're happy to remain in ignorance as to which rocks are really electro-magnetic tuning forks vibrating in harmony with Alpha Centauri, there's no great need to take a commercial tour.

The closest **vortex** to town is on **Airport Mesa**. Turn left up Airport Road from Hwy-89A as you head west, about a mile past the

South of
Flagstaff

"Y," and the vortex is at the junction of the second and third peaks, just after the cattle grid. Further up, beyond the precarious airport, the **Shrine of the Red Rocks** looks out across the entire valley.

Three and four miles further along Hwy-89A, two successive turnings to the left mark the Upper and Lower sections of the seven-mile **Red Rock Loop Road**, all of which is paved barring a bumpy but not too difficult mile or so in the middle. Its prime attraction is reached via a spur road a couple of miles down Lower Red Rock Loop Road. **Red Rock State Park** (daily: summer 8am–6pm; winter 8am–5pm; $5 per vehicle or $1 per person) may be the obvious name for a park in the Sedona area, but it's not in fact the best place to see red rocks. Instead it preserves a sweeping curve of **Oak Creek**, both of whose banks at this point used to belong to a private ranch. The riparian environment thus survives reasonably intact – its flora and fauna are explained in the prominent, well-equipped **visitor center** (same hours), which holds stuffed hawks and owls and some live fish in tanks – and can be explored on an assortment of short trails. Two miles from the highway on Upper Red Rock Loop Road, the site known as **Red Rock Crossing** is a small picnic area beside a picturesque ford in Oak Creek that has featured in many movies (daily 9am–8pm; $2). **Cathedral Rock**, on the far side of the stream, is another vortex.

Dry Creek Road, which heads north off Hwy-89 a mile closer to town, runs north past **Capitol Butte** to reach **Boynton Canyon**. The presence of the lavish *Enchantment Resort* has spoiled some of the magic of Boynton Canyon itself – which has its own vortex – but several neighboring canyons are still perfect for short desert hikes. The resort office can provide trail maps showing the locations of Sinagua ruins in **Red Canyon**, while climbing **Doe Mesa**, or up into **Loy Butte Canyon**, gives great views of the whole Sedona valley.

South from the "Y," Hwy-179 is soon barreling through the Coconino National Forest. Turn left as soon as you cross Oak Creek, onto the unpaved **Schnebly Hill Road**, to enjoy the area's most spectacular scenic drive. In summer, the road remains open all the way to I-17, twelve rough miles east. Alternatively, continue south for three miles and then take Chapel Road to the left, which soon brings you to the **Chapel of the Holy Cross**. This tall and very narrow concrete chapel, whose facade is shaped like a massive cross, is squeezed into a cleft in the red cliffs (daily 9am–5pm). Another two miles down the highway, **Bell Rock**, on the east as you enter the village of Oak Creek, is Sedona's fourth major vortex.

Eating

Sedona is bursting with expensive Southwestern-style **restaurants**, not all of which are particularly good, and still has a smattering of old-fashioned diners. There's a shortage of places where you can just sit and watch the world go by over a coffee and a sandwich; most of its cafes are twee little places intended mainly to entice tourists into pastel-trimmed gift stores.

Coffee Pot Restaurant, 2050 W Hwy-89A; ☎520/282-6626. Sedona's largest, oldest diner, open daily from 6am until late, has a sports lounge, a hundred kinds of omelette, and all the burgers, Mexican dishes and fried specials you could hope for.

Dylan's, 1405 W Hwy-89A; ☎520/282-7930. American diner where sandwiches and quesadillas are served all day for under $10, while a complete steak or seafood dinner costs more like $20. Open daily for all meals.

El Rincon, Tlaquepaque Shopping Center, Hwy-179; ☎520/282-4648. Authentic Mexican food in classy surroundings, with entrees costing up to $15 and indoor and outdoor seating. Tues–Sat 11am–9pm, Sun noon–5pm.

Fournos, 3000 W Hwy-89A; ☎520/282-3331. Lovely little Greek restaurant, offering traditional dishes with all the right ingredients – feta cheese, *kalamata* olives and so on. Open Thurs–Sat, when dinner is served at 6pm and 8pm, and Sun for brunch at noon; reservations compulsory, no credit cards.

Heartline, 1610 W Hwy-89A; ☎520/282-0785. Tasteful white-table-linen restaurant, with an attractive courtyard, that serves determinedly healthy – though not exclusively vegetarian – Southwestern cuisine. Open Mon–Sat for lunch and dinner, and dinner only on Sun.

L'Auberge, *L'Auberge de Sedona*, 301 L'Auberge Lane; ☎520/282-1667. Exquisite, riverview French dining at sky-high prices; individual entrees are around $30, a full set menu is $60. Open daily for all meals.

The Muse Literary Café, Artesania Plaza, 251 Hwy-179; ☎520/282-3671. Not desperately literary, but delicious fluffy breakfast *beignets* and coffees, salad lunches, and pizzas and pasta for around $10 in the evening – plus live music nightly. Opposite Tlaquepaque, just down from the "Y", with patio seating overlooking the creek. Open daily for all meals.

Sedona Coffee House & Bakery, 293 N Hwy-89A; ☎520/282-2241. Popular breakfast hangout near the "Y," serving espresso coffees and pastries, and graduating to soup and salad later on. Open daily 8am–5pm.

Thai Spices, 2986 W Hwy-89A; ☎520/282-0599. West of downtown, near the road out to Boynton Canyon; tasty, healthy Thai food, with meat or seafood green or red curries or Pad Thai noodles for under $10, plus vegetarian and even macrobiotic choices. Open daily for lunch and dinner.

Yavapai Dining Room, *Enchantment Resort*, 525 Boynton Canyon Rd; ☎520/282-2900. Showcase resort restaurant, serving top-class Southwestern cuisine at up to $25 per entree; plenty of beans and chile to go with the freshest meats and fish. Open daily for lunch and dinner.

Cottonwood

Describing **COTTONWOOD**, eighteen miles southwest of Sedona in the heart of the Verde Valley, the 1930s WPA guide to Arizona wrote that "Familiar figures in the town are the cowboys from the range and the prospector or 'desert rat' who wanders in from his camp in the mountains to break the monotony of his lonely life." Today's Cottonwood is not nearly so romantic, though it has grown much larger thanks to an influx of retirees. It's not really even the same

place, as the former downtown is stranded a couple of miles north of
Hwy-89A, now lined by modern strip development.

Cottonwood does, however, make an inexpensive base for trips to
Sedona and Jerome, and its old main street still possesses a certain
charm. Tucked around a flower-filled courtyard, the *Sundial Motel*,
1034 N Main St (☎520/634-8031; ②), is a pretty – albeit pretty basic
– old-style motel, while latterday desert rats break the monotony with
a coffee or snack at the friendly *Bell'Espresso* nearby, housed in a
small gallery at 1025A N Main St (closed Wed; ☎520/634-3300). If
you prefer dependable chain lodgings, the *Best Western Cottonwood
Inn* is on Hwy-89A at 993 S Main St (☎520/634-5575 or 1-800/350-
0025 in AZ, fax 520/634-5576; *cottonwoodinn@verdenet.com*; winter ③, summer ④).

Tuzigoot National Monument

At the start of the fourteenth century, the Verde Valley held around
fifty major pueblo sites, occupied by the ancient Indian people now
known as the **Sinagua**. One of the largest, which now constitutes
TUZIGOOT NATIONAL MONUMENT, perches on a hillock across
the Verde River from **CLARKDALE**, three miles west of Cottonwood.

The ground floor alone had 86 rooms, and shows signs of repeated additions; with fifteen more rooms on the upper level, it may have
been home to some 225 people. Some archeologists think it was a
final enclave, where the Sinagua gathered against encroaching
drought before abandoning the area early in the fifteenth century.
Artifacts at the **visitor center**, where you pay your entrance fee
(daily: summer 8am–7pm; spring & fall 8am–6pm; winter 8am–5pm;
$2; ☎520/634-5564) include turquoise mosaics and shell jewelry.

Unfortunately, Tuzigoot is one of the least satisfying such sites in
the Southwest. When it was restored as part of a 1930s make-work
program, a little too much work was done, and its authenticity was
all but destroyed by laying a broad cement trail over, across and
through the pueblo. Furthermore, while the river, lined with cottonwoods, still flows past the pueblo, the "fields" below are just a sickly
orange mass of tailings from the nearby copper mines.

Jerome

The former mining town of **JEROME**, once the fourth largest community in Arizona, stands high above the Verde Valley on Hwy-89A.
It's conspicuous from quite a distance; not only is an enormous letter "J" etched deep into the hillside above it, but a large chunk of that
hillside is missing altogether, having been blown apart for **opencast
copper mining**. This land abounds in mineral wealth – thick veins of
copper are interspersed with gold and silver, and an endless supply
of limestone is still extracted for cement – but serious exploitation
only started in 1876, The **United Verde** mine was partly financed by

New Yorker Eugene Jerome (a cousin of Winston Churchill's mother, Jennie Jerome), who insisted that the new town bear his name. The United Verde has been called "the richest mine ever owned by an individual"; it made William Clark $100 million, and by 1953, had produced enough copper to give a thirteen-pound lump to every person on earth. Until the tortuous highway was built, the only way up to Jerome was the rail line that corkscrewed down from the mine to the world's largest copper smelter, at Clarkdale.

With its disproportionate population of young males, Jerome was known as a hard-drinking, hard-living town. The young **Pancho Villa** started out in life by supplying its drinking water, using a relay of two hundred burros, and for a brief period the International Workers of the World (the "**Wobblies**") were a strong presence; several hundred miners and "outside agitators" were literally railroaded out of town in July 1917 and dumped unceremoniously in the remote deserts of southwest Arizona.

Harsh economic realities have always determined local fortunes. Plenty of copper remains in the earth; although the Depression hit hard, the mine was only closed in the early 1950s, when cheap imported copper made it uneconomic to continue, and there's every possibility that as prices rise, it will reopen. To keep the mineral rights from reverting to the state, the present owners are obliged to keep on researching and prospecting; in fact, they do more than they have to, and reportedly find enough gold to cover their expenses.

As recently as the 1970s, Jerome was a **ghost town** in which it was possible to turn up and move into an empty house. Many of those who did so are still here, making a living from arts and crafts, and the town itself has made a dramatic recovery. It's a bit of a tourist trap, but is nonetheless fascinating to explore.

Arrival and information

Though on paper at least Hwy-89A is a direct through route between **Sedona**, thirty miles northeast of Jerome, and **Prescott**, thirty miles southwest, the formidable **Mingus Mountain** makes reaching Jerome a slow business. Coming from Cottonwood, it's a painstaking switchback climb; if you approach from Prescott, you're descending back down by the time you come to Jerome, with gorgeous views of the valley spread out below.

Jerome's zip code is AZ 86331.

Hwy-89A branches in two in the heart of town, where a one-way system takes westbound traffic along **Hull Avenue**, and eastbound along **Main Street**. The local **visitor center** is housed in a makeshift hut at Hull and First avenues (daily 10am–4pm; ☎520/634-2900).

Accommodation

There's no room to build **motels** on Jerome's uncertain slopes, so accommodation is restricted to a couple of c.1900 hotels and a few former homes that have been converted into **B&Bs**.

Ghost City Inn, 541 N Main St; ☎520/634-4678 or 1-888/634-4678. Century-old house, at the entrance to town as you come up from Cottonwood, with huge views from its wooden veranda. Four of the themed rooms share baths, one is en suite; one is crammed with hot-air balloon memorabilia. ④.

The Inn at Jerome, 309 N Main St; ☎520/634-5094 or 1-800/634-5094. Atmospheric eight-room hotel in the heart of town, offering accommodation with and without en-suite bathrooms. ③.

*The price
codes used
here are
explained on
p.15.*

Jerome Grand Hotel, 200 Hill St; ☎520/634-8200, fax 639-0299. Restored vintage hotel, spilling down five stories from the highest point in town; the views are fabulous, but the accommodation is atmospheric rather than luxurious. ④.

Surgeon's House B&B, 101 Hill St; ☎520/639-1452 or 1-800/639-1452; *surghouse1@juno.com*. Smart, upmarket B&B with dramatic views from the top of town; the en-suite rooms are especially plush. ⑤/⑥.

The Town

Thanks to the steep angle of the hillside, Jerome's streets are effectively stacked one on top of the other, and its stone houses – it was far too expensive to haul timber up here – tend to have two stories at the front and four or five at the back. Under the repeated concussion of over two hundred miles of tunnels being blasted into the mountainside, the whole town used to slip downhill at the rate of five inches per year, and the **Sliding Jail** on Hull Avenue came to rest 225 feet from where it was built (it's still there, but not open to the public).

Built for mine owner "Rawhide Jimmy" Douglas in 1917, the **Douglas Mansion**, on Mine Museum Road below town, is now open as **Jerome State Historical Park** (daily 8am–5pm; $2.50). Given the sweeping views over the valley, it can be hard to concentrate on the displays that detail the history and workings of the mines, and the lifestyles of the bosses.

Up in town, the **Mine Museum** is housed beneath the pressed-tin ceiling of the former *Fashion Saloon* at 200 N Main St (daily 9am–4.30pm; $1). Its amateurish but enjoyable collection of oddities include paintings that record different eras in mining, a chicken-wire stretcher once used for accident victims, and the primitive calculator used to calculate the United Verde Copper Company's payroll.

Many of the **shops** only stock souvenirs, but there are some interesting **crafts** showrooms around, such as the Knapp Gallery on Lower Main Street and Made in Jerome Pottery next door.

Eating and drinking

Day-trippers tend to fill the tearooms and snackbars of Jerome at lunchtime – especially on weekends – but come the evening you can still get a faint sense of its riproaring past.

English Kitchen, 119 Jerome Ave; ☎520/634-2132. Built in 1899, this claims to be Arizona's oldest restaurant. Under Chinese ownership, it was an opium den; later the Wobblies held meetings downstairs. Now it's open for breakfast and lunch Tues–Sun, and its terrace offers a commanding view of the valley.

Flatiron Cafe, 416 N Main St; ☎520/634-2733. Small, friendly joint at the apex of the one-way system. Espresso coffees, scrambled-egg breakfasts and fancy salad-and-sandwich lunches for around $7. Daily 7.30am–5pm.

Paul & Jerry's Saloon, 206 N Main St; ☎520/634-2603. Old-style saloon dating from 1889, with glorious ornate pool tables and a fine old bar with period trimmings. Open daily.

Wedge on the Edge, 412 N Main St; ☎520/634-5554. Homemade sourdough pizzas for $10 and upwards, plus views out to both sides and off down the mountains. Tues–Thurs & Sun 11am–7pm, Fri & Sat 11am–9pm.

Montezuma Castle National Monument

Towards the east end of the Verde Valley, two dramatic ancient sites jointly constitute **Montezuma Castle National Monument**. Roughly five miles apart, each now stands a short way east of I-17, around forty miles south of Flagstaff and twenty miles southeast of Sedona.

The northernmost of the two, **Montezuma Well**, is a natural lake that measures 368 feet across by 55 feet deep. Set like a volcanic crater into a small hill, it was formed when the roof of an underground cave collapsed 11,000 years ago. It's still fed by a spring that produces a phenomenal 1.9 million gallons of warm water per day, naturally heated to a constant 75°F.

Not surprisingly, the well was sacred to Native Americans; the **Yavapai** people (see p.344) say that this was where they emerged into the world. The **Hohokam** are thought to have moved here around 600 AD, and were the first to divert its water for irrigation, while the **Sinagua** replaced them in 1125 AD. Traces of ruined Sinagua pueblos can be discerned on the hilltop, reached by a five-minute walk from the parking lot, and a more complete **cliff dwelling** is set into the inner crater wall. It's now inaccessible, though you get a good view from the foot of the staircase that leads down to the lakeside. A couple more dwellings stand at ground level here, next to the hole or "swallet" through which the water spills out of the lake and flows through the hillside to join Beaver Creek outside.

Five miles south, **Montezuma Castle** itself is a superbly preserved **cliff dwelling** in an idyllic setting above Beaver Creek. Filling an alcove in the hillside with a wall of pink adobe, and originally reached by three separate ladders from the valley floor, its five stories taper up to fit the contours of the rock. Apparently, the sycamore beams are still in place, and the fingerprints of the masons are still visible on the bricks, but visitors are not permitted to climb up.

The ruins of a much larger, though now much less photogenic, dwelling "next door" were exposed to view by a fire in around 1400 AD. Once again you can't go inside, but the exposed honeycomb of holes in the limestone rock show that it had around 45 rooms, as well as little "cupboards" recessed into the walls, and might have housed as many as a hundred people.

The **visitor center** at the castle, where you pay your entry fee (daily: summer 8am–7pm; winter 8am–5pm; $2; ☎520/567-3322) has informative displays on the Sinagua, including a macaw skeleton which suggests trade with the Mexican civilizations thousands of miles to the south. There is no connection with the Aztec ruler Montezuma, though the well is said to appear on a deerskin map that belonged to Cortes himself.

Camp Verde

The scrappy little town of **CAMP VERDE**, a mile or so east of I-17 and another two miles south of Montezuma Castle, is noteworthy only as the site of **Fort Verde**. Built in 1871 to succeed a neighboring fort established in 1865, it served as headquarters for General George Crook's campaign against the Tonto Apaches. Crook failed to grasp the fact that the Yavapai and the Apache were separate peoples, but his massacre of the Yavapai at Skeleton Cave convinced the Apache to surrender. Both groups were rounded onto a reservation at Camp Verde, and later marched east to the San Carlos Reservation. Some ultimately returned, and a few pockets of land are now set aside for Yavapai-Apache joint use.

*For a history
of the Apache
Wars, see
p.541.*

Fort Verde was damaged by fire in 1881, and decommissioned ten years later. The four crumbling adobe buildings that remain are now the **Fort Verde State Historic Park** (daily 8am–4.30pm; $2), with an interesting museum in the commanding officer's house and a few more exhibits – stuffed birds, old wheelchairs, fearsome medical instruments – in the former doctor's quarters. The fort was never walled, the Apaches always preferring to ambush soldiers in the mountains than attack defensive positions, so it bears little resemblance to movie depictions of Wild West military outposts.

Practicalities

While there's no great reason to spend a night in Camp Verde, the *Best Western Cliff Castle Casino*, 333 Middle Verde Rd (☎520/567-6611 or 1-800/528-1234; ④), is a classic Southwestern hybrid: a luxury hotel built in what might conceivably have been Ancestral Puebloan style, had they ever felt the urge to build enormous hotels, and now run as a casino by the Yavapai-Apache Nation, featuring 24-hour slots. Cheaper rooms can be had at the *Super 8*, at the Montezuma Castle exit off I-17 (☎520/567-2622 or 1-800/800-8000; ③).

*Hwy-260
climbs east of
Camp Verde
towards Pine
and
Strawberry, in
the woods
thirty miles
up; see p.281.*

Arcosanti

Two miles east of the interstate at **Cordes Junction**, 25 miles south of Camp Verde, the space-age project known as **ARCOSANTI** is gradually rising from the rim of a beautiful high desert canyon. Designed (someday) to be a self-sufficient community of five thousand people, Arcosanti is the clearest embodiment of **Arcology**, an ideal blend of architecture and ecology created by Italian architect **Paolo Soleri**, a former student of Frank Lloyd Wright.

Though far from any sizeable settlement, Arcosanti is intended as a model of future urban environments. Part construction site, part theme park, with buildings shaped to maximize the benefit of the sun's energy, it can be seen on hour-long guided tours (daily 9am–5pm; hourly tours 10am–4pm; $5; ☎520/632-7135). A spacious **cafe** serves healthy and tasty meals, and you can stay in the on-site **motel** for as little as $25 for a basic double room; if you like what you see, you can even sign up for one of the month-long workshops and help out with the construction. In summer, Arcosanti also hosts a very popular series of outdoor **concerts**.

South of Flagstaff

Paolo Soleri's bell foundry at Cosanti, near Phoenix, is described on p.224.

Prescott

The neat little Victorian town of **PRESCOTT** makes an unlikely sight in the Arizona wilderness, a hundred miles north of Phoenix by way of Hwy-69, which leaves I-17 at Cordes Junction, and fifty miles south of Ash Fork on I-40. In 1863, when President Lincoln acceded to pressure from mining interests in the central mountains and granted Arizona territorial status, he chose to establish a new capital well away from Tucson, which he saw as a hotbed of Confederate sympathizers. His first choice, **Fort Whipple**, was replaced in 1864 when gold was discovered near Prescott nearby, which became the site of both fort and capital. It was named in honor of William H. Prescott, the author of the classic *A History of the Conquest of Mexico*.

Though Tucson duly supplanted it as capital within three years, Prescott survived, with cattle ranchers joining the gold miners to make it the rowdiest, hardest-drinking town within a hundred miles. Those days are long gone, however, and while Prescott refused to die, it hasn't grown either. Its downtown, focused around the kind of **courthouse square** you'd expect to find in the Deep South, now feels prettified for tourists rather than the heart of a living community. For out-of-state visitors, Prescott doesn't really merit a substantial detour, but if you're passing this way anyway it makes a far more characterful halt than a typical interstate truckstop.

To get a feel for Prescott's past, head to the **Sharlot Hall Museum**, 415 W Gurley St (April–Oct Mon–Sat 10am–5pm, Sun 1–5pm; Nov–March Mon–Sat 10am–4pm, Sun 1–5pm; $4 donation). Sharlot Hall, a former official historian of Arizona who arrived in Prescott with her pioneer parents in 1882, at the age of twelve, put together the nucleus of this collection, which has expanded since her death to fill a dozen buildings and an entire city block. As well as the modern museum headquarters, it includes the 1864 Governor's Mansion – more of an oversized log cabin – plus a blacksmith's shop and a garage filled with vintage vehicles.

Practicalities

Prescott's **visitor center**, on Courthouse Plaza at 117 W Goodwin St
(Mon–Sat 9am–5pm, Sun 10am–4pm; ☎520/445-2000 or
1-800/266-7534), has listings of around twenty **B&Bs** in Victorian
homes. Among the nicest are the rambling *Victorian Inn*, 246 S
Cortez St (☎520/778-2642 or 1-800/704-2642; ⑤–⑦), which offers
a Teddy Bear Room and lavish breakfasts, and the Queen Anne-style
Marks House, 203 E Union St (☎520/778-4632; ④–⑥). The
restored *Hotel St Michael*, 205 W Gurley St (☎520/776-1999 or
1-800/678-3757, fax 520/776-7318; winter ②, summer ③), is an
inexpensive but atmospheric – some say haunted – old downtown
hotel, while the *Hassayampa Inn*, 122 E Gurley St (☎520/778-
9434 or 1-800/322-1927, fax 520/445-8590; *inn@primenet.com*;

*Prescott's zip
code is AZ
86303.*

winter ⑤, summer ⑥), is a grander Art Deco alternative.

The finest **dining** in town is at the *Siena Restaurant*, 111 Grove
Ave (closed Mon; ☎520/771-1285), which offers exquisite Italian
cuisine in an elegant former private home. For an experience more
in keeping with Prescott's early days, try the *Prescott Brewing
Company* instead, at 130 W Gurley St (☎520/771-2795), where as
well as home-brewed beers they have a bakery and a full menu. The
Caffe St Michael in the *Hotel St Michael* (see above) serves
espresso coffees.

Wickenburg

WICKENBURG, sixty miles southwest of Prescott and the same distance northwest of Phoenix, is another former mining and ranching
town now kept ticking over by tourism. It's only a little higher, and a
little cooler, than Phoenix, so the main visitor season is in winter,
between November and April.

*Hassayampa
means "river
that runs
upside down"
in Apache, a
reference to
the fact that it
often flows
underground.*

Wickenburg stands beside the **Hassayampa River**, on the "pumpkin patch" where Prussian prospector Henry Wickenburg built a mill
in 1864 to process the gold he'd discovered in the Vulture
Mountains, fifteen miles south. Though it yielded substantial quantities of gold, the **Vulture Mine** was seldom profitable thanks to geological peculiarities and its general inaccessibility. After years of
passing from hand to hand, it finally closed down in 1942. By then,
however, Wickenburg had established a successful sideline in running **dude ranches**, where well-heeled Easterners could dabble with
the Wild West lifestyle for a few carefree days.

In general, Wickenburg these days is a spruce and prosperous-
looking place, with little sense of a desert outpost, though the
wooden sidewalks and falsefront stores along **Frontier Street** in the
heart of town must look much as they did in Wickenburg's heyday.
You can still see the mesquite tree that served as the original town
"jail"; miscreants were simply chained to its trunk. Local history is
recalled at the **Desert Caballeros Western Museum**, 21 N Frontier
St (Mon–Sat 10am–5pm, Sun 1–4pm; $5), which as well as paintings

by Remington and Russell, several little dioramas and the usual
barbed-wire collection, features a re-created 1900s street scene.

Three miles south, the **Hassayampa River Preserve** (mid-May to
mid-Sept Wed–Sun 6am–noon; mid-Sept to mid-May daily 8am–5pm;
$5 donation) marks a spot where the river bubbles from its sandy
streambed to irrigate a lush stretch of woodland that's home to innu-
merable bird species.

The **Vulture Mine** itself can also be visited (May–Aug Mon &
Thurs–Sun 8am–4pm; Sept–April daily 8am–4pm; $5). Its long-aban-
doned workings rear up from the streets of the well-preserved ghost
town of **Vulture City**. Stick to the walking trail as you wander round;
the various buildings, which include a blacksmith's shop and the
mine's head office, are not as sturdy as they appear.

Practicalities

Wickenburg's **visitor center** is housed in the former railroad station at 216 N Frontier St (summer Mon–Fri 9am–5pm; winter
Mon–Fri 9am–5pm, Sat 10am–1pm, Sun 1–4pm; ☎520/684-5479
or 1-800/942-5242).

*Wickenburg's
zip code is AZ
85358.*

Only one working cattle ranch now accepts paying guests, the
Flying E Ranch, 2801 W Wickenburg Way (Nov–May only;
☎520/684-2690 or 1-888/684-2650, fax 520/684-5304; *flyinge
@primenet.com*; ⑦). *Rancho de los Caballeros*, at 1551 S Vulture
Mine Rd, is a purpose-built luxury resort, complete with its own golf
course and stables (Oct to early May; ☎520/684-5484, fax 684-
2267; ⑨). Of conventional **motels**, the *Best Western Rancho
Grande*, 293 E Wickenburg Way (☎520/684-5445 or 1-800/854-
7235, fax 520/684-7380; summer ③, winter ④), is the most attractive, part genuine adobe and part Spanish colonial mock-up, while
La Siesta, 486 E Wickenburg Way (☎520/684-2826; ②) is a budget
alternative. For a slap-up ranch-style **meal**, head out to *Charley's
Steakhouse*, 1187 W Wickenburg Way (Oct–April only, closed Mon;
☎520/684-2413); the *House Berlin*, 169 E Wickenburg Way
(closed Mon; ☎520/684-5044) serves German and other European
specialties.

Joshua Forest Parkway

Northwest of Wickenburg, US-93 runs for 108 dramatic miles
across some of Arizona's wildest and most scenic mountains, to
meet I-40 twenty miles east of Kingman (see p.312). If you're heading up from Phoenix, this slow two-lane highway serves as a
reminder of just how much of the state remains given over to wilderness. Apart from the hamlet of **NOTHING** – which might sound
enticing on the map, but really is nothing, other than the home base
of a towing company that rescues unfortunate stranded motorists –
there's almost no sign of human life along the way. Instead, the vegetation provides the main source of interest, with saguaro and

ocotillo **cactuses** scattered across the slopes of the impressive
rocky outcrops. Above all, these eastern fringes of the Mojave
Desert are one of the few places in Arizona where you'll encounter
an abundance of **Joshua trees** – hence the road's official designa-
tion as the **Joshua Forest Parkway**.

West of Flagstaff

Though the two hundred miles of I-40 that run **west from Flagstaff**
to California are kept busy by traffic heading to, from and between
the Grand Canyon and Las Vegas, few of the towns along the way are
especially interesting in themselves. However, most became reliant
on tourism during the heyday of **Route 66**, and driving through any
one of them can bring on a frisson of that era's romance.

If you have the time to indulge your 1950s fantasies, then take the
120-mile side trip on the longest surviving section of what John
Steinbeck called the "**Mother Road**," which starts at **Seligman**, loops
back down to **Kingman**, and then crosses some wild and mountainous country to the ghost town of **Oatman**. Otherwise, it makes little
difference where or even if you choose to take a break from the interstate.

Williams

Although Flagstaff is generally regarded as the obvious base for visitors to the Grand Canyon, **WILLIAMS**, 32 miles west, is in fact the
closest interstate town to the national park. It's also a nice little place
in its own right, filled with Route 66-era motels and diners but retaining a certain individuality despite the constant stream of tourists. Its
setting helps, cupped in a high grassy valley amid pine-covered hills;
the largest peak is the 9264-foot **Bill Williams Mountain** to the
south, which was named after pioneer trapper and "mountain man"
Bill Williams (1787–1849), and gave its name in turn to the town,
founded thirty years after his death.

Like Flagstaff, Williams originally based both its architecture and
its economy on the ponderosas of the surrounding forests. Ever
since 1901, however, when the Santa Fe Railroad first connected it
with the canyon rim, sixty miles due north, Williams has lived off
tourism. Though the railroad was driven out of business in 1968, it
reopened again in 1989 as the Grand Canyon Railway, promoted as
a fun ride rather than a serious means of transportation, and most
people who spend the night in Williams are here to take the morning
train up to the canyon.

Practicalities
Schedules and prices for the Grand Canyon Railway (☎520/773-
1976 or 1-800/THE-TRAIN) are listed on p.325; when it's running,

which is daily in summer, the train sets off from the station in the center of town at 9.30am. Williams' **visitor center**, at 200 W Railroad Ave (daily 8am–5pm; ☎520/635-1418 or 1-800/863-0546), hands out all the usual brochures, including one detailing a town walking tour, and doubles as an entertaining **museum** of neighborhood history.

West of
Flagstaff

*Note that
Amtrak trains
do not stop at
Williams.*

The two main streets, Railroad Avenue and Bill Williams Avenue, form a one-way loop through town, incorporating all of Williams' former Route 66 frontage. Several **motels**, such as the *Downtowner Motel*, 201 E Bill Williams Ave (☎520/635-4041 or 1-800/441-8828; *www.thegrandcanyon.com/downtowner*; winter ①, summer ③), stretch between the two. Other inexpensive options include the British-owned *Norris Motel*, 1001 W Bill Williams Ave (☎520/635-2202 or 1-800/341-8000; *www.thegrandcanyon .com/norris*; winter ①, summer ③); two *Super 8*s, including one at 2001 E Bill Williams Ave (☎520/635-4700 or 1-800/800-8000; winter ②, summer ④), a mile north of town near the interstate; and two *Motel 6*s. There are also plenty of **B&Bs**, like the plush *Red Garter*, 137 W Railroad Ave (☎520/635-1484 or 1-800/328-1484; ④), above the downtown Bed and Bakery, which sells fresh-baked goods (daily 6–11am & 4–6pm), and the *Johnstonian*, a little way south at 321 W Sheridan Ave (☎520/635-2178; ③–⑤).

*The zip code
for Williams is
AZ 86046.*

The cheapest alternative of all, assuming you have the transportation to reach it, is the *Red Lake Hostel*, a slightly run-down, red-painted converted motel en route towards the Grand Canyon (☎520/635-4753 or 1-800/581-4753; ①). Located nine miles north of town up Hwy-64 (also known as the Bushmaster Memorial Highway), it charges $11 for a dorm bed in summer, $8 in winter, and also offers tent and RV space. Otherwise, if you're **camping**, ask at the Chalender Ranger Station, 501 W Bill Williams Ave (☎520/635-2676), for details of secluded mountain sites in the Kaibab National Forest.

The most authentic of the Route 66 **restaurants** to survive is *Rod's Steak House*, 301 E Bill Williams Ave (☎520/635-2671). By contrast, *Grand Canyon Coffee & Cafe*, 125 W Bill Williams Ave (☎520/635-2080), serves espressos, juices, pastries and sandwiches.

Twin highlights of Williams' annual calendar are **Rendezvous Days**, on the Memorial Day weekend, when locals dress up as pioneer "buckskinners," and the **rodeo** on Labor Day.

Ash Fork

The ranching community of **ASH FORK**, another twenty miles west of Williams, is smaller, less picturesque and far less involved in catering to travelers. By this point I-40 has pulled clear of the forests, and downtown Ash Fork is characterized by buildings constructed with the yellowish local sandstone rather than timber.

The major **motel** chains haven't bothered to set up shop here, but there are still a few homespun alternatives, including the *Stage Coach*, 823 Park Ave (☎520/637-2551; ②), and the *Hi Line*, 124 E Lewis Ave (☎520/637-2766; ②).

Seligman

Starting a few miles west of Ash Fork, the old Route 66 parallels its modern replacement at a discreet distance for the twenty or so miles to **SELIGMAN**. This flyblown desert halt now feels more than a little stranded, a mile or two north of the interstate, but if you're in the mood to be seduced by its kitsch diners and drive-ins, it makes a mildly diverting stop in a long day's drive.

You might even choose to follow Route 66's original course as it curves northwards, through a dozen fading villages and part of the **Hualapai Indian Reservation**, and back south to Kingman. That's a total drive of 88 miles, as opposed to the dreary 65-mile run west on I-40. It also provides access to **Havasu Canyon**, in the depths of the Grand Canyon – one of the Southwest's least-known marvels.

For a full account of the wonders of Havasu Canyon, see p.342.

Whichever way you drive, Seligman has the only **accommodation** between Ash Fork and Kingman, though motels like the *Historic Route 66*, 500 W Chino Ave (☎520/422-3204; ②), and the *Romney*, 122 W Chino Ave (☎520/422-3294; ②), are all much of an indifferent muchness. The *Copper Cart*, in the former railroad station on Chino Avenue (☎520/422-3241), is the most popular **diner**, while the theory behind the *Snow Cap* (☎520/422-3291), further east at the interstate exit, is that it looks so tacky you simply have to stop and take a look.

Kingman

With a population of over thirty thousand, **KINGMAN**, 65 miles on from Seligman and thirty miles short of California, ranks second to Flagstaff among Arizona's I-40 towns. As all traffic between Phoenix or the Grand Canyon and **Las Vegas** – a mere hundred miles northwest on US-93 – is obliged to pass this way, Kingman also welcomes enough tourists to keep thirty or more motels busy year-round. The best that can be said for it, however, is that it's not particularly ugly, and it's not lifeless; apart from that, it's a humdrum little pit stop with a slight tinge of Route 66 quaintness.

Carole Lombard and Clark Gable were married in Kingman on March 29, 1939.

Kingman's main street, curving alongside the railroad tracks, is named in honor of native son **Andy Devine**, the actor who drove the eponymous *Stagecoach* in John Ford's 1939 movie. As the town's promotional brochure puts it, "there must be somebody who hasn't heard of Andy Devine, but that person sure doesn't live in Kingman." His career, the culture and basketwork of the Hualapai Indians, and sundry other unlikely components of Mohave County's heritage, are explored in the **Mohave Museum of History & Arts**, 400 W Beale St (Mon–Fri 10am–5pm, Sat & Sun 1–5pm; $2).

Practicalities

Kingman's large new **Powerhouse visitor center** stands at the western edge of downtown, at 120 W Andy Devine Ave (daily 9am–6pm; ☎520/753-6106); as well as the usual brochures, it displays and sells lots of Route 66 memorabilia, and also has its own diner, *Memory Lane*, complete with soda fountain and deli. The old station in the center of town still sees Amtrak **trains** between Flagstaff and LA, but only at unearthly hours of the night, while regular Greyhound **buses**, between Phoenix and Las Vegas as well as east–west, use a terminal up near the interstate at 3264 E Andy Devine Ave (☎520/757-8400).

Motels in the heart of town include the basic *Ramblin' Rose*, 1001 E Andy Devine Ave (☎520/753-5541; ②). More comfortable chain options, a couple of miles northeast near I-40 exit 53, range from the *Super 8*, 3401 E Andy Devine Ave (☎520/757-4808 or 1-800/800-8000; ②), to the *Best Western A Wayfarer's Inn*, 2815 E Andy Devine Ave (☎520/753-6271 or 1-800/548-5695, fax 520/753-9608; winter ③, summer ④). Timothy McVeigh spent a week at the very *un*-seedy *Hill Top Motel*, 1901 E Andy Devine Ave (☎520/753-2198; ②), shortly before he bombed the Alfred P. Murrah building in Oklahoma City, in April 1995. There's beautiful **camping** in the hills southeast of town in the county-run **Hualapai Mountain Park** (☎520/757-0915), which also holds the *Hualapai Mountain Lodge Resort* (☎520/757-3545; ③).

The most conspicuous **restaurant** in Kingman is *Mr D'z Route 66 Diner*, opposite the visitor center at 105 E Andy Devine Ave (closed Mon; ☎520/718-0066); it may be new, but its lurid neon signs are in the best traditions of Route 66, and so too are its burgers, shakes and fries. The *Old Town Coffeehouse*, on the eastern fringes of downtown at 616 E Beale St (closed Sun; ☎520/753-2244), is a more refined affair, serving espressos, soups and sandwiches on its small outdoor patio.

Chloride

Fifteen miles northwest of Kingman, as US-93 tears through the flat, prosaically-named **Detrital Valley** towards Las Vegas, a paved road climbs away into the mountains to the right. Its goal is the former silver mining center of **CHLORIDE**, four miles up, which was established in 1864 and boasts Arizona's oldest still-functional post office. As well as silver, vast quantities of gold, copper, lead and turquoise were also extracted from the roadless **Cerbat Mountains** beyond, but Chloride these days lives by its wits, exploiting its ramshackle Wild West appearance to attract tourists. You may be encouraged to drive another couple of miles down a dirt road to see the local **murals**, painted onto huge boulders during the 1960s by artist Roy Purcell; his semi-psychedelic meanderings aren't hard to find, but neither are they really worth the bother.

Some of Chloride's erstwhile neighbors – such as **CERBAT** and
MINERAL PARK – have foundered altogether, to become genuine
ghost towns. In tiny Chloride itself, the epicenter of the visitor
industry is *Shep's* (☎520/565-3643; ②), an antiques store that doubles as a four-room **B&B**.

Bullhead City and Laughlin

While both the old Route 66 and the interstate head southwest from
Kingman, Hwy-68 barrels due west for thirty miles to **BULLHEAD
CITY** on the Colorado. Built as a work camp for the construction of
nearby Davis Dam, Bullhead City somehow survived the dam's completion in 1953, and has prospered recently due to its proximity to
the casinos of **LAUGHLIN**, Nevada, just across the river.

In terms of temperature, **Bullhead** is the hottest town in the US,
exceeding 120°F on day after day each summer. In most other
respects, however, it's not the least bit hot. Nearly thirty thousand
people now live along a ten-mile riverfront stretch of Hwy-93; why
on earth you'd join them, even for a night, is hard to imagine.

Not that **Laughlin** is much better, despite the endless hype of its
tourist authorities. If you've never been to Las Vegas, you may well
be impressed by the sheer size of the dozen or so glittering **casinos**
that jostle for position beside the Colorado. They lack the panache of
their Vegas counterparts, however, as well as the will to cater to anyone other than hardened gamblers.

Practicalities

Both Tri State Super Shuttle (☎520/704-9000 or 1-800/801-8687)
and Best-Way Shuttle (☎520/758-1200 or 1-800/248-8744) run
daily **bus services** between Bullhead City, Laughlin and Las Vegas,
for around $25 one way. Several companies, such as Guaranteed
Tours (☎702/369-1000) also run free day-trips to Laughlin from
Las Vegas, subsidized by the casinos.

*For general
information
on Laughlin,
call
☎702/298-
3321 or 1-
800/452-8445;
Las Vegas is
described in
Chapter 8.*

At least eight casinos in Laughlin offer well over a thousand rooms
each, with weekday rates that drop as low as $15 per room, plus half
a dozen restaurants ranging from buffet joints whose all-you-can-eat
specials start at well under $5 to dimly-lit Italian schmoozeries. The
oldest of the casinos, which traces its ancestry all the way back to an
eight-room motel that opened in 1966, but has consistently kept
pace with the rest, is *Don Laughlin's Riverside Resort Hotel*, 1650
S Casino Drive (☎702/298-2535 or 1-800/227-3849; Sun–Thurs ①,
Fri & Sat ②). Neighbors include the counterfeit Mississippi steamboat that is the *Colorado Belle*, 2100 S Casino Drive (☎702/298-
4000 or 1-800/477-4837; Sun–Thurs ①, Fri & Sat ③); the sleeker
Edgewater Hotel, 2020 S Casino Drive (☎702/298-2453 or 1-
800/677-4837; Sun–Thurs ①, Fri & Sat ②); the spruced-up, railroad-
themed *Ramada Express*, 2121 S Casino Drive (☎702/298-4200
or 1-800/243-6836; Sun–Thurs ①, Fri & Sat ③); and the top-of-the-

range *Golden Nugget*, 2300 S Casino Drive (☎702/298-7222 or 1-800/950-7700; Sun–Thurs ①, Fri & Sat ③).

Oatman

If you're in no great hurry to get to California from Kingman, following Route 66 over the **Black Mountains** is much more enjoyable than skirting south then west on I-40. While **Needles**, California, is only fifty miles away on the "Mother Road," however – as opposed to 64 on the interstate – it's a long, slow drive, and you need to be confident that your vehicle can handle tricky mountain bends.

The eastern approaches to the mountains, at the edge of the Sacramento Valley, are guarded by a splendid solitary rock pinnacle that served as a beacon to early travelers. Following a laborious climb up to a gap between the peaks, the road twists down the far side and eventually enters **OATMAN**. This former gold-mining community, which was established in 1906, and went bust in 1942, is one of Arizona's most appealing **ghost towns**; a second career as an all-purpose movie backdrop and tourist stop-off has ensured that it's never truly been abandoned. The streets are still roamed by semi-wild burros descended from animals left by the miners.

Oatman is built on such a slope that the raised wooden boardwalk is a necessity to keep your footing as you browse its gift and craft stores, pausing perhaps to snack on rattlesnake at *Cactus Joe's* (☎520/768-3242). The *1902 Oatman Hotel* (☎520/768-4408; ②) – a restored adobe that was in fact rebuilt after a fire in 1920 – still rents out basic **rooms**, including the one where Clark Gable and Carole Lombard spent their wedding night in 1939.

Lake Havasu City

Forty miles southwest of Kingman on I-40, ten miles from the California border, a twenty-mile detour south on Hwy-95 brings you to the most incongruous sight of the Southwestern deserts. At **LAKE HAVASU CITY**, the old gray stones of **London Bridge** reach out across the stagnant waters of the dammed Colorado River.

Californian chainsaw manufacturer **Robert P. McCulloch** moved his factory to this unlikely spot – occupied by a disused military airstrip – in 1964, so he could try out his new sideline in outboard motors on the waters of Lake Havasu. Three years later, he heard Johnny Carson mention that London Bridge was up for sale; in the words of the nursery rhyme, it really was falling down, unable to cope with all those new-fangled automobiles. McCulloch bought it for $2,460,000, and painstakingly shipped ten thousand numbered blocks of granite across the Atlantic. Lacking anything for the bridge to span, he dug a channel that turned a riverbank promontory into the island of **Pittsburg Point**. Despite the jibes that McCulloch thought he was buying picturesque Tower Bridge – the turreted one that opens in the middle – instead of merely the latest in a long line of London Bridges, dating only from 1831, his investment paid off handsomely. The bridge now ranks second among Arizona's tourist attractions, after the Grand Canyon, and Lake Havasu City has become a major vacation resort and retirement center, with a population of thirty thousand.

That said, it's not often you see anything quite as **boring** in Arizona as London Bridge; unless you've never seen a bridge before, it's one to miss. Once again, Lake Havasu City is one of those places with an undeniable attraction for the parched urbanites of Phoenix, who flock to fish on the lake, or charge up and down in motorboats and on jet skis, but minimal appeal for travelers from further afield.

London Bridge is listed in the Guinness Book of Records *as the largest antique ever sold.*

Only when you cross the bridge onto the island, and then look back, do you appreciate how large Lake Havasu City has grown, sprawling up the gentle slope away from the river. Most of those broad hillside streets are lined with condo blocks and minor malls; the only place tourists bother to visit is the **English Village**, a mock-Tudor shopping mall, which also holds a handful of riverview restaurants, at the base of the bridge. Out on the island, if you head south from the bridge past the *Island Inn Resort*, you'll soon come to **London Bridge Beach**. The "beach" is more grit than sand, and few people swim from it. With its bizarre fringe of date palms, however, and its panorama of weird desert buttes and the Chemehuevi Mountains, it does at least linger in the memory.

Practicalities

The local **visitor center** is up from the river at 1930 Mesquite Ave (Mon–Fri 9am–5pm; ☎520/453-3444 or 1-800/242-8278); there's also an information kiosk at 420 English Village (daily 10am–4pm; ☎520/855-5655).

Several operators, such as Dreamcatcher (☎760/858-4593) and Dixie Belle Cruises (☎520/453-6776), offer short **river cruises** from the quayside of the English Village, charging around $12 for an hour-long trip focusing on the bridge, or $20 for a two-hour excursion to see rock formations upriver. Companies renting **jet skis** (at around $40 per hour) and the like include Arizona Jet Ski (☎520/453-5558 or 1-800/393-5558) and Fun Time Boat Rentals (☎520/680-1003 or 1-800/680-1003).

Lake Havasu City's zip code is AZ 86403.

Lake Havasu City has a good 25 or so **motels**, though relatively few of them are immediately obvious from Hwy-95. They range from the perfectly adequate *Windsor Inn Motel*, 451 London Bridge Rd (☎520/855-4135 or 1-800/245-4135; winter ①, summer ②), by way of the fancier, all-suite *Ramada at Lake Havasu*, 271 S Lake Havasu Ave (☎520/855-5169 or 1-800/528-5169; ③), to the frankly ridiculous riverfront *London Bridge Resort*, 1477 Queen's Bay Rd (☎520/855-0888 or 1-800/624-7939; ④), where everything has a British-royalty theme.

As for **nightlife**, most of Lake Havasu City seems to be tucked up in bed by 9pm. For a night out, the districts at either end of London Bridge are your best bet. The *London Bridge Brewery* (☎520/855-8782) is a lively **microbrewery** in the English Village on the mainland, while *Shugrue's* (☎520/453-1400), across the bridge in the **Island Fashion Mall**, serves good fresh fish and even sushi, plus salads and pasta.

Chapter 6

The Grand Canyon

Although five million people come to see the **GRAND CANYON OF THE COLORADO** every year, it remains beyond the grasp of the human imagination. No photograph, no set of statistics, can prepare you for such vastness. At more than one mile deep, it's an inconceivable abyss; varying from four to eighteen miles wide, it's an endless expanse of bewildering shapes and colors, glaring desert brightness and impenetrable shadow, stark promontories and soaring never-to-be-climbed sandstone pinnacles. Somehow it's so impassive, so remote – you could never call it a disappointment, but at the same time, many visitors are left feeling peculiarly flat. In a sense, none of the available activities can quite live up to that first stunning sight of the chasm. The **overlooks** along the rim all offer views that shift and change unceasingly from dawn to dusk; you can **hike** down into the depths on foot or by mule, hover above in a **helicopter** or raft through the **whitewater rapids** of the river itself; you can spend a night at **Phantom Ranch** on the canyon floor, or swim beneath the waterfalls of the idyllic **Havasupai Reservation**. And yet that distance always remains – the Grand Canyon stands apart.

Admission to the national park, valid for seven days on either rim, costs $20 per vehicle or $10 per pedestrian or cyclist. All the park-service passes detailed on p.21 are both valid and sold.

Mapping and defining precisely what constitutes the "Grand Canyon" has always been controversial; **Grand Canyon National Park** covers a relatively small proportion of the greater Grand Canyon area. Only in the last 25 years has it included the full 277-mile length of the Colorado River from Lees Ferry in the east to Grand Wash Cliffs near Lake Mead in the west, and even now it's restricted for most of that way to the narrow strip of the inner gorge. Ranchers whose animals graze in the federal forests to either side, mining companies eager to exploit the mineral wealth hidden in the ancient rocks, engineers seeking to divert the river to feed the deserts of southern Arizona, and Native Americans who have lived in the Canyon since long before the first Europeans reached North America, have combined to minimize the size of the park.

The vast majority of visitors arrive at the **South Rim** – it's much easier to get to, there are far more facilities (mainly at **Grand**

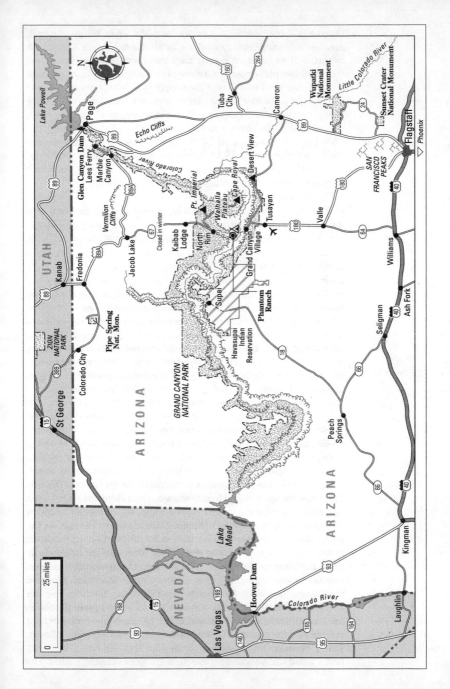

Canyon Village, inside the park), and it's open all year round. Another lodge and campground are located at the **North Rim**, which by virtue of its isolation can be a lot more atmospheric, but at one thousand feet higher this entire area is usually closed by snow from mid-October until mid-May. Few people visit both rims on a single trip; to get from one to the other demands either a two-day hike down one side of the canyon and up the other, or a 215-mile drive. On both rims, the main activity consists of gazing over the gorge from lookouts placed at strategic intervals along the canyon-edge roads. Whereas in the 1920s the average visitor stayed for two or three weeks, these days it's more like two or three hours – of which forty minutes are spent actually looking at the canyon.

Finally, there's a definite risk that on the day you come the Grand Canyon will be invisible beneath a layer of **fog**; many people blame the 250 tons of sulfurous emissions pumped out every day by the Navajo Generating Station, seventy miles upriver at Page.

A history of the Grand Canyon

It may look forbidding, but the Grand Canyon is not a dead place. All sorts of desert **wildlife** survive here – sheep and rabbits, eagles and vultures, mountain lions and, of course, spiders, scorpions and snakes. The earliest signs of any **human** presence are twig figurines of animals, found hidden in caves in the canyon walls. Dated to around 2000 BC, they were probably created to insure successful hunting. Remains of later dwellings built by the **Ancestral Puebloans** are scattered throughout the canyon – the most accessible to modern visitors is Tusayan Ruin (see p.335) – while the **Havasupai** (see box, p.344) are thought to have arrived around 1300 AD.

In 1540 – less than twenty years after Cortés conquered the Aztecs of Mexico – the first **Spaniards** reached the Southwest. At the Hopi mesas, a detachment of Francisco Vázquez de Coronado's company were told of a great river not far to the west, inhabited by people with very large bodies (presumably the Havasupai, who tend to be significantly bigger than the Hopi). A small party, led by García López de Cárdenas, was dispatched to investigate. Their Hopi guides led them to a spot somewhere near Grandview Point, but chose not to reveal the trails down to the river. The Spaniards spent three days on the South Rim, only appreciating the scale of the Canyon after an abortive attempt to reach the river. They identified the Colorado as being the Tíson or "Firebrand" River, up which a simultaneous naval expedition was attempting to sail (it managed 225 miles, reaching what's now the site of the Hoover Dam).

When jurisdiction over the Grand Canyon passed from Mexico to the United States in 1850, it had never been surveyed, and did not even have a fixed **name**. To the Havasupai, it was Wikatata ("Rough Rim"); Spanish maps showed it as Río Muy Grande ("Very Big River"); and trappers and prospectors knew it as the Big Cañon. The

The Formation of the Grand Canyon

Although the Grand Canyon could be called the world's clearest geological textbook, scientists continue to argue over how to read the story
written in the stone. Layer upon layer of different rocks, readily distinguished by color, and each with its own fossil record, recede down into
the canyon and back through time, until the riverbed lays bare some of
the oldest exposed rocks on earth. Almost all of the successive strata of
sandstone and limestone were deposited during periods when the entire
region was submerged beneath shallow primeval seas. The bottom
layer, the two-billion-year-old **Vishnu Schist**, is so ancient that it contains no fossils; it dates back to the Precambrian era, when life had
barely begun.

That same tale of sedimentation, of course, holds true for much of the
planet. What until five million years ago was an unremarkable landscape
was transformed into the Grand Canyon thanks to two major factors. First
of all, it was a **desert**; the chronic shortage of rain prevented the development of vegetation to bind the brittle surface together. Second, there was
the fast-flowing **Colorado River**, cascading down from the Rocky
Mountains with a gradient over 25 times steeper than the Mississippi. In
full flood, charged with mighty boulders, it can blast deep crevices into the
earth.

However, a crucial mystery remains. The Colorado Plateau is not flat at
this point; it's an enormous hill, known to the Paiute Indians as the
Kaibab, or mountain with no peak. Why, or how, the Colorado River cuts
straight through that hill, rather than flowing around it, has long taxed the
imaginations of geologists. The hypothesis currently in favor, "**stream
piracy**," suggests that until five million years ago, the river did indeed skirt
the Kaibab. Having reached what's now the eastern edge of the national
park it flowed southeast along the present channel of the Little Colorado
River. Then the headwaters of a minor stream that flowed west down the
Kaibab cut their way back sufficiently to breach a gap in the mountain,
through which the Colorado was able to surge.

Crudely speaking, while the river is responsible for the **depth** of the
canyon – and continues to scour its way ever deeper – it did little to create
its **width**. The fantastic pyramids and mesas that tower above the central
gorge are the result of erosion by wind, and extreme cycles of heat and
cold; in particular, vast slabs of stone are chiseled away when water that
trickles into cracks in the earth later freezes and expands. Some layers are
much harder than others; thus the solid Tapeats Sandstone of the **Tonto
Platform**, a mile-wide shelf above the river that runs through most of the
national park, was left behind when the weaker Bright Angel Shale above
it eroded away. Because the general slope of the Kaibab runs from north
to south, rain that falls north of the canyon flows down towards the gorge,
while rainfall to the south flows away. As a result, the **North Rim** is deeply
cut by tributary streams, and pushed back further from the Colorado,
while the lower **South Rim** is much more regular.

The most striking features were named for their supposed resemblances
to the great temples of India and China – **Brahma Temple**, **Shiva Temple**,
Vishnu Temple, and so on – by Clarence Dutton, a student of comparative
religion who wrote the first Geological Survey report on the canyon in
1881. The tradition was followed by later cartographers such as François
Matthes, who named **Krishna Shrine** and **Walhalla Plateau**.

name Grand Canyon, first used on a map in 1868, was popularized by the one-armed Civil War veteran **John Wesley Powell**, whose expeditions along the fearsome and uncharted Colorado, in 1869 and 1871–72 – see p.441 – captured public imagination.

As the Grand Canyon was being recognized as the most extraordinary natural wonder in the US, American settlers arrived in the vicinity in ever greater numbers. Tensions have arisen ever since between this new permanent population, determined to survive in such an unforgiving environment, and visitors hoping to find unspoiled wilderness. Broadly speaking, **logging** and **grazing** interests have retained control of the plateau forests, while in the canyon itself most attempts at **mining** were defeated by the difficulty of the terrain, and **tourism** soon proved a far more lucrative proposition.

When the **railroad** first crossed northern Arizona in 1882, visitors were taken by stagecoach from the nearest station to the Grand Canyon, at **Peach Springs**, to stay at the *Diamond Creek Hotel* by the river. With the growth of the timber towns to the east, that soon declined; by the 1890s, **Flagstaff** was the main terminus, connected with the canyon by three weekly stages. The railroad reached the canyon itself, via a branch line from **Williams**, in September 1901. That triggered the growth of **Grand Canyon Village**, built under the auspices of the Fred Harvey Company, a subsidiary of the Santa Fe Railroad, and dependent on water carried in 120 miles by rail from Del Rio. The company's grand *El Tovar Hotel* – still the showpiece canyon-edge lodging – opened in January 1905, and its early marketing strategies influence the experience of Canyon visitors to this day. Following an internal memo to "get some Indians to the Canyon at once," the Hopi House souvenir store was built, modeled on the Pueblo village of Old Oraibi (see p.534), and staffed with Hopi craftspersons. Similarly, Navajo weavers were exhorted to produce rugs to suit tourist tastes, using previously unfavored "earth" colors such as brown. Pseudo-Pueblo architecture became the dominant theme, with a single architect, Mary Jane Colter, designing such structures as Hermit's Rest (1914), the Desert View Watchtower (1932; see p.336) and *Bright Angel Lodge* (1935).

Nineteenth-century schemes to run a transcontinental railroad beside the river at the bottom of the Grand Canyon were thwarted not by the engineering problems but by the lack of towns – and therefore customers – along the way.

Late nineteenth-century proposals to create a **Grand Canyon National Park** aroused vigorous local opposition. In due course, however, naturalist **John Muir** – who had earlier championed Yosemite Valley in California, and declared the Grand Canyon to be "unearthly . . . as if you had found it after death, on some other star" – found a powerful ally in President **Theodore Roosevelt**. Only entitled to protect sites of historical, rather than geological, interest, Roosevelt used the pretext of preserving Ancestral Puebloan ruins to proclaim Grand Canyon National Monument in 1908. Having failed to persuade the Supreme Court to overrule the president, Arizonan politicians finally came round to the idea after Arizona achieved statehood in 1912. Even then, by the time the boundaries of the

Grand Canyon National Park were fixed in 1919, they had trimmed away large tracts of grazing land. The new park covered around 1000 square miles, and included just 56 miles of the actual canyon.

Since 1890, **Ralph Cameron** had been accumulating bogus mining claims along the South Rim, which enabled him to charge a toll of $1 to use the Bright Angel Trail. In 1905, he built his own hotel alongside the railroad terminal, thereby forcing the Fred Harvey Company to relocate the station out of sight of the upstart rival. Cameron continued to be a thorn in the side of the new national park. Elected to the US Senate in 1920, he spent a few years hacking at its budget before his mining claims were eventually invalidated. His presence had by then spurred the development of the **Kaibab Trail**, stretching from rim to rim of the canyon by way of the Kaibab suspension footbridge (see p.340). Plans to pave the route never materialized, but a small enlargement of the park in 1927 permitted the construction of a road east to Desert View, which with the completion in 1928 of the Navajo Bridge across Marble Canyon reduced the previous 600-mile drive between the rims to a more feasible 215 miles.

In the early years of the national park, the role of the park system in protecting the environment had yet to be defined, and techniques of **wildlife** management were in their infancy. Bitter rivalry over grazing lands pitted the park service against the forest service, while the decision to eliminate mountain lions on the North Rim during the 1920s resulted in ecological disaster. Free from predators, the deer population boomed from 4000 to 100,000, stripped the Kaibab Plateau bare, then starved to death en masse.

The first **automobile** arrived at the Canyon in 1902, despite running out of gas twenty miles short. By 1926, more visitors were coming by car than by train, and Flagstaff was once again the major point of access. Advance reservations for both mule rides and lodging have been necessary since 1938; annual visitor numbers first exceeded a million in 1956, and now run at over five million, with over 800,000 in each of June, July and August.

Green activists horrified by the damming of Glen Canyon (see p.428) forced the abandonment of proposals to dam the Colorado within the park itself during the 1960s, and commercial logging and mining were finally banned when its boundaries were redrawn and enlarged in 1975. With the exception of the Indian reservations, the Grand Canyon is now run exclusively for the benefit of visitors, though maximizing their enjoyment while minimizing their environmental impact is an all but impossible task.

The South Rim

The **South Rim** of the Grand Canyon is separated from the I-17 interstate by the sixty-mile expanse of **Coconino Plateau**, which is covered by the largest **ponderosa pine forest** in the world. Crossing this undramatic landscape, you get no sense of the impending abyss until you reach the very edge of the canyon.

In September 2000, the process of denying private vehicles access to the rim began. The park service's ultimate goal is to oblige all visitors to see the South Rim using a new integrated system of **light rail** and **shuttle buses**. However, at the time this book went to press, it was impossible to predict when these changes would be fully implemented. While you can assume that you won't be able to drive at will through the park, be sure to contact the park service in advance for the latest information (☎520/638-7888; *www.nps.gov/grca*) if you need to plan your visit in great detail.

The basic plan is that all drivers except those with overnight accommodation reservations in the rim-edge **Grand Canyon Village** (whether in a lodge or a campground) will be required to leave their cars at the **Grand Canyon Transit Center at Tusayan**, just outside the park boundary six miles south. From there, they'll be ferried by rail on the seven-minute journey up to the new **Canyon View Information Plaza**, a mile or so east of Grand Canyon Village near Mather Point, which serves as the park headquarters and visitor center. Your first glimpse of the canyon will therefore almost certainly come from one of the **overlooks** on the rim-edge pathway just beyond.

To the west, the central area of Grand Canyon Village holds the park's main concentrations of lodges, restaurants and stores, as well as its own light rail station, the **Village Transit Center**. In addition to further canyon panoramas visible from the village itself, the eight-mile **West Rim Drive** and 23-mile **East Rim Drive** offer countless differing vantage points. **Hiking trails** set off down into the canyon from trailheads scattered along the way.

Getting to the South Rim

The vast majority of visitors make their own way to Tusayan via either **Williams** (52 miles south; see p.310) or **Flagstaff** (75 miles southeast; see p.283), both on I-40. Flagstaff is served by Amtrak trains, while a separate **rail** service connects Williams with the canyon itself. If you're traveling by **road**, AZ-64 from Williams, also known as the Bushmaster Memorial Highway, joins US-180 from Flagstaff at **Valle**, thirty miles south of the canyon itself. The route from Flagstaff, by way of the San Francisco Peaks (see p.289), is the more scenic of the two, and it's also the one followed by most commercial **buses**.

It's also possible to drive to Grand Canyon Village from the east, by turning onto AZ-64 from US-89 at Cameron, (see p.349), while there are direct **flights** to Tusayan from Las Vegas and other points in the Southwest.

By train

Amtrak services from Chicago and points east arrive at Flagstaff at 8.43pm daily, and from Los Angeles at 5.46am daily. **Bus** connections are detailed below.

The restored **steam trains** of the **Grand Canyon Railway** (☎520/773-1976 or 1-800/THE-TRAIN; *www.thetrain.com*) run for 64 miles from **Williams** to the picturesque station at Grand Canyon Village. Most of that route is through the forest, however, so it has few scenic delights to offer. As visitors start to appreciate that they're no longer able to drive all the way to the rim itself, it's anticipated that rail services from Williams will become more frequent. For the moment, though, in **February**, the train runs on Friday, Saturday and Sunday; in **March** it runs from Wednesday to Sunday; from **late March until October** it's daily; in **November** it reverts to Friday, Saturday and Sunday; and in **December** it runs on Saturday and Sunday only, except for the week from December 26 until January 1, when it's daily again. Services leave Williams at 9.30am, arriving at Grand Canyon Village at 11.45am, and Grand Canyon Village at 3.15pm to arrive back in Williams at 5.30pm. The standard round trip costs **$50** for adults, $25 for ages two to sixteen, but there are also two higher classes of service; club costs $20 extra, first class $50 extra. Note that Amtrak passes are not accepted.

By bus

Nava-Hopi **buses** (☎520/774-5003 or 1-800/892-8687) run twice daily between **Flagstaff** (departing from both the Amtrak station and the nearby Nava-Hopi terminal at 114 W Route 66) and the Village Transit Center in Grand Canyon Village. The first leaves Flagstaff at 7.30am, calls at **Williams** at 8.20am, and arrives at the canyon at 9.45am; the second runs straight from Flagstaff to the canyon, departing at 2.30pm and arriving 4.30pm. Return trips leave the Village Transit Center at 10.30am – a direct service to Flagstaff, arriving at 12.15pm – and 5pm, reaching Williams at 6.15pm and Flagstaff at 6.50pm. The fare to and from Flagstaff is $12.50 one way, $25 round-trip; for Williams it's $9 and $18; and under-sixteens travel half price.

Nava-Hopi also operate **one-day tours** to the Canyon from Flagstaff, costing $38 (under-16s $19) for a bus-only tour, and $64 (under-16s $32) for a combined bus–train tour.

By air

The small **airport** at Tusayan – just outside the park boundary, and used primarily by "flight-seeing" tour companies (see box, p.327) – also welcomes scheduled services, especially from **Las Vegas**. Unlike the tours, these flights do not pass directly above the park, but they still give good views, and can cost as little as $60 one-way, or $100 for a day-trip.

The South Rim

A full account of the town of Williams appears on p.310.

These bus schedules are liable to change to fit in with the park's new transportation system; call to confirm. For more on Flagstaff, including details of car rental outlets, see p.283.

For taxi service in and around Grand Canyon Village, call ☎520/638-2822.

GRAND CANYON TOURS

FRED HARVEY

For details of, and reservations for the tours below, run by the Fred Harvey Company, contact the "transportation desks" in the lodges, or call ☎520/638-2631 ext 6015, or 303/297-2757.

Park Bus Tours

Desert View 3hr 45min rim tour east of the village (3 daily, including a sunset tour; $24.50, under-16s free).
Hermit's Rest 2hr rim tour west of the village (3 daily; $13.50, under-16s free).

Sunrise and Sunset Tours 1hr 30min tour to watch the sun rise or set near Yavapai Point (late April to Sept only, 2 daily; $10, under-16s free).

Horse Riding

Apache Stables (☎520/638-2891), based at *Moqui Lodge*, charges $25 for a 1hr **trail ride** through the Kaibab Forest, and $40 for 2hr, and in the evening offers **campfire rides** on horseback for $30, or by wagon for $8.50. To see the canyon itself, you have to take the 4hr **East Rim ride**, costing $65.

Smooth-Water Rafting

Good-value full-day excursion, including an 8hr round trip to Marble Canyon by bus, plus 4hr floating through the spectacular gorge on an inflatable raft, with a picnic lunch. Probably your only chance of a trip along the river at short notice (April–Oct daily .7am from *Maswik Lodge*; $86, under-12s $50).

Long-distance Bus Tours

Ancient Ones 10–11hr bus tour to Flagstaff and nearby national monuments (1 daily; $80, under-12s $50).
Monument Valley All-day, 360-mile excursion, available year-round; 11–13hr in off-road vehicle ($80, under-12s $50), or 6hr

30min with flight and ground tour ($245 per person).
Railroad Express Round-trip excursion to Williams, by bus one way and on the Grand Canyon Railway the other (2 daily; $40, under-17s $20).

Mule Rides

Mule rides down the Bright Angel Trail tend to be reserved up to a year in advance. A one-day round trip to Plateau Point, including lunch, costs $107; the round trip to *Phantom Ranch*, beside the river, takes a full day in each direction. A one-night trip, including cabin accommodation and all meals, costs $295 for one person, $524 for two persons; two-night trips, available mid-November to March only, cost $410 for one, $686 for two. For more on *Phantom Ranch*, see p.340.

GRAND CANYON FIELD INSTITUTE

*The Web site
for The Grand
Canyon Field
Institute is
www.grand
canyon.org/
fieldinstitute/*

Between April and November each year, the Grand Canyon Field Institute (PO Box 399, Grand Canyon, AZ 86023; ☎520/638-2485, fax 638-2484), co-sponsored by the Grand Canyon Association and the National Park Service, offers an extensive program of guided tours and hikes in and around the canyon. Different tours, some restricted to women only, specialize in geology, history, natural history, photography and wilderness techniques, among other topics. Some involve camping and backpacking, others include lodge accommodation; all are graded according to the difficulty of any hiking involved. A four-day backpacking tour costs around $275.

FLIGHT-SEEING TOURS

Controversy has surrounded air tours of the Grand Canyon in recent years. An alarming safety record has led to a ban on all flying below rim level, while restrictions on the total number of overflights are being introduced to limit the barrage of noise within the park. Nonetheless, for many visitors such flights remain the highlight of their trip. Prices range from $65 ($30 child) for 30min in an airplane, or $95 ($70 child) for 30min in a helicopter, up to as long as you like for as much as you've got; all are subject to an additional $6 Federal Airspace Fee. All the operators below are based in Tusayan, though some helicopter companies take off from their own landing fields rather than using the airport proper.

Air Grand Canyon; ☎520/638-2686 or 1-800/247-4726.
AirStar Airlines; ☎520/638-2139 or 1-800/962-3869.
AirStar Helicopters; ☎520/638-2622.

Grand Canyon Airlines; ☎520/638-2463.
Kenai Helicopters; ☎520/638-2764 or 1-800/541-4537.
Papillon Grand Canyon Helicopters; ☎520/638-2419.

Papillon also run excursions to the Havasupai reservation; see p.342.

WHITEWATER RAFTING

As the park service only allows around twenty thousand people to float through the canyon of the Colorado River each year, and there's a waiting list of almost ten years for permission to do so in your own boat, places on commercial whitewater rafting trips tend to be reserved as much as a year in advance. These vary in length from three days to three weeks, with the main choice being whether to cut the 300-mile voyage from Lees Ferry to Diamond Creek in half by leaving or joining the expedition at *Phantom Ranch*. An estimated 161 sets of rapids interrupt the full route.

Lobbyists for the industry have so far defeated park plans to ban motorized rafts, so you can also choose between a quieter, slower oar-powered trip or a motorized expedition; both tend to cost around $220 per person, per day. In addition to the operators listed below, virtually all of whom offer trips of both kinds and of varying lengths, the tribal-run Hualapai River Runners (☎520/769-2219 or 1-800/622-4409) arrange one- or two-day Colorado float trips on the Hualapai Reservation, starting at Diamond Creek.

Aramark-Wilderness River Adventures; ☎520/645-3296 or 1-800/992-8022.
Arizona River Runners; ☎602/867-4866 or 1-800/477-7238.
Canyon Explorations; ☎520/774-4559 or 1-800/654-0723.
Canyoneers; ☎520/526-0924 or 1-800/525-0924.
Diamond River Adventures; ☎520/645-8866 or 1-800/343-3121.

Grand Canyon Expeditions; ☎435/644-2691 or 1-800/544-2691.
Moki Mac River Expeditions; ☎801/268-6667 or 1-800/284-7280.
Outdoors Unlimited; ☎520/526-4546 or 1-800/637-7238.
Tour West; ☎801/225-0755 or 1-800/453-9107.
Western River Expeditions; ☎801/942-6669 or 1-800/453-7450.

All the white-water rafting operators listed in this box can be accessed on the Internet via links at www.the canyon.com/ river.htm.

The South Rim

The major Vegas operator is Scenic Airlines (☎702/739-1900 or 1-800/634-6801), which also offers day-trips from Las Vegas that include a half-hour Papillon Helicopters flight for $269 per person (under-12s $230). Others include Air Vegas (☎1-800/255-7474) and Eagle Canyon Airlines (☎1-800/446-4584).

Arrival and Information

Canyon View Information Plaza, set slightly back from the rim near Mather Point, a mile or so east of the center of Grand Canyon Village, serves as the main park headquarters and **visitor center** (daily 8am–8pm; ☎520/638-7888). As well as providing up-to-date information on the park's intricate network of trains and shuttle buses, the ultrapatient rangers are happy to advise on how to make the most of your visit, and hand out free brochures and details of an extensive program of **talks** and ranger-led **tours**. They also rent out **bicycles** for use on the 45-mile **Greenway Trail**, which follows the rim edge both east and west.

For details of the Backcountry Office, which issues permits for backpacking and camping in the canyon, see box, p.337.

Further information desks, with similar hours, operate at Kolb Studio, Yavapai Observation Station (see p.333), Tusayan Museum (see p.335), and Desert View (see p.336).

Most of these places, as well as several of the lodges and souvenir stores, sell a wide range of **books** about the canyon, including invaluable guides to the various hiking trails. None of the free **maps** on

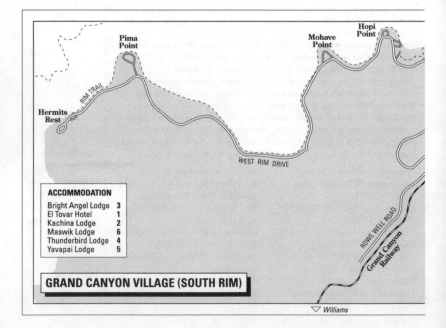

ACCOMMODATION

Bright Angel Lodge   3
El Tovar Hotel   1
Kachina Lodge   2
Maswik Lodge   6
Thunderbird Lodge   4
Yavapai Lodge   5

GRAND CANYON VILLAGE (SOUTH RIM)

▽ Williams

offer is adequate for backcountry hiking, so invest in the detailed hiking maps produced by Earthwalk Press ($3.95) or Trails Illustrated ($8.95). Canyon-related books and maps can be ordered from the Grand Canyon Association, PO Box 399, Grand Canyon, AZ 86023 (☎1-800/858-2808, fax 520/638-2484).

For free copies of the information-packed **newspapers**, *The Guide* and the *Trip Planner*, write to Grand Canyon National Park, PO Box 129, Grand Canyon, AZ 86023; the park also has an **Internet** homepage: *www.nps.gov/grca*.

Grand Canyon Village

For the century following the arrival of the railroad in 1901, **GRAND CANYON VILLAGE** was the main center for tourism at the South Rim. If you only have the time for a fleeting visit, though, it makes little difference these days whether you see Grand Canyon Village at all. Oddly enough, it's not an especially good vantage point from which to admire the canyon itself. Because it's set at the inward end of a vast curved recess, with long rocky promontories reaching out to either side, you won't be able to see any distance to the east or west. Neither will you see the Colorado itself, as it's buried too deep within the Inner Gorge. Nonetheless, a paved, railed **terrace** follows the rim for the length of the village. Far below, the Bright Angel Trail can clearly be seen as it heads out to Plateau

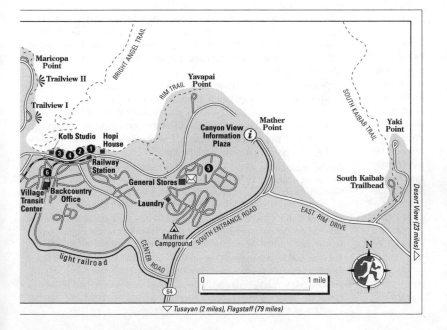

The South Rim

Point (see p.338), while at night you can usually pick out the few lights over on the North Rim.

Whether most visitors will continue to come to the village after their initial stop at the new information plaza remains to be seen. Certainly it still holds all the South Rim's in-park facilities for overnight visitors, and access is easy enough. The village has its own light rail station – the **Village Transit Center**, alongside *Maswik Lodge* – with direct connections to both Tusayan and the information plaza, and is served by shuttle buses as well.

The original early twentieth-century core of Grand Canyon Village, consisting of self-consciously rugged log-and-boulder buildings such as the *El Tovar* hotel and the Kolb photographic studio, has since been joined by a plethora of less attractive but stylistically similar structures, and the whole place is carefully laid out to avoid seeming too crowded. Tucked away in the woods across the road, well back from the canyon, lie several more lodges, stores, restaurants, and the campground, together with the well-hidden residential area used by park employees.

The closest youth hostels to the park are in Flagstaff (see p.285) and outside Williams (see p.311).

As explained on p.15, accommodation prices, excluding taxes, are indicated throughout this book by the following symbols:
① *up to $30*
② *$30–45*
③ *$45–60*
④ *$60–80*
⑤ *$80–100*
⑥ *$100–130*
⑦ *$130–175*
⑧ *$175–250*
⑨ *$250+*

Accommodation

Unless you're prepared to spend well over $150 for a deluxe room at the *El Tovar*, or $100 for a rim-side cabin at the *Bright Angel*, the **accommodation** available in Grand Canyon Village is not all that special. Neither does the village itself make a very stimulating place to spend the night. However, the Fred Harvey-run "lodges" are not bad value, and since prices in **Tusayan** (see p.332) and **Valle** (p.333) are much the same, there's no cheaper accommodation within sixty miles. If you are stuck, other possibilities include **Cameron** (see p.349), **Flagstaff** (p.284), and **Williams** (p.310).

Remember that staying in a lodge or campground in Grand Canyon Village entitles you to drive your own vehicle to your accommodation, but not to take pleasure jaunts along the South Rim. As for seeing the canyon, it makes little difference where in the village you stay. Even in the "rim-edge" places, few rooms offer much of a view, and in any case it's always dark by 8pm.

Bright Angel Lodge. Individual "rustic" but comfortable log cabins, clustered around an imposing 1935 lodge that also holds some more basic rooms. Its fireplace displays all the principal types of rock found in the Grand Canyon, in the correct chronological sequence. Rooms ④, rim-side cabins ⑤.

El Tovar Hotel. Canyon-edge hotel, named for an early Spanish explorer, that still displays the same combination of rough-hewn charm and elegant sophistication that made it the very peak of fashion when it opened in 1905. ⑥.

Kachina Lodge. Anonymous but perfectly adequate rooms in newer block, near the rim and run in conjunction with *El Tovar Hotel*. ⑥.

Maswik Lodge. Larger complex, a few minutes' walk from the rim at the west end of the village. A wide range of rooms, plus some basic summer-only cabins, some of which can sleep up to four guests. ④.

> All in-park **accommodation reservations**, including those for *Phantom Ranch* and for RV camping, are handled by Amfac Parks & Resorts, 14001 East Iliff, #600, Aurora, CO 80014 (same-day ☎520/638-2631; advance ☎303/297-2757, fax 303/297-3175; *www.amfac.com*). The best rooms are often booked as much as a year in advance, and your chances of turning up without a reservation and finding a place in summer are minimal.

The South Rim

For details of staying at Phantom Ranch, *at the bottom of the canyon, see* p.340.

Thunderbird Lodge. Long, low, boxlike lodge that shares the lobby of, and is run with, *Bright Angel Lodge*. Well-equipped if characterless rooms, separated by twenty yards of grass from the canyon edge. ⑤.

Yavapai Lodge. 350 reasonable rooms in two motel-type buildings, well back from the rim in the woods near the visitor center. Open mid-March to Oct. ⑤.

Eating and drinking

There's a reasonably wide choice of places to eat in Grand Canyon Village, and the prices in the budget cafeterias are not bad considering the canyon's remoteness and lack of water. However, summer crowding can lead to endless queuing, and it's worth bringing at least some food with you. A few stores – notably Babbitt's, near *Yavapai Lodge*, which has a deli counter – sell basic supplies.

Both the *Bright Angel* and the *El Tovar* have atmospheric traditional **bars** open until 12.30am nightly, while *Maswik Lodge* has a "sports lounge" with big-screen TV.

Arizona Steakhouse, *Bright Angel Lodge*. Informal, good-quality restaurant, only a few yards from the rim but without views to speak of, and specializing in conventional meat and seafood entrees costing $15–20. No reservations accepted, so you may have to wait 2 hours or more. Dinner only, daily 4.30–10pm.

Bright Angel Restaurant, *Bright Angel Lodge*. All meals of the day, and pretty much anything you might want, from snacks and salads for under $10 to steaks at over $20. No reservations, daily 6.30am–10pm.

El Tovar, *El Tovar Hotel*; ☎520/638-2631 ext 6432. Very grand, enormously expensive dining room, looking right out over the canyon; reservations are accepted for dinner only, and tend to be grabbed days in advance. The sumptuous menu includes such unlikely desert dishes as a mixed plate of lobster, mussels and scallops. Breakfast is the most affordable option; lunch and dinner can easily cost upwards of $40 per person. Daily 6.30am–10pm.

Maswik Cafeteria, *Maswik Lodge*. Self-service fast food; breakfast for under $5, Italian and Mexican specialties later on at around $7. Daily 6am–10pm.

Yavapai Cafeteria, *Yavapai Lodge*. Large family cafeteria, with attractive glassed-in seating area, which sells burgers for around $3 and chicken dinners for more like $6. Mid-March to mid-Nov daily 6.30am–10pm.

Other in-park facilities

Bank Near *Yavapai Lodge*. Mon–Thurs 10am–3pm, Fri 10am–5pm.

Camping Equipment Can be bought or rented at Babbitt's General Store, near *Yavapai Lodge*.

Disabled Travelers Pick up the *Accessibility Guide* at the visitor center, or call ☎520/638-2631 for advice and details of wheelchair tours.

Laundromat Near *Mather Campground*; (daily: summer 6am–11pm; winter 8am–6pm).

Medical Help Call ☎911 for emergencies; ☎520/638-2551 for the village clinic; ☎520/638-2460 for the pharmacy; and ☎520/638-2395 for dentist.

Post Office Near *Yavapai Lodge* (Mon–Fri 9am–4.30pm, Sat 11am–1pm).

Tusayan

Standing a full six miles south of the canyon itself, **TUSAYAN** offers no views or atmosphere whatsoever, but it's the nearest alternative if all the park accommodations are booked up. Until it suddenly seized on Tusayan as the answer to its growing transit nightmare, the park service had always rather looked down on the place as a messy, over-commercialized sprawl. Ironically, its new role is liable to make the town even less appealing as a destination in itself, but more and more visitors are likely to start choosing to stay here rather than Grand Canyon Village. So far, its one tourist attraction is an **IMAX Theater** specializing in stomach-lurching footage of the canyon (daily: March–Oct 8.30am–8.30pm; Nov–Feb 10.30am–6.30pm; $8).

Reservations for the large *Moqui Lodge* (mid-Feb to Nov; ⑤), set back in the woods just outside the park entrance, are handled by Amfac Parks & Resorts (see box, p.331). Otherwise, most of Tusayan's **hotels** are cast from the same anonymous but reasonably pleasant mold. The most appealing is the new *Grand Hotel* (☎520/638-3333; ⑥), built in a modern style with nods to traditional park-lodge design, and home to the *Canyon Star* restaurant, while the least expensive is the plain *Seven Mile Lodge* (☎520/638-2291; ④). Alternatives include the pastel-painted *Quality Inn* (☎520/638-2673 or 1-800/221-2222; ⑤), the *Grand Canyon Squire Inn* (☎520/638-2681 or 1-800/622-6966; ⑦), the *Red Feather Lodge* (☎520/638-2414 or 1-800/538-2345; ⑥), and the *Holiday Inn Express* (☎520/638-3000; ⑦). Each has its own **restaurant**, while Tusayan also holds the self-explanatory *We Cook Pizza and Pasta* (☎520/638-2278) and *Jennifer's Coffeehouse and Bakery* (☎520/638-3433).

Finally, if even Tusayan is booked up, it's worth considering the large new *Grand Canyon Inn* at the road junction in **VALLE**, another twenty miles south (☎520/635-9203 or 1-800/635-9203; ④), which has a heated outdoor pool.

Camping

For details of backcountry camping in the park, see box, p.337.

Sites at the year-round **Mather Campground**, south of the main road through Grand Canyon Village, can be reserved up to five months in advance through BIOSPHERICS (☎1-800/365-2267), and cost $12 per night. Rangers at park service areas and visitor centers have details of daily availability both here and at the summer-only, first-come, first-served **Desert View Campground** ($10), near the look-

out 26 miles east (see p.336). Reservations for **RV hookups** at the
Trailer Village alongside *Mather Campground* are handled by
Amfac Parks & Resorts (see box on p.331), and cost $20 per night
for two people.

In addition, the forest service runs the minimally equipped, first-
come, first-served **Ten-X Campground** (May–Sept; $10 per night) in
the Kaibab National Forest, outside the park entrance near Tusayan,
and there's a commercial campground, **Camper Village** (☎520/638-
2887; some RV hookups; $15–23), in Tusayan itself. Twenty miles
further south, in **VALLE** at the junction of Hwys 64 and 180,
Flintstone's Bedrock City (mid-March to Oct; ☎520/635-2600;
some RV hookups; $12–16) has its own prehistoric theme park.

Exploring the South Rim

The fact that visits to the South Rim start these days at Canyon View
Information Plaza, at **Mather Point**, rather than in Grand Canyon
Village, doesn't mean you're missing out. In fact, the canyon panorama
that spreads out below Mather Point is more comprehensive than any
obtainable from the village. The views to the east in particular are
consistently stupendous, and it's hard to imagine a more perfect position from which to watch the **sunrise** over the canyon.

*On average,
three or four
people fall into
the Grand
Canyon each
year; the
record is ten,
of which seven
were accidents
and three sui-
cides.*

The Colorado is visible from various vantage points along the rim-
edge footpath near Mather Point. In addition, if you walk west for around
ten minutes – that is, turn left along the rim from the information plaza
– you'll come to **Yavapai Point**. From here, you can see two tiny, separate segments of the river, one of which happens to include both the suspension footbridge across the Colorado and Phantom Ranch (see
p.340). Nearby, if you can tear your eyes away from its panoramic bay
windows, the **Yavapai Observation Station** (daily 8am–6pm; free) has
illuminating displays on how the canyon may have been formed.

Continue walking along the rim beyond Yavapai Point for another
delightful half-hour, and you'll come to Grand Canyon Village. The
easiest way to get there from Mather Point, however, is by bus or
light rail from the information plaza.

The **West** and **East Rim Drives** extend along the South Rim for
several miles in either direction from the information plaza and
Grand Canyon Village, paralleled by the paved **Greenway Trail** on
the very lip of the canyon. No one overlook can be said to be the
"best," but there are far too many to stop at them all. Obvious short
walks include an excursion to see the **sunset**, which is particularly
magical at Hopi Point, to the west.

The West Rim

Though the West Rim is closed to private vehicles, walking makes an
easy, pleasant alternative to the shuttle buses listed in the box overleaf. The four-mile round-trip from the village to Hopi Point, for
example, takes under two hours.

The first two viewpoints along the way, known as **Trailview I** and
II, let prospective Bright Angel Trail hikers (see p.338) see exactly
what they're in for, with its red-dirt switchbacks clearly etched
against the canyon walls below. After just over a mile, as you round
the corner to pass out of sight of Grand Canyon Village, the railed,
rocky overlook at **Maricopa Point** commands an almost 360° view,
though only the tiniest sliver of the churning Colorado is visible.
This is a prime spot for identifying the majestic buttes on the far
side of the river, such as the Brahma and Zoroaster "temples," each
with its capping layer of hard red-sandstone. It's also easy to see
from here why Bright Angel Canyon, cutting deeply in from the
north, provides the best hiking route to the river from the North Rim
(see p.352).

Beyond Maricopa, road and trail alike detour inland around a high
fence, festooned with solemn radiation warnings. In the heart of this
enclosure stands the hulking headframe of the **Orphan Mine**, which
started out mining copper in 1893 but became America's largest uranium producer in the 1950s. Production stopped in 1969, and the
mine was acquired by the park in 1988. However, there are still sig-

*For more on
John Wesley
Powell, see
p.44.*

nificant uranium deposits in the vicinity, located by no coincidence
at all in areas that remain outside the protection of the park. At the
far end, **Powell Point** marks the spot where the park was officially
dedicated on April 30, 1920, and holds a memorial to the crews of
John Wesley Powell's two Colorado expeditions.

Beneath the curved terrace at **Hopi Point**, two miles out from the
village, several distinct stretches of the Colorado are exposed to
view. The most dramatic lies immediately below Plateau Point (see
p.338), the last few yards of the trail to which are also visible. It's
hard to believe that the river is 350 feet wide down there, lying at the

---

PARK SHUTTLE SERVICES

The park's system of free shuttle buses was due to be greatly expanded as
this book went to press. At the time of writing, however, three routes were
in operation.

West Rim Loop
Runs between Canyon View Information Plaza and Hermit's Rest, ten miles
west, starting an hour before sunrise and stopping an hour after sunset.
Every 10min between 7.30am and sunset, every 30min otherwise.

Village Loop
Loops around all Grand Canyon Village hotels and campgrounds, and out
to Canyon View Information Plaza. Every 30min from one hour before sunrise until 6.30am, and every 10min between 6.30am and 10.30pm. The full
loop takes 50min.

Yaki Point/South Kaibab Loop
The only way to reach Yaki Point and the start of the South Kaibab Trail,
running from Canyon View Information Plaza every 30min from an hour
before sunrise until an hour after sunset.

---

foot of gnarled and impossibly ancient walls of black schist, streaked through with vertical pink faults.

By the time you reach **Mohave Point**, another three-quarters of a mile along, huge views have opened up to the west. The river threads its tortuous way towards the ocean between interleaved spurs of red rock, and a maze of lesser canyons twists among the mighty buttes.

Pima Point is four miles further on, beyond another sheer-walled recess known as The Abyss. The river is by now less than two miles from the South Rim – look almost straight down to admire the three-quarter-mile Granite Rapids – but from the far bank it's another twelve labyrinthine miles to the North Rim.

The West Rim Drive ends one mile down the road, at **Hermit's Rest**, where you'll find a small, summer-only snackbar and the trail-head for the rudimentary Hermit Trail (see p.342).

The East Rim Drive

While it's still possible to drive along the 23-mile **East Rim Drive**, which runs east from the information plaza, all the parking lots (with the exception of Desert View at the far end) are now open to shuttle and tour buses only. In order to appreciate the equally dramatic viewpoints located on or just off the route, therefore, you'll need to stay away from your vehicle a little longer.

The first of these, **Yaki Point**, commands prospects of several inner canyon hiking routes, including the South Kaibab Trail, which can be spotted switchbacking down an exposed scree slope of red rock between two buttes, far below – a long way from its trailhead near the parking lot (see p.341). Across the canyon, Vishnu Temple is silhouetted against the skyline, while the Watchtower at Desert View (see overleaf) stands stark on its promontory almost fifteen miles east.

Grandview Point, nine miles out from the village, is thought to have been where Europeans first saw the Grand Canyon, in 1540 (see p.320). For the ten years after 1895, the *Grandview Hotel*, a mile or so from the existing overlook, was a major tourist destination. Long views both east and west make this in many ways a better site than Grand Canyon Village, but the railroad swiftly drove the hotel out of business, and little trace of it now remains.

Tusayan Ruin, ten miles further east, in the forest just south of the highway (and not to be confused with modern Tusayan), is an open-air archeological site that centers on the remains of a genuine **Ancestral Puebloan pueblo**. One of two thousand such sites so far identified in the Grand Canyon area, it may not be comparable in scale to relics found elsewhere in the Southwest, but its very existence enabled President Teddy Roosevelt to accord National Monument status to the entire Grand Canyon (see p.322). Only low stone walls survive of the original complex of buildings, thought to have been occupied for perhaps 25 years by a group of up to thirty

*For more on
the Ancestral
Puebloans –
and an expla-
nation of why
the term
"Anasazi" is no
longer in com-
mon usage –
see p.520.*

people, around 1185 AD. A small museum (daily 9am–5pm; free), staffed by park rangers, holds displays on the contemporary Navajo and Hopi peoples, as well as 4000-year-old twig figurines and Ancestral Puebloan pottery found nearby.

Desert View, 23 miles out from the village and three miles east of Tusayan Ruin, is the highest point on the South Rim at 7500 feet. That's still lower than the North Rim, but as you look across you at least get a real sense of the tree-covered plateau on the far side. Down in the canyon, the Colorado River can be seen four miles away, flowing in from the north and just about to make its sudden westward turn, at the point where the "stream piracy" described on p.321 may have taken place. Just north of the last visible curve lies the confluence of the Colorado and Little Colorado rivers. A little further up the Little Colorado River from here lies the legendary *sipapu*, the hole through which the Hopi believe that human beings first entered this, the Third World (see p.534). You won't find this natural dome, topped by a permanent spring, marked on any map; only the Hopi are allowed access, or even know where it is.

Groups of tarantulas are often seen in the evenings at Desert View, scuttling back into the warmth of the canyon for the night.

The flat summit of **Cedar Mountain**, perched above the rim just east of Desert View, marks the original, pre-erosion ground level of this entire vast landscape. Beyond it, the north wall of the Little Colorado Canyon, running east, is the one stark break in the endless flatlands of the Navajo Nation, which stretch right to the horizon. Ninety miles northeast, beyond the Vermillion and Echo Cliffs, lies the gray bulk of Navajo Mountain.

The road east of Desert View, to Cameron and beyond, is described on p.349 onwards.

Desert View has its own small information center (daily 9am–6pm), but the odd-looking cylindrical construction on the very lip of the canyon is **Desert View Watchtower**, built for Fred Harvey by Mary Jane Colter in 1932. Beneath the Ancestral Puebloan-style masonry exterior it's held together by a solid framework of steel and cement, but it's still attractive, and well worth visiting. Pay 25¢ at the turnstile in the gift store at its base (daily 8am–7pm) to climb through three successive circular chambers, decorated with authentic murals by the Hopi artist Fred Kabotie, as well as reproduction petroglyphs.

South Rim hikes; into the canyon

Hiking any of the trails that descend into the Grand Canyon offers something more than just another view of the same thing. Instead you pass through a sequence of utterly different landscapes, each with its own distinct climate, wildlife and topography. However, while the canyon can offer a wonderful wilderness experience, it's essential to remember that it can be a hostile and very unforgiving environment, grueling even for expert hikers.

More detailed advice on desert hiking can be found on p.23 of Basics.

Park rangers have one simple message for all would-be hikers: **don't try to hike to the river and back in one day.** It might not look far on the map, but it's harder than running a marathon. Up to fifteen

Biosphere 2, AZ

Sedona, AZ

Blue Mesas, Petrified Forest National Park, AZ

San Xavier del Bac Mission, AZ

Havasupai Indian Reservation, AZ

Grand Canyon, AZ

Saguaro cactus, AZ

Zion National Park, UT

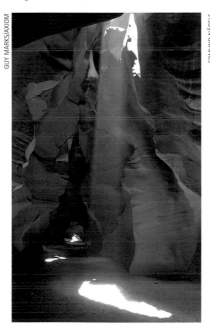

Antelope Canyon, AZ

Double Arch, Arches National Park, UT

Las Vegas, NV

Las Vegas, NV

Bryce Canyon National Park, UT

hikers each year die in the attempt, and several hundred more receive emergency medical treatment. If you do want to reach the Colorado, it's best to reserve campgrounds for two nights, so you have a day to recover before the trek out.

The South Rim is 7000 feet above sea level, an altitude which for most people is fatiguing in itself. Furthermore, all hikes start with a long, steep descent – which can come as a shock to the knees – and unless you camp overnight you'll have to climb all the way back up again when you're hotter and wearier. As a rule of thumb, keep track of how much time you spend hiking down, and allow twice that much to get back up again. Average summer temperatures inside the canyon exceed 100°F; to hike for eight hours in that sort of heat, you have to drink an incredible thirty pints of water. Always carry at least a quart per person, and much more if there are no water sources along your chosen trail. You must have food as well, as drinking large quantities without also eating can cause water intoxication.

Several trails lead into the canyon from the South Rim, but most either start from inaccessible places or are in poor condition. Traffic is heaviest on the **Bright Angel** and **South Kaibab** trails, the two "Corridor Trails" that link up in the gorge to lead to *Phantom Ranch*, and can be combined with the North Kaibab Trail to form a continuous route between the South and North rims. These trails also offer the best **day-hikes** in the canyon; down the Bright Angel Trail as far as **Indian Garden**, or at most out to **Plateau Point**, and down the South Kaibab Trail to **Cedar Ridge**.

The South Rim

The best seasons to hike in the Grand Canyon are spring and fall.

In summer, Trans Canyon Shuttle (☎520/638-2820) operate shuttle buses between the South and North rims.

Backcountry camping

To camp overnight below the canyon rim, or at undeveloped campsites on the rim, you must have a **permit** issued by the **Backcountry Office**, in the Maswik Transportation Center near Grand Canyon Village's *Maswik Lodge* (daily 8am–noon & 1–5pm; ☎520/638-7875). Each permit costs $20 for the entire party, with an additional charge of $4 per person per night; numbers are restricted, so approximately one in every three applications is turned down. If you put your name down as soon as you arrive at the canyon there's a chance of getting a cancellation, but it's best to reserve as far in advance as possible. Guests with reservations at *Phantom Ranch* do not need permits; anyone else found in the canyon without a permit is subject to a heavy fine.

Mailed applications (Backcountry Office, PO Box 129, Grand Canyon, AZ 86023) are accepted for dates until the end of the fourth month following the date of the postmark; thus in January you can apply for nothing later than the end of May. Telephone applications are not accepted, and all applications have to specify the number in your party, its leader, and an exact itinerary with named campgrounds; alternative dates and routes can be suggested. The office has full lists of campgrounds; much the most popular are the three along the rim-to-rim "Corridor Trails" – *Indian Garden* on the Bright Angel Trail, *Bright Angel Campground* near the river, and *Cottonwood Campground* on the North Kaibab Trail.

Note that overnight hikers are allowed to **drive** to, and leave their vehicles at, certain East Rim trailheads, including those for the Grandview, Hance and Tanner trails (the latter two of which are not detailed in this book). Day-hikers can either cycle, ride the park shuttle buses, or use a taxi (☎520/638-2631).

The Bright Angel Trail

The **Bright Angel Trail**, followed on foot or mule by thousands of visitors each year, starts in Grand Canyon Village, alongside the wooden shack that once served as the Kolb photographic studio. An old Havasupai route, it was improved by miners a century ago, and then operated as a toll trail when the mines failed to prosper.

Although the side canyon immediately below the village makes access to the Tonto Platform relatively straightforward, it's still a long, hard climb. Most **day-hikers** content themselves with walking to either of the two resthouses in the first three miles, but with an early start you should be able to manage the round trip of nine miles to Indian Garden, or even twelve miles to Plateau Point. In summer, you can obtain water along the trail, and only need to carry one quart of water per person; in winter, when there is none, you should carry two. Only try to reach the river – 7.8 miles from the trailhead, with *Phantom Ranch* almost two miles beyond that – if you've reserved a campsite for the night.

The trail begins with a long, exposed set of switchbacks down the dry rocky hillside, which changes in color from pale pink to sheer red. There are two short tunnels in its first mile. After another mile, you start to see more wildlife around – deer, rodents and the ubiquitous ravens – while rock surfaces at various points along the way hold a few pictographs, all but obscured by graffiti. Basic **resthouses**, built in the 1930s, are located after 1.6 and 3.1 miles. Both have water in summer (mid-May to Sept) and emergency phones, but only the 1.6-mile one has restrooms.

Beyond the second resthouse, a set of switchbacks known as **Jacob's Ladder** carry you down the sheer Redwall cliff, a major obstacle throughout almost the entire canyon. Then, finally, the trail starts to level out, and the vegetation gets greener, with a scattering of yellow- and red-blossomed cacti to either side. Soon you hear the astonishing sound of trickling water in Garden Creek, lined by dazzling green trees.

The spring at **Indian Garden**, 4.6 miles from the rim, is the reason this trail exists. Native peoples really did have a garden here, originally planted in prehistoric times and continuously used by the Havasupai from around 1300 AD until the nineteenth century. Now this unexpected little oasis holds a ranger station, restrooms, separate camping and day-use areas, and a staging post for mules.

Plateau Point

From Indian Garden, the Bright Angel Trail continues to the river (see p.340) while the **Tonto Trail** runs both east and west along the

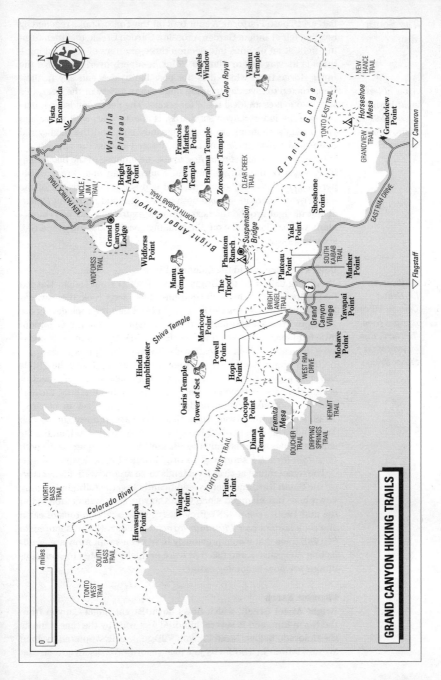

GRAND CANYON HIKING TRAILS

N

Vista
Encantada

Angels
Window

Cape Royal

Vishnu
Temple

NEW
HANCE
TRAIL

*Walhalla
Plateau*

Francois
Matthes
Point

Brahma Temple

Deva
Temple

Zoroaster Temple

Granite Gorge

Horseshoe
Mesa

Grandview
Point

TONTO EAST TRAIL

GRANDVIEW TRAIL

Bright
Angel
Point

KEN PATRICK TRAIL

UNCLE
JIM
TRAIL

CLEAR CREEK
TRAIL

NORTH KAIBAB TRAIL

Bright Angel Canyon

Shoshone
Point

EAST RIM DRIVE

Grand
Canyon Lodge

WIDFORSS TRAIL

Widforss
Point

Phantom
Ranch

Suspension
Bridge

Yaki
Point

Manu
Temple

The Tipoff

Plateau
Point

SOUTH
KAIBAB
TRAIL

Mather
Point

Shiva Temple

Maricopa
Point

*Hindu
Amphitheater*

Osiris Temple

Tower of Set

Powell
Point

Hopi
Point

BRIGHT ANGEL TRAIL

Grand
Canyon
Village

Yavapai
Point

Mohave
Point

Cocopa
Point

*Eremita
Mesa*

WEST RIM DRIVE

HERMIT
TRAIL

Diana
Temple

BOUCHER
TRAIL

DRIPPING
SPRINGS
TRAIL

TONTO WEST TRAIL

Piute
Point

Colorado River

Walapai
Point

NORTH
BASS
TRAIL

Havasupai
Point

SOUTH
BASS
TRAIL

TONTO
WEST
TRAIL

0   4 miles

▽ *Cameron*

▽ *Flagstaff*

The South Rim

Allow at least eight hours for the day-hike to Plateau Point and back.

flat, arid Tonto Platform. A spur trail off the Tonto Trail – reached by heading left at Indian Garden, crossing Garden Creek, and then turning right at an obvious intersection three-quarters of a mile along – threads its way out to **Plateau Point**, a superb overlook above the Inner Gorge from which it is not possible to descend any further. Constructed to give day-tripping mule riders a view of the river, this trail also makes an ideal route for hikers. The desert landscape, barren even by inner-canyon standards, is spectacular, with agave and yucca plants shooting up from the sandy soil, and the mighty red buttes and mesas of the canyon now framed against the blue sky.

Shortly after you get your first awesome glimpse of the black tumbling walls of the gorge, the trail comes to an end. Precariously perched on the rocky outcrops, you can see a long stretch of the dark-green Colorado, though both the bridges and *Phantom Ranch* lie out of sight around the next promontory to the east. With binoculars, you can just make out the buildings back at the top of the rim, six miles away.

Devil's Corkscrew and the Colorado River

All the water for Grand Canyon Village is piped from the North Rim, by way of the Silver Bridge.

The continuation of the Bright Angel Trail beyond Indian Garden first drops through the fertile margins of Garden Creek, then switchbacks down the **Devil's Corkscrew**, hacked into the rock during the 1930s to create a shortcut to the river. Once beside the Colorado, dwarfed beneath thousand-foot walls of dark-gray granite, it undulates through sand dunes scattered with yucca and prickly pear.

Hikers can cross the river around a mile along, using the 1960s **Silver Bridge**; mules, which quite sensibly balk at the prospect of seeing the river between its slats, have to continue a little further. The 400-foot **suspension bridge** they prefer was set in place in 1928, hanging from twin cables that were carried down the Kaibab Trail on the shoulders of 42 Havasupai. Close to the bank on the far side are the mule corral and Bright Angel Campground, with *Phantom Ranch* a short way up Bright Angel Creek beyond.

The temperature at river level tends to be around 20°F higher than on the South Rim, and there's significantly less rainfall. The **ecology** down here has changed since Glen Canyon Dam was completed in the mid-1960s (see p.428). Previously, up to a million tons of earth and rock hurtled past *Phantom Ranch* each day. Now it's more like 80,000; trees that would previously have been swept away are establishing themselves, and fish that were perfectly adapted to such conditions are now becoming extinct.

Phantom Ranch

Bright Angel Creek, which flows down Bright Angel Canyon from the North Rim, and is several hundred feet wide by the time it meets the Colorado below Grand Canyon Village, was first spotted by John Wesley Powell in 1869. His journals record "We discover a stream entering from the north, a clear beautiful creek coming down through a gorgeous red canyon"; he named it to contrast with the muddy Dirty Devil upriver in Utah.

Since then, the terrain just east of the confluence has been landscaped to create the welcoming glade now occupied by **Phantom Ranch**, the only accommodation option inside the canyon itself. Clustered around a central lodge, its various cabins, corrals and outbuildings stand amid huge cottonwoods and fruit orchards. These were planted early in the twentieth century, to shade *Rust's Camp*, renamed *Roosevelt's Camp* after a visit by Theodore Roosevelt in 1913. That in turn was replaced by *Phantom Ranch* itself, designed by Mary Jane Colter for the Fred Harvey Company in 1922, using uncut river stone to blend in with the surroundings.

The fully-equipped individual **cabins** at *Phantom Ranch* are reserved for the use of riders on Fred Harvey mule trips – full details, including prices, appear on p.326. In addition, there are four ten-bunk **dormitories**, intended for hikers, which cost $22 with bedding provided. Do not hike down without a reservation; even if you do have one, you must **reconfirm** before 4pm on the day before your stay, either at the *Bright Angel* transportation desk or by calling ☎520/638-3283. *Phantom Ranch* tends to be booked way in advance, but cancellations for dorm beds and, conceivably, cabins, are handed out first-come, first-served at the *Bright Angel* early each morning. Check what time they'll be opening the night before – it can be as early as 6am. All supplies reach *Phantom Ranch* the same way you do, so **meals** are expensive, a minimum of $12 for breakfast and $17 for dinner.

South Kaibab Trail

The **South Kaibab Trail**, the most direct route from the South Rim to *Phantom Ranch*, is never as busy as the Bright Angel Trail. And no wonder – taking just six miles to drop to the river, it's an even steeper haul, while the trailhead lies roughly three miles walk east of the information plaza. Set aside the time for a short day-hike, however, and you'll be rewarded by superb views.

The trail starts by descending slightly west of **Yaki Point**, but once past the end of the promontory it runs along the top of **Cedar Ridge**. This high crest surveys a thirty-mile stretch of the canyon in both directions, and also faces straight up Bright Angel Canyon towards the North Rim. In the absence of any water en route, most hikers turn back after 1.5 miles. If you keep going, down a precipitous and very exposed slope, you meet the **Tonto Trail** 4.4 miles down. A long if level trek east enables backpackers to connect with the Grandview Trail (see overleaf) but the obvious way to go is west. At a spot known as the **Tipoff**, a few hundred yards along, you're poised to plunge down into the Inner Gorge. The river, and the 1928 suspension bridge that leads to *Phantom Ranch*, are little more than a mile away.

The South Rim

Reservations for Phantom Ranch *are handled by Amfac (☎303/297-2757, fax 297-3175; www.amfac. com); see box p.331.*

An account of the North Kaibab Trail, which connects Phantom Ranch *with the North Rim, appears on p.356.*

If you're combining the Bright Angel and South Kaibab trails, the Kaibab is the one to descend.

Alternatively, continue on the Tonto Trail for four miles to **Indian Garden** (see p.338), and climb back up to the village from there.

Grandview Trail

The **Grandview Trail**, which starts from the parking lot at Grandview Point (see p.335), was built during the 1890s to aid copper mining at the Last Chance mine, out on **Horseshoe Mesa**. One of Ralph Cameron's less fictitious claims (see p.323), the Last Chance was nonetheless played out by 1907, and the trail was used by guests at the nearby hotel until that too folded in 1916.

Overnight hikers using the Grandview Trail are permitted to leave their cars at the trailhead.

Now officially an "unmaintained" trail, it's a very demanding hike, on which some of the most difficult switchbacks consist of wooden walkways pegged to the rock face. The chief appeal is to camp overnight on the mesa, three miles down, and explore (with care) the derelict mine workings, but it is possible to descend the far side to reach the Tonto Trail. Too hot and dry in summer, the Grandview Trail gets icy in winter, so the best months to come are April, May and October.

Hermit Trail

Before hiking unmaintained trails such as the Hermit, ask at the park visitor center about current conditions.

Named in honor of Louis Boucher, a nineteenth-century prospector, the **Hermit Trail** is another unmaintained trail that dates from the days when the obstreperous Ralph Cameron controlled access to most of the prime rim-edge sites (see p.323). Built in 1912 by Fred Harvey, for mule riders from the *El Tovar*, and abandoned in 1931, much of its engineering remains in good shape. Once more, it's used mainly by solitary types, setting off on long backcountry camping expeditions away from the crowds.

From the Hermit's Rest parking lot at the end of West Rim Drive (see p.335), the trail drops into a side canyon, then switchbacks into Hermit Gorge and slowly descends a high rock wall far above Hermit Creek. Rockfalls tend to make for slow progress, but eventually views of the Inner Gorge start to open up. *The Hermit Camp* **campground** is not far west of the junction with the Tonto Trail, 12.6 miles along. Turning right (north) shortly before the campground brings you to the Colorado itself, just over fourteen miles from the trailhead, at **Hermit Rapid**, where the wave-like surge of the river can reach over twenty feet high.

The Havasupai Reservation

Havasu Canyon, one of the most spellbindingly beautiful places in the entire southwest, nestles deep in the Grand Canyon a mere 35 miles west of the park headquarters. The only approach is from the east, however, so it's a road trip of almost two hundred miles; once you leave the interstate, the last ninety miles are across the endless Coconino Plateau.

Those visitors who brave the eight-mile desert hike down into the canyon are rewarded by a stunning oasis of turquoise waterfalls and lush vegetation, a Shangri-La that has been home for centuries beyond record to the same small group of Native Americans. They're here thanks to a geological fluke; although the canyon receives only nine inches of rain each year, all the water that falls for three thousand square miles around funnels down into this one narrow gorge, to create the year-round torrent of Havasu Stream.

Havasu Canyon forms the heart of the **Havasupai Reservation**, said by a 1930s anthropologist to be "the only spot in the United States where native culture has remained in anything like its pristine condition." Since then, tourism has become the mainstay of the tribal economy, but visitor numbers are kept deliberately low, at around 35,000 per year. Suggestions of building a road – or even a tramway – down into the canyon have always been rejected, to minimize the impact on the traditional way of life. Instead the five hundred or so Havasupai earn their keep by ferrying non-hikers up and down the trail on horses and pack mules, and operating a thriving **campground** beside the stream as well as a comfortable lodge in the village of **Supai**. While visitors should not expect sweeping views of the Grand Canyon itself – or to have much interaction with the tribal members – for spectacular desert scenery, and sheer romance, the Havasupai Reservation is beyond compare.

Getting to the reservation

The only way to reach the Havasupai Reservation by road is from I-40, turning off at **Seligman** if you're coming from Flagstaff or Grand Canyon Village, or at **Kingman** from Las Vegas or California. Stock up with food, water and gas when you leave the interstate, then follow AZ Hwy-66 to the poorly marked intersection with **Arrowhead Hwy-18**, six miles east of **Peach Springs**. The new *Hualapai Lodge* in Peach Springs itself (☎520/769-2230 or 1-888/255-9550; ④), makes a comfortable overnight stop if you want to make an early start on the trail.

Seligman and Kingman are described on p.312.

AZ Hwy-66 is the only surviving segment of Route 66 not to have been superseded by newer roads.

Hwy-18 runs for sixty miles with barely a building in sight, across bare sagebrush desert interrupted by patches of thick ponderosa forest. Despite maps to the contrary, it's paved throughout, and there's no possibility of losing your way. Eventually it starts to wind down through burgeoning canyonlands, coming to an end at the large plateau known as **Hualapai Hilltop**. Although this is no more than a small cluster of dilapidated shacks, there are usually far more vehicles parked here than you might anticipate for such a remote spot.

Do not set off from Hualapai Hilltop unless you have already reserved accommodation; see p.347.

Hualapai Hilltop commands a long view of the white-walled **Hualapai Canyon**, cutting into the tablelands as it stretches off to the north. The trail from the end of the parking lot zigzags steeply down the hillside to the right, and can then be seen threading its way across the valley floor below. **Hikers** are free to set off whenever

The
Havasupai
Reservation

The Havasupai

The Havasupai – the "people of the blue-green water" – can trace their occupation of Havasu Canyon back at least as far as 1300 AD. The word "Pai" means people, and refers to a Yuman-speaking group that reached the Southwest via California well over a thousand years ago. They soon quarreled, splitting to form the **Hualapai** ("Pine-clad Mountain People") of northwest Arizona, and the **Yavapai** ("Almost-People," who no longer quite deserved to be regarded as people) who settled along the Colorado further south. The Hualapai established close links with Pueblo groups such as the Hopi and Zuni, from whom they eventually acquired the art of raising sheep and horses, as well as the seeds and skills to grow imported crops such as peaches. Until the Havasupai were allocated their own reservation towards the end of the nineteenth century, they regarded themselves not as a separate "tribe" but as just another band of Hualapai.

Although the Havasupai took their name from the turquoise river that watered their fields, they only lived on the canyon floor in summer, in houses of hide-covered branches. In winter, the canyon made a cold, miserable home, lacking big game and wood for fuel and receiving as little as five hours of sunlight per day. Instead the Havasupai moved up onto the plateau to hunt deer, elk and antelope, using artificial water holes to lure them closer. Their territory extended beyond the San Francisco Peaks (near modern Flagstaff) and took in the region now occupied by Grand Canyon Village.

In the summer of 1776, as the Declaration of Independence was being signed in Philadelphia, the Havasupai welcomed their first white visitor. **Father Francisco Tomás Garcés**, a missionary from San Xavier del Bac near Tucson (see p.248), was greeted by five days of feasting. Describing the Grand Canyon as a "calaboose of cliffs and canyons," he dubbed it the Puerto de Bucareli; more enduringly, he was the first to name the Río Colorado. Meanwhile, as Garcés explored the canyon, the rest of his expedition blazed a trail to California, where they founded San Francisco.

The Havasupai then remained undisturbed for a further eighty years, before Anglo prospectors and surveyors began to enter the region. Conflict arose in 1866, when to encourage the spread of the railroads Congress granted the Atlantic and Pacific Railroad company ownership of swaths of land adjoining its tracks across northern Arizona. Native resistance soon escalated into **war**, and the defeated Hualapai spent several years confined to a reservation near Ehrenberg on the Colorado. Because the Havasupai did not participate in the fighting, they were allowed to remain in their traditional territory. In negotiations over the extent of a permanent Havasupai reservation, the US government was as usual only prepared to acknowledge Native American "ownership" of land that held permanent settlements and cultivated fields. Areas used for hunting, gathering or even grazing, especially if use was shared by more than one band, was never included in reservations. Fearful of being deported themselves,

they choose. If you prefer to **ride** down – which costs $50 per person one-way to the village, or $80 round-trip, and $110 round-trip to the campground – enquire either at the trailhead, or in the temporary cabins near the entrance to the parking lot. Riders' baggage weighing over ten pounds has to be carried separately – one animal can the Havasupai settled in 1882 for a tiny 518-acre plot at the bottom of Havasu Canyon. Restricted to a fraction of their former range, they were obliged to farm what little land they were granted as intensively as possible.

A century of hardship was to follow, during which the Havasupai repeatedly petitioned to have their reservation enlarged. Suffering great spiritual uncertainty, both the Havasupai and Hualapai took part in the **Ghost Dance** movement in the 1890s, when Native Americans throughout the West joined in trance-like rituals designed to insure that white men would vanish from the land and the old ways would return. The Havasupai also briefly adopted the rain-making *kachina* dances of the Hopi (see p.60), until a catastrophic **flood** on January 1, 1910 destroyed their village, which then stood half a mile from its current site.

At first, the creation of **Grand Canyon National Park** placed yet more restrictions on Havasupai use of traditional lands. One early supervisor avowed that the "Grand Canyon should be preserved for the everlasting pleasure and instruction of our intelligent citizens as well as those from foreign countries; I therefore deem it just and necessary to keep the wild and inappreciable Indians from off the Reserve." Although Coconino National Forest takes its name from the Hopi word for the Havasupai, tribal members could only graze animals there by annual permit. The Havasupai survived largely through disobeying whatever unenforceable regulations outsiders sought to impose, continuing to spend their winters up on the plateau. Many Havasupai in due course found jobs in Grand Canyon Village, while tourism to Havasu Canyon itself became an important element in the tribal economy.

After endless legal battles, and a lobbying campaign to persuade environmentalist groups that Native Americans could look after wilderness lands every bit as well as the Park Service, the Havasupai finally won their battle in 1975. Almost 200,000 acres were added to the reservation, the largest tract of land ever returned to Native Americans. It came only just in time; almost immediately, the Grand Canyon region experienced a boom in **uranium** mining, with over 3500 claims filed in the Arizona Strip during the ensuing decade.

In 1988, Energy Fuels Nuclear, a Denver-based corporation, was granted rights to develop a uranium mine at a sacred Havasupai site in the Kaibab National Forest, known as *Mat Taav Tijundva*. Despite fears that it could contaminate the stream, Havasu Canyon, and ultimately the Colorado itself, federal courts denied Havasupai attempts to stop the mine. Although Energy Fuels only offered to pull out in return for $50 million, the worldwide glut of uranium has forced an indefinite postponement of their plans. As that threat recedes, another grows; there are fears that the construction of Canyon Forest Village will deplete the water table for hundreds of miles around, and that Havasu Stream may finally run dry.

The
Havasupai
Reservation

carry up to four packs, again for $50 one-way, $80 round-trip – while many hikers also arrange to have their bags carried. There's a $15 surcharge for leaving the hilltop after noon, or Supai after 10am.

Helicopter flights between Hualapai Hilltop and Supai village, run by Action Helicopter of Arizona (☎520/282-7884) cost $55 each way. As a rule they're only available on Fridays and Sundays, but there's no harm in calling at other times.

Finally, it is also possible to take a helicopter to Havasupai from **Grand Canyon Village**. Papillon Grand Canyon Helicopters (☎520/638-2419; see also p.327) operate day excursions, including a horse ride to Havasu Falls but not meals, for $440 per person, and one-night trips, staying at the lodge, for $482.

The trail to Supai

Apart from its initial switchbacks, the **Hualapai Trail** is not especially difficult. It is, however, a long eight-mile walk, with no shade for the first three miles and no reliable water source until very near the end. Allow around three hours to reach the village (and four or more to come back up again), and be sure to carry all the food and water you will need for a day in the desert.

The route is very obvious, and kept busy throughout the day with small supply trains of mules and horses. Once on the valley floor, it follows the bed of a dry wash between red-rock walls that slowly but inexorably climb to form a deep, narrow canyon. The sand underfoot is so thick that it splashes at every step, but the potential for flash floods is clear from the much-scoured rocks to either side. Mighty boulders occasionally all but block the path, while solitary cottonwoods reach up towards the thin strip of sky overhead.

No one visits Havasu Canyon as a day-trip; quite apart from the drive to the hilltop, the twenty-mile hike to the falls and back takes well over ten hours.

After almost seven miles, the trail reaches the intersection where Havasu Canyon comes in from the right; until 1910, this was the site of Supai village (see below). Do not continue straight ahead into Cataract Canyon at this point – it took three weeks to find a dehydrated camper who did so in 1975. Bear left instead, at a dense cluster of small trees. The sound of rushing water soon signals the emergence of Havasu Stream from hidden crevices in the rock, and before long it's flowing through the parched landscape in all its blue-green splendor.

Not far beyond, you cross a low rise to be confronted by the meadow that holds the modern village, and the two red-rock pillars that watch over Supai from the high canyon wall on the far side. Known as the **Wigleeva**, these twin sentinels are regarded as the guardian spirits of the Havasupai.

Supai

Though located in a superb natural setting, a wide flat clearing surrounded on all sides by forbidding walls of red sandstone, the village of **SUPAI** is not in itself attractive. The Havasupai were only obliged to build a year-round settlement down in the canyon by the loss of their lands on the plateau above (see box, overleaf) and this site was their second choice after the first proved prone to flooding. It too was seriously damaged by floods in both January 1990 and February 1993, and consists of just a scattering of basic timber-frame houses and prefabricated cabins. The name itself is also a flimsy fabrication; "Supai" is a meaningless abbreviation of "Havasupai," invented by the US Post Office.

The
Havasupai
Reservation

Once the Hualapai Trail, running alongside a line of irrigation ditches, has shepherded you into the village, the first building you come to holds the tribal **registration office**. Only campers need to pay the reservation **entrance fee** here (April–Oct $15; Nov–March $12); for lodge guests, it's added to their bill. A back room holds a small **museum** (daily 7am–7pm; $1), with a random but reasonably interesting assortment of c.1900 photographs and newspaper cuttings. Although the Havasupai are famous for crafts such as basketmaking, ancient artifacts have become too expensive for the museum to afford.

The finest old Havasupai baskets to be seen in Arizona are in the Heard Museum in Phoenix; see p.223.

Fifty yards further on, beyond the only post office in the US still to receive its mail by pack mule, lies Supai's dusty, fly-blown **plaza**. Benches outside the village's one **grocery store** on the right form its main social center, where the older Havasupai gather each evening. The younger set, together with a vast population of dogs, are more likely to be found on the terrace of the **cafe**, opposite. Once past that the trail skirts the edge of the village school, then branches off left down towards the campground. Visitors are forbidden to wander away from the main trail into the farmlands around the village.

Practicalities

All visitors, whether planning to camp or stay in the lodge, should make advance reservations by calling either Havasupai Tourist Enterprises (☎520/448-2141) or the lodge. Space is at a premium in summer, and is often fully reserved several months in advance.

All prices on the Havasupai Reservation are subject to an additional five percent tribal sales tax.

Havasupai Lodge (☎520/448-2111; April–Oct ⑤, Nov–March ③), is located slightly apart from things on the edge of the village, close to the canyon wall behind the school. It's a simple two-story structure, much like a typical national park lodge, where the reasonable motel-style rooms are without phones or TVs. All sleep four people, with an $8 surcharge per additional guest.

The *Lodge* has a pleasant little garden, but the only place to get a meal in Supai is at the *Tribal Cafe* (daily 7am–6pm; ☎520/448-2981). Here the food is far from exciting, with fried breakfasts, and a lunch or dinner of beef stew, Indian fry-bread or burritos; pretty much everything seems to cost $5, or more if you want grated cheese on top. The grocery store has a limited selection of processed items, all carried in by mule and priced accordingly.

Spending a night at the **campground** – see overleaf – costs $10 per person in summer, and $9 in winter.

Below Supai

All the **waterfalls** for which the Havasupai Reservation is famous lie further down the canyon beyond Supai. Much of the riverbed immediately below the village remains cluttered with fallen trees and undergrowth deposited by the floods of 1990 and 1993, but after a mile and a half a thundering from the left betrays the presence of **Navajo Falls**. Plummeting down the far wall of the canyon, intervening trees make it hard to spot from the main trail, but hardy hikers can reach it by picking their way down below the path. Once there, clamber across a minor fork of the stream and you'll come to the foot of the falls, which tumble through a series of pools. The falls were named for Chief Navajo, who led the Havasupai at the time the reservation was first established, and died in 1900.

Havasu Falls

*A short horse-
back tour from
Supai village
down to
Havasu Falls
costs $45;
contact
Havasupai
Tourist
Enterprises –
see p.347.*

*Walking bare-
foot on the
sharp traver-
tine is not rec-
ommended.*

The trail beyond Navajo Falls – which was washed away completely in 1993, and has been reconstructed to follow a course higher up the canyon wall – soon reaches the stupendous double cascade of **Havasu Falls**. First seen from an overlook more or less level with the top, this is an absolutely breathtaking sight. The stream foams white as it hurtles over a 150-foot cliff, to crash into shallow terraces filled with limpid turquoise water. The rock formations all around are formed from water-deposited limestone known as **travertine** – the same stuff that creates the stalactites of Carlsbad Caverns, and clogs the inside of domestic kettles. It's the light travertine coating on the riverbed that gives the water its astonishing blue-green glow.

Havasu Falls used to be a long, broad expanse of water, which explains the solidified sheets and curtains of travertine that run right across its wide brim. Then a flash flood punched out a notch right in the center, through which the falls now gush to either side of a small outcrop that's knitted together by a frail cottonwood sapling. Side trails off the main path lead down to an idyllic shaded "beach" beside the largest, deepest pool, where the ceaseless roar makes conversation difficult, but swimming is all but irresistible. On the far side of the natural travertine dams that divide the various terraces – partially reconstructed after the 1993 flood, using artificial groynes that are now buried beneath new deposits – picnic tables stand in a cottonwood grove at the mouth of a side canyon.

The campground

A short distance beyond Havasu Falls, two miles down from Supai village, you finally reach the Havasu **campground**, set in an especially narrow and high-walled segment of the canyon. Although this site was once a tribal burial ground, it was only added to the reservation in 1975, having originally been considered to be too rich in mineral deposits to be left to the Indians.

The campground stretches for almost a mile, with tents pitched in clearings in the woods to either side of the stream. Facilities are primitive in the extreme, but it's a wonderful spot, with safe drinking water provided by fresh springs in the canyon wall. Villagers are barred from the area in summer, but groups of horses stand tethered at the entrance, waiting to carry campers back up the hill.

Mooney Falls and the Colorado River

Havasu campground is brought to an abrupt end by the 200-foot **Mooney Falls**. This natural barrier was long regarded as virtually impassable; it was named for an unfortunate prospector who dangled here for three days in the 1890s, after a rope snagged as he was being lowered to the bottom. As rescuers frantically tunneled through the travertine to reach him, the rope frayed and broke, and he fell to his death.

The trail to the bottom is little better today. Having scrambled down the travertine ledges to reach two successive tunnels that drop through the cliff face, you come to a sheer section that was blasted away in the flood of 1993, and now consists of a vertical series of footholds aided by an iron chain fixed into the rock.

A further set of swimming holes leads down from the bottom of the falls, while a good day-hike from the campground continues on for three miles to **Beaver Falls**. Negotiating a route beyond this quick-fire set of rapids involves climbing up to and along a high ledge, but keep going for four more miles and you'll eventually reach the Colorado itself. Quite possibly, you'll be greeted by river-runners who preferred to get here the easy way, shooting 157 miles of white water from Lees Ferry (see overleaf).

The road between the rims

In the absence of a road across the Grand Canyon, the shortest possible driving route between the South and North rims takes 215 miles, or at least four hours. From Canyon View Information Plaza, follow AZ-64 – the East Rim Drive – to meet US-89 at **Cameron**, head north to cross **Marble Canyon** on Navajo Bridge, and then double back east to **Jacob Lake** to join the 44-mile summer-only AZ-67 south to the North Rim.

Although there are very few towns along the way, the scenery is seldom less than spectacular. Beyond Desert View, AZ-64 runs close to the gorge of the **Little Colorado**; Navajo trinket stalls are dotted along the roadside and at a couple of overlooks, around ten miles west of Cameron.

Cameron

The junction of AZ-64 and US-89 is marked by the small **Cameron Visitor Center**, offering information on the Navajo Nation (June–Sept daily 8am–5pm; Oct–May Mon–Fri 8am–5pm). **CAMERON** itself, which amounts to little more than a handful of buildings, lies a mile or so north, on the south side of the suspension bridge spanning the Little Colorado River.

The **Cameron Trading Post** here, established in 1911, stocks a huge array of Southwest arts and crafts, from mass-produced trinkets and jeans to genuine Hopi *kachinas* and museum-quality Navajo rugs. While busy with tourists in summer, it remains at heart a trading center for the Navajo Nation, with some of its business still conducted by barter. Part of the main building houses a **cafeteria** serving reasonable food (daily 6am–10pm); accommodation is in the two large **motel** buildings alongside, which look out across the Little Colorado to the open desert (PO Box 339, Cameron, AZ 86020; ☎520/679-2231 or 1-800/338-7385; ④).

There's further accommodation at **GRAY MOUNTAIN**, ten miles south of Cameron, in the shape of the *Anasazi Inn* (PO Box 29100, Gray Mountain, AZ 86020; ☎520/679-2214; ④).

Marble Canyon and Navajo Bridge

Fifteen miles north of Cameron, US-160 branches off northeast via **Tuba City** (which also has motels; see p.349) towards Monument Valley and Colorado. Continuing north, after another forty miles of emptiness US-89 climbs away up the mesa to the right, heading for Page and Glen Canyon Dam (see p.433). US-89A, however, presses on at the foot of the **Echo Cliffs**, to reach **Navajo Bridge** after a further fifteen miles.

There are in fact two Navajo Bridges. The original, which opened in 1929, is now reserved for pedestrians only; a wider facsimile opened 150ft downstream in 1995. The Colorado at this point cuts through the chasm of **Marble Canyon**, such a narrow interruption in the vast flat plains that you can't tell it's there until you're right on top of it.

On the west bank of the river, *Marble Canyon Lodge* (☎520/355-2225 or 1-800/726-1789; ④) has over fifty conventional motel-style rooms, and can arrange river and fishing trips. In the atmospheric *Lodge* itself, there's a reasonable **restaurant** that's open for all meals daily, with a 6am start to meet the needs of the crowds of river-runners.

Lees Ferry

*Thanks to an
Act of
Congress,
there is no
apostrophe in
Lees Ferry.*

Before the construction of Navajo Bridge, ferries struggled across the river at **LEES FERRY**, six miles north. Mormon elder Jacob Hamblin was guided to this remote spot – the only place within hundreds of miles to offer easy land access to both banks of the Colorado – by Naraguts, a Paiute, in 1858.

Thirteen years later, **John Doyle Lee** was sent here to set up a ferry service to help Mormon missionaries en route south into Arizona. Lee was on the run after the **Mountain Meadows Massacre** in Utah in 1857, when a wagon train of would-be settlers was slaughtered by an armed white band clumsily disguised as Indians (see p.367). He remains a hero to some Mormons (a local plaque calls him "a man of good faith, sound judgment and indomitable courage"); those who have read Mark Twain's account of the massacre in *Roughing It* may disagree. He was finally arrested in 1874, and executed in 1877, but his (seventeenth) wife Emma remained here, at the place they knew as **Lonely Dell**.

The ferry service was always perilous, with the boats in constant danger of being swept downstream, and was finally abandoned after a fatal accident in June 1928. A crucial piece of equipment needed to finish the bridge on the left bank was stranded on the right bank; the only way to get it across was to take it eight hundred miles by road, via Las Vegas.

The reason you can get down to the water at Lees Ferry is because it marks the confluence of the Paria River with the Colorado; **Paria River Beach**, at the foot of the gently sloping road from Marble Canyon, is the official start of the Grand Canyon. To the south, the broad Colorado picks up speed as it squeezes into Marble Canyon. A few hundred yards north, across the Paria, you come to a large parking lot and launching ramp. This is where **whitewater rafting** expeditions set off into the Grand Canyon – the first point where boats can get out again is at Diamond Creek, twelve days away by muscle power – and Fred Harvey's smooth-water trips from Glen Canyon Dam (see p.326) come to an end. A fairly basic **campground** ($10; ☎520/355-2334) is located nearby.

From the far end of the lot, a trail leads within a couple of hundred yards to the well-preserved remains of buildings from the ferry era, built not surprisingly with slabs of red sandstone. They're interspersed with lumps of mangled machinery from a steamboat that was hauled here from San Francisco in 1911, and abandoned as a failed experiment after only five trips. It's possible to walk along the tranquil riverside for another mile or so upstream.

Lee's Lonely Dell Ranch was located on the fertile banks of the Paria, away to the west, an area that now forms part of the **Paria Canyon-Vermilion Cliffs Wilderness**. This can be explored along an extensive network of trails, including one four- to six-day epic that traces the full length of the Paria Canyon.

The Vermilion Cliffs

West of Marble Canyon, US-89A curves beneath the southernmost section of the **Vermilion Cliffs**. These soaring sandstone walls glow a magnificent red at sunrise and sunset, but the road itself is all but featureless. Only a couple of small **motels** offer any incentive to get out of your car. Both *Lees Ferry Lodge* (☎520/355-2231; ③) – three miles west of Marble Canyon, and smaller and slightly lower-priced than the *Marble Canyon Lodge* (see opposite) – and the mock-

Watch out for the awesome wingspan of the mighty Californian condor, which has recently been reintroduced to the Vermilion Cliffs.

Anasazi *Cliff Dweller's Lodge* (☎520/355-2228; summer ③, winter
②), half a dozen miles beyond, have their own stores and restaurants.

Once past the southernmost promontory of the cliffs, the highway is free to run as straight as an arrow across the broad sagebrush desert. Forty miles from the river, it hits the Kaibab
Mountains, and climbs through thick forest for the final eleven
miles to Jacob Lake.

Jacob Lake and DeMotte Park

The crossroads community of **JACOB LAKE**, deep in the pine forest 44 miles north of the North Rim, looks more like a Canadian
logging camp than anything you'd expect to find in Arizona. In
winter, when AZ-67 down to the Grand Canyon is closed by up to
140 inches of snow, Jacob Lake goes into hibernation; in summer,
however, it makes a good living from the constant stream of
tourists.

As well as a gas station and general store, the *Jacob Lake Inn*
(☎520/643-7232) offers simple **motel** rooms and log cabins (cabins
mid-May to Nov ④, Dec to mid-May ③; rooms mid-May to Nov ⑤,
Dec to mid-May ③); there are also **campgrounds** for tenters (mid-
May to mid-Oct; $10; ☎520/643-7395) and RVs (May to mid-Oct;
☎520/643-7804). The **Kaibab Plateau Visitor Center** (daily
8am–5.30pm; ☎520/643-7298) provides information on the surrounding area.

Jacob Lake is named for Jacob Hamblin, a Mormon missionary to
the Paiutes and Navajo. The Mormons made little use of the forests
to the south, however, apart from grazing their cattle in the large
meadow-like clearings that punctuate the road to the canyon. One of
these, **DEMOTTE PARK**, 27 miles from Jacob Lake, is now the site
of the *Kaibab Lodge* (☎520/638-2389 in summer, 520/526-0924
in winter, or 1-800/525-0924; ④), whose rudimentary cabins
remain open in winter for the use of cross-country skiers. The **gas
station** nearby is the last before the canyon; the park entrance is
another five miles down the road, with visitor facilities nine miles
beyond that.

The North Rim

*The exact clo-
sure dates of
the road to the
North Rim
depend on the
weather; as a
rule, it's open
mid-May to
late October.*

Higher, bleaker, and far less accessible, the **North Rim** of the Grand
Canyon receives less than a tenth as many visitors as the South Rim.
While that doesn't mean you'll have the place to yourself, it can still
make you feel as though you're venturing into unexplored wilderness. The basic principle, however, is the same as at the South Rim,
with a cluster of venerable park-service buildings where the main
highway reaches the canyon, and a handful of rim-edge roads where
drivers can take their pick from additional lookouts. Only one **hiking**

trail sees much use; the North Kaibab Trail, which follows Bright Angel Creek down to *Phantom Ranch*.

Tourist facilities on the North Rim, concentrated at **Bright Angel Point**, open for the season on May 15 and close on October 15. The park itself remains open for day-use only after October 15, but no food, lodging or gas is available, and visitors must be prepared to leave at a moment's notice. It's shut down altogether by the first major snowfall of winter, which usually comes towards the end of October.

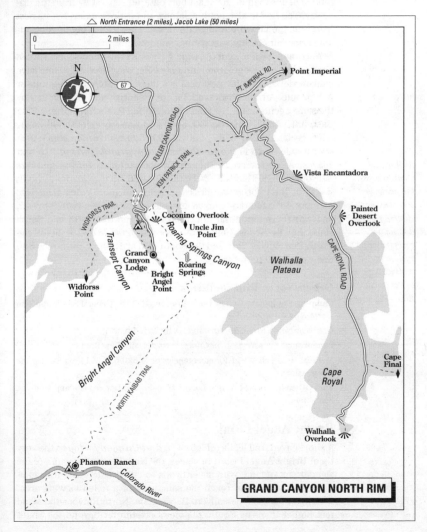

North Rim practicalities

Visitor activity on the North Rim focuses on the glorified log cabin known as **Grand Canyon Lodge**, perched above the canyon at **Bright Angel Point**. As you enter the main lobby, the park **information desk** (daily 8am–6pm; ☎520/638-7864) is on the left, together with a small **bookstore** that stocks detailed trail guides. To the right is the main **Dining Room**, open daily for all meals (☎520/638-2612 ext 160; dinner reservations required); the prices aren't bad, and the food is better than in the **snackbar**, entered separately from the driveway. The *Lodge* also holds a **saloon** and **espresso bar**, but its best feature is the **viewing lounge** downstairs, with an array of comfortable armchairs facing vast picture windows.

Accommodation at the *Lodge* (⑨) is in the cabins that spread back along the ridge from the entrance, very few of which have canyon views. The cheapest deal is a Pioneer Cabin, holding four or five people. Advance reservations are essential, and are handled by the same agents as for the South Rim; Amfac Parks & Resorts, 14001 East Iliff, #600, Aurora, CO 80014 (same-day ☎520/638-2631; advance ☎303/297-2757, fax 297-3175; *www.amfac.com*). Just over a mile north is the *North Rim Campground*, where $15 tent spaces can be reserved – though it's not necessary for backpackers – through BIOSPHERICS (☎1-800/365-2267).

Ask at the information desk for details of **mule rides** (1hr $15, half-day $40, full-day canyon expeditions $95; ☎435/679-8665), and **van tours** along the rim. **Buses** between the North and South rims, run by Trans Canyon Shuttle (☎520/638-2820) leave the North Rim daily at 7am and the South Rim at 1.30pm; the fare is $60 one-way, $100 round-trip.

As this book went to press, the park service was considering introducing a reservation system to restrict access to the North Rim.

Other North Rim facilities

Camping Equipment Can be bought or rented at the General Store, opposite *North Rim Campground*.

Gas Near *North Rim Campground*. Daily 7am–7pm.

Laundromat Near *North Rim Campground*. Daily 7am–9pm.

Medical Help Call ☎911 for emergencies or ☎520/638-2611 ext 222 for the village clinic.

Post Office In *Grand Canyon Lodge*. Mon–Fri 8–11am & 11.30am–4pm, Sat 8am–2pm.

Bright Angel Point

A short paved trail leads off left of *Grand Canyon Lodge* to the very tip of **Bright Angel Point**. In places, the trail fills the full width of the slender spit of land, with sheer drops to either side. After four hundred level yards, you reach the sanctuary of a railed viewing area, looking out across the canyon. Because the North Rim is a thousand feet higher than the South, the views stretch far beyond the South

Rim to the plateaus of Arizona and the San Francisco peaks, but it's
hard to spot a sign of life at Grand Canyon Village, eleven miles distant. As usual, the Colorado is too deeply buried in the canyon to be
seen; if you hear the sound of rushing water, it's coming from
Roaring Springs, much closer to hand, which supplies all the water
used by the park on both rims (see overleaf).

To either side, trees somehow cling to the near-vertical red ridges,
while high buttes in the canyon proper reach almost to the level of
the rims; most prominent of all is the neat-capped **Brahma Temple**
straight ahead, framed between two lesser specimens.

Cape Royal Scenic Drive

Apart from Bright Angel Point, all the **canyon overlooks** along the
North Rim are ranged along the eastern edge of the **Walhalla
Plateau**, a considerable drive from *Grand Canyon Lodge*. This long
high headland, to the east of Bright Angel Point, is reached by turning east onto **Fuller Canyon Road**, three miles north of the *Lodge*.
Five miles along, you come to a junction where **Point Imperial Road**
branches off to the left, while **Cape Royal Road** winds off into the
cool dense woods to the right.

Even if your time is limited, it's well worth making your way right
to the end of Cape Royal Road – fifteen miles from the junction – to
Cape Royal. From the unremarkable parking lot at the end of the
highway, an even, paved footpath leads first of all to the **Angels
Window**, a natural archway just below the top of a rocky spur. As
you approach, you can look down through it all the way to the
Colorado River. An extremely narrow railed pathway that detours off
the main trail a little further along leads onto the top of the "window,"
for views across to the flatlands of the Navajo reservation. Two
broad, green-trimmed stretches of the river are visible from this
point, including the foaming Unkar Creek rapids.

Views from **Cape Royal** itself, a couple of hundred yards further
along the main trail, extend much farther west, though the intervening ridge immediately west obscures Bright Angel Point. The canyon
is much narrower here, so flat-topped **Cedar Mountain** is very conspicuous, standing out just above the South Rim.

Other possible halts along Cape Royal Road include the **Walhalla
Overlook**, a mile or so back from the end of the road, where a very
short forest trail ends at the foundation walls of a small **Ancestral
Puebloan dwelling place**, and the **Painted Desert Overlook**, which
looks across Marble Canyon towards the Echo Cliffs.

Point Imperial

Turning left at the intersection of Fuller Canyon and Cape Royal
roads (see above) brings you after a gradual three-mile climb to
Point Imperial. Although at 8803 feet this is the highest spot along
either rim of the entire canyon, to reach the actual overlook you have

to descend a short distance from the parking lot. A long red sandy ridge pokes out just below the viewing area, with a stark butte at the end, while to the right is the thickly wooded ridge that ends at Cape Royal. Looking down, the landscape is as dry as dust, a labyrinth of spurs and buttes in which it's virtually impossible to guess which is the main gorge of the Colorado.

The plateau of the Navajo reservation on the far side is almost three thousand feet lower, so it spreads for miles at your feet, pierced by further chasms and gorges. To the southeast, the Little Colorado emerges from its own canyon to join the main onward rush of the Colorado.

North Rim hikes

Hikers on the North Rim of the Grand Canyon should take the same precautions, and be as aware of their physical capabilities, as their counterparts on the South Rim (see p.336). However, there tends to be less scope for getting into difficulties here, as almost all the North Rim trails suitable for day-hiking stay on top of the plateau. On the only route that descends into the canyon itself, the **North Kaibab Trail**, hiking to the river and back in a single day is completely out of the question – it's a 28-mile round trip with a 6000-foot change in elevation.

As on the South Rim, **permits** are required for all overnight hiking expeditions (see box, p.337). The same office handles advance requests, but you can also turn up at the North Rim Backcountry Office, in the Ranger Station (daily 8am–noon & 1–5pm).

The North Kaibab Trail

Some version of the **North Kaibab Trail**, following Bright Angel Creek down to the Colorado, has been in use for over a thousand years. Its current route, which starts by descending through Roaring Springs Canyon from a roadside trailhead two miles north of *Grand Canyon Lodge*, was established in the late 1920s. Parking at the trailhead is limited, but a **hiker shuttle** runs here on request from *Grand Canyon Lodge* (daily 6am–8pm; $5 for one person, $2 each additional passenger).

When planning a day-hike on the North Kaibab, it's easy to be over-ambitious; the mileages may not seem that great, but the gradient is steep from the word go. Many people go no further than the **Coconino Overlook**, just 1.4 miles down through the fir forests, a high rocky vantage point from which you can see the junction of Roaring Springs and Bright Angel canyons. The **Roaring Springs** themselves come after another 3.6 miles, during which the trail burrows through the **Supai Tunnel** and then crosses the precarious **Redwall Bridge**. Water from this open cascade is pumped up to the *Lodge*, and also piped over to the South Rim, but there's enough left over to keep alive the "gardens" just downstream that were originally planted by the Ancestral Puebloans.

The well-shaded **Cottonwood Campground**, 2.5 miles beyond the springs, is a major waystation for trans-canyon hikers. The highlight of the final seven-mile segment to **Phantom Ranch** (see p.340) is the lacy **Ribbon Falls**, reached via a short spur trail a mile past the campground.

Rim-edge trails

The best canyon-edge trail near Bright Angel Point, the ten-mile **Ken Patrick Trail**, alternates dramatic views with stretches of dense forest as it leads from the North Kaibab trailhead all the way to Point Imperial. The five-mile **Uncle Jim Trail** branches off it to reach a viewpoint that overlooks the North Kaibab Trail, while the **Widforss Trail** heads the other way, west from the inland end of Bright Angel Point out to the tip of the next headland along.

The Arizona Strip

By any logic, you'd expect the **Arizona Strip** – the anomalous area that's sandwiched between the North Rim of the Grand Canyon and the Utah state line – to belong to Utah rather than Arizona. In 1864, Mormon leader Brigham Young called on Congress to grant the Mormons all territory that lay within two degrees of latitude of either side of the Colorado; the boundary was drawn instead along the 37th parallel, and that remains the Utah–Arizona border. Repeated attempts to incorporate the Strip into Utah failed, largely because this remote region became a stronghold of renegade Mormons who didn't accept their church's reversal of doctrine on multiple marriage (see p.531). Effective isolation from the state authorities of both Utah and Arizona suited these die-hard polygamists just fine.

The Arizona Strip is not at all a tourist destination. Virtually no roads cross it, and those that do hold just a few semi-derelict hamlets. The only visitors who pass through tend to be making their way as fast as possible between the national parks of southern Utah – particularly Zion, a dozen miles north of the state line (see p.532) – and the Grand Canyon.

Fredonia

The largest town on the Arizona Strip, **FREDONIA**, stands thirty miles northwest of Jacob Lake. With the bigger and much more interesting community of **Kanab** a mere seven miles north, across the Utah border (see p.390), it's hard to see why anyone would choose to spend the night here, but Fredonia does hold a few small **motels**. Options include the very plain but reasonably new *Crazy Jug*, 465 S Main St (☎520/643-7752; ④), and the cheaper but somewhat rundown *Blue Sage*, 330 S Main St (☎520/643-7125; ②), which also has space for RVs.

Jacob Lake is 3000 feet higher than Fredonia, and as the highway climbs up into the forests of the Kaibab Plateau, roughly halfway between the two, you get some tremendous views across southern Utah. Tier upon tier of cliffs rise one behind the other into the distance, making it abundantly clear why the entire region is known to geologists as the **Grand Staircase**. First comes the red sandstone of the Vermilion Cliffs, the formation pierced by Zion Canyon (see p.377); next are the White Cliffs, which form the Kolob Canyons district of Zion National Park; and beyond them, forty miles away, stand the softer Pink Cliffs, sculpted into the hoodoos of Bryce Canyon (see p.396).

Pipe Spring National Monument

Thirteen miles west of Fredonia, just off AZ-389, **PIPE SPRING NATIONAL MONUMENT** (daily 8am–5pm; ☎520/643-7105; $2) marks the site of one of the very few water sources on the Arizona Strip. Not surprisingly, ownership of this precious spring has been much contested; a Mormon rancher, Dr James Whitmore, appropriated it from the Paiutes in 1863, and was killed three years later by a party of Paiute and Navajo raiders. The Mormons subsequently enclosed the spring in a fort, known as **Winsor Castle** after its first superintendent. They retained control until it was declared a national monument in the 1920s, as much because it stood halfway between the Grand Canyon and Zion national parks as for any intrinsic interest.

Pipe Spring now stands adjacent to the Kaibab Paiute Indian Reservation, and is largely staffed by Paiute rangers. The buildings remain in good condition, and serve as a rather unenthralling museum of early ranching life, of most appeal to students of Mormon history.

A couple of miles further off the highway, on reservation land, the Paiute run a small **casino** stuffed with low-stake slot machines.

Colorado City

AZ-389 continues northwest from Pipe Spring, and serves as the most direct connection from the North Rim to the I-15 interstate, between Las Vegas and Salt Lake City. A mile or so before it reaches Utah, a spur road to the right runs up to the staunchly traditional Mormon community of **COLORADO CITY**. Set beneath the towering bluffs of the Vermilion Cliffs, this is a surreal-looking place, laid out with a small grid of extremely broad streets that see very few cars but plenty of gingham pinafores. Everyone will assume you're a magazine journalist hoping to write a sensational article about polygamy, and there's no encouragement to linger.

Chapter 7

Southern Utah

S outhern Utah represents a peculiar combination of the mind-boggling and the mundane. Its **scenery** is stupendous, a stunning geological freakshow where the earth is ripped bare to expose cliffs and canyons of every imaginable color, unseen rivers gouge mighty furrows into endless desert plateaus, and strange sandstone towers thrust from the sagebrush. The tiny **Mormon towns** scattered across this epic landscape, on the other hand, are almost without exception boring in the extreme. Each has its cluster of characterless motels and dull-as-ditchwater diners; they're not unfriendly places, but finding ways to while away your evenings can be a supreme test of the imagination.

For a full account of the Mormons, and the history of Utah, see Contexts, on p.530 onwards.

Most visitors therefore spend as much time as possible **outdoors**. Southern Utah has the greatest concentration of **national parks** in the US; in fact there have been serious proposals for the entire area to become one vast national park. The five parks that currently exist are not necessarily the most beautiful or spectacular spots in the state – their boundaries are the result of devious behind-the-scenes wrangling, and exclude lands prized by the ranching and mining conglomerates. Taken together, however, they make an ideal focus for a first tour of Utah, each with its own well-maintained infrastructure of hiking trails and scenic overlooks.

The time in Utah is one hour later than Nevada all year round, and one hour later than Arizona from April to October; from November to March, it's the same as Arizona.

In southwest Utah, **Zion National Park** centers on an awe-inspiring and richly fertile canyon, backed by barren highlands of sun-scorched white sandstone, while **Bryce Canyon** is a roaring inferno of flame-like orange pinnacles. Over to the east, **Arches** holds an eroded desertscape of graceful red-rock fins and spurs, all on a more manageable scale than the astonishing hundred-mile vistas of neighboring **Canyonlands**. Both lie within easy reach of **Moab**, the disheveled former mining town that has suddenly become Utah's hippest destination. The fifth park, **Capitol Reef**, stretches down the massive rainbow-tinted Waterpocket Fold in the middle of the region, pierced by slender, ravishing canyons.

Lesser-known but equally dramatic wildernesses include **Dead Horse Point** and **Muley Point**, on the eastern side of the state, and

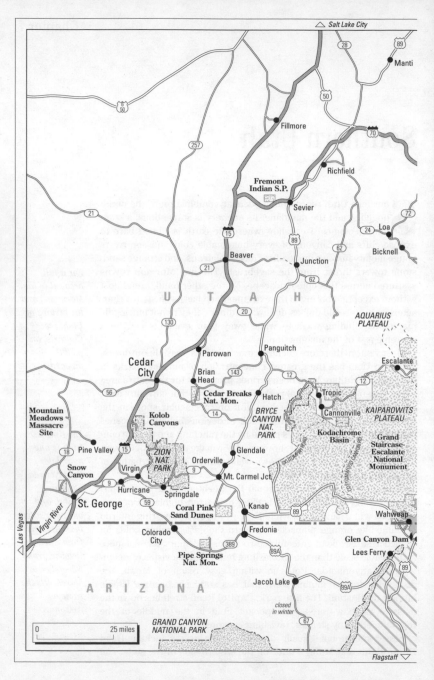

89

28

● Manti

50

50

257

● Fillmore

70

Richfield ●

Fremont Indian S.P.

Sevier ●

72

89

24

Loa ●

62

Bicknell ●

15

Beaver ●

Junction ●

AQUARIUS PLATEAU

21

21

20

62

U T A H

130

Panguitch ●

Escalante ●

Parowan ●

12

12

Cedar City

Brian Head ●

143

Tropic ●

56

Cedar Breaks Nat. Mon.

Hatch ●

KAIPAROWITS PLATEAU

Cannonville ●

Mountain Meadows Massacre Site

Kolob Canyons

14

BRYCE CANYON NAT. PARK

Kodachrome Basin

Grand Staircase-Escalante National Monument

18

Pine Valley ●

ZION NAT. PARK

Glendale ●

Orderville ●

SKUTUMPAH ROAD

Snow Canyon

Virgin ●

9

Mt. Carmel Jct. ●

COTTONWOOD CANYON RD.

9

Hurricane ●

Springdale ●

St. George

59

Kanab ●

89

Wahweap ●

Virgin River

△ Las Vegas

Coral Pink Sand Dunes

Glen Canyon Dam ▼

Colorado City ●

Fredonia ●

Lees Ferry ●

389

89A

89

Pipe Springs Nat. Mon.

A R I Z O N A

Jacob Lake ●

89A

closed in winter

67

0 ————— 25 miles

GRAND CANYON NATIONAL PARK

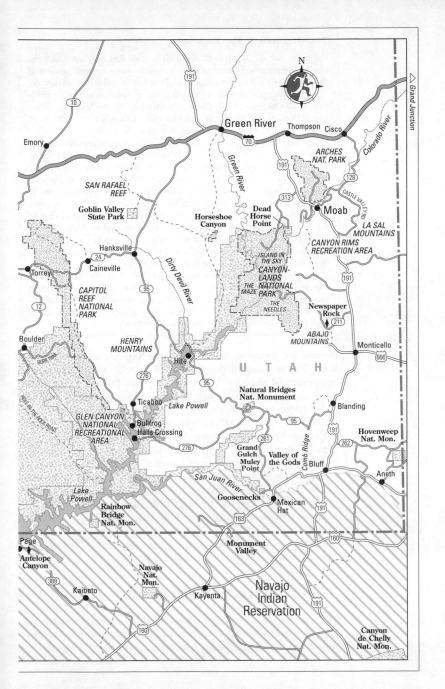

the vast new **Grand Staircase–Escalante National Monument** to the west. The most spellbinding wonder of them all, **Glen Canyon**, has been drowned since the 1960s beneath **Lake Powell**, an elongated reservoir whose turquoise waters, lapping desultorily against the red desert rocks, are a playground for houseboaters and jet-skiers.

The defining topographical feature of southwest Utah is the **Grand Staircase**. Named by pioneer river-runner John Wesley Powell, it consists of a series of plateaus, stacked tier upon tier, that climb from the North Rim of the Grand Canyon. The **Chocolate Cliffs**, near the border with Arizona, are followed by the dazzling **Vermilion Cliffs**, then the **White Cliffs** – a 2000-foot wall of Navajo Sandstone, best seen at Zion Canyon – the **Gray Cliffs**, and finally the **Pink Cliffs** of Bryce Canyon. Although it took a billion years of sedimentation for these rocks to form, the staircase itself has only been created in the last dozen million years, by the general upthrust of the **Colorado Plateau**, which stretches away to the east.

The southwest corridor

That the far southwestern corner is now the most accessible and densely populated area of southern Utah makes it easy to forget how forbidding it seemed to early explorers. In October 1776, close to modern Cedar City, fathers Domínguez and Escalante despaired of finding their way to California, and headed back towards Santa Fe. Not until 1830 did the **Old Spanish Trail** establish a permanent route west, and it was another twenty years before Brigham Young ordered Mormon settlers to establish a string of towns at the foot of the **Hurricane Cliffs**.

The largest of those towns, **St George** and **Cedar City**, stand fifty miles apart on I-15, the busy interstate that links Las Vegas with Salt Lake City. Both now depend on tourism for their livelihood – catering especially for visitors to Zion National Park – despite lacking any great appeal themselves. Only devotees of Mormon history bother to tour their humdrum array of museums and pioneer sites before heading into the wilderness that lies to the east.

St George

Spreading beneath a long sandstone escarpment, nine miles north of the Arizona state line, the venerable Mormon town of **ST GEORGE** is southern Utah's major population center. Its broad thoroughfares and sturdy well-spaced homes may still hold fewer than fifty thousand inhabitants, but that's five times the 1970 figure. Most of the newcomers are retirees from elsewhere in the Southwest, attracted by the mildness of the winters at this low elevation of just 2880 feet. They've done little to change the essential character of St George, however, which may be cosmopolitan by Utah standards but anywhere else would seem like a conservative country backwater, albeit with a surprising number of motels. Year on year, the town sprawls another few hundred meters further alongside the interstate, with another mall or two to mark its latest limits.

St George was named not for England's dragon-slaying patron but for a Latter-Day saint. Apostle George A. Smith hand-picked the 309 families who were sent to establish a colony here in 1861. The plan was to make Utah self-sufficient in **cotton**, supplies of which were threatened by the Civil War; thus this appropriately southern region became known as **"Utah's Dixie."**

The cotton-growing era ended when cotton from the Deep South reappeared after the war, made cheaper than ever by the coming of the railroads. St George, however, quietly prospered growing other crops, and became the winter refuge of Brigham Young and other ageing Mormon elders. Young's much-restored adobe **Winter Home** still stands at 200 North 100 West, complete with contemporary furnishings and artifacts (daily 9am–dusk; free).

The gleaming white **Mormon Temple**, 440 South 300 East, was the only LDS temple to be completed during Brigham Young's lifetime. Half fortress, half cathedral, it was a defiant statement that the settlers were here to stay. Young presided over its dedication shortly before his death in 1877, and it remains a powerful symbol to all Mormons. As usual, Gentiles can't go inside; there is a visitor center, however, where the problem is getting out rather than getting in. If you're sufficiently captivated, ask about guided tours of the smaller red-brick **Mormon Tabernacle** on Main Street, of similar vintage and modeled on the meeting houses of New England.

Arrival and information

Travelers driving up I-15 can call in at the **Utah Visitor Center**, just inside the state line (daily: summer 8am–9pm; winter 8am–5pm; ☎435/673-4542). Information on St George is also available from the town **visitor center** in the old County Courthouse at 97 E St George Blvd (Mon–Sat 9am–5pm; ☎435/628-1658; *www.colorcountry.org*).

Greyhound **buses** between Las Vegas and Salt Lake City stop outside *McDonald's* at 1235 S Bluff St, while the St George Shuttle (☎435/628-8320) connects with Las Vegas on request. Skywest Airlines (☎1-800/453-9417) operates daily **flights** to Salt Lake City and Las Vegas from an airport perched on the mesa high above town to the west, which is also used by Scenic Airlines (☎435/628-0481) as a base for aerial tours of the national parks.

Southern Utah Scenic Tours (☎435/867-8690) run all-day **bus tours** to Zion and/or Bryce, and also down to the Grand Canyon North Rim, for around $70 per day. **Mountain bikes** can be rented from Swen's Cyclery, 1060 E Tabernacle St (☎435/673-0878).

Accommodation

In principle, finding a **room** in St George should be no problem. At the last count, the town had 36 motels, most of them along the main drag, St George Boulevard, as well as several B&Bs tucked away on the back streets. On busy summer weekends, however, everywhere fills up early, and there's enough traffic on the interstate year-round for room rates to remain pretty constant. Watch out too for the sudden influx of students for Spring Break, in late March.

Best Western Coral Hills, 125 E St George Blvd; ☎435/673-4844 or 1-800/542-7733, fax 435/673-5352; *www.coralhills*.com. Very central *Best Western* property, quite large but still characterful, and boasting two pools. ③.

Claridge Inn, 1187 S Bluff St; ☎435/673-7222 or 1-800/367-3790, fax 435/634-0773. Modern, inexpensive motel southwest of the center; all rooms are non-smoking, most have two queen beds. Sun–Thurs ②, Fri & Sat ③.

Dixie Palm, 185 E St George Blvd; ☎435/673-3531. The cheapest motel in town, but not the worst. Some rooms have showers not baths, and there's no pool, but the price and central location may make up for that. ②.

Greene Gate Village, 76 W Tabernacle St; ☎435/628-6999 or 1-800/350-6999, fax 435/628-6989. Ten century-old structures, most brought by the current owners to this site, facing the Tabernacle. Individual rooms and entire houses for rent; one sleeps 22. All rooms are en-suite with TVs and phones, some have jacuzzis and/or fireplaces. ③–⑥.

Sands Friendship Inn, 581 E St George Blvd; ☎435/673-3501. Appealingly old-fashioned budget motel, with a reasonable pool. ②.

Seven Wives Inn, 217 North 100 West; ☎435/628-3737 or 1-800/600-3737, fax 435/673-0165. Two neighboring historic houses in central St George, one

The zip code for St George is UT 84770.

The best place to camp near St George is Snow Canyon; see opposite.

As explained on p.15, accommodation prices, excluding taxes, are indicated throughout this book by the following symbols:

① *up to $30*
② *$30–45*
③ *$45–60*
④ *$60–80*
⑤ *$80–100*
⑥ *$100–130*
⑦ *$130–175*
⑧ *$175–250*
⑨ *$250+*

built for a sevenfold polygamist, run jointly as a comfortable, period-furnished B&B inn. All rooms are en suite, with TVs and phones. ③–⑥.

Eating

Dining out in St George is a question of which highway steakhouse or fast-food outlet catches your eye; there's plenty of choice, but not much excitement. The only area you might stroll around looking for a restaurant is right in the center, where the small, slightly faded **Ancestor Square** mall holds a handful of lively options.

Basila's, Ancestor Square, 2 W St George Blvd; ☎435/673-7671. Classy restaurant in the heart of town, a bit dimly lit for lunch but romantic in the evening, and serving a welcome menu of Greek specialties with a few Italian options for the less adventurous. Open Tues–Sat only, with a liquor licence.

Dick's Cafe, 114 E St George Blvd; ☎435/673-3841. St George's longest-standing diner has an enjoyable small-town ambience, and you'd be pushed to spend $10 before you burst. Open for all meals daily.

Pizza Factory, Ancestor Square, 1 W St George Blvd; ☎435/628-1234. This friendly pizza-and-pasta joint seems to be inexorably taking over its neighbors in Ancestor Square; its terrace makes a nice spot for a light lunch, and things get lively later on. Closed Sun.

Sullivan's Rococo, 511 S Airport Rd; ☎435/628-3671. Upmarket steakhouse, poised on the bluff west of town, where half the customers have come for the panoramic views of town and the other half for the liquor licence. Steak, ribs and seafood entrees cost up to $35 in the evening, but the lunchtime sandwiches are well under $10.

From St George to Cedar City

Much the most direct route between St George and Cedar City is to follow the interstate northeast, but taking Hwy-18 due north leads you through an interesting stretch of mountainous high country. If you're heading for Zion National Park (see p.374), turn right onto Hwy-9 seven miles out of St George on I-15.

Snow Canyon State Park

One of Utah's most attractive state parks, focused on a classic red-rock canyon, lies within ten minutes' drive of downtown St George. **SNOW CANYON STATE PARK** was named for two of St George's leading pioneers, Lorenzo and Erastus Snow, so don't expect to see snow. Instead, its most distinctive feature is the layer of jet-black lava that flakes off the tops of its sun-baked sandstone pinnacles, left by a ten-thousand-year-old volcanic eruption.

The road through Snow Canyon remains open day and night; there are no fixed hours.

The park's six-mile **scenic drive** drops left from Hwy-18 seven miles north of St George, shortly beyond a viewpoint that looks out across most of the canyon. Winding down past a succession of overlooks and rounded monoliths, it reaches the **park headquarters** after a couple of miles. There's no visitor center, but this is the place to pay the $5-per-vehicle entrance fee and pick up hiking details. It's

*Horse rides in
the park, rang-
ing from one
hour to
overnight
trips, are
offered by
Snow Canyon
Stables
(☎435/628-
6677).*

also the site of the pleasant, shaded 36-space *Shivwits
Campground* (☎435/628-2255 or 1-800/322-3770; Mon–Fri $11,
Sat & Sun $12). Reservations are recommended in spring and fall,
but things get quieter during the hottest months.

The **Hidden Pinyon Trail**, an excellent hour-long (1.5-mile)
round-trip hike, starts a hundred yards further on. After cutting
between the craggy outcrops into a peaceful meadow, it zigzags up
and over a ridge to enter a heavily eroded landscape reminiscent of
Canyonlands' Needles District (see p.452). Vegetation en route
includes Utah junipers, creosote bushes and assorted cactuses.

If it's too hot to hike, pull off another two miles on instead, where
a cluster of lurid **red sand dunes** threatens to drift across the road.
Kids especially will enjoy sliding down the slopes, which had a bit
part in *Butch Cassidy and the Sundance Kid*. The dunes also doubled for central Asia in Howard Hughes' movie *The Conqueror*,
which starred John Wayne as Genghis Khan. It was filmed in 1954,
when the Nevada Test Site, just ninety miles west, was at its busiest;
Wayne, Hughes and three-quarters of the cast probably died from
cancers caused by fall-out from the explosions.

Leaving the park at its southern end enables you to complete a 24-
mile loop back to St George, but if you want to press on north, double back when you've had enough of the scenic drive.

Pine Valley

Sixteen miles north of Snow Canyon, a dead-end right turning off
Hwy-18 leads for ten miles into **PINE VALLEY**. By the time you
reach the valley's eponymous village, you're at 6500 feet, so Pine
Valley serves as a summer retreat for the sweltering citizens of St
George. Travelers from further afield may well feel that this gentle
alpine landscape is not what they came to Utah to see, but it's undeniably pretty. There's basic **accommodation** in the *Pine Valley
Lodge* (☎435/574-2544; ②), and a steakhouse nearby, plus a handful of small forest-service **campgrounds** – and plentiful hiking trails
– in the Dixie National Forest beyond.

Along the interstate: Silver Reef and Fort Harmony

In the course of the fifty-mile drive from St George to Cedar City,
I-15 climbs three thousand feet, passing between the Pine Valley
Mountains to the west and the Hurricane Cliffs to the east.

Fifteen miles northeast of St George, a spur road to the left leads
to the ghost town of **SILVER REEF**. Silver mining never came any
easier than here, the only spot in the West where silver was found
mixed in with ordinary sandstone. It took two decades, the 1880s
and 1890s, to scour the hills bare of metal, during which time Silver
Reef reveled in a reputation for very un-Mormon hell-raising. Relics
of the era, together with a scale model of town, can be admired in the
Silver Reef Museum, at 3200 Wells Fargo Rd (Mon–Sat 9am–5pm;

The Mountain Meadows Massacre

The lonely high-mountain valley known as **Mountain Meadows**, five miles beyond the turnoff into Pine Valley on Hwy-18, was the scene of one of the most infamous incidents in Western history.

In the summer of 1857, tensions between the ten-year-old Mormon kingdom of Deseret and the rest of the United States were at their peak. With a large detachment of US soldiers known to be advancing on Utah, the long-expected "Mormon War" was seen as inevitable. When the **Fancher Company**, a California-bound wagon train of settlers from Arkansas and Missouri, reached Salt Lake City in early August 1857, the locals refused to sell any of the supplies they were stockpiling for the winter. In retaliation, the migrants raided Mormon farms, taunting that they'd soon return in force. One claimed to be carrying the very gun with which Joseph Smith had been killed in Missouri.

The Fancher party then headed south to Mountain Meadows, a fertile, well-watered halt on the Old Spanish Trail where travelers often stopped to gather strength for the final haul across the desert. Within days, the wagon train was **ambushed** by warriors dressed as Indians. Several of its members were killed before the rest barricaded themselves behind earthwork defenses. Whether the attackers were genuine Utes, or white Mormons in disguise – as Mark Twain reported in *Roughing It* – remains controversial to this day. Clearly, however, the Mormon militia responsible for protecting southern Utah saw the hostile wagon train as a threat to be eliminated. Their commander, **John D. Lee**, rode up to the beleaguered Gentiles on September 11, claiming to have negotiated a truce with the "Indians," and stated that if they laid down their guns they would be allowed to proceed west in peace.

Desperately short of ammunition, the migrants agreed. Each was assigned a Mormon escort, and together they set off west. Within a mile, Lee called the order "**Halt! Do your duty!**," whereupon the Mormon militiamen killed the entire group, amounting to 120 unarmed men, women and children. Some sources allege that Utes also took part in the slaughter. The only survivors were seventeen infants, who were at first adopted by local Mormons but eventually returned to relatives.

When reports of the massacre reached the rest of the country, it was widely believed to have been carried out on Brigham Young's orders. No serious legal investigation ever took place, however, with the authorities in southern Utah almost certainly complicit in a cover-up, and the federal government too preoccupied with the Civil War to intervene. Most of the perpetrators laid low in remote desert outposts; most famously, John D. Lee established a ferry service across the Colorado (see p.350). In time, Young bowed to national pressure and first excommunicated Lee from the church in 1870, and then delivered him for trial. Lee was executed by firing squad in Mountain Meadows on March 23, 1877, bitterly claiming that "Young has sacrificed me through his lust for power." He remains a hero to some Mormons; one plaque in Lees Ferry calls him "a man of good faith, sound judgment and indomitable courage."

A monument to the massacre was erected in 1990 near the highest point on Hwy-18, a bleak, windswept spot overlooking the entire valley. Each of the victims is listed by name, but the inscription simply states that the party "was attacked," without mentioning Mormon involvement. More explicit graffiti is scrubbed away as soon as it appears.

$2.50). Only stunted walls remain of the town itself, however, and few visitors can summon up the energy on a red-hot Utah summer's day to find them of any interest.

There's even less to see at the site of **FORT HARMONY**, another eighteen miles north, just beyond the Kolob Canyons turnoff and fifteen miles south of Cedar City. **John D. Lee**, of Mountain Meadows fame, established a fortified outpost to guard this high pass in 1852. It was finally abandoned ten years later, after torrential rain caused its earthen walls to cave in, killing two of Lee's children.

A full account of the Kolob Canyons district of Zion National Park appears on p.388.

Cedar City

CEDAR CITY, 53 miles northeast of St George and now half its size, has a similar history to its upstart rival. It too was founded in Mormon Utah's precarious early years, as part of the church's bid for self-sufficiency. The Mormons urgently needed **iron**, so when scouting parties discovered iron ore in southern Utah, the *Deseret News* published an appeal in July 1850 for "fifty or so good effective men, with teams and waggons" to establish an **Iron Mission**.

Cedar City was established in November 1851, between the iron in the hills to the west and the coal deposits of Coal Creek Canyon to the east. Most of its first inhabitants were British miners; they succeeded in smelting iron within a year, but the venture ultimately failed, and was abandoned in October 1858. Since then, ore mined in the area has been shipped out for processing.

The Cedar City story is told in full at **Iron Mission State Park**, on the main highway a mile or so north of downtown (daily: June to Labor Day 9am–7pm; Labor Day to May 9am–5pm; $5 per vehicle or $2 per person). Apart from rusty nuggets, the warehouse-like museum is filled with nineteenth-century horse-drawn vehicles, including wagons, sleighs and hearses (one of which bears the slogan "Why walk around half dead when we can bury you for just $22?"). There's also a small and somewhat dull display of Native American artifacts, plus some homespun craft items – mostly carved vertebrae and crocheted doilies – and 380 individually tagged samples of barbed wire. Several more wagons are parked in sheds at the back, if you feel up to braving the heat.

Otherwise, there's little to see in Cedar City. It's not a place you're likely to want to tour on foot, despite the lure of historical markers detailing the former locations of the town's social hall, hospital, brick yard and flour mill.

Tourists do arrive in droves during the summer, however, drawn by the annual **Utah Shakespeare Festival**, a semi-professional event organized by Southern Utah State University since 1962. Running around June 20 until mid-October, it usually features six productions, with three or four Shakespeare and a couple of other classics. Three theaters are used, the most prestigious being the Adams

Memorial Shakespearean Theater, a replica of the original Globe, and tickets range from $19 to $40 (reservations on ☎435/586-7878 or 1-800/752-9849; *www.bard.org*). Peripheral activities include a regular mock-Elizabethan Medieval Feaste, costing $30.

Arrival and information

Cedar City's large new **visitor center** stands next to Iron Mission State Park at 581 N Main St (summer Mon–Fri 8am–7pm, Sat 9am–1pm; winter Mon–Fri 8am–5pm; ☎435/586-5124 or 1-800/354-4849); that isn't construction debris outside, but huge boulders of natural ferrous rock.

Greyhound **buses** (☎435/586-9465) call at 1355 S Main St, while the airport on the northwest fringes of town is used by Skywest Airlines (☎1-800/453-9417) for **flights** to Salt Lake City.

The zip code for Cedar City is UT 84720.

Accommodation

While Cedar City doesn't have quite the range of **accommodation** to match St George, around twenty motels and hotels line up along Main Street, including several right in the heart of town. Rooms are liable to be booked well in advance for the Shakespeare festival. The **All Utah Free Reservation Center** (☎1-800/776-4685) handles room bookings for Cedar City and the rest of the state.

There's a large *KOA* **campground** at 1121 N Main St (☎435/586-9872); for more seclusion head for the public sites that start around a dozen miles east of town, along Hwy-14 towards Cedar Breaks (see overleaf). For full details, call in at the **Dixie National Forest Ranger Station**, 82 North 100 East (☎435/865-3200).

Bard's Inn B&B, 150 South 100 West; ☎435/586-6612. Central B&B, open for the Shakespeare Festival and at other times by arrangement, with five en-suite rooms in the main house and two more in the adjoining cottage. ④.

Best Western El Rey Inn, 80 S Main St; ☎435/586-6518 or 1-800/688-6518, fax 435/586-7257. Very central *Best Western* hotel – one of the first ever – an easy walk away from the Festival events, with rooms of all sizes, plus pool, sauna and spa. ③–⑤.

Best Western Town and Country Inn, 189 N Main St; ☎435/586-9900 or 1-800/528-1234, fax 435/586-1664; *tcinn@tcd.net*. Large, smart and very central option, this time with *two* pools and spas. ④.

Super 8, 145 North 1550 West; ☎435/586-8880 or 1-800/800-8000. Reliable budget motel, with little seasonal variation in price. Well out of town, west of I-15 at exit 59. ③.

Willow Glen Inn, 3308 N Bulldog Rd; ☎435/586-3275; *www .willowglen.com*. Farm-set B&B, five miles northwest of downtown, near exit 62 off I-15. Rooms with and without baths in main house, and some luxurious suites in garden cottages. ③–⑥.

The price codes used here are explained on p.15.

Eating

A quick-fire succession of chain diners and fast-food outlets punctuates the main highway through Cedar City. For more characterful alternatives, head for the student-oriented places near the university, in the blocks immediately southwest of downtown.

Adriana's, 164 South 100 West; ☎435/865-1234. Wide-ranging menu, from soup and salad to steak, served for lunch and dinner amid pseudo-English decor. Most entrees cost $14–18, and they also offer good-value buffets and have a liquor licence. Open daily in summer, when it's always very busy, and closed Sun in winter.

Godfather's Pizza, 241 N Main St; ☎435/586-1111. Fills the spruced-up former railroad station opposite the visitor center, serving good pizzas in all sizes ($7–19) plus all-you-can-eat lunch and dinner buffets.

Pancho & Lefty's Cafe, 2107 N Main St; ☎435/586-7501. Lively dinner-only Mexican option, a fair way north of downtown, with a sideline in chunky steaks, and an open-air veranda that's a midsummer night's dream of a spot for a margarita.

Sullivan's Cafe, 301 S Main St; ☎435/586-6761. Popular breakfast place, a cornucopia of eggs and pancakes, that also has a fully-fledged (and licensed) steak and seafood restaurant upstairs.

Cedar Breaks National Monument

Cedar City stands at an elevation of 5800 feet, but the densely-wooded plateau to the east rises a further five thousand feet. **Hwy-14**, the most direct route to Bryce Canyon, climbs steadily onto the plateau from the narrow gorge east of town. The scenery along the way is rarely short of spectacular, with views that stretch south to encompass all of Zion National Park.

Around fifteen miles along, shortly after the highway enters the **Dixie National Forest**, you can't fail to spot the pink, white and orange rocks of **CEDAR BREAKS NATIONAL MONUMENT**, immediately below the forest that tops the high ridge to your left. Cedar Breaks is a sort of pocket version of Bryce, where erosive forces have scooped a natural amphitheater into the hillside and filled it with brilliantly colored limestone formations. While it lacks Bryce's opportunities for hiking, it's well worth seeing if you're in the area.

*For a full
account of
Bryce Canyon,
see p.396.*

The road through the monument – **Hwy-148**, which branches north from Hwy-14 19 miles out of Cedar City – is snowbound between late October and mid-May. When it's clear, you can choose between four similar cliff-edge viewpoints. The southernmost, **Point Supreme**, is the best, with pinnacles rising from the orange canyon floor at your feet and sweeping views to the south and west. The small **visitor center** just behind is only staffed in summer (May–Sept daily 8am–6pm; ☎435/586-0787); if you make it here in spring or fall, you can visit without paying the usual $4 fee. Overnight temperatures only rise high enough to make the adjoining **campground** ($10) an appealing proposition between July and September.

You can hike for short distances along the rim at both Point Supreme and **Chessmen Ridge**, a mile or so north, but no trails descend into the formations.

Panguitch Lake and Brian Head

Near the northern end of Cedar Breaks, Hwy-148 meets Hwy-143 where it turns sharply east towards Panguitch (see p.394). If you're heading for Bryce, it makes little difference whether you continue this way or return to Hwy-14. **Panguitch Lake**, in the heart of the forest halfway to US-89, appeals mainly to local trout fishermen, though the **campground** at *Panguitch Lake Resort* ($7; ☎435/676-2657) is nice enough.

Alternatively, keep going north on Hwy-143 and you'll come to tiny **BRIAN HEAD** within a couple of miles. Utah's highest town, at 9700ft, this remains accessible year-round from the north, via a steep fifteen-mile climb from Parowan. It's the site of southern Utah's only **downhill ski resort** (mid-Nov to May; lift tickets around $35 per day; information on ☎435/677-2035 or 1-800/272-7426). Despite offering slopes to suit all levels of competence – and the closest skiing to Las Vegas – Brian Head is not exactly thriving, so don't expect a heady whirl of post-piste partying. In summer, it verges on being a ghost town, but makes a peaceful overnight stop.

In the largest **hotel**, the year-round 200-room *Brian Head Hotel*, at 223 Hunter Ridge Drive (☎435/677-3000; summer ④, winter ⑥), the *Columbine Cafe* serves good-value breakfasts and lunches, while dinner at the swisher, health-conscious *Summit Dining Room* costs around $20. Most of the smaller condo complexes nearby, a few of which have their own restaurants, only open in ski season. The *Bump and Grind* at 259 S Hwy-143 (☎435/677-2864) is a convenient spot for coffee and a sandwich.

The road to Zion

The main road **east** to Zion National Park – **Hwy-9**, which leaves the interstate seven miles northeast of St George – makes a lovely thirty-mile drive. None of the pioneer villages along the way is especially exciting, but the scenery is great, with the cottonwood-fringed Virgin River to the south and gigantic sandstone cliffs to the north.

Hurricane

The westernmost town along Hwy-9 is **HURRICANE**, ten miles off the interstate at the junction with Hwy-59. While not actually on the Virgin River, it's connected to it by a seven-mile canal, conceived in 1863 but not completed until 1906. Only then was the townsite settled, and it's still much the same agricultural community a hundred years on.

With the recent spurt in tourism, however, Hurricane's early timber-frame homes have been joined by a number of **motels**, including a *Super 8*, at 65 South 700 West (☎435/635-0808 or 1-800/800-8000, fax 435/635-0909; ③), and two shiny new options on the hilltop west of town, the *Days Inn*, 40 North 2600 West (☎435/635-0500, fax 635-0272; ③), and the *Comfort Inn*, 43 N Sky Mountain

*The zip code
for Hurricane
is UT 84737.*

Blvd (☎435/635-3500 or 1-800/635-3577, fax 435/635-2425; ③)). There's also a central **youth hostel**, known as *HI-Hurricane, the Dixie Hostel*, at 73 S Main St (☎435/635-8202), which offers $15 dorm beds and a few private rooms (①/②), with rates including continental breakfast. Nearby, the *Cast and Crew Deli Juice Bar* serves snacks and drinks.

Southeast from Hurricane, incidentally, Hwy-59 takes twenty miles to reach the Arizona border, marked by the traditional Mormon community of **Colorado City** (see p.358). The **North Rim** of the Grand Canyon is another hundred miles beyond (see p.352).

Virgin, Rockville and Grafton

You'll probably barely notice either **VIRGIN**, seven miles east of Hurricane, or **ROCKVILLE**, ten miles beyond that; in fact it's hard to keep your eyes on the road at all as you come closer to the wonders of Zion. Rockville is nevertheless a pretty little town, with several small-scale **B&Bs** along its tree-lined central avenue, such as the *Hummingbird Inn*, 37 W Main St (☎435/772-3632 or 1-800/964-2473; ④).

Kolob Terrace Road, which heads north into the Zion backcountry from Virgin, is described on p.387 onwards.

If you can spare the time, follow Bridge Road south across the river from Rockville, turn right onto an unpaved track, and in five minutes you'll reach the photogenic little **ghost town** of **GRAFTON**. Mormon farmers abandoned the struggle against floods and Indians around 1900, but residents of Rockville have kept an eye on it ever since. It's also been touched up by Hollywood crews shooting movies like *Butch Cassidy and the Sundance Kid*; this is where Robert Redford rode a bicycle and sang *Raindrops Keep Falling On My Head* at one and the same time.

Just beyond Rockville, Hwy-9 veers north at the confluence of the North and East forks of the Virgin River, and heads for the maw of Zion Canyon.

Springdale

SPRINGDALE, the last town before Zion, spreads along a leafy three-mile stretch of the Virgin River just south of the park entrance. Rounding the final corner into town gives you your first stupendous view of Zion Canyon itself. Settled at the same time as the canyon, in the early 1860s (see box p.378), Springdale is now devoted almost exclusively to pampering tourists. By the time you've driven up and down the only road, **Zion Park Boulevard**, a couple of times, you'll have seen everything Springdale has to offer, but spending three or four nights in this lively, friendly community is no hardship whatsoever.

Arrival and information

Springdale has its own **visitor center**, in the Old Church at 868 Zion Park Blvd (summer only, Mon–Fri 9am–5pm; ☎435/772-3072), but for information on Zion you'd do better to go straight to the park (see p.379). You can also learn more about Zion by whiling away an evening at **The Grand Circle**, a multimedia show held in the open-air Obert C. Tanner Amphitheater just outside the park (late May to early Sept, nightly at dusk; $4; ☎435/673-4811) or watching **Treasure of the Gods** at the Cinemax Theater, at 145 Zion Park Blvd (daily: March–Oct 9am–9pm; Nov–Feb 11am–7pm; $7; ☎435/772-2400).

Bike Zion, at 445 Zion Park Blvd (☎435/772-3929), offers **bike rental** and guided bike tours, while the Zion Adventure Company, based near the Tanner Amphitheater at 36 Lion Blvd (☎435/772-1001), rents out gear for prospective Narrows hikers – see p.385 – such as ropes, tents and booties, runs a shuttle-van service for hikers, and also offers **guided hikes** (from $50 per day per person) and **canyoneering**, though park regulations mean that such tours can only be outside park boundaries.

The southwest corridor

The zip code for Springdale is UT 84767.

Accommodation

As Zion Park Boulevard runs straight between the burgeoning canyon walls towards the park, all the **motels** and **B&Bs** along the way offer the same attractive views. A couple of new properties appear each year, so except at the height of summer you should have no difficulty finding a room to suit your budget.

The shaded *Zion Canyon Campground*, half a mile outside the park at 479 Zion Park Blvd (☎435/772-3237), offers year-round tent **camping** ($15) and RV hookups, and has its own laundry and pizzeria.

For details of staying at the in-park Zion Lodge, *and of camping in* Zion, *see p.379.*

Motels

Best Western Zion Park Inn, 1215 Zion Park Blvd; ☎435/772-3200 or 1-800/934-7275; *www.zionparkinn.com*. Modern convention-style hotel at Springdale's southern end, offering spacious rooms with panoramic windows, and a heated swimming pool. Winter ④, summer ⑤.

Bumbleberry Inn, 897 Zion Park Blvd; ☎435/772-3224 or 1-800/828-1534, fax 435/772-3947. Central but very peaceful motel, set well back from the highway, with large rooms and a pool. ③.

Cliffrose Lodge and Gardens, 281 Zion Park Blvd; ☎435/772-3234 or 1-800/243-8824, fax 435/772-3900; *www.cliffroselodge.com*. The closest motel to the park has been slightly outclassed, and outpriced, by its newer rivals, but still makes a pretty place to stay, set in the cottonwoods alongside the Virgin River, with its own pool. Winter ⑤, summer ⑥.

The price codes used here are explained on p.15.

Desert Pearl Inn, 707 Zion Park Blvd; ☎435/772-8888 or 1-888/828-0898, fax 435/772-8889; *www.desertpearl.com*. Smart, attractive new motel, offering very good rates considering the high standard of accommodation, the huge pool and the riverside setting. ④.

El Rio Lodge, 995 Zion Park Blvd; ☎435/772-3205 or 1-888/772-3205; *elrio@infowest.com*. Small, very friendly and good-value motel, in walking distance of several restaurants. ③.

B&Bs

Harvest House, 29 Canyon View Drive; ☎435/772-3880, fax 772-3327; *www.harvesthouse.net*. Classy, nonsmoking B&B in modern home, tucked beneath the sandstone cliffs. Four en-suite rooms, an outdoor hot tub, and gourmet breakfasts. ⑤.

Zion House, 435 Zion Park Blvd; ☎435/772-3281; *www.zionhouse.com*. Rambling, cozy home run as a friendly well-maintained B&B inn. Three guestrooms – one has a private bath, the other share – plus a plusher suite. Rooms ④, suite ⑤.

Eating

Springdale lacks the national chains, offering instead a refreshing choice of individually-styled **restaurants**. If you prefer a light breakfast, there are also a couple of **espresso cafes** just before the park entrance.

Bit & Spur Saloon, 1212 Zion Park Blvd; ☎435/772-3498. Hectic Mexican restaurant and bar, across from *Zion Park Inn* at the south end of town, where the food is surprisingly delicious and the margaritas top-notch. Open for lunch and dinner daily in summer, Thurs–Mon in winter.

Flanigan's Inn Restaurant, 428 Zion Park Blvd; ☎435/772-3244. Traditional, relatively formal steak-and-seafood place not far from the park, serving all meals daily in summer, dinner only in winter.

The Shonesburg, *Bumbleberry Inn*, 897 Zion Park Blvd; ☎435/772-3522. Smart, high-ceilinged, but unatmospheric restaurant. Standard meat and fish entrees for around $15, excellent salads, and tasty *Bumbleberry* (mixedberry) pie. Closed Sun.

Switchback Grille, 1149 Zion Park Blvd; ☎435/772-3700. Clean, bright, upmarket restaurant at the south end of town beside the *Zion Park Inn*, with a panoramic dining room and patio seating. Wood-fired pizzas, well-prepared meat and fish dishes like smoked ribs and spit-roasted chickens, at above average but not extortionate prices, plus inexpensive lunchtime burgers and sandwiches. Open daily for all meals.

Tsunami Juice and Java, 180 Zion Park Blvd; ☎435/772-3818. Small, bright cafe immediately outside the park entrance, with smoothies, espressos and $5 wraps served hot or cold. Open daily, all day.

Zion National Park

With its soaring cliffs, riverine forests and cascading waterfalls, **ZION NATIONAL PARK** is the most conventionally beautiful of Utah's parks. On first glance, it's also the least "Southwestern"; its centerpiece, **Zion Canyon**, is a lush oasis that feels far removed from the otherworldly desolation of Canyonlands or the downright weirdness of Bryce. Like California's Yosemite Canyon, it's a spectacular gorge, squeezed between mighty walls of rock and echoing to the sound of running water; and also like Yosemite, it can get claustrophobic in summer, its one road clogged with traffic and its limited facilities crammed with sweltering tourists.

Too many visitors see Zion Canyon as a quick half-day detour off the interstate, as they race between Las Vegas (158 miles southwest) and Salt Lake City (320 miles northeast). Beautiful though the **Scenic Drive** through the canyon may be, Zion deserves much more of your time than that. Even the shortest **hiking trail** within the canyon can help you escape the crowds, while a day-hike will take you away from the deceptive verdure of the valley and up onto the high-desert tablelands beyond. In addition, two less-used roads – **Kolob Canyons Road** and the **Kolob Terrace Road** – lead into remoter sections of the park.

With elevations varying from under 4000 feet at the visitor center to almost 9000 feet at Kolob Peak, Zion is home to a bewildering array of **flora and fauna**. Its vegetation ranges from the cottonwoods and box elders along the Virgin River to the ponderosa pines and stunted piñons that cling to the high sandstone mesas. Desert flowers and cactuses provide unexpected flashes of color in the uplands, as do darting hummingbirds. Animals include the bank beaver (so named because it doesn't build dams) and the generally retiring Western rattlesnake. Mountain lions have been reintroduced since a disastrous experiment of the 1930s, when their extermination

Zion
National
Park

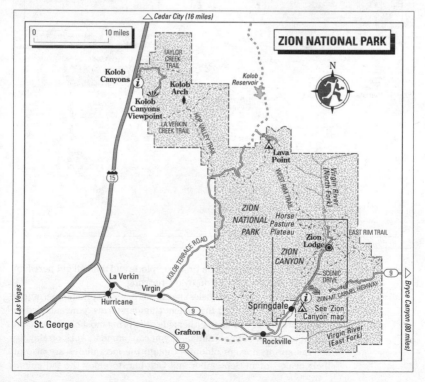

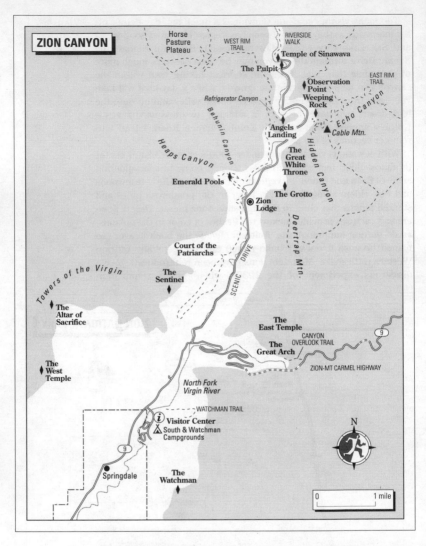

allowed the deer population first to explode and then all but perish in a terrible famine brought on by overgrazing.

Summer is by far the busiest **season**. That's despite temperatures in excess of 100°F, and the violent thunderstorms, concentrated in August and a week or so to either side, that bring most of Zion's scant fifteen inches of annual rainfall. If you can, come in April or May, to see the spring flowers bloom – though the mosquitoes are also at their peak – or in September and October, to enjoy the fall colors along the river. The park remains open throughout the winter, but daytime highs drop below 40°F in January, while the nights tend to be freezing from November to March.

Zion Canyon

It has taken thirteen million years for the North Fork of the **Virgin River** to carve **Zion Canyon** into the southern edge of the Markagunt Plateau. For most of the year, the Virgin meanders placidly along the valley floor, en route to the Colorado. After summer thunderstorms, however, run-off from the mesa-tops is channeled down into the canyon, turning it into a torrent that carries as much as 600,000 cubic yards of rock and sand – a good-sized city block – in a single day. Each winter, the canyon walls grow further apart, as water that seeps through the porous sandstone turns to ice, and shears mighty chunks off the cliffs.

*In Paiute,
Markagunt
means "high-
land of trees."*

As you approach from the south, the **Markagunt Plateau** – one of the seven high plateaus that make up the Colorado Plateau in southern Utah – is clearly the next rung of the **Grand Staircase** (see p.358). Zion Canyon serves as a handy cross-section to display the different layers of rock. At the lowest level, around the South Entrance, the thick red **Vermilion Cliffs** rise from a barely discernible bed of the even older and darker Moenave and Kayenta formations. These strata were deposited at the bottom of swampy seas around 200 million years ago, while the 2000-foot walls of the canyon itself are composed of rusty **Navajo Sandstone**, once a mass of drifting sand dunes.

The first of the colossal peaks that crown the chasm look down from either side of the South Entrance. The **West Temple** is one of two similar mountains here whose summits consist of neat little box-shaped mesas crowned with pine trees, while the **Watchman** stands guard to the east. At this point, the walls are well over a mile apart; officially the canyon doesn't begin for another few miles, but within just ten miles north it dwindles to a mere twenty feet wide.

Most visitors assume Mormon settlers gave Zion's pinnacles and promontories their portentous names – the **Court of the Patriarchs**, the **Great White Throne**, **Angel's Landing**, and so on – but in fact they were coined by a Methodist minister who visited in 1916.

Getting to Zion Canyon

Zion Canyon is 43 miles northeast of St George and sixty miles south of Cedar City, reached by following **Hwy-9** beside the Virgin River for thirty miles east of I-15. Not far beyond the park's South Entrance, just north of Springdale (see p.372), Hwy-9 finally abandons the river, tunneling its way out of the canyon and continuing east to meet US-89. Bryce Canyon, often seen in conjunction with Zion, is a total of 86 miles northeast.

Between March and October, all visitors to Zion Canyon, other than guests staying at *Zion Lodge* (see p.379), are obliged to leave

Zion
National
Park

A History of Zion Canyon

Zion Canyon may seem like an oasis in the Utah wilderness, but it has
never held much of a **human** population. Its earliest inhabitants were probably semi-nomadic hunter-gatherers, who from 500 AD onwards grew
rudimentary crops beside the Virgin River. Known to archeologists as the
Virgin Anasazi, they are regarded as less sophisticated cousins of the
Ancestral Puebloan groups to the east; living in small bands, they never
built the "cliff palaces" or pueblos for which their neighbors are renowned.
By 1250 AD, drought had driven them out of Zion, leaving isolated pictographs on the canyon walls to serve as their only monument.

During the centuries that followed, **Paiute Indians** migrated seasonally
throughout southern Utah, harvesting the few resources the desert could
offer. They saw Zion, however, as the abode of Wai-no-Pits, the evil one,
who cursed them with disease, and Kainesava, the God of Fire, whose
lightning blazed from its high peaks. When the young **Mormon missionary** Nephi Johnson arrived in 1858 to explore the Upper Virgin River, the
Paiute would lead him no further than Oak Creek, at the entrance to the
canyon.

Isaac Behunin, who set up a log cabin in 1862 where *Zion Lodge* now
stands, dubbed the canyon "**Little Zion**," in the hope that it would be a
place of refuge for beleaguered Mormons. Some of his fellow farmers were
soon taking things too easy; Brigham Young thundered that their indul-
gence in tobacco and wine made the name "**Not Zion**" more appropriate.
In the long run, Zion Canyon proved too narrow to support efficient farming, and its main commercial role was simply as a route through which timber sawn on the high mesas could be shipped out to the plains. Between
1900 and 1930, logs lowered from "Cable Mountain" built the fine homes
of such towns as St George.

Meanwhile, **John Wesley Powell**'s second Colorado expedition in 1872
(see p.441) had brought the scenery of Zion to national attention, under
the Paiute name of "Mukuntuweap Canyon." The canyon itself was set
aside in 1909 as Mukuntuweap National Monument; a larger area became
Zion National Park in 1919, and the Kolob Canyons district was added in
1956.

In its first full year, 1920, the park attracted fewer than four thousand
visitors. With numbers now approaching three million per year, and trails
and campgrounds little changed since their construction during the 1930s,
Zion has been showing the strain. In an attempt to reduce the damage, a
new federally-funded system of shuttle buses was introduced in 2000 (as
detailed opposite), and private vehicles were banned from using the
Scenic Drive in summer.

*For advance
information,
write to Zion
National Park,
Springdale,
UT 84767, or
access* www
.nps.gov/zion.

their vehicles either in Springfield or at the main park visitor center,
and use the park's network of shuttle buses (see opposite). The
Scenic Drive within the canyon is accessible to private vehicles during the winter only, while Hwy-9 remains open to through traffic all
year. Vehicles measuring over 7ft 10in wide or 11ft 4in high – which
includes virtually all RVs – pay $10 on top of the usual park fees to
use the Zion–Mount Carmel tunnel on Hwy-9, and in summer can
only do so between 8am and 8pm. Cyclists are forbidden to ride

through the tunnel altogether, but park rangers can arrange for bicycles to be transported by other vehicles.

Arrival and information

The **admission charge** for Zion National Park, valid in all sections of the park for seven days, is $20 per vehicle, or $10 for motorcyclists, cyclists and pedestrians. All nationwide passes, including the Golden Eagle pass (see p.21), are both sold and accepted.

You can also pay your fee and pick up the basic brochures at the kiosk that marks the park's East Entrance (daily 8am–5pm), while a separate, smaller visitor center serves the Kolob Canyons district (see p.388).

The park's large new **visitor center** is set to the right just beyond the South Entrance (daily: April–Oct 8am–7pm; Nov–March 8am–5pm; phone enquiries ☎ 435/772-3256 Mon–Fri 8am–4.30pm). Free handouts include park maps and the useful *Sentinel* newspaper, while the bookstore stocks detailed guides, and permanent displays explain the park's geology and history. As well as a full timetable of talks and slide shows, the park service runs Junior Ranger programs for 6–12-year-olds in summer.

Park Transportation

Between March and October, park **shuttle buses** run on two separate loops – one between Springdale and the visitor center, with nine stops en route, and the other between the visitor center and the end of the Scenic Drive, with six stops including *Zion Lodge*. Only guests at the *Lodge* are allowed to drive any further into the canyon than the visitor center; visitors staying overnight in Springdale can choose whether to leave their vehicles there and ride the shuttle to the park, or park at the visitor center and pick up the shuttle there. In **winter**, only the Scenic Drive loop operates, and it's no longer compulsory. Both loops are always free – or rather, the fares are included in the park admission fee – and you can get on and off as often as you like.

Zion Canyon practicalities

The only **food** and **lodging** available within the canyon is at *Zion Lodge*, an appealing if often overcrowded complex of low-slung wooden buildings set amid well-shaded lawns a couple of miles up the Scenic Drive. **Reservations** for its motel-style rooms and more characterful cabins (both ⑤), and larger studios (⑥), are handled by Amfac Parks & Resorts, 14001 East Iliff Ave, #600, Aurora, CO 80014 (☎303/297-2757, fax 297-3175; *www.amfac.com*). The lodge remains open all year, but to get a room in summer you need to call several months in advance.

Motels, B&Bs, campgrounds and restaurants in nearby Springdale are listed on p.373 onwards.

Whether or not you stay at the lodge, it's well worth stopping to eat in its bright, cool, upstairs **dining room** (☎ 435/772-3213). The river views will probably linger longer in your mind than its standard breakfasts (daily 6.30–10am) and lunches (daily 11.30am–3pm), both costing around $7. Dinners are slightly more sophisticated (daily 5.30–9pm), featuring entrees such as steak or trout for more like $15. A snackshop near the main entrance (daily 7am–9pm) serves burgers, sodas and ice creams.

It's also possible to arrange **horse rides** from the lodge (March–Oct; 3hr rides at 8.30am & 1.30pm daily, $40, minimum age 8; four 1hr rides daily, $15, minimum age 5; ☎435/772-3967; *www.onpages.com/canyonrides/*).

Camping

The *Watchman* and *South campgrounds*, which hold around four hundred sites between them, are alongside the visitor center; one or other stays open all year. *South* is first-come, first-served, while *Watchman* accepts advance reservations (☎1-800/365-2267; *http://reservations.nps.gov*). Basic sites at either cost $14 per night, or $7 with a Golden Age or Golden Access pass, while *Watchman* also offers sites with electricity for $16. Arrive early in summer, when they tend to fill by noon daily. Campers can walk alongside, and occasionally across, the river to meet the Scenic Drive on the easy two-mile paved **Pa'rus Trail**, also open to cyclists.

To camp in the **backcountry**, pick up the necessary permits, costing $5 per person per night – and a copy of the park regulations – from the visitor center. **Commercial campgrounds** nearby include *Zion Canyon Campground* in Springdale (see p.373), and the *Zican Campground* (☎435/648-2154) just outside the East Entrance, where there's also a cafe and a gas station.

Zion Canyon by road

Whether you access Zion Canyon using the park shuttle buses, or visit in winter when you're free to use your own vehicle, your first impressions of the place are going to be garnered from the highway. The main road, **Hwy-9**, passes plenty of dramatic formations as it climbs east towards Bryce, but Zion's most memorable monoliths are ranged to either side of the dead-end **Scenic Drive**, which runs for six miles north alongside the Virgin River.

The Scenic Drive

For half a mile north of the visitor center, Hwy-9 follows the west bank of the river. The highest of the peaks to the left, collectively known as the **Towers of the Virgin**, is the **Altar of Sacrifice**, named somewhat macabrely for the blood-like streaks of rust that seem to flow from its flat crest.

The highway doglegs right to cross the river just beyond its confluence with **Pine Creek**. Guarded by the **Sentinel** to the west and the **East Temple** to the east, this marks the start of Zion Canyon proper. The **Scenic Drive** branches left on the far side of the bridge, while Hwy-9 heads on east (see opposite).

Full details of Zion Lodge appear overleaf

From here on north the canyon is so narrow, and the walls so steep, that there's barely room to squeeze in a road. Erosion is continuing as fast as ever, and a 200-yard segment of the Scenic Drive had to be rebuilt after a landslide in April 1995. The first major roadside pull-out comes after 1.7 miles, facing the **Court of the Patriarchs**, where peaks named for Abraham, Isaac and Joseph stand arrayed around a small canyon west of the river. A mile further on you reach the meadows of *Zion Lodge*. In the height of summer the crowds here can be overwhelming, but for most of the year it's a pleasant, shady place to break the day, and it's also the trailhead for the popular **Emerald Pools Trail** (see p.383).

Zion Canyon's one designated picnic spot is the **Grotto**, less than a mile beyond the lodge near the foot of the **West Rim Trail** (see p.383). To one side stands **Red Arch Mountain**, named for a natural archway created in 1880 when a vast chunk of the mountain suddenly collapsed and obliterated a newly planted cornfield. To the other is the long western flank of the **Great White Throne**, which from this angle looks neither white nor especially dramatic.

During the next mile the road passes the trailhead for **Weeping Rock** (see p.385) and the **East Rim Trail** (see p.385), as well as a number of unnamed pull-outs where paths lead down to the river. The best views of all come just under five miles from the start of the Drive, as it completes its long curve around the "Big Bend" in the river. The lookout here faces the northern face of the **Great White Throne**, framed between the slender neck of **Angels' Landing** (see p.383) to the right and the pipe-like formations of the lesser **Organ** to the left. Glowing at sunset, the throne is utterly majestic.

A mile or so on, the Scenic Drive – and the shuttle-bus route – comes to an end at a large parking lot that marks the start of the mile-long hike towards the Narrows along the **Riverside Walk** (see p.384). This general area is known as the **Temple of Sinawava**, after a wolfish deity of the Paiute Indians; the most prominent single rock is the **Pulpit**, standing alone near the west bank of the river.

The Zion–Mount Carmel Highway

The side canyon formed by Pine Creek, half a mile north of the visitor center (see p.379), makes it possible for Hwy-9 to continue east, a route known as the **Zion–Mount Carmel Highway**. At first it heads straight for the **East Temple** – like its larger twin, topped by a forested mesa – but it's soon forced to start tacking its way up the hillside. At the eastern end of each extravagant switchback comes a better view of the enormous **Great Arch** at the head of the canyon. Measuring 720 feet wide by 580 feet high, this is not in fact an arch at all, but simply a deep alcove, or what's known as a "blind arch."

Finally the highway burrows into the rock, entering the first and longer of two remarkable tunnels blasted through the canyon walls in the late 1920s. Five "windows" punctuate its one-mile length to allow air and light into the passageway, but you can't stop to admire the views. All the rubble from the excavation was allowed to tumble into

Traffic regulations for the tunnels on Hwy-9 are summarized on p.378.

Zion
National
Park

*For accounts
of Mount
Carmel, Kanab
and points
east, see p.389
onwards.*

Pine Creek far below; the river may seem innocuous, but it cleared the whole lot away in the space of a single year.

Easily seen on the enjoyable **Canyon Overlook Trail** (see p.386), the hot dry plateau beyond the eastern end of the main tunnel feels far removed from the lushness of Zion. These pale, smoothly undulating rocks, capped here and there by strange beehives and hoodoos, are the lithified remains of ancient sand dunes. One huge specimen, crisscrossed with stress lines from eons of erosion and resembling some long-abandoned pyramid, is known as the **Checkerboard Mesa**. It looms south of the highway at a clearly marked turnoff around five miles beyond the second tunnel, just a quarter of a mile short of the park's East Entrance.

Hiking in Zion Canyon

Every visitor to Zion Canyon should **hike** at least one of its many clearly marked and signposted trails; that's the only way to see the canyon in anything approaching its natural state. However, all trails except the short Riverside Walk require a stiff climb away from the canyon floor, and with summer temperatures in excess of 100°F and elevations of well over 6000 feet, it's all too easy to overdo things. Carry plenty of food and drink, and don't imagine that because you have no trouble walking five miles at home you can do it here, straight up a cliff. Water is available on most trails – although not until around five miles along the West or East rim trails – but must be purified before use.

*For more
detailed advice
on desert hik-
ing, see p.23.*

As for specific **routes**, it makes sense to avoid the sun by hiking the east side of the canyon in the morning and the west in the afternoon. If you're reasonably fit and have just one day, the best combination is probably an hour or two along the **Riverside Walk** and a longer climb either to **Angels Landing** on the West Rim Trail or **Hidden Canyon** on the East Rim Trail.

*No pets are
allowed on
any of Zion's
trails.*

All the trails detailed below set off from either Hwy-9 or the Scenic Drive, but some of the longer ones leave the canyon altogether and end up on backcountry dirt roads. If you're planning a one-way hike, look at the **shuttle board** in the visitor center, to see if you can swap vehicles with hikers coming in the opposite direction. Both *Zion Lodge* and the Zion Adventure Company (see p.373) also operate commercial **hiker shuttle services**.

Watchman Trail

*Allow around
two hours to
complete the
two-mile
round-trip
hike on the
Watchman
Trail.*

Just inside the South Entrance, a right turning leads across the river to the *Watchman* campground (see p.380) and the start of the **Watchman Trail**. This steep mile-long climb switchbacks up a side canyon below Bridge Mountain, then heads back south to loop around a flat promontory below the Watchman itself. Thankfully, it doesn't go right to the top, but its views up the canyon, as well as across to the West Temple and back down to Springdale, tucked among the trees, are a good way to get your bearings when you first arrive. Until around 10am, the canyon walls keep most of the route in shade; later on, it's liable to be baking hot.

Emerald Pools Trail

The **Emerald Pools Trail**, which starts conveniently from *Zion Lodge*, is every bit as pretty as the name implies. It's also suitable for walkers of all levels, as the lowest of the three pools can be seen on a gentle round-trip stroll of little more than a mile, while the highest makes a good objective for a more energetic hike.

On the far side of the footbridge that crosses the Virgin River from the lodge, the pink-paved trail to the right is the direct route to the **lower pool**. After an easy climb through the forest, with views straight up the main canyon, it cuts left into Heaps Canyon, and soon reaches a huge overhang of red rock, streaked black by deposits from a broad cascade of water. The almost constant flow collects in pools that tend be a muddy red rather than an emerald green; the overhang is deep enough for the trail to circle inside them, running behind the waterfall.

From this point, the trail becomes confusing, with several alternative routes and countless "trails of use" made by lost or blundering hikers. If you're pressed for time, head back the way you came; alternatively, continue straight ahead, along the shelf on the canyon wall, and in just over half a mile you'll drop back to cross the river at the Grotto picnic area, half a mile north of *Zion Lodge*.

Most hikers head instead for the **higher pools**, by following a narrow path through the cleft in the gigantic split boulder to the left. Having first doubled back to the top of the waterfall, where the stream bubbles out of the woods to spill across a lip of slickrock, take the spur trail to the right on the far side.

The complete loop to the uppermost pool and back takes between two and three hours.

A hot hard climb of not much more than five minutes is rewarded by a delightfully cool seep-fed pool at the foot of the monumental outer walls of the canyon. Climbing any higher is out of the question, but this is a good place to linger, with a small sandy "beach" and plenty of shade. Once back on the main trail, head right while still above the main falls to complete a loop back to the lodge.

Angel's Landing and the West Rim Trail

Serious hikers and backpackers rate the **West Rim Trail** as Zion's most compelling challenge. Even if you have nothing to prove, its views and variety make it well worth attempting, but it's not to be undertaken lightly. The first couple of miles involve a grueling 1500-foot climb out of Zion Canyon, while to reach the obvious day-hike destination, **Angel's Landing** – a five-mile round trip from the valley floor – you have to brave a terrifying knife-edge ridge.

The trail starts across the river from the Grotto picnic area, half a mile north of the lodge. As it winds ever more steeply towards the sheer canyon wall, it seems impossible that there's any way on, but in the end it switchbacks several times and cuts back into a crack in the rock. Unless you've made a very early start, you'll have been out in the sun for a long time by now, and the cool shade of this narrow crevice – **Refrigerator Canyon** – comes as a merciful relief.

Soon however things get worse: beyond the brief flat stretch of the canyon you're confronted by a severe set of switchbacks known as **Walter's Wiggles**. Constructed during the 1920s and named for the park's then superintendent, these serve as a ladder up what would otherwise be an impassable cliff. At the top lies **Scout Lookout**, a tranquil patch of sand with views up and down Zion Canyon and a population of scavenging chipmunks that feast on the remains of countless well-earned picnics.

Daredevil day-hikers are invariably drawn to the spur trail from Scout Lookout to **Angels' Landing**. What you're letting yourself in for is obvious from the outset; the trail sets off along the top of the steep promontory straight ahead, with awesome drop-offs to either side, and only token stretches of metal chain to offer the illusion of security. The end is a hideous half-mile on, with a quarter-mile drop to the canyon floor at your feet and the Great White Throne towering a further thousand feet above you on the far side of the river.

The round-trip hike to Angel's Landing takes a good four hours.

Beyond Scout Lookout, the West Rim Trail climbs steadily out of the canyon. After crossing an expanse of slickrock, marked by small cairns and perilously close to the rim, it descends into a spectacular high-country valley. This is another side of Zion altogether, rimmed with white cliffs, "checkerboarded" by the erosive formation known as cross-bed hatching, and scattered with rounded outcrops of layered sandstone. For a couple of miles, the trail picks its way gingerly across the valley and up the far side, twice crossing streambeds that even when not visibly flowing nurture forest glades. Finally it runs into the monumental wall of red sandstone that marks the head of **Behunin Canyon**, a huge side canyon off Zion Canyon (itself by now way out of view). Doubling back, it clings to the cliff face on a long exposed switchback that comes out on top of **Horse Pasture Plateau**.

Just to set foot on Horse Pasture Plateau is a stiff target for a day-hike from the floor of Zion Canyon, a total round-trip of something over eleven miles. In the full heat of summer even that would be too much to take on, but the trail continues north for another ten miles, to **Lava Point** off the Kolob Terrace Road (see p.387), with plenty of optional scenic detours en route. This is Zion's most popular back-packing trip, usually done as a two-day expedition, starting from Lava Point and working down, and camping near the southern edge of Horse Pasture Plateau.

Backcountry camping in Zion requires a permit; see p.380.

Riverside Walk

Not least because it involves no climbing, the mile-long **Riverside Walk** at the end of the Scenic Drive is Zion's best-loved trail. Having watched the canyon walls converge ever closer, the urge to find out what happens beyond the end of the road is all but irresistible. You may well have more company than you'd prefer, but the views from the gentle paved footpath are too beautiful for that to matter.

Walls of deep red sandstone soar to either side of the river, which is flanked by shimmering cottonwoods that turn a rich gold in the fall. There are even patches of low-lying "desert swamp", where bull-frogs bellow in the rushes and willows thrust from the mud.

Until recently, Riverside Walk was known as the "Gateway to the Narrows Trail," as it ends where the Virgin emerges from **the Narrows**, overlooked by the mighty **Mountain of Mystery**. For eight miles upstream from this sandy little beach, the river fills the entire gorge, often less than twenty feet wide and channeled between vertical cliffs almost a thousand feet high. Conditions are so treacherous that it's now illegal to hike any distance upstream into the Narrows, against the current – hence the change of name. However, assuming you'll want to cool your feet, you're free to wade out from the beach, helped by one of the discarded walking sticks usually to be found nearby.

When the danger of flash floods is considered minimal, hikers are allowed to wade *downstream* through the Narrows from the far end. The trailhead is at **Chamberlain's Ranch**, a thirty-mile drive from Zion Canyon, reached by turning left 1.7 miles east of the East Entrance (just east of milepost 46 on Hwy-9), and then following North Fork Road, which in due course becomes a rough dirt track, for around seventeen miles north. Permits for the next day are issued from 8am onwards at the visitor center, and cost $5; eighty people per day are allowed to make the ten-hour trip as a day-hike, while 68 are permitted to camp for one night only en route. It's no easy jaunt, with the water often icy cold and thigh- or even neck-deep, but at least you may be lucky enough to spot the unique Zion Snail, the size of a pinhead and found only in the Narrows. Specialist equipment for the hike can be rented in Springdale, from outfitters such as the Zion Adventure Company (see p.373).

Weeping Rock

One of the easiest short walks in Zion Canyon – and thus prone to be overcrowded in summer – is the half-mile round-trip hike to **Weeping Rock**. Eaten from the canyon wall by a perennial spring, this damp alcove is filled with ferns and tiny flowers; while it comes as a surprise in the desert, however, it's not as beautiful as you may be led to expect. The paved trail up starts from the parking lot at the mouth of Echo Canyon, halfway between *Zion Lodge* and the end of the road.

Hidden Canyon and the East Rim Trail

Rewarding hikes of almost any length can be enjoyed by taking the **East Rim Trail**, which sets off from the Weeping Rock trailhead but

Zion National Park

It's easy enough to complete the Riverside Walk in under an hour, but you'll enjoy it more if you allow much longer.

The trail through the Narrows is usually passable during June, July, September and October only; all hikers must register at the visitor center.

*Hidden
Canyon is a
three-mile,
three-hour
round-trip
hike from the
Scenic Drive.*

branches right rather than left on the far side of Echo Canyon Creek. Only backpackers who camp overnight on the mesa-top attempt its full 10.5-mile length, and they normally prefer to start from the far end, near the park's East Entrance. However, the strenuous two-mile climb out of Zion Canyon is its most exhilarating segment, and offers several spur trails for day-hikers.

One possible goal for a half-day hike is **Hidden Canyon**, a "hanging canyon" that has yet to cut its way down to the floor of Zion. By the time the relevant spur trail leaves the East Rim Trail, you've switchbacked about half a mile up the face of Cable Mountain, but are still only halfway to the top. Hidden Canyon itself is a further half-mile on, beyond a brief stretch of forest and a hair-raising segment, where the trail clings to a wall of rock, which is enough to deter most would-be canyoneers. The broad "lip" of the canyon, perched 700 feet above Zion, turns into a waterfall after heavy rain, while the rounded holes scoured into the slickrock fill with water and life. Strictly speaking, the trail ends here; it's just about feasible to press on into the canyon, but only expert rock climbers have any hope of approaching its head.

*Allow six
hours for the
seven-mile
round-trip
hike to
Observation
Point.*

If Hidden Canyon sounds too intimidating, you may prefer to keep on switchbacking up the East Rim Trail beyond the Hidden Canyon turnoff. A mile or so further on, deep in wafer-thin Echo Canyon, the **East Mesa Trail** climbs steeply off to the left. A two-mile walk through the woods on top of the plateau brings you to **Observation Point**, which commands views all the way down Zion Canyon. The massive cliffs of Cable Mountain and the Great White Throne stare you full in the face, while Angels Landing towers proudly on the far side.

Assuming you stay on the East Rim Trail rather than taking the **East Mesa Trail**, it takes a good mile or more to drag yourself up out of Echo Canyon, and there may be streams to negotiate en route. Atop the mesa, walking becomes much easier, as the trails simply follow former logging roads. **Stave Spring**, the only perennial water source on the East Rim Trail, is roughly halfway between Zion Canyon, five miles west, and the East Entrance, slightly further southeast. Overnight campers can at this point head southwest, along a trail that soon forks to the summits of **Cable Mountain** – where you can take a closer look at the century-old workings that hauled timber down into Zion (see p.378) – or Deertrap Mountain. Either hike is a six-mile detour from Stave Spring.

Canyon Overlook Trail

Opposite the ranger station at the eastern end of the long tunnel on the Zion–Mount Carmel highway (see p.381), steps cut into the rock mark the start of the **Canyon Overlook Trail**. So long as you don't mind edging along the brink of a precipice – at one point the trail consists of wooden planks braced against the cliff-face – this offers a fascinating variety of terrain in the space of just half a mile. It's also the only trail described in this section for which the trailhead is accessible in your own vehicle year round – though there's so little parking that you may find that makes little difference anyway. The scenery en route ranges from fern-filled grottoes fed by seeping water to a bare slickrock mesa topped by tiny hoodoos. An informative booklet, usually available at the trailhead, explains the flora and fauna you may spot.

The trail ends at a railed viewing area at the head of Pine Creek Canyon; you can't see it, but you're directly above the Great Arch. Only one of the tunnel's five "windows" is visible in the rock wall to your left, but the road emerges below to zigzag into the valley. Straight ahead of you is the west wall of Zion Canyon; a helpful sign labels the peaks ranged along the far side of the river, from the ruddy tree-capped West Temple to the paler Sentinel.

Kolob Terrace Road

The only road access to the central uplands of Zion National Park is along **Kolob Terrace Road**, which branches inconspicuously north from Hwy-9 at the hamlet of **Virgin**, fifteen miles west of the park's South Entrance (see p.372). Especially in its earlier stages, it's a dramatic drive, deservedly proclaimed a Scenic Byway, but unless you have a high-clearance 4WD vehicle, you won't manage the full 43 miles to meet I-15 just south of Cedar City. Ordinary cars have to turn back after just over twenty miles, so only long-distance hikers or tourists with a spare afternoon to kill tend to come this way.

The road starts by climbing through a dry desert valley, dotted with pine trees, heading for two pyramidal mountains that dwarf the cliffs on the horizon. It dips repeatedly in and out of the park boundaries, reaching Zion after just over seven miles, only to exit almost immediately. As it next reenters the park, you get superb views north across **Hop Valley** to the russet and white pinnacle of **Burnt Mountain**. Keen backpackers can hike to Kolob Arch from here along the **Hop Valley Trail**, but it's not as easy as it looks; you have to plough through thick sand for most of the way, so the fifteen-mile hike is even more difficult than the route described on p.388.

Soon after you leave the park yet again, twenty miles up from the highway, a dirt road to the right leads 1.7 miles to **Lava Point**, back within the park. As well as being the trailhead for the West Rim Trail, which takes fourteen miles to drop down into Zion Canyon (see p.383), this is a superb vantage point in its own right. Park rangers use the cabin at **Fire Lookout**, a short walk from the end of the road, to keep a vigilant eye on the forests of the Markagunt Plateau. Poised four thousand feet higher than the visitor center, it overlooks a panorama that stretches north to Cedar Breaks and southeast to the Kaibab Mountains, with the monoliths of Zion Canyon mere incidental details in the foreground. There's a **picnic area** and a free six-site primitive **campground** (with no water) nearby.

Assuming you can grab one of the few parking spots, it takes around an hour to walk the full length of the Canyon Overlook Trail and return to the road.

The Kolob Terrace Road is closed to all traffic in winter.

Kolob Terrace Road is paved for just under two miles beyond the Lava Point turnoff, passing a village of pastel cabins before it turns to dirt for the last mile to **Kolob Reservoir**. Locals flock to this drab little lake to cool off and play with their boats, but it holds no great interest for tourists.

Kolob Canyons

Located just off I-15, twenty miles south of Cedar City, the **Kolob Canyons** have formed part of Zion National Park since 1956. Although easier to reach than Zion Canyon, they remain far less famous and receive far fewer visitors. In all honesty, neither are they as immediately impressive as Zion Canyon, and you'll only get the most out of the area if you can spare the time and energy to hike. If you stay in your car, you can drive to the end of the five-mile road, admire the view of the red-rock canyons, and be back on the interstate within the hour, wondering what the fuss is about.

Information on the Kolob Canyons can be picked up from the small **visitor center** at exit 40 off I-15 (daily: May–Sept 8am–7pm; Oct–April 8am–6pm; ☎435/586-9548). As well as providing free hiking advice, rangers also allot 24 numbered backcountry **campsites** ($5). No gas or food is available.

Beyond the visitor center, **Kolob Canyons Road** twists alongside Taylor Creek and then up through Lee Pass, with countless trailheads and roadside viewpoints en route. It ends at a parking lot that faces across the riverbed to a succession of narrow, red-walled **"finger" canyons** cut into the west rim of the Markagunt Plateau. Each was carved by a separate tiny stream; one, Hanging Valley, is interrupted by a sheer 1500-foot cliff, stranding an isolated patch of thick forest far above the valley floor. In the distance, you may just be able to make out the West Temple, above Zion Canyon.

Footpaths on the far side of the lot lead to a picnic spot in the woods. From here, the half-mile **Timber Creek Overlook** trail runs through low trees along the top of the ridge, to end at a rocky promontory with views over the endless rolling forests.

Hiking the Kolob Canyons

The two main **hiking trails** in the Kolob Canyons leave from earlier along Kolob Canyons Road. Starting two miles from the visitor center, **Taylor Creek Trail** follows the Middle Fork of Taylor Creek on a five-mile round-trip to **Double Arch Alcove**, passing long-abandoned cabins built by early homesteaders en route. The trail grows progressively less and less distinct before it culminates by climbing into the lush hollow in the canyon wall that lies beneath the Double Arch itself.

The **Kolob Arch Trail**, which ranks among Zion's very finest trails, leads down from Lees Pass along the drainage of Timber Creek. It can be muddy going at times, but at least there's usually plenty of water

It takes around four hours to hike to Double Arch Alcove and back.

en route (though it must be purified before drinking). The first couple of miles, heading south, feature superb close-up views of the finger canyons; you then veer east to meet **La Verkin Creek** just above a waterfall. The goal for most hikers is **Kolob Arch**, seven miles along, which may or may not be the world's longest natural rock span. Like Landscape Arch, in Arches National Park (see p.461), it's in the region of 300 feet across; no one agrees how to measure arches any more precisely, so they're generally considered equals. Camping somewhere nearby (by prior arrangement at the visitor center) makes for a less grueling hike, and gives you the option of exploring the remote regions that lie farther along La Verkin Creek.

Zion National Park

At fourteen miles, the day-hike to Kolob Arch and back is only for confident, experienced desert hikers.

East from Zion: US-89

As soon as you leave Zion National Park via its eastern entrance (see p.382), you're out in flat, open ranching country. Eleven nondescript miles further on, Hwy-9 meets **US-89** at Mount Carmel Junction. Turn **north** from here, and once across a mountainous ridge you'll find yourself driving up the broad **Long Valley**, where the **Sevier River** cuts between the Markagunt and Paunsaugunt plateaus. After just over forty pretty but uneventful miles, punctuated by the occasional tiny Mormon settlement, you can choose between keeping straight on towards Salt Lake City, or veering east towards Bryce Canyon and the other national parks.

The only real point in heading **south** on US-89 is to reach Arizona, with the North Rim of the Grand Canyon (see p.352) almost exactly a hundred miles away. A century ago, when Mormons from Arizona would come this way to be married in the temple at St George, this route was known as the **Honeymoon Trail**. The largest town along the highway, **Kanab**, retains a strong Mormon identity, but it also has a genuine back-of-beyond frontier feel to it, and makes the best overnight stop in the vicinity.

Mount Carmel and Mount Carmel Junction

The eastward progress of Hwy-9 stops when a north–south wall of red cliffs rears up on the far side of the Virgin River. It's a bucolic spot, with cottonwoods lining the river and horses grazing in the meadows to the north. Unless you're ready to stop for the night, however, there's precious little reason to get out of the car.

MOUNT CARMEL JUNCTION, where Hwy-9 intersects with US-89, consists of a couple of fairly upscale and reliable **motels**, both with licensed **restaurants**. The *Best Western Thunderbird* (☎435/648-2203 or 1-888/848-6358, fax 435/648-2239; winter ③, summer ④), which boasts a pool, spa and even half a golf course, has a considerable edge over the *Golden Hills* (☎435/648-2268 or 1-800/648-2268; winter ②, summer ③).

Hwy-14 from Cedar City and Cedar Breaks (see p.370) joins US-89 halfway between Mount Carmel and the Bryce turnoff.

In the parent community of **MOUNT CARMEL**, a mile or two
north, the summer-only *Mount Carmel Motel* (☎ 435/648-2323; ①)
offers half a dozen rudimentary rooms and an unappealing RV site.
It's nonetheless gigantic compared to its neighbor, a one-room motel
that looks suspiciously like a garden shed.

South from Mount Carmel: Coral Pink Sand Dunes State Park

Few areas in the Southwest conform so exactly to the popular notion
of a desert – graceful dunes of fine sand, their parallel crests sweep-
ing towards the horizon – as **Coral Pink Sand Dunes State Park**.
This pseudo-Saharan landscape, a dozen miles south of Mount
Carmel Junction, is reached by two separate paved roads that leave
US-89 four and nine miles southeast of town respectively.

*The park
remains open
24 hours, with
a $5 day-use
fee; informa-
tion is on
☎ 435/874-
2408.*

The only dune field in the Colorado Plateau lies at the foot of a
seven-mile bluff of the Vermilion Cliffs, which here unusually face
the northwest. Its sand grains are so uniformly small because they've
already been sifted at least twice by the winds that still keep them
swirling; the Navajo Sandstone from which they've eroded was itself
originally deposited in the form of dunes.

Hikers who launch themselves from the boardwalk near the
entrance station usually find that a few minutes of wading knee-deep
in sand sates their *Lawrence of Arabia* fantasies. However, in
marked contrast to Utah's federal parks, **off-road vehicles** are posi-
tively encouraged. The park was created in response to campaigns
by local off-road enthusiasts, and plays host to countless formal and
informal **dune buggy races**, most notably each July 4.

The well-shaded **campground** ($11; for summer-only reserva-
tions, costing $5 extra, call ☎ 1-800/322-3770) remains open all
year, though it only has water in summer. Spending a night here
offers the enticing prospect of seeing not only kangaroo rats but,
more to the point, the snakes that prey on them.

Kanab

Until new roads were pushed through the region in the 1950s,
KANAB, seventeen miles southeast of Mount Carmel Junction and
just two miles from the Arizona state line, was renowned as perhaps
the most inaccessible town in the US. Now it's a significant tourist
halt, thanks to a position halfway between the Grand Canyon, eighty
miles southeast, and Bryce Canyon, 83 miles northeast.

Kanab started life as **Fort Kanab**, a frontier outpost so prone to
Indian attacks that it only survived from 1864 until 1866. The town
itself was founded by Jacob Hamblin in 1870, as a God-fearing
ranching community with a sideline in harboring Mormons who fell
foul of the federal government, such as the perpetrators of the
Mountain Meadows Massacre (see p.367). That lawless image was

later cultivated by pulp novelist Zane Grey, who set many of his Westerns here, while Kanab's rugged surroundings made it a focus for Western movie-makers from Tom Mix, who filmed *Deadwood Coach* here in 1924, to Clint Eastwood.

East from Zion: US-89

Ranching in southern Utah has long been in decline, but the citizens of Kanab would still much prefer to wrest their living from the earth. Their biggest payday came in the late 1950s, when this was the original base for the construction of Glen Canyon Dam (see p.428). During the eighteen months it took to upgrade the 72-mile dirt road to the dam site, and build the new town of Page, locals scurried to grab their share of the 200 million federal dollars that were pumped into the project. In November 1958, the workers decamped for Page, and the boom was over.

Since then, Kanab has pinned its hopes on the prospect of large-scale coal-mining on the **Kaiparowits Plateau** to the northeast. The environmentalists and national politicians who thwarted such plans in the 1970s were burned in effigy on the streets of Kanab, while the town closed down in protest for an hour in October 1996 when President Clinton's declaration of Grand Staircase–Escalante National Monument (see p.409) precluded that possibility forever.

"Green" actor Robert Redford was among those burned in effigy in Kanab in 1976, which may explain why fewer movies are filmed here these days.

Kanab has thus been left to survive by catering for tourists, which it does with reasonably good grace. US-89 is lined with an above-par assortment of motels and restaurants, with the greatest concentration where it briefly doglegs to run east–west along **Center Street**. A few blocks south, US-89 proper branches off east towards Page, while US-89A continues south into Arizona.

Apart from some large Western-themed souvenir stores, such as Denny's Wigwam, opposite *Parry Lodge* at 78 E Center St (☎435/644-2452 or 1-800/854-8549), there's almost nothing to do in Kanab. Hikers may enjoy the views from the **Squaw Trail**, which leads up the cliffs a few blocks north of downtown, but if you're looking to fill the southern Utah equivalent of a rainy afternoon your best bet is to drive fifteen miles east on US-89 to **Johnson Canyon**. A bizarre local legend says this red-rock canyon conceals a fortune in Aztec gold, smuggled out of Mexico as their empire fell. More prosaically, it's home to a mock-Western township built for the TV series *Gunsmoke*, and also featured in movies such as *How The West Was Won* (daily dawn–dusk; $3, under-18s free).

For an account of Fredonia AZ, seven miles south of Kanab, and the route to the Grand Canyon, see p.357 onwards.

Information

Kanab's **visitor center** – slogan, "The Greatest Earth on Show" – is just south of Center Street at 78 South 100 East (Nov–Feb Mon–Fri 9am–5pm; March, April & Oct Mon–Sat 8am–6pm; May–Sept daily 8am–6pm; ☎435/644-5033 or 1-800/733-5263; *www.kaneutah .com*). The local **BLM** office, 318 North 100 East (Mon–Fri 8am–4.30pm; ☎435/644-2672) carries full information on Grand Staircase–Escalante National Monument.

The zip code for Kanab is UT 84741.

Accommodation

Kanab holds a number of good-value budget **motels**, so don't feel compelled to pay extra for a fancier name. All are within easy walking distance of downtown, but since there's no reason to walk anywhere, that makes little difference.

Best Western Red Hills, 125 W Center St; ☎435/644-2675 or 1-800/830-2675, fax 435/644-5915. Strangely ugly, somewhat overpriced, but very central motel. Large modern rooms plus a pool and whirlpool. Winter ③, summer ④.

Canyonlands International Hostel, 143 East 100 South; ☎435/644-5554. Friendly private hostel, a block east of the highway near the visitor center, that offers $10 dorm beds plus kitchen, library and laundry. ①.

National 9 Aiken's Lodge, 74 W Center St; ☎435/644-2625 or 1-800/524-9999, fax 435/644-8827. The ideal budget motel: crisp and clean, right in the heart of town, and with its own pool. ②.

The price
codes used
here are
explained on
p.15.

Parry Lodge, 89 E Center St; ☎435/644-2601 or 1-800/748-4104, fax 435/644-2605. Opened in 1931, Kanab's oldest motel has an undeniable air of romance, with its lobby and restaurant festooned with photos of movie-star guests and nameplates to tell you which rooms they (officially) slept in. You can even bathe in John Wayne's extra-large bathtub. *Parry's* isn't *that* great, though, and some of the newer rooms are both dingy and noisy, even if you can get room service from the restaurant. Winter ③, summer ④.

Shilo Inn, 296 West 100 North; ☎435/644-2562 or 1-800/222-2244, fax 435/644-5333. Large but very presentable motel, at the north end of town. Some rooms have kitchens, and there's a pool and spa. Winter ③, summer ④.

Super 8, 70 South 200 West; ☎435/644-5500 or 1-800/800-8000, fax 435/644-5576. Dependable budget motel, with large pool and hot tub, in a quiet location a block south of Center St. Winter ②, summer ③.

Eating

Around twenty formulaic **restaurants** cling to the edge of the highway as it passes through Kanab, safe in the knowledge that however bad they may be, there's not a better place to eat for a hundred miles in any direction.

Four Seasons Fifties-Style Restaurant, 36 North 300 West; ☎435/644-2635. Fun mock-Fifties diner, with a 10¢ jukebox and a menu of burgers, sandwiches and fried meats, to be washed down with (nothing stronger than) copious malts and shakes. Closes 7pm in winter.

Houston's Trails End, 32 E Center St; ☎435/644-2488. Western-themed family diner, serving chicken-fried steaks, fish and fried breakfasts. Open daily for all meals, but closed Jan to mid-Feb.

Nedra's Too, 310 South 100 East; ☎435/644-2030. Informal local place on the south side of town at the junction of US-89 and US-89A. The unifying factor of the Mexican/American menu is the frier; even the ice cream comes deep-fried, while if you're a newcomer to this neck of the woods you might want to sample the first Navajo taco (see p.26) of your life. Open daily for all meals.

Parry Lodge, 89 E Center St; ☎435/644-2601. This atmospheric dining room is as close as Kanab comes to having a gourmet restaurant, with a menu that occasionally hints at the healthy, in the form of dishes like poached salmon, and a licence to sell alcohol. Open for all meals in summer, breakfast and dinner only in spring and fall, and closed Nov–March.

North from Mount Carmel: Orderville

If you turn north on US-89 at Mount Carmel (see p.389), you'll arrive at **ORDERVILLE** within four miles. From 1875 onwards, this now-negligible settlement was the scene of the longest-lasting of several experiments in communitarian living organized by the **United Order**, a Mormon group that believed all property should be held in common. Each family had its own cabin inside a stockade, but meals were eaten en masse, and each member received the same pay. A man earned $1.50 per day and a woman 75¢, as credit at the village store; money left unspent returned to the pool. In 1886, when Orderville's children were drifting away in search of better-paid work, their parents gave up and shared out their assets.

As well as boasting two gas stations and two rock shops, Orderville has a couple of shabby motels, but neither is worth recommending.

Glendale

Five miles beyond Orderville, the almost equally insignificant hamlet of **GLENDALE** nestles amid a cluster of apple orchards. A white-clapboard house that looks much like the rest – complete with a large upstairs veranda – is grandly designated the *Smith Hotel*, and holds seven pleasant en-suite B&B rooms (☎ & fax 435/648-2156; April–Oct only; ③). The *Home Place*, 200 S Main St (☎435/648-2194; ③), is similar, smaller but slightly more upscale.

Hatch

Long Valley steadily dries out north of Glendale, so travelers from Cedar City who pick up US-89 at the east end of Hwy-14 – see p.387 – encounter further upland forests rather than farmland.

At 7000ft up, little **HATCH**, 25 miles on, makes a cool overnight stop in summer, but that's the only time its handful of motels are at all busy. Both the central *Mountain Ridge Motel* (☎435/735-4258 or 1-800/870-4258; ②), and the *Riverside Motel*, a mile north (☎435/735-4223, fax 735-4220; ③), have half a dozen basic but reasonable rooms, plus **camping** facilities for $14 per night. The somewhat smarter *Bryce–Zion Midway Resort*, 224 S Hwy-89 (☎435/735-4199 or 1-888/299-3531; ③), offers a choice of cabins or ordinary motel rooms, and also a decent **restaurant**.

The zip code for Hatch is UT 84735.

Red Canyon and the road to Bryce

The only road in a hundred miles that manages to climb through the wild country east of US-89 is **Hwy-12**, which was blasted into the rocks ten miles north of Hatch to provide a route to **Bryce Canyon** and beyond. Another seven miles' drive from here brings you to the town of Panguitch, but there are a couple of modern, comfortable motels right at the intersection, in the shape of *Bryce Junction Inn* (closed Nov–March; ☎435/676-2221 or 1-800/437-4361, fax 435/676-2291; ③) and *Harold's Place* (closed Nov–April; ☎435/676-2350; ③).

Hwy-12 climbs away from US-89 by way of **Red Canyon**. For information on this small precursor of the joys ahead, call in at the Dixie National Forest **visitor center** (☎435/676-8815), a few miles along on the left. This parking lot marks the start of the short Pink Ledges **hiking trail**; longer trails leave from the forest service's *Red Canyon* **campground** ($8, no showers; ☎435/865-3700), half a mile further on. Immediately beyond that, the highway tunnels through two artificial red-rock arches, before topping out on top of the Paunsaugunt Plateau, with another ten miles to go before Bryce.

Panguitch

The squeaky-clean Mormon town of **PANGUITCH** – 24 miles from Bryce, and fifty from Mount Carmel Junction – was established in 1864, and named for no good reason after the Paiute for "Big Fish." After an uncertain start, when like so many of its neighbors it was abandoned in the face of Indian attacks, Panguitch prospered. It became, and remains, the largest town along the Upper Sevier Valley. That was originally due in part to the brick factory responsible for the distinguished brick homes that still adorn its streets, but Panguitch today depends heavily on tourism for its bread and butter. It's a bit too chilly to linger in the off-season, but in summer, the pumps at the eight local gas stations rarely stop spinning (one, Todd's Truck Stop, stays open 24hr), and twenty-odd budget motels and restaurants are kept busy.

The zip code for Panguitch is UT 84759.

Panguitch's **visitor center**, a roadside cabin at 800 N Main St (May–Oct daily 9am–5pm; ☎435/676-2311 or 1-800/444-6869), doles out details of a **walking tour** of the town's historic homes. You'd have to be more than a little weird, however, to spend your morning doing that rather than setting off into the wondrous deserts on your doorstep.

Accommodation

An invisible network seems to connect Panguitch's many **motels**, meaning their rates can vary minute by minute according to demand. Broadly speaking, however, peak season runs from late spring to early fall, and you should be able to find a seriously inexpensive room at most other times, although a few winter skiers choose to stay here rather than in Brian Head (see p.371).

The price codes used here are explained on p.15.

Best Western New Western Motel, 180 E Center St; ☎435/676-8876 or 1-800/528-1234. Panguitch's largest and most luxurious motel, with an outdoor pool. Winter ③, summer ④.

Color Country Motel, 526 N Main St; ☎435/676-2386 or 1-800/225-6518, fax 435/676-8484; *www.infowest.com/ccmotel/*. Refurbished motel, with around twenty traditional rooms on two stories and a large pool. Winter ②, summer ③.

Marianna Inn, 699 N Main St; ☎435/676-8844 or 1-800/331-7407, fax 435/676-8340. Scrupulously clean, well-run motel on the northern edge of town, near several restaurants, with units ranging from one to four beds. Operated by the same management as the *Panguitch Inn*. Winter ②, summer ⑤.

Panguitch Inn, 50 N Main St; ☎435/676-8871 or 1-800/331-7407, fax 435/676-8340. Restored inn in the very heart of town, open May–Oct only and offering good clean rooms at low rates and a huge covered parking area. Spring and fall ②, summer ④.

Eating

The number of **restaurants** in Panguitch must run into double figures, though it feels more like there's just one restaurant that's repeated at fifty-yard intervals along the highway. You could always pig out on Pringles in your motel room instead.

Buffalo Java, 47 N Main St; ☎435/676-8900. Summer-only student hangout, serving espresso coffees plus soups and snacks.

Country Corner Cafe, 80 N Main St; ☎435/676-8851. Predictable family diner, right in the heart of town, and open Mon–Sat from 6am.

Cowboy's Smokehouse Bar-B-Q, 95 N Main St; ☎435/676-8030. Feast on barbecued meats and huge fruit pies under the impassive gaze of generations of stuffed elk heads. Open Mon–Sat for lunch and dinner, with Western music at weekends.

Flying M, 580 N Main St; ☎435/676-8008. Stacks of breakfast pancakes, and the usual diner-style meals later in the day. Up at the north end of town, and the only place in Panguitch licensed to sell beer.

Grandma Tina's Spaghetti House, 523 N Main St; ☎435/676-2377. As well as the pasta the name implies, this Italian diner, open for all meals daily, also serves a mean espresso.

North of Panguitch: Fremont Indian State Park

US-89 keeps going **north of Panguitch**, following the course of the Old Spanish Trail beside the Sevier River. Travelers heading for **Salt Lake City**, a total of 230 miles distant, can join **I-15** by cutting northwest after ten miles, or stay on US-89 until it meets **I-70** around sixty miles north.

There's no room in this book to cover the myriad small towns along the way, and Utah's mountainous heartland is in any case a far cry from the deserts to the south. However, if you're interested in native cultures of the Southwest, you may want to visit **Fremont Indian State Park**, just off I-70 eight miles east of US-89 (daily: summer 9am–6pm; winter 9am–5pm; $5 per vehicle; ☎435/527-4631). Although the park preserves the site of a large Fremont village, occupied around 1100 AD and discovered during the construction of the interstate, you soon find out that the village has in fact been completely destroyed. However, easy, short trails lead through canyons

filled with rock art, and the artifacts and arrowheads in the excellent
little museum bring the Fremont peoples to life.

The most convenient overnight base nearby is **RICHFIELD**, twenty
miles northeast, where budget **motels** include a good *Super 8*, 1575 N
Main St (☎435/896-9204 or 1-800/800-8000, fax 435/896-9614;
winter ②, summer ③). The *Little Wonder Cafe*, 101 N Main St
(☎435/896-8960) is an appealing local **diner**.

Bryce Canyon National Park

Few more freakish landscapes can exist than those confined within
BRYCE CANYON NATIONAL PARK. From the safety of the park's
rim road, visitors gaze down upon a throng of red, yellow and orange
pinnacles of rock, eating like the flames of a forest fire into the thickly wooded plateau. Braver souls can hike down into the inferno and
thread their way between the top-heavy towers, to explore a barren
desert that's aglow with almost psychedelic colors.

Paiute Indians, who hunted in the vicinity for many generations,
had an elegantly precise word for it: *Unkatimpe-wa-Wince-
Pockich*, "red rocks standing like men in a bowl-shaped recess." The
current name comes from the Mormon settler **Ebenezer Bryce**, who
established a short-lived homestead nearby in 1874, and memorably
declared that it was "a helluva place to lose a cow." In fact, however,
"Bryce's Canyon" is not a canyon at all, but a row of crescent-shaped
amphitheaters, hollowed into a twenty-mile stretch along the eastern
edge of the **Paunsaugunt Plateau**. At up to 9000ft above sea level,
this marks the final and most spectacular rung of the Grand
Staircase's ascent of southern Utah (see p.359). Between sixty and
forty million years ago, the **Pink Cliffs** were deposited in layers of
varying thickness and strength on the beds of shallow lakes. Some
are limestone, some siltstone; all were dyed and stained with combinations of red, white, orange, blue or yellow by different concentrations of minerals, especially iron.

Conditions at Bryce are perfect for rapid erosion, with ice forming
overnight and thawing in the morning over 200 times per year.
Water seeps into cracks in the ground, then expands as it freezes, to
wedge the cracks ever wider. Spurs emerge from the cliff-face as it
recedes, then dwindle to slender fins and eventually break into separate standing columns. When the topmost rock of a column is hard
enough, lower levels erode away beneath it at a much faster rate. A
mighty boulder left precariously perched on a tall, narrow pillar is
known as a **hoodoo**. At Bryce, thousands upon thousands of hoodoos
are crammed into each successive amphitheater, to form a
menagerie of multihued, contorted stone shapes. The best known,
and most precarious, is **Thor's Hammer**, near Sunset Point.

Since it became a national park in the 1920s – with its irregular
boundaries designed to minimize the impact on local ranchers –

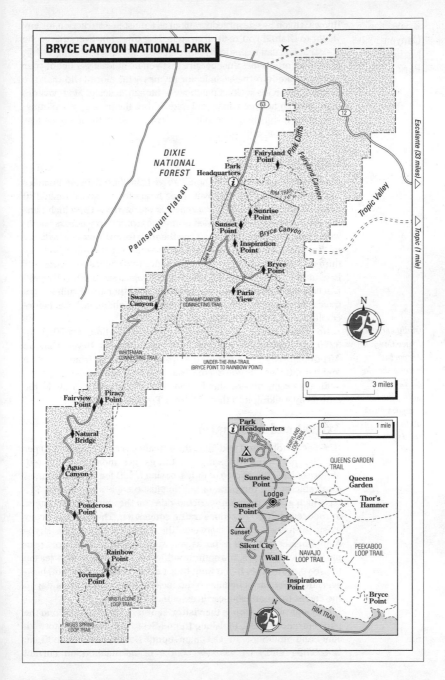

BRYCE CANYON NATIONAL PARK

DIXIE
NATIONAL
FOREST

Paunsaugunt Plateau

Pink Cliffs

Fairyland Canyon

Escalante (33 miles)

Tropic (1 mile)

Tropic Valley

63

12

Park
Headquarters

Fairyland
Point

RIM TRAIL

Sunrise
Point

Sunset
Point

Bryce Canyon

Inspiration
Point

See Inset

Bryce
Point

Paria
View

Swamp
Canyon

SWAMP CANYON
CONNECTING TRAIL

WHITEMAN
CONNECTING TRAIL

UNDER-THE-RIM-TRAIL
(BRYCE POINT TO RAINBOW POINT)

N

0 _____ 3 miles

Fairview
Point

Piracy
Point

Natural
Bridge

Agua
Canyon

Ponderosa
Point

Rainbow
Point

Yovimpa
Point

BRISTLECONE
LOOP TRAIL

RIGGS SPRING
(LOOP TRAIL)

Park
Headquarters

FAIRYLAND
LOOP TRAIL

0 _____ 1 mile

QUEENS GARDEN
TRAIL

North

Sunrise
Point

Lodge

Queens
Garden

Thor's
Hammer

Sunset
Point

Sunset

Silent City

Wall St.

NAVAJO
LOOP TRAIL

PEEKABOO
LOOP TRAIL

Inspiration
Point

Bryce
Point

RIM TRAIL

N

Bryce Canyon National Park

Bryce Canyon has deservedly ranked as a must-see attraction for any visitor to Utah. If you're at all stretched for time, however, this is one park that you can realistically hope to see in the space of a single day, or even an afternoon. Just be sure that you do at least get out of your car, and **hike** into the technicolor ravines – far more vivid than the Grand Canyon, as well as much more human in scale. Most visitors pass through between June and August, but the park is, if anything, even more inspiring in the stillness of winter, when the hoodoos rear their heads from a blanket of snow.

Getting to Bryce

Bryce Canyon is around two hours' drive from Zion Canyon, 86 miles southwest, and something over three hours from Capitol Reef, 120 miles northeast. The only approach is along **Hwy-12**, which runs within the northern boundaries of the park on its way across southwest Utah. However, you won't see the rock formations – or be liable for the entrance fee – unless you turn south off the main highway thirteen miles east of US-89 (a total of 20 miles southeast of Panguitch), or eight miles northwest of Tropic (see p.402). **Hwy-63** reaches the park entrance station after a further three miles, then traces the rim of the Paunsaugunt Plateau for eighteen miles before coming to a dead end at Rainbow Point.

No public **buses** serve Bryce, but Scenic Airlines (☎702/638-3270 or 1-800/634-6801) fly from Las Vegas to **Bryce Canyon Airport** on Hwy-12. Once on the ground, rent a car from, or join a tour with, Bryce Canyon Scenic Tours (see opposite).

Finally, keen **hikers** should note that it's possible to avoid the crowds by walking into the park from **Tropic** (see p.402).

Oddly enough, Bryce Canyon Airport is among the oldest in the US, with pine-log hangars built by the WPA in the 1930s.

Arrival and information

Between October and mid-May, the **entrance fee** to Bryce is $10 per vehicle, per week. In summer, things get more complicated. Motorists have the choice of either paying a $20 fee and taking their own vehicles into the park, or parking just outside and paying a $15 fee which grants them unrestricted rides on the **shuttle bus** system, introduced in 2000 to reduce traffic congestion. The buses basically exist to ferry visitors between the park entrance and Bryce Amphitheater. If that's as far as you want to go – and for most people, even keen hikers, it's entirely sufficient – then there's no reason to use your own car. If you want to get as far as Rainbow Point, however, the irregular schedules often include just one service a day to the end of the road, so a car is essential.

The logical first stop is the **visitor center**, a short way beyond the park entrance (daily: mid-June to mid-Sept 8am–8pm; May to mid-June and mid-Sept to Oct 8am–6pm; Nov–April 8am–4.30pm; ☎435/834-5322). A valuable source of information on current weather and hiking conditions, this is also the place to pick up back-country permits (see overleaf).

For information on **guided tours**, call at either *Bryce Canyon Lodge*, inside the park, or *Ruby's Inn*, outside it to the north (see below). The *Lodge* is the base for Bryce Tours, which operates a busy schedule of **driving tours** in summer (☎435/834-5361; adults $6, under-13s $3), and also Canyon Trail Rides (☎435/679-8665; *www.onpages.com/canyonrides/*), which arranges **horseback** expeditions (2hr rides starting at 9am & 2pm, $26.50; half-day rides at 8am & 1pm, $40). Bryce Canyon Scenic Tours (☎435/834-5200 or 1-800/432-5383), at *Ruby's Inn*, runs a **shuttle service** in summer between the visitor center, campgrounds and the major stops on the rim road ($5 for an all-day pass), as well as two-hour driving tours ($18), while Ruby's Outlaw Trail Rides (☎435/679-8761), has a similar program of **horse** rides to those mentioned above.

Flight-seeing companies based at Bryce Canyon Airport and other nearby spots include Aladdin Air (☎435/834-5555 or 1-800/914-3215) and Bryce Canyon Helicopters (contact via *Ruby's Inn*; ☎435/834-5341), whose rates start at $55 for a 17-minute flight.

Bryce
Canyon
National
Park

All the national park passes detailed on p.21 are valid in Bryce.

For advance information, write to Bryce Canyon National Park, Bryce Canyon, UT 84717, or visit the Web site (www.nps.gov /brca).

Bryce Canyon practicalities

Accommodation within the park itself is restricted to the venerable *Bryce Canyon Lodge*, located one hundred yards from the rim between Sunrise and Sunset points, and open between April and October only. This atmospheric stone-and-timber affair offers a handful of luxurious suites (⑥), a row or two of rough-hewn but very comfortable individual cabins (⑤), and about fifty rather ordinary motel rooms (⑤). All tend to be reserved several months in advance, through Amfac Parks & Resorts, 14001 East Iliff Ave, #600, Aurora, CO 80014 (☎303/297-2757, fax 297-3175; *www.amfac.com*).

The main lobby of the *Lodge* holds a fascinating large-scale relief model of the park, and leads to a good-quality **dining room**, open for all meals, plus several souvenir stores.

A few minutes' walk away, slightly north of Sunrise Point, the **General Store** stocks basic groceries, snacks and camping equipment, and holds a laundromat and public showers.

The closest towns offering a range of motels are Panguitch (see p.394) and Tropic (p.402).

Motels near the park

Bryce Canyon Lodge can only hold a tiny proportion of Bryce's summer influx, and is closed altogether in winter. However, half a dozen alternative options loiter just outside the park along highways 12 and 63; the cluster at the intersection is loosely known as **Pink Cliffs Village**, though there's no village to speak of. All remain open year-round, with considerably reduced rates in winter, and have their own unenthralling restaurants.

Best Western Ruby's Inn, PO Box 1, Bryce, UT 84764; ☎435/834-5341 or 1-800/468-8860, fax 435/834-5265; *www.rubysinn.com*. Large motel complex – something of an eyesore, if truth be told – a mile or so outside the park on Hwy-63. Fifty of the 350 rooms feature whirlpool baths, and there's a full program of tours. Nov–March ②, April & last two weeks of Oct ③, May & first two weeks of Oct ④, June–Sept ⑤.

Bryce Canyon Pines, PO Box 43, Bryce, UT 84764; ☎435/834-5441 or 1-800/892-7923, fax 435/834-5330. Reasonable, modern, anonymous motel, three miles west on Hwy-12, with a strangely shallow swimming pool in a separate shed. Winter ②, summer ④.

Bryce Canyon Resorts, PO Box 640006, 13500 E Hwy-12, Bryce, UT 84764; ☎435/834-5351 or 1-800/834-0043, fax 435/834-5256. Simple budget motel at the intersection in Pink Cliffs Village, three miles from the park entrance, with basic summer-only cabins and slightly more comfortable rooms. Cabins mid-April to mid-Oct ②; rooms Nov–April ②, May & Oct ③, June–Sept ④.

Bryce View Lodge, PO Box 640002, Bryce, UT 84764; ☎435/834-5180, fax 834-5181. Big, new and misleadingly-named motel, opposite *Ruby's* on Hwy-63 and run by the same management. The rooms are a pretty high standard for the price. Mid-Oct to May ②, June to mid-Oct ③.

Foster's Motel, Star Route, Panguitch, UT 84759; ☎435/834-5227, fax 834-5304. Cheap if somewhat shabby motel, just under two miles west of the park turnoff on Hwy-12. Winter ②, summer ②.

Camping

Both of the in-park **campgrounds** are first-come, first-served, and cost $10 per night. The *North Campground* stretches alongside the Rim Trail a short walk from the visitor center, while *Sunset Campground* is a mile or so south, across the highway from the lodge near Sunset Point. They're usually open, weather permitting, from early May until late October; in summer, all 216 sites tend to be filled by early afternoon. Neither campground offers RV hookups, and the closest showers are by the General Store.

Backcountry campers can choose from several designated sites, all south of Bryce Point below the rim and well away from the main trails. Pick up a $5 permit at the visitor center, and take lots of water.

The nearest **commercial campground** to the park is the slightly more deluxe area adjoining *Ruby's Inn*, a mile north (see overleaf; $14 per site), which also caters for RVs. If your heart is set on a night in the woods, head instead for the roadside campground at **Red Canyon**, ten miles west on Hwy-12 (see p.394).

Seeing the park

Most visitor activity at Bryce is concentrated around **Bryce Amphitheater**, the largest and most accessible of the indentations in the Pink Cliffs. Whether you park your own car off the loop road that leaves Hwy-63 half a mile south of the visitor center, or get dropped off by the shuttle bus, a brief walk will bring you to the brink of the crescent-shaped depression.

Quite where along the Rim Trail you get your first blast of the incandescent rocks makes little difference. Of the two official overlooks, around five hundred yards apart, **Sunrise Point** to the north gets slightly less of the tour-bus crowds than **Sunset Point** to the south. Neither name is particularly appropriate; both face east, so you won't see the sun set, while the best place to catch the dawn is **Bryce Point**, a mile or more further south. Here at the southernmost tip of the amphitheater, you can look back west as the first rays of the sun strike the toy soldiers below. At any time of day, the views to the east and north are astonishing, ranging as much as a hundred miles to encompass the Aquarius Plateau and the Henry Mountains.

Beyond Bryce Amphitheater, Hwy-63 – also known as the **Scenic Drive** – meanders south for another fifteen miles. It's a slow drive, passing a succession of substantially similar viewpoints; no one stops at them all, though each has its merits. Look out in particular for the **Natural Bridge**, which spans a steep gully around halfway along. Suspended far above the forest, it doesn't cross running water, so technically it's not a bridge but an 85-foot arch.

Hwy-63 climbs steadily as it continues south, until finally the ridge it's following narrows to a slender neck, and the road is forced to end at the highest viewpoint of all, **Rainbow Point**. Both this and nearby **Yovimpa Point** command sweeping views south, to Navajo Mountain and the Kaibab forest that fringes the Grand Canyon.

Hiking

The **Rim Trail** follows the lip of the plateau for just over five miles, skirting Bryce Amphitheater between Sunrise and Sunset points; die-hard backpackers can continue beyond its ending at Bryce Point all the way to Rainbow Point, 22.6 miles on, along the **Under-the-Rim Trail**. By far the most popular trails in the park, however, are those that drop into **Bryce Amphitheater** itself. With several alternative routes to the bottom, and a choice of connections once you're there, you can tailor a hike to suit whatever time you have, from a couple of hours to a full day.

The basic experience is much the same whichever trail you take. The rock stratum that has eroded to form the hoodoos, just below the rim, averages from 300 to 500ft thick, so hiking consists of descending between them until you reach the flatter pine forest beyond, walking through the woods, and then climbing back up again. At an elevation of almost two miles, even a brief hike involves considerable effort; you'll need good footwear and plenty of water.

For a concentrated burst of Bryce at its best, the **Navajo Loop Trail** is ideal. The shortest and busiest trail of all, it plummets abruptly from Sunset Point into a group of formations known as the **Silent City**, then circles back up to complete a hike of 1.4 miles. Taking its steeper right-hand branch as you set off makes for an easier hike, and also brings you, by way of a precipitous set of switchbacks, straight into the cool crevice of **Wall Street**. In places this awe-inspiring gulf of orange rock is less than twenty feet wide, but

*Bryce
Canyon
National
Park*

Dawn and dusk are the prime times to take photos at Bryce.

Fairyland Point, reached via a separate turnoff north of the visitor center, is one of Bryce's quietest yet most scenic viewpoints.

Allow two hours to enjoy the Navajo Loop Trail without exhausting yourself in the process.

it's too deep for the 800-year-old Douglas firs that grow from its sandy floor to poke their heads above the cliffs.

Beyond Wall Street, you swiftly reach a small sandy wash. The return leg of the Navajo Loop Trail starts a short way to the left, and follows a slightly gentler incline back to Sunset Point, passing **Thor's Hammer** and other humungous hoodoos en route. Alternatively, continue northwards on the level footpath just above the wash, pausing perhaps to rest in the shade of the pines and junipers. The basin known as the **Queen's Garden** is something over a mile along. Named for an almost translucent fin that's topped by a rocky pile bearing a vague resemblance to Queen Victoria, it's connected by a mile-long trail up the hillside to **Sunrise Point**. During its climb, the path cuts repeatedly through limestone fins and spurs, with each tunnel framing another irresistible photograph. Most of the horseback expeditions in the park – see p.399 – pass this way. Dwarfed beneath the ludicrous, multicolored spires and turrets, the horses make an especially surreal spectacle.

East of Bryce

By continuing east from Bryce Canyon, you're leaving civilization firmly behind. This central region of southern Utah is almost entirely given over to wilderness, and there's barely time to draw breath after Bryce before you plunge into Grand Staircase–Escalante National Monument. A few tiny communities cling to the fringes, however, and **Tropic** offers a few creature comforts as you gird your loins ready for what lies ahead.

Tropic

As described on p.398, it's possible to hike straight into the most spectacular parts of Bryce Canyon from Tropic.

The zip code for Tropic is UT 84776.

The first community east of Bryce along Hwy-12 is **TROPIC**, eight miles from the park turnoff. Among the migrants from Panguitch who settled this tiny hamlet in the 1880s – naming it for its allegedly superior climate – was Ebenezer Bryce himself (see p.396). His restored log cabin is now the centerpiece of the *Pioneer Village* motel.

Tropic may turn its back on the flamboyance of Bryce Canyon, ranged along the ridge above it, but it has little appeal of its own; the main street consists of a row of motels and drive-ins, and strolling around the center is unrewarding. However, the unmarked road that leads west from Bryce's cabin reaches the park boundary in a couple of miles, from where it's a further two-mile hike up to the main formations.

Accommodation

You don't gain much by staying in Tropic rather than the motels closer to the park, but it does have quite a reasonable range of

accommodation. None of the motels expects you to hang around during the day; they don't have pools, for example.

Bryce Pioneer Village, 80 S Main St; ☎435/679-8546 or 1-800/222-0381, fax 435/679-8607. Complex of dull but adequate motel rooms, with showers not baths, and more atmospheric individual cabins, transplanted from the park and equipped with two double beds as well as either baths or showers. Cabins ②–④, rooms ④.

Bryce Point B&B, 61 North 400 West; ☎435/679-8629. Cheerful family-run B&B attached to private house; all of the five large rooms have picture windows facing Bryce Canyon, plus their own baths and TVs, and there's also a shared deck with hot tub. ③.

Bryce Valley Inn, 199 N Main St; ☎435/679-8811 or 1-800/442-1890, fax 435/679-8846. Plain, large motel, with an on-site restaurant and a souvenir shop. Nov–March ②, April–Oct ④.

Country Inn Motel, 141 N Main St; ☎435/679-8600 or 1-800/993-6847, fax 435/679-8605. Conspicuous modern motel beside a gas station in the heart of town, with its own store and diner. Nov–March ③, April–Oct ④.

Francisco's Farm B&B, 52 Francisco Lane; ☎435/679-8721 or 1-800/642-4136. Three not especially fancy en-suite B&B rooms in a log-built home, located a block off the main street half a mile south of the center, and serving all-you-can-eat breakfasts. ④.

Grand Staircase Inn, 105 N Kodachrome Drive, Cannonville, UT 84718; ☎435/679-8400 or 1-877/472-6346; *www.grandstaircaseinn.com*. Simple but adequate highway motel five miles south of Tropic, attached to a grocery store and gas station. Mid-Oct to mid-April ②, mid-April to mid-June & first half of Oct ③, mid-June to Sept ④.

East of Bryce

As explained on p.15, accommodation prices, excluding taxes, are indicated throughout this book by the following symbols:

① *up to $30*
② *$30–45*
③ *$45–60*
④ *$60–80*
⑤ *$80–100*
⑥ *$100–130*
⑦ *$130–175*
⑧ *$175–250*
⑨ *$250+*

Eating

No one would make a special trip to eat in Tropic's limited array of restaurants, but once you're here it's not worth driving anywhere else either.

Doug's Place, *Country Inn Motel*, 141 N Main St; ☎435/679-8632. Bustling diner attached to large convenience store, which gets really busy at breakfast time and doesn't make all that romantic a rendezvous for dinner.

Hungry Coyote, *Bryce Valley Inn*, 199 N Main St; ☎435/679-8811. Fully licensed Western-themed restaurant, open for all meals but specializing in giant evening steaks.

The Pizza Place, Hwy-12; ☎435/679-8888. Quick, functional pizza joint, which also does takeouts and deliveries.

Kodachrome Basin State Park

At the village of **CANNONVILLE**, five miles south of Tropic, Hwy-12 veers east across the Paria River. Continue south along Paria Valley instead, on Cottonwood Canyon Road, and the pavement runs out after eight more miles at **Kodachrome Basin State Park**. This assortment of contorted rocky columns, tucked beneath the cliffs that climb to Kaiparowits Peak, was named in honor of the latest Kodak film by a *National Geographic* photographer in

1948, who felt that the area's existing name of Thorny Pasture was
too prosaic.

The main focus of the park is a unique geological phenomenon,
not found anywhere else on earth: its 67 **sand pipes**. Each of these
misshapen pillars was formed as an underground geyser, created by
an earthquake, which was then blocked with tough calcite sediment.
When the softer rock that surrounded them eroded away, they were
left towering as much as 150ft above the scrubby plain.

*To arrange a
horse ride
through
Kodachrome
Basin, contact
Scenic Safaris
in Cannonville
(☎435/679-
8536).*

Having paid the $5-per-vehicle day-use **fee** at the entrance station,
follow the road for a couple of miles to the left to reach the park's
attractive **campground** (Sun–Thurs $9, Fri & Sat $10; ☎435/679-
8562). Various trailheads along the way mark the start of short hikes
among the formations. Alternatively, the unpaved road that forks
right from the entrance station ends after a little over a mile at the
trailhead for **Shakespeare Arch**. A pleasant quarter-mile walk brings
you to a small high natural arch, named for the park manager who
first noticed its existence in 1976, from where you can get good
views across the valley to the Pink Cliffs of Bryce Canyon.

Grand Staircase–Escalante National Monument

Brought into being by a controversial and unexpected presidential
decree in September 1996, **Grand Staircase–Escalante National
Monument** is, at 1.9 million acres, the largest US national monument
outside Alaska. Though its staggering landscape unquestionably
merits such recognition, it's not so much a homogenous entity as the
final piece in a jigsaw puzzle, placing the leftover lands between
Bryce, Capitol Reef, the Dixie National Forest and the Glen Canyon
NRA under federal control. From the Aquarius Plateau in the north –
as the highest segment of the Colorado Plateau, the top rung of the
"staircase" – to Lake Powell in the south, only the farming valleys
around towns such as Tropic, Escalante and Boulder remain in private ownership.

*Trails
Illustrated
publish an
excellent*
Canyons of the
Escalante *topo-
graphical map
of the monu-
ment region.*

Although **Hwy-12** dips in and out of its northern flanks, **US-89**
runs briefly through its southern extremities, and the rudimentary
Burr Trail leads into Capitol Reef from its eastern end (see p.419),
no paved roads cross this magnificent wilderness. True, a handful of
dirt tracks provide limited access to the backcountry, but even they
don't begin to penetrate the extraordinary canyon country at its
heart, and all are in any case swiftly rendered impassable by poor
weather conditions. What's more, there's only one maintained hiking
trail in the whole huge expanse.

While certain issues concerning the monument's future remain to
be settled, it was created specifically in order to "maintain the
unspoiled nature" of the region, rather than "develop" it for tourism.

Grand Staircase–Escalante is unique among national parks and monuments in being administered not by the National Park Service but by the Bureau of Land Management. No new paved roads are going to be built, and all administrative and tourist facilities will be constructed in existing towns, with **Escalante** itself as the prime beneficiary.

The immediate effect of the monument's proclamation was to boost local tourism by fifty percent. Of the million visitors who now pass this way each year, however, many still arrive with little idea of what to do other than simply drive the hundred-mile stretch of **Hwy-12** between Bryce Canyon and Capitol Reef. Only completed in 1980, thanks to the difficulty of the terrain and the lack of towns en route, this is indisputably the most scenic of southern Utah's fifteen or so designated "Scenic Byways." No driver could fail to be awed by the highway's ever-changing panoply of red-rock canyons, crystal-clear rivers and shimmering oases. It's a shame, however, that in the absence of easily accessible information as to what lies beyond the road, most visitors have, until recently, remained firmly in their cars.

The **Escalante River**, which drains this whole region, was the last river to be named, let alone explored, in the continental US, and to this day most maps show the area as a vast blank. As government agencies, commercial publishers and local businesses compete to fill the information gap, however, the back roads and trails are starting to bustle with venturesome tourists. Visitors now tend to stay two or three nights rather than just one, spending perhaps one day exploring rugged **Hole-in-the-Rock Road**, which holds some remarkable **slot canyons**, and another in and around delightful **Calf Creek**. For backpackers, the options are all but infinite, though the sandstone bridges and arches on the lower reaches of **Coyote Gulch** and the Escalante River itself are the prime attraction.

Information

Much the best place to obtain up-to-date information on the public lands both in and around Grand Staircase–Escalante National Monument is the multiagency **visitor center** on Hwy-12 at the west end of **Escalante** (mid-March to Oct daily 7.30am–5.30pm; Nov to mid-March Mon–Fri 8am–4.30pm; ☎435/826-5499). The helpful staff here are happy to suggest detailed hiking or mountain biking itineraries, and issue free permits for **backcountry camping**. You can also pick up information from the BLM office in **Kanab**, 318 North 100 East (Mon–Fri 8am–4.30pm; ☎435/644-2672), or on-line at *www.ut.blm.gov*.

There is no admission fee for Grand Staircase–Esca-lante National Monument.

Skutumpah and Cottonwood Canyon roads

Two long, lonely dirt roads cut north–south trajectories through the western end of Grand Staircase–Escalante, branching off from the paved road to Kodachrome Basin (see p.403). Be sure to check current conditions with rangers before setting off – even slightly adverse

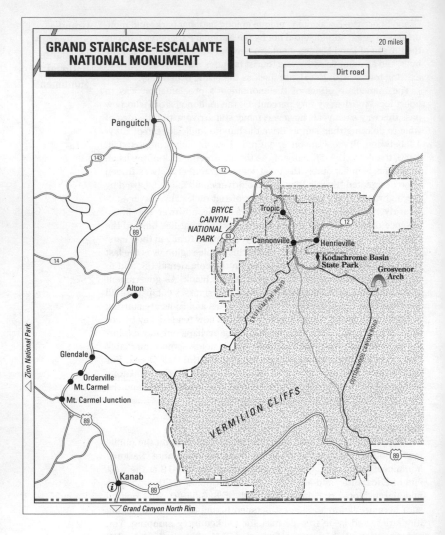

GRAND STAIRCASE-ESCALANTE NATIONAL MONUMENT

0   20 miles

——— Dirt road

Panguitch

143

12

BRYCE CANYON NATIONAL PARK

Tropic

12

63

Cannonville

Henrieville

Kodachrome Basin State Park

Grosvenor Arch

89

14

SKUTUMPAH ROAD

COTTONWOOD CANYON ROAD

Alton

Glendale

Orderville

Mt. Carmel

Mt. Carmel Junction

VERMILION CLIFFS

89

89

△ Zion National Park

ⓘ Kanab

89

▽ Grand Canyon North Rim

weather can make the going impossible – and unless you have 4WD, don't base your itinerary on the assumption you'll be able to get through.

Skutumpah Road, the better maintained of the two, starts three miles south of Cannonville and takes 52 miles to reach US-89, nine miles east of Kanab. The last sixteen of those miles are paved (as Johnson Canyon Road), but that still leaves 36 difficult unpaved miles, as the road picks its way across **Bull Valley Gorge** and through the **White Cliffs**. One of the best hikes comes early on,

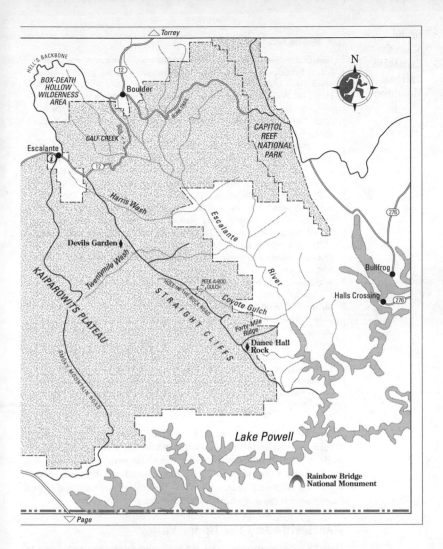

before the terrain becomes difficult, in the shape of a five-mile round-trip stroll though the narrows of **Willis Creek**. From the **trailhead**, six miles down Skutumpah Road, it only takes a few minutes' walking before canyon walls begin to climb to either side of the wash, and they swiftly close in to stand just a few feet apart.

Much of **Cottonwood Canyon Road**, which heads east from Kodachrome Basin, runs across bare **slickrock**. That makes it extremely dangerous after rain, but during drier periods, it's well worth continuing for ten miles beyond the park to see the intricate

A Monumental Affair

The first proposal to create **Escalante National Monument** was submitted to Franklin Roosevelt in 1940 by Secretary of the Interior Harold Ickes. Its boundaries would have enclosed 4.5 million acres, stretching from Lees Ferry as far as Moab and Green River, and taken in 280 miles of the Colorado River, 150 miles of the Green River, and 70 miles of the San Juan. That vast area was then crossed by just one road, and no bridge spanned the Colorado.

In principle, Roosevelt saw himself as an environmentalist, but the greenery of the Hudson River Valley was far more to his taste than the red rocks of the West. In the face of vociferous Mormon opposition in Utah, not to mention the coming of war, the idea was quietly dropped.

When Canyonlands National Park was created in the early 1960s (see p.443), it included only a small proportion of Ickes' suggested tract. Glen Canyon on the Colorado River was by now submerged beneath Lake Powell (see p.428), while the **Kaiparowits Plateau**, which stretches south of Escalante all the way to the lake, remained outside federal protection. That was thanks to pressure from economic interests in southern Utah, acutely aware that what they call Fifty-Mile Mountain stands on top of the world's largest known deposits of **coal**.

Plans to mine the Kaiparowits Plateau have been the focus of repeated rumors and campaigns for well over fifty years. The closest any came to fruition was in the 1970s, when the Southern California Edison company announced its intention to open a 6000-acre mine, complete with a network of new roads and an on-site electricity generating plant. Controversy over the scheme pitted the so-called **Sagebrush Rebels** – an informal but powerful grouping of Utah's Mormon-dominated business elite, plus the workers whose livelihoods were at stake – against environmentalists from across the nation. Although the abandonment of the project in 1976 was

double **Grosvenor Arch**. At that point, the road turns south, to meet US-89 thirty miles on, roughly halfway between Kanab and Page. En route it threads its way between the dark pyramidal fins of the **Cockscomb**, a bizarre geological oddity resembling the armor-plated back of a stegosaurus that forms the boundary between the Grand Staircase and the Kaiparowits Plateau.

Henrieville and the Upper Valley

Hwy-12 climbs northeast from Cannonville, passing through the speck that is **HENRIEVILLE** and then ascending the clay cliffs known as "The Blues." Once atop the cliffs you're confronted by the unexpected sight of the high but fertile **Upper Valley**, kept well watered by snowmelt from the Aquarius Plateau.

Escalante

A group of Mormon militiamen who pursued Indian raiders through the Upper Valley in 1866 noted the potential of the meadowland largely due to a slackening of demand for electricity in California, communities such as Kanab, desperate for jobs, took out their anger by burning effigies of green activists in the streets.

In 1980, a study commissioned by Congress showed that almost 400,000 acres on the Kaiparowits Plateau had already been logged to clear the way for mines. Much of that timber was processed at a mill in Escalante, and when green opposition resulted in a moratorium on tree-felling, Escalante too witnessed its own share of public "hangings." During those years, any stranger with licence plates from the notoriously tree-hugging state of California could expect a frosty welcome in the diners of Hwy-12.

Hopes that mining money might revitalize the economy of Escalante rose once more in the mid-1990s, with the news that a Dutch conglomerate was considering strip-mining the Kaiparowits. By now, however, many observers felt that the pro-mining lobby had become merely a vociferous minority, and President Clinton decided that a grand gesture designed to appeal to environmentalists in every state was more important than appeasing the business community in Utah. On September 18, 1996 – little more than a month before his reelection – he therefore took the stage at the Grand Canyon to declare the creation of the **Grand Staircase–Escalante National Monument**.

Utah legislators promptly condemned it as "the mother of all land grabs" and "a monumental blunder – pun intended," while the ropes came out once again, this time to "hang" both Clinton and his Interior Secretary Bruce Babbitt. However, the move was welcomed in the rest of the nation, and now that the die has been cast, even Escalante seems to have accepted it. After years of insisting that they'd rather be farming, logging and mining than running motels, the predominantly Mormon local population do at least seem to have been guaranteed a secure economic future, even if it's not quite the one they anticipated.

beyond, and dubbed the region "Potato Valley" in honor of its abundant wild sweet potatoes. Within ten years, acting on their own initiative rather than Church pressure, several returned to establish a ranching and farming community. They called it **ESCALANTE**, on the suggestion of a passing member of John Wesley Powell's second expedition, despite the fact that the Spanish explorer-priest Fray Silvestre de Escalante never came within a hundred miles of here.

The story of John Wesley Powell's two Colorado-River expeditions is told on p.441.

Life was harsh during Escalante's early years; the pioneers spent their first winter, 1875–76, huddled in primitive dugouts. Then came a period of deceptive ease, as their sheep and cattle multiplied on the open range. By 1910, however, it was becoming apparent that the native grasses on which they grazed were not growing back. The land has never recovered, and Escalante has remained frozen at much the same size and appearance ever since.

Escalante is a neat enough little town, with its main street gently sloping down from west to east and a couple of blocks of four-square brick and timber homes to either side. It's also a screamingly dull place to spend the night, though the wilderness that stretches away in every direction more than makes up for that.

If you do find yourself here in the daytime, **Escalante State Park**, beside an artificial lake a mile northwest of town, holds Utah's largest concentration of **petrified wood** ($5 day-use fee; information on ☎435/826-4466). Two short but very steep trails lead through a miniature "forest" of lithified logs, and there's a fully equipped **campground** (Sun–Thurs $9, Fri & Sat $10; for reservations, costing $5 extra, call ☎1-800/322-3770). It has to be said, however, that it takes a lot of effort before you see anything, and even then it isn't a patch on Arizona's Petrified Forest National Park (see p.274).

Information

A summer-only kiosk at 100 E Main St (mid-May to mid-Sept daily 10am–6pm; ☎435/826-4810), next to the *Padre Motel*, handles enquiries about Escalante itself. For information on hiking and camping in the surrounding region, head for the **visitor center** of the Grand Staircase–Escalante National Monument, at 755 W Main St (see p.405).

Accommodation

The price codes used here are explained on p.15.

Escalante's half-dozen tiny **motels** are comprehensively outclassed by the more sizeable *Prospector Inn*. Public **campgrounds** nearby include those at Escalante State Park (see above) and Calf Creek (see p.416).

Bunkhouse Motel, Escalante Outfitters, 310 W Main St; ☎435/826-4266, fax 826-4388. Hikers' and campers' supply store that has seven attractive little log cabins out back, rented for $29.50 per night to backpackers who don't mind roughing it. Each has heating but no water, phones or TV, and they share use of a bathhouse. ①.

The zip code for Escalante is UT 84726.

Circle D Motel, 475 W Main St; ☎435/826-4297, fax 826-4402. Basic old-style motel, perched at the west end of town, where the identikit units share a long wooden veranda; ask for one of the newer rooms. ②.

Escalante's Grand Staircase B&B, 280 W Main St; ☎435/826-4890. Simple two-room B&B inn that also rents out mountain bikes. ③.

Moqui Motel, 480 W Main St; ☎435/826-4210. Mundane motel and RV park on the edge of town, as the highway sweeps away westwards. ②.

Prospector Inn, 380 W Main St; ☎435/826-4653, fax 826-4285. Escalante's newest and largest motel, the first in town to boast a second story, offers spacious, comfortable twin-bedded rooms. ③.

Rainbow Country B&B, 585 East 300 South; ☎435/826-4567 or 1-800/252-8824. Small, friendly B&B; comfortable en-suite rooms share use of a hot tub, a large common room and a mountain-view veranda. Local tours available. ③.

Eating

Though **restaurants** have traditionally struggled to survive in Escalante, the *Ponderosa* seems to be thriving in the face of competition from a handful of nondescript diners where it's hard to stretch a night on the town much beyond twelve and a half minutes.

Circle D Restaurant, 425 W Main St; ☎435/826-4550. Dull diner/steakhouse, with a Mexican flavor and a few vegetarian alternatives. Open for all meals daily in summer but closed for much of the winter.

Esca-Latte, Escalante Outfitters, 310 W Main St; ☎435/826-4266. Small-scale daytime-only espresso bar that, unfortunately, doesn't open until 9am, to serve coffee, smoothies and light lunchtime snacks.

Golden Loop Cafe, 39 W Main St; ☎435/826-4433. Typical small-town diner, smack in the middle of downtown Escalante.

Ponderosa Restaurant, 400 West 50 North; ☎435/826-4658. An unexpected pleasure, behind the *Prospector Inn*, this Hungarian-owned restaurant serves high-quality European-influenced food daily for all meals. As well as dishes like *paloc goulash*, (beef soup), *stroganoff fricassee* and *wiener schnitzel*, they offer good steaks and ribs for around $17, and even Oysters Rockefeller for $8.

Hell's Backbone

While Hwy-12 is by far the quickest route between Escalante and Boulder, summer thrillseekers can choose instead to take a two-hour, forty-mile trip across the top of the Aquarius Plateau, along the old "Upper Road." Turn north on the 300 East block in Escalante, and the paved **Forest Road 153** heads up Pine Creek Canyon, to reach the appealing mountain-set **Posey Lake** fourteen miles on.

Turn east at the lake, onto Hell's Backbone Road, and the fun begins. Having crawled up the flanks of the 10,000-foot Roger Peak, this dirt track teeters along the slender ridge known as **Hell's Backbone**, with sheer drops down to Sand Creek on one side and Death Hollow on the other. The best views come at the hair-raising bridge halfway along. The bizarrely named **Box-Death Hollow Wilderness** far below can only be penetrated on foot, and is southern Utah's most difficult hiking region. Tracing its full length necessitates 18 miles of wading in ice-cold water, and takes between four and seven days; don't even consider setting off without talking first to the rangers at the visitor center in Escalante.

For the last ten miles, as it descends through the woods to Boulder, Hell's Backbone Road is paved, but the backcountry section is usually closed by snow between October and late May.

Hole-in-the-Rock Road

These days, **Hole-in-the-Rock Road**, which turns south from Hwy-12 five miles east of Escalante – just beyond a scenic turnout heralding Grand Staircase–Escalante National Monument – is emphatically a dead end. More than fifty slow, hard miles from the highway, its progress is halted by a landslide of tumbled boulders, high above the waters of Lake Powell. When it was created, however, over a century ago, it was intended to become the most direct route across southern Utah.

Be sure to carry water and emergency supplies if you're driving Hole-in-the-Rock Road.

In November 1879, the 230 Mormon pioneers of the **San Juan Mission** gathered outside Escalante. Intent on reaching their new home, almost 200 miles east, they were convinced they'd find a short cut along the uncharted east flank of the Kaiparowits Plateau and across the Colorado. Even when confronted with the abyss of Glen Canyon, their faith saw them through. In the space of six weeks, they dynamited a narrow slit in a fifty-foot cliff – the **Hole in the Rock** – until it was wide enough to squeeze through. Despite snow and ice, they then used ropes to lower 83 wagons down a precipitous "road" that descended 1800ft to the river in less than three quarters of a mile. Once there, they ferried the whole lot across the Colorado on makeshift rafts, and then repeated the entire process to escape the canyon on the far side. A mere hundred more miles of desert brought them to the townsite of **Bluff** – see p.483 – which they established on April 6, 1880. All 230 members of the party had lived through the trek, and they'd been joined by three babies born en route.

Hole-in-the-Rock Road has never been paved, but its first forty miles are passable for ordinary vehicles for most of the year, and it now constitutes the most popular route into Grand Staircase–Escalante National Monument. It's a long, slow drive, however – expect to take a good three hours to get as far as Dance Hall Rock and back – and despite the build-up it's not nearly as dramatic as Hwy-12. The reason to make the effort is to enjoy the various **hiking trails** that branch away from it, of which the best for day-trippers is the loop down to the Peek-A-Boo and Spooky **slot canyons**. Staff at the visitor center in Escalante (see p.405) can provide leaflets and simple maps, but if you're planning anything substantial, equip yourself with a proper topographical map, such as the Trails Illustrated one recommended on p.404.

Devils Garden

For its first five miles, Hole-in-the-Rock Road crosses mundane, level ranching country. It then climbs to reveal a first glimpse of the red rocks of Escalante Canyon away to the east, and the surface changes from gravel to mud. As you continue across a sagebrush-strewn plateau, there's no real incentive to get out of your car before **Devils Garden**, twelve miles along. Designated as the one official picnic area en route, this small valley, set below the highway to the west, is scattered with clusters of rounded, clayey hoodoos and arches, reminiscent of those at Goblin Valley State Park (see p.438). Countless trails and footpaths weave among the excrescences; none leads anywhere in particular, but it's a great place for a game of hide-and-seek.

The Slot Canyons of Dry Fork

Apart from crossing the occasional bouncy, sandy wash, Hole-in-the-Rock Road remains relatively uneventful as you continue beyond Devils Garden. Now and then, vistas of the color country open up, and 24 miles along you begin to see rounded slickrock domes perched above the canyon. Just as the thought of what lies to the east is becoming seriously frustrating, however, you finally get the chance to see what's down there.

Head east on **Dry Fork Road**, 26 miles (or something over 45 minutes) along Hole-in-the-Rock Road, and after five hair-raising minutes you'll come to a makeshift parking lot on the edge of a shallow canyon. A steep, sandy and rather hard-to-follow trail takes roughly twenty minutes to switchback down from here into the Dry Fork of Coyote Gulch, where you'll find a couple of Utah's most accessible **slot canyons**. Scoured by fierce desert storms, these kind of impossibly slender and delicate canyons have become hugely popular tourist destinations in the last few years, mainly because they look so unutterably gorgeous in photographs. In real life, they're breathtaking; but be warned that they're also very dangerous. If there's the slightest threat of rain anywhere nearby, don't go in.

The first of the pair, **Peek-a-Boo Gulch**, is the gem. Although it's facing you as soon you reach the canyon floor, you might not recognize it. It's *not* the sandy-bottomed canyon heading off to your left, which may be narrow but isn't quite narrow enough to count as a "slot." Peek-A-Boo instead is on the far side, with its mouth at first glance appearing to be blocked by a "chimney" of slickrock. Just to enter it, you have to haul yourself up a couple of chest-high ledges, and they serve as a foretaste of several more to come. Exploring is irresistible, however, as each twist and turn reveals some new arch, bridge or tunnel to scramble through or over. The walls to either side are never all that high, and it doesn't take long to get all the way through, but the elegant swirls and patterns in the storm-gouged rock make it a constant delight.

As if they weren't dangerous enough, both Peek-A-Boo and Spooky are home to midget rattlesnakes.

Spooky Gulch, which lies another fifteen minutes' walk down Dry Fork, is by contrast downright intimidating. It starts narrow, and just keeps on getting narrower, growing darker as it does so. To keep going at all, you have to crawl early on beneath a big fallen boulder, and after that it becomes a very tight squeeze indeed. Soon it's only possible to walk sideways, with serious pressure on your rib cage and back, and sandpaper rasping at your clothes.

Another slot canyon, **Brimstone Gulch**, lies further still along Dry Fork. However, penetrating it is only possible using technical climbing gear, and even to reach it you have to negotiate a huge boulder that's very difficult indeed to get back up again.

Coyote Gulch

Shortly after Dry Fork, the surface of Hole-in-the-Rock Road becomes sandier and more uneven, and progress is that much slower. A mile or so after the solitary finger of **Chimney Rock** first appears on the edge of the mesa, and a total of 33.5 miles from the highway, a parking lot on the right signals your arrival at **Hurricane**

Wash. This is the starting point for the monument's single most popular **backpacking** route, the three- to four-day round-trip hike down through **Coyote Gulch** to the Escalante River.

Strictly speaking, the trail proper begins a quarter of a mile down a dirt track to the left of Hole-in-the-Rock Road, but even if your vehicle can get that far, there probably won't be space to park. From there, it's five miles' walk along the sandy but ever-narrowing bed of Hurricane Wash before you reach Coyote Gulch, and then a further eight miles until that meets the Escalante in turn.

Coyote Gulch itself is a spellbinding creek, cutting through a slickrock canyon that's lined with gorgeous sandstone bridges and arches, and punctuated by dramatic waterfalls. By contrast, the Escalante River is simply the obvious place to turn back, rather than being a goal in its own right; its confluence with Coyote Gulch roughly coincides with the high water mark of Lake Powell, and thus the point where the Escalante as a river comes to an end. In fact, most of Coyote Gulch lies within the Glen Canyon National Recreational Area (see p.430), but you can only reach it on land by way of Grand Staircase–Escalante.

*Get detailed
advice in
Escalante
before attempt-
ing Coyote
Gulch. Above
all, never
climb down
unless you're
certain you
can climb up
again.*

Starting from Hurricane Wash, there isn't time to hike to any of the significant features of Coyote Gulch and back in the space of a single day. However, it is possible to snatch a glimpse on a **day-hike** from the end of **Forty-Mile Ridge**, an almost pure-sand "road" that leaves Hole-in-the-Rock Road another couple of miles further on. The first snag is that if you don't have 4WD, you'll probably only be able to drive the first five miles of Forty-Mile Ridge, and thus face an extra two-mile hike to reach the trailhead at its far end. The second snag is that the trail itself enters Coyote Gulch, two miles along, through the **Crack In The Wall**, an incredibly tight squeeze between sandstone boulders perched above a towering cliff that is every bit as alarming as its name suggests. And the final snag: it's much more difficult coming back the other way.

Assuming you can cope with those obstacles, the rewards are tremendous. Before you drop down into the gulch, you cross some fabulous slickrock slopes with colossal views out over the wilderness. Once there, Cliff Arch, Coyote Natural Bridge and the huge Jacob Hamblin Arch all lie within reach.

Dance Hall Rock

Under normal conditions, two-wheel-drive vehicles should go no further along Hole-in-the-Rock Road than **Dance Hall Rock**, a mile beyond Forty-Mile Ridge and 36 miles from the highway. The 1879 Mormon party (see p.412) camped alongside this superb natural amphitheater while they worked out how to get across the Colorado, presenting evening entertainments to keep up their spirits. An easy walk from the roadway enables you to tread the same stage, and it's also worth exploring the rolling slickrock hills that lie immediately behind. In a couple of places, natural tanks have been scooped deep into the rock, each sheltering a solitary tree on its sandy floor.

The Hole in the Rock

Beyond Dance Hall Rock, the gravel surface gives way to bare slickrock, only negotiable in high-clearance vehicles. The original **Hole in the Rock** lies just past the last parking lot, fifteen miles on. Keen hikers can scramble over the rocks that block it and pick their way down to the lake, which has obliterated the final thousand feet of the pioneers' primitive pathway.

The Upper Escalante River

While driving Hole-in-the-Rock Road certainly offers the thrill of venturing into the back of beyond, several wonderful hikes start from right alongside Hwy-12. If your time is at all limited, and you'd rather spend it on the trails than behind the wheel, there's a lot to be said for staying on the main road until it reaches the **Escalante River**. The first sighting of the Escalante system comes from a roadside lookout at an extravagant curve five miles on from the Hole-in-the-Rock turnoff. From there, it takes five more miles for the highway to drop down to the river itself, which it crosses on a low bridge that's designed to allow floodwaters to flow harmlessly over. Immediately on the far side, a parking lot serves as the trailhead for exhilarating hikes both up- and downstream.

It would be possible to make this the starting point for major **backpacking** trips in either direction. The town of Escalante is around two days' walk upstream, while Lake Powell lies a good ten days' hike away downstream. Fortunately, however, intriguing natural features much closer at hand serve as obvious **day-hike** destinations. Whichever way you go, trailside notices announce "Yup, You Gotta Get Wet," so be prepared to ford the river several times. The great thing is, if you're just going a short distance there's no great need to keep pulling your boots on and off – the riverbank is sandy enough to walk barefoot.

Upstream: Escalante Natural Bridge

The shorter of the two potential day-hikes from Hwy-12 heads **upstream** for just 1.6 miles, as far as **Escalante Natural Bridge**. Having started by following the river away from the highway bridge, you're soon obliged to wade over to its south bank. The canyon here is broad and open, and the trail gentle. Once you've crossed the river four times, meaning that you're now back on its northern side, you'll see the bridge open up on its southern wall. Although it's 100 feet wide, and 130 feet high, it spans a mere trickle, dribbling down from a little side canyon.

Downstream: Maverick Bridge and Phipps Arch

The trail **downstream** from Hwy-12, accessed by walking beneath the road bridge and then crossing a footbridge over Calf Creek, is slightly heavier going. Much of the valley floor remains in the hands of private farmers, so it takes a bit of scrambling and dodging to stay outside their fences, but it's still a lovely walk.

The best day-hike in this direction is twice as long as its upstream equivalent, at nearly seven miles for the round-trip. The route leaves the Escalante 1.6 miles along, heading south into sandy **Phipps Wash**. There are no signs or marked trail, so look for footprints and carry a good map (see p.404). After another half mile, you'll see two prominent knobs of Navajo Sandstone rising from the top of the canyon wall to your right. A hundred yards before you reach the larger of the two, head right again, up a sandy slope into a side canyon. One hundred yards along, you'll have to pick your way onto a ledge on your left to avoid a deep sink hole; another hundred yards after that, you'll come to **Maverick Bridge**, spanning the wash in front of another round cavity.

Back on Phipps Wash, keep going south for half a mile until another side canyon opens up to your left. Now things get difficult; to reach the stark, mesa-top **Phipps Arch**, you have to scramble up a steep slickrock ledge, and there's no way of knowing whether you've got the right one until you're up there. The views are so good it doesn't really matter, in the end, but make sure you keep track of how to get down again.

Calf Creek Falls

*Allow around
four hours to
hike to Calf
Creek Falls
and back;
there's a day-
use fee of $3.*

A mile or so north of the Escalante River bridge on Hwy-12, and a total of sixteen miles from Escalante, look out on your left for the parking lot at **Calf Creek**. There's a nice little **campground** right here, with minimal facilities ($5 per night), but most visitors simply come for the day to enjoy the magnificent six-mile round-trip walk to the 125-foot **Lower Calf Creek Falls**. Summer sun and deep sand can make it more effort than you might expect, but in principle it's a day-hike to rank with the very best Utah has to offer.

The clearly-marked trail heads upstream between the high red walls of Calf Creek Canyon, following a perennial creek, interrupted at intervals by beaver ponds, that feeds a lush riparian environment. Fremont pictographs along the way testify to a longstanding human presence. It takes around ninety minutes to reach the falls themselves, which are absolutely stupendous. Spilling over the pouting lip of a crevice in the center of a vast sandstone amphitheater, they spread over a mossy slope of golden stone, iridescent with permanent rainbows. The water that collects in the pool below is utterly freezing, and is fringed by a shaded beach where you can rest before you hike back out again.

The **Upper Calf Creek Falls** do exist, but you can't reach them from here. Instead, you start from a trailhead another six miles along

Hwy-12, and make your way for a mile across exposed open slick-rock in search of the stream. The slope can seem intimidating, but with good boots it's not too hard, and the views are amazing. Eventually, the trail forks, with one strand going to the top of the 50-foot falls, and the other to the bottom, where once again a lovely pool awaits.

Boulder

BOULDER, thirty miles beyond Escalante, is not so much a town as a group of farms scattered across a pleasant high-mountain valley. Cattle ranching in this remote spot started in 1889, but it was another fifty years before it was connected by road with the outside world, and in that time it acquired a reputation as Utah's own little Shangri-La. Now that it's just another stop on the highway, what magic it may once have had has largely gone.

As the western terminus of the controversial **Burr Trail**, Boulder is an ideal launching point for explorations into the backcountry of Capitol Reef, but few visitors spend much time in the valley itself. On a shallow knoll beside Hwy-12 in the heart of town, the small **Anasazi State Park** holds the excavated and partly reconstructed remains of an ancient Indian pueblo (daily: mid-May to mid-Sept 8am–6pm; mid-Sept to mid-May 9am–5pm; $2). Its 83 rooms were occupied by the Kayenta Anasazi, a subgroup of the peoples now generally known as the Ancestral Puebloans, between 1129 AD and 1169 AD, when the whole complex was destroyed by fire. A six-room replica at the end of the short ruins trail illustrates their daily life, which revolved around farming along Boulder Creek.

For a full account of the Burr Trail, most of which lies within Grand Staircase–Esca -lante, see p.424.

Practicalities

Boulder offers pretty minimal facilities for visitors, though the new *Boulder Mountain Lodge*, where Hwy-12 meets the Burr Trail (☎435/335-7460 or 1-800/556-3446, fax 435/335-7461; *www .boulder-utah.com*; ④), has twenty comfortable rooms and a reasonable restaurant. There's an **information kiosk**, open erratic hours in season, outside the *Burr Trail Cafe* (☎435/335-7432), a summer-only diner nearby. Otherwise, *Pole's Place*, opposite the state park at 465 N Hwy-12 (☎435/335-7422 or 1-800/730-7422; ③), is a summer-only **motel** with its own cafe and store, while the *Circle Cliffs Motel* nearby (☎435/335-7353; ①/②) is in fact a pink-painted family house that offers three far-from-fancy guestrooms.

The zip code for Boulder is UT 84716.

North to Capitol Reef

Although Hwy-12 leaves Grand Staircase–Escalante for good as it heads north of Boulder, the scenery remains every bit as sublime. The 35-mile link between Boulder and Torrey is the highway's newest section, and

*Boulder
Round-up
(☎435/335-
7377) orga-
nizes horse
riding on
Boulder
Mountain,
from $35 for a
2-hr trip.*

takes around an hour to drive. This eastern segment of the Aquarius Plateau is also known as **Boulder Mountain** or Boulder Top. Once Hwy-12 has climbed out of Boulder Valley, a succession of roadside lookouts survey fabulous vistas to the east, across a sea of gold- and red-sandstone outcrops to the Waterpocket Fold and beyond.

Primitive Forest Service **campgrounds** en route, costing $9 per night, include those at **Oak Creek**, fifteen miles along, and a little further on at **Pleasant Creek**, where a ranger station can provide full details.

Torrey

Poised at the intersection of highways 12 and 24, eleven miles west of Capitol Reef National Park, **TORREY** has thrown its lot in firmly with the tourist trade. As a result, it has quietly prospered while so many of its neighbors have faltered, though it still consists of little more than one tree-lined central avenue plus a handful of slightly stark brick motels on a ridge to the west. However, for visitors who see their evenings as opportunities to meet other travelers, Torrey is the most exciting prospect for at least a hundred miles.

In summer, you can pick up local **information** from a hut (open irregular hours) in the forecourt of the gas station that faces the highway intersection.

Accommodation

The zip code for Torrey is UT 84775.

Torrey holds well over a hundred **motel** rooms, with rates that range across the full spectrum. If you'd rather **camp**, there are a few private campgrounds in town, but the public sites along Hwy-12 (see above), or in the national park (see p.422), are far more attractive.

Austin's Chuck Wagon Motel, 12 W Main St; ☎435/425-3335 or 1-800/863-3288, fax 435/425-3434; *www.austinschuckwagonmotel.com*. Well-kept two-story "log cabin" motel, beside a tiny church in the town center, with a couple of cheaper rooms. Winter ②/③, summer ③–⑤.

Best Western Capitol Reef Resort, 2600 E Hwy-24; ☎435/425-3761 or 1-800/528-1234, fax 435/425-3300. Well-equipped modern motel, three miles east of Torrey, with great views and a good pool. The closest option to the national park, and the base for trail rides into it. Nov–March ③, April–Oct ④.

Capitol Reef Inn & Cafe, 360 W Main St; ☎435/425-3271; *www.capitolreefinn.com*. Long established but crisply maintained motel, just off the highway in the heart of town, looking south to Boulder Mountain. On-site restaurant (see opposite) and small bookstore. Winter ②, summer ③.

The price codes used here are explained on p.15.

Days Inn, 675 E Hwy-24; ☎435/425-3111 or 1-888/425-3113; *www.capitolreefdaysinn.com*. Clean, modern and friendly chain motel, facing the intersection at the east end of town. Winter ③, summer ④.

Sand Creek Hostel & Bunkhouse, 540 E Hwy-24; ☎435/425-3577 or 1-877/425-3578. Newly cleared park area near the highway intersection, with RV facilities, camping for $9, dorm beds in the large wooden bunkhouse for $10, and a coffee bar. ①.

Skyridge B&B, 950 E Hwy-24; ☎435/425-3222. Six nonsmoking en-suite B&B rooms in tasteful, imaginatively furnished modern home on the way towards central Torrey from the intersection, plus use of hot tub and very large grounds. ⑤.

Super 8, 600 E Hwy-24; ☎435/425-3497 or 1-800/800-8000, fax 435/425-3496. New chain motel, with indoor pool and all facilities. ③.

Wonderland Inn, PO Box 750067; ☎435/425-3775 or 1-800/458-0216, fax 425-3212; *www.capitolreefwonderland.com*. Attractive property, consisting of several spruce modern buildings and a separate covered pool, all perched on a bluff just above the highway intersection. Winter ③, summer ④.

Eating

Whether it's the pressure of competition or just a little local pride, the **restaurants** and **diners** of Torrey make considerably more effort to please than you may have come to expect of southern Utah.

Brink's Burgers Drive-In, 165 E Main St; ☎435/425-3710. Summer-only burger bar; a slap-up feed that's a notch or two above the usual standard.

Cafe Diablo, 599 W Main St; ☎435/425-3070. Surprisingly inventive restaurant, offering a slight Southwestern twist to the usual meats and fish. Closed for breakfast, and open mid-April to Oct only.

Capitol Reef Inn & Cafe, 360 W Main St; ☎435/425-3271. Bright cafe that serves some of Torrey's best food, using fresh ingredients like just-caught local trout. The amazing ten-vegetable salad can form part of a real vegetarian feast, and there are sumptuous banana pies to follow. Avoid the coffee, though.

Robbers Roost, 185 W Main St; ☎435/425-3265. Central bookstore that's an invaluable resource for information on the parklands, and also serves great coffee. Closed Mon.

Wonderland Restaurant, PO Box 750067; ☎435/425-3775. Large, efficient diner at the *Wonderland Inn*; the best item on the menu is the halibut.

Capitol Reef National Park

Capitol Reef National Park, the second largest of Utah's five national parks, is also the least visited. Life might be different if it bore the name originally proposed by locals – **Wayne Wonderland**, this being Wayne County. As it is, that word "reef" seems to confuse visitors. It refers to the fact that the hundred-mile rock wall thrust up by the **Waterpocket Fold** presented an almost impenetrable obstacle to nineteenth-century travelers, who therefore likened it to a reef on the ocean. Add the resemblance of the rounded "knobs" of white sandstone that top its central section to the dome of the US Capitol in Washington, and you have "Capitol Reef."

Apart from the unusual name, Capitol Reef is very much of a piece with the Southwest's other national parks. Within its 378 square miles lie hidden canyons, verdant valleys and strange rock formations whose colors are drawn from an extravagant palette of golds and greens, reds and whites. Despite stretching for over a hundred

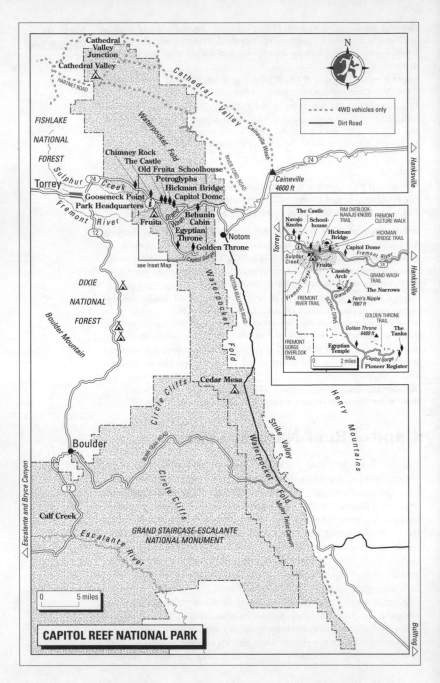

CAPITOL REEF NATIONAL PARK

miles north to south, the park is often less than ten miles wide. The one east–west highway, **Hwy-24**, crosses it in under twenty miles, following the gorge of the Fremont River. It's an impressive drive, but that's nothing rare in southern Utah, and you could easily pass straight through Capitol Reef without feeling any great urge to stop. Only if you take the time to explore will you get a sense of the magic of the place, and why it fully deserves its national-park status.

Even a couple of hours is enough to admire the western cliffs from the dead-end **Scenic Drive**, south of the park headquarters at **Fruita**. Given half a day or more, you could venture all the way south to Lake Powell on the unpaved **Notom–Bullfrog Road**, tracing the eastern flank of the Waterpocket Fold, or loop back westward via the **Burr Trail**, halfway along. With **hiking trails** of all lengths and levels setting off into the wilderness, it would be easy to spend a week in this one park.

The best **seasons** to visit Capitol Reef are spring, when the fruit trees blossom and the wildflowers bloom, or fall, when the crowds have gone, the cottonwoods change color, and hiking conditions are at their peak. Midsummer temperatures can reach 100°F, and August in particular is prone to flash-flooding, but so long as you set your sights appropriately low – say, to lazing on your back in the orchards, eating fresh fruit – a summer visit is not such a bad idea.

A history of Capitol Reef

Although traces of human occupation date back ten thousand years, the first known inhabitants of the Capitol Reef region were the **Fremont Anasazi**. This Ancestral Puebloan subgroup farmed along the valley of the Fremont River between 700 AD and 1300 AD, when changes in the climate forced them to move on. Archeologists

---

The Geology of Capitol Reef

The **Waterpocket Fold**, which slopes from north to south for the full hundred-mile length of Capitol Reef National Park, is what geologists call a **monocline**, created when layers of sedimentary rock buckled under pressure roughly sixty million years ago. Within the last ten million years, it has in turn been lifted a mile or so above sea level by the general raising of the Colorado Plateau. Most of the original fold has long since eroded away; the reef itself is just the rump. Its western face consists of a long, jagged cliff of hard rock; it rises more gently from the east, in multicolored waves of sandstone that the Navajo called the "Land of the Sleeping Rainbow."

Here and there, the Fold is pierced right through by deeply incised canyons. Often hundreds of feet deep but less than twenty feet wide, these slender gorges were mostly blocked by fallen rocks until Mormon pioneers cleared a way through. After summer thunderstorms, rainwater can cascade through the canyons in fearsome flash floods. At other times, it collects in depressions worn into the rock – the "**waterpockets**" for which the whole mighty edifice is named.

For more
about the
Ancestral
Puebloans of
the Colorado
Plateau, see
p.520.

distinguish them from their more sophisticated cousins to the south-east by the fact that they lived in pithouses dug into the hillsides, rather than in brick houses, and the lack of domesticated dogs or turkeys. The most enduring signs of their presence are the intriguing **petroglyphs** still to be seen on the canyon walls.

After many centuries when only the occasional Paiute hunter passed this way, a small group of Mormons established a permanent settlement beside the Fremont in 1878. The orchards they planted transformed the landscape, and when the post office insisted they gave their community a proper name, a few years later, **Fruita** seemed the perfect choice. The population of the fledgling town never rose above fifty, however, and it was soon suggested that the region had more future as a park than a home. The immediate vicinity of Fruita became Capitol Reef National Monument in 1937, and that was upgraded to national park status when it was enlarged to include the entire Waterpocket Fold in 1971. Former Fruita towns-people and their heirs are still entitled to graze cattle within the park, but ranching is slowly being phased out.

Arrival and information

The closest gas
station to
Capitol Reef is
at the junction
of hwys 12 and
24 in Torrey.

The defunct village of **Fruita**, at the heart of the park, ranges for a mile or so around the intersection of Hwy-24 and the Scenic Drive, eleven miles east of Torrey. Bryce Canyon is 120 miles southwest, the I-70 town of Green River a hundred miles northeast; no **public transport** passes this way.

The **visitor center**, right at the road junction (daily: summer 8am–7pm; winter 8am–4.30pm; ☎435/425-3791), has the usual exhibits and handouts. In addition to the free *Cliffline* newspaper, pick up the $1 driving guide to Cathedral Valley.

For advance
information,
write to
Capitol Reef
National Park,
HCR 70 Box
15, Torrey, UT
84775, or
access
www.nps.gov
/care. Tourist
facilities near-
by are detailed
at www.xmis-
sion.com/~cap
reef.

Only visitors who embark on the Scenic Drive, beyond the visitor center and campground, become liable for the **admission fee** of $4 per vehicle, $2 for motorcyclists, cyclists and pedestrians. All the nationwide passes detailed on p.21 are both sold and accepted.

There are no motels or lodges inside the park; the closest **accom-modation** is in Torrey (see p.418). Torrey is also the place to rent a **bike** (Pedal Pusher, 151 W Main St; ☎435/425-3378 or 1-800/896-5773) or to arrange a **4WD** or **horseback** tour of the park (Hondoo Rivers & Trails; ☎435/425-3519 or 1-800/332-2696). Wild Hare Expeditions (☎435/425-3999 or 1-888/304-4273), who also run jeep tours, organize **guided hiking** expeditions, from a couple of hours at $20 per person up to multiday trips at around $150 per night.

Camping

All three **campgrounds** in Capitol Reef are first-come, first-served and do not take reservations. By far the largest and most popular is the *Fruita Campground* ($10), which makes a good overnight stop even if you never see the rest of the park. Set amid the orchards, a mile south of the visitor center, it remains open all year, but has no showers and in winter can be without water altogether.

Both the **backcountry** campgrounds – much smaller and more primitive, and free – are 35 miles from the visitor center. *Cedar Mesa* is 22.5 miles south of Hwy-24 along the Notom–Bullfrog Road, while *Cathedral Valley* is 25 miles north of Hwy-24 along either the Hartnet Road (which requires you to ford the Fremont River) or the Caineville Wash Road. To camp elsewhere in the backcountry, you must have a free permit from the visitor center.

Driving through the park

At its simplest, driving through Capitol Reef on **Hwy-24** takes well under half an hour. However much of a hurry you may be in, it's worth pausing once or twice en route. Rather than a token pit stop at the visitor center, try taking a five-minute hike from one of the clearly-marked trailheads.

The first of these lies a short distance south of the highway, rough- *An even more* ly three-quarters of the way from Torrey to the visitor center. The *stupendously* brief climb to **Gooseneck Point** is rewarded with a 500-foot view *sinuous gorge* down into the canyon of Sulphur Creek, an "entrenched meander" *can be seen in* that once curved across a flat floodplain but has been etched deep *Goosenecks* into solid rock by the uplifting of the Colorado Plateau. *State Reserve,*

*An even more
stupendously
sinuous gorge
can be seen in
Goosenecks
State Reserve,
in southeast
Utah; see
p.482.*

Hwy-24 passes the visitor center on the right a couple of miles fur- *in southeast* ther along, though the huge, fluted red-rock butte known as the *Utah; see* **Castle** to the left is bound to catch your eye first. Whether you fork *p.482.* right to join the Scenic Drive, or continue on the main highway, you'll reach the heart of the village of **FRUITA** within a few hundred yards, where Sulphur Creek meets the **Fremont River**. You may want to peep into Fruita's former **schoolhouse**, just north of the highway. Built in 1896, it hasn't had a pupil for over fifty years; park rangers, not a Mormon schoolmarm, keep it spick and span.

The village's old **orchards**, however, are Capitol Reef's crowning glory. A waxy, luxuriant green against the towering red cliffs, they hold almost three thousand trees planted by the pioneers. The cherries and peaches **blossom** in the first half of April, the apples slightly later, while the **harvest** lasts from the second half of June until well into October. So long as you stay in the orchards, you can eat as much fruit as you like; you only pay for what you take away.

A short distance further down the highway beyond the schoolhouse, the **Fremont Culture Walk** is an easy amble along a raised boardwalk that leads beside a canyon wall crammed with ancient **petroglyphs**. As well as stylized representations of goats and Bighorn sheep, some show how the Fremont people (see p.395) may have seen themselves – unless of course these strange helmeted figures, with triangular bodies and massive shields, really did come from other planets.

*Other rock art
sites in Utah
are described
on p.450 and
p.452.*

Hwy-24 crosses the Fremont two miles east of the visitor center, near the start of the longer **Hickman Bridge Trail** (see p.427). Only beyond this point does **Capitol Dome**, high above the north bank another half-mile ahead, resolve itself into a dome; so far you've seen it from the side, as a slender fin. By now Fremont Canyon is at its deepest, and it's joined within the next couple of miles by **Chimney Rock Canyon** from the north and **Grand Wash** from the south (see p.426). A mile past Grand Wash stands the sandstone cabin of one of Fruita's earliest settlers, **Elijah Behunin**, with the eastern boundary of the park another 2.5 miles down the road.

The Scenic Drive

Other than Hwy-24, the only paved road in Capitol Reef is the **Scenic Drive**, which parallels the golden cliffs of the Waterpocket Fold for twelve miles south from the visitor center. The first couple of miles lead through Fruita, where a cluster of restored barns and houses serve as homes for park employees, while overnight visitors camp out in the orchards.

Beyond the village, and the fee station where your $4 admission charge is collected, the road undulates through the desert, dipping into dry sandy washes and then climbing scrubby rolling hillocks. Successive individual pinnacles, such as **Fern's Nipple** and the **Egyptian Temple**, line the crest of the red-rock battlements to the east. Until Hwy-24 was pushed through the Fremont Canyon in 1962, this unlikely route was southern Utah's main east–west thoroughfare. For a century, traffic squeezed its way between the narrow walls of **Capitol Gorge**, at the far end. The gravel Capitol Gorge Road now peters out after a mile or two, but hikers can continue on foot, to see the Pioneer Register where early wagon-drivers carved their names (see p.427).

The Notom–Bullfrog Road

If you'd rather survey the Waterpocket Fold from the comfort of your car than sweat it out on foot, the long drive south along the **Notom–Bullfrog Road** is Capitol Reef's best option. Just be sure to stock up on gas and water; you'll have to drive at least seventy miles to find any facilities.

The road leaves Hwy-24 nine miles east of the visitor center, not far outside the park. Only its first four miles are paved, as far as the tiny but well-irrigated settlement of **NOTOM**, now home to perhaps half a dozen ranchers. Thereafter, its rough surface repeatedly ripples into a "washboard" as it follows a dry-as-dust bench above Sandy Creek, with the eerie badlands of the Waterpocket Fold to the west and the volcanic **Henry Mountains** to the east.

Ordinary vehicles should have no problem negotiating the full length of the Notom–Bullfrog Road, which reenters the park twenty miles along, and then leaves it again in the southeast corner fifteen miles on. Seventy miles from the highway, after a final 25-mile segment where you find yourself constantly stopping to swoon at the turquoise expanse of Lake Powell on the southern horizon, you come to the modern marina at **Bullfrog** (see p.435).

The Burr Trail

These days, most drivers who set off south on the Notom–Bullfrog Road don't make it to Bullfrog, but complete a loop around the Waterpocket Fold by branching onto the **Burr Trail**. This is the only road actually to cross the fold, rather than slice through it, and it does so by means of a fearsome set of switchbacks that climb west from the Notom–Bullfrog Road, roughly halfway down.

The Burr Trail began life as a rutted wagon trail, which was upgraded by uranium prospectors in the 1940s and 1950s. The four miles within the national park remain unpaved, but the remaining thirty, running west to Boulder on Hwy-24, were paved during the late 1980s. Wilderness advocates argued that increased road use would irreparably damage one of Utah's least-spoiled regions; Garfield County authorities, keen to grab a piece of the Capitol Reef action from their neighbors in Wayne County, went ahead anyway. From their point of view, they were just in time; the area has since been incorporated into the Grand Staircase–Escalante National Monument, which will probably preclude further road construction.

If all that leaves you feeling too guilty to take the Burr Trail, you're missing out. The panorama that unfolds as you ascend the switchbacks and head west is out of this world. Looking back across the Notom–Bullfrog Road, you see the top of Swap Mesa – whose coal deposits may well be the next target of the mining companies – and the stark Henry Mountains. Just past the topmost ridge, the Upper and Lower sections of **Muley Twist Canyon** stretch to north and south through the heart of the Fold. Both provide excellent opportunities for multiday backpacking expeditions, starting from near the highway. Where the pavement begins, as you leave the park and enter the National Monument, an extraordinary procession of reefs marches south, with the white canyons of the Waterpocket Fold in the foreground and four or five craggy red cliff-faces beyond, leading on to Lake Powell.

The oval plain just west of the park, ringed by the Circle Cliffs, was described by the nineteenth-century geologist Clarence Dutton as "a spot which is about as desolate as any on earth." The Burr Trail leaves it by way of the deep **Long Canyon**, then struggles on to reach Hwy-24 immediately south of Boulder (see p.417).

Cathedral Valley

Capitol Reef's least accessible section is **Cathedral Valley**, north of the highway. Like the Notom–Bullfrog Road, it parallels the eastern side of the Waterpocket Fold, but the territory here is much more forbidding than the sagebrush plain to the south. In among the heavily eroded red, blue and gray hills lie deep canyons and primeval gardens, populated by strange stone monoliths. Unless you have your own 4WD or high-clearance vehicle, however, you'll only see it by joining one of the 4WD tours detailed on p.422.

Two roads run north into the backcountry from Hwy-24, 11.5 and 18.6 miles east of the visitor center. The first, **River Ford Road**, traverses the Fremont River by means of a crude ford a few hundred yards along. If you're planning a loop drive, come this way first – it's not safe to cross when the water's more than a couple of feet deep, and you wouldn't want to find that out at the end of a sixty-mile drive. The second route, the **Caineville Wash Road**, meets the first – by now Hartnet Road – at the far end of Cathedral Valley. Several more dirt roads leave the park at this northern extremity, connecting with I-70 to the north or joining Hwy-72 above Loa to the west.

Hiking in Capitol Reef

You probably won't drive far in Capitol Reef before the backcountry starts to beckon. Choosing which of the many, mostly short **trails** to hike is largely a matter of whether you feel up to climbing; only a few, such as the walks through the Capitol Gorge or Grand Wash, remain on level ground, while the rest demand mountain-goat-style scrambling up the slickrock.

If you do choose to stick to the canyon floors, bear in mind the danger of **flash floods** after rain, and try not to pause anywhere where there's no clear escape route.

Grand Wash

The busiest Capitol Reef trail connects the Scenic Drive with Hwy-24, by way of the gravelly bed of the **Grand Wash**. Both trailheads are roughly four miles from the visitor center, one at the end of the unpaved Grand Wash Road, which leaves the Scenic Drive a mile past Fruita, and the other on the south bank of the highway a mile or two beyond Capitol Dome.

As a one-way walk, the **Grand Wash trail** is just over two miles long and takes around an hour, but unless you arrange a pick-up at the far end you'll have to double back. In the half-mile stretch known as **The Narrows**, the vertiginous 800-foot canyon walls close in to a mere sixteen feet apart. **Butch Cassidy** and his gang are said to have used the tangle of side canyons that lead off Grand Wash as hideouts, but there's no evidence that Butch ever saw **Cassidy Arch**, reached by a short steep climb from near the southeast end of the trail.

Capitol Gorge

The **Capitol Gorge trail** at the end of the Scenic Drive is every bit as claustrophobic as the Grand Wash. In the space of a mile, it inches all the way through a crack in the Waterpocket Fold, though hikers have to turn back when they reach the private land on the far side. From 1871 onwards, this "**Blue Dugway**" was a major trans-Utah thoroughfare, as the painstaking inscriptions on the **Pioneer Register**, carved into the canyon wall halfway along, will testify.

A couple of twists of the canyon past the Register, side canyons open up to both left and right. The one on the left looks more promising, but is blocked a short way along; to the right, you have to start climbing almost immediately, but within a few hundred yards you'll come to some typical **waterpockets**. Early travelers would break off from the laborious haul through the gorge, in the hope of finding fresh water in these clifftop "tanks."

A separate two-mile, one-hour trail from the Capitol Gorge trailhead launches itself straight up the hillside to the north. The slickrock flatlands that cap the Waterpocket Fold enjoy huge views to Boulder Mountain in the east and the Henry Mountains in the west. The dominant feature up here, however, is the glowing Navajo Sandstone butte of the **Golden Throne**, at the foot of which the trail ends.

Hickman Bridge

The **Hickman Bridge Trail** may not be the easiest of Hwy-24's roadside trails – the Fremont Culture Walk, detailed on p.423, is far less demanding – but it makes a supremely rewarding two-mile, two-hour hike. Setting off along the north bank of the Fremont River, two miles east of the visitor center, it meanders briefly through the cottonwoods before climbing a brisk stairway out of the canyon to the shadeless heights up top.

Once you've marveled at Capitol Dome, off to the east, fork left at the junction ahead. Pockmarked black boulders strewn on all sides, incongruous against the red, pink and cream sandstone, testify to ancient lava flows. Three-quarters of a mile along, the path loops around and through the arching span of **Hickman Bridge**. A hundred feet high, a hundred feet wide, it's a genuine natural bridge, worn through the rock by a side channel eager to reach the Fremont below. The rocky chaos beneath somehow complements the grace of the bridge itself.

Taking the right rather than the left fork at the junction lets you in for a nine-mile round trip on the **Rim Overlook Trail**. Highlights include a towering overview of the orchards of Fruita, and the **Navajo Knobs** at its furthermost point.

Lake Powell

Until the early 1960s, it was all but impossible to travel between southwest and southeast Utah. In the unseen heart of the endless desert, the mighty Colorado River churned its way towards the Pacific through a succession of yawning canyons. Here and there boatmen might ferry the occasional passenger across, and a few

Lake Powell

Lake Powell: Controversy and Compromise

The western half of the United States would sustain a population greater than that of our whole country today if the waters that now run to waste were saved and used for irrigation.

President Theodore Roosevelt,
State of the Union address, 1901.

The twentieth-century growth of the American West is largely the story of the "taming" of the **Colorado River**. If the Colorado ran dry, Los Angeles, Las Vegas and Phoenix would die, and the exodus from the Southwest would dwarf anything from the Dustbowl era. In terms of volume, the Colorado does not rank among the top 25 rivers in the US. However, the sheer aggression with which it hurtles from 13,000ft up in the Rockies makes it the fastest and fiercest of them all. That's why it's responsible for so many magnificent canyons; and that's also why civil engineers can't bear to leave it alone. They yearn to harness its energy with hydroelectric dams, and divert its flow to irrigate the desert instead of rushing uselessly to the sea.

Early in the twentieth century, the sparsely populated Southwestern states began to fear that southern California's ever-increasing thirst might one day drain them dry. The **Colorado River Compact**, signed in 1922, divided the river between an **Upper Basin**, consisting of Utah, Wyoming, Colorado and New Mexico, and a **Lower Basin** – Arizona, Nevada and California. Each was to receive 7.5 million acre-feet of the estimated annual flow of 16.8 million, with the dregs left over for Mexico. This was the first of fifteen such agreements in fifty years, largely because the estimates were wrong; the correct figure was more like 13.9 million acre-feet.

The task of distributing the water fell to a new federal agency, the **Bureau of Reclamation**, and the main tool at its disposal was the **dam**. Its engineers saw their mission as being to reshape the West, to "reclaim" it to the way it ought to be. They began in 1935, by damming Black Canyon, on the doorstep of California, with what came to be known as the **Hoover Dam** (see p.500). That project inspired a spree of dam-building, in the US and all over world. Though critics argued the American dams were supplying far more hydroelectric power than the nation needed, it was all soon absorbed into feeding the war effort, and fueling the economic boom of the 1950s. According to the Bureau of Reclamation, yet more dams were needed; its plans for the Colorado Plateau were clear from the subtitle of one report: *A Natural Menace Becomes A Natural Resource*. Proposals included damming the Green River in northwest Colorado, the San Juan in New Mexico, and the Colorado itself in both Bridge Canyon in Arizona and Utah's Glen Canyon.

Almost a century earlier, in 1869, John Wesley Powell had been entranced by the idyllic canyon that lay below the confluence of the Green and Colorado rivers: "A curious ensemble of wonderful features – carved walls, royal arches, glens, alcove gulches, mounds and monuments . . . We decide to call it **Glen Canyon**." Those few river-runners who had seen it since knew it as a cool, tranquil haven, bursting with luxuriant vegetation and desert wildlife, and a far cry from the cataract-filled canyons both up- and downstream. Theirs were lone voices in the wilderness, however; too little known to have been granted federal protection, Glen Canyon's remoteness was to work against it. As a campaigning force, the environmental movement was in its infancy in the 1950s, and its strategy concentrated on defending national parks at all costs. The Green River dam-site being within Dinosaur National Monument, **David Brower**, the executive director of the Sierra Club, argued before a Congressional committee that damming Glen Canyon was a far better idea – in fact he originally endorsed the construction of a dam in the Grand Canyon *on condition* that a dam was built at Glen Canyon as well. Conservationists prided themselves on a job well done when it was eventually decided to dam the Green River outside Dinosaur, at Flaming Gorge to the northwest, and to go ahead with damming Glen Canyon. The one concession to "the abominable nature lovers," as one Utah senator termed them, was that water would not be allowed to encroach upon Rainbow Bridge National Monument.

The first blast at the dam-site was detonated on a signal from President Eisenhower in September 1956. Meanwhile, with Glen Canyon doomed but not yet drowned, archeologists, artists and photographers set out to chronicle its disappearing treasures. These included the glowing, fern-dripping alcove known as the **Cathedral-in-the-Desert** – described in Eliot Porter's best-selling *The Place No One Knew* as "the single most spectacular place I ever visited" – and the **Crossing of the Fathers**, where the Spanish priests Domínguez and Escalante forded the river in 1776, which now lie far beneath buoys no. 68 and no. 21 respectively. Floyd Dominy, the gung-ho head of the Bureau of Reclamation, preferred to dwell on the future, writing in the glossy coffee-table volume *Lake Powell, Jewel of the Colorado* that "like a string of pearls, ten modern recreation areas will line Lake Powell's shores."

The Colorado River was stopped for the first time in its history on January 21, 1963. That same day, President Kennedy's Secretary of the Interior, Stewart Udall – the great-grandson of John D. Lee, of Lees Ferry (see p.350 – announced plans to build two further dams within the Grand Canyon. By now, the Sierra Club had realized its mistake; and it promptly made another. This time it argued for building coal-burning power stations instead of hydroelectric dams. The Navajo Nation, imagining that nuclear power might soon render its mineral resources worthless, decided to cash in by permitting the strip-mining of Black Mesa (see p.44), and the hideously polluting Navajo Generating Station was constructed outside Page.

It took seventeen more years – and a Supreme Court decision that Congress could ignore its own previous rulings and allow the lake to lap against Rainbow Bridge – before Lake Powell was filled to the brim, on June 22, 1980. David Brower, who left the Sierra Club to found Friends of the Earth in 1969, was by now calling his support for Glen Canyon Dam "the greatest sin I have ever committed." As recently as November 1996, the 84-year-old "Archdruid" was back in the headlines with a call for Lake Powell to be drained so the canyon could regenerate. One of the original arguments for the dam had been that the Colorado's phenomenal load of silt would otherwise fill Lake Mead, behind the Hoover Dam, within a few years; Brower now says that the floodgates at Glen Canyon should remain open until that really does happen, perhaps two hundred years from now. Other activists would go much further. The central fantasy of Edward Abbey's *The Monkey-Wrench Gang* involved dynamiting the dam, and Abbey was among the demonstrators who in 1981 signaled the birth of the **Earth First!** movement by suspending a 300-foot strip of plastic down its face to simulate an almighty crack. To some extent, the argument has been won; no major dam has been built since the 1960s, and the general consensus is that Glen Canyon Dam will be the last.

adventurous souls even rafted down the river itself, but there was no highway for two hundred miles north of Arizona.

Now the Colorado has gone, submerged beneath the huge, docile **Lake Powell**. For many people – especially those who knew the sublime **Glen Canyon** that it destroyed – the new lake is a loathsome abomination. Many more see it as a thing of beauty, and Lake Powell has become Utah's number-one tourist attraction, drawing around four million visitors per year and matched in popularity in the Southwest only by the Grand Canyon. It is, undeniably, an extraordinary spectacle, its lurid turquoise waters rippling against its stark red-rock rim, and cradling islands that once were buttes and mesas. No one could ever mistake this for a natural landscape, however, and you don't have to be an out-and-out green to be disturbed by the transformation of America's last great wilderness into a playground. The concessionaires of the **Glen Canyon National Recreational Area** invite you to "think of Lake Powell as a 160,000-acre bathtub and consider our boats, floats, boards and tubes as your toys."

Lake Powell's success as a wet'n'wild theme park has been a surprise spin-off from its real purpose. Glen Canyon Dam was constructed to regulate the flow of water along the Colorado River. Half is kept back to irrigate the deserts of the plateau, while the rest gushes through its turbines, generating electricity as it goes, and makes for Arizona and California. Demand is so precisely monitored that the level of the lake fluctuates according to whether it's dinnertime in Phoenix. Hence its closest resemblance to a bathtub – the scummy dirty-bath tidemark, up to thirty feet above the water, which sullies the sandstone around its edge.

The whole vast engine cost $300 million to build. Lake Powell is 550 feet deep at the dam, and holds enough water to cover all Arizona five inches deep. It stretches back up 186 miles of the Colorado River and 72 miles of the San Juan River, as well as inundating 96 side canyons formed by rivers such as the Escalante and the Dirty Devil. The total shoreline of 1960 miles is longer than the entire US Pacific coast.

Four of the five **marinas** so far built around Lake Powell are accessible by road. Three of those – **Bullfrog**, **Hall's Crossing** and **Hite** – are in Utah, while the largest, **Wahweap**, lies just across the border in Arizona, not far from the dam itself and the purpose-built town of **Page**. There's surprisingly little accommodation on land; it's assumed you'll want to join the armada out on the water, either in your own vessel or in a rented **houseboat**. For a quick taste, you can join a **guided tour** at either Wahweap or Bullfrog – the half-day trips to **Rainbow Bridge** are by far the most popular – or take the **ferry** service that plies between Bullfrog and Hall's Crossing.

Page

Home to over seven thousand people, **PAGE**, Arizona, is now the largest community in a 720-mile stretch of the Colorado River.

Before Glen Canyon Dam was constructed four miles west, this all but barren mesa belonged to the Navajo Nation. Thanks to a small spring, however, it made the best site to house the dam's workforce. The Navajo agreed to swap it for a similar-sized chunk of desert between Bluff and Hatch in Utah, a new road was blasted through the Echo Cliffs, and the town was born on Thanksgiving Day 1958.

At first, Page seemed destined to wither away once the dam was completed. Ironically, it gained a new lease of life when Congress decided that instead of building more dams, the Southwest could meet its power needs by burning coal instead. The **Navajo Generating Station**, which creates electricity using coal from Black Mesa, and pumps water from Lake Powell to Phoenix, went up four miles southeast of town. It may have had a catastrophic effect on the air quality at the Grand Canyon, but it's kept Page in work.

The view as you drop down towards Page, whether from Utah or Arizona, is utterly surreal. The five power-station chimneys stand silhouetted amid the sandstone outcrops, with lines of pylons marching off across the desert and the misty hump of Navajo Mountain rising in the distance. As you get lower, the waters of Lake Powell emerge from the haze, with drowned buttes poking their heads here and there above the surface.

The story of John Wesley Powell's Colorado expeditions is told on p.441.

Page itself, on the other hand, resembles a dull suburban mall writ large. Most of its original trailer homes have been replaced by more permanent structures, but the only sight of any interest is the **John Wesley Powell Memorial Museum**, 6 N Lake Powell Blvd (Nov to mid-Dec and mid-Feb to April Mon–Fri 9am–5pm; May–Oct daily 8am–6pm; donations). As well as charting the exploits of the first man to raft down the Colorado, this celebrates later river-runners and also recounts Page's own brief history.

On the first weekend of October each year, Page hosts a spectacular air show known as the Air Affaire.

Arrival and information

Page's **visitor center** is in Dam Plaza at 644 N Navajo Drive (summer Mon–Sat 8am–7pm, Sun 10am–6pm; winter Mon–Fri 8.30am–5pm, Sat 9am–5pm; ☎520/645-2741). Brochures on local attractions can also be picked up at the Powell Museum (see above).

Arizona Stage Lines, 55 S Lake Powell Blvd (☎520/645-9356 or 1-888/253-7420) run an intermittent **shuttle van** service between Page and Flagstaff, while the local **airport**, a mile east on Hwy-98, is connected with Las Vegas and Phoenix by Scenic Airlines (☎1-800/445-8738).

Bus tours to Antelope Canyon are detailed on p.433, and boat trips from Wahweap Marina on p.434.

Accommodation

While no one would choose to spend much time in Page itself, Lake Powell is enough of an attraction to keep its **motels** busy for most of the year, and to hike their rates higher than you might expect.

Best Western Arizonainn, 716 Rim Drive; ☎520/645-2466 or 1-800/528-1234, fax 520/645-2053. Standard upmarket motel on the outskirts of Page,

*The zip code
for Page is AZ
86040.*

*For further
accommoda-
tion options
near Page, see
Wahweap,
p.434.*

commanding a massive desert panorama from the poolside. Mid-Oct to March ④, April to mid-Oct ⑤.

Best Western at Lake Powell, 208 N Lake Powell Blvd; ☎520/645-5988 or 1-800/528-1234, fax 520/645-2578. Large, good-value motel perched above downtown Page, with a pool. Mid-Oct to mid-May ③, mid-May to mid-Oct ④.

Courtyard by Marriott, 600 Country Club Drive; ☎520/645-5000 or 1-800/321-2211, fax 520/645-5004. Page's most incongruous splash of luxury – complete with golf course – is located down below the mesa in view of the dam. Nov–Feb ④, March–Oct ⑥.

Lake Powell International Hostel, 141 Eighth Ave; ☎520/645-3898 or 1-800/545-5405. Welcoming, central budget hostel, offering dorm beds (with bed linen) from $12, plus basic private rooms. Boat tours can be arranged. ①–②

Navajo Trail Motel, 800 Bureau St; ☎520/645-9508; *http://pages.ivillage .com/pp/navajotrailmotels/*. Inexpensive motel, near the museum. Nov–Feb ①, March–Oct ②.

Eating

Page offers the usual range of **diners** and **fast-food** outlets. If you're just racing through, *Beans Gourmet Coffeehouse* at 644 Dam Plaza, next to the visitor center, serves espressos and light snacks. The *Gunsmoke Saloon* alongside offers live country music – and beer – nightly.

Bella Napoli, 810 N Navajo Drive; ☎520/645-2706. Classy, dinner-only Italian cuisine, with lots of shrimp and seafood entrees – even Alaskan lobster – plus less expensive pastas and pizza. Closed mid-Nov to Feb.

Cactus & Tropicals Gardens and Cafe, 809 N Navajo Drive; ☎520/645-6666. Breakfast coffees, and lunchtime sandwiches and salads, in the center of town. Closed Sun.

Pepper's Restaurant, *Courtyard by Marriott*, 600 Country Club Drive; ☎520/645-5000. Upscale hotel restaurant as you approach town from the dam, with a varied if not wildly exciting menu that ranges through salads, pasta, sandwiches and dinner specials.

Porter's Sunset Grille, 125 S Lake Powell Blvd; ☎520/645-3039. Mexican and Southwestern specialties, from fajitas and tacos to T-bone steaks. They also do big breakfasts and lunchtime sandwiches.

Antelope Canyon

A couple of miles southeast of Page, milepost 299 on Hwy-98 marks the trailhead for **Antelope Canyon**, the most famous "slot canyon" in Arizona. There are actually two entirely separate parts of the canyon, located to either side of the highway. Both are on Navajo land.

The **Lower** section achieved worldwide notoriety in 1997, when the tragic deaths of eleven hikers in a flash flood proved just how dangerous such places can be. Nevertheless, they're also irresistibly, astonishingly beautiful. In the last few years, the Navajo have begun to appreciate what an invaluable tourist asset Antelope Canyon represents, and to control all access. If and when the Lower canyon is reopened to visitors, it's likely to be on guided tours only.

In summer, the **Upper** canyon, to the south of the highway, can be seen simply by turning up at the parking lot (May–Oct daily 8am–5pm; ☎520/698-3384). However, not only is there a $5 fee, but you also have to pay an outrageous $12.50 more to ride in a shuttle van down to the canyon entrance, a matter of perhaps two miles. You're deposited just outside a slender, unprepossessing crack in a wall of red sandstone. Stepping inside is like entering both a cathedral, in that you find yourself in a majestic chamber adorned with delicate glowing colors, and a pinball machine, in that you can just imagine that any second some mighty and unavoidable boulder will come thundering down the narrow passageway ahead. Walking the full length of the canyon and back takes barely twenty minutes, even with constant pauses to admire the interlacing fins of many-hued rock that swirl overhead, to a height, in places, of 120 feet.

*Antelope Canyon may be transformed by the time you read this by the opening of a Navajo-owned **marina** near its intersection with Lake Powell*

Companies running frequent **tours** to Antelope Canyon from Page, at a typical price including all fees of between $25 and $30, include Scenic Tours, 48 S Lake Powell Blvd (☎520/645-5594); Lake Powell Jeep Tours, 104 S Lake Powell Blvd (☎520/645-5501); and Roger Ekis' Photographic Tours (☎520/645-8579).

Glen Canyon Dam

Glen Canyon Dam plugs **Marble Canyon** (see p.350) not at its narrowest point, but at its northern end, just downstream from Wahweap Creek. As US-89 crosses Glen Canyon Bridge four miles outside Page, the vast curve of the dam is to the north, while Marble Canyon drops 700ft below you. An east-bank spur road tunnels through the cliffs to reach the river; it's used mainly by river-rafters setting off on the gloriously lazy fifteen-mile float down to Lees Ferry (see p.434).

There's no stopping on the bridge, so if you want a better look, call in at the ultramodern **Carl Hayden Visitor Center** (daily: Oct–April 8am–5pm, May–Sept 7am–7pm; ☎520/608-6404; *www.nps.gov /glca*) on the west bank, which doubles as the main source of information on the **Glen Canyon National Recreational Area**. With half an hour to spare, you can take a **free tour** of the actual dam, dropping via two elevators first to the walkway along the top, and then a further 500ft to the generating station at the bottom. Beneath the roar of the 1.3-million-kilowatt turbines, a digital counter steadily ticks off the billions of dollars so far earned by the sale of power.

Wahweap

Unlike Page, **WAHWEAP**, a couple of miles west of Glen Canyon Dam, has never become a town. Lake Powell's principal **marina** has, however, grown steadily since it was established in 1963, coordinat-

Lake Powell

ing most of the boat rental and tour business and also offering several hundred motel rooms.

To the fury of the federal authorities, the first man to appreciate Wahweap's potential did so long before the dam was ever built. Art Greene, the owner of the *Marble Canyon Lodge* (see p.350), ran boat trips upriver to Rainbow Bridge from the 1940s onwards; when he got wind of plans to dam Glen Canyon, he shrewdly leased the land at the mouth of Wahweap Creek at a knockdown rate. Knowing it made the perfect site for a marina, Greene refused to budge, and wound up making a killing as official concessionaire.

Accommodation

Only half the rooms in the plush *Wahweap Lodge* (☎520/645-2433 or 1-800/528-6154, fax 520/331-5258; *www.visitlakepowell.com*; Nov–April ⑥, May–Oct ⑦) overlook Lake Powell. Its *Rainbow Room* restaurant, however, has huge lakeside windows, and serves good food daily for all meals.

The same management also operates the summer-only *Lake Powell Motel*, three miles west on US-89 (April–Oct; ☎520/645-2477; ⑤), and a first-come, first-served **campground** ($12).

Boat tours from Wahweap

These same Marble Canyon float trips are offered by the Fred Harvey Company at the Grand Canyon; see p.326

Lake Powell Resorts and Marinas (see box, below) run tours to **Rainbow Bridge** from Wahweap all year round, with a **full-day** rate of $92 for adults, $62 for under-12s, and **half-day** rates of $69 and $49 respectively. Other tours from Wahweap range from a one-hour paddlewheeler trip (adults $10, under-12s $7) up to a dinner cruise ($53, no reductions), and there are also ninety-minute cruises to Antelope Canyon.

In addition, Wahweap is the base for **rafting trips** down Marble Canyon to Lees Ferry. Half-day trips, available all year, cost $49 for

---

Renting a Houseboat

To rent a **houseboat** on Lake Powell, contact Lake Powell Resorts and Marinas, PO Box 56909, Phoenix, AZ 85079 (☎520/645-2433, 602/278-8888 or 1-800/528-6154, fax 602/331-5258; *www.visitlakepowell .com*). Between mid-May and mid-October, the smallest houseboat, capable of sleeping six, costs $1009 for three days or $1616 for a week. For the rest of the year, the price drops to $605 or $970 respectively. Throughout the year, rates for the luxury ten-berth Admiral class of boat are well over double.

Any number of **package deals**, offering different combinations of time spent on houseboats, in the marina lodges, and on guided tours, are also available.

Many houseboat users like to **camp** overnight on-shore; NRA regulations insists that anyone who camps within a mile of the lake must carry and use portable toilets.

adults, $42 for under-12s, while the full-day version (April–Oct only) costs $69 for adults, $62 for under-12s.

Rainbow Bridge National Monument

Millions of tourists have Lake Powell to thank for providing effortless access to the world's largest natural bridge, the magnificent **RAINBOW BRIDGE NATIONAL MONUMENT**. The Navajo, seeing this formerly sacred site swarming with visitors, are far less enthusiastic, though at least the height of Glen Canyon Dam, and thus the level of the lake, was mandated to ensure that Rainbow Bridge was not drowned – unlike the nearby and equally revered confluence of the Colorado and San Juan rivers.

Boat tours to Rainbow Bridge from Wahweap and Bullfrog are detailed opposite and overleaf.

Both the Navajo and the Paiute knew of Rainbow Bridge before the first university-sponsored expedition reached it in 1909. Within a year, it was declared a national monument, but it remained far off any beaten track until the coming of Lake Powell. The bridge now lies a mile or two down Forbidding Canyon, a side canyon located just under forty miles by water from either Wahweap or Bullfrog.

Forbidding Canyon twists away from the lake until it peters out at a jetty that floats in a morass of pond scum. A ten-minute walk from there leads to the astonishing sandstone gateway, which springs up nearly 300 feet from just above the waterline. It's also almost 300 feet wide, with Navajo Mountain visible through its superbly smooth curve. The upper section, including the forty-foot-thick span, is composed of Navajo Sandstone, while the base belongs to the harder Kayenta formation, not as easily cut by flowing water.

With a great deal more difficulty, Rainbow Bridge can also be reached on **foot**. Two fourteen-mile trails start respectively 38 and 42 miles up Arrowhead Hwy-16, which runs north from Hwy-98 from a junction 57 miles southeast of Page. They loop to either side of Navajo Mountain, before joining for the last half-mile. This hike should only be attempted by experienced canyoneers, all of whom must obtain **permits** from the Navajo Nation (Parks & Recreation Dept, Box 9000, Window Rock, AZ 86515; ☎520/871-6647 or 871-6636).

Bullfrog

The marina at **BULLFROG** is slapped atop the slickrock on the west side of Lake Powell, seventy miles upstream from Wahweap, or seventy miles southeast of Capitol Reef National Park on the Notom–Bullfrog Road (see p.424). It's the focus of a small community that now proudly boasts its own high school, as well as a spanking new Glen Canyon NRA **visitor center**, so far open in summer only (March Sat & Sun 8am–5pm, April–Oct daily 8am–5pm; ☎435/684-7400).

A houseboat on stilts above the road serves as a sign for the *Defiance House Lodge* (☎435/684-2233, 602/278-8888 or 1-

Lake Powell

The Lake Powell Ferry

The *John Atlantic Burr* takes 25 minutes to cross between **Bullfrog** and **Hall's Crossing**, and leaves at the following times daily:

	From Hall's Crossing	From Bullfrog
mid-April to mid-May	8am, 10am, noon, 2pm & 4pm	9am, 11am, 1pm, 3.30pm & 5pm
mid-May to Sept	8am, 10am, noon, 2pm, 4pm & 6pm	9am, 11am, 1pm, 3pm, 5pm & 7pm.
Oct	8am, 10am, noon, 2pm & 4pm	9am, 11am, 1pm, 3.30pm & 5pm
Nov to mid-April	8am, 10am, noon & 2pm	9am, 11am, 1pm & 3.30pm

Fares: Foot passengers $2, age 5–11 $1, under-5s and over-65s free; bike $2, motorbike $3, ordinary car $9. Increased rates for larger vehicles. Call ☎435/684-4000 to check the boat's current state of repair.

800/528-6154; mid-Oct to mid-May ④, mid-May to mid-Oct ⑥). The best place to enjoy the big lake views from this pricey mesa-top **motel** is its *Anasazi* restaurant, but the food is indifferent. The park concessionaires also have some fully furnished but deeply unatmospheric **housekeeping units** for rent (☎ as above; mid-Oct to mid-May ⑤, mid-May to mid-Oct ⑦).

Boat tours from Bullfrog and Hall's Crossing

All-day boat **tours** from Bullfrog and Hall's Crossing to **Rainbow Bridge** run between April and October only, and cost $92 for adults, $62 for under-12s. The *Canyon Explorer* also sets off from both Bullfrog and Hall's Crossing in summer on 2hr 30min cruises to nearby lesser-known canyons such as Forgotten Canyon, home to the Defiance House Ruin Ancestral Puebloan site (adults $35, under-12s $27), and half-day trips up Escalante Canyon (adults $69, under-12s $49).

Hall's Crossing

HALL'S CROSSING, on the east shore of Lake Powell, now plays second fiddle to its larger neighbor of Bullfrog to the west. As the name suggests, it was the base of a ferry operator long before the lake existed. **Charles Hall** started out by building his own boat at Hole-In-The-Rock, 35 miles downstream (see p.415), in 1870. Business there was so bad that he moved here instead in 1881, only to give up altogether when the transcontinental railroad rendered his service redundant. Hall charged $5 per wagon, and 75¢ per passenger; the going rate these days for a family car is $9 (see box above).

The NRA Ranger Station above Hall's Crossing marina is rarely staffed; call ☎1-800/582-4351 in emergencies. **Accommodation** possibilities are limited to housekeeping units in a glorified trailer park (phone number and rates as for Bullfrog), while if you're looking for a meal you can either take your pick from a small assortment of Twinkie bars on sale at the local gas station, or a marginally wider range of groceries at the marina store. There's nothing at all at the **ferry ramp**, just over a mile beyond the marina.

When they finally get round to colonizing Mars, the first settlement should look much like the airstrip on top of the bare red mesa that rises above Hall's Crossing. Hwy-276 to the east makes an exhilarating drive, dropping down the **Clay Cliffs** with views across the red plains to Monument Valley, and running for forty empty miles to meet Hwy-95 near Natural Bridges (see p.479).

Ticaboo

Hwy-276 sets off bravely into the desert northwest of Bullfrog, passing a series of unlikely-looking warehouses used to store boats during the winter. Twelve miles up, well past the turning to Notom and only a few miles short of the red-tinged peak that marks the southernmost point of the Henry Mountains, the grandiose resort development of **TICABOO** stands to the left of the highway.

An optimistic venture that still hasn't quite paid off, Ticaboo consists of the comfortable *Ticaboo Lodge* (☎435/788-2110 or 1-800/987-5253, fax 435/788-2118; Oct–April ④, May–Sept ⑤), plus the *Ticaboo Cafe*, which is – in theory – open all day, serving steak and pasta, the *Wild Hare* bar and a Conoco gas station.

Hite

The fourth and northernmost of the road-accessible marinas on Lake Powell, at **HITE**, is reached via **Hwy-95**, which branches off Hwy-24 halfway between Capitol Reef and I-70 to run for 122 miles southeast to Blanding. The only highway to cross the Colorado between the Glen Canyon Dam and Moab, Hwy-95's most dramatic segment is the twenty-mile stretch as it approaches the river from the west, rattling along beside the North Wash.

Soon after Lake Powell first laps at the canyon walls, the road climbs to **Hite Overlook**. Signboards on this windswept hilltop point out the patch of water that covers the short-lived gold-mining town of Hite itself, which flourished for thirty years from 1883. It takes a while before your eyes stop scouring the buttes on the horizon and pick out the ramshackle **Hite Marina** that has replaced it.

Once past the overlook, Hwy-95 loops north to cross first the Dirty Devil River and then the Colorado. Reaching Hite Marina involves a detour of a couple of miles on the far side; unless you need gas or groceries, or are boating, there's no point going out of your way. Renting a **housekeeping unit** here (phone number and rates as for Bullfrog) would be a seriously bad idea.

Between Capitol Reef and Canyonlands

No direct route crosses the tract of craggy sandstone and eroded clay that stretches for a hundred miles east of Capitol Reef. Travelers making the circuit of Utah's parks are obliged to make a giant detour to the north or south, either crossing Lake Powell at Hite, or taking Hwy-24 up to meet I-70 and then looping back down to Moab – a total drive of around 150 miles.

The scenery along Hwy-24 is consistently awesome, beginning with the **badlands** twenty miles beyond Capitol Reef, where the 1500-foot **Factory Butte** rises above corrugated humps of grayish-blue clay reminiscent of Arizona's Painted Desert (see p.276). Only small sections of the backcountry are at all accessible, however, and there's only one town of any size en route, **Green River**.

Hanksville

Forty miles from the Capitol Reef visitor center, Hwy-24 turns sharply north towards the interstate, while Hwy-95 runs south towards Lake Powell. The tiny farming community of **HANKSVILLE** stands at the intersection, a few miles south of the confluence where the Fremont and Muddy rivers join to form the Dirty Devil.

Hanksville is only a spot on the map, but with the next spot a good fifty miles away in any direction, it draws in enough weary drivers to keep it ticking over. The most appealing overnight options are a couple of **B&Bs**: *Fern's Place*, 99 East 100 North (☎435/542-3251; ③), which consists of a cluster of blue cottages, and the friendly, three-room *Joy's*, 296 S Center St (☎435/542-3252; ③), which is open to couples only. There's also a large commercial **campground**, the *Red Rock*, at 226 East 100 North (March–Nov; $10; ☎435/542-3235 or 1-800/452-4971), which has a reasonable restaurant. Otherwise your choice is restricted to a handful of run-down little **motels**, like the *Desert Inn*, 197 East 100 North (☎435/542-3241, fax 542-3231; ②), and the *Whispering Sands*, 140 S Hwy-95 (☎435/542-3238, fax 542-3456; ③). *Blondie's Eatery* (☎435/542-3255), poised on a low bluff close to the intersection, is better than it looks.

Goblin Valley State Park

To see Goblin Valley inhabited by bona-fide space goblins, catch the 2000 movie Galaxy Quest.

Utah's quirkiest park, **Goblin Valley State Park**, nestles at the foot of the San Rafael Reef, a short distance west of Hwy-24 just over twenty miles north of Hanksville. This small patch of barren desert became a park for the simple reason that its rock formations are funny. The man who first noticed them, in the 1940s, called it Mushroom Valley, but "goblin" is as good a name as any.

To reach the park, branch west from Hwy-24 near mile post 137 and drive for five miles along Temple Mountain Road, then turn south onto a seven-mile paved spur road. Past the entrance kiosk ($4 day-use fee, open 24 hours; ☎435/564-3633), the road ends beside a sheltered overlook, poised above a slim valley whose sandy floor is completely devoid of vegetation. It's filled instead with parallel fins of pale Entrada sandstone, each topped by a ridge that's indented with weird eroded figures. Some hoodoos also stand alone, while larger buttes and columns loom around the periphery.

A couple of formal trails lead down into the valley, but no one bothers to follow them, preferring to slither at random from one mis-shapen masterpiece to the next. Once you're on the valley floor, a typical monster in the maze will rise a few feet over your head; some really do look like goblins, complete with eyes and ears.

Away from the main valley, but still engulfed by stunted sandstone sprites, the park has a well-equipped **campground**, open year-round ($9; reservations on ☎1-800/322-3770).

Between Capitol Reef and Canyonlands

The Goblin Valley turnoff is half a mile north of the dirt road that leads to the Horseshoe Canyon subsection of Canyonlands National Park; see p.448.

The San Rafael Swell

The **San Rafael Swell**, fronted by the "reef" that soars immediately northwest of Goblin Valley, is one of southern Utah's least known but most tantalizing wilderness areas. With so many named, mapped and tamed parklands available to explore in the region, for such instant and abundant rewards, few out-of-state visitors have time to add this difficult, mountainous terrain to their itineraries. A sight of it from I-70, as the interstate plunges east down its craggy foothills towards Green River, has to suffice.

The main deterrent to casual sightseeing is that, as a rule, the swell is only safely accessible in a 4WD vehicle. Ask in Green River or Goblin Valley for current conditions, however; the dirt roads tend to be regraded each spring, to repair damage wrought during the harsh winters, and thus may be passable to ordinary vehicles in early summer.

If you can get through, possible destinations include **Little Wild Horse Canyon**, a slot canyon that cuts into the reef roughly seven sandy miles west of Goblin Valley; the summit of **Temple Mountain**, which can be reached or circled with a six-mile hike that starts a mile up Temple Mountain Road beyond the Goblin Valley turnoff; and the swell's highest point, the **San Rafael Knob**, a four-hour round-trip hike from the end of Copper Globe Road, which heads south from I-70 at exit 114.

Green River

Hwy-24 joins I-70 44 miles north of Hanksville just as the interstate completes a dramatic descent from the uplands of the San Rafael Swell to slope gently east through a landscape of soaring buttes. Within a few miles, a ribbon of green vegetation becomes visible ahead, cutting through the desert at the bottom of a long broad valley

– the line of the **Green River**. To the north stand the forbidding **Uintah Mountains**, to the south the stream burrows into a labyrinth of twisting canyons, so this is the best place to ford the river for hundreds of miles.

The town of **GREEN RIVER** has long straddled crucial cross-country routes. For east–west travelers, it remains the major waystation between Colorado and Utah, while river-runners from John Wesley Powell onwards have launched themselves south from here towards the Colorado. The first bridge was built to serve the Denver & Rio Grande Railroad in 1883.

While Green River is a welcome oasis, however – fertile enough to be considered the "melon-growing capital of east Utah" – it still amounts to little more than a strip of motels, gas stations and fast-food outlets. Given a sensible reluctance to erect permanent structures too close to the river, there's a gap where you might expect downtown to be; most of the built-up strip lies to the west.

The east bank of the river, however, is noteworthy as the site of the **John Wesley Powell River History Museum**, at 885 E Main St (daily: summer 8am–8pm; winter 8am–5pm; $2). This recounts the epic journeys of the Canyonlands region's first true explorer, whose second voyage started at Green River on May 22, 1871. Powell made that trip partly because he lost the notes from his first, so the second time around he ensured that his every movement was fully recorded, in photos that now make marvellously evocative viewing. A twenty-minute multimedia show and several rooms of exhibits cover developments in river navigation since then, ranging through several c.1900 steamers – none managed more than a handful of voyages – up to the army-surplus rubber inflatables that triggered the postwar boom in whitewater rafting. Spare a moment to glance out of the panoramic windows, and you'll see that the river here is not green at all, but a dark muddy brown.

South of Main Street, sandwiched between the river's west bank, the railroad tracks, and Green River Boulevard, a cluster of fine old cottonwoods marks the attractive waterfront **Green River State Park**. This makes a good spot to break your journey with a picnic, and also holds the area's nicest **campground** (day-use $5, camping $10 on weekdays or $11 on weekends; ☎435/564-3633; for summer reservations, costing $5 extra, call ☎1-800/322-3770).

Arrival and information

The Powell museum at 885 E Main St doubles as Green River's **visitor center** (hours as above; ☎435/564-3526), which can advise you on driving local backcountry roads. Greyhound **buses** between Denver and points west call at the *Rodeway Inn*, 525 E Main St, but although Amtrak trains pass through town, the closest stop is 25 miles east, at **Thompson**.

*The zip code
for Green River
is UT 84525.*

John Wesley Powell

Until **John Wesley Powell** led the first expedition to float down the full length of the Green and Colorado rivers, the Colorado Plateau was a vast blank at the heart of maps of the American West. No one knew how the mountains and waterways of the region fitted together, or whether falls larger than Niagara might prevent river traffic completely.

Powell was born in Ohio in 1834, the son of a traveling preacher, and spent his youth making solo forays along the Ohio, Mississippi and Illinois rivers. He lost his right arm fighting for the Union at Shiloh, where he formed a lasting friendship with the future president Ulysses Grant. Once the Civil War was over, the veteran major headed west, and decided to explore the Colorado Plateau at his own expense.

Powell, his brother Walter, and eight frontier types who volunteered to serve as an unpaid crew, set off from Green River, Wyoming, on **May 24, 1869**. They had four flat-bottomed wooden boats, purpose-built in Chicago; Powell was lashed to an upright wooden chair in the leading vessel. Not long after entering the Uintah Mountains, by way of **Flaming Gorge**, they were reduced to three boats, when one was smashed to smithereens in Lodore Canyon. They then whisked through Green River, Utah, and plunged into the desert, encountering their biggest challenge so far in the shape of **Cataract Canyon**, soon after the Green met the Grand to form the Colorado. Wherever possible, they carried their boats around the fiercest rapids, and with prodigious energy Powell repeatedly climbed out of the canyon to get his bearings. After several terrifying days, they burst out of the gorge, for an idyllic period of respite in **Glen Canyon**.

Three members of the party became demoralized in the depths of the **Grand Canyon**, when the blackness of the walls to either side seemed to presage further ferocious rapids ahead. They decided to hike their way out, only to be murdered by Shivwits Indians who mistook them for a group of trappers who had recently attacked an Indian woman. Powell, however, made it through the remainder of the canyon with unexpected ease. He arrived at the **Grand Wash Cliffs**, at the confluence of the Colorado and Virgin rivers (now beneath Lake Mead) on August 30. Two of his crew continued all the way to the Pacific, but Powell and his brother left the river, after almost a hundred days afloat.

Now a national celebrity, Powell returned for a better funded and much more leisurely trip two years later. Starting this time from Green River, Utah, he documented his experiences in much greater detail, and used them as the basis of a best-selling book. During the voyage, he left the canyon at every opportunity, and even returned to Washington DC for the winter, while his crew holed up in Kanab.

In later years, Powell became director of the Smithsonian Institution's **Bureau of Ethnology** in Washington, and of the **US Geologic Survey**. His forceful opinions as to how the federal government should administer the limited resources of the West – and especially its water – are now regarded as prophetic. Refusing to accept the then current adage that "rain follows the plow," he argued that state boundaries should be drawn along natural watersheds, to prevent water issues from bedeviling the region's political future. It was his advocacy of federally funded water projects that led the bureaucrats to name **Lake Powell** in his honor, but one can't help imagining that Powell himself would prefer Glen Canyon as it was in the beginning.

Companies running **rafting trips** from Green River include Moki Mac River Expeditions (☎801/268-6667 or 1-800/284-7280; *www .mokimac.com*), and Holiday River Expeditions, 1055 E Main St (☎801/266-2087 or 1-800/554-RAFT; *www.bikeraft.com*). Every Memorial Day, hundreds of boats set out on weekend-long convoy trips that cruise down to the Colorado confluence, and then chug back upriver to Moab.

Accommodation

Although Green River is not much of a destination in its own right, it has almost four hundred **motel** rooms. They tend to fill by early evening in summer, partly with the overspill from Moab and partly with long-distance interstate travelers. The best camping in town is at Green River State Park (see p.440).

Best Western River Terrace, 880 E Main St; ☎435/564-3401 or 1-800/528-1234. Green River's top option, with a pool, river views and adjacent restaurant. Winter ④, summer ⑤.

Budget Host Book Cliff Lodge, 395 E Main St; ☎435/564-3406 or 1-800/493-4699. Low, sprawling complex, set back from the highway west of the river, and holding 100 pretty basic motel rooms, a diner, souvenir stores, a gas station and a crazy golf course. Winter ②, summer ④.

Mancos Rose Motel, 20 W Main St; ☎435/564-9660. Basic but bearable motel that counts as Green River's cheapest option. Winter ①, summer ②.

Super 8, 1248 E Main St; ☎435/564-8888 or 1-800/800-8000, fax 435/564-8890. Reliable, reasonably new budget motel, perched on a slight eminence at the east end of town. Winter ②, summer ④.

The Green River

But for political shenanigans in the 1920s, the **Green River** might rank among the most famous rivers in the world. It starts by flowing north to loop around the Wind River Mountains of central Wyoming, then heads south into Utah, briefly ducks into the northwest corner of Colorado, and then crosses Utah to meet the Colorado after a 730-mile journey. The only thing is, the "Colorado" at that point – originally known as the **Grand River** – has come a mere 430 miles from the central Colorado Rockies. By geographical convention, the Green River should be regarded as the main course of the Colorado River, and thus renamed.

Until 1859, when Captain J.N. Mancomb discovered the confluence deep in the heart of the canyonlands, no one knew that the Green and Grand rivers met to form the Colorado. The Colorado had been named by the Spanish founder of New Mexico, Juan de Oñate, in 1606, while the Green River was identified by Fray Alonso de Posada in 1686 as the boundary between the territories of the Ute and the Comanche. French trappers stumbled across the Grand perhaps a century later.

Colorado's legislators were mortified to learn that the "Colorado River" did not after all flow through Colorado, as had always been assumed. When apportioning its waters became a major issue in the 1920s (see p.428), they therefore renamed the Grand the Colorado, which fortunately dovetailed with a vote in conservative Utah against changing the name of the Green River.

Eating

As well as the usual fast-food places and a couple of local cafes, several of Green River's motels have their own restaurants.

Book Cliff Restaurant, 395 E Main St; ☎435/564-3650. Pick from a large menu of diner food – mostly under $10, from chicken fried steak to fish and chips – as you gaze across a gas station forecourt. Open daily for all meals.

*The price codes
used here are
explained on
p.15.*

Tamarisk Restaurant, 870 E Main St; ☎435/564-8109. Brisk, busy restaurant, overlooking the river opposite the museum and open daily for breakfast, lunch and dinner. The food isn't bad, and the evening buffets (adults $9, kids $6) are pretty good value.

West Winds Restaurant, 545 E Main St; ☎435/564-8240. A 24-hour licensed diner, near the river's west bank, where breakfast is available nonstop and burgers, sandwiches, steaks and Mexican dishes are served until 2am.

Canyonlands National Park

CANYONLANDS NATIONAL PARK, the largest and most magnificent of Utah's national parks, is as hard to define as it is to map. Its closest equivalent, the Grand Canyon, is simply an almighty crack in an otherwise relatively flat plain; the Canyonlands area is a bewildering tangle of canyons, plateaus, fissures and faults, scattered with buttes and monoliths, pierced by arches and caverns, and penetrated only by a paltry handful of dead-end roads.

*Advance information on
Canyonlands is
available from
2282 S West
Resource Blvd,
Moab, UT
84532;
☎435/719-
2313; or
www.nps.gov
/cany.*

The 527 square miles of the park are just the core of a much larger wilderness that stretches to the horizon in every direction. To nineteenth-century explorers, this was the epitome of useless desolation; only since uranium prospectors blazed crude trails across the trackless wastes in the 1950s has it become at all widely known. Even after Canyonlands park was created in 1964, it took a couple of decades before tourists arrived in appreciable numbers.

Canyonlands focuses upon the Y-shaped confluence of the Green and Colorado rivers, buried deep in the desert forty miles southwest of Moab. There's only one spot from which you can see the rivers meet, however, and that's a five-mile hike from the nearest road. With no way to get down to the rivers, let alone cross them, the park therefore splits into three major sections. The **Needles**, east of the Colorado, is a red-rock wonderland of sandstone pinnacles and hidden meadows that's a favorite with hardy hikers and 4WD enthusiasts, while the **Maze**, west of both the Colorado and the Green, is a virtually inaccessible labyrinth of tortuous, waterless canyons that presents a stiff challenge even to expert climbers and backpackers. In the wedge of the "Y" between the two, the high, dry mesa of the **Island In The Sky** commands astonishing views across the whole park and beyond, with several overlooks that can easily be toured by car. Getting from any one of these sections to the others involves a drive of at least a hundred miles. Both the Needles and the Island In The Sky are reached via long approach roads that leave US-191 north

*A full list of
operators who
run tours into
the
Canyonlands
backcountry
appears on
pp.468-469.*

Canyonlands National Park

Canyonlands Fees and Permits

The entry fee for Canyonlands National Park, levied between March and October only, is $10 per vehicle, $5 for cyclists or hikers, and is valid for seven days in all sections of the park. All the usual passes (see p.21) are sold and accepted.

Only limited numbers of visitors are allowed to spend a night or more in the backcountry, and all such groups are required to have permits. Backpacking permits, covering a maximum party of seven persons in the Needles and Island In The Sky districts, or five persons in the Maze, cost $10. Vehicle campsite permits, issued for groups of up to three vehicles (carrying fifteen people in the Island In The Sky, ten in the Needles or nine in the Maze), are $25. Day-use permits, costing $5, are also required for bikes and 4WD vehicles that enter Salt Creek, Horse or Lavender canyons in the Needles district.

Though not compulsory, reservations are essential for the most popular areas, especially in the peak seasons of spring and fall. They must be purchased at least two weeks in advance, and are issued for dates throughout each calendar year from the first Monday of August in the previous year. Permits must be picked up in person – with every member of the group present – from the appropriate park visitor center, at least one hour before it closes.

For application forms, and full details of the park's complex regulations, write to the National Park Service Reservations Office, 2282 S West Resource Blvd, Moab, UT 84532-8000; call ☎435/259-4351 (Mon–Fri 8am–4pm); or contact a park visitor center. You can also download the forms from the park Web site (www.nps.gov/cany).

and south of Moab respectively; the Maze is an endless jolting ride on dirt tracks from either Hwy-24 or the town of Green River.

The rivers themselves count as Canyonlands' fourth major component. A rafting expedition from Moab, with the operators detailed on p.468, is the best way to experience the eerie stillness of the deep canyons, at once exhilarating and supremely restful. However, since there's no way out before Lake Powell, you'll need to set aside several days, and several hundred dollars – and be prepared to face the awesome power of Cataract Canyon, just beyond the confluence, which contains some of the most intense whitewater rapids in the US.

The largest selection of motels near Canyonlands is in Moab (see p.466); park campgrounds are detailed on p.446 and p.454.

Finally, there's one last subsection of the park: Horseshoe Canyon in the west, which was added in 1971 to preserve the Southwest's finest collection of ancient rock art.

Canyonlands is not a place that lends itself to a short visit. With no lodging and little camping in the park, and no loop road to whisk you through it, it takes a full day to have even a cursory look at a single segment. If you're among the many visitors who find the conditions too grueling to spend much time out of your car – summer temperatures regularly exceed 100°F, and most trails have no water and little shade – then the Island In The Sky is the most immediately rewarding option. On the other hand, if you fancy a long day-hike you'd do better to set off into the Needles.

The Island In The Sky

It's not obvious from most maps, but like the Colorado River confluence over which it looms, the mesa known as the **Island In The Sky**
is itself shaped like a "Y." After a steady climb of around 25 miles,
Hwy-313, which heads southwest from US-191 eight miles north of
Moab, enters the park across the slender **Neck** that forms the right-
hand fork of the Y. It then branches to the northwest, to run as far as
the crater of **Upheaval Dome**, and to the south, where it ends at the
overwhelming **Grand View Point**.

Most visitors to the Island In The Sky content themselves with driving from one overlook to the next. Some also walk one or two of the
short, easy trails that cross its thin capping of Kayenta sandstone, to
gaze over the brink of the sheer Wingate cliffs that hold it up. It is
also possible, however – either in a sturdy 4WD vehicle, or by some
very strenuous hiking – to make your way down to the pale plateau
of the **White Rim**, prominent a thousand feet below.

*Contrary to the
official Utah
state map,
ordinary vehi-
cles cannot
reach the
Island In The
Sky from Moab
by way of Hwy-
279, the Potash
Road.*

Dead Horse Point State Park

Shortly before you reach the national-park boundary, twenty miles in
from US-191, a turning to the east leads in four miles to the smaller

---

The Geology of Canyonlands

In a land with so little water, the sheer *effort* that went into creating the
splendor of Canyonlands is almost impossible to conceive. As you look out
from the park's highest point, atop the Island In the Sky, the cliffs drop
away a thousand feet, with the rivers a thousand feet below that. For a hundred miles to the south, successive plateaus, benches and tablelands
diminish into the distance, studded with the occasional butte. And yet
twelve million years ago, this entire landscape was one vast plain, level
with where you're standing. Bit by bit, at the rate of two inches every thousand years, the topsoil has crumbled to silt and been carried away by the
rivers. Most of it was deposited at the edge of the Pacific, but these days
it's gradually filling up Lake Powell instead.

Canyonlands was not literally carved by the rivers, however. Both the
Green and the Colorado began life as gentle streams that ran across the
plains. In the last twelve million years, as the Colorado Plateau pushed its
way up, they have remained in their original courses, ever more deeply
entrenched into the earth. Meanwhile, ice produced in a ceaseless cycle of
freezes and thaws has chiseled away at the rocks that surround them, tumbling boulders into the water to be swept away.

Canyonlands is unique in resting on a mile-thick bed of **salt**, which was
deposited on the bottom of an ancient sea three hundred million years ago
and now fills the **Paradox Basin**. That salt was covered by later layers of
sediment, themselves interspersed with further deposits of salt. Under the
pressure of thousands of feet of harder rock, the salt layers are squeezed
like toothpaste until they flow far underground, then bubble up towards
the surface. As they do so, they push up fins and spurs of rock that crack
and split to create phenomena such as the Needles, or they may hit ground
water and dissolve, leaving gaping caverns behind.

---

*Dead Horse
Point is also a
death trap for
unwary pet
dogs; the cur-
rent record is
three drop-offs
in a month.*

but equally breathtaking **Dead Horse Point State Park**. This miniature version of the Island In The Sky stands at the tip of another narrow mesa, poised two thousand feet above a stupendous "gooseneck"
loop in the Colorado. Off to the east, the turquoise evaporation
ponds of Moab's potash plant (see p.472) make a garish contrast
with the red rocks, while the Anticline Overlook (see p.473) stands
guard above the far side of Meander Canyon.

Dead Horse Point's **visitor center**, two miles short of the main
overlook, has recently been completely remodeled, and incorporates
a **Desert Museum** of human and natural history (daily: summer
8am–6pm; winter 8am–5pm; ☎435/259-2614). Displays here
explain the name: nineteenth-century cowboys used the mesa as a
natural corral, herding wild horses behind the piñon fence that
blocked its ninety-foot neck. One band of horses is said to have been
too scared to cross the gap even when the gate was left open, and
perished of thirst.

Day-use of the park costs $5, and its *Kayenta* **campground** ($11;
reservations mid-March to mid-Oct only, costing $5 extra, on ☎1-
800/322-3770) makes an excellent – and much better equipped –
alternative if there's no room in Canyonlands.

Island In The Sky Visitor Center

A couple of miles south of the turnoff to Dead Horse Point, and a mile
or so in from the entrance to Canyonlands National Park, the modern
visitor center for the Island In The Sky district stands to the right of
the highway (daily: summer 8am–6pm; winter 8am–4.30pm;
☎435/259-4712). Rangers have full details on road and trail conditions as well as campsite availability.

Mesa Arch Trail

Four miles past the visitor center, just short of the fork in the road,
the **Mesa Arch Trail** is the Island In The Sky's best short hike. During
a mile-long loop around the mesa-top hillocks, it runs right to the rim
of the abyss, where long, shallow **Mesa Arch** frames an extraordinary view of the La Sal Mountains, 35 miles northeast. Admiring
Washer Woman Arch and Monster Tower, closer at hand, it would be
easy to stumble right through the gap – there's no barrier.

Grand View Point Overlook

Grand View Point Overlook, at the southern end of the road, is the
Island In The Sky's definitive vantage point, and a real agoraphobic's
nightmare. It commands a hundred-mile prospect of layer upon layer
of naked sandstone, here stacked thousands of feet high, there frac-
tured into bottomless canyons.

The most conspicuous feature is the plateau formed by the **White
Rim** layer, a thousand feet below, whose faint smattering of grass is
crisscrossed by abandoned mining trails and ends at the White Rim

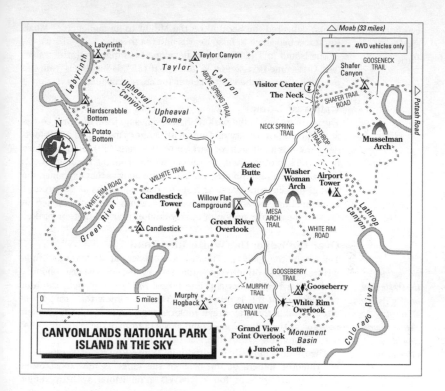

itself. That peters out in the mass of white-capped red-rock pillars known as **Monument Basin**, where the **Totem Pole** may be 305ft tall but looks the size of a pencil. Neither river can be seen; the Colorado River is tucked out of sight another thousand feet down, while the equivalent canyon of the Green River is hidden by the twin buttes to the west. Everything is however mirrored by an identical chaos on the far side, rising towards the snow-capped peaks of the **Abajo Mountains**, forty miles south.

A stroll along the two-mile **Grand View Trail**, starting from the overlook, enables you to contemplate the whole jigsaw puzzle from countless additional angles. Every now and then, you may spot the silhouette of the Needles, far to the south.

Green River Overlook and Willow Flat campground

A couple of hundred yards north of the fork in the park road, a reasonable 1.2-mile dirt road leads to the **Green River Overlook**. The clearer, flatter expanse of the White Rim that spreads below is pierced by the green-trimmed meandering course of the river itself, as it flows through placid **Stillwater Canyon**. At this very spot, in the biblical epic *The Greatest Story Ever Told*, Max von Sydow (aka

Jesus) delivered the Sermon on the Mount to an audience of Moab Rotarians bedecked in false beards and tea towels.

The Island In The Sky's only developed **campground**, the water-less, first-come first-served *Willow Flat* ($5), is just back from the overlook. Contact the visitor center for current availability.

Upheaval Dome

The northern end of the park road, five miles up from the fork, comes at the geological oddity of **Upheaval Dome**. This jagged 1500-foot-deep crater is a highlight of park air tours (see p.469), but from close up, at the end of the steep ten-minute climb from the parking lot, it's something of a disappointment. Elaborate theories that explained the prongs of pale stone bursting from its darkest depths as the product of undulating subterranean salt have recently been abandoned in favor of the simpler notion of a sixty-million-year-old **meteor strike**.

Over the Edge: the White Rim Road

The reason the Island In The Sky is accessible at all, and that crude dirt tracks strike off into the wilderness almost everywhere you look, is that this region was a prime target for the freelance **uranium prospectors** of the 1950s (see p.464). They knew that uranium is often found in the gray-green rocks of the **Chinle formation**, which here forms the talus slopes found at the bottom of the Wingate cliffs, not far above the White Rim.

No sections of the White Rim, Shafer Trail or Mineral Bottom roads should be attempted in ordinary vehicles.

The rough-and-ready hundred-mile **White Rim Road**, scraped out by would-be miners at the base of the cliffs, is now most often explored on three- or four-day **4WD expeditions**, with overnight stops at various primitive campgrounds en route (by permit only; see p.444). Only the hair-raising **Shafer Trail Road**, which drops from just south of the visitor center, connects the mesa-top with the White Rim; otherwise drivers join the White Rim Road by means of the **Potash Road** from Moab (see p.471), or along **Mineral Bottom Road**, which runs west from Hwy-313 a couple of miles north of the Dead Horse Point turnoff.

Hikers can however clamber between the Island In The Sky and the White Rim along various trails. All are too demanding for a round-trip day-hike down to the White Rim – let alone to either river – to be a good idea. Register with the park service before you set off on a multiday trip. Options include the **Lathrop Trail**, an utterly exhausting nine-mile route that makes it all the way to the Colorado, passing close to abandoned but potentially toxic uranium mines; the **Upheaval Canyon Trail**, which drops down to the Green River from the far side of Upheaval Dome; and the **Shafer Trail Road** itself.

Horseshoe Canyon

Remote **Horseshoe Canyon**, a detached chunk of Canyonlands National Park located well northwest of its main body, is home to the most extraordinary **rock art** to be found anywhere in North America. No one now knows the meaning of the mysterious, haunting figures that line the sandstone walls of the **Great Gallery**; although to the modern eye they suggest an astonishing sophistication, they are among the **oldest** such images to survive.

Even if you're not a rock-art enthusiast, the six-mile round-trip hike down to the gallery – there's no road access – is one of Utah's most beautiful. With either forty miles of dirt road to negotiate south of Green River, or 34 miles east from Hwy-24, before the trail even starts, few visitors come this way, so you may well get the gorgeous red-rock canyon, rustling with wildlife, to yourself.

The San Rafael Desert: the road to Horseshoe Canyon and the Maze

Unless the weather has been dreadful – check at the Green River visitor center (see p.440) for current conditions – ordinary vehicles should have no problem driving to Horseshoe Canyon. From the center of Green River, follow signs for the airport until you cross the railroad tracks. Once the surface has turned to gravel, fork left at a BLM sign pointing towards the San Rafael River.

After an initial flat section, the road pushes through painted-desert badlands formed by the fossil-rich Morrison Formation, and then winds down to a glorious panorama of Monument Valley-style buttes. It crosses the **San Rafael River** on a rickety wooden bridge after nineteen miles, then climbs again to offer views that stretch to the Henry Mountains in the west and the La Sals in the east.

Just over forty miles south of Green River, beyond **Antelope Valley** – home to one of Utah's few surviving herds of pronghorn antelope – an easily-missed spur road branches off to the east. The **Horseshoe Canyon trailhead** is at its far end, at the edge of the plateau two miles along.

As the road veers west, a junction 5.5 miles past the Horseshoe Canyon turnoff marks the start of the 21-mile drive south to **Hans Flat Ranger Station**, the main point of access for the Maze (see p.450). Keep going west, and a total of thirty miles from Horseshoe Canyon you'll finally meet **Hwy-24**, just south of Goblin Valley (see p.438). This last stretch crosses Sweetwater Reef before dropping into the **San Rafael Desert**, where it insinuates itself between two impressive buttes known as Little Flat Top and Big Flat Top.

The hike to the canyon

The only route into **Horseshoe Canyon** picks its way down from the trailhead described above, marked by cairns as it crosses patches of deep sand alternating with slickrock. Once you reach the bottom, follow the dry sandy wash to your right, and in ten minutes you'll come to the **Horseshoe Shelter**, nestled beneath an overhanging cliff. When Harvard archeologists excavated this site in 1930, it held

Canyonlands National Park

Between April and October, rangers lead six-hour guided hikes into Horseshoe Canyon, starting at 9am on Sat & Sun; call ☎ 435/259-2652 to check.

If you're heading east from Capitol Reef, it's much quicker to reverse the route described here; just be sure you have enough gas.

Canyonlands National Park

The Rock Art of Horseshoe Canyon

At the time it was first studied, Horseshoe Canyon was called **Barrier Canyon**, and that name still defines the style of art for which it's famous. It's characterized by anthropomorphic figures, roughly life-sized but tending to be weirdly elongated, and often lacking both arms and legs. Those that have eyes have large round ones, or simply empty sockets, and many seem draped in stylized robes; for most visitors to this lonely desert backwater, the cumulative effect is to suggest ghosts or spirits from another, different time.

While spearpoints found in Horseshoe Canyon date back as much as twelve thousand years, archeologists believe that the pictographs were produced by people of the **Archaic** culture, which flourished between 7500 BC and 500 AD. At the start of that period, the climate was much wetter, and the canyon held lakes, ponds and plentiful game. When conditions dried out, it was briefly abandoned, but then reoccupied.

Life was now far more difficult, and **shamanastic rituals** were increasingly used in the attempt to insure successful hunting. These involved the creation first of clay statuettes, from 5000 BC onwards, and later of figurines made out of split willow-twigs, which have been found here and in the Grand Canyon (see p.320). Many represent what seem to be deities or shamans as well as animals; and the pictographs of the Great Gallery are thought to depict those same entities.

As for **technique**, the Great Gallery is very literally rock art. To produce the paint, different colored rocks were ground up, dissolved in water and bonded with saliva produced by chewing seeds. The red is hematite, heavy with rust; the white is gypsum or chalk; even the blue comes from a local stratum. Some figures were produced with brushes, others by blowing or flicking paint at a stencil.

Experts estimate the gallery to be anything from 1600 to 6000 years old. Carbon-dating tests that suggested extreme antiquity have recently been discounted, but certain sites do seem to have been rendered inaccessible by rock falls that occurred a very long time ago indeed. All that's certain is that none dates from later than 400 AD, when the Archaic people acquired the bow and arrow – not shown in any of the images – and began to transform into the **Fremont** culture. Fremont art, as seen elsewhere in Utah (see p.395) as well as here in Horseshoe Canyon, has its own very distinct style.

The round-trip hike to the Great Gallery takes at least five hours; start early, or sit out the midday sun down in the canyon.

several rooms; all that remains is a vivid band of **pictographs** in the palest stratum of the rock, which was above the roofs of the shelters and is thus now out of reach. The animals, squiggles and triangular figures – many with strange protuberances on their heads – date from the Fremont era, but the scattering of ghostly footless figures are in the earlier Barrier Canyon style.

The **Great Gallery** is a good forty minutes' walk on, beyond several twists and turns in the canyon walls, and another small collection of pictographs in a massive sandy alcove. As you round the final bend, suddenly apparent beneath a lesser overhang, the Gallery takes your breath away. Framed between the cottonwoods, a long row of dark, hollow-eyed, otherworldly entities stands stark against the pale rock. Though the details grow clearer the closer you get, somehow a sense of vast, alien distance remains.

Apart from a couple of well-shaded stone benches, there are no facilities for visitors. Look out, however, for two army-issue metal boxes, marked PLEASE OPEN ME: one holds a set of powerful NPS binoculars, the other photostats of relevant academic papers.

The Maze

The name of Canyonlands' **Maze** district is no exaggeration. This brain-teaser of convoluted canyons and barren desert washes, west of the Green and Colorado rivers, must be the least explored region of the United States. If you're determined to get away from it all, the Maze is the place for you; getting back to it all when you've finished is more of a problem.

Somewhere in the heart of the Maze is the legendary **Robbers Roost**, a canyon fastness used as a hideout by nineteenth-century cattle rustlers and bandits such as **Butch Cassidy** and his Wild Bunch. They'd escape the long arm of the law by riding the Outlaw Trail up from the Green River near Mineral Bottom; lacking their familiarity with the terrain, pursuing posses had no choice but to turn back defeated. No roads entered the region until uranium prospectors bulldozed their way in during the 1950s.

Even today, you'll need a high-clearance 4WD vehicle to get any further than **Hans Flat Ranger Station** (daily 8am–4.30pm; ☎ 435/259-2652), which stands 21 miles south of the road through the San Rafael Desert to Horseshoe Canyon, described overleaf. That makes it 46 miles east of Hwy-24, and 66 miles south of Green River. An even worse sixty-mile dirt track also runs south, to connect it with Hite on Lake Powell. Technically the ranger station is in Glen Canyon National Recreation Area, but it's the main source of information for hikers and drivers setting off into the Maze.

The **jeep roads** beyond Hans Flat take another twenty or thirty miles to jostle and switchback into the actual Maze. There are two main routes in, one ending at the **Maze Overlook**, and the other at **Doll House Butte**, which marks the far end of the **Land Of Standing Rocks**, above the west bank of Cataract Canyon and straight across from the Needles.

Having come this far, most backpackers launch themselves into the wilderness for days or weeks at a time. There are few formal trails, but favored destinations include **Pictograph Canyon**, not far beneath the Maze Overlook, where Barrier Canyon-style pictographs (see box above) seem to record the moment when the Archaic people first acquired the skills of agriculture. However, unless you're extremely self-sufficient, a workhorse when it comes to carrying vast quantities of water, and a fearless, fully-equipped rock-climber, you're never going to see them.

Canyonlands National Park

No camping is permitted in Horseshoe Canyon itself, but there's a basic site beside the parking lot at the trailhead.

*Confusingly,
the Needles
Overlook is not
in the national
park at all, but
in the BLM's
Canyon Rims
area; see p.473.*

The Needles

Thanks to its intricate tracery of backcountry trails, which offer the chance to engage with the landscape as opposed to merely marveling from a distance, the **Needles** district is Canyonlands National Park's most satisfying segment for hikers, bikers and 4WD drivers. While it has its share of long-range vistas – including the park's only **Confluence Overlook** – the Needles is noted primarily for its namesake thickets of candy-striped **sandstone pillars**. Clustered on scrubby rock outcrops, concealing pockets of incongruous grassland, these intriguing formations can be explored on brief forays or multiday backpacking expeditions.

The **Needles** area is a very long way from civilization, at the far end of the stunning **Hwy-211**, a total of 75 miles from Moab and fifty from Monticello. If you're planning a number of successive dayhikes, it makes sense to camp overnight in the park, so reserve a spot at *Squaw Flat* or in one of the backcountry sites as soon as you know you're coming (see p.444).

*More detailed
advice on
desert hiking
appears on
p.23.*

Ordinary mortals, as opposed to obsessive canyoneers, should also be warned that even casual **hiking** in the Needles area may well be the hardest thing you've ever done. Carry a good map and a *lot* of water, stick to the trails, and above all be very careful how far you climb – it's much easier to go up than it is to come down, and you run the risk of getting "rim-rocked."

The road to the Needles: Squaw Flats Scenic Byway

*The mountain
road from
Monticello,
described on
p.474, meets
Hwy-211 just
west of
Newspaper
Rock.*

The 35-mile **Hwy-211** – also known as the **Squaw Flats Scenic Byway** – heads west of US-191 forty miles south of Moab. You can't miss the turning; it's marked by a colossal butte immediately opposite, which, if you happen to be hungry, may well seem to resemble a giant brioche.

As it winds lazily into the park, between cottonwood-lined **Indian Creek** stream and canyon walls of rich red sandstone, and overlooked by the twin castellated **Sixshooter Peaks**, the byway seems to carry you back a century, into the unspoiled Wild West. Much of the route lies through open grazing country, making this one of the few spots in the Southwest where you're still likely to see genuine **cowboys** riding the range. The Dugout Ranch, halfway along, was established in 1885, and later amalgamated with its neighbors to form the Indian Creek Cattle Company, Utah's largest cattle outfit.

Newspaper Rock

Newspaper Rock Recreation Site, next to Hwy-211 twelve miles west of US-191, preserves a panel of black desert varnish that's inscribed, like some prehistoric newspaper, with literally hundreds of **petroglyphs**. Ancient peoples clearly recognized this as a perfect site, sheltered by a protective rock lintel beneath a hillock at a narrow bend in the valley immediately north of the Abajo Mountains. As

CANYONLANDS NATIONAL PARK
NEEDLES DISTRICT

well as abstract designs, the images include helmeted human figures, buffalo and bighorn sheep, plus lots of six-toed footprints and what look like bear pawprints. Some are probably symbols left by clans who performed particular ceremonies here, or simply passed by. With the obvious exception of recent graffiti, it's hard to say when they were executed, but you have to suspect that most are not in fact all that old; nineteenth-century Ute are thought to be responsible for the mounted riders, shown hunting with bows and arrows.

The riverside woods across the road from the rock hold a lovely if basic **campground**, free but waterless.

The Needles Outpost

Up a short spur road just outside the park boundary, the privately owned **Needles Outpost** (mid-March to Oct daily 8am–7pm; ☎435/979-4007 or 259-8545) is a summer-only grocery store and gas station that has its own small **campground**, and also arranges **4WD rentals** and **tours**, plus **scenic flights** over the park.

Driving into the Needles

Rangers at the **Needles visitor center**, a mile inside the park (daily: summer 8am–6pm; winter 8am–4.30pm; ☎435/259-4711), can provide up-to-date hiking information, with a handy model of the whole park to make things clearer. They issue 34 **backpacking permits** per night, each for a group of up to seven people; in high season, if you don't have a reservation (see p.444) the chances are none will be available. Day-hikers don't need permits.

4WD users venturing into the remote Salt Creek, Horse and Lavender canyons – which there isn't room to describe in this book – require $5 day-use permits.

Roughly three miles along from the visitor center, a left turning leads to the first-come, first-served *Squaw Flat* **campground**, where space is at an absolute premium in spring and fall ($10 Feb–Nov, when water is available; otherwise free). Ordinary vehicles can continue beyond the campground, on an uneven dirt road, for three more miles to **Elephant Hill**.

The main park road presses on past the Squaw Flat turnoff for another four miles, ending where the **Big Spring Canyon Overlook** confronts an array of mushroom-shaped hoodoos. Of the short hiking trails along the way, the half-mile **Pothole Point Trail** is an easy stroll to the top of the roadside ridge, while the longer 2.5-mile **Slickrock Trail** provides an enjoyable orientation to the region, following a cairned footpath from one sandstone knoll to the next, each with its own long-distance mountain-and-mesa views.

The much-photographed Angel Arch can only be reached by hiking from the 4WD road through Salt Creek Canyon.

The Chesler Park Loop Trail

Chesler Park, the high grassy meadow whose stubby sandstone pinnacles gave the Needles its name, makes a great destination for a long day-hike. Simply to reach it requires a six-mile round-trip trek from Elephant Hill, or a ten-mile one from Squaw Flat campground, while looping around the "park" itself adds another five miles.

As you climb across the cairned stretches of slickrock that rise from both Elephant Hill and Squaw Flat, look north for sweeping views to the Island In The Sky, with the White Rim neatly etched beneath it. The two trails meet half an hour up from Elephant Hill, then dip west to cross the wash that runs through **Elephant Canyon** – it may look dry, but there's usually water flowing far beneath the sand – before the final ascent to Chesler Park.

Allow seven hours for the complete hike from Elephant Hill, even longer if you start from Squaw Flat.

For the most part, the **Chesler Park Loop Trail** undulates around the edge of the 600-acre clearing, on the slopes below the red-and-white barber-pole Needles. On the eastern flank, however, it runs straight across the lavender-tinted grassland, while in the far southwestern corner it disappears into an extraordinary mini-canyon whose blackened walls are seldom as much as three feet apart. This claustrophobic segment, almost a mile long and known as the **Joint Trail**, is the highlight of the trip. A ledge perched above its eastern end, a 500-foot detour off the main trail, provides a superb overview of Chesler Park. Through a gap to the west, the gigantic Doll House Butte (see p.450), across the Colorado River, can also be glimpsed.

As an alternative to circling Chesler Park, consider following the spur trail that branches south along Elephant Canyon. It takes just over three miles of steady climbing to reach **Druid Arch**, named for its resemblance to the rough-hewn monuments of Stonehenge.

Several more trails can be used to connect Chesler Park and Elephant Canyon with Squaw Flat, including routes through **Squaw Canyon** and the upper reaches of **Big Spring Canyon**. Backcountry **camping** is however only allowed at specific sites along the jeep road that runs west and north of Chesler Park, of which the closest to the main trails is at Devils Kitchen Camp – and you'd be lucky to get one of the necessary permits (see p.444).

Canyonlands National Park

With a 4WD vehicle, you can join the Chesler Park Loop near the Joint Trail, and walk the loop alone as a five-mile hike.

The Confluence Overlook Trail

According to writer Edward Abbey, the local business community only agreed to the creation of Canyonlands park in 1964 on the understanding that its different parts would be linked by a loop drive, of which the focus would be the **Confluence Overlook**. It was even anticipated that this would be the site of a Junction Dam, which would create an even larger lake than Lake Powell. In the absence of either road or dam, however, the demanding eleven-mile round-trip hike from **Big Spring Canyon Overlook** remains the only way to see the spot where the Green River meets the Colorado.

The trail starts with a steep drop down into Big Spring Canyon, then laboriously climbs out again. After twenty exhausting minutes you emerge through a natural portal between two huge nodules to be greeted by long-distance views of the red-rock wilderness ahead – and cool shade closer at hand. A short metal ladder brings you out onto a level plateau, but you're soon descending again into **Elephant Canyon**, at this point several miles north of, and considerably broader than, the segment near Chesler Park (see opposite). Each time you climb back onto the slickrock mesa-top, new views open up, either south to the Needles, or north to Junction Butte beneath the Island In the Sky.

Clambering from rock to rock beyond Elephant Canyon, you pass through several lifeless valleys known as **grabens**, from the German for "ditches." Thought to be a mere 55,000 years old, these were created when shifting underground salt beds caused landslides. At times, the scrambling is hard going, and you have to haul yourself up onto head-high ledges, but it always stops short of actual rock climbing. Finally, after a half-mile section of jeep road – 4WD drivers can get this far via a nine-mile drive from Elephant Hill – you teeter out to the edge of the plateau and see the confluence for the first time.

A thousand feet below the **Confluence Overlook**, the Green River flows in from the west, and the Colorado from the northeast. They're

The round-trip hike to the Confluence Overlook takes a good seven hours.

never the same color. Sometimes the Green really is a pale green, and the Colorado almost red, tinted with dissolved red sandstone; at other times the Green is more of a yellow, and the Colorado a muddy chocolate. In any case, the two hues remain distinct for the first mile or two after the rivers combine, intermeshing like a zipper as they flow parallel but separate towards the fearsome Cataract Canyon.

Arches National Park

ARCHES NATIONAL PARK seems to have become the national park for people who aren't quite sure whether they like national parks. It's not too hard to get to, just five miles out of Moab; it's not too big, with just twenty miles of paved roads; and it has a catchy name, to tell you what to expect. A million visitors a year drive in, tick off however many arches they feel they have time for, and drive on to their next destination.

Thanks to *Desert Solitaire*, **Edward Abbey**'s lyrical evocation of his year as an Arches ranger, the park is also dear to the hearts of environmentalists and wilderness enthusiasts. The irony is that when Abbey was here, during the 1950s, there was no road into the body of the park, and the only way to explore it was to blaze your own trails. Now you can cruise round in a couple of hours, and barely step out of your vehicle.

For all that, Arches remains well worth visiting. The **Colorado River** here is literally peripheral, running unseen along the park's southern boundary. The emphasis instead is on the stark, strangely disjointed **sandstone scenery** of the higher ground to the north. As at Canyonlands, these rocks rest on an unstable layer of salt. **Salt Valley**, which slopes down across the park towards the Colorado, was formed by the collapse of an underground salt dome. That massive subsidence left high ridges to either side, which cracked along vertical fault lines to create long parallel "fins" of orange-pink Entrada sandstone.

Contact the Pack Creek Ranch (☎ 435/259-5505; see p.467), for horseback trips through Arches; other Moab-based tour operators are listed on p.468.

Over the eons, water collects in pores in the fins, and scours them into potholes; piece by piece, the stone flakes away, until a hole is worn right through. Estimates of how many such "arches" the park holds vary from the eighty or so named on maps to the official count of over two thousand. No one has bothered to define whether a "window" is a type of arch or just another word for one, but it's agreed that an arch or window has to be at least three feet wide. Both are distinct from "bridges," which span running water.

As far as Edward Abbey was concerned, the arches themselves were a "small and inessential" feature of the park's landscape. Unless you're a real obsessive – in which case, you can buy specialist arch-and-bridge magazines – the appeal of hunting down arch after arch soon palls. The park's short, straightforward **hiking trails** are enjoyable enough in their own right, however, so you're bound to see a good number of them. **Delicate Arch** is by far the most impressive, in that it's a freestanding crescent of rock. Most of the rest are just holes, though **Landscape Arch** is such a big one it would be a shame not to see it.

Apart from one solitary cabin, testament to a failed attempt at cattle ranching, very few traces of human occupation remain in this forbidding desert. It became a national monument after the Klondike

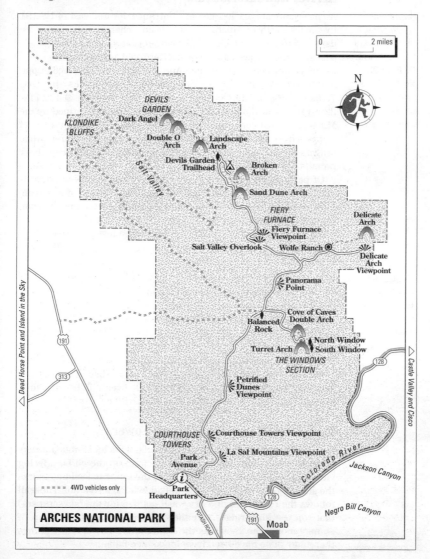

Bluffs area was found by a wandering prospector in the 1920s, and was enlarged into a national park in 1971.

Most visitors now arrive in **midsummer**, despite blazing temperatures than can reach 110°F. Hiking conditions are much more bearable in spring – when the wildflowers blossom – or fall.

Arrival and information

For advance information, write to Arches National Park, PO Box 907, Moab, UT 84532, or access www.nps.gov /arch.

Arches National Park has just one **entrance**, located east of US-191 five miles north of Moab. The **admission charge**, valid for seven days, is $10 per vehicle, or $5 for motorcyclists, cyclists and pedestrians. All the passes detailed on p.21 are sold and accepted.

The **visitor center** (daily: mid-April to early Oct 7.30am–6.30pm; mid-March to mid-April, and middle two weeks in Oct, 7.30am–5.30pm; late Oct to mid-March 8am–4.30pm; ☎435/719-2299) stands at the base of a long, tall escarpment, formed by the Moab Fault, that conceals the bulk of the park from the highway. Its displays help to make the geology of the place a bit clearer, while rangers provide advice on hiking conditions and issue backcountry permits (see below).

Of **park regulations** you'll need to know, the most important is that each **parking lot** along the road is designed to hold a specific number of vehicles, to limit the number of hikers on any one trail. Park illegally, and there's a $25 on-the-spot fine. No vehicles, or bikes, are allowed on the trails, but there are a few **4WD roads**.

Camping

The nearest motels to Arches are in Moab; see p.466.

Rangers at the visitor center will know whether there's room at Arches' only **campground**, at the far end of the road across from the **Devil's Garden** trailhead ($10 mid-March to Oct, when water is available; $5 otherwise; no showers). Throughout most of the summer, all its 51 first-come, first-served sites are taken by early morning.

So long as you pick up a free **permit** at the visitor center, you can camp anywhere in the **backcountry** that's out of sight of roads, trails and named arches. In fact, Arches sees little overnight backpacking, as most people do all the hiking they want within a day.

Park Avenue and Courthouse Towers

Beyond the visitor center, the park road begins its 18-mile journey north to Devil's Garden with a steep climb up the cliffs, offering views across to Moab. A parking lot at the top, a mile along, marks the start of the simple one-mile walk down **Park Avenue**. The trail follows the rocky bed of a dry wash, named for the "skyscrapers" that top the high ridges to either side. It ends amid a group of chunky monoliths known as the **Courthouse Towers**; any arches there may once have been have long since fallen.

Unless you arrange to be met at the northern of its two trailheads, you'll have to walk Park Avenue as a two-mile round-trip. The road in between the two passes the **La Sal Mountains Viewpoint**, which offers the first glimpse of the peaks to the east.

The Windows Section

In the heart of the park, almost ten miles up from the visitor center, the fifty-foot **Balanced Rock** rests precariously on its slanted pedestal. Immediately beyond, a spur road to the right leads in three miles to the **Windows Section**. Several fine arches can be admired from the parking lot at the end, the largest in the park, which is also the starting point for a couple of very popular short trails.

North and South Windows

The busy one-mile loop trail to the North and South Windows ambles gently upwards for a couple of hundred yards towards **North Window**, the only one of the pair that's visible from the road. Take the steeper spur trail that leads right up to it, gaze through, and you'll appreciate why the word "window" is so appropriate. So far the gaping aperture has framed only blue sky, but now a magnificent desert panorama comes into view.

South Window is just a few yards away, though you have to rejoin the main trail and round one last pinnacle to see it properly. You can't climb right up to it, though a much rougher trail continues around the back and leads eventually back to the parking lot. Alternatively, you'll have noticed by now that the lone fin across the main trail is pierced by **Turret Arch**. Wander over there, then look back for a shot of the two windows side by side – a pair of dazzling blue eyes, separated by a bulbous snub nose.

Double Arch

A shorter, half-mile, trail leads from further around the Windows parking lot to **Double Arch**, where the roof of a wedge-shaped arch has fallen in to create either a skylight, or two separate arches, depending on your point of view. On the far side, the **Cove of Caves** is packed with incipient future arches, burrowing into the cliffs.

Delicate Arch

As befits the state's single most remarkable natural phenomenon, **Delicate Arch** has become a symbol of Utah. Oddly enough, its sturdy bow-legged form, familiar from automobile licence plates and millions of tourist brochures, is not in fact all that delicate. It was originally called "Landscape Arch," for the view of the La Sal Mountains it so neatly frames, and only swapped names with what's now Landscape Arch (see p.461) due to a map-maker's mistake.

For photographs, Delicate Arch Viewpoint is best in early morning, while the Delicate Arch Trail is better in the afternoon.

A side road towards Delicate Arch leaves the park road shortly beyond **Panorama Point**. The arch itself can only be reached via the grueling **Delicate Arch Trail**, which leads up from Wolfe Ranch 1.2 miles along. If you lack the time or energy for that, you can see it from afar from the **Delicate Arch Viewpoint**, at the end of a level hundred-yard trail that begins a mile further on.

The Delicate Arch Trail

Hikers in Arches should take especial care to avoid walking on the cryptobiotic crust; see p.23.

The **Delicate Arch Trail** may be just 1.5 miles long, but the three-mile round-trip to the arch and back involves a steep climb across bare slickrock that can take the wind out of the hardiest hiker's sails. It starts just short of **Wolfe Ranch**, where Civil War veteran John Wolfe built a cabin in 1906, using cedar and cottonwood logs hauled seven miles from the Colorado. His cattle had by then been denuding the nearby slopes for almost twenty years; when sheep-farmers began to graze their animals on this impoverished soil as well, Wolfe gave up and moved back to Ohio.

Allow a good two hours for the round-trip hike to Delicate Arch.

Beyond the cabin, a footbridge crosses the shallow perennial **Salt Wash**, and the trail begins its determined ascent. Considering that fewer than ten inches of rain fall here each year, the terrain is surprisingly varied, from the scrubby riverbanks, choked with tamarisk, by way of a small-scale piñon-juniper forest, up to the naked rock three-quarters of a mile up. An alcove off to the left, just below the hilltop, cherishes "hanging gardens" of rushes and even orchids, fed by a spring that stains the rocks.

It's easy to lose the sparsely-cairned trail at the top of the mesa; the trick is to follow a narrow ledge in the rock that leads around the back of a high fin. Suddenly, from a viewing area neatly fenced off by a natural rock parapet, you're confronted by the full glory of **Delicate Arch**. Standing in superb isolation on the high lip of a canyon, it looks taller than its 45 feet. Quite how much closer you dare to approach depends on your confidence walking across the steeply inclined slickrock. There's no physical reason to stop you standing right under it.

The Fiery Furnace

No backcountry camping is permitted in the Fiery Furnace.

An uninspiring overlook three miles on from the Wolfe Ranch turn-off gives little idea of the labyrinthine complexity of the **Fiery Furnace**. Named not for any exceptional heat but for its golden late-afternoon glow, this warren of high-walled dead-end gullies and parallel fins is so disorientating, and so fragile, that you can only enter it on ranger-led **guided hikes**. These take place daily in high season at 10am and 4pm, at 10am and 2pm in spring and fall, and on weekends only in winter, again at 10am and 2pm. Numbers are restricted, so you should register at the visitor center as soon as you arrive, and pay the fee of $6 for adults, $3 for ages seven to twelve. The hikes don't involve walking all that far – most of the time goes on explaining the various rock formations and signs of life along the way – but they're fascinating if you're at all interested in learning more about the desert.

The Devil's Garden

The park's largest concentration of arches is found in the **Devil's Garden**, beyond the far end of the road eighteen miles up from the visitor center. The prime target here is the 300-foot **Landscape Arch**, reached by a graveled, reasonably level one-mile trail. This slender span is so frail that hikers are not allowed up to or through the arch itself; a sixty-foot-long slab dropped off it in 1991, and lesser rock falls happen all the time. Arch aficionados will probably still be debating whether this or Kolob Arch in Zion National Park (see p.389) is the world's longest arch when it finally disintegrates.

What's now Landscape Arch was originally Delicate Arch, and vice versa; see p.459.

If your appetite for high-desert hiking has been whetted, press on beyond Landscape Arch on a trail that immediately becomes far cruder. After another mile – during which a one hundred-yard section obliges you to totter along the top of a narrow sandstone fin – you round a corner to see **Double O Arch** on the skyline. At first, only its large upper oval is visible; as you approach, you'll see the much smaller ring beneath it as well. The pallid alkali wastelands that stretch away to the east were once prime uranium territory, and one heavily polluted section is still known as the **"Poison Strip."**

The four-mile round-trip hike to Double O Arch also leads past half a dozen other named arches, and assorted minor pin-pricks and peepholes. Real gluttons for punishment can turn it into a seven-mile loop, by circling back on the Primitive Loop Trail, but that route is every bit as demanding as its name implies.

Moab

Boom-and-bust cycles are a recurring theme in Western history, but few communities can have experienced quite such a rollercoaster ride as **MOAB**. Within the last sixty years, it has gone from an insignificant backwater in the 1940s to being celebrated as "The Richest Town in the USA" by *McCalls* magazine in the 1950s, only to become what one journalist called "one of the most economically depressed towns in Utah" by 1986, and then find itself transformed, almost against its will, into the Southwest's number-one adventure-vacation destination.

Through it all, Moab has never been a large town – the population still hasn't reached ten thousand – and neither is it an attractive one. The **setting** is what matters. With two national parks on its doorstep, plus millions more acres of public land, Moab is an ideal base for **outdoors enthusiasts**. The first to turn up were **jeep** drivers, taking advantage of the remote dirt roads cleared by the uranium

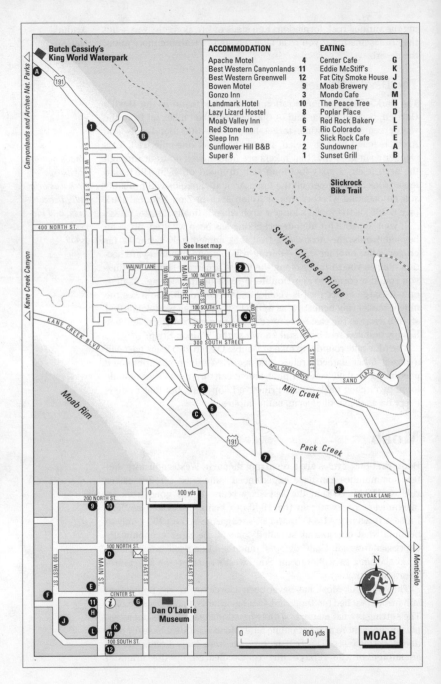

ACCOMMODATION

Apache Motel	4
Best Western Canyonlands	11
Best Western Greenwell	12
Bowen Motel	9
Gonzo Inn	3
Landmark Hotel	10
Lazy Lizard Hostel	8
Moab Valley Inn	6
Red Stone Inn	5
Sleep Inn	7
Sunflower Hill B&B	2
Super 8	1

EATING

Center Cafe	G
Eddie McStiff's	K
Fat City Smoke House	J
Moab Brewery	C
Mondo Cafe	M
The Peace Tree	H
Poplar Place	D
Red Rock Bakery	L
Rio Colorado	F
Slick Rock Cafe	E
Sundowner	A
Sunset Grill	B

Butch Cassidy's
King World Waterpark

Slickrock
Bike Trail

Swiss Cheese Ridge

Canyonlands and Arches Nat. Parks

Kane Creek Canyon

500 WEST STREET

400 NORTH ST.

Walnut Lane

See Inset map

200 NORTH STREET

MAIN STREET

100 WEST STREET

100 NORTH ST.

CENTER ST.

100 EAST ST.

100 SOUTH ST.

200 SOUTH STREET

300 SOUTH STREET

KANE CREEK BLVD

Moab Rim

Mill Creek Drive

USHER STREET

SAND FLATS RD

Mill Creek

Pack Creek

Holyoak Lane

Monticello

Moab Rim

200 NORTH ST.

100 NORTH ST.

Main Street

100 WEST ST.

100 EAST ST.

200 EAST ST.

Center St.

100 SOUTH ST.

Dan O'Laurie
Museum

0   100 yds

0   800 yds

N

MOAB

prospectors. Then the **whitewater rafting** companies moved in, and the town swiftly became a mecca for **mountain-bikers** too, lured by the legendary **Slickrock Bike Trail**. These days, Moab is almost literally bursting, all year, with legions of lycra-clad holidaymakers from all over the world.

Perhaps the main reason Moab has grown so fast is that out-of-state visitors tend to find Utah's rural communities so irredeemably boring. As soon as Moab emerged from the pack, it became a beacon in the desert, attracting tourists ecstatic to find a town that stayed up after dark. Moab amounts to little more than a few miles of motels, restaurants and bars, but that's enough to make it the only southern Utah town where you can stay for a week and still feel that you haven't seen everything, and everyone, a dozen times.

A history of Moab

Moab stands just south of the Colorado River, at the north end of a long valley created by the collapse of an underground salt dome. Because a similar valley slopes down to the river on its northern side, it's the best place to cross the Colorado in all Utah. Ute Indians passed this way for generations, but the site was first recorded by Juan de Rivera in 1765, and a ferry service later helped travelers on the **Old Spanish Trail**. The **Elk Mountain Mission**, set up in 1855, had to be abandoned after Indian attacks, but Mormon pioneers returned in the 1870s to establish a farming settlement. They named it for the biblical wilderness of Moab, located at the edge of Zion.

Until Charlie Steen discovered **uranium** in 1952 – the first of a series of major finds in the region – the biggest thing ever to hit Moab was when **Butch Cassidy** hijacked the Colorado ferry on his way home from a bank job. The uranium boom lasted well into the 1970s, but as it petered out, the local political scene turned very sour. Moab was a major focus of the **Sagebrush Rebellion** (see p.408), which pitted mine-owners and Utah businessmen, together with their fearful workforce, against the burgeoning national coalition of **environmentalists**, and the federal government that seemed to support them. Grand County commissioners repeatedly defied federal legislation by smashing bulldozers into neighboring **Negro Bill Canyon**, administered by the BLM, in the hope of opening it and other protected wilderness areas for mineral exploitation.

While they may have won the bitter **Bulldozer Wars** – Ronald Reagan came to power proclaiming that he too was a "Sagebrush Rebel" – Utah's conservatives were no match for the world economy. The uranium market crashed in 1980, thanks partly to the accident at Three Mile Island in 1979, and partly to the discovery of vast deposits of high-grade uranium in Canada in 1980. At the same time, the bottom also fell out of oil, coal and potash. Unemployment in Moab rocketed, and the population dwindled.

Charlie Steen: The Uranium King

In the early 1950s, as the Cold War gathered steam and nuclear power stations seemed to hold infinite promise, the US government was desperate to locate a reliable domestic source of **uranium**. The Atomic Energy Commission therefore offered a $10,000 reward to anyone who discovered a mineable uranium deposit – even on public land – and guaranteed to buy whatever it produced for the next ten years.

Freelance prospectors converged on the Colorado Plateau, where uranium had been found and mined as early as 1912. Their war-surplus jeeps piled with provisions, they set off into Utah's uncharted backcountry, waving their Geiger counters at whatever likely-looking rocks might catch their eyes. Most knew which strata offered the best odds, and searched for places along the cliffs and canyon walls where they might be exposed.

Charlie Steen, a geologist from Texas, was mocked for insisting that he could find uranium by **drilling**. He would project the angle of the canyonlands' crazily tilted slopes deep underground, and calculate where the precious mineral might have accumulated atop layers of harder rock. Concentrating his efforts on the **Lisbon Valley**, thirty miles southeast of Moab, he staked out countless claims, and gave each a Spanish name.

In July 1952, the 31-year-old Steen broke his last drill bit in a 200-foot bore on the **Mi Vida** ("my life") claim. Driving back to his trailer home in despair, he pulled into a gas station in Cisco, Utah. The attendant offered to test the final plug of rock on the bed of Steen's pick-up; his Geiger counter went straight off the scale.

Following his $60-million strike, Steen opened a processing mill in Moab that became Grand County's largest employer. As the "**Uranium King,**" he built himself a hilltop mansion above town, and threw a lavish annual party for all its citizens. He had his own plane, in which he'd circle above Moab at night to improve the reception on his TV, and was even a celebrity guest on *I Love Lucy*. In quick succession, he was elected to the Utah senate, then resigned after failing to change the state's liquor laws. Selling Mi Vida, he moved to Nevada, only to fritter his entire fortune away, losing $250,000, for example, on a pickle factory.

By the early 1970s, Steen was back in Utah, once more searching the canyon country as a penniless prospector. This time he traveled in disguise and under a false name, in order both to avoid media attention and to protect any discoveries he might make. Success eluded him, however, and he eventually conceded defeat and moved to Colorado, where he still lives.

The wilderness devotees who saw the region's future as resting with **tourism** now seized the chance to prove their case. They succeeded beyond their wildest dreams; out of nowhere, Moab became the West's hottest new destination, the desert equivalent of chic mountain hideaways like Aspen and Telluride in Colorado.

Sadly, almost everyone agrees that things have now gone too far. Most of the old-timers have left, driven out by rising real-estate prices and none too keen to swap mining for motel clerking at a third of the wages. Low-impact eco-tourism seemed a real possibility when only the select few had even heard of Moab, but the canyonlands now seem to be taking as hard a battering from the fat-tyre brigade as they ever did from the mining conglomerates.

Getting to Moab

No scheduled **buses** connect Moab with the outside world, but Bighorn Express (☎435/587-3061 or 1-888/655-RIDE) offers a daily **shuttle service** between Salt Lake City airport and Green River, Moab, Monticello and Blanding. Sunrise Air (☎435/259-3422 or 1-800/842-8211) offers at least one commuter **flight** daily between **Canyonlands Airport**, twenty miles north of Moab on US-91, and Salt Lake City, for a round-trip fare of around $150. Arriving passengers can rent a car through Redtail Aviation (☎435/259-7421 or 1-800/842-9251), or take a $15 **taxi** ride into town with West Tracks (☎435/259-7317) or Roadrunner Shuttle (☎435/259-9402). Both of the latter also provide shuttle services for bikers, rafters, and hikers.

Information

The superb new **visitor center** for Moab and Grand County stands right in the heart of town at Center and Main (daily: summer 8am–9pm; winter 8am–5pm; ☎435/259-8825 or 1-800/635-6622; *www.canyonlands-utah.com*). As well as stacks of information on Moab itself, it carries brochures and maps for the nearby parks and public lands, and is the venue for the *Canyon's Edge* multimedia **show**, held twice nightly in summer.

The zip code for Moab is UT 84352.

Other good sources for news and information include Moab's **coffee shops** (see p.470) and the excellent Back of Beyond **bookstore**, 83 N Main St (☎435/259-5154), all of which should have copies of the free *Canyon Country Zephyr*, which keeps a critical eye on local goings-on. Detailed topographical **maps** can be picked up from TI Maps, across from the visitor center at 29 E Center St (☎435/259-5529).

Accommodation

If you've already been in Utah for a while when you reach Moab, the glittering neon signs of **motels** like the *Greenwell* and the *Landmark* will come as a big surprise. At the last count, there were 27 motels in town, but every one of the thousand-plus rooms is taken on many nights between mid-March and October, so **reservations** are strongly recommended. If you arrive without having booked anything, call in first at the visitor center, where the free *TravelHost* guide contains useful discount coupons. In addition, organizations such as Moab/Canyonlands Central Reservations (☎435/259-5125 or 1-800/748-4386; *www.moab.net/reservations*) or Moab Realty Property Management (☎435/259-6050 or 1-800/897-7325; *www.moabutah.com*) can help. In winter, **room rates** can drop as low as $25 per night, but you'd be lucky to find anything much below $50 in high season.

Campgrounds

Moab's dozen commercial **campgrounds** can be a godsend, considering the dearth of sites in the national parks, but they do tend to be dominated by family parties.

Canyonlands Campground, 555 S Main St; ☎435/259-6848 or 1-800/522-6848. Large, year-round site in the heart of town, catering mainly to RVs but equipped with tent sites at around $15 per night.

Sand Flats Recreation Area, 1924 S Roadrunner Hill; ☎435/259-6111. Barely developed BLM campground, along the top of the mesa to the east of town near the Slickrock Bike Trail, intended primarily for mountain bikers and costing $8 per night.

Campgrounds in Canyonlands are described on p.446 and p.454, and in Arches on p.458.

Slickrock Campground, 1301 N-Hwy 191; ☎435/259-7660 or 1-800/448-8873. Moab's biggest site, a mile north of town, but it's a pleasant enough and well-shaded spot charging $15 per tent per night, and comes with all mod cons.

Hostels, motels and B&Bs

Apache Motel, 166 South 400 East; ☎435/259-5727 or 1-800/228-6882, fax 435/259-8989. Long-established, two-story traditional motel on a quiet back street east of the center. John Wayne stayed here while filming *Rio Bravo* in the nearby canyons. Winter ②, summer ③.

Best Western Canyonlands Inn, 16 S Main St; ☎435/259-2300 or 1-800/528-1234, fax 435/259-2301; *www.canyonlandsinn.com*. Standard, dependable *Best Western*, across from the visitor center. Winter ③, summer ⑤.

Best Western Greenwell Motel, 105 S Main St; ☎435/259-6151 or 1-800/528-1234, fax 435/259-4397; *www.moab-utah.com/bestwesternmoab*. Central, modern and very comfortable motel. Winter ③, summer ⑤.

Bowen Motel, 169 N Main St; ☎435/259-7132 or 1-800/874-5439; *www.moab-utah.com/bowen*. Renovated 1940s motel, offering good value for such a central location. Winter ②, summer ④.

Castle Valley Inn, 424 Amber Lane, Castle Valley; ☎435/259-6012, fax 259-1501; *www.castlevalleyinn.com*. Large, tasteful, beautifully furnished B&B, set in spacious grounds in magnificent Castle Valley, twenty miles east of town (see p.472). Five en-suite rooms and three separate bungalows, dinner served five nights weekly. ⑤–⑦.

Gonzo Inn,100 West 200 South; ☎435/259-2515 or 1-800/791-4044, fax 435/259-6992; *www.gonzoinn.com*. Luxurious if rather self-consciously "hip" inn, complete with kitsch retro furnishings, gecko doorhandles, quirky artworks and in-house espresso bar. ⑥.

Lazy Lizard International Hostel, 1213 S Hwy-191; ☎435/259-6057. Amiable, very laid-back private hostel, well south of the center (just beyond a bowling alley), with $8 beds in six-person dorms, $6 campsites, and private cabins for up to six people at $22, plus a hot tub and kitchen facilities. No membership necessary. ①

Moab Valley Inn, 711 S Main St; ☎435/259-4419 or 1-800/831-6622, fax 435/259-4332; *www.moabvalleyinn.com*. Large and well-equipped new motel at the south end of downtown, with indoor and outdoor pools, hot tub and on-site car and 4WD rental. Winter ④, summer ⑤.

Pack Creek Ranch, PO Box 1270; ☎435/259-5505, fax 259-8879. Large guest ranch, with individual cabins plus assorted pools and tubs, twenty miles southeast of town, just off the lower reaches of the La Sal Mountain Loop Road (see p.472). Summer rates of around $125 per person include all meals and trail rides on horseback. Winter ⑥, summer ⑧.

Red Stone Inn, 535 S Main St; ☎435/259-3500 or 1-800/772-1972, fax 435/259-2717; *www.moabutah.com/redstoneinn*. New, bargain-rate motel, a few blocks south of the center. Winter ②, summer ④.

Sleep Inn, 1051 S Main St; ☎435/259-4655 or 1-800/753-3746, fax 435/259-5838. Upmarket but reasonably priced motel at the south end of town, with a pool and an indoor spa. Winter ③, summer ④.

Sunflower Hill B&B, 185 North 300 East; ☎435/259-2974 or 1-800/662-2786, fax 435/259-2470; *www.sunflowerhill.com*. Antique-furnished former farmhouse, now an 11-room B&B, away from the bustle on a dead-end side street. All units are en suite, some are in separate cottages. Winter ③, summer ④.

Super 8, 889 N Main St; ☎435/259-8868 or 1-800/800-8000, fax 435/259-8968. Moab's largest motel, kitted out in *Super 8*'s normal drab colors but offering good value for money, at the north end of town not far from the Colorado. Winter ②, summer ④.

The Town

Main Street, the broad five-mile section of **US-191** that sweeps through the center of Moab, is lined with all the gas stations, diners, motels and other businesses that you'd expect. For two blocks north and south of **Center Street**, which crosses it at the visitor center in the middle, window-shopping pedestrians stroll the sidewalk and browse the menus. Elsewhere, everybody drives or cycles. Squeezed between Swiss Cheese Ridge to the east and the Moab Rim to the west, the town has little room to expand, but you can still see a few pioneer homes, and the occasional apple orchard, if you venture down the side streets.

Local history is enjoyably recalled at the **Dan O'Laurie Museum**, also known as the Canyon Country Museum, at 118 E Center St (summer Mon–Sat 1–8pm; winter Mon–Thurs 3–7pm, Fri & Sat 1–7pm; free). Displays start with a mammoth tusk dredged from the Colorado, and the replica of an ancient petroglyph claimed to show the "Moab mastodon." Then follows the usual small-town assortment, ranging from an Ancestral Puebloan basket to Moab's first telephone switchboard, plus plenty of souvenirs from the uranium days. A **gallery** upstairs holds separate exhibitions of contemporary art.

Seen by some critics as the final straw in the commercialization of the local scenic splendors, the **Moab Skyway** is a chairlift that climbs one thousand feet up the Moab Rim from a terminus on Kane Creek Boulevard at the south end of town (summer daily 9am–10pm,

As explained on p.15, accommodation prices, excluding taxes, are indicated throughout this book by the following symbols:

① *up to $30*
② *$30–45*
③ *$45–60*
④ *$60–80*
⑤ *$80–100*
⑥ *$100–130*
⑦ *$130–175*
⑧ *$175–250*
⑨ *$250+*

The highspots of Moab's calendar are the Jeep Safari at Easter, and the Fat Tire mountain-bike festival in late October.

ADVENTURE TRAVEL OUTFITS IN MOAB

As southern Utah's main center for wilderness activities, Moab is filled with companies that specialize in guiding and equipping adventurous travelers. The visitor center can provide full lists of tour operators and rental outlets, plus free maps and route suggestions for bikers and 4WD drivers. Another list, with links to most operators, appears on the National Park Service Web site at *www.nps.gov/cany/comm.htm*.

Colorado River Trips

Virtually everyone who goes **rafting** on the Colorado River does so with one of Moab's **river-running operators**. All those listed below offer motorized one-day trips for around $45, plus half-day tasters for $30 or so; most also offer multiday expeditions, and day-trip combinations such as jeep-and-raft or horse-and-raft.

Shorter trips start northwest of Moab, near Fisher Towers, and arrive near town in the afternoon; many companies give passengers the chance to float quieter stretches in two-person kayaks. While there are enough stretches of small-scale whitewater to whet the appetites of first-timers, a little romance is lost by the fact that the road runs alongside the river for much of the way. **Longer** (2–7-day) trips head through Cataract Canyon and other wild Canyonlands spots. **Oar-powered rafts** are slower but much quieter, and less expensive than motorboat trips.

Mountain Biking

While the Moab area is ideally suited to **mountain-bike touring**, only experienced riders should attempt its most famous route, the **Slickrock Bike Trail**. Originally laid out as a motorbike trail in 1969, this challenging ten-mile loop explores the sandstone knobs east of Moab, skirt-

Adrift Adventures, 378 N Main St; ☎435/259-8594 or 1-800/874-4483
Canyon Voyages, 211 N Main St; ☎435/259-6007 or 1-800/733-6007
Canyonlands by Night & Day, 1861 N Hwy-191; ☎435/259-5261 or 1-800/394-9978
Chili Pepper Bike Shop, 702 S Main St ☎435/259-4688 or 1-888/677-4688
Dreamrides, 600 N Main St; ☎435/259-6419 or 1-888/662-2882
Farabee Adventures, 401 N Main St; ☎435/259-7494
Kaibab Mountain Bikes, 391 S Main St; ☎435/259-7423 or 1-800/451-1133
Lin Ottinger Tours, 600 N Main St; ☎435/259-7312
Navtec Expeditions, 321 N Main St; ☎435/259-7983 or 1-800/833-1278
Nichols Expeditions, 497 N Main St; ☎435/259-3999 or 1-800/648-8488
North American River Expeditions, 543 N Main St; ☎435/259-5865 or 1-800/342-5938
Pack Creek Ranch, PO Box 1270, La Sal Mountain Rd; ☎435/259-5505
Poison Spider Bicycles, 497 N Main St; ☎435/259-7882 or 1-800/635-1792
Rim Tours, 1233 S Hwy-191; ☎435/259-5223 or 1-800/626-7335
Slickrock 4x4 Rentals, 284 N Main St; ☎435/259-5678 or 1-888/238-5337
Tag-a-Long Expeditions, 452 N Main St; ☎435/259-8946 or 1-800/453-3292
Western River Expeditions, 1371 N Hwy-191; ☎801/942-6669 or 1-800/453-7450
Western Spirit Cycling, 478 Mill Creek Drive; ☎435/259-8732 or 1-800/845-BIKE

ing the rim of Negro Bill Canyon with views to the La Sal Mountains and the Colorado River. Following the white dotted line around this exposed expanse of lithified red dunes, up steep inclines and along narrow ledges, takes at least four hours. Be sure to allow enough daylight, and carry two gallons of water – far more than you can take in bike bottles alone.

To reach the trail, which lies within the **Sand Flats Recreation Area**, climb Salt Flats Road up from Millcreek Drive, which branches off 400 East Street four blocks south of Center Street. There's a fee of $1 per cycle and $3 per vehicle for trail users, but spectators can go in for free.

If you're simply cycling for pleasure, you may prefer to try the red-rock side canyons east and west of Moab, such as **Kane Creek**.

JEEP TOURS AND RENTALS

The dirt roads that crisscross the backcountry to all sides of Moab – most created by 1950s uranium prospectors – make perfect goals for **4WD** explorations. The roads described on p.471 onwards are good for half-day trips, while obvious destinations further afield include the Island In the Sky and Needles districts of Canyonlands. Jeep **rental** rates are in the region of $100 per day; full-day guided tours cost $50–80 per person.

SCENIC FLIGHTS

From Canyonlands Airport (see p.465), **Redtail Aviation** (☎435/259-7421 or 1-800/842-9251) run unforgettable flights over Canyonlands and beyond. A one-hour reconnaissance costs $75 per person, 2hr 30min trips are $150. **Slickrock Air Guides** (☎435/259-6216 or 1-800/332-2439) have similar rates, while **Classic Helicopters** (☎435/259-4637) are rather more expensive at around $250 for a 2hr flight.

River Tours	River Rentals	Jeep Tours	Jeep Rentals	Bike Tours	Bike Rentals	Horses
•		•				
•	•	•				
•	•	•				
				•	•	
		•		•	•	
		•	•			
				•	•	
		•				
•		•		•		
				•		
•		•				
						•
					•	
				•	•	
			•			
•	•	•				
•	•					
				•		

shorter hours off season; $7). During its swaying twelve-minute ascent up the face of a red-rock column known as the Portal, you emerge above the green fields of Moab to views of the full curve of the Colorado River, with the fins of Arches National Park visible on the far horizon. A mile-long trail at the top provides a chance to get your breath back, and to look down on the much lower cliffs of the Swiss Cheese Ridge on the other side of town, topped by the Slickrock Bike Trail (see p.468).

On a hot summer's day, you might prefer a quick wallow at **Butch Cassidy's King World Waterpark** (mid-April to mid-Sept daily 10am–10pm; adults $8.50, under-13s $6.50). This complex of water slides and swimming pools is tucked into a side canyon at the north end of town, said to have been used as a hideout by the Wild Bunch.

Eating

While Moab has yet to acquire the range of **restaurants** you might find in a major resort, it offers by far the greatest choice in southern Utah, and for once most places make a serious effort to cater for **vegetarians**. Full menus appear in the *Moab Menu Guide*, available free at local motels. There's also no problem getting a **drink** – Moab even has two pubs and its own winery – while **coffee bars** are springing up all over town. Several bike shops have espresso counters for early-morning customers.

Amid much local controversy, certain restaurateurs, arguing that foreign visitors seem unfamiliar with the American custom of **tipping**, have taken to adding a fifteen percent service charge to all checks. Be sure you don't end up paying twice.

Center Cafe, 92 E Center St; ☎435/259-4295. This expensive but exquisite restaurant, offering gourmet dining with a Pacific twist, serves far and away the best food in Moab. Appetizers for around $9 include Thai shrimp satay and grilled eggplant pizza; entrees, at more like $24, range through Asian barbecue salmon and rack of lamb. Open for dinner nightly, plus brunch on Sun, 9am–1pm; closed Dec–Feb.

Eddie McStiff's, 57 S Main St; ☎435/259-2337. Central pub, next to the visitor center, which has some interesting beers, including raspberry and blueberry. The restaurant serves a varied menu from 6.30am daily, with inexpensive salads, fancy Southwestern pizzas (with toppings like sundried tomatoes and jalapeño peppers) from $8, plus pasta and steak dinners, but the service can leave a lot to be desired.

Fat City Smoke House, 36 South 100 West; ☎435/259-4302. Informal Texas-style open-pit barbecue, serving tangy chicken, pork and ribs, and vegetarian sandwiches. Mon–Sat 11am until late, Sun 5–9pm.

Moab Brewery, 686 S Main St; ☎435/259-6333. Moab's newest microbrewery, a cavernous place a good way south of the center. The beers aren't bad, but the food is. Open from 11.30am daily.

Mondo Cafe, 59 S Main St; ☎435/259-5911. Groovy all-day hangout next to *Eddie McStiff's*, serving espresso coffees and the odd pastry or sandwich. Daily 7.30am–10pm.

The Peace Tree, 20 S Main St; ☎435/259-8503. Very central juice bar and cafe, that serves good sandwiches, wraps and smoothies to take out or eat on the small outdoor patio. Daily 9am–9pm.

The Poplar Place, First North and Main St; ☎435/259-6018. Friendly, classy adobe bar with Ancestral Puebloan-themed ironwork, serving draft beers and good pizzas. Daily 11.30am–11pm.

Red Rock Bakery & Cafe Y2K, 74 S Main St; ☎435/259-5941. Small cafe-bakery opposite the visitor center, which also offers Internet access from a back room.

Rio Colorado Restaurant and Bar, 2 South 100 West; ☎435/259-6666. Private club – the formalities are minimal – that serves substantial portions of inexpensive but not particularly good Mexican food, and only has much atmosphere on Friday and Saturday nights, when there's live music. Open daily from 3pm, plus Sun 11am–2pm.

Slickrock Cafe, 5 N Main St; ☎435/259-8004. Central, modern cafe which gives every meal of the day a Southwestern flavor. Omelettes, burritos, burgers and sandwiches earlier on, and some good chicken and pasta entrees, for $10–18 in the evening. Daily 7am until late.

Sunset Grill, 900 N Hwy-191; ☎435/259-7146. Charlie Steen's luxury hilltop home (see box p.464) is now one of Moab's finest restaurants, with tasty meat and seafood entrees for $13–20, great desserts, and stunning views across the valley. The tortuous if short approach road from the north end of town (lit at night) means it's no place to drink and drive.

Around Moab

Although most visitors head straight for the national parks, several lesser-known areas in the Moab region are well worth exploring. Both upstream and downstream, minor roads run alongside the **Colorado River**, while the **La Sal Mountains** to the east make a snowy contrast to the aridity of the desert.

The Potash Road

The dead-end **Potash Road**, Hwy-279, which doubles back southwest along the Colorado's west bank from just north of the bridge on US-191, passes a number of intriguing **rock art** sites, and provides a great close-up view of the river. In this stretch the Colorado is broad and lazy, tinted the same reddish brown as the Navajo Sandstone cliffs that tower above it.

The Potash Road cliffs are often busy with rock climbers; if you fancy a lesson, contact the Moab Climbing Shop (☎435/259-2725).

Seven miles down the road, you reach a group of **petroglyphs** a dozen feet up on the canyon wall to the right. Scraped into the dark "desert varnish" by Fremont Indians, some time between 700 and 1300 AD, they depict animals and anthropomorphic figures, including a chain of linked humans resembling paper dolls.

A mile further on, two mounted metal tubes tucked among the roadside bushes point to a group of barely discernible **dinosaur tracks**. More petroglyphs can also be seen, this time higher on the cliffs. The signposted **Jug Handle Arch**, seven miles on, is not all that spectacular, while a smaller and even less enthralling arch is located on the western flank of the same side canyon.

Just past the arches, seventeen miles from US-191, the valley floor widens. The road officially ends here, at the ugly green plant where Moab Salt produces salt and **potash**, accompanied by billowing clouds of white smoke. It is possible to drive on, but how much further you go probably depends on whether you own the vehicle you're driving. The surface is paved for another 1.3 miles, while 1.7 bumpy miles beyond that you get your first glimpse of the 23 vinyl-lined **evaporation ponds** where the potash is prepared. Dyed a lurid bluey-turquoise to speed evaporation, they're a real eyesore, clearly visible from Dead Horse Point far above (see p.445).

Only **4WD** vehicles can continue past the ponds, and the nearby boat-launch ramp. *Thelma and Louise* freeze-framed their way into the final credits from the mesa-top a few miles further up, and in due course the Potash Road meets up with the White Rim Road in Canyonlands (see p.448).

Castle Valley and the La Sal Mountains

Fisher Towers were originally "Fissure Towers"; there was no "Fisher."

Turning northeast off US-191 just south of the bridge takes you onto **Hwy-128**, which follows the Colorado's east bank for 35 miles, then crosses the river to meet I-70 ten miles further up. In summer, this superbly scenic section of the river is busy with one-day rafting trips, which can be watched from several roadside lookouts. Roughly twenty miles along, the three-pronged red butte of **Fisher Towers** rises to the right of the road.

Snow usually closes the La Sal Mountain Loop Road from November until April. In summer, it takes four hours to complete the loop.

For an excellent sixty-mile **loop trip** back to Moab, turn right, southeast, fifteen miles along the river road, onto Castle Valley Road. **Castle Valley** is a verdant cleft that boasts some quintessentially Western scenery, with red-sandstone walls and buttes such as the **Priest and Nuns** to the east, and high dark hills to the west. At its far southern end, eleven miles along, another right turn sets you climbing up the volcanic 10,000-feet **La Sal Mountains**. A couple of narrow single-file gravel stretches and some hair-raising hairpins later, you reach a vantage point commanding views across the Colorado to Arches and Canyonlands. Beyond that, the road runs through the high mountain landscape of the **Manti–La Sal National Forest**. A few campgrounds are tucked into the woods, but you won't see another building before the road eventually drops back towards Moab Valley.

Hole N" The Rock

Don't confuse the Hole N" The Rock with the Hole In The Rock pioneer river crossing near Escalante; see p.415.

The peculiarly punctuated **Hole N" The Rock**, 15 miles south of Moab on US-191 (daily 9am–6pm; $2.75), is a classic piece of 1950s Americana. Having started out with a roadside diner at the foot of a cliff, Albert Christensen and his wife Gladys ended up hollowing an entire home deep into the red sandstone. Albert was a dreadful taxidermist – his unfortunate donkey Henry has to be seen to be believed – and painter – cross-eyed Christs a specialty – but his cool, well-lit house is a masterpiece. He died in 1957, without completing the

spiral staircase that was planned to lead 65ft up to a roof-top patio.
In the fine tradition of the "jewelry" Gladys made from broken beer
bottles, the gift store is stocked with tacky souvenirs.

Canyon Rims Recreation Area

The vast and almost completely empty mesa west of US-191, which
separates Moab from the Needles district of Canyonlands National
Park (see p.452), is largely taken up by the BLM-run **Canyon Rims
Recreation Area**. Not much recreation goes on up here, although it
has the usual jeep roads and a scattering of hiking trails; there are
also two basic, waterless **campgrounds**, *Hatch Point* and
Windwhistle (both April–Oct only; $6; ☎435/259-6111).

Only consider visiting the two main overlooks if you have a lot of
time to spare – it involves a two-and-a-half-hour detour from the
highway – or if you're not going to get to the Needles district, in
which case the **Needles Overlook** provides a (relatively) quick
overview that's as dramatic as any in Canyonlands itself.

The Needles Overlook

The paved road into the Canyon Rims Recreation Area leaves US-191
32 miles south of Moab. Its dreary 22-mile course westwards comes
to an abrupt halt at the windswept **Needles Overlook**, where a short
railed footpath gives eagle's-eye views across the canyonlands.
Specific landmarks are hard to pick out amid the orange-sandstone
ledges that spread below, but looking south you should spot the twin
Sixshooter Peaks, and Hwy-211 winding alongside Indian Creek
towards the Needles district (see p.452). Further west, the Needles
themselves poke from the hillocks, while the Colorado loops its way
from the north towards its confluence with the Green River.

The Anticline Overlook

Fifteen miles in from US-191, or seven miles short of the Needles
Overlook, forking right onto an even, broad gravel road commits you
to the 25-minute drive across the tumbleweed-strewn sagebrush
desert to the **Anticline Overlook**. You probably won't pass another
vehicle before the final parking lot, from which a five-minute walk
leads to a high promontory that faces the potash evaporation beds
(see opposite) and **Dead Horse Point** across the Colorado.

Some people call this the Anti-climax Overlook, disappointed to
realize that they've driven almost all the way back to Moab. As you'll
see if you follow the fence around the headland, only **Kane Creek
Canyon** – where the creek is the tiniest of green slivers in the red
wasteland – intervenes. You'll almost certainly hear motorbikes
scrambling across the slickrock of the Moab Rim on the far side. To
the northeast, silhouetted above a brief stretch of the Colorado, you
also get a remarkable view of the fins of **Arches** National Park, with
the line of sight passing straight through the South Window.

Southeast Utah

It may lack big-name national parks, but Utah's **southeast corner** is every bit as scenic as the neighboring regions. The desert here is so unforgiving that only a handful of widely separated settlements cling to life, and large tracts remain entirely without roads.

Culturally as well as geographically, southeast Utah has much in common with the Four Corners area, covered in Chapter One. The **Ancestral Puebloans** were here in force, as countless abandoned pueblos can testify. They're thought to have moved off to the south and east around 1250 AD, but even now almost half the population of **San Juan County**, which covers the bulk of the region and is larger than several states, is Native American. A few are Utes, but most are **Navajo**, many of them descended from families who hid here during the 1860s to escape the Long Walk (see p.539).

The first **Mormons** to reach this far-flung corner were the Hole-in-the-Rock pioneers (see p.412), who established **Bluff** in 1880 and went on to found **Blanding** and **Monticello** as well. All those towns make viable bases, but the real attraction, as ever, is the landscape, with hikers heading for **Natural Bridges National Monument**, more ambitious backpackers for **Grand Gulch**, and drivers rattling across the desert to the unbelievable **Muley Point, Goosenecks State Park** and the **Valley of the Gods**.

Monticello

*The local pro-
nunciation of
Monticello is
"monti-sello."*

The first fifty miles of US-191 south of Moab are so desolate that it comes as a major shock, on climbing some straggling foothills, to find yourself confronted by plowed green fields. To Mormon pioneers, this terrain resembled Thomas Jefferson's country home in Virginia – hence the name of **MONTICELLO**, six miles further on. Farming has never been all that easy here, however, and the economy has only recently been put on a steadier footing by the growth of tourism.

The normal route to the Needles District of Canyonlands, fifty miles northwest, is to take Hwy-211 west from US-191, roughly 22 miles north of town. In summer, it's also possible to take a very different approach, through the volcanic **Abajo Mountains**, which rise west of town to over 11,000ft. The road up, from the west end of 200 South, is pretty straightforward, and passes through some lovely quasi-alpine meadows where you may spot browsing deer. You then veer north and drop down a much rougher track, to meet Hwy-211 near Newspaper Rock (see p.452)

To the east of Monticello, US-666 heads off to Colorado through what looks like a segment of the Great Plains that has wandered astray, complete with grain silos and fields of wheat and beans.

Arrival and information

Information on Monticello, and on the parks and public lands in the vicinity, can be picked up from the multiagency **visitor center**, in San Juan County Courthouse at 117 S Main St (April–Oct Mon–Fri 8am–5pm, Sat & Sun 10am–5pm; Nov–March Mon–Fri 8am–5pm; ☎435/587-3235 or 1-800/574-4386; *www.southeastutah.org*).

From the airstrip three miles north of Monticello, Midway Aviation (☎435/587-2774) run $59 one-hour scenic flights over Canyonlands.

Southeast Utah

The zip code for Monticello is UT 84535.

Accommodation

Monticello is not nearly as lively a place to spend the night as Moab, but it does have a reasonable set of **motels** to choose from.

Best Western Wayside Inn, 197 E Central Ave; ☎435/587-2261 or 1-800/633-9700, fax 435/587-2920. Comfortable upscale motel, with pool and spa, a few yards down US-666 towards Colorado. Winter ③, summer ④.

Canyonlands Motor Inn, 197 N Main St; ☎435/587-2266 or 1-800/952-6212, fax 435/587-2883. Roadside motel, on the north side of town, that has seen better days; fairly decrepit rooms at reasonable rates. Winter ②, summer ③.

Days Inn, 549 N Main St; ☎435/587-2458, fax 587-2191. The biggest, smartest and newest motel around, on the brow of the hill at the north end of town. Winter ③, summer ④.

Grist Mill Inn, 64 South 300 East; ☎435/587-2597 or 1-800/645-3762, fax 435/587-2579; *gristmill@hubwest.com*. Restored 1930s flour mill with six en-suite B&B rooms. There are three more in an adjoining building, plus a converted railroad caboose. ③–⑤.

Super 8, 649 N Main St; ☎435/587-2489 or 1-800/800-8000. Monticello's northernmost motel, with a pool, clean rooms and friendly managers. Winter ③, summer ④.

Triangle H Motel, 164 E Central Ave; ☎435/587-2274 or 1-800/657-6622, fax 435/587-2175. Neat, unexciting but inexpensive single-story motel, with some two-bedroom units. Winter ②, summer ③.

The price codes used here are explained on p.15.

Eating

Like any self-respecting farming town, Monticello abounds in wholesome if unexciting **diners**, plus a few fast-food outlets.

Lamplight Restaurant, 655 E Central St; ☎435/587-2170. Dinner-only joint on the eastern edge of town, offering steaks, burgers and meat in general, with plenty of options below $10, and a salad bar. Mon–Sat 4–11pm.

MD Ranch Cookhouse, 380 S Main St; ☎435/587-3299. Attractive wood-themed restaurant, with attached gift store. Grilled breakfasts and sandwich lunches, but the real *raison d'être* is to serve big steak dinners, including T-bones for $15 and buffalo for $17, all in; they also have fish, shrimp, ribs and veggie burgers. Live music Fri & Sat.

Mesa Java, 518 N Main St; ☎435/587-2601. Espresso coffees and fresh pastries from 7am, on the open-air terrace of a gift store. Oct–April Thurs–Tues, May–Sept daily.

Wagon Wheel Pizza, 164 S Main St; ☎435/587-2766. Homemade pizzas of all sizes and one shape, plus deli sandwiches.

Blanding

BLANDING, just over twenty miles southwest of Monticello, was established as "Grayson" in 1905, when a new irrigation channel brought water to this site from the Abajo Mountains. In 1915, **Thomas Bicknell**, an East Coast millionaire, offered to give a library to any Utah town that would change its name to his own. Two jumped in; Thurber, near Torrey, became Bicknell, while Grayson took his wife's maiden name, Blanding. Each got a new library, though it's said they didn't get as many books as they'd expected.

Having skirted the Abajos, US-191 is running due west as it enters Blanding, and makes a sharp dogleg turn south at the four-way stop in the center of town. That brief pause is as much time as most travelers give Blanding, whose broad avenues seldom seem to display much sign of life. However, head north at the central junction, then west, and you'll come to the interesting **Edge of the Cedars State Park**, 660 West 400 North (daily: mid-May to mid-Sept 8am–8pm; mid-Sept to mid-May 9am–5pm; $5 per vehicle or $2 per person; ☎435/678-2238). An excellent museum here, primarily intended as an educational resource for local kids, holds displays that range from the Ancestral Puebloans to the Anglos. In a town with a notorious reputation for illegal pot-hunting by profit-seeking amateurs – known locally as "Moki poachers" – it emphasizes the role and techniques of proper archeology. Some of the Ancestral Puebloan artifacts are truly remarkable, including pots and pendants, stylish wooden plates, and a complete loom dated to around 1150 AD. Outside, a footpath leads around an Ancestral Puebloan pueblo occupied between 700 and 1220 AD. In the one section to have been excavated, visitors can climb down a ladder into a musty, haunting *kiva*. Signs point out that all the buildings face south, probably to maximize sunlight, whereas Navajo dwellings always face east.

For more about the Ancestral Puebloans, including explanations of the terms used here, see p.520.

Several blocks further south, the **Nations of the Four Corners Cultural Center**, 707 West 500 South (open 24hr; free) is a small park holding reconstructions of a Navajo *hogan*, a Ute tepee, a Mormon cabin and an Hispanic *hacienda*. It occasionally hosts cultural events on summer evenings.

Accommodation

The zip code for Blanding is UT 84511.

Traffic between Lake Powell to the west and Moab to the north keeps Blanding's motels busy enough in summer, but they're not a very inspiring bunch.

Blanding Sunset Inn, 88 W Center St; ☎435/678-3323. Inexpensive, basic motel on the quieter section of Center St, west of the four-way stop. Winter ②, summer ③.

Cliff Palace, 132 S. Main St; ☎435/678-2264 or 1-800/553-8093. Small, slightly run-down 1960s motel that advertises itself with the slogan "Watching Your Pennies? Stay At The Cliff Palace." ②.

Southeast
Utah

*The price codes
used here are
explained on
p.15.*

Comfort Inn, 711 S Main St; ☎435/678-3271 or 1-800/622-3250, fax 435/678-3219. Characterless chain motel well south of the center, with an indoor pool and complimentary continental breakfasts. Winter ③, summer ④.

Four Corners Inn, 131 E Center St; ☎435/678-3257 or 1-800/574-3150, fax 435/678-3219. Large, modern, two-story motel, just after the highway doglegs to the right, with free continental breakfasts. Winter ③, summer ④.

Super 8, 755 S Main St; ☎435/678-3880 or 1-800/800-8000, fax 435/678-3780. New, white-painted chain motel at the south end of town, with a strict non-smoking policy. Winter ③, summer ④.

Eating

Eating in Blanding is indeed bland eating.

Elk Ridge Restaurant, 120 E Center St; ☎435/678-3390. Blanding's busiest diner, open for all meals with a standard menu of chicken, liver, steak and a few Mexican dishes. Daily 6am–10pm.

Homestead Steak House, 121 E Center St; ☎435/678-3456. Ribs, burgers, chicken and steaks, served for lunch and dinner in the throbbing epicenter of downtown Blanding.

Old Tymer, 735 S Main St; ☎435/678-2122. Conventional tourist diner, next to the *Comfort Inn* at the south end of town.

West of Blanding

A mile or so south of Blanding, at a junction marked only a by solitary gas station, **Hwy-95** heads west from US-191, to embark on a magnificent 120-mile trans-Utah journey to Hanksville. Until it was completed in 1976 – which is why it's also known as the **Bicentennial Highway** – east–west travel was effectively barred by the massive monocline of **Comb Ridge**, ten miles west of Blanding. To the Navajo, this thousand-foot wall of red rock, which stretches over eighty miles from north to south, was the backbone of the earth, as well as one of four "arrowheads" protecting their homeland. To Mormon pioneers, it was a definitive "reef" (see p.419); and to the modern highway builders, it was an obstacle they simply had to blast their way through.

No towns interrupt Hwy-95 apart from the speck that is **Hite**, 87 miles along at Lake Powell (see p.437). Humans have at times occupied the region, however. Several side canyons off Hwy-95 bear traces of an Ancestral Puebloan presence, while the cattle ranchers who tried their hands here a century ago were later succeeded by uranium miners in the 1950s.

The Butler Wash Ruins

Ten miles west of the highway intersection, a short spur road climbs west of Hwy-95 to the parking lot for the **Butler Wash Ruins**, a stimulating Ancestral Puebloan site that's located on BLM land (24hr; free). A ten-minute hike, much of it up steep bare rock, leads to an overlook into a side canyon just short of the crest of Comb Ridge. The ruins are located in the topmost of three natural rock alcoves; a long stone ledge to the left leads down to the fertile wash where the inhabitants farmed. Archeologists see them as combining elements from what are usually regarded as distinct subgroups of the Ancestral Puebloans, in that the complex includes one Kayenta-style square *kiva* and three Mesa Verde-style round *kivas*.

Comb Ridge

Immediately beyond Butler Wash, Hwy-95 picks its way down the lurid red wall of **Comb Ridge** to a cottonwood-rich valley, watered by **Comb Wash**. Confronted by the ridge on their endless journey east, the Hole-in-the-Rock party decided to head south at this point, which explains why they ended up at Bluff (see p.482). Don't copy them, however; a tempting dirt road does branch south from the highway beside the stream, with a nice little campground a short way along, but it soon succumbs to deep drifts of sand no ordinary vehicle could hope to overcome.

Mule Canyon

Roughly seven miles west of Comb Wash, after Hwy-95 has climbed laboriously back up onto the plateau, a dirt road to the north, signed for Texas Flat, leads to two separate trailheads for **Mule Canyon**. The northern sides of each of this shallow canyon's two forks hold several small but well-preserved Ancestral Puebloan **cliff dwellings**. Both forks are around six miles long, but the most interesting ruins are roughly one mile and three miles along the South Fork, so a six-mile day-hike is enough for most visitors. In itself, it's not a difficult walk, but as few hikers pass this way it's important to be prepared for all eventualities. For current advice, ask at the Kane Gulch Ranger Station (see p.480)

A separate paved turnoff, half a mile along from the Texas Flat road, leads in a few yards to **Mule Canyon Ruin**, a partly restored Ancestral Puebloan pueblo that dates from around 1000 AD. This small site, a bit too near the highway to be very evocative, is similar to Boulder's Anasazi State Park (see p.417). Its most conspicuous features – a round *kiva* that has been roofed over for preservation, and a two-story masonry tower – are connected by an underground tunnel, perhaps used for surprise appearances during religious ceremonies.

Through the Bear's Ears

Before Hwy-95 was constructed, the main road west of Blanding – and the principal access to Natural Bridges (see opposite) – was a dirt track that climbed across the southern fringes of the Abajo Mountains. In reasonable weather, ordinary vehicles can still follow this attractive route, by turning north from Hwy-95 seven miles from the intersection. The 32-mile detour takes well over an hour.

After a cool, pleasant drive through the mountain-top woodlands, the road crosses a razorback ridge above Arch Canyon and then descends between two rounded outcrops known as the **Bear's Ears**. This prominent landmark is regarded by the Navajo as the embodiment of a bear, guarding the northern limits of their territory. The road eventually switchbacks down a sheer red cliff to join the approach road that leads into Natural Bridges.

Natural Bridges National Monument

Three of the world's largest natural bridges span the streambeds of the small, unspectacular White and Armstrong canyons, which cut through the white sandstone of **Cedar Mesa** southwest of the Abajo Mountains. **NATURAL BRIDGES NATIONAL MONUMENT** was the loneliest of spots when prospector Cass Hite stumbled across it in the 1880s, and remained pretty isolated until it was made Utah's first federal park in 1908. Now, however, it can be easily accessed by a four-mile spur road off Hwy-95, forty miles west of Blanding.

Originally dubbed Edwin, Augusta and Caroline, the bridges were given Hopi names when it was realized that much of the rock art found on the canyon walls represented Hopi clan symbols. It's thought this was one of the many places that the Ancestral Puebloan ancestors of the Hopi passed through during their migrations, departing around 1270 AD after a stay of perhaps six hundred years.

Each bridge can be seen from overlooks along the one-way, nine-mile **Bridge View Drive** that loops through the monument. With considerably more effort, you can clamber down into the canyons for closer inspection, and also follow the stream from one to the next for a potential hike of up to nine miles.

Practicalities

Admission to Natural Bridges costs $6 per vehicle or $3 per person; the gates to the loop drive are open from dawn until dusk daily. The **visitor center** – which is solar-powered, being so far from any other source of energy – stocks free trail guides and other background material (daily: March–Oct 8am–5pm; Nov–Feb 9am–4.30pm; ☎435/692-1234). Excellent displays show how the bridges were formed, pointing out that natural bridges occur throughout the US, from West Virginia to Illinois. The visitor center is the only source of water for the first-come, first-served **campground** nearby ($6).

The closest **motel** to the monument is the romantically isolated *Fry Canyon Lodge & Cafe* (PO Box 200, Fry Canyon, UT 84533; ☎435/259-5334; Dec–Feb ②, March–Nov ③), twenty miles west at mile marker 71 on Hwy-95, which has its own **campground** ($14).

The monument visitor center holds the only public payphone in the 122 miles between Hanksville and Blanding.

Bridge View Drive

The first and largest bridge, **Sipapu Bridge**, was named for the "hole" through which the Hopi emerged into this world. Standing at 220 feet high by 268 feet wide, it is surpassed only by Rainbow Bridge (see p.435). Although the roadside overlook provides a good straight-on view as it thrusts from a tangle of rocks, you'll only really appreciate Sipapu's size if you hike down from the trailhead half a mile further on. This is the most difficult trail in the monument, involving three short ladders, two metal staircases and a couple of stretches of slickrock with steep drop-offs. The best photos come from a ledge halfway down; by the time you're amid the trees directly beneath it, it's too big to fit in most viewfinders.

The next parking lot on the road is the start of a half-mile mesa-top trail that leads to a vantage point above **Horsecollar Ruin**. This small Ancestral Puebloan site, tucked into an alcove low on the canyon walls, is not visible from below.

Even after a 4000-ton rock fall in 1992, **Kachina Bridge**, the next stop, is much thicker than Sipapu, being more of a tunnel beneath a broad span of desert-varnish-stained sandstone. Seen from the over-look, it's far less distinct, with rocks rather than sunlight visible through the gap. On the trail down, railings guide you across the slickrock, and there's a crude staircase made from sandstone slabs. The stream at the bottom is lined by splendid cottonwoods, while pictographs near the base of the bridge resemble the *kachinas* of Hopi religion (see p.60).

Allow five hours for the full 8.6-mile hike from Sipapu Bridge to the two others and back across the mesa.

Natural bridges are short-lived phenomena. Even the oldest in the monument – **Owachomo**, two miles beyond Kachina by road – is a mere 5000 years old, and it's unlikely to last much longer. Though 180ft across, it tapers to just nine feet thick. It now stands slightly to one side of the streambed of Armstrong Canyon, reached by an easy half-mile round-trip hike. *Owachomo* means "flat-rock mound," a reference to the hummock at the left end of the span.

The **streambed trail** that connects the three bridges makes a delightful walk, meandering along the sandy wash beneath the trees. However, unless you double back, returning to your starting point involves a long hike across the mesa top, which is not as flat as you'd imagine and offers very little shade. One idea would be to start from Owachomo or Kachina and hike back towards Sipapu, hoping you'll meet up with someone who can give you a ride back to your vehicle.

Grand Gulch Primitive Area

If you share a passion for archeology with the stamina for long-distance hiking, an expedition into the **GRAND GULCH PRIMITIVE AREA**, south of Natural Bridges, can make you feel like a real-life Indiana Jones. Every twist and turn of this deep, dramatic gorge seems to be filled with relics of its thousand-year occupation by the Ancestral Puebloans, although they abandoned the canyon six centuries before it was named by the Hole-in-the-Rock pioneers.

Grand Gulch gouges across Cedar Mesa for just over fifty miles, dropping 2700ft to meet the San Juan River. There's no access for vehicles; the only path in starts from **Kane Gulch Ranger Station** (March to mid-Nov; no phone), five miles south of the point where Hwy-261 leaves Hwy-95, two miles east of the Natural Bridges turnoff. Typical backpacking expeditions last as long as a week, and you can only camp overnight in the gulch with a $5-per-night permit, obtainable up to six months in advance from the San Juan Resource Area office in Monticello's visitor center (see p.475; ☎435/587-1532). Don't turn up at the trailhead without a reservation, but do register there before you set off, even if you're just day-hiking.

The trail begins by dropping steadily down Kane Gulch, a side canyon that deepens as it goes, and joins Grand Gulch proper four miles along. **Junction Ruin** here, the largest ruin in the canyon system, makes a popular day-hike destination, though **Turkey Pen Ruin**, at 4.7 miles, and **Stimper Arch** just beyond, are also within round-trip reach. If you're making a longer trip, it's possible to leave Grand Gulch via **Bullet Canyon** to the east – in which case a total hike of 23 miles brings you back to Hwy-261 roughly seven miles south of the ranger station – or **Collins Canyon** to the west further along – a 38-mile hike that ends at a dirt road south of Hwy-276. For either of those routes, you'll need a car shuttle to get back to your vehicle, but that's probably easier to arrange than fixing for someone to meet you by boat on the San Juan, which is the only way out if you hike all the way to the end of Grand Gulch. Most visitors find it simpler just to double back at some point en route.

Kane Gulch Ranger Station can also provide details on day-hikes that head **east** from Hwy-261, into remote side canyons on Cedar Mesa. Road conditions are often treacherous, so don't set off without obtaining up-to-the-minute advice.

Muley Point

South of Kane Gulch, Hwy-261 crosses Cedar Mesa for its remaining seventeen miles. Before you take the plunge on the **Moki Dugway**, **MULEY POINT**, exactly five miles west of its top along an unmarked red-dirt road, is an absolute must-see.

When they finally get around to declaring all of southern Utah to be one vast national park, Muley Point will surely be the centerpiece. Quite simply, these are among the most stupendous views in the world. You're now at the southernmost tip of Cedar Mesa and the eastern extremity of Glen Canyon National Recreational Area. Far below, the San Juan River goosenecks its way west, while the Navajo Nation stretches off on the far side. Features on the horizon include Monument Valley in all its glory, the Sleeping Ute in Colorado, Navajo Mountain, and the cliffs above the west shore of Lake Powell.

The Moki Dugway

Hwy-261 doesn't stand on ceremony when it needs to get down off Cedar Mesa; it just plummets over the edge. The unpaved **MOKI DUGWAY**, which drops 1100ft in little more than two miles, is a terrifying but exhilarating ride, switchbacking through repeated hairpin

The views from Muley Point are reminiscent of those from Dead Horse Point, poised at a similar elevation ninety miles north; see p.445.

*Soon after the
pavement
resumes at the
bottom of the
Moki Dugway,
another dirt
road marks
the western
end of the
Valley of the
Gods; see
opposite.*

*Goosenecks
State Reserve
has no visitor
center and no
opening hours,
and charges
no fee.*

*The full story
of the Hole-in-
the-Rock expe-
dition is told
on p.412.*

*In late
October, Bluff
plays host to
the three-day
Utah Navajo
Fair.*

bends on a "washboard" strip of gravel. This ancient trail was improved by mining companies during the 1950s; you'll just have to hope you don't meet a truck-load of uranium coming the other way. If you have the nerve, the pull-outs for vehicles to pass make great viewpoints, but it's best to do all your sightseeing at the top.

Goosenecks State Reserve

Just before Hwy-261 meets US-163, six miles from the foot of the Moki Dugway and five miles north of Mexican Hat, the inconspicu-ous **Hwy-316** branches off to the west, to end 3.5 miles along at the extraordinary **GOOSENECKS STATE RESERVE**. Although the railed viewing area here stands a thousand feet below Cedar Mesa, the **San Juan River** is still another thousand feet down.

The river is an amazing sight, looping between huge pyramidal buttes in a textbook example of what geologists call an "entrenched meander." Its serpentine coils – once meanders on a muddy plain, later fixed in stone by the uplifting of the Colorado Plateau – are so extravagant that it flows six miles while advancing little more than one mile west. Above the distant sliver of riverbank greenery, alter-nate layers of grey limestone and red sandstone stripe the cliffs, while Monument Valley once again stands out on the skyline.

Bluff

BLUFF, 23 miles south of Blanding on US-191, is a pretty little river-side settlement whose somewhat humdrum present belies the extra-ordinary efforts its founders made to get here. The 230 **Hole-in-the-Rock** pioneers who reached this site on April 6, 1880 had trekked right across the heart of Utah, literally blasting their way through the canyons of the Colorado.

Once they arrived, they settled down to a life of ranching and agri-culture, made difficult by the San Juan River's propensity to flood. The back streets still hold a dozen or so of their original sturdy homes, making Bluff the least spoiled, most authentic town in the region. Its setting is consistently stunning, from the red-rock pinnacles known as the **Navajo Twins**, which mark the mouth of the narrow **Cow Canyon** gorge through which US-191 drops in from the north, to the cotton-woods that line the San Juan River, glinting against the sheer red bluff that rises on the far side. **Ancestral Puebloan** remains abound, including petroglyphs along Hwy-163 to the east, and the unexca-vated mound, thought to conceal a buried pueblo, beside the town cemetery on a hillock just north of the center.

Bluff is also a center for **river-running** on the San Juan, with rafts putting in at **Sand Island Recreation Area**, three miles west. The chief local operator, Wild Rivers Expeditions (☎435/672-2244 or 1-800/422-7654), runs one-day float trips to Mexican Hat (adults $85, under-13s $65), plus a range of longer voyages.

Accommodation

Bluff may not be the fanciest place in the world, but its genuine small-town feel makes it a nicer prospect than any of its neighbors.

Bluff B&B, PO Box 158; ☎435/672-2220. Homely two-room B&B in a 1960s brick house, on the edge of the desert northeast of town. ④.

Desert Rose Inn, 701 W Hwy-191; ☎435/672-2303 or 1-888/475-7673, fax 435/672-2217. Smart new timber-built motel at the west end of town, with thirty attractively designed and well-furnished rooms plus individual cabins of similar standard. Winter ③, summer ④.

Kokopelli Inn, PO Box 27, US-191; ☎435/672-2322 or 1-800/541-8854, fax 435/672-2385. Friendly, quiet roadside motel, adjoining a gas station and grocery with a deli counter. Winter ②, summer ③.

Recapture Lodge, PO Box 309; ☎435/672-2281, fax 672-2284. Pleasantly rural wooden motel, reaching back toward the river, plus a few rooms in two old pioneer homes. For groups, the owners can arrange area tours, including Monument Valley expeditions and llama treks. Winter ②, summer ③.

River House Inn, 500 West and US-191; ☎435/672-2448. Ramshackle seven-room motel at the west end of town, beyond the Cottonwood Wash. Winter ②, summer ③.

Eating

Despite its size, Bluff has a good range of **restaurants**, but they're a bit too spread out to walk from one to the next comparing menus.

Cottonwood Steakhouse, US-191; ☎435/672-2282. Open-air barbecue at the west end of town, with wooden tables arranged around a giant cottonwood. A great place to enjoy beer and steaks beneath the stars, though the menu's a bit short if you're not a beef-eater. One corner of the pseudo-Western stockade serves as Fort Crapper. Dinner only, from 5pm in spring and fall, 6pm in summer. Closed mid-Nov to Feb.

Cow Canyon Trading Post, Hwy-163; ☎435/672-2208. Former trading post, where Hwy-163 leaves US-161 and heads for Colorado, that's now an imaginative local restaurant. If you've had your fill of Navajo tacos, this is the place to sample a Navajo quiche. Usually open in summer only, Thurs–Mon.

K&C Trading Post Deli, US-191; ☎435/672-2221. Grocery deli that sells pizzas, sandwiches and fried chicken until 11pm in summer, 9pm in winter.

Turquoise Restaurant, US-191; ☎435/672-2433. The full gamut of Utah cuisine, from ham and eggs in the morning to steak at night. Mon–Sat 7am–9pm, Sun 8am–8pm.

Twin Rocks Cafe, Navajo Twins Drive; ☎435/672-2341. Glass-fronted diner, set against the rocks north of town, just west of US-191. Breakfast bagels and muffins, then salads and sandwiches, and chicken or fajita dinners for around $10. Daily 8am–10pm.

The Valley of the Gods

Bluff is very much at the edge of the desert; driving west you soon descend the southern end of **Comb Ridge** (see p.478) into vintage red-rock badlands, with the buttes of Monument Valley silhouetted above the horizon.

Bluff makes a handy overnight stop for Hovenweep National Monument, forty miles northwest; see p.66.

The zip code for Bluff is UT 84512.

Similar, smaller-scale monoliths can be toured closer at hand, with no restrictions or admission fees, in the **VALLEY OF THE GODS**. This "garden" of isolated sandstone columns – said by the Navajo to be petrified warriors – holds no fixed hiking trails. Drivers can see it all from a winding **seventeen-mile dirt road**, which leaves US-163 on the far side of Lime Creek, roughly eighteen miles west of Bluff, and meets Hwy-261 near the foot of the Moki Dugway (see p.481), 10.6 miles northwest of Mexican Hat.

It's a rough road, which gets impassable when wet, but so long as you don't mind a few bangs on the bottom as you cross dry stony washes you should be able to make it in a rental car. The east side holds the best of the "monuments," and the most difficult terrain, but there's something to be said for driving in from the west, which offers great views all the way along.

The only building en route is the *Valley of the Gods* **B&B** (PO Box 310307, Mexican Hat, UT 84531; ☎970/749-1164, fax 435/638-2292; ⑤), which squats in superb isolation half a mile in from the west. All its four rooms have baths, dinner is served by prior arrangement, and the owners can also fix backcountry **tours**.

Mexican Hat

MEXICAN HAT, the last halt in southeastern Utah before the start of the Navajo Indian Reservation across the San Juan River, is an appealingly fly-blown outpost that has never amounted to the status of a town. It first sprang into being in 1901, following false reports that gold had been discovered nearby, and was kept going by a genuine oil strike in 1908, and the uranium boom of the 1950s. For tourists, it now makes a convenient base for **Monument Valley**, twenty miles south (see p.45).

Mexican Hat Rock, the sandstone sombrero for which the settlement was named, looks down on the San Juan a mile north. The highway passes a few hundred yards west, but a gravel road permits closer inspection. It's at its best in the afternoon, when the sun strikes the amazing zigzag striations of the gray and white cliffs across the river. This pattern, known as the **Navajo Blanket**, is said to show the skin markings of a giant bullsnake that lives in the river below, and carved out the "goosenecks" to the west (see p.482).

Accommodation and eating

*The zip code
for Mexican
Hat is UT
84531.*

All Mexican Hat's four **motels**, except the budget *Canyonland*, have their own restaurants and stores, and are substantially the same. There are virtually no other buildings around.

Burch's Trading Co & Motel, PO Box 310337, US-163; ☎435/683-2221, fax 683-2246. Modern, timber-built motel, 100 yards up from the river, with an atmospheric cafe, *Burch's*. There's also a separate $12 campground, plus a grocery and a Conoco gas station. Winter ②, summer ④.

Canyonland Motel, PO Box 310187, US-163; ☎435/683-2230. Very basic ten-room motel, on the higher side of the highway next to the Texaco gas station, and open in summer only. ②.

Mexican Hat Lodge, PO Box 310175, US-163; ☎435/683-2222, fax 683-2203. Mexican Hat's northernmost motel, with a pool and a nice open-air steakhouse. Winter ②, summer ④.

San Juan Inn & Trading Post, PO Box 310276, US-163; ☎435/683-2220 or 1-800/447-2022, fax 435/683-2210. The number-one choice; solid, long-established motel perched fifty feet above the north bank of the San Juan, beside the highway bridge. The *Olde Bridge Bar and Grill* serves a full menu from 7am daily, ranging from Navajo tacos to steaks, plus cold beers. Winter ②, summer ④.

Chapter 8

Las Vegas and Salt Lake City

Together with Phoenix and Albuquerque, **Las Vegas** and **Salt Lake City** hold the most convenient major **airports** for travelers who plan to explore the Southwest. Las Vegas is just a couple of hours' drive from Zion National Park in southwest Utah, and a quick flight from the Grand Canyon; Salt Lake City is half a day by car from Moab and Canyonlands. Apart from being handy places to rent a car and set off into the wilderness, however, it's hard to imagine two cities with less in common. Which one suits you best depends whether you rank yourself among the Saints – in which case you can have a good night's sleep in straight-laced Salt Lake City before you hit the road – or the sinners, and fancy a lost weekend in loose-living Las Vegas.

Las Vegas

Little emphasis is placed on the gambling clubs and divorce facilities – though they are attractions to many visitors – and much is being done to build up the cultural attractions. No cheap and easily parodied slogans have been adopted to publicize the city, no attempt has been made to introduce pseudo-romantic architectural themes or to give artificial glamor or gaiety. Las Vegas is itself – natural and therefore very appealing to people with a wide variety of interests.

WPA Guidebook to Nevada, 1940

Shimmering from the desert haze of Nevada like a latter-day El Dorado, **LAS VEGAS** is the most dynamic, spectacular city on earth. At the start of the twentieth century, it didn't even exist; now it's home to over one million people, with enough newcomers arriving all

---

For an exhaustive account of Las Vegas, see the separate *Rough Guide to Las Vegas*, also by Greg Ward.

the time to need a new school every month. Boasting fourteen of the world's fifteen largest hotels, it's a monument to architectural exuberance, where flamboyant, no-expense-spared **casinos** lure in over thirty million tourists each year. Las Vegas has been stockpiling superlatives since the 1950s, but never rests on its laurels for a moment. Long before they lose their sparkle, yesterday's showpieces are blasted into rubble to make way for ever more extravagant replacements. A few years ago, when the fashion was for fantasy, Arthurian castles and Egyptian pyramids mushroomed along the legendary Strip; now Vegas demands nothing less than entire cities, and

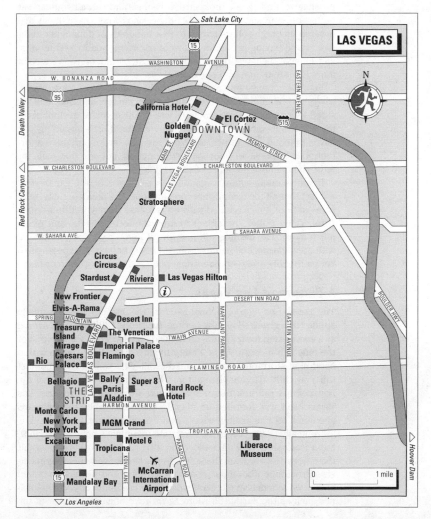

Las Vegas has already acquired pocket versions of New York, Paris, Monte Carlo and Venice.

While Las Vegas has certainly cleaned up its act since the early days of Mob domination, there's little truth in the notion that it's become a **family** destination. In fact, for kids, it's not a patch on Orlando. Several casinos have added theme parks or fun rides to fill those odd non-gambling moments, but only five percent of visitors bring children, and the crowds that cluster around the exploding volcanoes and pirate battles along the Strip remain almost exclusively adult. Neither is Vegas as consistently **cheap** as it used to be. It's still possible to find good, inexpensive rooms, and the all-you-can-eat buffets offer unbeatable value, but the casino owners have finally discovered that high-rollers happy to lose hundreds of dollars per night don't mind paying premium prices to eat at top-quality restaurants, and some of the latest developments are budgeting on room rates of more like $300 than $30 per night.

Your first hours in Las Vegas are like entering another world, where the religion is luck, the language is money, and time is measured by revolutions of a roulette wheel. Once you're acclimatized, the whole spectacle can be absolutely exhilarating – assuming you haven't pinned your hopes, and your savings, on the pursuit of a fortune. Las Vegas is an unmissable destination, but one that palls for most visitors after a couple of (hectic) days.

If you've come solely to gamble, there's not much to say beyond the fact that all the casinos are free, and open 24 hours per day, with acres of floor space packed with ways to lose money: **million-dollar slots**, video **poker**, **blackjack**, **craps**, **roulette** wheels, and much much more. The casinos will just love it if you try to play a system; with the odds stacked against you, your best hope of a large win is to bet your entire stake on one single play, and then stop, win or lose.

A history of Las Vegas

The name *Las Vegas* – Spanish for "the meadows" – originally applied to a group of natural springs that from 1829 onwards served as a way station for travelers on the Old Spanish Trail. For the rest of the nineteenth century, the Paiute Indians shared the region with a handful of Mormon ranchers, and the valley had a population of just thirty in 1900. Things changed in 1905, with the completion of the now-defunct rail link between Salt Lake City and Los Angeles. Las Vegas itself was founded on May 15 that year, when the railroads auctioned off lots around what's now Fremont Street.

Ironically, Nevada was the first state to outlaw gambling, in 1909, but it was made legal once more in 1931, and the workers who built the nearby Hoover Dam flocked to Vegas to bet away their pay-packets. Providing abundant cheap electricity and water, the dam amounted to a massive federal subsidy for the infant city. Hotel-casinos such as the daring 65-room *El Rancho* began to appear in the early 1940s, but the Midwest Mafia were the first to appreciate the potential for profit. Mobster Bugsy Siegel raised $7 million to open the *Flamingo* on the Strip in December 1946; early losses forced him to close again in January, and although he swiftly managed to

Getting Married in Las Vegas

Second only to making your fortune as a reason to visit Las Vegas is the prospect of **getting married**. Over a hundred thousand weddings are performed here each year, many so informal that bride and groom just wind down the window of their car during the ceremony, and a Vegas wedding has become a byword for tongue-in-cheek chic. What's more surprising, however, is that most marriages are deeply formal affairs. Both the casinos and a horde of independent wedding chapels compete to offer elaborate ceremonies with all the traditional trimmings, from white gowns and black limousines, to garters and boutonnieres. Especially busy days include New Year's Eve, which gives American couples the right to file a joint tax return for the preceding year, and Valentine's Day.

You don't have to be a local resident or take a blood test to get wed here. Assuming you're both at least eighteen years old and carrying picture ID, and not already married, simply turn up at the Clark County Marriage License Bureau, downtown at 200 S Third St (Mon–Thurs 8am–midnight, and continuously from 8am on Fri to midnight on Sun; ☎702/455-4416), and buy a marriage license for $35 cash.

Wedding chapels claim to charge as little as $50 for basic ceremonies, but at that sort of rate even the minister is an "extra" costing an additional $40. Reckon on paying at least $100 for the bare minimum, which is liable to be as romantic a process as checking in at a hotel, and to take about as long. The full deluxe service ranges up to around $500. Novelty options include taking your vows perched on a tiny platform at A.J. Hackett Bungy at *Circus Circus* (☎702/385-4321), then plummeting on an 18-story bungee jump, while Las Vegas Helicopters (☎702/736-0013) can provide a ceremony either hovering over the Strip or on the rim of the Grand Canyon.

Candlelight Wedding Chapel, 2855 Las Vegas Blvd S; ☎702/735-4179 or 1-800/962-1818. Busy little chapel across from *Circus Circus*, where you get a garter with the $169 wedding package, or two white T-shirts with the $499 option.

Graceland Wedding Chapel, 619 Las Vegas Blvd S; ☎702/474-6655 or 1-800/824-5732. Home of the King – an Elvis impersonator will act as best man, give the bride away or serenade you, but unfortunately he can't perform the service.

Little Church of the West, 4617 Las Vegas Blvd S; ☎702/739-7971 or 1-800/821-2452. Once part of the *Last* *Frontier* casino, this fifty-year-old chapel is on the National Register of Historic Places, and has moved progressively down the Strip to its current site south of *Mandalay Bay*. Among the more peaceful and quiet places to exchange your Vegas vows – if that's really what you want.

Little White Chapel, 1301 Las Vegas Blvd S; ☎702/382-5943 or 1-800/545-8111. Where Bruce Willis and Demi Moore married each other, and Michael Jordan and Joan Collins married other people. Open all day every day, with the "The One & Only 24hr Drive-Up Wedding Window," if you're in a major hurry.

Elvis married Priscilla at the Aladdin on May 1, 1967, nine months to the day before the birth of Lisa Marie, and eight years before Michael Jackson met Lisa Marie at a Jackson Five gig in Vegas.

re-open in March, his erstwhile partners were dissatisfied enough with their returns to have him murdered in LA in June.

By the 1950s, Las Vegas was booming. The military had arrived – mushroom clouds from **A-bomb tests** in the deserts were visible from the city, and visitors would drive out with picnics to get a better view – and so too had big guns like **Frank Sinatra**, who debuted at the *Desert Inn* in 1951, and **Liberace**, who received $50,000 to open the *Riviera* in 1955. As the stars gravitated towards the Vegas honeypot, nightclubs across America went out of business, and the city became the nation's undisputed live-entertainment capital.

The beginning of the end for Mob rule in Vegas came in 1966, after reclusive airline tycoon **Howard Hughes** sold TWA for $500 million and moved into the *Desert Inn*. When the owners tired of his non-gambling ways, he simply bought the hotel, and his clean-cut image encouraged other entrepreneurs to follow suit. **Elvis** arrived a little later; the young rock'n'roller had bombed at the *New Frontier* in 1956, but started a triumphant five-year stint as a karate-kicking lounge lizard at the *International* (now the *Las Vegas Hilton*) in 1969.

Endless federal swoops and stings drove the Mob out of sight by the 1980s, in time for Vegas to reinvent itself on a surge of junk-bond megadollars. The success of Steve Wynn's *Mirage* in enticing a new generation of visitors, from 1989 onwards, spawned a host of imitators. The 1990s kicked off with a spate of casino building, including *Excalibur* and the *MGM Grand*, that has barely let up since, with *Luxor* and *New York–New York* followed as the millennium approached by the opulent quartet of *Bellagio*, *Mandalay Bay*, the *Venetian* and *Paris*. Beneath the glitz, however, **gambling** remains the bedrock, and Las Vegas' preeminence seems little dented by the spread of casinos elsewhere in the US. City boosters point out that only fifteen percent of Americans have so far seen Vegas, and they're confidently expecting the rest to turn up any day now.

Arrival, information and getting around

National and international flights to Las Vegas are detailed on p.3 onwards.

Las Vegas' busy **McCarran International Airport** is a mile east of the southern end of the Strip, and four miles from downtown (☎702/261-5743). Some hotels run free shuttle buses for guests, while Bell Trans (☎702/739-7990) run a **minibus** service to the Strip ($3.50) and downtown ($5), and a **cab** to the Strip costs from $9 for the southern end up to $15 for casinos further north.

If you plan to see more of Vegas than the Strip – and even there, it's too hot in summer to walk more than a couple of blocks in the daytime – a **car** is invaluable. All the rental companies listed on p.20 have outlets at the airport; Allstate (☎1-800/634-6186) is an inexpensive local alternative. **Public transport** does exist, however. The oak-veneered streetcars of the **Las Vegas Strip Trolley** (☎702/382-1404) ply the Strip between *Mandalay Bay* and the *Stratosphere*, for a flat fare of $1.40, while the similar **Downtown Trolley**

(☎702/229-0624) loops between the *Stratosphere* and downtown for 50¢. CAT buses (☎702/228-7433) serve the whole city; #301 and #302 connect the Strip to downtown ($1.50). Greyhound's long-distance buses use a terminal at 200 S Main St downtown. Several Strip casinos are also connected by free **monorail systems**, but these don't link up with each other, and most require you to walk through the full length of the casinos in order to use them.

Any number of local freesheets and magazines – usually bursting with discount vouchers – provide local information. There are also **visitor centers** at 3150 Paradise Rd (Mon–Fri 8am–6pm, Sat & Sun 8am–5pm; ☎702/892-0711 or 1-800/332-5333), half a mile east of the Strip inside the vast Convention Center, and 711 E Desert Inn Rd (Mon–Fri 8am–5pm; ☎702/735-1616). There can be no easier city in which to change money: the casinos gladly convert almost any currency, and their walls are festooned with every conceivable ATM machine.

Accommodation

Although Las Vegas has well over 100,000 motel and hotel rooms (most of them hitched to casinos), it's best to book accommodation ahead if you're on a tight budget, or arriving on Friday or Saturday; upwards of 200,000 people descend upon the city every weekend. Whatever you may have heard, Las Vegas hotels no longer offer incredibly cheap deals at the drop of a hat; with occupancy rates averaging ninety percent year-round, they don't need to. It is true that serious gamblers can get their accommodation free, but to count as "serious" you'd have to commit yourself to gambling several thousand dollars, which is a pretty strange definition of "free."

Precise **room rates** are entirely dictated by supply and demand. Even if you stay in the same room for several consecutive days, you'll be charged a different rate for each day, depending not only on the day of the week but also which conventions or events may be happening in town, and the hotel's general level of business. Whatever rate you're quoted for a particular day, it's always worth trying a little negotiation; you may get a discount if you're attending a convention, or simply for belonging to a motoring organization such as the AAA or the British AA. However, the only sure-fire way to get a cut-price room is to **visit during the week** rather than the weekend. Rates everywhere rise enormously on Friday or Saturday; expect to pay perhaps $30 extra per night in a lower-end property, more like $50 to $100 extra in the big-name casinos. On top of that, many hotels won't accept Saturday arrivals. The Convention & Visitors Bureau runs a reservation service on ☎ 1-800/332-5333.

If you're planning a trip from elsewhere in North America, check local newspaper advertisements for the latest Vegas bargains – virtually all hotels and motels offer discounts and food vouchers.

Las Vegas

Amtrak trains no longer serve Las Vegas, but a new high-speed service between LA and Las Vegas is rumored to be coming soon.

For details of flights and tours from Las Vegas to the Grand Canyon, see p.328.

Unless otherwise noted, the zip code for all properties listed here is NV 89109.

Most of the casino-hotels reviewed here are described in detail on p.495 onwards.

Las Vegas

As explained on p.15, accommodation prices, excluding taxes, are indicated throughout this book by the following symbols:

① *up to $30*
② *$30–45*
③ *$45–60*
④ *$60–80*
⑤ *$80–100*
⑥ *$100–130*
⑦ *$130–175*
⑧ *$175–250*
⑨ *$250+*

Bear in mind that room rates shown here rise during major events.

The Strip

Bellagio, 3600 Las Vegas Blvd S; ☎702/791-7111 or 1-888/987-6667, fax 702/792-7646; *www.bellagiolasvegas.com*. The very top of the spectrum. Extremely luxurious rooms, with plush European furnishings and marble bathrooms; amazing pool complex; and the best restaurants in town. Sun–Thurs ⑦, Fri & Sat ⑧.

Caesars Palace, 3570 Las Vegas Blvd S; ☎702/731-7222 or 1-800/634-6661, fax 702/731-6636; *www.caesars.com*. Right in the heart of the Strip, the epitome of 1960s luxury has recently trebled in size, and offers the last word in pseudo-Roman splendor, with top-class restaurants and shops. Sun–Thurs ⑤, Fri & Sat ⑥.

Circus Circus, 2880 Las Vegas Blvd S; ☎702/734-0410 or 1-800/444-2472, fax 702/734-5987; *www.circuscircus-lasvegas.com*. Venerable Strip hotel that's popular with budget tour groups. Kids love the theme park and circus acts, adults love the low room rates. The rooms in the Manor section at the back are pretty grim; pay a little more to stay in the Tower section. Sun–Thurs ③, Fri & Sat ④.

Excalibur, 3850 Las Vegas Blvd S; ☎702/597-7700 or 1-800/937-7777, fax 702/597-7040; *www.excalibur-casino.com*. This fantastically garish fake castle offers plenty to amuse the kids while the adults gamble away their college funds, but its four thousand rooms are pretty poor in quality, and only minimally themed. Few have views to speak of – many face in rather than out – and they have showers not baths. Thanks to an endless stream of tour groups and families, the whole place tends to be uncomfortably crowded. Sun–Thurs ③, Fri & Sat ④.

Flamingo Hilton, 3555 Las Vegas Blvd S; ☎702/733-3111 or 1-800/732-2111, fax 702/733-3353; *www.hilton.com*. The latest round of renovations has put Bugsy Siegel's *Flamingo* back in the premier league of Vegas casinos, with over 3600 well-appointed rooms and a great tropical-themed pool. Sun–Thurs ④, Fri & Sat ⑤.

Imperial Palace, 3535 Las Vegas Blvd S; ☎702/731-3311 or 1-800/634-6441, fax 702/735-8578; *www.imperialpalace.com*. Behind its hideous facade, this is one of the best-value options in the heart of the Strip. Its standard rooms are adequate if not exciting – all have balconies – while the irresistible "luv tub" suites, at $30 extra, offer huge beds, even bigger sunken baths, and mirrors absolutely everywhere. Sun–Thurs ②, Fri & Sat ④.

La Concha, 2955 Las Vegas Blvd S; ☎702/735-1255, fax 369-0862. Quintessential space-age motel opposite the *Stardust*, holding over three hundred very ordinary rooms and a couple of swimming pools. What you lose in glamour and comfort you gain in convenience. Sun–Thurs ②, Fri & Sat ③.

Luxor Las Vegas, 3900 Las Vegas Blvd S, NV 89119. ☎702/262-4000 or 1-800/288-1000, fax 702/262-4406; *www.luxor.com*. A night in this vast smoked-glass pyramid is one of the great Las Vegas experiences. All the 2000 large rooms in the pyramid itself face outwards, with tremendous views. Unlike the additional 2000 rooms in the new Tower next door, however – some of which have jacuzzis next to the windows – most have showers not baths. All are enjoyably Egyptian-themed. Sun–Thurs ③, Fri & Sat ⑥.

Mandalay Bay, 3950 Las Vegas Blvd S, NV 89119. ☎702/632-7777 or 1-877/632-7000, fax 702/632-7190; *www.mandalaybay.com*. Young-adult playground that can feel a little far removed from the central Strip. Each of its luxurious rooms has both bath and walk-in shower; the theming varies, and the floor plans can be a bit odd, but some have great Strip views. Guests have exclusive access to the spectacular wave pool. Sun–Thurs ⑤, Fri & Sat ⑦.

MGM Grand, 3799 Las Vegas Blvd S; ☎702/891-7777 or 1-800/929-1112, fax 702/891-1000; *www.mgmgrand.com*. The downsides of staying at the world's largest hotel, with 5005 rooms and more on the way, are that waiting for any kind of service, especially check-in, can be horrendous, and that walking from one end to the other can take half an hour. There are plenty of positives, however, including the standard of accommodation you get for the price, and the on-site presence of several of Las Vegas' finest restaurants. Sun–Thurs ④, Fri & Sat ⑤.

The Mirage, 3400 Las Vegas Blvd S; ☎702/791-7111 or 1-800/627-6667, fax 702/791-7446; *www.themirage.com*. The glitzy *Mirage* is not the market leader it was, and its generally smallish rooms seem less distinctive now they've lost their tropical theming. Even so, the public areas downstairs remain impressive, and the weekday rates for staying in one of Las Vegas's most prestigious addresses aren't at all bad – plus, of course, you get to watch the volcano from your bedroom window. Sun–Thurs ⑤, Fri & Sat ⑦.

New York–New York, 3790 Las Vegas Blvd S; ☎702/740-6969 or 1-800/NYFORME, fax 702/740-6920; *www.nynyhotelcasino.com*. Sheer attention to detail makes *New York–New York* the most exuberantly enjoyable casino on the Strip. It's also small enough that guests don't have to spend half their visit shuffling down endless corridors. The rooms themselves are very nice, if a bit small, and filled with Art Deco furnishings and flourishes. Sun–Thurs ⑤, Fri & Sat ⑦.

Paris-Las Vegas, 3645 Las Vegas Blvd S; ☎702/967-4611 or 1-888/BON-JOUR, fax 702/967-4288; *www.parislasvegas.com*. Flamboyant new casino, where the rooms and services are pitched slightly below those of Las Vegas' most upscale Vegas joints, but the location, views and general ambience are superb. Sun–Thurs ⑤, Fri & Sat ⑦.

Stratosphere, 2000 Las Vegas Blvd S, NV 89104; ☎702/380-7777 or 1-800/99-TOWER, fax 702/383-4755. The *Stratosphere* has confounded the skeptics by surviving at all, despite its unfashionable location at the far north end of the Strip, thanks largely to low room rates and a steady flow of budget tour groups. Its rooms are large but not fancy in any way, and only have small windows. None of the accommodation is in the hundred-story tower, so don't expect amazing views, but otherwise it's not a bad deal. Sun–Thurs ②, Fri & Sat ④.

Treasure Island, 3300 Las Vegas Blvd S; ☎702/894-7111 or 1-800/944-7444, fax 702/894-7414; *www.treasureisland.com*. Sister hotel to the neighboring *Mirage*, geared towards young, affluent parents with their kids in tow; the theming is fun, but the (smallish) rooms are quite subdued in a pastel-toned sort of way. Stay on the Strip side for a great view of the pirate battle, even though the balconies are just for show. Sun–Thurs ④, Fri & Sat ⑦.

Tropicana, 3801 Las Vegas Blvd S; ☎702/739-2222 or 1-800/634-4000, fax 702/739-2469. Jungle-themed casino, recently spruced up to compete with its giant neighbors, but still offering swim-up gaming tables around the world's largest indoor–outdoor swimming pool. Sun–Thurs ④, Fri & Sat ⑦.

The Venetian, 3355 Las Vegas Blvd S; ☎702/414-1000 or 1-888/283-6423, fax 702/733-5560; *www.venetian.com*. Even the standard rooms at this upscale behemoth are split-level suites, offering antique-style canopied beds on a raised platform, plus roomy living rooms. Each also has a marble bath and walk-in shower. Sun–Thurs ⑦, Fri & Sat ⑨.

Accommodation elsewhere

California Hotel, 12 Ogden Ave at First St, NV 89101. ☎702/385-1222 or 1-800/634-6255, fax 702/388-4463. Almost all the guests in this mid-range downtown casino are Hawaiian, and Hawaiian food and drink dominate the bars and restaurants. The actual rooms are plain but adequate. Sun–Thurs ③, Fri & Sat ④.

El Cortez Hotel, 600 E Fremont St, NV 89102; ☎702/385-5200 or 1-800/634-6703, fax 702/385-1554. Veteran downtown casino, where the cut-price rooms in the main building are a little better than the rather dismal gaming area downstairs might suggest. The mini-suites in the new tower are really good value at $40, and the bargain-basement accommodation in *Ogden House* across the street costs just $18. ①.

Golden Gate Hotel, 1 E Fremont St, NV 89101. ☎702/385-1906 or 1-800/426-1906. The oldest joint in town, founded in 1906 when Las Vegas was just a year old. With 100 retro-furnished rooms, it's tiny by Vegas standards, and likes to call itself a B&B, but really it's a hotel-casino much like its downtown neighbors. Sun–Thurs ②, Fri & Sat ③.

Hard Rock Hotel, 4475 Paradise Rd; ☎702/693-5000 or 1-800/693-ROCK, fax 702/693-5010; *www.hardrockhotel.com*. Thanks to the high profile of the Hard Rock name, you might assume that "the world's only rock'n'roll casino" is the best in town; it isn't. Over a mile east of the Strip, it's a pale and overpriced imitation of Las Vegas' showcase giants. That said, the guestrooms are well above average, with French windows that actually open, and the pool is great. Sun–Thurs ⑤, Fri & Sat ⑦.

Las Vegas Backpackers Hostel, 1322 E Fremont St, NV 89101; ☎702/385-1150 or 1-800/550-8958, fax 702/385-4940; *www.hostels.com/us.nv.html*. Well-kept private hostel in a grim neighborhood ten blocks east of downtown, offering dorm beds for $15 and private double rooms for $45, plus use of a good pool. ①–③.

Las Vegas International Hostel, 1208 Las Vegas Blvd S, NV 89104; ☎702/385-9955; *www.hostels.com/us.nv.html*. Bare-bones AAIH hostel in a small, dilapidated former motel, in an insalubrious area on the fringes of downtown not far north of the *Stratosphere*. Dorm beds cost $14, rooms with shared bath under $30, which for two or more visitors is little cheaper than some Strip and several downtown hotels. Nonetheless, demand is heavy, especially in summer. ①.

Main Street Station, 200 N Main St at Ogden, NV 89101. ☎702/387-1896 or 1-800/713-8933; *www.mainstreetcasino.com*. Downtown's best-value option, two short blocks from Fremont St, holds four hundred large guestrooms plus a brewpub and an assortment of good restaurants. ③.

Motel 6 – Tropicana, 195 E Tropicana Ave; ☎702/798-0728, fax 798-5657. Despite its 880 rooms, the largest *Motel 6* in the country is much the same as the rest – a low-rise straggle of very routine lodgings. The location is good, just ten minutes' walk off the Strip, and may well mean that it gets redeveloped shortly. Sun–Thurs ②, Fri & Sat ③.

Rio, 3700 W Flamingo Rd, NV 89103. ☎702/252-7777 or 1-800/PLAY-RIO, fax 702/253-6090; *www.playrio.com*. The only Vegas casino not on the Strip or downtown that seriously attempts to rival the Strip giants. The restaurants, bars and buffets are all excellent, and the rooms are large and luxurious, with floor-to-ceiling windows and great views. However, the prices are not cheap, and whatever the *Rio* likes to pretend, the Strip stands half a mile away to the east, along a highway no one would ever dream of walking. Sun–Thurs ⑨, Fri & Sat ⑦.

Super 8, 4250 Koval Lane; ☎702/794-0888 or 1-800/800-8000, fax 702/794-3504. The closest of Vegas' three *Super 8*s to the Strip offers three hundred rooms, a pool, its own little casino and a reasonable restaurant. Sun–Thurs ②, Fri & Sat ③.

The City

Though the Las Vegas sprawl measures fifteen miles wide by fifteen miles long, most tourists stick to the six-mile stretch of Las Vegas Boulevard that includes both the downtown area, slightly southeast of the intersection of I-15 and US-95, and the Strip, home to the major casinos. In between lie two somewhat seedy miles of gas stations, fast-food drive-ins and wedding chapels, while the rest of town is largely residential, and need barely concern you at all.

The Strip

For its razor-edge finesse in harnessing sheer, magnificent excess to the deadly serious business of making money, there's no place like the Las Vegas Strip. It's hard to imagine that Las Vegas was once an ordinary city, and Las Vegas Boulevard a dusty thoroughfare scattered with the usual edge-of-town motels. After five decades of capitalism run riot, with every new casino-hotel setting out to surpass anything its neighbors ever dreamed of, the Strip seems to be locked into a hyperactive craving for thrills and glamour, forever discarding its latest toy in its frenzy for the next jackpot.

Each casino is a self-contained fantasyland of high camp and genuine excitement. Almost against your will, huge moving walkways sweep you in from the sidewalk; once inside, it can be almost impossible to find your way out. The action keeps going day and night, and in this sealed and windowless environment you rapidly lose track of which is which. Even if you do manage to get back onto the streets during the day, the scorching heat is liable to drive you straight back in again; night is the best time to venture out, when the neon's blazing at its brightest.

As the Strip pushes deeper into the desert, the newest casinos tend to rise at its southern end, not far west of the airport. The procession kicks off with the glowing gilded tower of *Mandalay Bay*, which opened in 1999 and boasts a vaguely Burmese theme. Financed through the profits from its neighbors, *Luxor* and *Excalibur*, *Mandalay Bay* is more upmarket than either, though all it has to offer the casual sightseer is the "Treasures of Mandalay Bay" museum (daily 9.30am–11pm; $7), a dull collection of old coins and banknotes. With an excellent assortment of restaurants as well as the *House of Blues* music venue, however, it's lively at night, while guests are kept happy during the day by the huge wave pool at the back.

Hotel accommodation in Mandalay Bay *and the other major casinos is reviewed on pp.492-3, while selected restaurants are described on p.502 onwards.*

Next door stands the 36-story smoked-glass pyramid of *Luxor*. From the palm-fringed avenue of sphinxes guarding the entrance, to the reconstruction of Tutankhamun's tomb inside, the whole building plays endless variations upon the theme of Egyptian archeology. In Las Vegas' closest approximation to Disneyland, three separate simulator rides and 3-D movies combine to reveal the Secrets of the Luxor Pyramid, a confusing saga of derring-do that's overpriced at $21. Meanwhile, the most powerful artificial light beam ever created shines up from the pyramid's apex; visible from planes circling over LA, 250 miles west, it supposedly pays tribute to the ancient Egyptian belief that the soul of a dead Pharaoh would rise directly into the skies.

Luxor's architect, Veldon Simpson, had previously designed *Excalibur*, immediately north. A less-sophisticated mock-up of a medieval castle, complete with drawbridge, crenellated towers and a basement stuffed with fairground-style sideshows for the kids, it's usually packed out with low-budget tour groups. Its brief reign as the world's largest hotel, from 1990 to 1993, ended when the five-thousand-room *MGM Grand* – another Simpson creation – opened across the street. At that time, the *MGM Grand* sold itself on the strength of having its own **theme park**. Not a patch on the theme parks of Orlando or LA, however, that theme park has long since been scaled down, but the *Grand* is prospering nonetheless. As well as boasting a fine crop of restaurants, it has become the most prestigious big-fight venue in town. Turnover in the casino is so phenomenal that when the crowds after the Holyfield–Tyson debacle in June 1997 mistook the popping of champagne corks for gunfire, and the resulting panic forced the tables to close down for two hours, the loss was estimated in millions of dollars. Its latest attraction, the **Lion Habitat**, is a shameless mix of elements from *Caesars Palace* and the *Mirage*, being a walk-through wooded zoo near the front entrance where real lions lounge around a ruined temple beneath a naturally-lit dome. Admission is free (daily 11am–11pm), while for $20 you can have your photo taken with a cute little lion cub (daily except Tues, 11am–5pm).

Excalibur and the *MGM Grand* are not the only giants facing off across the intersection of Las Vegas Boulevard and Tropicana Avenue, said to be the busiest traffic junction in the US. The northwest corner, diagonally opposite the veteran *Tropicana*, is occupied by an exuberantly meticulous re-creation of the Big Apple, *New York–New York*. This miniature Manhattan – created, like the original, in response to space limitations – boasts a skyline featuring twelve separate skyscrapers, and is fronted, of course, by the Statue of Liberty. Unusually, the interior is every bit as carefully realized, with a lovely rendition of Central Park at dusk (not perhaps somewhere you'd choose to be in real life). In one respect, it even surpasses New York itself; for $5 you can swoop around the whole thing at 65mph on the hair-raising Manhattan Express **roller coaster**.

The original MGM Grand, further up the Strip, was renamed Bally's after it was devastated by a 1980 fire in which 74 people died.

This book went to press before the unveiling of the new *Aladdin*, which is designed to expand upon the Arabian Nights theme of the original 1966 version, and centers on a "Lost City" perched atop an artificial cliff. Its two major selling points are the **Desert Passage** – a shopping and entertainment mall intended to rival the Forum – and an as-yet-undefined "**Music Project.**"

Immediately north of that, *Paris* was the 1999 handiwork of the same team of designers as *New York–New York*. With a half-size Eiffel Tower straddling the Arc de Triomphe and the Opera, it all feels a little compressed, but once again the attention to detail is a joy. Beret-wearing bread-toting bicyclists whistle Gallic tunes as they scurry along its cobbled streets, dodging the stripy-shirted accordionists and smart gendarmes, and there's a fine assortment of top-notch French restaurants. Elevators soar through the roof of the casino and up to the summit of the Eiffel Tower, for stunning views of the city, at their best after dark (daily 10am–1am; $8).

The Eiffel Tower was cheekily positioned to enjoy a perfect prospect of *Bellagio*, opposite, *Mirage* owner Steve Wynn's 1998 attempt to build the best hotel in world history. *Bellagio* is undeniably a breathtaking achievement, and clearly a quantum leap ahead of its Las Vegas competitors, but Wynn set himself a pointless and self-defeating task. Traditionally, casino theming has always been playful – you're not supposed to think that being in *Luxor* is like being in ancient Egypt, just that it's fun to pretend. No longer, however, is it enough to create an illusion; *Bellagio* wants to be real, and somehow more authentic than its original models. The trouble is that *Bellagio* is not in Europe, it's in Las Vegas, and it's stuffed full of slot machines. Inlaid with jewel-like precision into marble counters, perhaps, but still slot machines. The main hotel block, a stately curve of blue and cream pastels, stands aloof from the Strip behind an eight-acre artificial lake. The mere presence of so much water in the desert announces the wealth at *Bellagio*'s disposal, but the point is rubbed in every half-hour at night when hundreds of submerged fountains erupt in Busby-Berkeley water-ballets, choreographed with booming music and colored lights.

Pedestrians enter *Bellagio* at its northeast corner, by means of the **Via Bellagio**, a covered mall of impossibly glamorous designer boutiques, while hotel guests sweep up along a grand waterfront drive to enter a separate sumptuous lobby. That leads in turn to *Bellagio*'s real showpiece, the opulent **Conservatory**. Beneath a *Belle Époque* canopy of copper-framed glass, a network of flowerbeds is replanted every six to eight weeks with ornate seasonal displays. Further back, near the pool, the thirty or so pieces on display at the **Bellagio Gallery of Fine Art** (daily 8am–10pm; $12) may form a very small "Greatest Hits"-style collection, and the admission fee is expensive, but they're uniformly excellent, ranging from an 1874 Renoir, via canvases by Picasso, Monet and Degas, to a Liechtenstein from

1995. All the art is for sale; a big enough win on the tables, and you could walk out with a painting tucked under your arm. To get the full benefits of *Bellagio*, which include a luxurious spa and beauty salon, and an array of six superb landscaped swimming pools, you need to stay at the hotel. For any visitor to Las Vegas, however, it has instantly become a must-see attraction in its own right, representing the best the city has to offer in almost any category you care to think of (with the obvious exception of parking spaces).

Across Flamingo Road from *Bellagio* – this is the intersection where rapper Tupac Shakur was gunned down in 1996 – the long-established **Caesars Palace** still encapsulates Las Vegas at its best. Here, the walkway delivers you past grand marble staircases that lead nowhere, and full-sized replicas of Michaelangelo's David, into a vast labyrinth of slots and green baize, peopled by strutting half-naked Roman centurions and Cleopatra-cropped waitresses. Above the stores and restaurants of the extraordinary **Forum**, the blue-domed ceiling dims and glows as it endlessly cycles from dawn to dusk and back again. The Forum is also home to **Race for Atlantis**, Las Vegas' only 3-D IMAX simulator ride (Sun–Thurs 10am–11pm, Fri & Sat 10am–midnight; $9.50). What you pay is expensive for what you get – shaken to smithereens in front of a short sci-fi B-feature – but few kids seem to leave disappointed. *Caesars* itself has its own giant-screen OMNIMAX movie theater ($7), as well as the elaborate Magical Empire, a dinner-cum-magic-show for which tickets cost $75.

Night-time crowds jostle for space on the sidewalk outside the glittering **Mirage**, beyond *Caesars*, to watch the somewhat half-hearted volcano that erupts every fifteen minutes, spewing water and fire into the lagoon below. Inside, near the main entrance, a couple of Siegfried and Roy's white tigers (see p.507) lounge dopily in a glass-fronted enclosure, and you can also pay to see more of them in the **Secret Garden & Dolphin Habitat** in the garden (Mon–Fri 11am–5.30pm, Sat & Sun 10am–5.30pm; $10, under-10s free). Next door, a pirate galleon and a British frigate, crewed by actors, do noisy battle outside *Treasure Island* (every ninety minutes, daily 4–11pm; free). Around the back, behind the Fashion Show Mall, the **Elvis-A-Rama** memorabilia museum at 3401 Industrial Road (daily except Mon 10am–6pm; $13) keeps the legend of the King alive. It's no Graceland, but you can admire (if not step on) Elvis' very own blue suede shoes, and enjoy regular free impersonator shows.

Opposite *Treasure Island*, another 1999 newcomer, the **Venetian**, incorporates loving facsimiles of six Venice buildings, plus the Rialto Bridge, the Bridge of Sighs, and a deliberately muddy stretch of phony Adriatic Sea. The main emphasis in the casino itself is on the **Grand Canal Shoppes** upstairs. Centered around a ludicrous re-creation of the Grand Canal, complete with gondolas and singing gondoliers ($10 a ride), it's quintessential Las Vegas. The second and third floors of the Venetian's library hold the first US out-post of Madame Tussaud's renowned waxwork museum, called the **Celebrity Encounter** (daily 10am–10pm; $12.50, ages 4–12 $10), because visitors can pose with, touch, and mock the effigies. Unless you've always dreamed of caressing a waxen chef (Wolfgang Puck) or an unresponsive Tom Jones, the whole experience is seriously over-priced, its token animatronic showpieces not a patch on the free shows at *Caesars*.

The family-oriented *Circus Circus*, another mile north, uses live circus acts to pull in the punters – a trapeze artist here, a fire-eater there – and also has an indoor theme park, **Grand Slam Canyon** (Sun–Thurs 10am–6pm, Fri & Sat 10am–midnight), where you pay separately for each roller coaster or river-ride. If you really want to cool off, you'd do better to head on to the flumes and chutes of Vegas' one purpose-built water park, **Wet'n'Wild**, 2601 Las Vegas Blvd S (summer daily 10am–8pm; $24).

Half a mile east of *Circus Circus*, the **Las Vegas Hilton**, at 3000 Paradise Rd, is home to the **Star Trek Experience** (daily 11am–11pm; $15). Visits start from the Space Quest Casino, a sort of Enterprise with slots, to which access is free. If you're lucky enough to arrive when the lines are short – expect to wait up to two hours on summer weekends – you might not realize that the ramp that spirals up from the ticket booths is a glorified queuing area. Glossy display panels recount a wordy chronology featuring high-lights such as World War III in 2053 and the birth of Spock in 2230. Museum-like artifacts and costumes abound, while diminutive Ferengi stroll among you. The whole thing culminates when you're caught up in a dramatic plot to prevent Jean-Luc Picard ever being born, and sent on a mildly vomitous motion-simulator ride through deep space to emerge in a shopping area you could have reached without paying, where memorabilia prices boldly go to well over $2000 for a leather jacket.

Circus Circus has traditionally marked the northern limit of the Strip, though the 1996 opening of the *Stratosphere*, half a mile towards downtown, tried to change that. At 1149 feet, the *Stratosphere* is the tallest building west of the Mississippi, and the outdoor deck and indoor viewing chamber in the sphere near the summit offer amazing city panoramas ($5). Two utterly demented thrill rides can take you even closer to heaven; the world's highest roller coaster swirls around the outside of the sphere, while the ludi-crous Big Shot shunts you to the very top of an additional 160-foot spire, from which you free-fall back down again ($5 each).

Downtown and the Liberace Museum

As the Strip has gone from strength to strength, **downtown** Las Vegas, the city's original core, has by comparison been neglected. Long known as "Glitter Gulch," and consisting of a few compact blocks of lower-key casinos, it has recently embarked upon a revival. Between Main Street and Las Vegas Boulevard, five entire blocks of Fremont Street, its principal thoroughfare, have been roofed with an open-air mesh to create the **Fremont Street Experience**. This "Celestial Vault" is studded with over two million colored light bulbs, choreographed by computer in dazzling nightly displays (hourly, 8pm–midnight; free), but there's a long way to go before the district as a whole can compete with the Strip once again.

The best of the rest of Las Vegas' museums, which are otherwise eminently missable, is the **Liberace Museum**, two miles east of the Strip at 1775 E Tropicana Ave (Mon–Sat 10am–5pm, Sun 1–5pm; $7). Popularly remembered as a beaming buffoon who knocked out torpid toe-tappers, Liberace, who died in 1987, started out playing piano in the bars of Milwaukee during the 1940s. A decade later, he was being mobbed by adolescents and hounded by the scandal-hungry press. All this is recalled by a yellowing collection of cuttings and family photos, along with electric candelabra, bejeweled quail eggs with inlaid pianos, rhinestone-covered fur coats, glittering cars and more. The music, piped into the scented toilets, may not have improved with age, but the museum is a satisfying attempt to answer the seminal question "how does a great performer top himself on stage?".

Red Rock Canyon

For a blast of sunlight and fresh air away from the casinos, and a sample of some classic Southwestern canyon scenery, head twenty miles west of the Strip along Charleston Boulevard to the **Red Rock Canyon National Conservation Area**. This BLM-run park consists of a cactus-strewn desert basin surrounded by stark red cliffs pierced repeatedly by narrow canyons accessible only on foot.

Red Rock Canyon's **visitor center**, which has displays about the canyon and a viewing window overlooking its main features (daily 8.30am–4.30pm; ☎702/363-1921), stands just before the start of the **Scenic Drive** (daily 7am–dusk; $5 per vehicle). As this thirteen-mile loop road meanders around the edge of the basin, it passes trailheads like the one for the cool, slender **Ice Box Canyon** (a 2.5-mile round-trip hike), and the three-mile **Pine Creek Trail**, which follows a flower-lined creek beyond a ruined former homesite towards a towering, red-capped monolith.

Lake Mead and the Hoover Dam

Contrary to popular belief, only four percent of Las Vegas' energy comes from the Hoover Dam.

Almost everyone who goes to Las Vegas visits **LAKE MEAD**, the vast reservoir thirty miles southeast of the city that was created by the construction of the Hoover Dam. As with the similarly incongruous Lake Powell (see p.427) it makes a bizarre spectacle, the blue waters a vivid counterpoint to the surrounding desert, but it gets excruciatingly crowded all year round.

Though the Lake Mead National Recreation Area straddles the border between Nevada and Arizona, the best views come from the Nevada side. Even if you don't need details of how to sail, scuba-dive, water-ski or fish from the marinas along the five-hundred-mile shoreline, call in at the Alan Bible visitor center (daily 8.30am–4.30pm; ☎ 702/293-8990), four miles northeast of Boulder City on US-93, to enjoy a sweeping prospect of the whole thing.

Eight miles on, beyond the rocky ridges of the Black Mountains, US-93 reaches the **Hoover Dam** itself. Designed to block the Colorado River and provide low-cost electricity for the cities of the Southwest, it's among the tallest dams ever built (760ft high), and used enough concrete to build a two-lane highway from the West Coast to New York. It was completed in 1935, as the first step in the Bureau of Reclamation program that culminated with the Glen Canyon Dam (see p.428). Informative half-hour guided tours of the dam leave from the **Hoover Dam Visitor Center** on the Nevada side of the river (daily 8.30am–5.45pm; $8, plus $2 parking; ☎ 702/293-1824).

Las Vegas

Bus tours to the dam from Las Vegas, with Gray Line (☎ 702/384-1234) or other operators, cost around $23 for a five-hour trip.

Eating

Barely ten years ago, the **restaurant** scene in Las Vegas was governed by the notion that visitors were not prepared to pay for gourmet food. All the casinos laid on both pile-'em-high buffets at knock-down prices and 24-hour coffeeshops offering bargain steak-and-egg deals, but the only quality restaurants were upscale Italian places well away from the Strip. Now, however, the situation has reversed, as the major casinos compete to attract culinary superstars from all over the country to open Vegas outlets. Many tourists now come to the city specifically in order to eat at several of the best restaurants in the United States, without having to reserve a table months in advance or pay sky-high prices. Which is not to say that fine dining comes cheap in Las Vegas, just that most of the big-name restaurants are less expensive, and less snooty, than they are in their home cities.

Nonetheless, almost every casino still features an all-you-can-eat **buffet**, open to guests and non-guests alike for every meal of the week. These are not quite as good value as they used to be, and you're no longer likely to wonder how they can possibly afford to keep going. However, even at the worst you're bound to find something you can keep down, and the cost is low enough that you won't feel ripped off. The better buffets tend to be in casinos that are neither on the Strip nor downtown, and depend on locals as well as tourists. These have been at the forefront of innovations like having separate named areas serving different cuisines, or offering "action cooking," where your stir-fry, omelette, fajita or whatever is cooked to your specific order. By contrast, the buffets at the largest casinos, like *Excalibur* and the *MGM Grand*, only have to be good enough to ensure that the crowds already in the building don't leave, while also coping with a daily deluge of customers.

Buffets

Bally's Big Kitchen Buffet, *Bally's*, 3645 Las Vegas Blvd S; ☎702/739-4111. Among the best of the old-style buffets, with breakfast at $9, lunch $10, and dinner $14. A classy spread of fresh meats and seafood – including shrimp at lunchtime – plus a wide-ranging salad bar. Other than a few Chinese dinner entrees, however, it's all rather homogenous. Bally's Champagne Sterling Brunch (Sun 9.30am–2.30pm), served in a separate room, is magnificent – as it should be, for $50.

The Buffet, *Bellagio*, 3600 Las Vegas Blvd S; ☎702/791-7111. Far and away Las Vegas' best buffet. With others, you may rave about what good value they are; with this one, you'll rave about what good food it is. The sheer range is extraordinary. For breakfast ($10), as well as bagels, pastries and eggs, you can have salmon smoked or baked, fruit fresh or in salads, and omelettes cooked to order. Offerings at lunchtime ($12.50) include sushi and sashimi, dim sum, four-cheese tortellini, game hen and quail, plus focaccia, fruit tarts, figs and grapes and fancy desserts. At dinner ($20), the stakes are raised again with the addition of lobster claws, fresh oysters and venison.

Carnival World Buffet, *Rio*, 3700 W Flamingo Rd; ☎702/252-7777. Excellent value, half a mile west of the Strip. The variety is immense, including Thai, Chinese, Mexican and Japanese stations as well as the usual pasta and barbecue, and even a fish'n'chip stand. $8 for breakfast, $10 for lunch, and $12 for dinner.

Feast Around The World, *Sunset Station*, 1301 W Sunset Rd; ☎702/547-7777. All four of the Stations chain of outlying casinos – *Sunset*, *Texas*, *Boulder* and *Palace* – offer similarly appealing, good-value buffets, and attract large crowds of loyal locals. At the large, colorfully themed, *Feast Around The World*, in the very center of *Sunset Station*, roughly seven miles southeast of the Strip, a wide range of international cuisines are dispensed by sections like Mama Mia's pizzas, Chinatown, Country Bar B Que, and Viva Mexico. Breakfast is $4, lunch $6.50, and dinner $9.

Garden Court Buffet, *Main Street Station*, 200 N Main St; ☎702/387-1896. Downtown's best-value buffet, ranging from fried chicken and corn at "South to Southwest," to tortillas at "Ole," and pork chow mein and oyster tofu at "Pacific Rim." Breakfast is $5, lunch $7, and dinner $10.

Le Village Buffet, *Paris*, 3655 Las Vegas Blvd S; ☎702/967-7000. Superb French-only cuisine, with great seafood, succulent roast chicken, and super-fresh vegetables. The setting is a little cramped, squeezed into a very Disney-esque French village, but the food is *magnifique*. Breakfast is $10, lunch $13, and dinner $20.

Restaurants on the Strip

America, *New York–New York*, 3790 Las Vegas Blvd S; ☎702/740-6451. Cavernous 24-hour diner, complete with vast 3-D "map" of the United States. Each menu item supposedly comes from some specific region; thus $4–7 appetizers include California sushi rolls, Cajun mini sticks, and super nachos, while entrees range from Maryland crab cakes ($17), via New York pizzas ($7–9), down to peanut butter sandwiches from Plains Georgia ($4). There really is something for everyone, and it's all surprisingly good.

China Grill, *Mandalay Bay*, 3950 Las Vegas Blvd S; ☎702/632-7404. Large, ultrafashionable Asian restaurant, featuring a $750,000 psychedelic light show. The food is delicious, with appetizers like a crackling calamari salad for $10 and tempura sashimi for $16, and entrees such as dry-aged Szechuan beef with sake and soy for $27.50, or pan-seared tuna for $26. Bizarrely, though, the dishes arrive as they are made; appetizers may appear before, after or simultaneously with entrees. In the more minimal *Zen Sum*, adjoining, diners pick plates of tasty dim sum from a conveyor belt. Dinner only, every night.

Chinois, Forum Shops, *Caesars Palace*, 3570 Las Vegas Blvd S; ☎702/737-9700. At Wolfgang Puck's postmodern Asian-fusion restaurant, the ambience is minimal; there are no tablecloths, ornaments, or even condiments, and the young black-clad staff are too busy posing to provide attentive service. Upmarket, *nouvelle*-tinged appetizers, at $7–10, include moo shu duck, while the best of the entrees, all priced under $20, is a delicious pepper-crusted red snapper in a mushroom-soy broth.

Coyote Cafe, *MGM Grand*, 3799 Las Vegas Blvd S; ☎702/891-7349. Long-established outpost of Mark Miller's definitive "Modern Southwestern" restaurant. The cheaper *Cafe*, open to the casino, offers good-value breakfasts and light lunches as well as much the same dinner menu as the quieter, more formal, *Mark Miller Grill Room* behind, which features appetizers like plantain-crusted sea bass ($11), and slightly less adventurous entrees at $25–30, such as steak and beans or grilled *ahi* (tuna).

The original Coyote Cafe, in Santa Fe, is reviewed on p.118.

Emeril's New Orleans Fish House, *MGM Grand*, 3799 Las Vegas Blvd S; ☎702/891-7374. An authentic slice of New Orleans in the heart of the *MGM Grand*. Cajun seafood with a modern (but never low-cal) twist is the specialty, with barbecue shrimp for $18 at lunchtime and redfish in red bean sauce for $25 at dinner. The menu also includes meat options such as three-way chicken ($21) and steak ($24). Oysters cost $18 per dozen. Daily for lunch and dinner.

Il Fornaio, *New York–New York*, 3790 Las Vegas Blvd S; ☎702/740-6403. This rural-Italian restaurant is the nicest place to enjoy the atmosphere of *New York–New York*. Grab a pizza for $10, or linger over a full meal of soft-shell crab ($9) or carpaccio of beef ($8) to start, followed by gnocchi with smoked salmon ($14), baked sea bass ($18.50), or rotisserie chicken ($14.50). Open daily for all meals.

Le Provencal, *Paris*, 3655 Las Vegas Blvd S; ☎702/946-6932. Bright, cheerful – rather than romantic – restaurant specializing in regional French cooking, with earthy wooden tables and crockery, and jerkin-clad staff who cavort intermittently in a mercifully brief floor show. Dinner entrees like lobster risotto or pepper-stuffed pork may seem expensive at $30–45, but the price includes a full meal of four appetizers, two hot and two cold, such as escargots or mushrooms with beef, and four delicious desserts. Breakfast and lunch are much humbler affairs, with lunchtime pastas and salads costing under $10. As everywhere in *Paris*, the breads are irresistible. Daily for all meals.

Margarita's Mexican Cantina, *New Frontier*, 3120 Las Vegas Blvd S; ☎702/794-8433. Appealingly old-fashioned bar-cum-restaurant that offers the best-value Mexican food on the Strip. Warm tortillas and dips are served as soon as you sit down, while the satisfyingly substantial tacos, burritos, or faji-

Las Vegas

tas cost $8–12, and a 12oz margarita to wash it all down is a mere $3.25. Daily for lunch and dinner.

The Noodle Kitchen, *The Mirage,* 3400 Las Vegas Blvd S; ☎702/456-4564. The inexpensive but top-quality dim sum, and the wide range of noodle dishes ($8–14), stand out on a largely Chinese menu that also extends to meaty plates of pork or duck. The odd location, tucked inside the larger *Caribe Cafe* diner – and sharing the same anonymous buffet-style decor – means you can order an all-American dessert to round it all off. Daily 11am–4am.

Olives, *Bellagio,* 3600 Las Vegas Blvd S; ☎702/693-8181. *Bellagio's* best-value gourmet restaurant is the kind of place that calls a $10 pizza an "individual oven-baked flatbread," and where your food is more likely to be arranged vertically than horizontally, but the largely Mediterranean menu is uniformly fresh and superb. It's a great spot for lunch, with $10–13 appetizers like tuna or beef carpaccio and crispy fried oysters on jumbo ham hocks, pasta dishes like Israeli couscous carbonara ($9.50), and specials such as barbecued yellow-fin tuna ($18.50). Dinner entrees are pricier, but at least they come with a platter of huge, delicious olives. Daily for lunch and dinner.

Spago's, Forum Shops, *Caesars Palace,* 3570 Las Vegas Blvd S; ☎702/369-6300. Surreal, space-age new-Californian restaurant that remains Vegas' premier site for star-spotting. Watch the world go by with a designer pizza or sandwich in the mall-level, all-day sidewalk *Cafe,* priced at $10–20, or sneak the odd peek at your elite co-diners in the exclusive (but noisy) interior dinner-only *Dining Room,* while you swoon over the tuna sashimi, steamed lobster, or Chinese duck, with entrees for $15–30.

Wolfgang Puck Cafe, *MGM Grand,* 3799 Las Vegas Blvd S; ☎702/895-9653. Designer-diner-cum-cafe, where they'll whisk you through your meal in the blink of an eye, but you won't be disappointed with the food. The large breakfast menu includes well-priced Benedicts and omelettes, and three eggs for $6. Later on, $10 buys one of Puck's signature postmodern pizzas or a delicious salad; Pad Thai noodles or meatloaf go for $13–15, and sesame seared *ahi* (tuna) with horseradish mashed potatoes costs $19. No reservations. Daily for breakfast, lunch and dinner.

Restaurants elsewhere

Binion's Horseshoe Coffee Shop, *Binion's Horseshoe,* 128 E Fremont St ☎702/382-1600. The 24-hour Las Vegas coffeeshop of your dreams. The setting is exactly right, in the basement of this veteran downtown casino, and the food is American-diner-heaven. Between 10pm and 5am, a steak dinner costs just $3, but even at prime time (4.45–11.45pm), a 16oz T-bone is only $6.75. Breakfast is highly recommended, and better value than any buffet; the $3 "Benny Binion's Natural," served 2am–2pm, consists of two eggs, bacon or ham, toast, tea or coffee, and magnificent home fries.

Costa Del Sol Oyster Bar, *Sunset Station,* 1301 W Sunset Rd; ☎702/547-7777. Pleasant, spacious casino restaurant, sadly seven miles southeast of the Strip, serving great seafood from around the world. Shellfish comes raw, with oysters or clams at $8 per half-dozen; steamed, with clams at $12 and New Zealand mussels at $13; in Mediterranean stews, like a French *bouillabaisse* or an Italian *cioppino,* and in gumbos or roasted, for around $16. Daily for lunch and dinner.

Enigma Garden Cafe, 918 S Fourth St; ☎702/386-0999. "Alternative" cafe in a pretty seedy area just south of downtown. All the coffees, teas and sodas you'd expect, plus deli sandwiches (not all vegetarian), hummus wraps, tortillas and so on for $5–7. The service is ramshackle, but it's a good place to pick up on non-mainstream local happenings. Closed Mon.

Mr Lucky's 24/7, *Hard Rock Hotel*, 4455 Paradise Rd; ☎702/693-5000. Very stylish 24-hour coffeeshop, with an open kitchen, faux-fur booths, and subdued tan-and-cream paint-job, where the food is well above average. As well as all the usual breakfast items, it serves burgers, sandwiches, pizzas and pasta dishes for $6–10, a 12oz steak for $14, and milkshakes or microbrews for $3.50.

Second Street Grill, *Sam Boyd's Fremont Hotel*, 200 E Fremont St; ☎702/385-3232. Downtown's most original fine-dining option, a dinner-only "Pacific Rim" restaurant that draws heavily on Chinese, Thai and Japanese traditions. Appetizers, mostly costing $10–12, are largely seafood, including *ahi* (tuna) sashimi and crab cakes; there are more meat entrees, such as steaks for $22–24 or Chinese duck for $19, but the signature dish is a whole red snapper, prepared Thai style, for $28.

Bars and Clubs

As the perfect fuel to turn a dithering gawker into a diehard gambler, alcohol is very easy to come by in Las Vegas. If you want a drink in a casino, there's no need to look for a bar; instead, a tray-toting waitress will come and find you. All the casinos do have actual **bars** as well, ranging from open-sided **lounges** in the heart of the gaming area to **brewpubs** and themed nightspots tucked well away from the action.

As for **live music**, check newspapers like *City Life* and the *Las Vegas Review Journal* to see who's appearing when you're in town, or call casinos like the *Grand* or *Caesars Palace*. In general, it'll help if your tastes are rooted in the 1960s or even earlier, but some of the newer breed of casinos are now orienting themselves towards younger audiences.

Angles / Club Lace, 4633 Paradise Rd; ☎702/791-0100. Two distinct 24-hour gay bars – *Angles* is predominantly for men, *Club Lace* is more mixed but has some women-only nights – devoted more to drinking and cruising than dancing.

The Beach, 365 Convention Center Drive; ☎702/731-1925. 24-hour dance club, just east of the Strip, which attracts a very young crowd to the massive dance floor downstairs, decked out with palm trees and coconuts, and sports bar upstairs.

Breathe . . ., 4750 W Sahara Ave, suite 32; ☎702/258-4502. Something really different, a couple of miles west of the Strip; an oxygen bar, where customers pay to be hooked up to canisters of pure oxygen flavored with aromatherapy oils. It costs a dollar a minute, for a minimum of ten minutes, and not everyone even notices it's happening, but still.

Gaudi Bar, *Sunset Station*, 1301 W Sunset Rd, Henderson; ☎702/547-7777. Las Vegas' most weird and wonderful casino lounge, seven miles southeast of the Strip. A billowing mosaic-encrusted toadstool of a tribute to Spanish architect Gaudi, complete with faux-sky underbelly.

Gipsy, 4605 Paradise Rd; ☎702/731-9677. High-profile gay dance club, whose success has spurred the emergence of the surrounding gay business district. There's normally some form of live entertainment to justify the $5 cover charge, and there are all-you-can-drink-for-$5 beer busts most evenings too. Nightly except Mon.

House of Blues, *Mandalay Bay*, 3950 Las Vegas Blvd S; ☎702/632-7600. The Strip's premier live music venue, the voodoo-tinged, folk-art-decorated *House of Blues* has a definite but not exclusive emphasis towards blues, R&B, and black music in general. Typical prices range from around $25 for medium names up to $65 for stars like BB King.

The Joint, *Hard Rock*, 4455 Paradise Rd; ☎702/693-5066. The venue of choice for big-name touring rock acts, not least because its affluent baby-boom profile enables someone like Ringo Starr to charge $127 for a ticket. Differing levels of admission for performers such as Elvis Costello or Neil Young range between around $40 and $80; cheaper rates are for the much less atmospheric balcony.

Monte Carlo Pub & Brewery, *Monte Carlo*, 3770 Las Vegas Blvd S; ☎702/730-7000. Massive microbrewery on the Strip that's better for an early-evening drink before it turns into a deafening retro dance club at 9pm.

Ra Nightclub, *Luxor*, 3900 Las Vegas Blvd S; ☎702/262-4400. Despite the gloriously camp Egyptian motifs, *Ra* feels like a real city nightclub, catering to a ferociously hip and very glamorous crowd. Cage dancers watch over a changing schedule of special nights, usually with playful quasi-erotic tinges. Nightly Wed–Sat.

rumjungle, *Mandalay Bay*, 3950 Las Vegas Blvd S; ☎702/632-7408. Part nightclub, part restaurant – open daily for dinner only – *rumjungle* is a fabulous experience, where the entire facade is a "fire wall" of erupting gas jets, semi-naked showgirls gyrate at the door, and there's a colossal list of good-value cocktails and specialty rums. The chic and beautiful crowd is mostly Latin, and stays up dancing until 2am on weekdays, 4am on weekends.

Triple Seven Brewpub, *Main Street Station*, 200 N Main St; ☎702/386-4442. Roomy, high-ceilinged downtown brewpub, with poor service but great beers and good food.

VooDoo Lounge, *Rio*, 3700 W Flamingo Rd; ☎702/252-7777. Las Vegas' hottest bar, with amazing 51st-floor views and super-cool atmosphere. The outdoor terrace boasts a fabulous prospect of the Strip, half a mile east, but most of the beautiful crowd prefer to admire their own reflections in the purple-tinted windows. The ersatz New Orleans voodoo-themed decor, and the "mixologists" diligently setting cocktails aflame, add to the ambience, the food is pretty good, and there's live music nightly except Mon.

Entertainment

There was a time when Las Vegas represented the pinnacle of any show-business career. In the early 1960s, when Frank Sinatra's Rat Pack were shooting hit movies like *Ocean's 11* during the day then singing the night away at the *Sands*, the city could claim to be the capital of the international entertainment industry. It was even hip. Now, however, although the money is still there, the world has moved on. As the great names of the past fade from view, few of the individual performers popular with traditional Vegas visitors are considered capable of carrying an extended-run show. The tendency instead is to rely on lavish stunts and special effects. A fair number of old-style Vegas revues are still soldiering on, but there are more stimulating contemporary productions than you might imagine.

Imagine, *Luxor*, 3900 Las Vegas Blvd S; ☎702/262-4400. Completely un-Egyptian, despite the wonderful Egyptian setting, and a prime example of post-Cirque du Soleil entertainment. Artfully tailored to offer similar thrills to *Mystère* at half the price, it crams in a stunning array of tumblers, acrobats and contortionists, some sexy showgirls and showboys, and lots of magical illusions, all accompanied by a barrage of thunderous semi-orchestral rock. Mon, Wed, Fri & Sat 7.30pm & 10pm, Sun & Tues 7.30pm. $40.

Lance Burton, *Monte Carlo*, 3770 Las Vegas Blvd S; ☎702/730-7160. Las Vegas' best family show, featuring the superb and very charming master magician Lance Burton. As well as traditional but very impressive stunts with playing cards, handkerchiefs and doves, Burton takes on Siegfried and Roy at their own game, with large-scale illusions like the disappearance of an airplane and a narrow escape from hanging. Tues–Sat 7.30pm & 10.30pm. $35 and $40.

Legends in Concert, *Imperial Palace*, 3535 Las Vegas Blvd S; ☎702/794-3261. Celebrity-tribute show, with a changing roster that ranges from the Righteous Brothers to Shania Twain. The slick Four Tops are unbeatable, but the surreal re-creation of Michael Jackson's *Thriller* is a joy to behold, and a tongue-in-cheek Elvis clowning through *Viva Las Vegas* makes a fitting finale. Check if they're giving away tickets on the sidewalk before you buy. Daily except Sun 7.30pm & 10.30pm. $34.50, ages 12 and under $19.50, including 2 drinks.

Mystère, *Treasure Island*, 3300 Las Vegas Blvd S; ☎702/894-7722. The Cirque du Soleil's original Las Vegas show is such a visual feast that it barely matters whether you see its dreamscape symbolism as profound and meaningful or labored and empty. Seen at first as being too "way-out" for Las Vegas, its success has redefined the city's approach to entertainment. Above all, it's a showcase of fabulous circus skills, with tumblers, acrobats, trapeze artists, pole climbers, clowns and strong men, but no animals apart from fantastic costumed apparitions. Wed–Sun 7.30pm & 10.30pm. $70, ages 12 and under $35.

O, *Bellagio*, 3600 Las Vegas Blvd S; ☎702/693-7722. Las Vegas' most expensive show; a remarkable testament to what's possible when the budget is barely an issue. Any part of the stage at any time may be submerged to any depth. One moment a performer walks across a particular spot, the next someone dives headfirst into it from the high wire. From the synchronized swimmers onwards, the Cirque du Soleil display their magnificent skills to maximum advantage. Highlights include a colossal trapeze frame draped like a pirate ship, and crewed by fearless acrobats and divers, and footmen flying through the air in swirls of velvet drapery. Mon, Tues & Fri–Sun 7.30pm & 10.30pm. $90 and $100.

Siegfried and Roy, *The Mirage*, 3400 Las Vegas Blvd S; ☎702/792-7777. Austrian magicians Siegfried and Roy have appeared well over four thousand times at the *Mirage*, and it shows, not just in their sheer professionalism but in their air of going through the motions. The highest-paid entertainers in Vegas history put on an impressive display of illusions, causing elephants and even dragons to vanish, and teleporting themselves across the arena, but even though you can't tell how it's done, you know they're basically technicians operating industrial machinery. When the stage fills up with their beloved white lions and tigers, Siegfried and Roy finally perk up enough to take a cloying, self-congratulatory bow; the narcissism of the whole thing is as breathtaking as the magic. Mon, Tues & Fri–Sun 7.30pm & 11pm. $89, including drinks.

Salt Lake City

Disarmingly pleasant and easy-going, **SALT LAKE CITY** is well worth a stopover of a couple of days. It may not be a particularly thrilling destination in itself, but its setting is superb, towered over by the mountains of the **Wasatch Front**, which mark the dividing line between the comparatively lush eastern and the bone-dry western halves of northern Utah.

That Salt Lake City today seems so quietly prosperous, even complacent, is a remarkable tribute to the energy and dedication of its **Mormon** founders. When established, in 1847, it lay beyond the boundaries of the United States. Brigham Young, who had led his persecuted flock westwards in search of a land that "nobody else wanted," emerged from the western flank of the Rockies and declared "This is the place." The city was thereupon laid out according to plans prepared for the "City of Zion" by the church's original Prophet, Joseph Smith, in 1833, with **Temple Square** at its heart. Within ten years, thanks to an extensive missionary program back East, its population had grown to fifty thousand, while the economy had been kick-started by its role in provisioning the Gold Rush wagon-trains that struggled through en route to California.

For a detailed account of Mormon history, see p.530.

Salt Lake City is now home to around 160,000 citizens, though thanks to the proximity of the further 600,000 who live in suburban areas ranged along the Wasatch Front, it feels a whole lot larger. Around seventy percent are Mormons, and it remains the worldwide headquarters of the Mormon church. The city's bid to raise its international profile by hosting the 2002 Winter Olympics has so far resulted in a major building program both in the city proper and in the surrounding ski valleys, plus an unwelcome notoriety following the taint of corruption that surrounded its selection. For the moment, however, people elsewhere in the US still tend to imagine Salt Lake City as one step away from *The Stepford Wives* in terms of spontaneous public fun, and they're not far wrong. There is a fundamental lack of things to do, in the way of museums or other cultural diversions, but if you're willing to switch gears and slow down, its unhurried pace, and the lack of pretence and positive energy of its people, can make for a surprisingly enjoyable experience. In addition, the proximity of the mountains means that the region offers great hiking or cycling in summer and fall, and some of the world's best skiing in winter.

For a note on the easy system of grid-reference addresses prevalent in Utah, see p.362.

Arrival, information and getting around

Salt Lake City International Airport (☎801/575-2400) is a mere four miles west of downtown. A cab into town costs around $12; slightly cheaper shuttle vans to downtown destinations are run by Xpress Shuttles (☎801/596-1600). If you're heading further afield,

*A light rail
system, TRAX,
is due to open
in the Salt
Lake Valley in
time for the
2002 Winter
Olympics.*

Canyon Transportation (☎801/255-1841) serves the ski areas, while Bighorn Express (☎801/328-9920 or 1-888/655-RIDE) offers daily **shuttle services** both southwest to Cedar City and St George and southeast to Green River, Moab, Monticello and Blanding. Long-distance Greyhound-Trailways **buses**, 160 W South Temple Blvd (☎801/355-4684), and Amtrak **trains**, 320 S Rio Grande Ave, also arrive downtown.

On the whole, Utah Transit Authority's **buses** are not wildly useful, but #50 serves the airport hourly (75¢), and there's a fairly restricted free-fare zone downtown (☎801/287-4636). In summer, the **Discovery Trolley** loops between the main visitor center (see overleaf), the downtown malls, the university museums, and This is the Place park (June to mid-Oct Mon–Sat 10am–6pm; $2).

Gray Line (☎801/521-7060) and Scenic West Tours (☎801/572-2717) both offer **bus tours** ranging from half- and full-day city jaunts to multiday trips to the various national parks. To reach the best parts of the surrounding mountains, however, you'll need a car – all the rental companies are represented at the airport – or a bicycle and strong legs. **Bikes** can be rented from Utah Ski Rental, 134 W 100 South St (☎801/355-9088).

Visitor centers supplying information on the city itself can be found downtown at 90 S West Temple Blvd in the Salt Palace Convention Center (Mon–Fri 8am–5pm, Sat & Sun 9am–5pm; ☎801/521-2822; *www.saltlake.org*), or in Terminal 2 of the airport (Sun–Fri 9am–9pm). For details on the rest of Utah, stop by the Utah Travel Council, across from the capitol at 300 N State St (Mon–Fri 8am–5pm, Sat & Sun 10am–5pm; ☎801/538-1030; *www.utah.com*). The downtown **post office** is at 230 W 200 South St (Mon–Fri 8am–5.30pm, Sat 8am–1.30pm; ☎801/978-3001; zip code 84101).

Accommodation

*Unless other-
wise stated,
the zip code
for all these
properties is
UT 84101.*

Salt Lake City is well equipped with accommodation, with downtown options that range via budget **motels** and **B&B** inns up to rather more luxurious **hotels**, and the usual mid-range places near the airport and along the interstates.

Brigham Street Inn, 1135 E South Temple Blvd, UT 84102; ☎801/364-4461 or 1-800/417-4461, fax 801/321-3201. Luxurious, peaceful – and rather inconspicuous – B&B a few blocks east of downtown towards the mountains. ⑨.

Cavanaughs Olympus Hotel, 161 W 600 South St; ☎801/521-7373 or 1-800/325-4000, fax 801/524-0354. Good-value mountain-view rooms downtown, convenient for Amtrak, airport and interstates. ⑨.

Deseret Inn, 50 W 500 South St; ☎801/532-2900. This downtown motor lodge is a real throwback to a bygone era; though far from smart, its rooms are clean and very inexpensive. ②.

Doubletree Hotel, 255 S West Temple Blvd; ☎801/328-2000 or 1-800/222-TREE, fax 801/532-1953. Plush modern high-rise, with indoor pool, in the Salt Palace complex downtown, offering good views of both the Temple and the mountains. ⑨.

Holiday Inn Airport, 1659 W North Temple Blvd, UT 84116; ☎801/533-9000 or 1-800/HOLIDAY, fax 801/364-0614. Well-equipped top-end hotel with reasonable rates, connected with the airport by free shuttle buses and not too far from downtown. ④.

Hotel Monaco, 15 W 200 South St; ☎801/595-0000 or 1-888/294-9710. Extremely hip, very upscale downtown hotel – as they'd have it, "elegant and edgy" – housed in the former Continental Bank building. ⑥.

Motel 6, 176 W 600 South St; ☎801/531-1252. Budget downtown motel, handy for the Amtrak station. ②.

Peery Hotel, 110 W 300 South St; ☎801/521-4300 or 1-800/331-0073, fax 801/575-5014. Refurbished 1910 downtown landmark, with small but characterful rooms. ④.

Pinecrest Bed and Breakfast Inn, 6211 Emigration Canyon Rd, UT 84108; ☎801/583-6663 or 1-800/359-6663. Top-quality accommodation in six-acre pine forest, high above the city, with massive breakfasts. ④.

Quality Inn-City Center, 154 W 600 South St; ☎801/521-2930 or 1-800/521-9997, fax 801/355-0733. Spacious downtown motel, with pool and free airport shuttle. ④.

Saltair Bed and Breakfast Inn, 164 S 900 East St, UT 84102; ☎801/533-8184 or 1-800/733-8184. Attractive B&B in historic downtown building, not quite as old as it looks but enjoyably modeled on the nineteenth-century Saltair resort beside the Great Salt Lake. ④–⑤.

Shilo Inn, 206 S West Temple Blvd; ☎801/521-9500 or 1-800/222-2244, fax 801/359-6527. Clean rooms in a downtown tower, with pool, sauna and gym. ⑤.

Travelodge – Temple Square, 144 W North Temple Blvd; ☎801/533-8200, fax 596-0332. Most central and least expensive of three local *Travelodges*. ③.

Ute Hostel, 21 E Kelsey Ave; ☎801/595-1645; *www.infobytes.com /utehostel*. Much the better of Salt Lake City's two hostels, this small private establishment, a few miles south of downtown, offers $15 dorm beds and a couple of private rooms, plus a hot tub and free pickup from the airport, Greyhound or Amtrak. ①/②.

*As explained
on p.15, accom-
modation
prices, exclud-
ing taxes, are
indicated
throughout this
book by the fol-
lowing sym-
bols:*
① *up to $30*
② *$30–45*
③ *$45–60*
④ *$60–80*
⑤ *$80–100*
⑥ *$100–130*
⑦ *$130–175*
⑧ *$175–250*
⑨ *$250+*

The City

Thanks to its straightforward grid of streets, it's so easy to get to grips with the layout of Salt Lake City that you start to feel like an expert after a couple of hours. It's also especially easy to negotiate by car; the sweeping one-way principal boulevards were designed to be "wide enough for a team of four oxen and a covered wagon to turn around," traffic is generally light, and parking spaces plentiful.

The snag is, there's not a hell of a lot to **do**. For Mormons worldwide, of course, Salt Lake City is something of a place of pilgrimage, and most Gentiles too enjoy at least a short visit to the main complex of church buildings, Temple Square. Apart from that, however, the city's crop of museums are unusually disappointing, and once you get behind the wheel you'll soon find yourself tempted to head out of town, and up into the mountains to the east.

Temple Square

The geographical – and spiritual – heart of Salt Lake City is **Temple Square**, the world headquarters of the **Mormon Church** (or Church of Christ of Latter Day Saints – LDS) and the only real public space in the city. Its focus is the monumental **Temple** itself, completed in 1893 after forty years of intensive labor. The multispired granite edifice rises to 210 feet above the city – it's not the tallest building on the mainly flat skyline but, thanks to its crisply angular silhouette, it's just about the only interesting one. Only confirmed Mormons may enter the Temple, and even they do so only for the most sacred LDS rituals – marriage, baptisms and "sealing," the joining of a family unit for eternity.

Wander through the gates of Temple Square, however, and you'll swiftly be snapped up by one of the many waiting Mormon guides,

*There's free
admission to
the Mormon
choir's 9.30am
Sunday broad-
cast, and its
rehearsals on
Thursday
evenings at
8pm.*

and shepherded to join a free 45-minute **tour** of the various sites within. As well as monuments to Mormon pioneers, and the sea-gulls who fortuitously saved them by consuming a plague of locusts that threatened their first harvest, you'll be ushered into the odd oblong shell of the **Mormon Tabernacle**. No images of any kind adorn its interior, which is home to the world-renowned **Mormon Tabernacle Choir**; a helper at the lectern laconically displays its remarkable acoustic properties by tearing up a newspaper and dropping a nail.

The primary aim of the tours is to awaken your interest in the Mormon faith; differences from Christianity are played down in favor of a soft-focus video of Old Testament scenes. The tour ends in the northern of the Square's two visitor centers, where an array of touch-screen computers provide woolly answers to questions like "What is the purpose of life?" and "Who was Joseph Smith?" In the southern visitor center, a surprisingly good free movie tells the story of the arrival of Salt Lake City's first Mormon settlers.

Capitol Hill

Quite why the Mormons chose not to put their Temple on the gentle hill that stands above today's Temple Square is anyone's guess. As a result, when Utah was finally granted statehood in 1896, it was free to become the site of the imposing, domed **Utah State Capitol** (summer Mon–Sat 6am–8pm; winter Mon–Sat 6am–6pm; free). Along with all the plaques and monuments you might expect, the corridors of power are packed full of earnest and rather diverting exhibits of great Utah moments. The basement area in particular holds a fine assortment of historical what-nots, ranging from mining dioramas to the 18-cylinder, 750-horsepower *Mormon Meteor*, raced by Ab Jenkins across the Bonneville Salt Flats in the 1950s.

Now called **Capitol Hill**, the neighborhood around the Capitol holds some of Salt Lake City's grandest c.1900 residences, with dozens of ornate Victorian houses lining Main Street and Quince Street to the northwest; walking-tour maps of the district are available from the Utah Heritage Foundation, 355 Quince St. Directly opposite the Capitol stands another architectural landmark, **Council Hall**, the old Territorial Legislature building that was dismantled and rebuilt here in the 1960s. The main chamber off the entrance has been restored to its period appearance, while the rest of the building houses the Utah Travel Council (see p.12).

Downtown Salt Lake City

A block east of Temple Square along South Temple Boulevard, the **Beehive House** (Mon–Sat 9.30am–4.30pm, Sun 10am–1pm; free) is a plain white New England-style house with wraparound verandas and green shutters. Erected in 1854 by church leader **Brigham Young**, it's now a small museum of Young's life, restored to the style of the period. Free twenty-minute tours, which you have to join to see much of the house, are given at least every half-hour.

The **Family History Library**, across West Temple Boulevard from Temple Square (Mon 7.30am–6pm, Tues–Sat 7.30am–10pm; free), is intended to enable Mormons to trace their ancestors, and then baptize them into the faith by proxy, but it's open to everyone. The world's most exhaustive genealogical library is surprisingly user-friendly, giving immediate access, through CD-ROMs and banks of computers, to birth and death records from over fifty countries, some dating back as much as five hundred years. All you need is a person's place of birth, a few approximate dates, and you're away; out of respect for the privacy of those still living, most of the information pertains to centuries prior to our own. Volunteers provide help if you need it, but leave you alone until you ask. Next door to the library, the **Museum of Church History and Art** (Mon–Fri 9am–9pm, Sat & Sun 10am–7pm; free) charts the rise of the Mormon faith in art and artifact.

The area southwest of Temple Square, now the site of the massive **Salt Palace** convention center and sports arena (home of the Utah Jazz basketball team), has undergone a rapid transformation. The surrounding district of brick warehouses around the Union Pacific railroad tracks is quickly filling up with designer shops and art galleries, signs that even Mormons can be yuppies.

Further west, the "other side of the tracks" around the interstate, remains one of the city's most run-down and forgotten areas, the last resort of transient winos and Utah's growing homeless population. The museum run by the **Utah Historical Society** in the Amtrak station, 300 S Rio Grande Ave (Mon–Fri 8am–5pm, Sat 10am–3pm; free), is too mediocre to make it worth passing this way.

The University Museums

Salt Lake City's two most interesting **museums** are located on the campus of the University of Utah, which sprawls across the Wasatch Front foothills a couple of miles east of downtown. The **Utah Museum of Natural History**, 1390 E Presidents Circle (Mon–Sat 9.30am–5.30pm, Sun noon–5pm; $5), focuses quite specifically on the geology, flora and fauna of Utah itself. Fortunately, the state ranks among the world's greatest repositories of dinosaur remains, so its allosaurus and stegosaurus fossils are first rate. There's also a full-size reproduction on canvas of the Great Gallery of rock art in Horseshoe Canyon (see p.450), though it has to be said that kids may find the displays too old-fashioned and low-tech to hold their attention for long.

The collection of the **Utah Museum of Fine Arts** (Mon–Fri 10am–5pm, Sat & Sun noon–5pm; free) – housed currently at 1530 East S Campus Drive but due in the lifetime of this edition to move to larger premises at 1650 East S Campus Drive – is much wider-ranging. Galleries named for various benefactors range from ancient Rome, Egypt and China up to Italian and Dutch demi-Masters and twentieth century, with plenty of pre-Columbian artifacts from the Americas for good measure. One highlight is William Holbrook Beard's *Lo The Poor Indian*, a sentimentalized Native American portrait whose title is drawn from an Alexander Pope line that continues "whose untotor'd mind sees God in clouds."

This Is The Place Heritage Park

The exact spot where Brigham Young proclaimed in 1847 that the 1300-mile trek of the Mormon pioneers had come to an end, just beyond the university at the mouth of Emigration Canyon, is now the site of the prosaically named **This Is The Place Heritage Park**. A huge monument erected for the centenary stands just outside the **visitor center** (Mon–Sat 9am–5.30pm; summer $8, winter $1), where exhibits tell the whole story in copious detail. Spacious grounds beyond hold **Old Deseret Village**, where buildings from the city's history have been arranged to form a model community complete with stores and workshops. In summer, it's brought to life by costumed volunteers (mid-May to mid-Oct Mon–Sat 9am–5pm); in winter, you can stroll around the complex, but the actual buildings remain locked.

Bingham Canyon Copper Mine

Roughly 25 miles south of downtown Salt Lake City on I-15, what looks at first like just another bizarre bit of Southwestern badlands, off to the west, is in fact the largest man-made hole in the world. Since 1906, the vast open-pit **Bingham Canyon Copper Mine** has yielded copper, gold, silver and molybdenum to a value greater than the entire Californian and Klondike gold rushes combined; two-thirds of all Utah's mineral production has come from this one mine. In doing so, it has replaced a mountain with a terraced hole that's 2.5 miles across and twice the depth of the world's tallest building. Briefly shut down in the 1980s, it is now owned by Rio Tinto Zinc, and hard at work again. The whole place glows in the dawn sunlight – not that glowing is an especially desirable attribute in a mine.

Visitors drive to the very top of the astonishing abyss, where a **visitor center** (April–Oct daily 8am–8pm; $3 per vehicle) does its best to stress the positive aspects of what in most eyes is an ecological hellhole, while the occasional disconcerting boom tells of ongoing blasting in its bowels.

Great Salt Lake

The **GREAT SALT LAKE**, in the barren desert west of Salt Lake City, is the last remnant of Lake Bonneville, a 20,000-square-mile inland sea that once stretched into Idaho and Nevada. The first outsider to see it was "mountain man" Jim Bridger in 1824; legends circulated that it was home to a monster, or even to a school of whales, and connected to the Pacific by a subterranean outlet. In the late nineteenth century, the lake's shores were lined with extravagant resorts, and steamboats and pleasure cruisers plied across its surface. After years of mysterious decline, when enough of its contents evaporated to make it the world's second-saltiest body of water, it started – equally mysteriously – to refill in the 1980s. Its level today is far higher than state planners ever bargained for, and has forced the raising of the adjacent I-80 interstate by several feet.

On the plus side, the lake's formerly abundant **wildlife**, and especially its migratory **birds**, have begun to reappear, but it's still not especially attractive to humans. **Great Salt Lake State Park**, sixteen miles west of town on I-80 (daily 8am–sunset), is the dingiest affair imaginable. It marks the site of the flamboyant 1890s Saltair pavilion, which closed down in 1968 when the waters receded, and was promptly destroyed by fire. A smaller version reopened in 1983, just in time to be flooded out; it's now pretty decrepit and threadbare, but still gamely showing videos of the lake, while gaudy railroad cars and a lake boat outside act as gift shops.

The largest of the lake's varying number of islands, **Antelope Island**, is also a state park that's home to a herd of six hundred bison (daily: summer 7am–10pm; winter dawn–dusk; $7). It's reached by a causeway near **Syracuse**; leave I-15 at exit 335, north of the city.

Eating

Though Salt Lake City has a perfectly good selection of **restaurants**, it lacks an atmospheric – let alone hip – dining district. If you like to compare menus, the only downtown area with much potential is the block or two to either side of West Temple Street, south and east of the Salt Palace; otherwise, for good food in scenic surroundings, head for *Ruth's Diner* or the *Santa Fe Restaurant*, in Emigration Canyon at the edge of the mountains, three miles east of downtown.

Bambara, *Hotel Monaco*, 15 W 200 South; ☎801/363-5454. Chic, post-Deco and pricey downtown restaurant, where the fabulous menu ranges from $10 appetizers like buffalo carpaccio or crab cakes, to entrees at $20–25 such as lamb sirloin on Puy lentils or grilled salmon on Israeli couscous. Daily for lunch and dinner.

Bill and Nada's Cafe, 479 S 600 East; ☎801/359-6984. All-American 1940s diner, open 24hr. Great for breakfast, but worth a visit anytime for its ace jukebox, the best west of Memphis – packed with Hank Williams, Patsy Cline, blues and bebop tracks.

Cafe Pierpoint, 122 W Pierpoint Ave; ☎801/364-1222. Large, downtown Mexican restaurant, open for lunch from Sunday to Friday and dinner daily, with top-quality *ceviche* and gourmet dishes plus the usual standards, all competitively priced.

Einstein Brothers Bagel Bakery, 147 S Main St; ☎801/537-5033. Downtown outlet of a citywide fast-food chain that has become a local institution, serving a wide range of espressos along with bagels and salads. Daily 7am–midnight.

Lamb's Restaurant, 169 S Main St; ☎801/364-7166. Great breakfasts, best eaten at the long shiny counter, and excellent-value set meals throughout the day in one of Utah's oldest restaurants. Open Mon–Sat 7am–9pm.

Market Street Grill, 48 Market St; ☎801/322-4668. As close as Salt Lake City comes to a New York City bar and grill. Fresh seafood, especially oysters, plus steaks in all shapes and sizes. Lunch specials at $8, full dinners $15–30. Open for all meals daily.

Oasis Cafe, 151 S 500 East; ☎801/322-0404. Classy but inexpensive cafe, open daily for all meals and serving very good food (dinner entrees $12–20), with plenty of appealing vegetarian options; there's also an espresso bar. Live acoustic music or jazz in the evening.

Rio Grande Cafe, 270 S Rio Grande; ☎801/364-3302. Spirited and stylish Mexican *cantina* housed in the old Denver and Rio Grande railroad station, still used by Amtrak, three blocks west of downtown. Mon–Sat 11.30am–2.30pm & 5–10pm, Sun 4–9pm.

Ruth's Diner, 2100 Emigration Canyon Rd; ☎801/582-5807. Good-value indoor and patio dining, often accompanied by live music, set in and around old railroad carriages in a narrow canyon just three miles east of town. Wide selection of fresh dishes, great salads and Utah's best breakfasts. Daily 8am–10pm.

Santa Fe Restaurant, 2100 Emigration Canyon Rd; ☎801/582-5888. Sophisticated upmarket sister restaurant to *Ruth's* (see above). Eclectic menu of the best of Southwest cuisine; brilliantly presented grilled meats and fish, and an excellent $12 Sunday brunch. Lunch and dinner daily.

Shogun Sushi, 321 S Main St; ☎801/364-7142. Central Japanese dining, tasty if rather upmarket, with American- and Japanese-style formal seating and a sushi bar. Lunch Mon–Fri, dinner daily.

Drinking and nightlife

Salt Lake City doesn't roll up the sidewalks when the sun goes down. As explained on p.362, many drinking venues are technically private clubs, in which a nominal membership fee entitles the cardholder and up to five guests to two weeks' use of the facilities. However, Salt Lake City now has a handful of **brewpubs**, for which membership is not required; they're distinguishable from their counterparts in other states only by the requirement that they can't sell beer with an alcoholic content of greater than 3.2 percent.

To find out about the city's broad range of fringe art, music and clubland happenings, pick up free papers such as *City Weekly* or the monthly *Catalyst*, or tune to radio station KRCL 91FM.

Dead Goat Saloon, 165 S West Temple Blvd; ☎801/328-4628. Raucous, semi-subterranean saloon, with live loud music most nights.

Squatters Pub, 147 W Broadway; ☎801/363-2739. Casual, friendly brewpub with a range of beers available until 1am every day.

Zephyr Club, 301 S West Temple Blvd; ☎801/355-2582. Salt Lake's premier live jazz and blues venue, with semi-famous names most nights. Upmarket clientele, elegant decor, cover $5–15.

The Contexts

A History of the Southwest

What is now the Southwest USA has been home to Native Americans for around twelve thousand years. Around four hundred years ago, they were joined by a small group of Hispanic colonists, who claimed the region for Spain as New Mexico. After over two hundred years of Spanish rule, it passed briefly into the hands of the newly independent nation of Mexico, before being taken over by the United States, which has now held it for a little over 150 years.

Throughout that long history, the Southwest has been either controlled, or at least heavily influenced, by distant powers. Its best-known ancient peoples, the Ancestral Puebloans and the Hohokam, drew their cultural inspiration from the civilizations of Mexico; the settlers of Santa Fe looked to Madrid and Mexico City for financial and spiritual support; and even the current status of the region owes much to federal funding from Washington.

What makes the history of the Southwest so fascinating is that so many of the different peoples who have migrated into the region are still there, and still inter-reacting with each other. In the words of an anthropologist from Zuni Pueblo, "the Anasazi are alive and well and living in the Rio Grande valley." The Navajo, relative latecomers, form the majority population in the Four Corners region, though they've never displaced the Hopi. Santa Fe remains a visibly Hispanic, Catholic city, while Utah is still seventy percent Mormon, and Phoenix and Las Vegas typify the Anglo impact.

The Paleo-Indians

No one knows when humans reached the American continent. While ancient campfires have been tentatively dated back as far as 30,000 BC, there's no firm evidence to suggest that the Southwest, or anywhere else in the modern United States, held a significant population until 10,000 BC.

These **Paleo-Indians** were originally Siberian nomads, who worked their way into Alaska along a **"land-bridge,"** exposed when the level of the ocean dropped, which followed the approximate line of what's now the Bering Strait. Though that entire region was treeless tundra, no more appealing than it is today, it supported sufficient quantities of large mammals to make hunting worthwhile. Quite possibly, a band of no more than fifty individuals completed the journey. Their descendants then spread so quickly across the new continent that they reached the southern-most tip of South America within a couple of thousand years.

Between 10,000 BC and 8000 BC, the Southwest was dominated by what archeologists call the **Clovis** culture, whose distinctive flaked-stone spear-points were first identified at Clovis, New Mexico. Living in small groups, constantly on the move, Clovis hunters pursued their prey across large distances. Their weapons have been found poking from the ribs of dead mammoths, and they seem to have been such successful killers that they drove the indigenous fauna – which also included giant sloths, camels and even horses – to extinction.

The Archaic culture

As the large animals died out, early Southwesterners had to adapt, and became **hunter-gatherers**. The people of the **Archaic** or **Desert** culture learned where and when particular plants would ripen, and migrated seasonally within relatively restricted areas – often between canyons or valleys and nearby hillsides – in search of fresh food. Hunting for small mammals such as rabbit and deer was still important, however. The development of shamanistic rituals is demonstrated by the clay statuettes and split-twig figurines, depicting what appear to be deities as well as animals, that have been found in remote locations in the Grand Canyon and elsewhere. Few substantial remains of their actual homes survive, however; it's thought they lived in caves wherever possible. The most remarkable manifestation of Archaic culture was the haunting, mysterious rock art of the **Great Gallery** in Canyonlands National Park (see p.450); they also constructed "intaglios," giant earthworks in the shape of enigmatic figures or snakes, in the deserts of southwest Arizona.

The Archaic era was brought to an end by the gradual infiltration of Mexican influences from the south. The first and most crucial was agriculture. **Corn** – in the shape of tiny fingers of maize, much smaller than today's strains – may have been cultivated in the highlands of southern Mexico as early as 5000 BC. The skill of growing it was then passed northwards from group to group, accompanied no doubt by the prayers and rituals necessary to insure a good harvest, and may have reached southern New Mexico around 1200 BC. However, anthropologists have noted a common reluctance among hunter-gatherers the world over to give up what they regard as a pleasant lifestyle, which offers individuals food in return for comparatively little effort, and lots of free time. The Southwest followed that pattern, in that a low level of farming – more like gardening – served at first to supplement the traditional diet, and communities only made the transition to intensive agriculture when forced to by increasing population levels.

The Basketmakers

Southwestern peoples embarked on the large-scale cultivation of crops – corn, together with a more recent arrival, **squash** – from around 100 BC onwards. The first such society was confusingly named **Basketmaker II** by early archeologists, who assumed that more primitive "Basketmaker I" sites would subsequently be found. The Basketmakers lived in extended family groups, in shallow **pithouses** – rectangular pits dug two to six feet into the ground, with earth-covered roofs that rose above ground level. They hunted using the *atlatl* – a lever-like spear-throwing device used throughout the Americas – and cooked by dropping hot rocks into yucca-leaf baskets that had a waterproof lining of pitch. By now they had also domesticated **dogs**, for hunting, and **turkeys**, used mainly for feathers rather than food.

Pottery is thought to have spread from Mexico, by way of the Mimbres region of southwest New Mexico (see p.210), in the first few centuries AD. All pots were made by women, using the technique of hand-coiling, which involves layering successive strips of rolled clay on top of each other and then smoothing them together. The use of fragile ceramic vessels presupposes a relatively sedentary society, but brings great benefits; it's much easier to boil **beans** in a pot than

a basket, so the Southwest acquired its third great staple food, and basketmaking declined.

By around 500 AD, the so-called **Basketmaker III** culture had emerged. As well as corn, squash and beans, they grew another Mexican import, **cotton** – originally cultivated mainly for its oil-rich edible seeds – and used **bows and arrows** for the first time. Sizeable **villages** (what the Spanish later called **pueblos**) started to grow up.

Each village soon focused around one specific pithouse that was larger than the rest, and was probably set aside for public or ritual use. Such buildings are recognizable as the first **kivas** – the ceremonial underground chambers that remain at the heart of Pueblo religion to this day. Each *kiva* was entered from above, via an opening that also served as the smokehole for the central firepit. A bench ran around its circumference, and there were also niches set into the walls where ritual objects may have been placed. A small depression in the floor in front of the firepit, known as the *sipapu*, symbolized the hole through which human beings emerged onto this earth.

The Ancestral Puebloans

By 700 AD, much of the Southwest was populated by the forerunners of the modern Pueblo Indians. This book follows contemporary practice among archeologists and Pueblo Indians alike in calling these people "**Ancestral Puebloans**" in preference to the previously common term "**Anasazi**." The Hopi in particular object to that name, which comes from a Navajo word meaning "enemy ancestors," (see p.534) and have championed the use of either their own word for "ancestors," **Hisatsinom**, or the more generally applicable "Ancestral Puebloans."

Over the course of six centuries, from 700 AD to 1300 AD, Ancestral Puebloan civilization spread beyond the **Four Corners** region to cover most of what's now northern Arizona and New Mexico, as well as southern Utah and Colorado, reaching as far as the depths of the Grand Canyon and into southern Nevada. At the start of that period, there was a steady increase in the size and sophistication of their villages, and also a crucial change. Individuals stopped living in pithouses, and instead built surface structures of mud plastered onto a framework of brushwood – a style known as wattle-and-daub. However, they continued to dig large subterranean *kivas*, which kept the pithouse form but were exclusively designed for communal or ceremonial use. Many such *kivas* could now be accessed not only through the roof, but also via concealed underground tunnels, which may have enabled costumed priests or dancers to make surprise appearances during rituals.

The Ancestral Puebloans were the first North Americans to use looms to weave cotton. In addition to cotton clothes, they made blankets and even socks from yucca leaves interwoven with turkey feathers, and wore yucca sandals. For a time, they seem to have deliberately flattened and broadened their skulls by binding the heads of babies against cradleboards. As you might imagine from their tiny doorways and cramped living quarters, they were on the small side, with women averaging five feet in height and men a few inches more. Life expectancy was thirty or less, although perhaps one in ten reached the age of fifty. Adults were plagued by the twin problems of arthritis, often exacerbated by years of carrying heavy loads, and loss of teeth. Their teeth were worn away by the grit in their food, the result of grinding corn between a hand-tool or *mano* and a flat slab known as a *metate*, both made from sandstone; in the words of a modern Hopi saying, "a person eats a rock in a lifetime." They also had some medical expertise, using cottonwood bark, which contains the main active ingredient of aspirin, as a painkiller, and the sap from piñon pines as an all-purpose antiseptic.

The Ancestral Puebloans of the Four Corners reached a cultural peak during the eleventh century. By that time, three main subgroups had emerged – centered on Chaco Canyon in what's now northwest New Mexico, Mesa Verde in southwest Colorado, and the Kayenta region of northeast Arizona – and there were also lesser concentrations such as the Virgin Anasazi of southern Utah.

The **Chacoans** seem to have been the most sophisticated of all, as witnessed not only by the architectural complexity of the multistory pueblos of Chaco Canyon, but by the fact that the canyon was so unsuited for large-scale occupation that they must have survived by extracting tribute from surrounding regions. A detailed account of the "Chaco Phenomenon" appears on p.86.

The wealth of Chaco demonstrates that by 1050 AD the Southwest was crisscrossed by extensive **trading routes**. In the absence of pack animals, most of the trade was in ritual or orna-

mental artifacts rather than the necessities of life. In exchange for **turquoise** from the mines of Cerrillos (see p.124), which passed from group to group all the way down to the Aztecs in central Mexico, the Ancestral Puebloans received silver and copper artifacts from Mexico, sea-shells from the Pacific Coast, and the most prized ceremonial objects of all – live **macaws**.

The decline of Chaco, during the first half of the twelfth century, was mirrored by a general decline in the Ancestral Puebloan population. Following a period of instability, and mass migrations, however, Ancestral Puebloan civilization had a majestic final flourish in the Four Corners. The thirteenth century – when they constructed the **"cliff dwellings,"** squeezed dramatically into narrow alcoves high on canyon walls, for which they're now celebrated – was also characterized by the widespread growth of major **towns**. Colorado's Montezuma Valley was typical in holding around eight large pueblo complexes, ranged across the valley floor and along neighboring ridges, each home to over a thousand people. The nearby cliff dwellings preserved in **Mesa Verde** National Park (see p.69) were home to a smaller, probably peripheral group; though compellingly beautiful to modern eyes, they represent a relatively minor aspect of Ancestral Puebloan life.

The disappearance of the Ancestral Puebloans

Between 1275 AD and 1300 AD, the Ancestral Puebloans vanished from the entire Four Corners region. Their **"disappearance"** is still widely presented as a great mystery, although the increasing use of the term "Ancestral Puebloans" in preference to "Anasazi" is in itself an indication that that the puzzle has largely been solved. Modern Pueblo peoples are so self-evidently their descendants that it's clear the Ancestral Puebloans migrated away rather than simply dying out. Why they did so is harder to explain. Traditional accounts say that a sustained **drought** forced them to leave, but it has now been demonstrated that such droughts were not uncommon, and that the region remained capable of producing enough food to support them.

It seems more likely that the drought coincided with a period of cultural upheaval. While archeologists argue as to whether individual Ancestral Puebloan cliff dwellings were intended for defence, there's no disputing the fact that the region as a whole was prone to violent conflict at this time. Recent proof of cannibalism in the Montezuma Valley has shattered notions of Ancestral Puebloan society as being utterly peaceful, and isolated groups appear to have banded together in larger settlements for mutual defence.

The influence of the blood-drenched civilizations of ancient Mexico was also at its height. As described on p.60, the *kachina* religion, which centered on supernatural entities that, at this formative stage, closely paralleled the warring deities of the Aztecs, spread rapidly across the Southwest. Recent discoveries at Chaco Canyon, as detailed on p.86, have even suggested to some archeologists that the *kachina* cult was introduced by cannibalistic warrior refugees from the south. Such theories remain very controversial, however, and do nothing to alter the fact that over time, in any case, religious emphasis shifted away from blood and sacrifice towards ceremonies designed to bring rain, and thus corn. The drought of the late thirteenth century may have seemed like the first crucial test of, or judgment upon, those rain-making powers, and it may be that charismatic religious leaders persuaded their followers that the failure of the harvest was a signal to move on.

In addition, the Ancestral Puebloans had severely depleted their **environment**. The need for fuel and building materials meant that the landscape for many miles around their settlements had been stripped bare; the pueblos of Chaco Canyon, for example, used over 200,000 large wooden beams. Cutting down trees not only made the search for firewood increasingly arduous, but led to the process known as *arroyo*-cutting, whereby, once the trees that held their banks together were removed, previously placid streams became savage torrents that destroyed prime riverside farmland. It may be no coincidence that the Four Corners remained all but deserted until the arrival of the Navajo during the sixteenth century (see p.538); it may have taken that long to recover from over-exploitation.

The Hohokam

While the Basketmakers and Ancestral Puebloans held sway further north, the deserts of southern Arizona and northern Mexico were home to the equally sophisticated **Hohokam** civilization. This region was not then so barren as it appears today – much of it was covered with grass until the Spanish allowed their cattle to overgraze – and the Hohokam were primarily **farmers**. They lived not in compact pueblos but in what the Spanish later called *rancherías* – sprawling farming communities, where each separate homestead consisted of a framework of timber and brush coated with mud. Thousands of such villages, most of which were occupied for many generations, were scattered across the desert, interspersed with larger "towns" that were probably ceremonial and trading centers rather than residential districts. The population was most heavily concentrated in the **Phoenix Basin**, where they compensated for the lack of rainfall by digging over three hundred miles of irrigation **canals**. Constructed without the use of metal tools, and requiring constant maintenance, these enabled the Hohokam to grow two crops each year – corn, beans and squash, and also cotton for trade.

Whether the Hohokam migrated into the region from central Mexico around 300 BC, as some archeologists believe, or simply evolved from indigenous desert peoples, they were clearly heavily influenced by Mexican culture. Each major town had at least one Mexican-style **ball-court**, where a ritual game with similarities to modern basketball was played with a rubber ball, and a raised-earth **platform mound** – a primitive pyramid – used for religious ceremonies. Like the Ancestral Puebloans, with whom they had little direct contact, the Hohokam traded commodities like cotton and salt for treasured ritual items from the south, such as copper bells, onyx, parrots and macaws.

During the eleventh century, the Hohokam trading complex known as **Snaketown**, at the confluence of the Gila and Salt rivers, rivaled Chaco as the largest settlement in the Southwest. Though Snaketown then declined, the Phoenix Basin became one of the most densely populated areas in North America, with perhaps eighty thousand inhabitants in the thirteenth century. However, the Hohokam **disappeared** from history at much the same time as the Ancestral Puebloans, around 1350 AD. The very word "Hohokam" means "all used up" in the language of the later **O'odham** people of southern Arizona (known to the Spanish as the Pima and the Papago), and reflects 'O'odham oral history that the Hohokam drained every possible drop of sustenance from the land. Archeologists agree, suggesting that they damaged the region's delicate ecological balance so extensively that their descendants were reduced to an impoverished subsistence lifestyle. In addition, the arrival of European diseases such as smallpox, measles and typhus reduced the population of the Phoenix Basin to less than five thousand by the end of the seventeenth century.

While no modern Native American group claims direct physical descent from the Hohokam, it's possible to trace certain cultural continuities. The *ranchería* style of dwelling endured until recent times among tribes such as the Yavapai, the Havasupai, and the 'O'odham themselves. Those peoples also follow an individualistic system of belief, without *kachinas* or *kivas*, and depending on shamans rather than priests, that seems to be in line with what little is known about Hohokam religion.

The Mogollon

Archeologists distinguish a third significant group among the pre-Columbian peoples of the Southwest – the **Mogollon**. Contemporaneous with the Ancestral Puebloans and the Hohokam, and sharing elements of both cultures, the Mogollon occupied an extensive area in what's now west-central New Mexico and east-central Arizona. The main geographical feature of the region is the **Mogollon Rim**, a 200-mile-long, 2000-foot-high escarpment that marks the southern limit of the Colorado Plateau. The Mogollon people lived on the cool plateau above the rim, farming the upland meadows and hunting in the adjacent mountains.

Being so close to Mexico, the Mogollon heartland, which focused on the valleys of the **Gila** and **Mimbres** rivers, was probably the first area of the Southwest to acquire the techniques of agriculture and pottery. The Basketmaker phase lasted longer here than in the Four Corners; the Mogollon only stopped building pithouses around the eleventh century, and the few pueblos they constructed, such as the one now preserved as Gila Cliff Dwellings National Monument (see p.211), were on a smaller scale than their Ancestral Puebloan counterparts. In one respect, however, Mogollon culture was unsurpassed – the extraordinary **pottery** produced by the **Classic**

Mimbres people, a Mogollon offshoot described in detail on p.210.

Much like the Four Corners, the entire Mogollon region became **depopulated** during the fourteenth century. As the Mogollon peoples had probably been instrumental in introducing the *kachina* religion to the Southwest, it makes sense to suppose that their descendants helped to create modern Pueblo culture. Specific Mogollon-descended pueblos may well have been the hardest hit by the arrival of both the Spaniards and the Apache, however, and if their inhabitants survived at all, they probably fled north as refugees.

The Pueblo world and the Spanish invasion

Although the Ancestral Puebloan era ended with their departure from the Four Corners, their immediate descendants created the Southwest's largest pre-Hispanic communities of all. In particular, the city of **Casas Grandes**, which flourished in what's now the northern Mexican state of Chihuahua between 1300 AD and 1400 AD, consisted of over two thousand rooms, and served as a major macaw-breeding center.

However, the most enduring legacy of the Ancestral Puebloan was the emergence of **Pueblo** communities throughout what had until the fourteenth century been relatively uninhabited areas of northern New Mexico. Most of the people of Mesa Verde migrated to the northern reaches of the **Rio Grande** valley, where they founded pueblos such as Taos and Santa Clara; their language, known as Tanoan, evolved into the Tiwa and Tewa languages spoken today. The Chacoans, on the other hand, who spoke the language that became Keresan, moved further south to establish pueblos like Cochiti and Santo Domingo, as well as Ácoma and Zuni to the west.

Other population centers – not so well known today, as they failed to survive the impact of the Spanish – included the **Galisteo Valley**, not far southeast of Santa Fe, which held around a dozen large pueblos, the **Chama Valley**, and the **Tigüex** region near modern Albuquerque.

By the time the Spanish arrived, the Southwest may have held as many as a hundred separate pueblos, with a total population approaching one hundred thousand. New forms of social organization had emerged, and individual pueblos consisted of alliances of either clans – each with its own religious or military responsibilities – or **moieties** – the technical term for a society divided into two halves, in which half the pueblo might belong to a *kiva* associated with winter ceremonies, and the other half to one connected with summer. However, pueblos did not have chiefs or leaders in the European sense, and neither was there any tradition of alliances between pueblos. That lack of political unity seriously weakened their ability to resist the Spanish invaders, who turned their attention northwards after completing the conquest of Mexico.

The coming of the Spaniards

The first Spanish expedition to reach what's now the USA, led by **Ponce de Leon**, sailed up the Atlantic Coast in 1513 and named **Florida**. The next Spanish voyage, in 1528, ended in shipwreck in Tampa Bay, but a junior officer, **Alvar Núñez Cabeza de Vaca**, survived. Together with three shipmates, he spent eight years on an extraordinary trans-continental odyssey. Living with various Native American groups – sometimes held as slaves, sometimes revered as seers – they made their way across Texas, following the Pecos River and the Rio Grande. It's unlikely that they reached modern New Mexico or Arizona, but while staying in the pueblo of the Jumano tribe, somewhere on the Rio Grande, they heard tales of larger pueblos further north, and in northern Mexico they were given emeralds that had been purchased with parrot feathers from a people who lived to the north.

Cabeza de Vaca's eventual arrival in Mexico City in 1536 created a sensation, and the Viceroy of New Spain resolved to investigate his tales of golden cities deep in the desert. One of Cabeza de Vaca's companions had been a black African from Azamor in Morocco, called **Esteban de Dorantes**. Rather than return to a life of slavery, he volunteered to map the route for a new expedition led by **Fray Marcos de Niza**. In 1539, Esteban set off ahead of Fray Marcos, and followed a long-established Indian trading route north across the Rio San Pedro into what's now Arizona.

A giant of a man, dressed like a shaman in jewelry and feathers, and accompanied by two colossal greyhounds, he amazed the native peoples he encountered, and soon acquired a large entourage. Having arranged to send a sig-nal back to Fray Marcos if he discovered anything to rival the marvels of Mexico, he duly did so as he approached the pueblo of **Zuni** (see p.90). Zuni at this time was a major trading center, where the trail from the south met others from the Pacific Coast to the west and the Rio Grande pueblos to the east. The Zuni villages were nonetheless simply clusters of adobe houses, not cities on the Mexican scale. According to the Zuni, Esteban's demands for tribute were incompatible with his claims to be a medicine man, and they punished his sacrilegious behavior by killing him, cutting him into strips, and distributing his flesh among their neighbors.

Fray Marcos reported that he was in sight of Zuni when he heard of Esteban's death and fled back to Mexico; it seems more probable that he never reached Arizona. Even so, he announced "this land . . . is the greatest and best of all that have been discovered." Rendering the Zuni name Shi:wona as Cíbola, he called the six Zuni villages the **Seven Cities of Cíbola**, and identified them with the legendary Seven Cities of Antilla, long sought by Spanish explorers.

On February 22, 1540, therefore, a further expedition, led by **Francisco Vásquez de Coronado**, set off into the Southwest from Compostela in northern Mexico. Consisting of over three hundred Spanish soldiers plus hundreds more Indian "allies" and servants, and accompanied by several thousand horses and cattle, they marched up through Arizona and reached Zuni on July 7. In front of the town of Hawikkuh, the Zuni drew a line of sacred cornmeal along the ground, which they forbade the Spaniards to cross. During the pitched **battle** that ensued – the first ever fought between Europeans and Native Americans – Coronado himself was knocked unconscious, but Spanish weapons prevailed. The town was taken, its storehouses revealing not gold, but something that by now seemed equally precious – food.

Within two weeks, news of the fall of Zuni spread throughout the Southwest. Coronado made his headquarters in the conquered pueblo, and dispatched exploratory parties in all directions. One such, under Pedro de Tovar, forced the "warlike" Hopi pueblos to surrender (see p.535), and reached as far as the **Grand Canyon**; another, commanded by Melchor Díaz, crossed the Colorado further south, and thus penetrated modern **California**. A detachment led by Hernando de Alvarado headed east, passing

Ácoma Pueblo – "the greatest stronghold ever seen in the world" – and reaching the pueblos of the Rio Grande.

Meanwhile, emissaries from the Pueblo world were traveling to Zuni. Peaceful overtures from two men from **Cicuyé** (now Pecos National Historical Park; see p.144), known to the Spaniards as **Cacique** (meaning Governor) and **Bigotes** (Whiskers), persuaded Coronado to move his expedition east. They camped for the winter beside the Rio Grande, in a region they called **Tigüex**, and commandeered an entire pueblo as their new base. This may have been Kuaua, now preserved as Coronado State Monument (see p.122) – it's hard to say, because relations with the Tigüex soon degenerated into full-scale war, and in a bloody succession of sieges and massacres, all the Tigüex pueblos were destroyed.

Coronado remained convinced that gold was somewhere to be found. In the spring of 1541, he decamped northeast to Cicuyé, which was a prosperous community where Pueblo peoples traded with nomads from the Plains. In what may well have been a deliberate plot, Cacique and Bigotes introduced him to "the Turk," a Pawnee captive, who knew of a city far to the east, **Quivira**, that was rich in gold. Details of the Turk's story suggest that he was familiar with the culture of the Mississippi Indians, but he was probably released by the leaders of Cicuyé in the hope that he'd lead the Spaniards into oblivion on the endless Plains.

In the event, the expedition wandered for three fruitless months across what they called "the domain of the cows," in honor of its vast buffalo herds. From the Llano Estacado or "Staked Plains" of **Texas**, where they drove wooden stakes into the ground to avoid losing their way, they veered northeast into **Kansas**, following the Arkansas River along the route of what later became the Santa Fe Trail. There they did indeed reach a land known as Quivira, but its inhabitants were nomadic and utterly gold-free buffalo-hunters. At that point, Coronado lost patience; the Turk was garrotted, and the Spaniards returned to the Rio Grande. After another beleaguered winter in Tigüex, they embarked on the long journey back to Mexico, leaving behind a handful of (swiftly martyred) missionaries and many of their Mexican-Indian allies. Popular myth has it that Coronado was disgraced on his return home, but while his expedition was certainly seen as a failure, the man himself held important offices in Mexico City for the rest of his life.

The colony of New Mexico

During the fifty years after Coronado's departure, unauthorized Spanish adventurers made occasional forays into the Southwest. Not until 1598, however, was **Don Juan de Oñate** granted royal permission to establish a permanent **colony** in the region. His expedition, consisting of 130 families and two hundred single men, crossed the Rio Grande near modern El Paso on May 1, and took possession of the land under the name of **New Mexico**. The geography of the region remaining unknown, the precise boundaries of the colony were not specified, but broadly speaking it extended from the Colorado River in the west to the Pecos River in the east, and included not only what's now New Mexico, but all of Arizona, plus parts of Utah, Colorado, Nevada and California. At that time, the name "Mexico" referred only to what we call Mexico City – the modern country was known as "New Spain" until 1821 – so "New Mexico" was named in the hope that it would match the riches of the Aztecs.

As Oñate's party traveled north along the river, each pueblo they came to turned out to have been hurriedly deserted by its inhabitants, fearful of being captured as slaves. Eventually, at the confluence of the Rio Grande and the Chama River near what's now Española, the settlers took over the pueblo of O'ke, renamed it San Juan, and made it their **capital**. Like Coronado before him, Oñate sent soldiers to all quarters of his new realm in search of gold; and like Coronado he soon found himself at war. After a group commanded by Oñate's nephew was all but wiped out, he launched a full-scale artillery onslaught on Ácoma Pueblo. Over eight hundred Acomans were killed, and eighty male prisoners had their feet chopped off in public ceremonies in the pueblos of the Rio Grande.

By the time Oñate returned to his capital, most of the colonists had given up and returned to Mexico. Oñate himself was recalled to Mexico City in disgrace once Franciscan missionaries reported his cruelty to their superiors. Meanwhile, however, Captain Pérez de Villagrá had trumpeted Oñate's "achievements" in an epic poem, *Historia de Nueva México*. In the face of all the evidence, Villagrá still insisted that New Mexico had the potential to become the greatest kingdom in the Spanish empire, and he was sufficiently believed in Madrid for another attempt at colonization to be launched. **Don Pedro de Peralta** was therefore sent to New Mexico with orders to found a new capital, and the city of **Santa Fe** was duly laid out in 1610.

The early Spanish colonists of New Mexico dreamed of emulating their predecessors in Mexico, who had accumulated both land and wealth in prodigious quantities. However, it soon became clear that New Mexico was the end of the road, with no access to the ocean and no rich neighbors for the Spaniards either to trade with or plunder. Santa Fe never grew into a mighty city, but remained a remote military outpost of crude adobe buildings. Enterprising colonists therefore dispersed up and down the valley of the Rio Grande, appropriating Pueblo farmlands – and often enslaving Pueblo peoples – to create **ranches** on which they raised sheep and corn, and planted orchards of peaches, plums and cherries. **Wheat** was the most significant of the new crops. Unlike the traditional triumvirate of corn, beans and squash, which have to be grown entirely in spring and summer, wheat can be planted in December for harvest in June.

At the same time, **Franciscan missionaries** set out to convert the Pueblo Indians to Catholicism. One or two friars would attach themselves to a specific pueblo, recruit Indian labor to build adobe mission churches, and set about persuading the Pueblos that their *kachina* cults and corn ceremonies were wicked.

Throughout the seventeenth century, the Spanish civil and religious authorities in New Mexico were at loggerheads. The church deplored violence against the Pueblos and yet demanded the eradication of their beliefs; the military governors preferred not to antagonize the Indians unnecessarily, but felt their authority ultimately rested on the sword.

Quite apart from any specific actions, the very presence of the Spaniards utterly disrupted the region. Settled communities like the villages of the Rio Grande were especially vulnerable to **epidemic diseases** such as smallpox, measles and typhus, which were unknown before the arrival of the Europeans. By 1640, the Pueblo population had dropped from a hundred thousand down to around thirty thousand, and more than half of all pueblos had been abandoned. Existing patterns of **trade** across the Southwest had also been shattered, and the Rio Grande valley became a prime target for Native American raiders who coveted Spanish arms and, above all, **horses**. Tribes such as the Navajo and the Apache – see p.538 – turned from wandering nomads into fearsome mounted warriors, and all too often it was the Pueblo peoples who bore the brunt of their attacks.

The Pueblo Revolt

In 1675, as it became ever more obvious that traditional Pueblo beliefs still endured beneath a veneer of Catholicism, the Spanish arrested 47 Pueblo religious leaders. Three were condemned as "witchdoctors" and hanged at Santa Fe; the rest were publicly horsewhipped. One of these, a man called **Po'pay** from San Juan Pueblo made his way to Taos Pueblo, and turned one of its *kivas* into the center of a campaign of resistance. A date was set for a concerted uprising against the Spanish, and knotted strings were sent out to all the pueblos, with the instruction to untie one knot each night until the last signaled the arrival of the great day. Somehow, the plot was betrayed, so the **Pueblo Revolt** began a day early, on August 9, 1680.

For the first and only time in their history, the Pueblos of the northern Rio Grande, plus their cousins in Ácoma, Zuni and the Hopi mesas, combined in unison; they were even joined by the Navajo and the Apache. Their anger fell especially upon the missionaries; 21 out of New Mexico's 33 priests were murdered, as were 375 men, women and children out of a total of 2350 Spanish colonists.

After a ten-day **siege of Santa Fe**, the Governor, the garrison and around one thousand citizens were allowed to retreat south. They were joined en route by the Christianized majority from Isleta Pueblo – the only modern pueblo not to join the attack – and all the Pueblo peoples who lived south of Albuquerque. For the next thirteen years, the refugees remained together at what's now Ciudad Juarez, across the Rio Grande from El Paso. Those Indians who had joined the exodus founded Ysleta and other pueblos in the neighborhood, while the former colonists, refused permission to continue any further south, awaited an opportunity to return north.

Back in Santa Fe, the doors and windows of the Palace of the Governors had been sealed up, and the building turned into a typical multistory pueblo. Po'pay was nominally in control, but the concept of a central political administration was alien to the Pueblos, and the alliance soon fragmented.

Not until 1692 did the Spanish crown appoint a new Governor of New Mexico, **Don Diego de Vargas**. His exploratory expedition encountered no opposition when it returned to Santa Fe that September. As a result, he set off again with a party of colonists the following year; this time they had to fight before they could re-enter the city, in December 1693. The return of the Spanish triggered mass migrations throughout the region – as described on p.83, modern Navajo culture originated with the intermingling of the ancestral Navajo with Pueblo refugees during this period – and there were further minor insurrections in the years ahead, but the **Reconquest** was completed by 1696.

The eighteenth century

Although Hispanic settlers continued to dominate the region for 150 years after the Pueblo Revolt, New Mexico was always a peripheral part of the Spanish empire. Separated from the rest of Mexico by vast tracts of empty desert, the colonists were obliged to be self-sufficient, and found themselves thrown into alliance with the Pueblo peoples to resist the threat of Ute and Comanche attack. The Spaniards and the Pueblos had much in common; the New Mexican landscape was similar to that of Andalucia in Spain, as indeed were its adobe hamlets or *pueblos*. The Pueblos had long been subsistence farmers who traded for rare luxuries with far-off civilizations to the south, and the Hispanic ranchers slotted into the same pattern. There was little intermarriage, although Pueblo communities came to acquire sizeable populations of *genízaros*, the bastard offspring of captured Plains Indians and their Spanish masters.

In the first half of the eighteenth century, the **French** established their own colony to the east, **Louisiana**. The immediate Spanish response was to set up missions among the Indians of what now became a separate province of New Spain, **Texas**. As the French and Spanish zones of influence expanded, there were armed clashes; thus a combined force of Spaniards and Pueblos was defeated by a French-Pawnee alliance near North Platte, Nebraska, in 1720.

In general, the French coexisted more amicably with Native Americans than did the Spanish; they were predominantly traders, eager to acquire beaver and other furs and not interested in converting Indians to Christianity. Unlike the Spanish, they were also prepared to supply Indians with **guns**. As a result, the Comanche, Ute and Apache, equipped with the latest European firearms, consistently raided along the Rio Grande at harvest time, seizing crops and livestock, while the Hispanic villagers, inadequately supplied from Mexico, could only offer minimal resistance with their bows and arrows. The colonists financed the occasional retaliatory expedition by selling Indian captives to work as slaves in the silver mines of Mexico, thereby incurring ever greater Indian hostility.

Louisiana having proved no more profitable to France than was New Mexico to Spain, Louis XV of France simply gave it to Spain in 1762. The Spanish frontier in North America was now the Mississippi river. Determined to resist encroachment by the infant United States, King Carlos III placed the entire region under his direct control from Spain in 1776. However, far too few Hispanic settlers moved in to make any difference, and in 1802, as the Spanish empire weakened, he handed Louisiana back to Napoleon. Carlos' hope that the French would serve as a buffer against the Yankees was misplaced; Napoleon sold his American territories to the US in the following year, in the **Louisiana Purchase**.

At the end of the century, Santa Fe was home to around two thousand Hispanic citizens, while the Pueblo population had dwindled to perhaps nine thousand, in a mere nineteen pueblos.

The settlement of Arizona

Before the Pueblo Revolt, the Spanish presence in New Mexico was confined to the valley of the Rio Grande and the scattered pueblos to the west. Under the names of **Pimería Alta** and **Papaguería**, what's now southern Arizona was left to peoples the Spaniards called the **Pima** and the **Papago**, known today as the **'O'odham**.

Around 1700, however, **Jesuit** missionaries conceived the notion of constructing a chain of missions all the way from New Spain to California, and built churches in a couple of 'O'odham villages. Hispanic ranchers and prospectors also drifted in. In 1736, a Yaqui Indian created a silver-mining camp, a few miles southwest of modern Nogales, called **Arizonac**. The name came either from the 'O'odham *ali shonak*, meaning "small springs," or from the Basque language of Spain, in which *arritza onac* means "valuable rocky places," and *aritz onac* means "good oaks."

After an 'O'odham rebellion killed several Jesuits, the Spanish installed a military garrison at **Tubac** (see p.250) in 1752. This *presidio* (fort) was relocated forty miles north to San Agustín de **Tucson** in 1776. Another Indian revolt in 1781, in which 150 settlers were wiped out during Mass at **Yuma**, dashed Spanish hopes of establishing a permanent trail to California, and Tucson, like Santa Fe, came to be seen as a remote and insignificant dead-end town. In 1804, by which time there were around a thousand Spanish colonists in the vicinity, its commander reported "we have no gold, silver, lead, tin, quicksilver, copper mines, or marble quarries . . . the only public work here that is truly worthy of this report is the church at **San Xavier del Bac**" (see p.248).

The end of the Hispanic era

The decline in New Mexico's importance to its Spanish rulers was mirrored by increasing contacts with the rest of North America. In the closing years of the eighteenth century, permanent trails were established both west to California – in the form of the **Old Spanish Trail**, painstakingly mapped across Utah by the Franciscan friars **Domínguez and Escalante** in 1776 – and east to St Louis, along the **Santa Fe Trail** blazed by French explorer Pedro Vial in 1792. After the Louisiana Purchase, expeditions sponsored by the US government also crossed the Plains, such as **Lewis and Clark**'s trek to the Northwest in 1804, and **Lt Zebulon Pike**'s incursion into New Mexico in 1807.

Within a few years, the Spanish grip on the New World was finally loosened; following a **revolution** led by General Agustín Iturbide, Mexico became an independent nation in 1821. Although their governors swiftly transferred allegiance to Mexico City, neither New Mexico nor California perceived any advantage in their new status as Mexican territories. As the flow of resources from the south – including the handouts that had started to keep the Apache relatively docile – dwindled to rock-bottom levels, the effect on the New Mexican economy was crippling.

For the authorities in Santa Fe, the only answer seemed to be to increase trade with the US. Traffic along the Santa Fe Trail swiftly turned New Mexico into an entrepôt through which American goods were shipped south into Mexico. No Americans were permitted to live in New Mexico, but free-booting Anglos began to make their way across the Plains to seek their fortunes in the West. Among them were fur-trapping "**mountain men**" such as **Bill Williams** and **Kit Carson**, who made extended forays along the region's rivers in pursuit of beavers (known as "hairy banknotes"). **Taos** became renowned for its annual rendezvous, gatherings of Anglo, Hispanic and Native American traders far from the authority of any government. Northern New Mexico was now also beyond the reach of the Catholic Church; devout Hispanics kept their faith alive by forming sects such as the **Penitentes** (see p.142), and established a tradition of religious folk art that endures to this day.

Meanwhile, enough Yankee newcomers had flocked into **Texas** to outnumber its loyal Mexican subjects. In 1836, after Texas fought to gain independence from Mexico and then voted for annexation by the US, the president of Mexico attempted to hold onto New Mexico by closing down the Santa Fe Trail. It was too late. The doctrine that it was the United States' "**Manifest Destiny**" to extend across the whole continent led the US government first to try to **buy** New Mexico and California, and then, when negotiations failed, to declare **war** on Mexico in 1846. American economic might was neatly illustrated when the US Army of the West took Santa Fe without a fight, in August 1846; the Mexican governor was simply paid $50,000 to leave, together with his garrison.

Territorial days: New Mexico and Arizona

Under the **Treaty of Guadalupe-Hidalgo**, signed in September 1847 after US soldiers had captured Mexico City, the United States took formal possession of New Mexico, Texas and California – seen as the real prize – in return for a payment of $18.25 million. New Mexico, which consisted of all those parts of modern New Mexico and Arizona that lie north of the Gila River, plus areas of Nevada and Utah, was generally regarded as an arid, worthless wasteland. General Sherman is said to have jibed that "We had one war with Mexico to take Arizona, and we should have another to make her take it back."

Ironically, only the discovery of **gold** in California in 1847 gave New Mexico any great value to the US – as a route west. Surveyors mapping possible courses for a southern transcontinental railroad soon realized that the best routes lay on the Mexican side of the border. The Mexican government accepted the least extensive of five suggested land deals, and in June 1854, the $10 million **Gadsden Purchase** gave the US what's now southern Arizona, including Tucson, Tubac and Tumacacori.

Another 25 years were to pass before the railroad reached the Southwest – during that time, **Yuma** on the lower Colorado River burgeoned as a major port – but prospectors trekking to and from California soon began to investigate the region more thoroughly. After gold was found near the confluence of the Gila and Colorado rivers, **miners** fanned out across central Arizona, and reports of rich silver and copper lodes lured ever more migrants in.

Feeling that they had little in common with the Hispanic farming communities of the Rio Grande, the new arrivals argued that the territory was too large to govern as a single unit, and should be split in two. Many came originally from the South, and they seized upon the start of the **Civil War** in 1861 to declare the formation of the Confederate Territory of **Arizona**, which consisted of all the Gadsden Purchase lands. Its capital was Mesilla, in what's now New Mexico. The Confederate cause in the Southwest was short-lived: a Confederate army sent to establish a military presence was turned back by Union forces at **Glorieta Pass** – outside Santa Fe, near modern Pecos – in March 1862. The federal government recognized the existence of Arizona in 1863, but to avoid giving it a built-in Confederate majority drew a north–south boundary rather than an east–west one, and thereby delineated the two modern states.

The Indian wars

In the early years of the Civil War, US Army outposts throughout the Southwest were abandoned when the troops were sent east. That spurred a new era of raiding by the **Apache** and **Navajo**, and the Anglo and Hispanic settlements of southern Arizona in particular became depopulated. By late 1861, there were only two significant non-Native settlements left in Arizona; two hundred citizens remained in Tucson, and a band of miners held out at Patagonia.

However, the Army soon returned in greater strength than ever, resolved to eradicate the Indian "menace" once and for all. As detailed on p.539 onwards, Brigadier General James Carleton and Kit Carson drove the **Navajo** into exile in New Mexico in 1865 – they were soon back in Arizona, but never again posed a military threat – while a long cycle of treaties, betrayals and guerrilla campaigns wore down **Apache** resistance by 1886.

Towards statehood

The progressive subjugation and confinement of the region's Native American population cleared the way for a large-scale influx of Anglo settlers. During the 1860s, ancient Hohokam canals in the Salt River Valley were cleared to irrigate the new city of **Phoenix**, which swiftly became the capital of Arizona. Mining camps in the mountains, such as **Silver City** in New Mexico, and **Tombstone** and **Jerome** in Arizona, turned into fully-fledged towns, while massive cattle ranches began to spread across the open desert.

At first, the Anglo newcomers were almost exclusively male, and married into Hispanic families. Spanish remained the lingua franca, Catholicism the dominant religion, and silver Mexican pesos the common currency. With the coming of the **railroad**, however, around 1880, things began to change, and the pattern of north–south links were replaced by commerce oriented towards the east and west. The Southwestern economy became increasingly **extractive**, digging up minerals and depleting natural resources for shipment to distant cities. Where Native Americans and Hispanics had farmed for self-sufficiency, the Anglos sought profit. During the 1880s, huge herds of sheep and cattle were introduced to marginal grasslands that swiftly proved incapable of supporting them; well over half a million cattle died in southern Arizona when drought hit in 1893.

Towards the end of the nineteenth century, tensions began to pit the large-scale mining or cattle-raising concerns, backed by wealthy eastern corporations and the federal government, against individual prospectors and cowboys. These swiftly became so acute, and so recurrent, that some historians speak of a **Western Civil War of Incorporation**. Many legendary Wild West incidents, like the **Gunfight at the OK Corral** in Tombstone, Arizona (see p.258), and the **Lincoln County War** in New Mexico, which brought Billy the Kid into the public eye (see p.188), stemmed more from behind-the-scenes political maneuvering than from the whims of trigger-happy outlaws.

As well as bringing an influx of cowboys, miners and other adventurers to the Southwest, the railroads also created new industries. Communities such as Flagstaff and Williams sprang up to exploit the vast ponderosa forests of northern Arizona – not least to build the railroads themselves – while the increased accessibility of the Grand Canyon, recently publicized by the voyages of John Wesley Powell (see p.441), meant that the first **tourists** began to arrive.

Meanwhile, in New Mexico, Hispanic villagers looked on helplessly as huge tracts of their lands were parceled out to newly arrived Anglo ranchers. New Mexicans had traditionally owned small plots for individual use, and shared all grazing lands in common, but American courts refused to recognize communal land rights. Families who had been farmers, ranchers and skilled laborers found themselves increasingly obliged to work as unskilled laborers.

To a considerable degree, it was anti-Hispanic Anglo racism that delayed **statehood** for both Arizona and New Mexico. For many years, Republicans in Washington clung to the idea that they should be reunited and admitted as a single state, in the hope that Arizona's larger Anglo population would help to "temper" the Hispanic majority in New Mexico. Arizonans overwhelmingly defeated that proposal in a referendum in 1906 (which passed in New Mexico), and both were finally admitted in 1912 – **New Mexico** in January as the **47th** state, **Arizona** in February as the **48th**, the last of what are now known as the "Lower 48."

Utah in the nineteenth century

Until the nineteenth century, the history of what's now the state of Utah forms a minor adjunct to the story of the Southwest as a whole. Its main Ancestral Puebloan groups, the Virgin and the more nomadic Fremont peoples, abandoned southern Utah at much the same time as their Four Corners brethren moved away. By the time Spanish explorers such as Domínguez and Escalante began to pass through, in search of a route to California, it had become the domain of Ute and Paiute Indians. An estimated twelve to thirty thousand of them were present in 1850; most had traditionally been farmers, but they had

recently acquired horses and were starting to raid travelers on the newly created Old Spanish Trail, which linked Santa Fe to Los Angeles.

The reports of men such as the fur trapper **Jedediah Smith**, who named the Virgin River, and **John C. Frémont**, who mapped much of southwest Utah in the early 1840s, attracted the first permanent white settlers to the region. By far the most important of these were the massed ranks of the Church of Jesus Christ of Latter-Day Saints, known to the outside world as the **Mormons**.

The Mormons

The Mormon church was founded by **Joseph Smith**, who was born to a family of itinerant farmers in Sharon, Vermont, on December 23, 1805. Smith was a farmhand in Palmyra, western New York, when he had his first vision of the **Angel Moroni** in 1823. On his third annual visit, Moroni led him to a set of golden plates hidden in a nearby hillside. Only Smith was ever to see them; concealed behind a curtain in his house, he translated them from the "reformed Egyptian" with the aid of two mysterious devices he called the Urim and the Thummim, and thus dictated the Book of Mormon. Harshly described by Mark Twain as "chloroform in print," this revealed that two Israelite families fled Jerusalem around 600 BC, and sailed east from the Red Sea to the "Promised Land," led by a man named Lehi. His sons later quarreled; Nephi remained loyal, and was rewarded by a visit from the risen Christ, while Laman and Lemuel led the dissident, cursed Lamanites, the ancestors of the Native Americans. After a thousand years of conflict, the Lamanites finally defeated the Nephites in a great battle at the hill of Cumorah. The one Nephite survivor – Moroni, son of Mormon – buried the plates close by.

Smith proclaimed his new church on April 6, 1830. He was not unique among contemporary frontier prophets in attracting thousands of followers. His vision of an ordered, communalistic society was clearly rooted in the economic uncertainty of his own life, and struck a deep chord with his peers. To their unconverted **"Gentile"** neighbors, on the other hand, leadership by divine revelation smacked of Catholicism, and like the Catholics the Mormons were suspected of owing their first loyalty to their church and not their country. Their most controversial trait was the practice of **polygamy**, or "celestial marriage." Smith denied this to outsiders, pointing to a passage in the Book Of Mormon that called polygamy "abominable." In private, however, he declared his disciples to have a sacred duty to marry and produce children, thereby freeing disembodied spirits from limbo by giving them bodily form. Preaching the salvation of the dead, which said that the dead could be baptized by proxy, he argued that Mormon marriage was different to the "until death do us part" Christian sacrament. Church elders had a duty to establish polygamous, patriarchal families that would endure into the afterlife. Smith also became a Mason, and many of his church's rituals were inspired by Masonic practices.

In the face of constant harassment, Smith moved his family to Kirtland, **Ohio** – where they built their first temple – and then on to **Missouri** in 1838. After bloody clashes between slaveholding Gentiles and the Mormon militia, the Sons of Dan, he was captured and sentenced to death, then allowed to escape by sympathetic guards. The Mormons were next given sanctuary by the governor of **Illinois**, who saw them as hard-working potential citizens, and their new settlement of **Nauvoo** swiftly became the largest city in that state, with a population of 25,000.

In 1844, when Joseph Smith announced that he was running for President, the Latter-Day Saints were being attacked not only by their neighbors, but also from within. When a group of anti-polygamy dissenters attempted to establish a rival church in Nauvoo, and set up their own newspaper, Smith ordered that its presses be destroyed. Together with his brother Hyrum, Smith was arrested and imprisoned in nearby Carthage. A "blackface" mob attacked the jail, and both men were shot.

It was widely assumed that the Mormon church would disintegrate after Smith's death. However, although one of his sons decamped to Missouri with his own monogamous splinter group, Smith's successor, **Brigham Young**, held the flock together. Young, who was also of Puritan Vermont stock, promised the governor of Illinois in 1845 that the Mormons would abandon Nauvoo the following year, and set about organizing a mass **westward migration**. In the winter of 1846, ten thousand Saints camped near modern Omaha, Nebraska, while Young scouted ahead. Descending the western flank of the Rockies, he declared "This is the place," and

in 1847 his followers founded **Salt Lake City**, as detailed on p.508.

At that time, the all but empty wilderness claimed by the Mormons as **Deseret** (a Mormon word meaning "honeybee," to denote industry), or the **Great Basin Kingdom**, still belonged to Mexico. As well as what's now Utah, its putative boundaries included almost all of modern Nevada, most of Arizona and southern California, and sizeable chunks of four other present-day states. Mormon dreams of establishing an independent theocracy, outside the United States, were dashed within a year, when the US government annexed the entire region and the Gold Rush wagon trains began to roll west. The Saints therefore petitioned Congress for Deseret to be granted statehood. Suspicious of its religious underpinnings, Congress instead recognized a smaller area as the **Territory of Utah** in 1850, and appointed Brigham Young as its first governor.

Recognizing that individual farmers could make little impact on the uncompromising terrain of the West, the Mormons embarked on a massive communal effort to irrigate the desert. They were joined over the next decade by thousands more converts recruited by missionaries throughout America and Europe, to reach a total by 1860 of over fifty thousand. Fifteen thousand arrived from England alone, of whom three thousand literally walked across America, pushing their belongings in handcarts ahead of them.

During the 1850s, and especially after Young, who felt no further need for diplomacy, publicly acknowledged the existence of polygamy in 1852, the federal government came to see the Mormons as a significant threat to the Union. The newly formed Republican party – whose presidential candidate in 1856 was John C. Frémont, the veteran Western explorer – railed against slavery and polygamy in equal measure, as "twin relics of barbarism." Congress decided to appoint a new non-Mormon Governor of Utah, and sent him west with a detachment of 2500 soldiers, representing one-sixth of the US army. Salt Lake City was temporarily abandoned, but thanks in large part to the secession of the Confederacy, the Mormon War never quite happened.

When the **Civil War** in the East cut off supplies of commodities such as cotton, Brigham Young redoubled his commitment to making the Mormons **self-sufficient**. Pioneer parties were dispatched to create "missions" throughout the

Southwest, but while many of the small farming communities they established still survive – especially in southern Utah, where examples include **Cedar City** and **St George** – they did little to diminish Utah's economic interdependence with the rest of the US. The advent of the railroads, and the arrival in Utah of ever-increasing numbers of non-Mormons – especially miners – exacerbated the situation.

As the Mormons set out to "tame" the wilderness, the **Ute** fought back. Reciprocal raids by Utes and whites escalated into the **Black Hawk War**, waged between 1865 and 1867, in which the Utes were eventually worn down and finally confined to reservations in the territory that by now bore their name. In an eerie postscript, the dying Ute leader, Black Hawk, insisted on making a personal tour of all the towns affected by the war, to apologize in person. With Indian resistance broken, the Mormons spread throughout southern Utah. The **"Hole-in-the-Rock"** party (see p.412), for example, made the grueling trek across the central deserts in the winter of 1879–80 to establish the community of **Bluff** in the east. Little now survives from simultaneous Mormon attempts to settle in **northern Arizona**, apart from a few tiny settlements along the Arizona Strip (see p.357).

Meanwhile the federal authorities renewed their attacks on polygamy. The **Morrill Anti-Bigamy Act** of 1862, which was upheld by the Supreme Court in 1878, subjected polygamists to disenfranchisement and the confiscation of their property; as one federal judge put it "we want you to throw off the yoke of the Priesthood, to do as we do, and be Americans in deed as well as name." Utah retaliated by giving women the vote, so Mormon women could consolidate the Church's hold on State power; the **Edmonds-Tucker Act** of 1887 hit back, dissolving the Church and confiscating its assets, and once more disenfranchising women.

Brigham Young had died in 1877, and the new Mormon leaders now sensed that they would do better to drop polygamy on their own terms before they were forced to do so. Polygamy was therefore formally renounced in 1890 – although a few dissidents still practice it to this day – and the way was cleared for Utah to become a **state** in **1896**. Mormons were now encouraged to participate in national politics; church authorities even suggested that half should become Democrats, and half Republicans.

The Southwest in the twentieth century

Arizona, New Mexico and Utah spent most of their first century of statehood battling to secure ever greater quantities of **water**. In the early years, the main objective was to prevent California – already undergoing rapid development – from grabbing the lion's share of the flow of the Colorado River. Later on, cities such as Phoenix fought for federal funds to build grandiose water-diversion schemes. The political machinations behind the construction of the **Hoover Dam** in the 1930s, and the controversial damming of **Glen Canyon** in the 1960s, are chronicled on p.428. Suffice it here to say that with the completion of the **Central Arizona Project** in 1991, John Wesley Powell's nineteenth-century prediction that "All the waters of all the arid lands will eventually be taken from their natural channels" has now all but come true.

While New Mexico at the start of the twentieth century remained much what it had always been – a cluster of farming towns along the Rio Grande Valley – Arizona was prospering on the large-scale exploitation of its mineral wealth. **World War I** saw a leap in copper prices, and in alliance with state politicians the mine-owners easily quashed labor disputes such as the one that led to the **Bisbee Deportation** in 1917 (see p.260). Arizonan employers could also take cynical advantage of the vast pool of potential workers just across the border. After the Wall Street Crash of 1929, for example – by which time the state was responsible for half of all US copper production – over 500,000 Mexican laborers, now surplus to requirements, were deported.

Though the **Depression** hit hard across the Southwest, the region also benefited from a massive injection of federal cash, in the form of make-work public projects such as dam- and road-building. **World War II** not only renewed demand for copper and other metals, but kick-started the phenomenon of **urbanization** throughout the Southwest. Partly to make them less vulnerable to attack, defence installations were relocated away from the coasts, presenting **Albuquerque** and **Phoenix** in particular with their first major industrial plants, as well as greatly increased numbers of consumers. A former school in **Los Alamos**, New Mexico, was transformed into the laboratory that developed the atomic bomb – hence, some say, the alien crash-landing at **Roswell** in 1947 (see p.196).

After the war, the defence and other industries stayed on, and the ensuing period of mass migration to the Southwest resulted in an extraordinary population boom. Arizona and New Mexico were home to around 500,000 people each in 1940; Arizona is now fast approaching five million, with half that number in the metropolitan Phoenix area alone, while New Mexico has around 1.8 million. Even more striking is the fact that whereas at the start of the century, Arizona was 84 percent rural, around ninety percent of the population are now city-dwellers. **Las Vegas**, Nevada, did not even exist until 1905; it now boasts well over a million inhabitants.

Meanwhile, though **Salt Lake City** has grown at a steady pace throughout the twentieth century, **southern Utah** has remained sparsely inhabited. Attempts at large-scale ranching in the late 1800s resulted in destructive overgrazing, and the region relied on subsistence farming

until the discovery of **uranium** in 1952 (see p.464) triggered a **mining bonanza** that sent prospectors scurrying into every nook and cranny of the wilderness. Local Mormon businessmen of southern Utah lobbied hard for mine and dam projects in the face of growing environmental opposition. Calling themselves the **"Sagebrush Rebels,"** they attracted support from President Reagan, but were ultimately defeated as much by the realities of world commodity markets as by the "tree-huggers" they despised. Since the collapse of mining in the early 1980s, **tourism** has finally been appreciated as a major industry, and towns like **Moab**, which formerly reveled in their isolation, have begun to develop facilities for travelers smitten by the lure of the desert.

Histories of individual cities such as **Albuquerque** (p.170), **Phoenix** (p.218), and **Las Vegas** (p.488) are scattered throughout the text of this book.

The Hopi

Nowhere in the Southwest is the continuity between the pre-Hispanic past and the present more apparent than on the three Hopi mesas, on the southern edge of Arizona's Black Mesa. The Hopi have lived here for at least one thousand years, preserving their culture despite repeated incursions from outsiders, and their history is sufficiently distinct to be worth relating as a separate narrative.

For a guide to visiting the Hopi mesas today, and an account of the *kachina* religion, see the section that starts on p.59.

The origin of the Hopi

According to Hopi mythology, this, the **Fourth World**, is inhabited by the righteous people who escaped the destruction of the Third World by climbing a reed through the dome of the sky. They emerged in the depths of the Grand Canyon, through a hole beside the Little Colorado River known as the *sipapu*. There they were greeted by the terrifying but nonetheless kindly disposed deity **Maasaw**, who explained the rules of life in this world and dispatched them on migratory journeys to the four points of the compass. Their wanderings ended with a return to the **Sacred Circle**, and the establishment of the villages on what are now the Hopi mesas.

Myth and history agree on a picture of the Hopi as a peripatetic people who became ever more sedentary as they learned the techniques of agriculture, pottery and so on. Archeologists and Hopi alike recognize the cultural continuity between the Hopi and the ancient peoples of the Southwest. The Hopi refer to their ancestors as the **Hisatsinom**, and have pressed for the use of the term "Ancestral Puebloans" in preference to the more familiar Navajo name **Anasazi**, which means "ancient enemies." There's no doubt that the earliest occupants of the Hopi mesas migrated here from nearby Kayenta Anasazi and Sinagua settlements, but whether they had previously wandered further afield – most obviously, into Central America, where the language and beliefs of the **Aztecs** show clear parallels to the Hopi – remains unproven.

The Hopi mesas were probably inhabited from around 700 AD onwards, but the process the Hopi describe as the "**gathering of the clans**" was at its peak between 1100 AD and 1300 AD, and thus coincided with the abandonment of the most famous Ancestral Puebloan sites. One by one, small groups of refugees arrived at the mesas and petitioned those who were already there for land and the right to settle. Each was required to demonstrate what it could offer the rest, with the crucial factor being the ceremonial power to produce rain. After being allowed to stay, each group – in reality, most were probably no more than individual families – was regarded as a separate **clan**.

The Bear clan, said to have come from Mesa Verde, was the first to arrive – which is why it retains precedence to this day – and established the Second Mesa's "mother village," at the foot of the mesa. Originally called Maseeba, this village changed its name to **Shungopavi** when it relocated to the mesa-top several centuries later. Similarly, **Walpi** on First Mesa, when founded by the Snake clan from Hovenweep, stood several hundred yards below its present, highly defensible mesa-top site. **Oraibi**, the "mother village" of Third Mesa, is generally regarded as the oldest of the Hopi villages because it has occupied the same spot since its foundation; beams used in its construction have been dated to 1260 AD, but earlier dwellings may be a century or more older.

By 1275 AD, the three mesas held 35 villages. The Fire, Water and Coyote clans had come from the cliff dwellings of Keet Seel and Betatakin, now in Navajo National Monument; the Flute clan from Canyon de Chelly; the Rabbit clan from the south, perhaps Casas Grandes in Mexico; and others had streamed in from Chaco Canyon, and the Sinagua sites of Wupatki and Walnut Canyon. While each village remained autonomous, this disparate community forged a common culture, adopting its own variation of the *kachina* religion as it spread throughout the pueblos of the Southwest (see p.522).

The coming of the Spaniards

Hopi prophecies have long predicted the return of *Pahaana*, the "True White Brother" who was separated from the Hopi at an early stage of their migrations. Assuming that he finds the Hopi living lives of purity and righteousness, he will help solve whatever problems they may be facing, and lead them in due course into the Fifth World. If the Hopi saw *Pahaana* in the first **Spanish** explorers to reach the mesas, in 1540 – a detachment of Coronado's expedition led by Lieutenant Pedro de Tovar (see p.524) – their illusions were soon shattered.

Exactly what happened is uncertain. Alerted by the Zuni, the Hopi greeted the party in the fields, signaling that they should not cross a line of sacred cornmeal sprinkled on the earth. According to the official Spanish report, a Franciscan friar, exasperated by the rigmarole, commented "To tell the truth, I do not know why we came here" – and that was enough to trigger a Spanish onslaught. By the next sentence, the two sides are at peace, and Hopi guides went on to lead a group of Spaniards to the Grand Canyon (see p.320). Some sources suggest that this encounter took place at a village called Kawaika-a, which was completely destroyed by the Spanish.

During that and subsequent sixteenth-century Spanish incursions, the Hopi seem to have taken care to make their lands – which the Spanish called **Tusayan** – appear as valueless as possible. As a result, the Spanish never bothered to leave either a garrison or any settlers in the vicinity. Franciscan **missionaries** did however return in 1629, and set about building churches in Awatovi, Shungopavi and Oraibi. The one at Awatovi was on a similar scale to the San Esteban del Rey mission that still survives at Ácoma (see p.96), and required a similar amount of forced Indian labor; others involved the filling-in and "rededication" of existing *kivas*. The missionaries also brought sheep and cattle to the mesas, so the Hopi were the first people to raise livestock in Arizona.

The Hopi were enthusiastic participants in the **Pueblo Revolt** of 1680, sacking the churches and killing four priests. Fearing a Spanish return, they welcomed Tewa-speaking Pueblo refugees from the Rio Grande, who founded the First Mesa village of Hano. By now, the **Navajo** – whom the Hopi called *Tasavuh* or "head pounders," as they were said to bash in their captives' skulls with a rock – had entered the picture. They too joined the Pueblo Revolt, but were also starting to crowd the Hopi away from their summer farming

and grazing lands, and to raid for animals. It was during this unsettled period that the villages of Walpi, Shungopavi and Mishongnovi moved to occupy fortified positions up on the mesa tops.

After the Spanish reconquered New Mexico, those Hopi who still regarded themselves as Christians gathered in **Awatovi**. When the other Hopi villages realized their willingness to invite the missionaries back to stay, they determined to eradicate the Christian menace once and for all. At the end of 1700, the men of Awatovi were betrayed by their headman, who called a pre-dawn meeting in the *kiva*. Warriors from all the other villages pulled up the ladder, rained arrows down on the trapped men, and then set light to the *kiva*; surviving women and children were shared out as booty.

That act of savagery probably spared the Hopi both from internal dissent and missionary interference for the remainder of the Spanish and Mexican era. The mesas were however increasingly beleaguered by mounted Navajo and Ute war parties, and slave raiders from the south.

The Hopi under the United States

By the time the Southwest was acquired by the United States, during the 1840s (see p.528), the Hopi were desperate for protection from the marauding Navajo. Hopi scouts eagerly participated in General Carleton's 1864 round-up which dispatched the Navajo on the Long Walk to Bosque Redondo (see p.539).

Within a few years, the Navajo were back, re-asserting their control over their former territory and raiding extensively to replenish their herds. Called upon to define who "owned" what land, the US government was inadequate to the task. The very concept of a "tribe" was a federal invention; neither Navajo nor Hopi recognized any overall authority above clan or village level. Moreover, the idea of a reservation only worked if one group or other had exclusive use of an area. Only villages and fields counted as the "possession" of land; hunting grounds were regarded as unoccupied. Because the San Francisco Peaks are sacred to, and used by, both the Navajo and the Hopi, they belong to neither.

The **Moqui Indian Reservation**, established in 1882, was a rectangle measuring seventy miles by 55 miles. It did not even include all the Hopi villages; the hundred Hopi at Moenkopi were excluded, while an estimated three hundred

Navajo lived within the boundaries. As was standard, the decree creating the reservation states that it was intended not only for the Hopi but for "such other Indians as the Secretary of the Interior shall settle thereon." The resultant disputes have simmered ever since.

Outsiders now appeared on the mesas in ever-increasing numbers. Mormon and Mennonite **missionaries** came and went, and **anthropologists** stuck their oars in; Jesse Walter Fewkes called the Hopi "the most primitive aborigines of the United States" in 1891. **Tourists** too came by bus and railroad, with two thousand or more turning up for the annual Snake Dances. Turn-of-the-century images of Hopi ceremonies make it clear why photography was soon barred altogether; the crowds and cumbersome equipment made it all but impossible to move. Above all, the federal agents of the **Bureau of Indian Affairs** caused the most grief, by such actions as ordering haircuts for all Hopi men, for whom long hair is a sign of initiation, and kidnapping Hopi children to attend distant boarding schools, from 1887 onwards. Nineteen elders who protested against compulsory Christian education were imprisoned on Alacatraz in 1894.

The twentieth century

At the start of the twentieth century, the Hopi were divided between what outsiders perceived as the "**Friendlies**," who if not well disposed towards the government at least felt resistance was futile, and the "**Hostiles**," who sought to defend and preserve the old ways. Their differences in fact had as much to do with tensions between clans, and a breakdown in the allocation of resources and land now that Hopi territories were so circumscribed. The split became explicit at **Oraibi**, where the two factions declared themselves unable to coexist any longer. On September 8, 1906, each lined up behind its leader, with each man's hands on the shoulders of the next, for a "pushing contest." The "Hostiles" were literally pushed out, and established their own village of **Hotevilla** nearby.

The dispute at Oraibi politicized the role of the ceremonial priest at each village, known as the **kikmongwi**. When the Hopi were obliged to adopt a Tribal Constitution in 1936, under the provisions of the New-Deal Indian Reorganization Act, the kikmongwis were automatically appointed as governors of their village. Part of their function was to endorse members elected to the new **Hopi Tribal Council**. Ever since then, however, many kikmongwis have refused to recognize the authority of the tribal council, and aligned themselves instead with the **Traditionalists**, the heirs of the "Hostiles."

Paradoxically, the Traditionalists, who regard themselves as the guardians of all that is truly Hopi (and speak of their opponents as the pensilhoyam, or "little pencil people"), have raised awareness of the Hopi throughout the world. Rather than waiting for a saviour to come to them, they have embarked on a "search for Pahaana." The movement started immediately after World War II, when certain Hopi elders announced that following the use of the atomic bomb it was time to reveal teachings and prophecies that were supposed to remain secret until "a gourd of ashes fell from the sky." Since 1948, the Traditionalists have written to every US President, and addressed the United Nations, with a message stressing Hopi sovereignty and religious integrity, and the importance of respecting the environment. Among their successes was the recognition of Hopi religion as a "peace religion," which excluded Hopi from military service.

In practical terms, the Traditionalist movement has been a focus for opposition to **mineral leasing**. Since the Hopi Constitution's definition of the role of the tribal council as being to prevent leasing was illegally overruled by the Secretary of the Interior in 1961, strip mining by the Peabody Company has devastated much of Black Mesa (see p.44). Almost all the income brought by the leases during the 1960s was invested by the tribal council in an unsuccessful bra factory near Winslow. Traditionalist lawsuits have however failed to put a stop to the mining, which has become more acceptable to most Hopi since the leases were renegotiated on much more favorable terms, including environmental stipulations, in the 1980s. Mineral leasing is now responsible for around seventy percent of the tribal budget, and four hundred Hopi work as miners. To some extent, Traditionalist resistance to modernization is based on a refusal to become dependent on external agencies. Thus while Hotevilla forcibly rejected the installation of public utilities, there is little objection to individual use of solar energy.

Meanwhile, the **Navajo–Hopi land dispute** has raged on. By 1958, the ranks of the Navajo living on Hopi lands had swollen to outnumber the Hopi by more than two to one, while the

Navajo reservation had completely surrounded the Hopi mesas. Much of the impetus to resolve the problem came from the federal authorities and the mineral companies, who could not commence mining operations until definite title to the land was established. Public sympathies, and court rulings, swayed back and forth for decades. A **Joint Use Area** was established in 1958, to be shared equally between the Hopi and the Navajo, but it soon became evident that 98 percent of it was being used by the Navajo alone. In the 1970s, therefore, separate Hopi and Navajo **Partitioned Lands** were defined, with Hopi living on the Navajo side of the line, and vice versa, being expected to relocate. More Navajo than

Hopi were affected, and the plight of the **Big Mountain** Navajo in particular, who were given five years to move in 1981, made them a national *cause célèbre*.

The latest solution, the **Navajo–Hopi Land Dispute Settlement Act**, was signed by President Clinton in October 1996. It allows Navajo residents of Hopi land to sign 75-year leases, after which ownership will revert to the Hopi. If enough Navajo sign, the Hopi will receive $50 million to buy land elsewhere in northern Arizona (though their water rights will be restricted, which goes against more than a century of Indian policy). Dissident Navajo argue that the problem has simply been postponed for another generation.

The Navajo and the Apache

The best known Native American peoples in the Southwest – mainly on account of the fierce resistance they put up against the US Army in the nineteenth century – are the Navajo and the Apache. Both are now largely concentrated in Arizona, though both also occupy parts of New Mexico, and the Navajo Nation also extends into southern Utah. They are also relative newcomers to the region, having moved into their current territories at much the same time as the first Spaniards were arriving, and their impact was every bit as devastating as that of the European colonists.

Although the Navajo and the Apache are now distinct peoples, their languages are, with patience, mutually comprehensible, and their paths have only diverged within the last five hundred years. Both are descended from **Athabascan** peoples, whose Asian ancestors crossed into Alaska seven or eight thousand years ago, long after the New World's first migrants. Other Athabascans remained in the north, becoming the **Dene** peoples of Alaska and northwest Canada, and the **Na** of what's now the northwest USA, who included the Haid and Tlingit. At some point, however, the ancestral Navajo and Apache migrated south, hauling their possessions on dog-sleds as they pursued bison down the eastern flanks of the Rockies.

Estimates of when they reached their first base in the Southwest – probably on the edge of the Plains, somewhere east of the Rio Grande – range from 575 to 1525 AD, with the most likely date being 1250 to 1300 AD. Like nomads the world over, they traded the fruits of their hunting and gathering, especially buffalo hides, for the agricultural produce of more settled communities like the Rio Grande pueblos. Chroniclers with the earliest Spanish venture into the Southwest, Coronado's expedition of 1540 (see p.524), drew no distinction between the Navajo and the Apache, referring to both as **Querecho**. However, by the time the Spanish returned at the end of the century, the Navajo, who called themselves the *Diné*, had separated off from the Apache, or *Ndee*.

The Navajo

It used to be thought that it was the arrival of the warlike Navajo in the Four Corners region that forced its previous Ancestral Puebloan occupants to leave at the end of the thirteenth century (see p.521). In fact, however, the Navajo only moved west to occupy the now-empty San Juan Basin well after the Ancestral Puebloans had gone. It's even suggested that it was the Ancestral Puebloans who ejected the Navajo, when the Chaco Canyon and Mesa Verde communities fragmented, and their inhabitants headed east to establish pueblos along the Rio Grande.

During the late sixteenth century, a region centered on Largo Canyon, east of modern Farmington – still the core of Navajo territory – became known as the **Dinétah**, meaning "Among the People." The *Diné* defined their new realm as lying between four **sacred mountains**: Blanca Peak, or *Sis Naajini*, away to the east in Colorado; Hesperus Peak (*Dibé Nitsaa*), also in Colorado but to the north, near modern Durango; Mount Taylor (*Tsoodził*), further south in New Mexico; and the San Francisco Peaks (*Dook'o'oosłííd*), near what's now Flagstaff, Arizona. Legends began to grow up that detailed how First Man and First Woman lived near **Huerfano Mountain**. They found a baby on **Gobernador Knob** whom they named Changing Woman, and she in turn gave birth to the Navajo Twins, Monster Slayer and Child Born for Water.

The Lords of the World

By the 1580s, the Navajo had started to impinge upon the pueblos of Ácoma, Zuni and Hopi. Their expansion was soon given a huge boost when the establishment of a permanent Spanish presence enabled them to start acquiring **horses**. From 1606 onwards, the Navajo embarked on a cycle of raiding Hispanic and Pueblo settlements along the Rio Grande, seizing livestock, new crops and metal artifacts. In the Tewa language, spoken in many pueblos, *apache* means "strangers" or "enemies," and *nabajú* means "big planted fields." The first Spanish mention of the *"Apaches de Nabajú"* appeared in 1626, and the name was soon truncated to "Navajo."

The Navajo and the Pueblos were not always at war, however, and some Navajo participated in the **Pueblo Revolt** of 1680 (see p.526), which briefly succeeded in expelling the Spanish from the Southwest. When the Spanish returned to reconquer the region a dozen years later, many Pueblo peoples escaped their revenge by retreating to join the Navajo. As detailed on p.83, the culture of the modern Navajo, which anthropologists regard as a hybrid of Athabascan and Pueblo elements, was forged in the remote fortresses known as the **"Pueblitos of Dinétah,"** in Largo and Gobernador canyons.

While any explicit Pueblo-Navajo alliance soon foundered, the Navajo had by the eighteenth century acquired Pueblo skills such as pottery and weaving, as well as Pueblo-influenced social and religious structures. Obtaining horses vastly increased their mobility, while their large flocks of **sheep** enabled them to live well on what had previously been considered marginal lands. They therefore expanded westwards to cover a much greater area, occupying most of northeast Arizona and encircling the Hopi.

To the Spanish, the Navajo at this time were *Los Dueños del Mundo*, the "Lords of the World" – feared horsemen with a solid economic base in their own lands who nonetheless continued to plunder the pueblos at will. For most of the eighteenth century, however, the Navajo and the Hispanic settlers of New Mexico were nominally at peace, united in resisting incursions by the allied **Utes** and **Comanches** of the north. Then the Navajo began to realize that in fact the Spanish were tacitly encouraging Ute and Comanche raiders, and buying their Navajo captives as slaves. After 1786, when the Spanish signed a formal treaty with the Comanche, they were at constant war with the Navajo.

With conversion to Christianity as an excuse, Navajo women and children were shipped into slavery in Mexico; the Navajo replenished their numbers by carrying off Pueblo villagers. Certain mission settlements had to be abandoned in the face of Navajo attacks. By and large, the Navajo heartlands remained impregnable, although **Lieutenant Narbona**'s party of 1805 penetrated the Canyon de Chelly and massacred over a hundred Navajo (see p.53).

War with the United States

Mexican independence in 1821 did nothing to diminish the conflict, and the Navajo and the Hispanic settlers of New Mexico were still at loggerheads when the US Army marched in and took control of the Southwest in 1846. The Navajo were amazed to find that the American invaders expected them to make peace with their old enemies, on the basis that the New Mexicans were now themselves considered to be Americans.

A major factor in the American failure to sign and keep treaties with the Navajo was the fact that the Navajo were not a single homogenous group. They did not have "chiefs" as the Americans understood the term, let alone a single paramount chief. No Navajo could speak for much more than his immediate family, or felt bound by a pact signed by another without his knowledge or consent. Even so, the Navajo remained broadly at peace with the Americans until a widely respected elder – who, confusingly, had taken the name **Narbona** – was murdered and scalped by US soldiers, under a flag of truce, in 1849. For the next fifteen years, Narbona's son-in-law, **Manuelito**, fought a running war with the US cavalry, based at **Fort Defiance**, near Window Rock. New Mexican slave raiders, meanwhile, continued to steal Navajo children.

In 1863, **General James Carleton** resolved that the Navajo should be removed from their lands altogether, partly so that they might "become an agricultural people and cease to be nomads" and partly to allow New Mexicans to expand beyond the Rio Grande valley and seize whatever agricultural and mineral wealth the *Dinétah* might hold. Aided by veteran scout **Kit Carson**, he launched a scorched-earth campaign that culminated early in 1864 with the destruction of the *hogans*, fields and peach orchards of the Canyon de Chelly. As the starving Navajo surrendered, they were dispatched to "Fair Carletonia," the **Bosque Redondo** reservation at Fort Sumner in eastern New Mexico (see p.183).

A total of nine thousand Navajo made the **Long Walk** of 370 miles to Bosque Redondo, where three thousand of them were to die. The reservation was utterly unsuitable for agriculture; far from being self-supporting, it became a burden on the federal government. Carleton was dismissed, and in 1868, after four years, twelve Navajo leaders – including **Barboncito**, who

■

pleaded "I hope to God you will not ask me to go to any other country except my own" – signed a treaty that allowed them to return home.

For a detailed guide to traveling in the Navajo Nation, see Chapter 1.

The Navajo Nation

By treating the Navajo as an independent people, the "**Old Paper**" formed the basis of the Navajo Indian Reservation – which the Navajo prefer to call the **Navajo Nation** – as it endures to this day. The original reservation of 1868 was, however, just a small rectangle of northeast Arizona and northwest New Mexico, which included Canyon de Chelly and Shiprock but not Window Rock. Here the survivors of Fort Sumner rejoined those Navajo who had evaded capture in the backcountry; some had hidden near **Navajo Mountain**, and now regarded it too as a sacred peak.

During the twentieth century, the Navajo **population** grew at a phenomenal rate, from 20,000 in 1900 to around 250,000 today. Similarly, in over a dozen different transactions, the boundaries of the reservation expanded from 6000 to 27,000 square miles. A formal Navajo **government** was only established in 1923, when the major oil companies needed to find someone who could sign leases allowing them to exploit the reservation's newly discovered oil reserves. The **chapter** system of local administration was set up soon afterwards, and Window Rock became tribal headquarters in 1927.

The most traumatic event of the twentieth century was the 1933 **stock reduction**, when the federal authorities killed off a million sheep and goats and reduced the total Navajo herd to half a million animals. They argued that overgrazing

was washing silt into the Colorado that threatened the new Hoover Dam; the effect was to force a change away from pastoralism towards wage labor.

Since World War II, the Navajo Nation has continued to modernize, acquiring its first paved road in 1947, and the first college ever built on an Indian reservation, Tsaile's Navajo Community College, which opened in 1969. While many families still manage to live a traditional Navajo lifestyle, the greatest change has been the increasing exploitation of **mineral** resources. Mines and generating stations have appeared all across the region, often just outside the reservation but dependent on Indian labor. Many projects have been deeply controversial. The **Four Corners** plant near Farmington has been described as the single worst source of pollution in the United States, while the Peabody Company's strip-mining of **Black Mesa** to feed the **Navajo Generating Station** at Page is widely regarded as an environmental tragedy. In 1979, **Church Rock**, northeast of Gallup, was the scene of the worst contamination in the history of the nuclear industry, when a dam burst at the United Nuclear Corporation mill released almost a hundred million gallons of radioactive water, and a thousand tons of radioactive mud.

In 1975, Tribal Chairman **Peter MacDonald** helped set up the Council of Energy Resource Tribes, which he described as a "domestic OPEC." While the mineral leases of the 1950s

Navajo Clans

The basis of Navajo society and family life is the **clan** system. Each Navajo child is said to be born "to" its mother's clan, and born "for" its father's clan. Navajo identify themselves to each other by the clans of their parents, and no one is supposed to marry a member of either their mother's or father's clan. Traditionally, all members of a clan were responsible for each other's crimes or debts.

Originally, there were just four clans, each descended from one of the four pairs of men and women said to have been created in the

west by Changing Woman. There are now more like sixty clans, with each new clan having arisen when a woman from another tribe, or another place, has married into the Navajo. While certain clan names identify the descendants of Zuni, Mescalero, Mexican, Ute and Jemez newcomers, most hark back to specific locations on the reservation, mythical incidents or other attributes – the Turning Mountain Clan, Salt Clan, the People That Have Fits Clan, the Rock-Extends-into-Water clan, and so on.

and 1960s paid pitifully low returns, more lucrative agreements have now strengthened the Navajo economy. Navajo opposition to the principle of mineral exploitation has however also grown, as its long-term effects become apparent. Many feel that the long-running **Navajo–Hopi land dispute** (see p.536) has been manipulated by federal politicians and mineral companies for their own ends.

Peter MacDonald's efforts to diversify the economic base ranged from computer software companies to *shiitake* mushroom farms, but suspicion that he was feathering his own nest in the process was confirmed by a fourteen-year jail sentence in 1989. Although found guilty by a federal court of bribery, corruption and conspiracy, MacDonald remains popular on the reservation; tribal elections since then have alternated between his opponents, and pro-MacDonald factions who have granted him "pardons" not recognized under federal law.

The Apache

Around 1600 AD, as the Navajo began to incorporate Pueblo elements and become an entirely distinct people, the Apache fragmented into several separate groups. The **Western** Apache occupied the mountains of central Arizona; the **Jicarilla**, regions of northwest New Mexico between the Chama Valley and the Four Corners, and the **Lipan** moved east onto the plains of west Texas. At the same time, in southern New Mexico the **Mescalero** started to range east of the Rio Grande, while the **Chiricahua** spread west as far as what's now southern Arizona.

Even these groups were not really "tribes" in the way outsiders like to imagine. Apache lived in nomadic, clan-based societies of between thirty and two hundred people, each of which would elect its own "chief." A chief's primary responsibility was to insure his band got enough food; his authority soon collapsed in the event of failure. Most groups raised a few seasonal crops, but they supported themselves above all by **raiding**, not only against settled Pueblo communities, but against the Navajo, and even each other.

The coming of the Spaniards gave the Apache **horses** for the first time. At first, they stole them solely to eat, but once they learned to ride they swiftly adapted to a regular calendar of raiding the villages of the Rio Grande at harvest time, while allowing them to continue largely unmo-

lested for the rest of the year. It was beneath Apache dignity even to breed their own horses, let alone sheep like the Navajo; they simply stole livestock as they required it.

The colonists of New Mexico, who remained confined for the whole period of Spanish and Mexican rule to a fragile ribbon of riverside land, knew the huge Apache-dominated territories that surrounded them as **Apachería**. As the Apache never united to engage in formal warfare – no Apache war party in history exceeded two hundred warriors – it was impossible to take concerted action against them. In the first half of the eighteenth century, the Apache were nonetheless forced to consolidate into smaller and more mountainous areas, as the even more aggressive mounted **Comanche** warriors swept in across the Plains with ever-increasing regularity.

Later in the eighteenth century, the Spaniards managed to pacify the Apache to some extent by establishing *presidios* or forts that supplied them with food, alcohol, and even guns that were adequate for hunting but not war. When Mexico became independent, however, in 1821, the new administration could no longer afford such subsidies. Instead it placed a bounty of $100 on each Apache scalp – male or female, young or old – that was brought into the *presidios*.

The Apache Wars

To the federal government of the United States, which took over New Mexico in the 1840s, the Apache way of life was utter anathema. As a group of Mescalero Apache acknowledged to a US Army quartermaster in 1850, "We must steal from somebody . . . if you will not permit us to rob the Mexicans, we must steal from you or fight you." In total, the Southwest held between six and eight thousand Apache. By far the strongest resistance came from a group of just over a thousand, the **Chiricahua**, led by a chief known as **Cochise**, meaning "Oak."

Conflict between the US Army and the Apache flared into war in 1861, when Cochise agreed to meet Lt George Bascom in southeast Arizona, and found himself falsely accused of kidnapping a child. Although Cochise managed to escape into the Dragoon mountains, his brother and two nephews were hanged. Cochise then rampaged across Arizona, killing miners, prospectors, stagecoach passengers and soldiers wherever he might find them. As Anglos packed up and fled the territory, he imagined he had driven them out forever. What he didn't realize was that his campaign coincided with the start of the **Civil War**, which meant that all US forces were withdrawn east.

Within a year, the Union army was back, under the leadership of General James Carleton (see p.529). His Apache policy was simple, though directed at first against the Mescalero rather than the Chiricahua: "All Indian men of that tribe are to be killed whenever and wherever you can find them." During the winter of 1862–63, the Mescaleros were rounded onto the **Bosque Redondo** reservation at Fort Sumner in eastern New Mexico, where they were later joined by the Navajo (see p.183).

In 1862, Cochise's group had been joined by another Chiricahua band, the **Warm Springs** Apache of New Mexico, under the veteran **Mangas Coloradas**. The treacherous murder of Mangas Coloradas the following year, by US soldiers at Pinos Altos, where he had been invited for peace negotiations, hardened Chiricahua resolve even further. Over the next ten years, the US Army spent an estimated $38 million on campaigns that killed a total of a hundred Apache; the Apache meanwhile accounted for over a thousand Americans.

It was during this period that the name of **Geronimo** became widely feared. He was born into the Bedonkohe subgroup of the Chiricahua Apache, near the Gila cliff dwellings in New Mexico (see p.211), around 1823. Named Goyahkla, meaning "One Who Yawns," he reached adulthood without seeing a white American. After his mother, wife and three children were killed by Mexican soldiers at Janos in northern Mexico, in March 1851, he sought revenge in repeated raids on Mexico for years to come. Somehow, the Mexican battle-cry to St Jerome, "Geronimo," became the name he used for the rest of his life. Although he became a respected healer and medicine man, he was never, strictly speaking, a "chief."

In the **Camp Grant Massacre** of 1871, a Tucson-based alliance of Tohono 'O'odham Indians, Hispanics and Anglos massacred 144 Apache – of whom no more than eight were men – supposedly under the protection of the US Army in Aravaipa Canyon, Arizona (see p.232). A public outcry back East led President Grant to adopt a new policy towards the Apache, under which the **White Mountain** (also known as the

Fort Apache Indian Reservation; see p.280) and **San Carlos** (see p.231) **reservations** were established in 1872.

Any Apache who failed to present themselves at the reservations, however, were deemed to be renegades. The task of hunting them down was given to **General George Crook**, who adopted the new scorched-earth strategy of "total war," developed during the Civil War. Employing White Mountain Apache scouts, on the basis that the best person to track an Apache was another Apache, he "overhauled" the Tonto Basin during the winter of 1872–73, killing around five hundred Indians.

Following an uneasy truce, the Chiricahua were granted their own reservation, a small square measuring roughly fifty miles in each direction that centered on what's now Chiricahua National Monument (see p.262). Within three years, however, renewed cross-border raiding after the 1874 death of Cochise caused the reservation to be disbanded. The Chiricahua were moved onto the San Carlos reservation, despite the fact that they traditionally regarded the San Carlos Apache as "Bi-ni-e-Dine," or "brainless people."

In 1877, another Chiricahua leader, **Victorio**, assembled a five-hundred-strong band of Apache from the many different groups who hated life at San Carlos. A lengthy guerrilla campaign across New Mexico and West Texas resulted in another thousand Anglo deaths before the Chiricahua were driven into Mexico and killed in Chihuahua in October 1880. The few survivors were sold into slavery.

Geronimo, who had not joined Victorio, now became the focus for dissident Apache. During the 1880s, he repeatedly burst out of the reservation and went on the warpath, with a dwindling band of followers each time. The first time was in 1881, when he passed within a few miles of Tombstone, and was pursued by Wyatt Earp and his brothers. In 1883, General Crook tracked him down in the Sierra Madre in northern Mexico, and was briefly captured by the Apache before Geronimo chose instead to surrender to him.

Geronimo fled the reservation again in May 1885, and surrendered to Crook once more in Mexico in 1886, on the understanding that he'd be exiled to the eastern United States for not more than two years. Before Crook could get him back to San Carlos, Geronimo got drunk and escaped yet again. Crook resigned his command, to be replaced by **General Nelson Miles**.

The Chiricahua's final five-month guerrilla campaign, in the summer of 1886, pitted a band of 37 Apache, of whom eighteen were warriors, against five thousand soldiers, a quarter of the entire US Army. General Miles eventually managed to contact Geronimo in Mexico, and falsely told him that all the Chiricahua who remained on the reservation had been shipped to Florida. In despair, Geronimo **surrendered** for the fourth and final time in Skeleton Canyon, Arizona on September 3, 1886. The general's lie now became the truth. Geronimo and five hundred Chiricahua – along with the Apache scouts who had fought on the side of the US army – were indeed dispatched to **Florida** by rail. Men and women were segregated in separate camps. In time, the Chiricahua were reunited on reservations in first Alabama, and then Oklahoma, but Geronimo never returned to the Southwest. Among many public appearances in his later years, he rode at the head of Teddy Roosevelt's inaugural procession in 1905; he died in 1909.

In 1913, the 261 surviving Chiricahua were allowed to choose between remaining in Oklahoma or joining the Mescalero Apache in New Mexico; around two-thirds made the trip. In addition, it's thought that perhaps ten Chiricahua never were rounded up by the Army, and stayed hidden in Mexico; free Apache were reported still to be fighting in the Sierra Madre as late as the 1930s.

The Apache today

A total of around twenty thousand Apache now live in the Southwest. Both their largest reservations are in Arizona: the **Fort Apache** reservation (see p.280), which has the third highest population of all Native American reservations in the US, and the neighboring **San Carlos** reservation (see p.231). The **Jicarilla** still live in northwest New Mexico, concentrated around the settlement of Dulce (see p.163).

Visitors are however most likely to come into contact with the **Mescalero** Apache, who share their lands with the descendants of the last Chiricahua in the mountains of southeast New Mexico. Among unlikely ventures here that have brought them a rare degree of economic security are the Ski Apache **ski resort** (see p.192), which the tribe bought for $1.5 million in 1962, and features the luxurious *Inn of the Mountain Gods* hotel/casino. More controversially, the Mescalero have also signed an agreement permitting the storage of high-level nuclear waste adjacent to the reservation.

Books

The following list is a personal selection of books that proved most useful, interesting or entertaining during the research for this guide. A large proportion are only available in the US, and most of those you'd be lucky to find anywhere outside the Southwest.

History and archeology

Donald A. Barclay, James H. Maguire, and Peter Wild (eds), *Into the Wilderness Dream* (University of Utah Press, US only). Gripping collection of Western exploration narratives written between 1500 and 1800; thanks to any number of little-known gems, the best of many such anthologies.

Pedro de Castañeda, *The Journey of Coronado* (Dover). An invaluable historic document; the eyewitness journals of a Spaniard who accompanied Coronado into the Southwest in 1540.

Fray Angélico Chávez, *My Penitente Land* (Museum of New Mexico Press, US only). Inspirational history of Hispanic New Mexico, written by a Franciscan friar, which stresses the parallels between the New Mexican landscape and pastoral lifestyle – and soul – of both Spain and ancient Palestine.

William Cronin, George Miles and Jay Gitlin (eds), *Under An Open Sky – Rethinking America's Western Past* (WW Norton). Enjoyable essays on different aspects of Western history.

Robert Gottlieb and Peter Wiley, *America's Saints* (HBJ). When it appeared in the 1980s, this study of the growth of Mormon economic and political power was considered controversial in Utah; if anything, it's surprisingly tame.

Paul Horgan, *Great River: The Rio Grande in North American History* (Wesley University Press, US only). Horgan's monumental study of New Mexican history makes weighty reading; his more accessible *The Centuries of Santa Fe* (University of New Mexico Press, US only) is a lightly fictionalized set of biographies drawn from different periods of history.

J. Donald Hughes, *In The House of Stone and Light* (Grand Canyon Natural History Association, US only). The human history of the Grand Canyon in words and pictures.

Clyde A. Milner II, Carol A. O'Connor, Martha A. Sandweiss, *The Oxford History of the American West* (Oxford University Press). Fascinating collection of essays on Western history, covering topics ranging from myths and movies to art and religion.

David Grant Noble, *New Light on Chaco Canyon* (SAR Press, US only). Accessible and informative overview of the latest research into New Mexico's most important Ancestral Puebloan site.

Stephen Plog, *Ancient Peoples of the Southwest* (Thames and Hudson). Much the best single-volume history of the pre-Hispanic Southwest, packed with diagrams and color photographs.

Caroll L. Riley, *Rio del Norte* (University of Utah Press, US only). Fascinating history of the upper Rio Grande valley from prehistoric times up to the Pueblo Revolt.

Thomas E. Sheridan, *Arizona – A History* (University of Arizona Press). Stimulating reassessment of 11,000 years of Arizona history.

Alex Shoumatoff, *Legends of the American Desert* (HarperCollins). Comprehensive, anecdotal and entertaining first-person survey of several centuries of Southwestern history.

Stewart L. Udall, *Majestic Journey* (Museum of New Mexico Press, US only). Lively, well illustrated chronicle of Francisco Coronado's 1540–42

Unless otherwise specified, all books are published by the same publisher in the US and the UK.

---

entrada into the Southwest, written by a former US Secretary of the Interior, plus an attempt to reconstruct the Spaniard's route.

Richard White, *It's Your Misfortune and None of My Own* (University of Oklahoma Press). Dense, authoritative and all-embracing history of the American West, that debunks the notion of the rugged pioneer by stressing the role of the federal government.

Charles Wilkinson, *Fire on the Plateau* (Island Press, US only). This authoritative examination of the recent history of the Colorado Plateau is good on environmental and legal issues, but a bit heavy on personal reminiscence.

Native Americans

Between Sacred Mountains (Sun Tracks & University of Arizona Press). Superb overview of Navajo history, culture and politics, written by Navajo teachers and parents as a sourcebook for Navajo students.

Richard O. Clemmer, *Roads In The Sky* (Westview). A history of the Hopi, with an emphasis on the twentieth century and the role of prophecy.

Angie Debo, *Geronimo* (University of Oklahoma Press, US; Pimlico, UK). Gripping full-length biography of the Apache medicine man who led the last Native American uprising against the US Army.

Paula Richardson Fleming and Judith Lynn Luskey, *The Shadow Catchers* (Laurence King, UK only). A history of nineteenth-century photographers of Native Americans, with some stunning images of the Hopi and Navajo.

Basil C. Hedrick, J. Charles Kelley and Carroll C. Riley (eds), *The Meso-American Southwest* (Southern Illinois University Press, US o/p). Intriguing essays exploring possible trade, cultural and religious links between the ancient Southwest and the "high cultures" of Mexico.

Robert H. Keller and Michael F. Turek, *American Indians and National Parks* (University of Arizona Press, US only). What happens when the federal park system appropriates land from its former indigenous inhabitants; Mesa Verde, Rainbow Bridge and the Grand Canyon are among examples considered in detail.

Raymond Friday Locke, *The Book of the Navajo* (Mankind, US only). Comprehensive history of the Navajo, from their mythic origins to the present day.

Jerry Mander, *In The Absence of the Sacred* (Sierra Club, US only). Intriguing diatribe that pits the endurance of Native American values – with much discussion of the Hopi and Navajo – against the shortcomings of modern technology.

Robert S. McPherson, *Sacred Land Sacred View* (Signature Books, US only). Intriguing anthropological account of how the Navajo perceive the Four Corners region.

David Roberts, *Once They Moved Like The Wind* (Simon & Schuster). Excellent, fast-moving history of the Apache.

Polly Schaafsma (ed), *Kachinas in the Pueblo World* (University of New Mexico Press, US only). Well-illustrated survey of the *kachina* cult in the Southwest (see p.60).

Stephen Trimble, *The People* (SAR Press, US only). Excellent introduction to all the Native American groups of the Southwest, bringing the history up to date with contemporary interviews.

Frank Waters, *The Book of the Hopi* (Viking Penguin, US; Penguin, UK). As authoritative an account of Hopi religion as it's possible to find, though it's said that Waters' informants were not themselves initiated into all the secrets of the *kiva*.

Travel

Kenneth A. Brown, *The Four Corners* (HarperCollins). Slightly dry but very comprehensive journalist's account of his wanderings in search of the geology and history of the Four Corners region.

Colin Fletcher, *The Man Who Walked Through Time* (Vintage Books). Enjoyable account by the first man to hike the full length of the Grand Canyon.

Susan Shelby Magoffin, *Down the Santa Fe Trail and into Mexico* (University of Nebraska Press, US only). Absorbing first-person account by a trader's wife who reached Santa Fe in August 1846 in time to witness the Yankee takeover of New Mexico.

Melanie McGrath, *Motel Nirvana* (St Martin's Press, US; Flamingo, UK). Entertaining account of a British traveler's experiences in the Southwest, with some enjoyable swipes at various New Age nonsenses.

John Wesley Powell, *The Exploration of the Colorado River and Its Canyons* (Dover). Powell is said to have adapted the details of his first epic journey down the Colorado – see p.441 – for public consumption, but his journals still make exhilarating reading.

Douglas Preston, *Cities of Gold* (University of New Mexico Press). Long but very readable account of a horseback journey in the steps of Coronado, which throws a lot of light on history both ancient and modern.

Robert Leonard Reid, *America, New Mexico* (University of Arizona Press, US only). Insightful if selective journal of travels across contemporary New Mexico.

David Roberts, *In Search of the Old Ones* (Touchstone Press). An engaging chronicle of one man's obsession with Southwestern archeology.

Mark Twain, *Roughing It* (Penguin). This rollicking account of Twain's peregrinations across the nineteenth-century West may well be the greatest story ever told, though only his account of the Mormons is of much relevance here.

Ted J. Warner (ed), *The Domínguez-Escalante Journal* (University of Utah Press, US only). The extraordinary diary of two Franciscan friars who crossed Utah in 1776 in search of a new route to California.

The contemporary Southwest

Atlas of the New West (Norton). Absorbing, well-illustrated compendium of changes and developments in the contemporary West, produced by the Center of the American West at Boulder.

Alan Hess, *Viva Las Vegas* (Chronicle). A comprehensive, beautifully illustrated survey of Las Vegas' architectural history, which consistently throws fascinating sidelights on the development of the city.

Scott Norris (ed), *Discovered Country* (Stone Ladder Press, US only). Anthology of essays focusing on the impact of tourism on the Southwest, with some interesting material on the repackaging of Native American culture for Anglo consumption.

Debra Rosenthal, *At the Heart of the Bomb* (Addison Wesley, US only). Intriguing reportage of what really goes on in New Mexico's vast defense laboratories.

Hal K. Rothman, *Devil's Bargains: Tourism in the Twentieth-Century American West* (University

Press of Kansas, US only). Thought-provoking assessment of how tourism has shaped the modern West, which overturns many a cozy historical myth about places such as Santa Fe and Las Vegas.

Hunter S. Thompson, *Fear and Loathing in Las Vegas* (Random, US; Paladin, UK). Classic account of a drug-crazed journalist's lost weekend in early-1970s Vegas; what's really striking is how much further over-the-top Las Vegas has gone since then.

Mike Tronnes (ed), *Literary Las Vegas* (Mainstream Publishing, UK only). Sin City, Nevada, as seen by Tom Wolfe, Joan Didion, Noel Coward and others.

Environment and natural history

Edward Abbey, *Desert Solitaire* (Simon and Schuster Trade, US; Robin Clark Ltd, UK). Abbey's classic evocation of his year as a ranger at Arches National Park was the first of his many volumes championing the wildernesses of the Southwest.

Donald L. Baars, *The Colorado Plateau: A Geologic History* (University of New Mexico Press, US only). Among the more readily comprehensible explanations of the geology of the Four Corners.

Philip L. Fradkin, *A River No More* (University of California Press). The story of the Colorado River, from John Wesley Powell to the water-management issues of today.

Edward A. Geary, *The Proper Edge of the Sky* (University of Utah Press, US only). Loving evocation of the history and topography of southern Utah.

Ed Marston (ed), *Reopening the Western Frontier* (Island Press, US only). In-depth articles on the changing Southwestern environment from the *High Country News* newspaper; particularly good on southern Utah.

Russel Martin, *A Story That Stands Like A Dam* (Henry Holt, US only). Meticulously chronicled indictment of the West's last great dam, which inundated Glen Canyon in the 1960s.

Barbara J. Morehouse, *A Place Called Grand Canyon* (University of Arizona Press, US only). Fascinating academic analysis of how the Grand Canyon has been defined and exploited.

Marc Reisner, *Cadillac Desert* (Penguin). The damning saga of the twentieth-century damming of the West.

Raye C. Ringholz, *Uranium Frenzy* (University of New Mexico Press, US only). Lively account of the 1950s uranium boom on the Colorado Plateau, with plenty of hard-hitting material on the health consequences for the miners.

Bette L. Stanton, *Where God Put The West* (Four Corners Publications, US only). Photo-packed history of movie-making in Monument Valley and Moab.

Ann Zwinger, *Wind in the Rock* (University of Arizona Press). An inveterate canyoneer's account of the natural history of southeast Utah.

The Southwest in fiction

Edward Abbey, *The Monkey Wrench Gang* (Ballantine Books, US; Robin Clark Ltd, UK). Classic wishful thinking from the wilderness advocate, this fast-paced novel centers on plans by environmental saboteurs to destroy the Glen Canyon dam.

Willa Cather, *Death Comes For The Archbishop* (Random, US; Virago, UK). Not as sensational as the title implies, but a magnificent evocation of the landscapes and cultures of nineteenth-century New Mexico. Cather's *The Professor's House* (Vintage) features an extended account of the discovery of Ancestral Puebloan remains on a remote New Mexican mesa.

Clyde Edgerton, *Redeye* (Viking Penguin, US; Penguin, UK). Brief, bumptious, Western, focusing on the discovery of Ancestral Puebloan cliff dwellings and the aftermath of the Mountain Meadows Massacre.

Natalie Goldberg, *Banana Rose* (Bantam, US only). Taos-based creative-writing guru – her *Wild Mind* (Bantam, US; Rider, UK) and *Writing Down the Bones* (Shambhala Publications) have inspired countless would-be writers – practices what she preaches in this evocative novel, set partly in New Mexico.

Zane Grey, *Riders of the Purple Sage* (Penguin). Gloriously purple prose, first published in 1912, from the doyen of Western writers.

Tony Hillerman, *A Thief of Time* (HarperCollins, US; Penguin, UK), *The Dark Wind* (HarperCollins, US; Sphere, UK o/p), and several others. Hillerman has written about a dozen entertaining, intricately-plotted detective novels set on and around the Navajo Nation, all packed with fascinating detail about Navajo, Hopi and Zuni culture and beliefs.

Barbara Kingsolver, *Pigs in Heaven* (HarperCollins, US; Faber, UK). Enjoyable romp through modern Arizona, by Tucson-based writer.

Cormac McCarthy, *Blood Meridian* (Random, US; Picador, UK). A disturbing portrayal of the West in all its bloody reality – the scenes at Yuma Crossing are horrendous – if a tad macho for some tastes.

N. Scott Momaday, *House Made of Dawn Time* (HarperCollins, US; Penguin, UK o/p). Pulitzer Prize-winning novel, written by a Kiowa Indian, about the spiritual crisis of a young Pueblo Indian.

John Nichols, *The Milagro Beanfield War* (Owl Books, US; Deutsch, UK o/p). Thanks to the Robert Redford movie, this entertaining saga of a water-rights rebellion by dispossessed Hispanic villagers in northern New Mexico is the best-known of Nichol's *New Mexico* trilogy (the others are *The Magic Journey* and *The Nirvana Blues*).

Michael Ondaatje, *The Collected Works of Billy the Kid* (Random, US; Picador, UK). Slim volume of poetry and contemporary accounts which add up to an evocative picture of New Mexico's most famous tearaway.

Simon J. Ortiz, *Men On The Moon* (University of Arizona Press, US only). Evocative contemporary short stories by an Ácoma Indian poet.

Leslie Marmon Silko, *Almanac of the Dead* (Penguin, US only). Epic novel, by a Laguna Pueblo Indian, of a Native American mother searching for her lost child on the fringes of the Tucson underworld; look out also for Silko's *Ceremony*.

Glossary

Adobe Construction material, consisting of bricks of mud, sand, and grass or straw, and by extension a building itself; see p.98.

Anasazi Formerly used term for the ancient people of the Four Corners region; see p.520.

Anticline Geological term for a dome or ridge shoved upwards by subterranean bulging.

Arroyo Flat, often dry desert streambed.

Atlatl Spear-throwing device – a sort of detachable, lever-like handle that gave extra power and accuracy – used by ancient Native Americans.

Backcountry Term used particularly in national parks to signify wilderness areas that cannot be reached by road (as opposed, occasionally, to frontcountry).

Bulto or *santo bulto* Carved wooden statue of a saint, characteristic of Hispanic New Mexico.

Butte Geological term for a flat-topped outcrop of rock that's taller than it is wide, usually formed by the erosion of a larger mesa.

Casita Cottage, now applied mainly to individual guest accommodations in upmarket B&Bs.

Cuesta Long sloping mesa terminated by an abrupt bluff.

Genízaros In colonial New Mexico, the mixed-race offspring of captured Plains Indians and their Spanish masters.

Graben Geological term, from the German for "ditches," applied to narrow valleys created by the erosion of underground salt beds.

Grand Staircase Topographical feature of southwest Utah, stretching from the Grand Canyon to Bryce Canyon; see p.358.

Great House Archeological term for a defensively oriented, multistory ancient pueblo with hundreds of rooms, as seen at Chaco Canyon; see p.85.

Great Kiva Archeological term for a *kiva* that was used by an entire community rather than an individual clan or family.

Heishi Necklace of threaded disks, usually cut from seashells, as made originally by Ancestral Puebloans and now by Santo Domingo Pueblo.

Hisatsinom The Hopi name for their Ancestral Puebloan forebears.

Hogan Navajo dwelling; see p.56.

Hohokam Ancient people of southern Arizona; see p.522.

Hoodoo Natural sandstone formation in which a boulder is left balanced on a slender pillar, as at Bryce Canyon; see p.396.

Kachina (also spelled *katsina*) "Spirit messengers," central to the religions of the Hopi and other Pueblo Indians; see p.60.

Kiva Chamber used for religious ceremonies by Pueblo Indians, usually located underground; see p.520.

Latilla Light pole used in the roof construction of adobe buildings.

LDS Abbreviation to denote the Latter-Day Saints, or Mormons.

Mano Hand-held stone traditionally used to grind and crush seeds.

Mesa From the Spanish for "table"; geological term for a large, broad flat-topped outcrop of rock.

Metate Stone slab or trough, used with a *mano* for grinding seeds.

Mimbres Ancient people of southern New Mexico, renowned for their pottery; see p.210.

Moki or **Moqui** The former name for the Hopi people of northern Arizona.

Monocline Geological term for an abrupt irregularity in the usual stratification of rocks, often resulting in a dramatic cliff.

Penitentes Catholic sect in nineteenth-century New Mexico; see p.142.

Petroglyph Ancient rock-art image carved or pecked into stone.

Pictograph Ancient rock-art image painted onto stone.

Presidio Spanish term for a fortress built during the colonial period.

Pueblo Spanish word meaning "village"; applied to ancient Native American dwellings and also to modern Indian communities and peoples.

Reef Word applied by early Anglo settlers to such natural barriers to their progress across the desert as Utah's Capitol Reef; see p.419.

Reredos Painted altarpiece, as seen in Hispanic churches at Chimayó (see p.140) and elsewhere.

Retablo Kind of Hispanic religious folk art, painted on tin or wood.

Ristra garland of chile peppers, sold as souvenirs in New Mexico.

Santo In Hispanic folk art, an image or holy object.

Sinagua Ancient people of central Arizona.

Sipapu In Pueblo religion, the hole through which humans reached this earth; see p.534.

Slickrock Pioneer term for smooth, undulating stretches of sandstone, as a rule only slick after rain.

Syncline The opposite of an anticline, a rock formation created by an underground collapse.

Talus Fallen rock debris which accumulates to form slopes at the bases of cliffs and canyon walls.

Viga A broad beam of ponderosa or fir, as used by the Ancestral Puebloans in roof construction, and prominent in adobe architecture today.

Index

Top Ten Museums

Top Ten Drives

The Apache Trail, AZ 229
The Burr Trail, UT 424
The High Road, NM 140
The Moki Dugway and Muley Point, UT 481
Monument Valley, AZ/UT 45
Salt River Canyon, AZ 280
Scenic Hwy-12, UT 405
Squaw Flats Scenic Byway, UT 452
Valley of the Gods, UT 483
Zion Canyon Scenic Drive, UT 380

Top Ten Small Towns

Bisbee, AZ 260	Moab, UT 461
Flagstaff, AZ 283	Ouray, CO 78
Jerome, AZ 302	Silver City, NM 207
Las Vegas, NM 145	Silverton, CO 77
Lincoln, NM 188	Taos, NM 146

ROUGH GUIDES: Travel

Amsterdam
Andalucia
Australia

Austria
Bali & Lombok
Barcelona
Belgium &
  Luxembourg
Belize
Berlin
Brazil
Britain
Brittany &
  Normandy
Bulgaria
California
Canada
Central America
Chile
China
Corfu & the
  Ionian Islands
Corsica
Costa Rica
Crete
Croatia
Cyprus
Czech & Slovak
  Republics
Dodecanese &
  the East Aegean

Dominican
  Republic
Ecuador
Egypt
England
Europe
Florida
France
French Hotels &
  Restaurants
  1999
Germany
Goa
Greece
Greek Islands
Guatemala
Hawaii
Holland
Hong Kong &
  Macau
Hungary
India
Indonesia
Ireland
Israel & the
  Palestinian
  Territories
Italy
Jamaica
Japan
Jordan

New England

Kenya
Lake District
Laos
London
Los Angeles
Malaysia,
  Singapore &
  Brunei
Mallorca &
  Menorca
Maya World
Mexico
Morocco
Moscow
Nepal
New England
New York
New Zealand
Norway
Pacific Northwest
Paris
Peru
Poland
Portugal
Prague
Provence & the
  Côte d'Azur
The Pyrenees
Rhodes & the
  Dodecanese
Romania

St Petersburg
San Francisco
Sardinia
Scandinavia
Scotland
Scottish
  Highlands &
  Islands
Sicily
Singapore
South Africa
South India
Southwest USA
Spain
Sweden
Switzerland
Syria

Thailand
Trinidad &
  Tobago
Tunisia
Turkey
Tuscany &
  Umbria
USA
Venice
Vienna
Vietnam
Wales
Washington DC
West Africa
Zimbabwe &
  Botswana

AVAILABLE AT ALL GOOD BOOKSHOPS

ROUGH GUIDES: Mini Guides, Travel Specials and Phrasebooks

MINI GUIDES
Antigua
Bangkok
Barbados
Big Island of
  Hawaii
Boston
Brussels
Budapest

Dublin
Edinburgh
Florence
Honolulu
Jerusalem
Lisbon
London
  Restaurants
Madrid
Maui
Melbourne
New Orleans
Rome
Seattle
St Lucia

Sydney
Tokyo
Toronto

TRAVEL SPECIALS
First-Time Asia
First-Time
  Europe
Women Travel

PHRASEBOOKS
Czech
Dutch

Egyptian Arabic
European
French
German
Greek
Hindi & Urdu
Hungarian
Indonesian
Italian
Japanese

Mandarin
  Chinese
Mexican
  Spanish
Polish
Portuguese
Russian
Spanish
Swahili
Thai
Turkish
Vietnamese

AVAILABLE AT ALL GOOD BOOKSHOPS

ROUGH GUIDES:
Reference and Music CDs

REFERENCE

Classical Music
Classical:
  100 Essential CDs
Drum'n'bass
House Music
Jazz
Music USA

Internet
Millennium

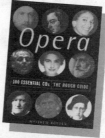

ROUGH GUIDE MUSIC CDs

Music of the
  Andes
Australian
  Aboriginal
Brazilian Music
Cajun & Zydeco

Opera
Opera:
  100 Essential CDs
Reggae
Reggae:
  100 Essential CDs
Rock
Rock:
  100 Essential CDs
Techno
World Music
World Music:
  100 Essential CDs
English Football
European Football

Classic Jazz
Music of
  Colombia
Cuban Music
Eastern Europe

Music of Egypt
English Roots
  Music
Flamenco
India & Pakistan
Irish Music
Music of Japan
Kenya & Tanzania
Native American
North African
Music of Portugal

Reggae
Salsa
Scottish Music
South African
  Music
Music of Spain
Tango
Tex-Mex
West African
  Music
World Music
World Music Vol 2
Music of
  Zimbabwe